THE COMPLETE ENCYCLOPEDIA OF
CRICKET

First published in 2006

This revised and updated edition published in 2011
by Carlton Books Ltd
20 Mortimer Street
London W1T 3JW

10 9 8 7 6 5 4 3 2 1

A CIP catalogue record of this book is available from the British Library

ISBN: 978-1-84732-867-0

Printed in China

All statistics are correct as of the end of the 2011 Indian Premier League.

Opposite: **The England team celebrate with the Urn and Trophy after winning the 2010/11 Ashes series 3–1 at the Sydney Cricket Ground in January 2011.**

THE COMPLETE ENCYCLOPEDIA OF
CRICKET

FOREWORD BY **STUART BROAD**

PETER ARNOLD AND PETER WYNNE-THOMAS

FOURTH EDITION

CARLTON
BOOKS

CONTENTS

INTRODUCTION

Cricket is not a game which stands still, and the two years or so which have passed since the previous edition of this encyclopedia have had their fair share of exciting cricket, shifts in power and scandal. Perhaps the euphoria of the wonderful Ashes series of 2005 has not been surpassed (will it ever be?) but the series in 2009 in which England regained the Ashes lost so emphatically in 2006-07, was not short of its exciting moments. It started when at the new Test ground of Cardiff, England's last pair found themselves desperately batting out time for a draw, and ended at the Oval with an emphatic win. It's a funny game, as the Aussies will ruefully agree, having outbatted England in the series by eight centuries to two, and taken 12 more wickets than England. And such are the uncertainties of cricket that England turned the statistics on their head in such an overwhelming manner in 2010-11 that they averaged 51.14 runs per wicket to Australia's 29.23.

But Indian and South African readers will be wondering what all the fuss is about the Ashes. In 2010 India became the leading Test power in the world according to the ICC ratings, and South Africa became their nearest challengers. The two countries fought it out in two series in 2009-10 and 2010-11, and both series ended as draws.

Meanwhile Bangladesh won a series in the West Indies, although this was due to a strike by West Indian players. Nevertheless the decline of the West Indies, sadly, continues. Some sort of resurgence is urgently required.

The betting scandals that have plagued cricket in recent years returned again in 2010, when a newspaper scam directed against Pakistan players touring England ended with claims that deliberate no-balls were being bowled in Test matches for the benefit of gamblers betting on such occurrences. Three players were banned by the cricket authorities following the allegations, including two young and very promising fast bowlers.

While Test cricket was providing excitement, and other county and state games lasting the traditional three or more days continued, the limited-overs game was still flourishing. Twenty20 cricket retained its appeal, and some great finishes and giant-killing in the 2011 World Cup kept audiences enthralled from beginning to end.

Cricket, however, is not a game that, over 450 years or so, has relied too much on instant excitement and great deeds. It is a contemplative game, bringing pleasures that seep into the consciousness rather than grabbing minute-by-minute attention. It is complex, with nuances that have produced better literature than that enjoyed by any other sport. Writers like Francis Thompson, Neville Cardus, R.C. Robertson-Glasgow, C.L.R. James, John Arlott and Alan Ross have helped give cricket an ambience, an attitude, and an atmosphere evoking summer days, sportsmanship and camaraderie.

Yet this is not the complete story, and things are not always what they seem. Even the phrase "It's not cricket" – frequently used to describe something underhand that could not possibly exist in the pure world of cricket is misleading. Robert Hendrickson, in *Encyclopedia of Word and Phrase Origins* (Fact on File Publications, New York and Oxford, 1987), suggests that the phrase was first used when, in 1622, villagers of Boxgrove, near Winchester, were prosecuted for breaking the law by playing the game of cricket on a Sunday, and tried to avoid fines by claiming the game they were playing "was not cricket", which puts a different light on the phrase altogether.

The idea of cricket being a byword for honesty, fair play and gallantry is comparatively recent and is best expressed in Sir Henry Newbolt's poem "Vitai Lampada", in which the schoolboy cricketer is imbued with the aforementioned qualities which he "bears through life like a torch in flame" after experiencing his captain's hand on his shoulder urging him to "play up! play up! And play the game!"

The mores of cricket have changed dramatically over its history. In the early days, it was a means for heavy betting, rivalling the equally aristocratic sports of horse-racing and the prize ring, and no doubt attracting many of the same unsavoury characters. After many years when it would have been unthinkable to bet on cricket, betting tents reappeared, and the conservative BBC quoted the latest odds.

So everything in cricket changes, except the delight it brings to its fans. We hope this book will bring them the pleasures of reminding them of games and heroes of the past and whet their appetites for more of the same in the future.

Left: **Lord's, the home of cricket, is bathed in sunshine during England's May 2009 Test match against the West Indies.**

FOREWORD

Cricket is one of the oldest professional sports and retains its position as one of the most distinctive and best-loved games in the world. It attracts millions of spectators around the globe from a wide variety of cultures and generates passions and talking points that become the stuff of legend.

Not only does cricket have an incredible history – something I feel every time I step out onto the pitch at Lord's or the MCG – but it keeps on reinventing itself. No other sport can exist in so many different formats, from the majesty of the full five-day Test, to the mixture of pace and patience needed for a One Day International win, to the all-out excitement of Twenty20 cricket. At the same time, it keeps everybody satisfied, from the purists of Test cricket to the kids who idolise their Twenty20 heroes.

Entering a sport with such a rich history meant that my own inspiration wasn't difficult to find. Tales of glorious wins, dramatic comebacks, stunning new records and amazing individual and team performances have entertained me and inspired me as my own career has grown.

Contained on these pages are the stories of cricketers I've watched and heard about all my life – some of them are now my contemporaries in the England teams, or part of opposing teams. Not only did I watch my father, Chris, play with the kind of passion and skill that made me want to follow in his footsteps, but throughout the game, right across the world, a string of names, with all the stories and achievements that will be forever associated with them, meant that I was never short of people to emulate. Ian Botham's heroics in the 1981 Ashes series, Shane Warne's 700th Test wicket, Don Bradman's unassailable batting record, Brian Lara's 501 not out, Sachin Tendulkar's record number of Test match runs – there's an embarrassment of riches here to choose from.

Recent years have added to these riches, in which I am proud to have played my part. The two magnificent Ashes series successes in 2009 and 2010–11, plus the great 2010 World Twenty20 win, has put England back at the forefront of world cricket. Against a backdrop of the massive amount of excitement that the creation of the Indian Premier League has injected into the game, plus the recent joy for India as they won the 2011 World Cup on home soil, cricket is in great health, and is celebrated for the wonderful game it is on the pages of this book.

Stuart Broad, Nottingham, 2011

Opposite: **Stuart Broad in action during a 2010 World Twenty20 match. In 2011, he was made captain of the Twenty20 team.**

1 THE HISTORY OF CRICKET

Cricket began in south-east England, and was taken up by the landed gentry. It reached the great public schools and Oxford and Cambridge Universities whence it was taken back by students to their home regions, rapidly gaining popularity in Nottinghamshire and Yorkshire in particular. By means of the army, cricket then spread across the British Empire.

Below: **A 1768 portrait of a young boy holding a cricket bat by the artist Francis Cotes (1726-1770).**

Cricket has been described as "casting a ball at three straight sticks and defending the same with a fourth", but one of the "three straight sticks", the middle stump, has been present in the wicket for only half the game's known existence. Strange as it may seem today, before then the ball frequently passed between the two stumps of earlier wickets without hitting either, and therefore without disturbing the bail, with the batsman remaining "not out".

The first definite mention of the game is in a statement by a witness recorded during a court case in 1598. John Derrick, aged 59, stated that when a schoolboy at the Free School in Guildford he played "creckett" with his friends on a disputed piece of land in Holy Trinity Parish in Guildford. This would mean that a game called cricket was being played at around 1550.

This first instance of a version of the word "cricket" appearing in written records was typical of many instances which followed in the 17th century, in that they were connected with breaking the law -- by playing on holy ground or on a Sunday.

The first attempt at tracing the history of the game was made by the Reverend James Pyecroft in 1851, in a book entitled *The Cricket Field*. Before that there were coaching manuals, the best known being *The Young Cricketer's* Tutor of 1833, supposedly written by John Nyren but actually by Charles Cowden Clarke, perhaps the first of cricket's host of ghost writers.

Cricket, meanwhile, had been taken abroad by English settlers and the military, with matches recorded in the 18th century not only in parts of the British Empire, but also in such places as Paris and New York. The first tour of English players took place in 1859 (to the USA) and by the end of the 19th century what are now known as Test matches were taking place between England and Australia and England and South Africa.

Opposite: **This painting of an early cricket match is in the Tate Gallery, London. The artist is unknown, but the period is clearly close to that of the portrait to the left. The fact that the wicket comprises only two stumps suggests it is from before the 1780s, when a third stump was introduced.**

1550
Cricket played by schoolboys in Guildford

1624
Jasper Vinall killed while playing cricket at Horsted Keynes, Sussex

1640
Cricketers found guilty of playing on Sunday in Maidstone

1694
Wager laid on cricket match at Lewes, Sussex

1706
First detailed description of cricket

1709
First known inter-county match – Kent v Surrey

1710
Cricket played at Cambridge University

1721
Mariners playing cricket in India

1737
Cricket in Georgia, North America

1739
First known depiction of cricket being played

Early History

Cricket as played in the Mary-le-bone Fields, c.1744 (oil on canvas) by Francis Hayman (1708-76).

In 1611, Randle Cotgrave's French-English Dictionary describes "crosse" as "a cricket staffe, or the crooked staff wherein boyes play at cricket". This is the first written record which gives a flavour of the game as we know it. There is one early mention in 1598 when a game called "creckett" is referred to during a court case in Guildford.

During the course of the next 60 years, every single reference to cricket occurs in the South East of England and broadly in or immediately adjacent to The Weald – the area between the North and South Downs. This firmly establishes the fact that the game was created in the South East of England. The rough geographical centre of this area is Horsted Keynes and on the Green in that town occurred the first fatality while playing cricket. A fielder in 1624 attempted to catch the ball, while the batsman tried to hit it away. The batsman in fact struck the fielder over the head with the bat with tragic consequences. Accidental death was the coroner's verdict.

Cricket was confined to Kent, Sussex, Surrey and the counties immediately bordering them through the whole of the 17th century, but when many of the nobility were forced to reside on their country estates during the Cromwellian period, those whose estates were in the South East adopted the game of cricket from the local population. This led to cricket being played at the principal Public Schools – Eton, Harrow, Charterhouse and Winchester – as well as at the colleges of Oxford and Cambridge.

Thus, the first real description of a cricket match was written by an Old Etonian, who had gone up to Cambridge University in 1700. His poem on cricket was published in 1706 – in Latin! Three years later comes the first newspaper reference to an inter-county match, Kent v Surrey at Dartford for £50. Nothing more is known of this match.

What is equally irritating is that no laws are still extant from this period. We know that laws must have existed, because of a document relating to three matches of 1727 between the Duke of Richmond's Team and Alan Brodricks's Team. The document lists a set of additional regulations made specifically for these games, because matches were being staged for increasingly large sums of money.

In the 1730s, the Honourable Artillery Company's ground of City Road in London became the

The Artillery Ground, Finsbury, London

Situated off City Road, opposite Finsbury Square, this ground was the principal venue for cricket matches in London from the 1730s until the 1770s. Its heyday came in the 1740s and '50s, when the principal entrance to the ground was beside the Pyed Horse Inn in Chiswell Street and the ground was run by George Smith, the innkeeper. Smith charged 2d admission and crowds of 7,000 or more turned up, but when he increased the charge to 6d in 1774 only 200 thought it worthwhile to pay. Be that as it may, the large crowds began to attract many undesirables, since betting was one of the major features of matches. In 1773, the Artillery Company had finally had enough and banned the playing of public matches there. Cricket is, however, still played there and, in recent years, benefit matches for a number of county cricketers have taken place on the ground.

1744
First extant Laws; first major match with detailed score, Kent v All England

1747
Cricket in New York

1751
First cricket reference in Yorkshire

1766
Cricket played in Paris

1767
Hambledon Club in Hampshire formed

1769
First individual century, by John Minshull

1772
Picture of boys playing at Harrow School

1774
Leg Before Wicket Law introduced

1787
First match on original Lord's cricket ground

1789
Proposed England tour to France abandoned

1794
First known inter-schools match: Charterhouse v Westminster

1790s
Matches played at Eden Gardens, Calcutta

principal venue for major matches. 'The Greatest Cricket Match ever known' thus described in the *London Magazine* of June 1744, was staged on the Artillery Ground with Kent challenging the Rest of England. Among the spectators were the Prince of Wales, the Duke of Cumberland and the Duke of Richmond, all keen supporters and promoters of cricket. Because of the amount of money resting on the outcome, a revised set of the Laws of Cricket were drawn up – these are the oldest set still in existence. Kent won by one wicket. The detailed score of the match is also preserved.

The nobility and landed gentry were taking up cricket and through the second half of the 18th century it spread via the major country estates to most counties in England. That was the good news. The bad news was that, in London at least, the game's reputation was becoming tarnished by the amount of gambling involved; this led to the bribing of players and the gathering together at major matches of the seamy underworld of the capital. As a result the Honourable Artillery Company closed its ground to public matches and respectable citizens were discouraged from attending games.

The cricketing elite were drawn away from London to an obscure village in Hampshire, where the Rev. Charles Powlett, educated at Westminster and Cambridge and the son of the Duke of Bolton revived the Hambledon Club in conjunction with Richard Nyren, who had learned his

cricket on the Duke of Richmond's estate at Goodwood.

By 1770, the Hambledon Club developed into the major cricket organization in England and for two decades raised the Hampshire team which, like Kent before it, was capable of beating the Rest of England. The venue for the Hambledon Club games was Broadhalfpenny Down, with the adjacent Bat and Ball Inn.

During Hambledon's time of pre-eminence, three major changes took place. Bowling, which was in those days under-arm switched from fast deliveries all along the ground to the ball being pitched in front of the batsman, enabling spin bowling to develop. Bats had been of a hockey-stick design to deal with the fast daisy-cutters, they now changed to the parallel-sided bats of today's type, though not before a batsman called White had used a bat as wide as the wicket, which immediately evoked a law making the maximum width of a bat $4\frac{1}{4}$ inches – the size it remains today. The third change was the introduction of a middle stump – it is alleged that a Hambledon bowler sent the ball between the then two stumps three times in succession, without dislodging the bail. In the 1780s, three stumps began to be used.

The major cricket activity in London in the 1780s was run from the Star and Garter Tavern in Pall Mall – the Jockey Club was founded there and, similarly, the Earl of Winchelsea ran the cricket club. In 1786, the Earl asked Thomas Lord,

the club's general factotum, to set out a private ground for the use of the Club. The first match was played on "Lord's", off Marylebone Road, in 1787. The Cricket Club then became described as "Marylebone Cricket Club".

Away from the South East, cricket was progressing rapidly in the Midlands. Major matches between Nottingham, Sheffield and Leicester took place regularly from 1771, but their standard was not up to that of the southern players, as was proved in 1791, when MCC played their first away games at Burley in Rutland and at Nottingham.

Thomas Lord.

Richard Nyren (1734-1797)

The landlord of the Bat and Ball Inn near Broadhalfpenny Down, he captained the Hambledon Club in its great years. He had come to Hambledon from the Sussex village of Slindon where, in the 1740s, his uncle, Richard Newland, had been the greatest batsman of the day – Newland had made the highest scores in the England v Kent match of 1744. Nyren learned his cricket from his uncle. The story of Hambledon and its players was related by Richard's son John and the book was one of the most popular ever published on the game. John Nyren stated that the Hambledon Club collapsed after 1791, when Richard Nyren and his family moved to London. However, the creation of Lord's cricket ground probably had a significant effect on the demise of Hambledon.

1801
First instructional book on cricket by T. Boxhall

1805
Eton v Harrow at Lord's, Lord Byron played for Harrow

1806
Gentlemen v Players match – the first of a series lasting until 1962

1814
Present Lord's cricket ground opened

1815
First record of a team being all out for 0 – in a village game in Norfolk

1816
Wide balls penalized in Laws

1817
William Lambert hit a century in each innings of a match – first known instance

1818
Cricket mentioned in Valparaiso, Chile

1819
Size of wickets increased to 26" x 7"

1820
William Ward hits 278 for the MCC – first recorded double century

1822
John Willes no-balled for bowling "round-arm"

1823
Size of wickets increased to 27" x 8"

1825
Kent and Sussex play matches home and away – the genesis of the present County Championship

1826
First known cricket club in Sydney, New South Wales

1827
Oxford University play Cambridge University for first time

1800-60

The effects of the long war against Napoleon, allied to the industrial revolution and the Enclosures Acts, were having dire economical and social consequences on England from 1795 through the next 20 years. Cricket's development was thus very much stunted through this period. The number of recorded matches dropped quite dramatically and recovery did not start until Napoleon was safely on St Helena. It was now that the popularity of the formation of cricket clubs really took off. Towns usually had clubs based on local hostelries, while the squire or vicar often led local village clubs. The aristocracy tended to retreat to private matches played within the estate and this, in time, led to the creation of "Country House" cricket, which reached its zenith in Edwardian England.

Entrepreneurs were always on the lookout for moneymaking ideas and, in 1821, George Steer built a ground in Sheffield to stage grand matches and to hire it out to local clubs. He was very successful and, within a few years, built a second, larger ground. Leicester had a similar ground laid out in 1825, but of even more historical importance, James Ireland leased the near-derelict Prince of Wales ground in Brighton in 1823. It was a multi-sport venue, but he determined that the major feature would be matches between Sussex

A scene from a match played between Kent and Sussex at Brighton in 1849, with the town and the church clearly visible in the background.

and Kent. It took him two years to negotiate the terms, then, in 1825, he staged the first Sussex v Kent match (it was indeed the first major inter-county match of the 19th century). His enterprise blossomed into the present County Championship. The matches continued on an annual basis and the press designated them as contests for the "Championship Belt" – taking the name from the boxing contests of the time.

By 1834, Nottingham had been the most successful Midland club, having beaten Sheffield, Leicester and Cambridge. In 1835, converting themselves to "Nottinghamshire" they challenged Sussex and then Kent. Surrey, founded in 1845 at

The Oval, joined in the battle for the Championship and gradually the other major counties formed County Clubs and took part in the contest.

The laws of cricket altered little from the 1790s until bowlers, seeing batsmen flourish more and more on slowly improving pitches, attempted to cast aside under-arm bowling in favour of round-arm. In under-arm, the hand delivering the ball had to be below elbow height. Round-arm raised the hand to shoulder height. In the 1820s, great arguments took place between the traditionalists and the round-arm fraternity. In 1835, the latter finally had the law changed. It should be noted that the lawmakers were now the MCC rather

John Willes (1777-1852)

When cricket recovered its popularity in the dying years of the Napoleonic era, pitches improved and batsmen found the under-arm bowling of the time easier and easier to score off. John Willes, a very enthusiastic cricketer who played for the Gentlemen v Players in the first match between the two sides in 1806, employed a professional, William Ashby, as a coach and also converted a barn on his estate at Fonford near Canterbury in order to practise during the winter months. He noticed the skill of his sister bowling at him "round-arm" (i.e. with the hand above elbow height) and, in 1822, while playing for Kent v MCC at Lord's, he copied his sister and bowled "round-arm"; the umpire called "no-ball", Willes threw down the ball in protest, mounted his horse and rode out of the ground, stating he would never play cricket again.

than the committee at the Star and Garter Tavern – the MCC still control the laws to this day.

Aside from the start of the County Championship, three other major contests of the period began. Eton played Harrow in 1805 (the latter had Lord Byron in their XI); the following year the amateurs challenged the professionals, creating the Gentlemen v Players fixture which continued until 1962; Oxford opposed Cambridge for the first time in 1827. These three fixtures, usually staged at Lord's, became an integral part of the social scene and, until 1939, attracted vast crowds.

However, for the lower classes another type of match was shortly to be born. William Clarke had followed Messrs Steer and Ireland by building his own ground – Trent Bridge in Nottingham – but he

did not find the idea financially worthwhile. That was in 1838; in 1845, he tried a second innovation: he signed up the top players of the day and invented the England XI. He arranged three fixtures, against Sheffield, Manchester and Leeds. The local sides were allowed several more than 11 men. The matches were three-day, two innings a side.

Cricket was the only team sport in England, and the top cricketers were stars. The public flocked in. Within a few years Clarke's England XI had more invitations to stage matches than they could squeeze into a full season; a second rival team was created, again the rivals had more fixtures than they could fit into their schedule. With, effectively, the top 22 England players touring the British Isles, county cricket took a back seat.

At a lower level there was a sea change in the attitude of school authorities to inter-school matches. One headmaster flogged the entire school team when he learned that they had organized a match. Thomas Arnold, headmaster of Rugby, with his "muscular Christianity" – healthy mind, healthy body – saw cricket as an ideal vehicle for his new school principals. The teaching of "fair play" became the maxim. The best-selling cricket book of the 1850s noted: "The game of cricket philosophically considered is a standing panegyric on the English character: none but an orderly and sensible race of people would so amuse themselves."

The many new Public Schools set out cricket grounds and employed cricket professionals as coaches, as did the colleges at Oxford and Cambridge. Cricket disciples flooded out of the system and took the game to the countries of the expanding Empire.

A brief look overseas. America had had cricket reported in New York in 1751; after the War of Independence there was a lull but, by the 1790s, the game on the eastern seaboard was growing. So much so that the first ever International was United States v Canada in 1844. Australia's first inter-colonial game came in 1851, Victoria v Van Diemen's Land; Victoria opposed New South Wales in 1856. Across the Tasman Sea, Wellington played Otago in the first inter-provincial game in 1860; while in India cricket was well established in Calcutta, Bombay and Madras

by the middle of the century. An important point is that the Parsees in India had adopted cricket. The Army and Navy spread cricket to all colonies, but on continental Europe, with very rare exceptions, cricket remained a game strictly for the "eccentric" English.

The All-England XI of 1847. At a time when cricket was the only team sport in England, the top players were real stars and the public flocked to see them perform in great numbers.

Fuller Pilch (1804-70)

"His style of batting was very commanding, extremely forward and he seemed to crush the best bowling by his long, forward plunge before it had time to shoot, or rise, or do mischief by catches." That is how Pilch was described by a contemporary. Pilch was one of three cricketing brothers from Norfolk and he played for his native county from 1820 to 1836, when he was paid £100 a year to move to Town Malling and play for Kent. He then dominated the Kent side for some 20 years. He is credited with scoring ten centuries, a small amount by today's reckoning, but quite outstanding in the middle of the 19th century. In addition, Pilch was a regular member of William Clarke's All England XI from its inception.

1861-62
First English team tours Australia

1862
England score 503 v Surrey, the highest total to date

1863-64
Otago play Canterbury - the first first-class match in New Zealand

1864
Over-arm bowling legalized; first edition of *Wisden's Cricketers' Almanac;* Western Province CC established in Cape Town

1865
First first-class match in West Indies, Barbados v Demerara (Guyana)

1868
Australian Aborigines Team tour England; E.F.S. Tylecote scores 404 not out in a match at Clifton College - a new record

1871
W.G. Grace scores 2,739 first-class runs in a season, including ten centuries - both figures are new records

1874
W.G. Grace becomes the first player in first-class cricket to achieve the "Double" of 1,000 runs and 100 wickets

1876-77
First ever Test match - Australia v England in Melbourne

1877
Kent CCC Cricket Annual first issued - the oldest continuously issued county annual in England

1878
First Australian tour of England - no Test matches played; the team also play matches in North America and New Zealand; proposed tour of England by Indian Parsees team falls through

1880
First Test match in England - v Australia at The Oval; first Canadian tour to England

1882
England beaten by Australia in England: genesis of "The Ashes"

1883
Surrey score 650 v Hampshire - a new first-class record

1861-1900

W.G. Grace was the most famous Englishman in the world in his time.

During the 40 seasons there were many changes of great historical importance in cricketing terms, but virtually the whole period was totally dominated by one man, who has claim to be the greatest figure ever to appear on the English sporting scene. That man was W.G. Grace. His first-class career spanned from 1865 to 1908. In the course of it he effectively created a host of records that dwarfed his predecessors and set high standards for all who have come after him. His presence at a cricket match guaranteed a good gate – in many cases a record attendance on his initial appearance. The fact that several biographies of Grace were published to celebrate the 150th anniversary of his birth in 1998 demonstrates the regard in which he is still held.

In the 1850s, America had been the main overseas cricketing country, but the American Civil War, allied to the rise of baseball, quickly altered that position during the '60s. Instead of building on England's 1859 venture to North America, the cricketing promoters of the day switched in 1861-62 to visiting Australia. The financial rewards of the trip were such that it was the first of a continuous line of such tours, many of which incorporated a visit to New Zealand at the same time. Australian cricket in those early tours could not compete with the strength of England and the tourists played "odds" matches – the local opposition being allowed more than 11 players, usually 14 or 16. A number of English professionals stayed in Australia as coaches and in 1876-77 Australian standards had

risen to match those of England. In March 1877, England met Australia at Melbourne on even terms for the first time. This match is considered the first Test match. Australia won.

An Australian side toured England in 1878, and in alternate years to 1890. In 1880, the first Test was staged in England – at The Oval – it's hardly necessary to add that W.G. Grace hit England's first Test century!

In Australia in the 1880s, five-match Test series became the norm, but not until 1899 was the first five-match series staged in England – the initial game of this series saw Grace's final Test appearance, at the tender age of 51.

The major alteration in the laws came in 1864 when over-arm bowling was finally legalized; in addition, to speed up matches, the number of balls per over, originally four, was increased to five in 1889 and six in 1900 – Australia jumped from four to six in one leap in 1887. In the

The First Test Match

James Lillywhite took an England team to tour Australia and New Zealand in the winter of 1876-77. The side initially played in Australia, then played in eight matches in New Zealand, before sailing back to Australia for a final round of games. The team had an extremely rough voyage, lasting six days, across the Tasman Sea, and the whole side were violently sea-sick. The day after their landing in Australia, they had been scheduled to play Victoria in Melbourne, but the Victorians picked a combined side of Victoria and New South Wales cricketers. The England team comprised only 12 men, but as the specialist wicket-keeper, Ted Pooley, had been detained in New Zealand owing to a fracas in a pub, England's side chose itself, with John Selby pressed into the wicket-keeping position. To many Australians' surprise, Australia won the game by 45 runs. A return match was hastily squeezed into the timetable. Unlike the first game, the betting was now in favour of Australia, but England won by four wickets amid accusations that the England players had deliberately lost the first match in order to make money by getting good odds on the second.

A team shot of the first Australian touring side to England in 1878. They may not have played any Test matches, but they set a precedent that continues to this day.

Journalists attempted to divide the counties into three divisions in the late 1880s, but confusion reigned when, in 1889, three counties were jointly tied at the top of the major league table. The secretaries of the counties met and, with the MCC, set down basic rules for a league.

Overseas, top-class domestic cricket was also in the process of regulation. The Sheffield Shield was introduced in Australia in 1892, the Currie Cup in South Africa in 1889-90; the Plunkett Shield in New Zealand in 1906-07. In the West Indies distance rather isolated Jamaica, but the other colonies competed against each other. In India, the Parsees challenged the Europeans in a major match for the first time in 1892-93. This was to develop into the Bombay Tournament, when Hindu and Muslim teams joined the competition. Over in the United States cricket became centred on Philadelphia, but players came from a very restricted section of society. On continental Europe the only countries to take any interest were Holland and Denmark.

Tours between England and the main cricketing countries became more and more commonplace in the closing decades of the 19th century. The Canadians came to England in 1880, the Philadelphians in 1883, the Parsees in 1886, the South Africans in 1894 and, in 1900, the first West Indian team arrived. England's cricketers first toured South Africa in 1888-89, India in 1889-90 and the West Indies in 1894-95.

1880s instances of tail-end batsmen throwing their wickets away led to captains, from 1889, being permitted to declare their innings closed.

In the middle of the 19th century, distinctive coloured shirts for a given team appeared; these died out in the 1880s to be replaced by the standard white shirt. Blazers with individual team colours were the vogue from the 1860s onwards and matching caps became common about the same time. Sweaters, again with the club colours, were worn from the 1890s.

So far as protection for the batsman is concerned, pads and batting gloves made a gradual appearance over a long period but, by 1900, it was rare to see batsmen without both sets of protection.

The arrival of regular Australian sides killed the last remnants of the England XIs that had toured the British Isles from 1846 and county cricket revived, to the extent that virtually every English shire possessed a county club, in Scotland and Wales they were common and even most of the Irish counties had some sort of county club.

From the 1860s the press began to publish a competitive "league" table for the major competing countries and each season a "Champion County" was proclaimed. There was, however, some disagreement on the status of the counties on the borderline of what was now being described as "first-class".

Lord Harris (1851-1932)

One of the most influential personalities ever to appear in the game, he played for Eton and Oxford before joining the Kent county side in 1870. His first determination was to resuscitate Kent cricket, which was in a sad state at the time. He was, at various times, captain, honorary secretary and president of the county club and, in 1906, at last saw Kent regain the County Championship. In 1878-79, he captained England in the first Test staged in England. He was a great stickler for the correct administration of the Laws and fought a winning battle against illegal bowling in the 1880s, by which time he was the major figure behind the scenes at Lord's. Harris set up the first proper body to govern county cricket but, just as it was being established, he was appointed Governor of Bombay. While in India, he greatly encouraged cricket there and believed that the game was a major bond in keeping the Empire together.

1901-14

The Golden Age of Cricket – or was it? Those who survived the First World War looked back with increasing nostalgia on the Edwardian cricket scene as perfection. Their memories were reinforced by the writings by a new genre of cricket journalists, spearheaded by Neville Cardus (*Manchester Guardian*). He romanticized the period to the extent that he quoted conversations between various professional players which never took place.

Undoubtedly the 50 years of intense cricket activity in the numerous Public Schools, where to play in the XI was the height of many pupil's ambition, had a very uplifting effect on the standard of amateur cricket. This also helped cricket professionals, with literally thousands of men employed as practice bowlers, coaches, groundsmen and so on – at the top no less than 55 men were employed on the ground staff at Lord's in 1909!

At amateur level a host of, mainly, batsmen emerged on the county and Test circuit – Stanley Jackson, Charles Fry, Pelham Warner, Gilbert Jessop, Archie McLaren, all automatic selections for England, are just a sample. Added to their number was Prince Ranjitsinhji, the Cambridge-educated Indian, who captained Sussex, played for England and, for five summers,

Lancashire's Archie MacLaren was an automatic pick for England at the turn of the century.

was the outstanding batsman in the entire country, amateur or professional.

The Ashes series of 1902 has since been hyped as the epitome of the whole of the long series of England-Australia matches. In reality, the first two games were rained-off draws; Australia won the next two and thus the rubber. The final Test, which was in theory meaningless, turned out to be sensational. Having been dismissed for 183 in their first innings, England required 263 in the final innings and collapsed to 48 for 5. Jessop, coming in at No. 7, then hit the fastest Test hundred recorded to date, but 15 runs were still wanted

when the final pair – Yorkshiremen, George Hirst and Wilfred Rhodes - joined forces. "We'll get them in singles," said Hirst. In fact, he never said it and they did not score the runs in singles, but England did win by one wicket.

One unforeseen, and in the long term disastrous, consequence of the multitude of talented amateurs, whose wealth meant they could idle their time away, was the doubling of the number of first-class counties taking part in the Championship - up from eight in 1890 to 16 in 1905. On the surface, everything was fine. The amateurs delighted the spectators by their carefree approach to the game – "style" was all-important. The division between "gentlemen" and "players" was accepted, reflecting English Edwardian Society – the "upstairs, downstairs" syndrome.

Even with half the players being "unpaid" labour, two or three counties only broke even, despite generous patrons: it was an ominous sign.

Meanwhile, the Australian top-class cricketers did not fit the English pattern at all. On tours to England they were handsomely paid, but were ranked as "gentlemen". In England, the MCC had taken control, rather reluctantly, of running cricket. The organizing of the County Championship had been thrust upon them in 1890; in 1903, MCC took over the running of major England

C.W. Alcock (1842-1907)

One of the most remarkable figures in English sporting history, Charles William Alcock has been described as the inventor of modern sport. Alcock was elected as honorary secretary of the Football Association in 1870 and not only suggested the FA Cup competition, but also captained the winning side, Wanderers, in the final. In the same year, he was appointed secretary of Surrey CCC and became editor of *Lillywhite's Cricket Annual*, the main rival to *Wisden*. In 1875, he played for England against Scotland in a soccer international staged at The Oval and, in 1880, arranged the first Test match to be held in England - again at The Oval. In 1882, he launched, and was the editor of, the first weekly magazine devoted solely to cricket, called *Cricket*. He remained as editor of the magazine and continued as secretary of Surrey CCC until his death in February 1907.

The England team in Australia, 1911-12. Second and third from the left, standing, are Frank Woolley and Syd Barnes. Wilfred Rhodes is seated on the left, with Jack Hobbs second from right.

tours overseas from the private entrepreneurs and latterly patrons. Lord Hawke (Yorkshire) and Lord Harris (Kent) held the levers of power and the occasional professional who was "awkward", found himself out of work. The lower classes kept their place. Australians, however, did not take kindly to being told what to do by an Australian "Board of Control". The situation exploded in 1911-12, when there was a punch-up at a Test selectors' meeting. The top players refused to tour England the following summer.

South Africa possessed the most forward-thinking cricket administrator of the period – Sir Abe Bailey. Due entirely to his efforts, the first organization to control world cricket was launched in 1909 – the Imperial Cricket Conference. At first, it included only England, Australia and South Africa, but now, under the same initials, it is still cricket's ruling body – International Cricket Council.

South Africa played their first Tests in England in 1907. Fatally, the country had already made a policy decision not to include Cape-Coloured cricketers in their touring sides.

In 1906, West Indies made their first first-class tour to England and in 1911, the Indians toured as a first-class side. Neither country played Test cricket until the inter-war period. New Zealand could not afford the cost of travel for an English tour, but they imported several noted English and Australian cricketers to act as coaches. The Philadelphians came as first-class tourists in 1903 and 1908 – in the latter year their best bowler, Barton King, topped the bowling averages for the whole country. It was a pity that the very name Imperial Cricket Conference precluded the United States. As it was, the 1908 team was the end of the line.

The New Zealanders formed a national body for cricket and the first country to tour the country at first-class level was Fiji in 1894-95! Another unexpected cricket outpost was South America. In 1900, a two-divisional league was set up in Buenos Aires and, in 1911-12, an MCC touring team played "Test matches" against Argentina. There were also cricket clubs in Brazil and Peru.

Cricket had a brief, one-match appearance at the Olympic Games - in Paris in 1900. England (represented by the not-too-daunting Devon Wanderers) beat France (one Frenchman and ten Englishmen) to take "gold". The only worthwhile cricket on the continent was in Holland and several Dutch sides of club standard toured England; one Dutchman, C.J. Posthuma, was good enough to play in five first-class games in England in 1903.

In 1912, at the investigation of Sir Abe Bailey, a Triangular Test Series was staged in England. Australia could only send their second-string players, then it rained all summer. A financial loss was incurred and the event was never repeated. No major cricket teams visited England in either 1913 or 1914, so the 1912 matches were the last English-based Tests before war was declared.

Test Match Grounds (1877-1914)

Melbourne Cricket Ground	**1877-1912**
Kennington Oval	**1880-1912**
Sydney Cricket Ground	**1882-1912**
Old Trafford	**1884-1912**
Lord's, London	**1884-1912**
Adelaide Oval	**1884-1912**
Port Elizabeth	**1889-1914**
Newlands, Cape Town	**1889-1910**
Wanderers, Johannesburg	**1896-1914**
Trent Bridge	**1899-1912**
Headingley	**1899-1912**
Edgbaston	**1902-1909**
Bramall Lane	**1902**
Lord's, Durban	**1910-1914**

Note: Of the above, Wanderers and Bramall Lane no longer exist as cricket grounds – Bramall Lane is a soccer venue and Wanderers has been replaced by the New Wanderers Ground.

1915
Death of W.G. Grace, his last appearance as a batsman had been in July when he scored 69 not out

1915-16
Eight-ball overs tried as an experiment in club cricket in New South Wales

1916
Sind Tournament instituted in northern India

1918-19
Plunkett Shield re-starts after war using eight-ball overs

1919
County Championship re-starts, matches confined to two days, but other first-class games generally three days. Worcestershire unable to play in championship because of financial problems

1919-20
Sheffield Shield re-starts in Australia using eight-ball overs

1920
Worcestershire rejoin championship; Combined Services organize representative team which plays occasional first-class matches until 1960s

1920-21
England lose all five Tests in Australia – a unique record up to that time

1921
Glamorgan join County Championship; *The Cricketer* magazine founded in England

1921-22
Plunkett Shield in New Zealand re-organized on a league basis

1922
Dublin University v Essex match ranked first-class; Brazil Cricket Association founded

1922-23
W.H. Ponsford scores a new record 429 for Victoria v Tasmania; Northern India Tournament in Lahore ranked as first-class

1915-39

Cricket in England came to an abrupt end when the declaration of war occurred in August 1914. The last fixtures of that summer were cancelled and by the time the 1915 season was due to begin, it was considered unpatriotic to play cricket while men were dying in the trenches of France.

This attitude slowly changed as the war dragged on, so that by 1918 some major games were being staged for war charities. When hostilities ceased in November of that year, the cricket authorities began the task of arranging inter-county matches for 1919, though it was agreed that counties only required 12 games to qualify for the Championship. For some inexplicable reason the contests were restricted to two days each, a decision hastily come to and just as hastily abandoned for 1920.

With Australia keen to resume Test cricket, an England side toured that country in 1920-21, then a return series was arranged in England in 1921. Australia won both series by an overwhelming margin, due to their brilliant pair of fast bowlers, Ted McDonald and Jack Gregory, allied to the spin of Arthur Mailey.

It was not until the Ashes series of 1926 that England finally regained the coveted trophy.

And then came Bradman. He made his debut in 1927-28 and, apart from one major hiccup, dominated cricket for the next 20 years.

Bradman was simply the greatest run-machine the cricket world has ever witnessed. In first-class cricket his batting average was 95.14 – the next best record for players with careers of any length is 56.83. That statistic says it all.

The major hiccup was, of course, the bodyline series of 1932-33, engineered by England's captain Douglas Jardine and aided by that splendid pair of fast bowlers, Harold Larwood and Bill Voce. Of the ten Ashes series between the wars, England came out on top just three times.

Just as Australia dominated the Test scene, Yorkshire held sway at county level. The White Rose county won the Championship in 12 of the 21 summers; Lancashire took the

Donald Bradman was undoubtedly the greatest player to have played the game, and England's determination to stop him in 1932-33 caused perhaps the sport's greatest controversy.

title five times, with Derbyshire and Notts having one trophy each; this meant that the Southern counties had just two years of success, 1920 and 1921 when Middlesex came on top. Northern grit won the day over the more amateur approach south of the Trent.

Sir Neville Cardus (1889-1975)

John Arlott, in a tribute to Sir Neville, noted that Cardus brought the qualities of personalization, literary illusion and imagery to the reporting of cricket matches. In fact he changed the face of cricket journalism forever. Before Cardus, reporters had been accurate and detailed in what they wrote, but there was no spark in the sentences delivered.

Cardus was brought up in poor circumstances in Manchester, but from an early age he had an immense interest in both literature and cricket – so much so that he obtained a post at Shrewsbury School as an assistant cricket coach and secretary to the headmaster. After the First World War, he joined the staff of the *Manchester Guardian* under the great C.P. Scott and, in 1920, began his stint as the paper's cricket correspondent. Later, he combined this post with being the paper's music critic and it is said that Cardus was one of a small band of journalists who raised the circulation of the paper by their writing alone. In addition, some 20 books of his writing were published during his lifetime and a number of reprints have appeared since his death.

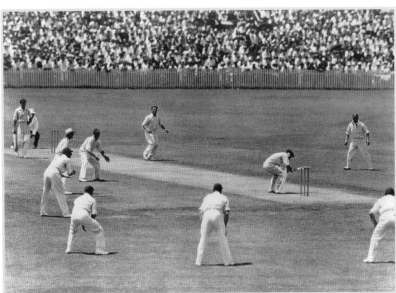

BILL WOODFULL TAKES EVASIVE ACTION FROM HAROLD LARWOOD IN 1933.

Bodyline

Of all the great controversies in cricket, none has fascinated the public as much as the 1932-33 row over the style of bowling adopted by the English team touring Australia. Indeed, books are still published on the rights and wrongs of the affair today. When Australia toured England in 1930 they brought with them a batsman who seemed invincible – Don Bradman. Douglas Jardine, who was asked to lead England on the 1932-33 visit "Down Under", was obsessed with one thought: how could the English attack dismiss the invincible Bradman? Having two remarkable fast bowlers, Harold Larwood and Bill Voce, in his squad, Jardine decided that Bradman's weakness was short, fast deliveries aimed at the leg stump and accompanied by a ring of close fielders on the leg side. The scheme worked – in broad terms: Bradman's batting average for the series halved from an unbelievable 100 to a mere-mortal 50. However, with short-pitched cricket balls hurling down at or near the leg stump, there was a great danger of the batsman being hit and several Australian batsmen were indeed injured. England won the series but, soon after, the type of bowling that had been used was outlawed from the game.

At club level there was a similar divide, since the North in general preferred competitive league cricket, while the South played "friendly" matches!

In Australia, club cricket remained, as it had done since the 1890s, a very serious business. Away from the two major cricketing countries, South Africa did beat England in two series, in 1930-31 and again in 1935, but made no headway against Australia, failing to win a single Test, never mind a rubber.

West Indies, New Zealand and India were all raised to Test status during the inter-war period, but with the exception of West Indies on their home grounds, rarely challenged the senior Test sides.

The two outstanding West Indian cricketers were Learie Constantine and George Headley. Constantine, the electric all-rounder, moved to England and delighted Lancashire League crowds, but despite qualifying by residence for Lancashire never played county cricket. Headley also went into English league cricket.

In the 1920s, Ted McDonald left Australia to play for Lancashire, but it was very rare to see overseas players in the County Championship, save for a handful who had been educated at Oxford or Cambridge. This number included two notable Indian batsmen, Duleepsinhji and the Nawab of Pataudi, both of whom played Test cricket for England. India might have developed its game more quickly if these two had devoted more time to the administration of cricket in their native country – both did in fact do so from the 1940s onwards, with Pataudi captaining India in 1946.

Lord Harris continued to dominate the running of cricket from Lord's – indeed it was largely due to his efforts that the Test arena was expanded by three countries – Harris had been born in Trinidad and had, in the 1890s, been Governor of Bombay.

In the United States, cricket was in terminal decline, despite several visits there by English sides and the appearance of the Australian team. In continental Europe, apart from Holland and Denmark, the game was confined mainly to expats, though a league did operate in Germany. Cricket was played in Britain's African colonies, but rarely by native Africans, though in Kenya the flourishing Asian community fostered the game. In Ceylon, the Ceylonese had an annual match against the Europeans and proved superior by the late 1930s. In sharp contrast in Burma, cricket seemed to hold no interest outside the European players – and it effectively died out once the British left.

The laws of cricket underwent few changes except for one major alteration. Due to the shirt-front wickets on which most first-class matches took place, the wicket was increased by an inch in both height and width – it made little difference to Don Bradman!

1940	**1941**	**1943**	**1944**	**1945**
British Empire XI created to play charity matches – a great success, it continues until 1945	Andrew Ducat, a double cricket and soccer international, collapses and dies while batting at Lord's	Members of the Royal Australian Air Force stationed in England play a number of charity matches, their fixtures continue in 1944 and 1945	Flying bomb apparently heading for Lord's causes all the players to lie on the grass until danger passes	England play Australia in five "Victory" Tests – these are not included in official Test match records
MCC play Rugby School – to mark the centenary of the match immortalized in Tom Brown's Schooldays	**1942-43** Some first-class matches in New Zealand and South Africa, but none in Australia	**1943-44** No first-class matches in either Australia or South Africa	**1944-45** First All India tour to Ceylon, a record 2,078 runs scored in the match, Bombay v Holkar	
1940-41 India continue competitive first-class cricket throughout the war, the only country to do so				

1940s

In contrast to the First World War, cricket playing was not considered unpatriotic during the wartime summer of 1940. In fact most of the county clubs tried to arrange some one-day games, either with sundry Service teams or with neighbouring counties, since travel restrictions prevented any games against distant counties. A 19-year-old called Desmond Donnelly created the British Empire XI which, in 1940, played 37 one-day games in aid of the Red Cross. Most of their games were in the Home Counties.

Perversely the counties, who had been in dire financial straits in the late 1930s, found their situations eased. Many county members continued to pay their subscriptions, which were now little more than "donations" and good crowds attended the one-day games.

Overseas, the Sheffield Shield in Australia and the Plunkett Shield in New Zealand were staged in 1939-40, but then were suspended for the duration. Nineteen first-class matches were played in South Africa in 1939-40, but not for the Currie Cup. Only in India was first-class cricket unaffected by the war, both the Ranji Trophy and the Bombay Tournament took place each season and with the added spice that several England Test players who were stationed in India were involved, notably Denis Compton and Joe Hardstaff.

Bill Edrich (left) and Denis Compton scored 7,355 runs in 1947 including 30 centuries.

The war in Europe ended in May 1945. The cricket authorities in England hastily arranged a series of five "Victory" Tests between England and a team picked from Australian servicemen then in England. The visitors possessed only one current Test player – Lindsay Hassett. He was picked as captain. The average daily crowd was 20,000. Very competitive cricket was played and the series drawn two wins each. The series discovered one new star, Keith Miller, an Australian all-rounder of tremendous talent. On their way home, the Australian side also played a number of matches in India.

1946 saw the resumption of Test and County Championship cricket in England. India were the tourists – the final "All India" team before the country was split in two. Australia were very keen to host an Ashes series, so England agreed to tour in the winter of 1946-47. The England v India series had unearthed two new notable players – Alec Bedser and Godfrey Evans, the former a very accurate pace bowler, the latter a wicket-keeper. Apart from Miller, Australia had discovered several new talents, including the tearaway fast bowler, Ray Lindwall. Bradman still overshadowed everyone and Australia predictably won easily.

The sun shone in England in 1947. The Middlesex twins, Denis Compton and Bill Edrich, broke numerous records – Compton's batting for the summer remains unbeaten to this day. His face seemed to decorate every billboard advertising the hair conditioner called "Brylcreem" – a new departure in advertising terms, at least for cricketers.

Thanks to Compton and Edrich, Middlesex broke the Yorkshire stranglehold on the Championship. The same pair of batsmen flourished just as brilliantly in the 1947 Test series as they had done for their county. England beat South Africa by three wins to nil. All seemed right with the world. 2,300,910 people paid to watch county matches that summer: a record which would never

John Arlott (1914-91)

The Hampshire burr of John Arlott's voice was suited to the game of cricket that was played during his period as a broadcaster – whether it would have been so apt for the frenetic hustle of today's game is purely academic. To the generations who listened to the wireless between 1946 and 1980, John Arlott was the sound of cricket. Just as important was the fact that Arlott was also a literary man. Unlike too many broadcasters, he could select just the right phrase or adjective to describe what was happening before his eyes.

A well-rounded individual, he appreciated and wrote poetry, twice stood for Parliament, wrote for newspapers and also had many books published. However, the listeners who relished his commentaries will always appreciate the fact that they lived at the right time to hear his harmonious voice gracing the airwaves.

be repeated. In addition there were well over 50,000 county members, whose attendance must surely have pushed the total watching to at least three million, if not four. No one knows, since members were not counted through the turnstiles.

In retrospect, it would have been prudent for the counties to increase the salaries of their players; as it was, too many talented youngsters chose safer jobs with the prospect of higher earnings. Top county men received £500 per annum; young hopefuls received £2 per week for just the summer season.

The selectors in England then made a complete hash of the team to tour the West Indies in 1947-48. The West Indian strength was totally underestimated. A virtual England Second XI was dispatched. They failed to win a single game Len Hutton was sent out as a reinforcement halfway through, but even his expertise couldn't produce a victory. Among other cricketers the West Indies had unearthed "the Three Ws" – Worrell, Walcott and Weekes – all of whom were destined to cause trouble in the next decade.

The England team returned home with a bloody nose just in time to see the Australians land, headed by Don Bradman. It was Bradman's farewell tour; the crowds flocked to cheer the master batsman for the last time. Bradman's Australians went through the season undefeated and made a profit of £75,000 – double the previous record. Bradman was knighted in the 1949 New Year's

Honours, the first time for a cricketer so soon after his career ended.

One curiosity of 1948 was that the Cinderella County, Glamorgan, won the County Championship. They had been promoted to first-class status in 1921, but in pre-war years had really struggled.

The revised Laws of Cricket came into operation for 1948. This revision by Col. R.S. Rait Kerr, MCC secretary, was the first such re-writing since 1884. The Laws themselves were not altered a great deal, but the revision removed the many cumbersome footnotes that had accrued. Also in 1948, as a result of the 1947-48 tour fiasco, new guidelines were set up for England touring parties, including wage rises for players and guarantees against financial loss by the country to be visited.

England had a successful tour of South Africa in 1948-49, but the New Zealand tour to England in 1949 was a farce, as Tests were limited to three days – all destined as draws from day one.

Elsewhere, India had broken new ground. They toured Australia for the first time in 1947-48 and then hosted West Indies in 1948-49. Fiji made their second major tour to New Zealand, their first having been in 1894-95. The appetite for cricket books increased. No less than 31 publications, were printed on the 1948 Australian tour! Pre-war visits had averaged half that number. Radio broadcasts were also popular, with such commentators as John Arlott, Rex Alston and Arthur Gilligan.

The 1948 Australians

One of the favourite pub arguments is to discuss which cricket team was the greatest of all time. The 1948 Australians are rapidly becoming a distant memory, but one fact about their tour to England that summer can never be disputed. They were the first Test-playing combination to tour England and return home undefeated. It is difficult to make such a comparison with more recent sides, because the number of matches played has reduced – in 1948, Australia played 34 and won 25, drawing the other nine; they also won four out of the five Tests.

Don Bradman captained the team, announcing beforehand that it would be his last visit to England as a cricketer. It seemed that his ambition was, in fact, not to be defeated. He possessed one of the greatest pairs of fast bowlers in Ray Lindwall and Keith Miller. The batting was also quite phenomenal, with seven of the touring party hitting over 1,000 runs and scoring 50 centuries between them. Sid Barnes and Arthur Morris opened the innings – both averaged over 80 in the Test series. Bradman came in first wicket down with Keith Miller at No. 4 and Lindsay Hassett at No. 5. The wicket-keeper was Don Tallon and the bowlers to come after Lindwall and Miller were Bill Johnston, Ernie Toshack and spinner Ian Johnson. England had no answer to this array of talent – the public flocked to watch the side and the profit from the tour was double that of any previous visit.

1950
West Indies win Test series in England for first time

1950-51
East African Cricket Conference founded

1951
First comprehensive book of cricket records published

1951-52
Currie Cup divided into two sections with promotion and relegation

1952
Pakistan elected to Imperial Cricket Conference; Uganda Cricket Association founded

1952-53
Pakistan play first Test matches - v India in India

1953
Kenya Cricket Association founded; England beat Australia in Test series for first time since 1932-33

1953-54
Gopalan Trophy established - annual contest between Ceylon and Madras; first New Zealand tour to South Africa

1954
First Pakistan tour to England and first Test series between the two countries; Canada tour England and play first-class matches there for the only time

1954-55
First Indian tour of Pakistan - all five Tests drawn

1950s

Ramadhin and Valentine spun West Indies to victory for the first time in England in 1950.

"With those two little pals of mine, Ramadhin and Valentine," so went the chorus of the Victory Calypso when West Indies beat England at Lord's for the first time in 1950. The old ground, which rang with West Indian music and Caribbean dancing, had never witnessed anything like the festival staged by West Indian supporters.

In the long history of Test cricket, the performances of the spinners - Ramadhin from Trinidad and Valentine from Jamaica - during the 1950 West Indian tour to England have never been equalled. Each had come to England as complete unknowns, with just four first-class matches between them and both under the age of 21. Valentine took 33 wickets in the series, Ramadhin 26; West Indies won three matches to one. What, however, was possibly more surprising, given those two

bowlers, plus Worrell, Weekes and Walcott, and then Gary Sobers from 1953-54, was that West Indies did not win another Test series against either England or Australia until 1963! No doubt the politics of picking a West Indies team from effectively so many separate countries played its part.

England gradually increased in stature as the '50s unrolled. In 1951, at Melbourne, they finally won a Test against Australia. At home in 1953, they at last regained the Ashes. New players were coming through - fast bowlers Fred Trueman, Brian Statham and Frank Tyson; Peter May and Colin Cowdrey as batsmen, and Jim Laker and Tony Lock supplying the spin. Laker created a record at Old Trafford in 1956 by capturing 19 Australian wickets, a very rare feat in any class of cricket.

In view of England's resurgence, it is curious that the numbers of spectators watching county cricket fell steadily through the decade. Experts blamed changing social habits and the motor car. Counties were losing money; the honeymoon period of the '40s was fast becoming a distant memory.

Leslie Deakins, the Warwickshire secretary, combated the decline by creating a vigorous Supporters' Association, making money from football pools. He rebuilt the rundown Edgbaston ground with

SURREY'S JIM LAKER BOWLS AUSTRALIA'S KEITH MILLER IN 1956.

Surrey

When Surrey became joint county champions with Lancashire in 1950, it was the first time that they had topped the table in 36 years, despite possessing such great players as Jack Hobbs, Douglas Jardine, Percy Fender and Alf Glover during the inter-war years. Although Surrey fell to sixth place in 1951, they then won the title a record seven times in succession. The initial inspiration behind their achievement was the fast bowler and brilliant close fielder Stuart Surridge – captain from 1952 to 1956. In Jim Laker and Tony Lock the county also had possibly the best pair of spin bowlers ever seen in county cricket – Laker, the supreme off-spinner and dour Yorkshireman – and Lock, left-arm medium or slow. England's premier medium-pace bowler of the immediate post-war era, Alec Bedser, opened the bowling initially with Surridge and later with Peter Loader, who also played for England. Arthur McIntyre, another Test player, kept wicket to this formidable group of bowlers. The star batsman was Peter May, who was soon to develop into the outstanding batsman in England - he also took over as captain when Surridge retired. Others who played a major role in Surrey's success were Alec's twin brother, Eric Bedser, David Fletcher and Bernard Constable. With the changing circumstances, it seems unlikely that any county can repeat Surrey's run of titles.

1955
Cricket ball reduced in size and used in some first-class matches in England – experiment abandoned as a failure

1955-56
New Zealand tour India and Pakistan for first time

1956
J.C. Laker takes 19 wickets in the England v Australia Test at Old Trafford, a world record for first-class cricket

1956-57
First West Indian Quadrangular Tournament with all matches on one ground in Georgetown

1957
Declaration of innings now permitted at any time during a match; boundaries reduced to a maximum of 75 yards in county cricket

1957-58
First MCC tour of East Africa; first Test series between the West Indies and Pakistan in the West Indies; G.S. Sobers hit new Test record of 365 not out West Indies v. Pakistan in Kingston, Jamaica

1958
Surrey win County Championship for record seventh consecutive season

1958-59
Hanif Mohammad hits new first-class record of 499 for Karachi v Bahawalpur

1959
First-class counties Second XI competition established

the pools profits and Test cricket returned to Birmingham in 1957 after a gap of 28 years. Other counties copied his ideas, but football pools weren't a long-term answer. Learned committees were set up, but failed to make any radical moves. Just as serious for the future was that teenage sports talent was being more and more attracted to the glamorous world of soccer.

At the other end of the scale, those talents nurtured at Fenner's or in The Parks could no longer afford to play county cricket as amateurs – the taxman had dug deep into parental pockets. That was the state in England. On the sub-continent cricket was booming.

Pakistan was raised to Test status in July 1952. Two seasons later, they toured England for the first time and won the final Test – no other country had beaten England during an initial Test visit. Pakistan's star was seam bowler Fazal Mahmood. One of the sub-continent's difficulties was the reluctance of Australia to tour there. Anthony de Mello, of the Indian Board of Control, solved the problem by inviting a Commonwealth team. Many experts thought the idea of players from different countries joining a multi-national touring side just wouldn't work. They were wrong. Under manager George Duckworth, three such teams went in the 1950s and were successful.

Ceylon was also cricket-mad. Several of their players moved to England and performed well in county cricket. First-class touring

Fazal Mahmood took 12 wickets in Pakistan's victory at The Oval in 1954.

sides visited the island, which aspired to Test status.

In South Africa, the racial divide increased. The black and Asian inhabitants formed their own cricket authority and ran their own competitions, while the white players exclusively ruled the Test and first-class arenas. South Africa did cause a major surprise in 1952-53 when a team of young hopefuls under Jack Cheetham toured Australia and tied the Test series – so doubtful had the Australian Board been as to the viability of the visit that they had demanded a £10,000 guarantee from South Africa against a possible loss. The tourists made a profit of £3,000.

In East Africa, cricket flourished in Kenya. The major fixture was still Europeans v Asians, but the two

teams combined as Kenya to oppose increasingly strong touring sides Unheralded, an Egyptian club side toured England in 1951, but the fall of the monarchy two years later saw cricket in that country in terminal decline.

Across the Atlantic, Canada looked most likely to go forward to Test Match status. A representative Canadian team toured England in 1951, but were outplayed in their first-class fixtures. Over the southern border, in the States, cricket was at an all-time low. Expatriot West Indians played the game in New York and around Hollywood some social cricket survived. MCC sent a side to South America in 1958-59 only to discover that a very modest standard of the game lingered on.

In Holland, a keen band of enthusiasts kept cricket alive. The principal problem was the total lack of exclusive cricket grounds. This meant that matting pitches were used on sports fields usually featuring soccer. The South African touring team to England in 1951 went briefly to Holland and other touring teams followed suit.

The closing years of the decade saw a revival in Australia's fortunes, with a young side astutely led by Richie Benaud. England were comprehensively beaten four matches to nil in 1958-59, though the series was marred by a re-surfacing of bowlers being accused of "throwing" – the problem of illegal bowling was destined to continue into the 1960s.

A.H. Kardar (1925-96)

Imran Khan commented: "After Kardar's retirement, Pakistan cricket was thrown to the wolves, the cricket bureaucrats whose progeny still rule the game." A.H. Kardar came to England in 1946 under the auspices of the Nawab of Pataudi's Indian tourists. It was just before the creation of Pakistan and Kardar appeared as Abdul Hafeez. A free hitting left-hander, he struggled on the soft English pitches of 1946, but still appeared in all three Tests. He remained in England after the tour and went up to Oxford, where he was in the XI for three years. Returning to Lahore, now in Pakistan, he captained his new country in their first 23 Test matches, including the initial tour to England in 1954, when Pakistan won their famous Test victory at The Oval. Later, he was the president of the Pakistan Board of Control. He ruthlessly modernized the running of cricket in Pakistan and was an early advocate of, among other things, neutral umpires in Test cricket. He ultimately resigned as president in protest over government interference in his country's cricketing matters.

1960s

It was a cruel irony that cricket's showpiece match – the annual Lord's Test match – had seen Ramadhin and Valentine's triumph, then, in 1960, saw the tragic humiliation of another young overseas Test bowler, Geoff Griffin of South Africa. The witch-hunt against "chuckers" in the 1950s continued into the '60s. Griffin in the 1960 Lord's Test was continuously no-balled until he had no option but to bowl under-arm in order to complete an over. It was the first time a bowler had ever been no-balled for throwing in a Test in England. His promising career was at an end.

The following year, for totally different reasons, a referendum in South Africa produced a majority in favour of leaving the Commonwealth. Technically, this move stopped South Africa's Test cricket, since only members of the Commonwealth could belong to the ICC and only ICC members could play Test cricket. England, Australia and New Zealand blithely ignored this regulation and Tests between those three countries and South Africa continued as if nothing had happened.

However, the campaign to cut any sporting ties with South Africa over their policy of apartheid was beginning to receive press publicity. In 1964, Basil D'Oliveira, the Cape-Coloured cricketer, began his career in county cricket with Worcestershire; two seasons later

THE LAST AUSTRALIAN BATSMAN IS RUN OUT AND THE TEST IS TIED.

The First Tied Test Match

It was not until the 502nd Test match that a game finished in a tie. The match was Australia v West Indies at Brisbane on 9-14 December 1960. The first two innings were high scoring with both sides evenly matched, with the West Indies, captained by Frank Worrell, batting first and making 453, with Gary Sobers being the one century maker and Alan Davidson taking five wickets. Norman O'Neill hit 181 as Australia replied with 505 all out. The West Indies struggled against Davidson in their second knock, making 284, so Australia required 233 to win. They collapsed to 92 for 6, then Davidson was joined by captain Richie Benaud. The pair took the total to 226: 27 runs wanted with 30 minutes' playing time left. At this point, Davidson was run out by Joe Solomon. Benaud was caught at the wicket off Wes Hall and Wally Grout was then run out. The scores were now level with two balls left and one wicket to fall. Ian Meckiff attempted a suicidal run and Solomon threw down the wicket. The match was tied.

he was in the England team. In 1968-69 England were scheduled to tour South Africa. The team was chosen, but one member, Tom Cartwright, had to withdraw due to injury. The selectors picked D'Oliveira to replace Cartwright. South Africa refused to allow D'Oliveira into their country. England refused to de-select him. The tour was switched from South Africa to Pakistan. That country was riven by student riots and the students used the England v Pakistan Tests as a focal point for their demands. The first Test was continually interrupted by rioters and England quit the tour during the third Test when rioting made it impossible to continue.

The financial problems, which had enveloped county cricket in the 1950s, grew worse in the new decade. A county Knock-Out Cup, first suggested in 1945, at last emerged in 1963 under the sponsorship of Gillette. This was very successful, but 16 one-day county games could not act as anything beyond a sticking plaster over the gaping financial hole. Counties began to schedule three matches to include play on Sundays in order to attract the public. It was illegal to charge spectators at the gate on Sundays, so the public were requested to buy expensive programmes! The next step to bring back the crowds was the introduction of "overseas"

Basil D'Oliveira's selection to tour South Africa in 1968-69 led to the tour's cancellation.

players into county cricket. With some exceptions, cricketers had either to be born in a county or reside there for two years in order to be allowed to play. In 1968, each county was allowed to sign a player without him being thus qualified. It is a moot point whether the counties profited – did the rise in gate receipts equal the cost of the player? In some counties, players' costs were sponsored and therefore there was a financial benefit. A year later, the counties, having got over the problem of gate receipts on Sundays, introduced the "John Player Sunday League". This proved to be of great financial benefit.

Having more or less let sport run itself independently over the years,

the government began to take an interest and, in 1964, the Sports Council was created, its job being to give government grants to individual sporting bodies, provided that each specific sport had a national governing body. To cope with this, cricket created the MCC National Cricket Association, but the Sports Council refused to recognize it. In its place, therefore, was substituted the Test and County Cricket Board and the National Cricket Association. government funding was available from 1968.

The five Test series of the decade between England and Australia saw some intriguing battles, but England failed to win a single one of them.

One tradition that disappeared during the 1960s was the distinction between amateurs and professionals at county level. The famous Gentlemen v Players contests, which had begun as far back as 1806, ended in 1962. In future, all players would be called simply "cricketers".

At a lower level, English schools cricket had always been split between Public Schools and the rest, but finally in 1965 a representative side combining both sections took to the field for the first time.

Another change in the '60s was the recognition of "league" cricket by the Home Counties. Surrey were the first county to set up a Surrey Club League, followed closely by Hertfordshire.

In the West Indies, another shibboleth fell in 1960 when, for the first time, the Test team was not led by a white

Gentlemen v Players (1806-1962)

The Gentlemen opposed the Players at Lord's for the final time in July 1962. It was the 137th such match at headquarters: the Players had won 68, the Gentlemen 41 and 28 were drawn. The Rev. David Sheppard (for the Gentlemen, of course) made the highest individual score; the captain of the Players side was Fred Trueman, who hit a whirlwind 63 to save his team from disaster. The contest ended in a draw.

Matches between Gentlemen and Players had been a feature of the end-of-summer Scarborough Festival since 1885.

In 1857, a match was arranged at The Oval for the first time, a few days prior to the traditional game at Lord's. In the 1930s, it became more and more difficult to gather representative sides for The Oval fixture and, after 1934, no more such matches were staged there.

Apart from Scarborough, other seaside resorts tried similar fixtures, notably Hastings, Bournemouth and Folkestone, but rarely could they be called full-strength representative games. The only double century on either side in the match at Lord's was C.B. Fry's 232 not out in 1903.

player. Frank Worrell was the first of the new line and created great excitement in his first Test as captain when the Test v Australia ended in a tie – a unique event, though no longer so. The era when Ramadhin and Valentine held sway was about to give way to the domination of a galaxy of fast bowlers, commencing with Wes Hall and Charlie Griffith. Griffith was particularly aggressive. His fast yorker was deadly, but in 1961-62 when the Indian team toured West Indies, a bumper from Griffith knocked the Indian captain, Nari Contractor, unconscious and it was touch and go whether he would recover, his skull being fractured –

fortunately, he did, though he never reappeared in Test cricket.

In 1965, the Imperial Cricket Conference changed its name to the International Cricket Conference. It was agreed that non-Commonwealth countries could join and a new type of membership was created – Associate – in order that non-Test-playing countries could also acquire membership. The first three to be elected were United States, Ceylon and Fiji. South Africa did not apply to rejoin. The Netherlands, Denmark, Bermuda and East Africa became Associates in 1966. It was the beginnings of a genuine world body to govern cricket.

1970
Proposed South African tour to England cancelled. Five matches between England and The Rest replace the Test series; Jamaica tour England and play four first-class matches

1971
First limited-overs international – Australia v England at Melbourne; East Pakistan (renamed Bangladesh) ceded from Pakistan

1972
Benson & Hedges limited-overs competition instituted; County Championship reduced to 20 matches per county

1973
New regulations defining first-class matches in Britain, which include the detail that Scotland v Ireland is first-class, but matches by Scotland or Ireland versus any county is not first-class

1974
New regulations limit the first two innings of a County Championship match to 200 overs

1970-71
Limited-overs competition instituted in New Zealand; batting and bowling bonus points introduced in Sheffield Shield and Currie Cup

1972-73
Currie Cup sponsored by South African Breweries; Ceylon is declared a republic and renamed Sri Lanka

1973-74
New Zealand play Test cricket in Australia for first time; Moin-ud-Dowlah ceased to be first-class after this season; Pakistan Under-25s tour Sri Lanka

1970s

The quiet rhythm of Test cricket was to be rudely shattered in the 1970s by a rather loud-mouthed Australian tycoon. While cricket professionals in England did earn a modest, but respectable, income from the game, overseas cricketers were still largely amateur and even Test players, except those who found "winter" employment in England, needed good non-cricketing jobs to survive. Yet Test matches were being given greater and greater publicity via television and the Boards of the Test-playing countries received largish sums from broadcasting rights, which were given almost automatically to the state-owned broadcasting companies – the BBC in the case of England.

In 1976 with the great spectacle of the Centenary Test match on the horizon, Kerry Packer, who ran an independent broadcasting company in Australia, approached the Australian Cricket Board about the right to televise Test cricket. His offer was much higher than the amount which the Australian Broadcasting Commission (ABC) paid. Despite this, the cricket authorities turned their backs on Packer. Packer's reaction, though typical of the man, was apparently unexpected. Secretly, his agents signed up the world's top players – including almost the entire current Australian Test team – to play in a series of "Super-Tests" that he intended to stage and televise during

the 1977-78 Australian summer. To the great embarrassment of the authorities in England and Australia, the two principal cricketers who had organized the signing up of players were Tony Greig and Greg Chappell, the Test captains of the two countries.

The ICC's reaction was to ban everyone who signed for Packer from official Test matches. Packer's company took the ICC to court claiming "restraint of trade" and, after a seven-week hearing, Packer won the court action.

In the season of 1977-78, Packer staged more than 40 matches in Australia, his players being split into three teams – Australia, West Indies and The Rest. The top Test grounds

refused to allow matches by Packer to be played there and he used mainly football stadia. His company had players dressed in coloured clothing and many of the games were floodlit.

Australia did not pick any Packer players for official Tests in 1977-78, so fielding a Second XI, Australia lost a series to India for the first time. The following season, 1978-79, England went to Australia and created a new record, winning no less than five Tests. That season Packer's squad played in the West Indies as well as in Australia and made a reasonable profit for the near-bankrupt West Indian Board. Packer's players had been contracted for three years, but on 30 May 1979, the Australian Board announced that they had granted

Kerry Packer (1937-2005)

Described as one of the toughest and shrewdest business brains of his day, he was regarded as the richest man in Australia who was worth, it was believed, about £3 billion. A compulsive gambler, he was reported to have lost £11 million at Crockford's in 1999 but, on another occasion, won £2.4 million playing blackjack. When his father died in 1974, Kerry Packer assumed control of a huge media empire. Not long afterwards, he determined to get exclusive rights to Test cricket for his television company. When the Cricket Board declined his generous offer, he confounded them by secretly signing up all the best players in Australia and a

goodly sprinkling of those abroad. When detailed talks between Packer and the Board failed to bring about a compromise, Packer walked out, saying, "Now it's every man for himself and the devil take the hindmost."

After two years, for an undisclosed sum of money, the Board conceded exclusive TV rights to Packer and the war was over. Packer continued on his way with bigger and greater business deals and more gambling. In 1991, he had a heart attack but recovered. In 2000, he had a kidney transplant – on both occasions he had been pronounced dead, only to survive. He died on Boxing Day 2005.

The Queen shakes hands with Derek Randall at the Centenary Test at Melbourne.

one of Packer's companies a ten-year contract to televise the official Tests. "Packer's Circus", as it had been dubbed, disbanded. The wages for Test cricketers were substantially increased and ideas such as coloured clothing and floodlighting were soon incorporated into "traditional" international cricket.

That was the major brouhaha in the second half of the decade but, in 1970, another crisis with even more political content occupied the cricket establishment. 1970 was in the schedule as a South African Test tour to England. Led by the Rev. David Sheppard and a young Peter Hain, a group in the autumn of 1969 began a "Stop the Tour" campaign. This anti-apartheid group gathered strength as autumn moved to winter and the government was lobbied. A second group supporting the tour was created. The cricket authorities stood their ground and insisted on the tour going ahead, to the extent that

barbed-wire barriers ringed cricket squares where matches were to be staged. In order to stop protesters interrupting play, matches were to be all-ticket. Finally, the government stepped in and more or less told the cricket authorities to abandon the tour.

In its place a series of "Test" matches between England and The Rest were played – The Rest contained five South Africans who had been on the touring party. This action brought an end to South African Test cricket (a tour to Australia was also aborted) and it was 20 years before South Africa came back into the fold.

With one-day cricket – first the Gillette Cup and then the Player Sunday League – proving so popular with the English public, a natural progression was to create international one-day matches. This occurred by accident rather than design. England toured Australia in

1970-71 with the usual Test matches on the fixture list. However, the first three days of the third Test match scheduled for Melbourne were completely washed out by rain. The officials on both sides met and decided to use the fifth day as a 40-over-a-side one-day game and to add an extra Test match at the end of the tour. This 40-over game is now considered the first one-day international.

When Australia came to England in 1972, three such one-day internationals, sponsored by Prudential, were on the fixture card. The one played at Lord's broke all ground receipt records and, in 1975, the ICC organized the first World Cup.

The matches were one-day 60-overs-a-side games. The six Test-playing countries were invited, together with Sri Lanka and East Africa, to make eight teams in all. West Indies beat Australia in the final at Lord's, another receipts record day. 1979 saw the second World Cup, again in England and again, West Indies won, but this time against England.

In between times, the other Test-playing countries devised one-day competitions to run alongside their traditional first-class fixtures. In England, the two one-day competitions, Gillette and Player League, had a third, sponsored by Benson and Hedges, added in 1972 – to fit this into the summer, the County Championship was reduced to 20 three-day matches per county.

Brian Johnston (1912-94)

Although Brian Johnston's broadcasting lacked the subtlety and depth of John Arlott's, he was, among the general public, the most popular of the broadcasters. Johnston was educated at Eton and Oxford, then served in the Grenadier Guards in the Second World War and made his name on the radio in such programmes as *In Town Tonight* and *Down Your Way*. He was an expert at interviewing ordinary people. His cricket commenting began in television. He lasted 25 years before being unexpectedly sacked in 1970. He then switched to radio on *Test Match Special* and began his endless prep-school jokes, puns and nicknames for his fellow workers. He acquired a considerable female fan base and became notorious for the receipt of chocolate cakes – the contrast to John Arlott could hardly have been greater, but the partnership functioned. Johnston died while on tour with his theatrical performance "An Evening with Johnners" in 1994.

1980

New Code of Laws published; Centenary Test played to mark 100 years of Tests in England

1980-81

Some Sheffield Shield matches arranged for three days; Castle Bowl in South Africa divided into two sections; West Indies v England in Georgetown cancelled for political reasons; Zimbabwe becomes an "independent" cricketing country

1981

Pitches fully covered for County Championship games

1981-82

Rebel England team tour South Africa and play three unofficial Test matches; Sri Lanka play their first Test match v England in Colombo

A colourful Australian side in the field during a one-day international against West Indies at the SCG in 1988.

1982

Fines for slow over-rates increased to £1,000

1982-83

Sheffield Shield now decided on challenge match between the top two states in the table; West Indies and Sri Lanka send "rebel" teams to South Africa; Lancashire and Essex tour South Africa

1983

Number of County Championship matches per team increased to 24

1983-84

Penalty points introduced for slow overs-rates in Ranji Trophy and Shell Cup; top four teams in Currie Cup play a knock-out section to decide champions

1980s

Ian Botham's performance against Australia at Headingley in 1981 has become legendary.

The flamboyant personality of Ian Botham dominated English cricket and indeed the English sporting scene to a greater extent than perhaps any cricketer since W.G. Grace. He was the subject of press headlines throughout his international career from 1977 to 1992. Botham reached the Test double of 1,000 runs and 100 wickets after just 21 Tests. He went on to become the first player to top both 5,000 runs and 300 wickets. In the 1985 season he hit a record 80 sixes and then walked from John O'Groats to Land's End, raising £600,000 for charity. England beat Australia in England in 1981 with Botham hitting the most runs and taking the most wickets. England were again successful against the old enemy in 1985, Botham taking most wickets in the series. Australia, however, were victorious in the 1982-83 series in Australia, but Botham was not fully fit, though no one took more wickets for England than he did and he also held many remarkable catches.

At the start of the decade, the revised Laws came into operation for only the fifth time in 200 years. One point that was altered was the "timed out" law. The rules regarding "unfair" play were also largely tightened. Thought was given to banning the wearing of helmets, which had become increasingly common at the end of the 1970s, both for batsmen and close fielders. However, it was thought that if helmets were banned and a player was seriously injured legal action might result. Matters such as players damaging the pitch, bowlers deliberately wasting time and players showing dissent, all trends that had developed in recent summers, were also brought into the new laws.

On the international stage, Sri Lanka was granted Test-match status in 1981 and played their first Test in the 1981-82 season, playing England in Colombo. England won by seven wickets.

A much greater event on the international scene in the 1980s was the start of unofficial "Test" tours to South Africa. In 1981-82 a party of English cricketers secretly left London for South Africa to play a series of eight matches. When they arrived in South Africa, the Test and County Cricket Board sent them a cable stating that it was not too late to abandon the tour and warning them of the consequences. The team was captained by Geoff Boycott. The players were rumoured to have been paid up to £40,000 each. The TCCB imposed a three-year Test ban on the 15 tourists, but most were offered contracts to play in South Africa for the period of their ban.

The following winter (1982-83), the South African authorities invited first a Sri Lankan team, then a West Indian team to tour. The Sri Lankan cricketers who took up the offer seriously weakened the official Sri Lankan team but, as with England, the financial rewards were enormous. The touring Sri Lankan side hardly offered more than token opposition to the full South African side in the two "Tests". The West Indian team,

C.E.B. Rice (1949–)

Undoubtedly the most talented cricketer of the 20th century not to appear in Test cricket, Clive Rice's career coincided almost exactly with South Africa's isolation from international cricket. He was picked for the South African team to tour Australia in 1971-72, but the tour was cancelled for political reasons. He opted for a career in English cricket, leading Nottinghamshire to the County Championship in 1981 and the Championship plus the NatWest Trophy in 1987. Back in South Africa, he led the most successful Transvaal side of all time: the side won the Currie Cup five times in the 1980s and the One-Day Trophy three times. A brilliant batsman and an excellent bowler, he proved that he was the world's finest all-rounder by winning the Silk Cut Challenge in Taunton in 1984, against such opposition as Kapil Dev and Ian Botham. When South Africa resumed Test cricket in the 1990s he was considered too old, but he did lead his country against India in their first one-day international.

1985
Minimum overs bowled per day in County Championship fixed at 112

1985-86
Goa, Himchal Pradesh and Tripura join Ranji Trophy; Australian "rebel" team tour South Africa; Ireland tour Zimbabwe

1986
Random dope testing introduced for county players

1986-87
Gloucestershire first county to tour Sri Lanka; programme of matches in West Indies Shell Shield reduced for financial reasons

1987
Pitches now only covered at ends and bowlers' run-ups

1987-88
Currie Cup divided into two sections; Australian tour to Sri Lanka cancelled owing to civil unrest; Red Stripe take over sponsorship of West Indies first-class competition

1988
Some County Championship matches arranged for four days

1988-89
Lakspray Trophy in Sri Lanka ruled first-class; England's tour to India cancelled for political reasons

It may have been more suited to some climates around the world than others, but floodlit cricket proved a real hit with the fans. Here is a shot of the SCG under lights.

which was captained by Lawrence Rowe and included the fearsome fast bowler Sylvester Clarke, was a different kettle of fish and their series was tied. This tour caused much controversy in the West Indies and all 17 players were banned for life both from Test cricket and first-class cricket in the West Indies.

Such was the overall strength of West Indian cricket in the mid-1980s, that the West Indies under Clive Lloyd toured England in 1984 and won the Test series five matches to nil. It was the first time such an overall success had been achieved by a touring side to England – even Botham, who took most wickets for England and came second in the batting table, could not save his country. The West Indian strength lay in their battery of fast bowlers – Joel Garner, Malcolm Marshall and Michael Holding. Sides had often contained a pair of formidable bowlers, but this trio – and they did have Courtney Walsh as back-up – had never been experienced before.

Between 1976 and 1990, England lost seven successive Test series against West Indies. Similarly, Australia lost five successive series between 1983 and 1993. It is perhaps surprising given this complete domination by West Indies that, having won the World Cup in 1979, they were beaten in India in the 1983 final and in 1987 they did not even reach the final.

Of the other Test-playing countries, the most successful was New Zealand, who possessed the great all-rounder Richard Hadlee. In 1983, New Zealand at last won a Test in England and in 1985-86 they were triumphant in Australia, winning a Test series against their neighbours for the first time – New Zealand and the other lesser Test-playing countries were catching up to the standard set by England and Australia.

On the English domestic front, it was agreed that all pitches should be covered for Championship matches – a move fiercely argued, since the batsmen would have greater advantage and to reinforce this notion, in 1989 it was announced that counties would be deducted 25 points if they produced a "poor" pitch. The campaign to change Championship games from three-day to four-day began and, in 1988, each county was instructed to play six four-day and 16 three-day matches.

In 1987, for the first time, the World Cup was not staged in England. The matches were played in India and Pakistan, with the final in Calcutta. Great excitement came when both Pakistan and India reached the semi-finals, but to the disappointment of the fans, neither reached the final.

MCC Bicentenary Match, 1987

This five-day game was arranged to celebrate the 200th anniversary of Thomas Lord opening his first cricket ground. The MCC opposed the Rest of the World, the former being selected from current players appearing in the County Championship. The Rest, captained by Allan Border, contained four West Indians, three each from Pakistan and India, and Border from Australia. The MCC XI comprised six English players, two from the West Indies and one each from New Zealand, India and South Africa. Two notable cricketers were absent: Ian Botham withdrew through injury and Viv Richards withdrew in order to play for Rishton in the Lancashire League. The MCC, batting first, made 455 for 5. Captain Gatting hit 179 and Gooch made 117. In response, Sunil Gavaskar, "The Little Master", hit 188, largely in partnership with the famous Pakistan captain, Imran Khan – the pair, of course, being deadly rivals when Pakistan oppose India. The Rest reached 421 for 7. In the second innings MCC scored 318 for 6, with Gordon Greenidge making 122 and, with one day to play, the Rest wanted 340 to win with nine wickets in hand. Unfortunately, rain washed out the final day. Despite the drawn result, the match was a testament to the fact that cricket can still be played keenly but with a sporting spirit – the world's finest cricketers entertained a knowledgeable crowd.

1990
R.J. Hadlee retires with record 431 Test wickets

1990-91
England A tour to Pakistan abandoned after one match because of the Gulf War; a court case between two teams delays Ranji Trophy for six weeks; the two racially divided governing cricket bodies in South Africa are merged

1991
Victoria come to England to play county champions Essex

1991-92
South Africa play their first one-day internationals; Zimbabwe enter Test cricket, playing India in Harare; South Africa tour West Indies for first time

1992
Durham admitted to County Championship

1992-93
Namibia tour South Africa for first time; New Zealand tour to Sri Lanka cut short owing to assassination of Sri Lankan naval commander

1993
County Championship altered to 17 four-day matches per team; no-balls counted as two runs in County Championship

1993-94
Duleep Trophy changed from knock-out to league basis; Logan Cup raised to first-class status in Zimbabwe; B.C. Lara creates new Test record, 375, for West Indies v England in St John's; A.R. Border retires with Test record 11,174 runs

1994
Square-leg umpires to inspect ball to prevent tampering; B.C. Lara (below) creates new first-class record, 501 not out, for Warwicks v Durham at Edgbaston

1990s

As the game of cricket lurched from one scandal to another through the 1990s, the England Test team sunk to its lowest point since Test cricket had expanded in the inter-war period. Of the 109 Tests played by the birthplace of cricket between 1990 and 1999, no less than 44 were lost and only 27 won. Only against New Zealand did wins exceed losses – against Australia there were five victories to measure against 16 defeats.

Radical solutions were required and, in 1994, discussions to create an English Cricket Board to replace the Test and County Cricket Board and the National Cricket Association began. On 1 January 1997 the change actually took place. Lord MacLaurin, the former head of the supermarket chain Tesco, became chairman of the ECB. A document called "Raising the Standard" was issued the following year – the blueprint for the future of English (and Welsh) cricket. Among the ideas was one to divide the counties into three "conferences". The programme for each county would involve 14 four-day matches and 28 one-day games. The scheme nose-dived before it put its head above the parapet. Dividing the counties into two divisions of nine – Durham had been created as the 18th first-class county in 1992 - was agreed, with the "Sunday" league being split in 1999.

At club level all counties were urged to create a "Premier" league with feeder leagues at a lower level. These came into being during the final years of the decade, despite major problems with the old established leagues in the north.

The Test arena also changed. South Africa were re-admitted to the ICC then, in 1992, Zimbabwe were given Test status. In 1997 both Kenya and Bangladesh were raised to the level of being able to play official one-day internationals. In fact one-day internationals became almost meaningless: in 1997 no less than 110 were staged and it was impossible for the general public to follow the results in any detail – apart from the usual venues, some games were played in Singapore and Toronto, adding to the annual one-day contests in Sharjah.

Australia succeeded West Indies as the unofficial champions of the game. Led by Allan Border and with batsmen such as the Waugh twins,

How the County Championship Grew

In 1992, Durham became the 18th county to compete in the County Championship, but few can name the county who dropped out and who were never reinstated. The details since 1864 are as follows:

1864	**The following counties were considered to be competing for the title: Cambridgeshire, Hampshire, Kent, Middlesex, Nottinghamshire, Surrey, Sussex and Yorkshire**
1865	**Lancashire joined**
1868-69	**Hampshire dropped out**
1870	**Gloucestershire joined, Hampshire rejoined, Cambridgeshire dropped out**
1871	**Derbyshire joined, Cambridgeshire rejoined, Hampshire dropped out**
1872	**Cambridgeshire dropped out**
1875	**Hampshire rejoined**
1879	**Hampshire dropped out**
1880	**Hampshire rejoined**
1882	**Somerset joined**
1886	**Hampshire and Somerset dropped out**
1888	**Derbyshire dropped out**
1891	**Somerset rejoined**
1895	**Derbyshire and Hampshire rejoined; Essex, Leicestershire and Warwickshire joined**
1899	**Worcestershire joined**
1905	**Northamptonshire joined**
1921	**Glamorgan joined**

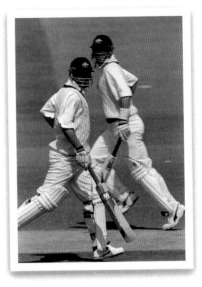

Twins Steve and Mark Waugh were outstanding for Australia in the 1990s.

Steve and Mark, plus Mark Taylor and David Boon, then the emergence of Shane Warne, the brilliant leg-break bowler, Australia brushed aside the opposition. As has been indicated, England lost every rubber against Australia in the 1990s.

Although West Indies cricket was largely in the doldrums, one outstanding cricketer appeared from Trinidad, Brian Lara. His Test debut was in 1990-91. In April 1994 in St John's, Antigua, Lara created a new Test record, scoring 375 against England. In June of the same year, playing for Warwickshire v Durham at Edgbaston, he broke the long-standing first-class batting record by hitting 501 not out.

Across the world in Sri Lanka another phenomenal cricketer was learning his trade – Muttiah Muralitharan. An off-spinner with a very flexible wrist action, he baffled the best of batsmen. Later in their careers, he and Warne were to chase each other for the honour of the most wickets in a Test career. However, Muralitharan's bowling caused eyebrows to be raised and, in 1995, he was no-balled for throwing in a Test at Melbourne. The ICC, however, studied his action and declared it legal.

Another area of bowling dispute was players roughening up one side of the ball in order to help "swing". This escalated to major proportions in 1994, when the England captain, Mike Atherton, was accused of forcing soil into the seam of the ball to help "reverse-swing".

During the early 1990s, rumours of bribery of players to affect match results and players betting on their own side to lose matches spread throughout the game. This exploded when three Australian Test players stated that Salim Malik, the then Pakistan captain, had tried to bribe them to fix a match. The ICC should have been the authority to deal with these allegations, but they took no action. An investigation was set up under a Pakistani judge, but the Australians refused to travel to Pakistan to give evidence. The enquiry failed to reach a satisfactory conclusion. A Code of Conduct was introduced banning players from betting. Gambling, however, was rife in the Gulf States and in Mumbai (Bombay) rumours and counter-rumours of misdeeds continued to surface.

Three World Cup competitions were held during the decade. Australia and New Zealand were the hosts in 1992. Nine countries took part – the eight Test-playing nations plus Zimbabwe. Pakistan beat England in the final, which was played on the recently revamped Melbourne Ground. A crowd of 90,000, the most ever to watch a one-day international, attended. Pakistan's success was largely due to Imran Khan, the captain, who handpicked the team – satisfyingly Imran hit the highest score in the game.

The 1996 World Cup was the second staged on the sub-continent but, unlike its predecessor, the logistics were muddled. The semi-

The Australians win the World Cup for the second time with victory in 1999, beating Pakistan in the final after a tie with South Africa in the semi-final.

final between India and Sri Lanka at Eden Gardens, Calcutta, ended in a serious riot. Sri Lanka made 251 for 8, batting first. India reached 98 for 1, then no less than seven wickets fell for the addition of 22 more runs. The crowd exploded, bottles were thrown and seating set alight. Later, an armed guard had to protect the house of the Indian captain. The players had left the field, an effort was made to continue the game, but then the referee decided to award the game to Sri Lanka and, amazingly, the ceremony of presenting medals to the winners went on as if nothing untoward had occurred. Sri Lanka beat Australia in the final in Lahore.

The 1999 competition returned to England. The first World Cup final in 1975 had lasted nearly ten hours. The 1999 final was a one-sided anti-climax. Pakistan were dismissed for 132 and Australia took just 20.1 overs to reach the target. Pakistan may have been embarrassed by their performance in the final, but the hosts, England, were even more so, since they did not enter the "Super-Six" stage, which involved the six most successful countries during the group matches. England, therefore, were ranked with Sri Lanka, Kenya, West Indies, Bangladesh and Scotland. If England Test fortunes were at the bottom, so were their one-day aspirations.

2000

New Code of Laws introduced; County Championship, sponsored by PPP Healthcare, is divided into two divisions of nine teams, each team playing 16 matches; Zimbabwe's first Test tour to England

2000-01

W.J. Cronje, South African captain, banned for life; C.A. Walsh retires with record 519 Test wickets; Bangladesh play first Test v India in Dhaka; Green Delta National League elevated to first-class status in Bangladesh

W.J Cronje

2001

England's National Cricket Academy founded; County Championship sponsored by CricInfo, Yorkshire win title after 33-year gap

2001-02

Sharjah stages Test cricket for first time, Pakistan playing West Indies in two matches; Pakistan tour Bangladesh for first time; ICC strips South Africa v India Test at Centurion of its status, when India refuse to allow M.H. Denness as referee

2002

Last season of Benson & Hedges Cup competition in England; Sri Lanka have full tour to England for first time

2002-03

World Cup staged in South Africa, Zimbabwe and Kenya, but England declined to play in Zimbabwe and New Zealand declined to play in Kenya; Bangladesh play Test matches in Australia for first time

2003

Chester-le-Street stages its first Test, England v Zimbabwe; Twenty/20 county competition inaugurated in England; first bowler officially recorded as bowling at 100mph, Shoaib Akhtar (right)

21st Century

After the depressing England record through the 1990s, the ECB began its campaign to turn fortunes around with the appointment of Duncan Fletcher as coach. A former Zimbabwe ODI player, he had successfully coached Western Province, South Africa A and Glamorgan. His initial job was to take England on tour to South Africa in 1999-2000, where they lost a close-fought series 2-1. For the summer of 2000, the ECB introduced the next plank of their strategy by bringing in "central contracts" for the top dozen England players. This effectively meant that international considerations took preference over any demands on the players by their individual counties. England won the 2000 home series against West Indies, 3-1, but West Indies cricket was in disarray. In the winter of 2000-01, England played Tests toured Pakistan and Sri Lanka and won both series. The major trial of Fletcher and central contracts came in 2001, when Australia visited England. Australia won 4-1. The ECB appointed the Australian Rod Marsh to run a National Academy, based on those in Australia and South Africa.

In the winter of 2001-02, there were tours to India and New Zealand. The 11 September attack made players edgy regarding plane travel and touring India. Players selected were given the option of withdrawing. In the event, Andy Caddick and Robert Croft were the only two who declined the trip. India won their series and the New Zealand series was drawn, with one win each. India came to England for the summer and this series was drawn, but England did beat Sri Lanka 2-0.

In the next serious encounter, in Australia, 2002-03, Australia won 4-1, but the atmosphere was soured by excessive "sledging" and two Australians were reprimanded for their conduct. McGrath, Warne and Gillespie were the home side's major weapons. South Africa came to England in 2003. An exciting series was drawn with two wins each. Shaun Pollock was the outstanding all-rounder of the year.

2004 saw the fruition of England's efforts over the last four or so summers. West Indies were beaten at home 3-0, with Graham Thorpe the star batsman, and Steve Harmison and Matthew Hoggard the principal bowlers. Brian Lara created a new Test record, hitting 400 not out at St Johns. New Zealand and West Indies then came to England – England won all seven Test matches, with Andrew Flintoff joining Harmison, Thorpe and Hoggard as England's triumphant players. The 2004-05 trip to South Africa saw another great series, this time England came out on top.

Having done well, could England beat Australia in 2005? The interest in the series was quiet extraordinary – tickets for the Tests were sold out well in advance. Australia won the first

England's Cricket Annuals

The 146th edition of *Wisden Cricketers' Almanack* was published in 2009. Wisden has the longest unbroken run of any sporting annual in the world. Occasionally rivals have been published, but in recent times they have quickly faded; that wasn't always the case, though. When John Wisden, a Sussex cricketer, opened a shop selling sports goods, he decided to issue a small book advertising his goods and containing some data on cricket and other matters. That was in 1864. He was not breaking new ground, since he was competing with *The Guide to Cricketers*, edited by Frederick Lillywhite. In 1864, the 19th edition of the *Guide* was being issued. However, Fred Lillywhite died in 1866. Two other Lillywhite annuals then emerged but, by 1901, both had gone. The secret of *Wisden*'s success lay in the fact that he published full scores of all major matches, whereas the rivals contented themselves with potted scores.

The other long-standing present day annual is *Playfair*, which began life in 1895 as the *Star and Morning Leader Annual* and which, later, was taken over as the *Daily News Annual* and then the *News Chronicle Annual*. The principal content of these annuals is, and was, a list of brief biographies of current English cricketers.

Andrew "Freddie" Flintoff with the Ashes urn and a cigar after the 2005 series.

2003-04
B.C. Lara creates new Test record, 400 not out, West Indies v England at St John's; Australian Cricket Board renames itself "Cricket Australia"; South Africa introduce Pro 20 Competition; England A take part in the Duleep Trophy

2004
ICC Intercontinental Cup founded, a first-class competition for 12 non-Test-playing countries. Scotland beat Canada in the final in Sharjah

2004-05
First Twenty/20 international, Australia v Pakistan

2005
ICC move their headquarters to Dubai; England regain Ashes (right) after what is considered best five-Test series ever

2005-06
B.C. Lara creates new Test career batting record, overtaking A.R. Border

2006-07
S.K. Warne becomes the first bowler to take 700 Test wickets; Australia beat England 5-0, the first Ashes whitewash since 1920-21

2007
Australia beat Sri Lanka in near darkness in final to retain ICC Cricket World Cup

2007-08
India launches new franchised team tournament, the IPL

2008
India defeat Pakistan in inaugural World Cup Twenty20 final

2008-09
England lose $20 million winner-takes-all Twenty20 match against Stanford All-Stars in Antigua

2010-11
England take the Ashes

Test by 239 runs, owing to the bowling of McGrath and Warne. McGrath was injured in the warm-up just before the second Test and couldn't take part. England won by two runs. The third game was a nail-biting draw, with the two captains showing their talents – Michael Vaughan hit 166 and Ricky Ponting 156. England dominated the fourth match, though some brilliant bowling by Brett Lee and Shane Warne nearly caused an upset as England hit off the 129 runs required in the final innings. Could Australia win the final Test and draw the series? The game was even after the first two innings. England's batsmen in general made a cow's heel of their second innings, saved by Kevin Pietersen's 158, which caused the game to be drawn, giving England back the Ashes. Andrew Flintoff and Shane Warne were deservedly joint Men of the Series. The England team toured central London in an open-topped bus the following day and vast crowds assembled in Trafalgar Square to cheer the team.

Following the Ashes success, England faced two tours in the winter of 2005-06. The first was to Pakistan. The squad which had beaten Australia suffered dramatic losses through injury and the series against Pakistan was lost. Then came the series against India – Michael Vaughan, the captain, and Marcus Trescothick, his deputy, both had to withdraw. Flintoff was appointed captain and inspired the team which, having lost one Test, won the final game in Mumbai to tie the series, their first win in India for 20

years. In 2006, England beat Pakistan, tied a series with Sri Lanka, but totally failed to make any impression in the 2006-07 Ashes series, with Australia winning all five Tests.

There were several scandals off the field. Two Test captains, Hansie Cronje of South Africa and Mohammad Azharuddin of India, were both investigated by a commission set up specifically to look at the matter. They were both found to have been involved in match fixing, working in conjunction with a bookmaker called M.K. Gupta. The ICC set up an Anti-Corruption Unit under Sir Paul Condon to check on any possible future problems with regard to players being bribed or betting on matches. "Referees" were appointed to monitor each international and to take appropriate action if players

breached the ICC Code of Conduct. The ICC itself was crawling out from under the shadow of the MCC at Lord's and decided for tax and cost reasons to move to Dubai in 2005.

England's domestic scene was becoming chaotic with the County Championship effectively cut into two, with the new Twenty20 taking out almost a month in midseason. This new competition was a huge success, with sell-out crowds everywhere, including 27,000 fans at Lord's for a night game between Middlesex and Surrey. But having led the way in this short form of cricket, the ECB was usurped by the Board of Cricket Control in India. The BCCI took the concept a step further and their IPL series - featuring regional franchises and players picked at auction - did everything the English

version did, but with more pizzazz. A team world championship was backed by the Indian, Australian and South African cricket authorities. The ECB prevaricated and lost out on a multi-million dollar bonanza.

On a less happy note, Zimbabwe's political situation resulted in the best players being ignored and the ICC excluded Zimbabwe from Test cricket. The limited overs teams took some fearful beatings too.

As the decade came to an end, the old order was changing. India and South Africa won Test series in Australia. The retirement of seven of the 11 regulars who dominated most of the previous dozen years proved to be too much to overcome for the Baggy Green. It set up the 2009 Ashes series nicely for an England win.

Betting Scandals

In the 1990s the cricket world was rocked by a series of betting scandals. These were severely dealt with by the authorities and several well-known cricketers including the South African captain, Hansie Cronje, were banned from the game for life. Others receiving life bans were Salim Malik, Azharuddin and Ajay Sharma, all in 2000. For a time the betting scandal problems died away, but in 2010 three Pakistani cricketers were accused of receiving money for "spot-betting" - bowling (or arranging to have bowled) no-balls at specific points in the England v Pakistan Test at The Oval. The three were found guilty in February 2011 and effectively each received a five-year ban. The players were Mohammad Asif, Mohammad Amir (pictured above) and the Pakistan captain, Salman Butt.

INDIAN PREMIER LEAGUE 2011

Right: **Chris Gayle of Royal Challengers Bangalore was the top scorer in the competition with 608 runs.**
Far right: **S.L. Malinga took a total of 28 wickets (av 13.39) for Mumbai Indians.**
Below: **Chennai Super Kings celebrate their 2011 IPL final win.**

Opposite: **Mike Hussey (left) and Murali Vijay set new standards with the bat, compiling an IPL record first wicket stand in the final.**

The four sides that topped the Indian Premier League in 2011 after playing 14 matches each were Bangalore, Chennai, Mumbai and Kolkata. Chennai Super Kings totally outplayed Royal Challengers Bangalore in the final to win their second title in as many years but did have two key advantages – they were playing on their home ground

and, only the evening before, Royal Challengers had played a gruelling game in the third qualifying match against Mumbai Indians.

Super Kings' openers, Mike Hussey and Murali Vijay, found no problems in the pitch and few in the bowling as the pair compiled a record first wicket stand of 159. Hussey was the first to go, with 63, while Vijay reached 95.

In fact, the first wicket did not fall until the fifteenth over.

Needing 206 to win, Royal Challengers's hopes rested on the prolific batting of Chris Gayle (the highest scorer in the IPL this season). When he was dismissed for a duck, the team seemed to lose heart and the game slipped away, much to the delight of the partisan crowd.

2011 FINAL

CHENNAI SUPER KINGS 205 FOR 5
(VIJAY 95, GAYLE 2-34)

ROYAL CHALLENGERS BANGALORE 147 FOR 8
(TIWARY 42 NOT OUT, ASHWIN 3-16)

CHENNAI SUPER KINGS WON BY 58 RUNS

PREVIOUS WINNERS:
2008   RAJASTHAN ROYALS
2009   DECCAN CHARGERS
2010   CHENNAI SUPER KINGS

2 DOMESTIC CRICKET

Wherever English people settled, cricket went with them. English soldiers, merchants and missionaries played the game in most countries of the world. In Europe, the locals ignored the strange rituals, as did the Chinese and Japanese in the Far East, but in India, Pakistan, Ceylon (now Sri Lanka) and the West Indies things were different.

ENGLAND

The owners of the great estates in the South East of England, when they became involved in cricket and staged matches against each other, named the sides they raised after the county in which they resided. At the same time, a town side opposing another, but from a different county, often entitled the match as one between two counties, rather than two towns, in order to bolster the standing of the match. The fashion of using county titles, therefore, was established long before such organizations as county clubs existed. With large sums wagered on these county matches, rules were established as regards the status of players qualified to play - bona fide resident or born inside the county boundaries was the usual agreed condition.

Following the famous Kent versus England match in 1744, county patrons' ultimate ambition for their team was to beat the Rest of England. Surrey, Sussex, Kent and Hampshire all aspired to this great achievement; so much so that in the first two decades of the 19th century a county versus the Rest was virtually the only major county contest - actual inter-county games were unfashionable.

In the early 1820s, however, James Ireland took over the old Brighton cricket ground, which had been laid out for the Prince of

Below: **Early forms of competitive cricket in England attracted large crowds.**

Opposite: **A Frizzell County Championship match between Worcestershire and Hampshire at the picturesque New Road ground in Worcester in 2003.**

In the 1830s, the Nottingham team, which had beaten every side in the Midlands, joined the inter-county contest by challenging Sussex. In 1845, Surrey finally got its act together, formed a county club and established its home at Kennington Oval. Sussex had become a county club in 1839 and Nottingham's county club first emerged in 1841. Thus individual patrons raising and running county sides had given way to groups of subscribers putting up money to pay for players and their expenses for away games. The extensive space the newspapers of the 1830s and 1840s devoted to

The Nottinghamshire XI of 1884. Increased newspaper coverage reflected the growing popularity of the inter-county games.

Wales (later George IV). He believed that money could be made staging matches between Sussex and Kent and, after much disappointment, he managed to set up home and away fixtures in 1825. With the Hambledon Club having folded in the 1790s and the famous cricketers who made up that club's Hampshire team all gone, and with Surrey lacking any central organization, Sussex and Kent were the only major cricketing counties which could field good-class teams. So Ireland's idea caught on and each season from 1825, Sussex and Kent battled it out for the County Championship.

these inter-county games gives an indication of their importance.

In 1846, however, William Clarke, captain of Nottinghamshire and founder of Trent Bridge, engaged the leading players of the day for a side which was to become known as the All England XI. At a stroke, he deprived the major counties of their "stars" and within a year or two had built up a full fixture list for his England team, playing what amounted to exhibition matches in whatever town would pay his expenses. The star players preferred Clarke's team to their county side simply because Clarke offered

full-time employment through the summer, whereas the county teams arranged only a handful of games.

It took a dozen or so years for the craze of what were called wandering professional XIs (there were in time rivals to Clarke's outfit) to reach its peak. Then inter-county cricket not only re-emerged but increased rapidly. The 1860s saw the creation of clubs for Glamorgan, Gloucestershire, Worcestershire, Lancashire, Middlesex, Somerset and Yorkshire (of the present day first-class counties) as well as a goodly number of clubs among the lesser counties.

Not that all the seven listed suddenly began to challenge Kent, Nottinghamshire, Surrey and Sussex for the title of "champion county" – only Lancashire, Middlesex and Yorkshire rose to first-class rank immediately on the creation of a county organization. The romanticism surrounding Hampshire, fuelled by tales of the great Hambledon days, meant that various patrons and groups made attempts to raise Hampshire sides, but usually with dire results. Derbyshire was created as a county club in 1871, but struggled to produce a worthwhile side; in contrast, Cambridgeshire had a worthwhile team in the 1860s, but failed to create a satisfactory county club.

With all these sides, it became impractical to decide which county was the best on a challenge basis, so the press began making up crude league tables.

COUNTY CRICKET

Since cricket at this time was the only popular team ball game with nationally, indeed internationally, recognized laws and in England was the major participatory game, both for playing and watching, the general public had an enormous interest in which county, in each season, was the best. In 1873, after some years of dispute, it was decided to lay down clearly the qualification rules for county cricketers; players had been taking advantage of the loose rule that they could play for county of residence or of birth and had in some cases played for both in the same season. This duality was stopped and a more careful record was kept to see that players genuinely resided in a county.

In the same year, the MCC decided to stage a knock-out county competition. Only one match was played, however, before the scheme collapsed. The two main reasons for its failure were, first that all matches were fixed to be played at Lord's and, second, that by the very nature of a knock-out competition players would not know whether they were required on a given match day until each round had been played. Most professional players had signed agreements with local clubs, which meant they could not be released willy-nilly to play for other teams, but only for set county and major matches on dates that were fixed.

The press continued to decide on the county champion and on how the league tables were presented each year, through the 1870s and into the 1880s. The situation was not very satisfactory, especially since there was no hard-and-fast rule as to which counties were included in the results as shown in a league table of top teams. Somerset, Hampshire and Derbyshire were the three sides which caused the press most problems.

In 1887, the editor of *Wisden's Cricketers' Almanack* decided to take a firm line. He cut out the three counties noted above and formulated a new "points" system. To his embarrassment, in 1889 his system resulted in a three-way tie at the head of a table which contained just eight counties: Gloucestershire, Kent, Lancashire, Yorkshire, Middlesex, Nottinghamshire, Surrey and Sussex. The counties themselves decided to act and, for 1890, devised a new "points" system, though they kept to the eight-county league. Somerset were particularly upset at being excluded; and the following year simply forced their way into the league by arranging matches with the top counties.

The *Wisden* editor then came up with the idea of creating three leagues of eight teams each with promotion and relegation, but any

England's legendary all-rounder Ian Botham moved from Worcestershire to Durham to aid the new county's cause when they gained first-class status in 1992.

hope of this sensible arrangement collapsed in 1895 when Derbyshire, Essex, Hampshire, Leicestershire and Warwickshire were all given a place in the "County Championship". All the other counties with teams that wanted to play competitive county cricket then joined together to form a separate Minor Counties' Cricket Association. The architect of this plan was Worcestershire's secretary, P.H. Foley, and it began in 1895.

In effect, this pattern of county cricket – First-Class County Championship and Minor Counties Championship – has remained unaltered ever since. No county has been demoted from first-class to minor, but Worcestershire (in 1899), Northamptonshire (six years later), Glamorgan (1921) and Durham (1992) have all joined the top grade.

For the first two decades of inter-county games, which involved only Kent, Nottinghamshire and Sussex, Kent was the predominant shire. Their supporters had persuaded the greatest batsman of the day, Fuller Pilch, to move from East Anglia and play for them. In the 1820s, bowling style switched from under-arm to round-arm and Pilch was the first batsman to master thoroughly the new style. The county also possessed the best bowler in Alfred Mynn. Sussex's answer to these players was William Lillywhite, uncle of the first England Test captain. Lillywhite was 30 years old before he came into his own as a slow-medium round-arm bowler – and he was 60 when he played his final game for his county. Nottinghamshire had cunning under-arm bowler William Clarke, and an elegant batsman in Joe Guy, but they were no match for Kent.

A combination of events in 1844 and 1845 led first to the conversion of a market garden into the Kennington Oval Cricket Ground and then to the formation of Surrey County Cricket Club. Within a few years, this new club had thoroughly shaken the three senior counties and the 1850s belonged to Surrey.

This Championship side was characterized by its all-round strength, rather than reliance on one or two stars. Tom Lockyer kept wicket, William Caffyn was the all-rounder and Julius Caesar of Godalming the principal batsman. Heathfield Stephenson, the captain of the first side to Australia, was another all-rounder, while George Griffiths was the tearaway fast bowler who hit sixes. In 1864, Surrey won six of their eight championship games, drawing the other two. No one seeing the side that year could dream that 23 years would elapse before Surrey regained the title.

Next it was the turn of Nottinghamshire to hold centre stage. Between 1865 and 1886, they were champions 14 times. In Alfred Shaw and Fred Morley they possessed the finest pair of bowlers in England; Billy Barnes and Wilfred Flowers were two all-rounders – the former was the first professional to achieve the "double" of 1,000 runs and 100 wickets in the same season. A succession of brilliant batsmen headed the run-getting. George Parr

of Radcliffe-on-Trent succeeded Fuller Pilch as the best professional batsman in England, then Richard Daft, born in Nottingham, took over the crown, to be followed in his turn by Arthur Shrewsbury, who was to become the first man to reach 1,000 Test runs. Rather like the Surrey side of 1864, the Nottinghamshire team of 1886, having won the Championship, faded away and, apart from the infamous triple tie of 1889, Nottinghamshire had to wait until 1907 for their next success.

THE THREE GRACES

In covering briefly the 20 years from 1865 onwards, one fact has been omitted and it is an Everest of an omission. A 16-year-old youth named William Gilbert Grace appeared in his first first-class match in 1865 – by the 1880s, he was to vie with W.E. Gladstone as the best-known Englishman.

Born in a village near Bristol, he effectively belonged to no major county – Gloucestershire did not really exist in cricketing terms in 1865. His family remedied this shortcoming by single-handedly creating Gloucestershire County Cricket Club. Grace had two brothers, E.M. and G.F., both by any standards brilliant cricketers, but both played in the shadow of W.G. – as did everyone else. Gloucestershire played their first first-class, inter-county game in 1870; in 1873 they were acclaimed as the joint champions with Nottinghamshire. The county of the Graces, as they were quickly christened, retained the title in 1874, lost it to Nottinghamshire in 1875, but regained it in 1876 and 1877. Too much depended on W.G. Grace and, though he continued to lead the county until deposed in 1899, Gloucestershire never again ended a season on top of the table. A peculiarity of the Gloucestershire side of the 1870s was that it contained only amateurs, whereas

Herbert Sutcliffe and Percy Holmes take the plaudits after breaking the first-wicket stand record. The pair put on 555 runs for Yorkshire against Essex at Lyton in 1932.

Nottinghamshire generally fielded a side made up of all-professionals.

Throughout this period, Sussex and Kent, the oldest counties, went through some hard times; Yorkshire could field a good side, but their professionals were a wayward lot; Lancashire tied for the title with Nottinghamshire in 1879 and captured it in their own right in 1881, when most of Nottinghamshire's top professionals were on strike; Middlesex, through their London connections, had some fine amateurs qualified by residence or

birth, but rarely managed to field a full-strength side; Derbyshire and Hampshire flirted on the fringes, without causing the top counties much trouble.

The late 1880s saw Surrey return to the fore. They were champions every year from 1887 to 1895 – except 1893. Walter Read and Maurice Read, unrelated, were Surrey's principal middle-order batsmen; Bobby Abel opened the innings, while George Lohmann, an outstanding medium-fast bowler, was partnered by Bill Lockwood in the attack. The

County Championship – especially in the years when Australia did not tour England – drew enormous crowds for the top matches. It was at this time that the tradition of Lancashire playing Yorkshire and of Nottinghamshire meeting Surrey over the Whitsun and August Bank Holiday weekends was established.

THE SLEEPING GIANT AWAKENS

The decade of the 1890s saw the sleeping giant of cricket finally realize its potential. In Lord Hawke, Yorkshire had found a leader who was capable of instilling some discipline into the professional ranks – one or two notable players were warned and then consigned to the scrapheap, but Yorkshire had ample reserves. Although, like all teams, the White Rose county had its less successful summers, for the next 70 years Yorkshire was the one side that was always feared.

Yorkshire's power base was founded on twin all-rounders: two complementary characters whose records were the equal of anyone (except of course W.G.) who had participated in the game of cricket. George Hirst of Kirkheaton is the only man to score 2,000 runs and take 200 wickets in a single summer – when asked what he felt like, having reached this peak, he is reported as saying "tired". Wilfred Rhodes, Hirst's partner, and fellow left-arm bowler – and also from Kirkheaton – is the only man to take more than 4,000 first-class wickets. His batting was almost as impressive with 39,969 runs. He achieved the "double" 16 times to Hirst's 14. Not satisfied with two outstanding all-rounders, the county possessed a third in the amateur F.S. Jackson, but business commitments and his service in the Boer War meant that he was not always available for his county. Jackson captained England to Ashes victory in 1905 but, with

The art of captaincy. Mike Brearley led England to Ashes success in 1981 and also Middlesex to four County Championships between 1976 and 1982.

Lord Hawke in office, was never Yorkshire's official leader.

In the period up to 1914, despite Yorkshire's great superiority, the county did not take the title in the way Nottinghamshire and Surrey had earlier. Lancashire and Middlesex were allowed their turn and Nottinghamshire won in 1907. Even Warwickshire took a turn in 1911, but the strongest rival to Yorkshire in the years leading up to the First World War was Kent.

Lord Harris, one of the greatest figures in English cricket, had devoted himself to the revival of Kent cricket. Cricketers such as Blythe and Woolley made the county once more a stronghold of the game. A comment must be made on Warwickshire's single success, due almost entirely to their captain Frank Foster who topped both batting and bowling averages.

The 21 years between the wars might be described as a second War of the Roses; Yorkshire won

12 championships, Lancashire five, Middlesex two, Nottinghamshire and Derbyshire once each. Yorkshire boasted a team of stars, from opening batsmen Herbert Sutcliffe and Percy Holmes through to Hedley Verity and Bill Bowes. In the late 1930s came Len Hutton and Ellis Robinson. Lancashire had Ernest Tyldesley as their batting stalwart, Dick Tyldesley as the principal slow bowler, as well as Eddie Paynter and Cyril Washbrook.

Middlesex's years were 1920 and 1921, with Patsy Hendren and Jack Hearne; Nottinghamshire, always a formidable batting side, won in 1929 when Harold Larwood and Bill Voce were at the top.

Derbyshire also owed their championship to the emergence of some sharp bowlers, Bill Copson and Alf Pope in particular. When cricket returned to normal after the Second World War, Yorkshire were again champions but, after years of modest returns, Surrey came back with a vengeance. Led by the inspiring Stuart Surridge, the county had a perfect attack. In 1953, for example, the four Surrey bowlers, Alec Bedser, Peter Loader, Jim Laker and Tony Lock, were all in the top ten in the English bowling averages. Laker (off spin) and Lock (left arm) were the slower bowlers, while Bedser and Loader opened. Surrey shared the title with Lancashire in 1950, then won it outright for seven successive years commencing 1952.

Yorkshire climbed back in 1959 and gained seven of the next ten titles. In those 20 or so post-war years, three of the former also-rans had their moments of glory: Glamorgan won in 1948 and 1969, Worcestershire in 1964 and 1965 and Hampshire in 1961.

The newest county, Durham, won the County Championship for the first time in 2008, thanks to some splendid bowling by Mark Davies, who topped the first-class averages.

TWENTY20 CUP 2010

FRIENDS PROVIDENT WINNERS 2010

The eighth Twenty20 Cup finals day took place at the Rose Bowl, Southampton, on 14 August 2010. the four qualifying teams were Essex, Hampshire, Somerset and Nottinghamshire.

Hampshire beat Essex in the first semi-final, with Essex scoring 156 for 7 and Hampshire getting the runs with four balls to spare to win by six wickets. In the second semi-final, Somerset scored 182 for 5 and Nottinghamshire were foiled by rain, finishing three runs short of their Duckworth-Lewis target with 117 for 4 in 13 overs.

There was an amazing finish to the final. Somerset scored 173 for 6 and Hampshire 173 for 5, thus winning by losing fewer wickets. But the match ended in a farcical manner. Dan Christian, facing the last ball with Hampshire one run short, called for a runner, having pulled a hamstring. Hampshire scrambled a leg-bye, with both Christian and the runner, Jimmy Adams running. Somerset could have thrown down the stumps and won, but didn't, even though the umpires waited for them to do so. Eventually the umpires removed the stumps and declared Hampshire the winners.

Above: **The Hampshire team celebrate their 2010 win over Somerset.**

2010 FINAL

SOMERSET 173 FOR 6
(KIESWETTER 71, TREGO 33)

HAMPSHIRE 173 FOR 5
(McKENZIE 72, ERVINE 44 NOT OUT, ADAMS 34, RAZZAQ 33)

HAMPSHIRE WON BY LOSING FEWER WICKETS

PREVIOUS WINNERS ARE LISTED ON PAGE 48.

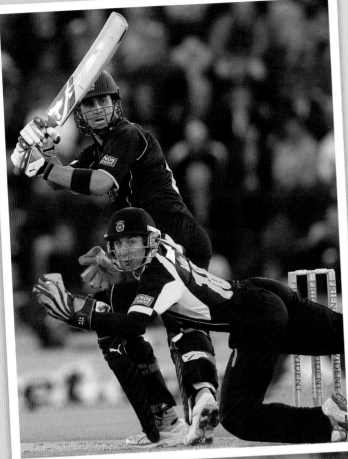

Top left: **Somerset's Craig Kieswetter looks on as Hampshire's Michael Bates dives for the ball. Kieswetter finished as Somerset's highest scorer on 71.**

Top right: **Hampshire's Neil McKenzie square drives a delivery. McKenzie finished top scorer in the match with 72 and was given the Man of the Match award.**

Left: **The sun sets over the Twenty20 final at the Rose Bowl, Southampton. The match didn't finish until 11pm.**

LIMITED-OVERS CRICKET

With county cricket in a parlous state financially in the late 1950s and early 1960s, the time had come for change. A one-day limited-overs knock-out competition – the Gillette Cup – began in 1963: in 1969 it was joined by a 40-overs-a-side Sunday League and a third – a 55-overs-a-side competition – started in 1972.

In 1968, the authorities broke with tradition by allowing counties to play overseas cricketers. The immediate effect of this was that the domination by the counties with large populations was broken.

Yorkshire alone decided to stick with players born within the county boundary.

Essex and Middlesex came to the fore in the 1970s. The former, led by Keith Fletcher, possessed a fine attack, with John Lever and Neil Foster the principal seam bowlers and Ray East and David Acfield as spinners. The batting line-up included the captain and Graham Gooch and Ken McEwan, while Derek Pringle was the all-rounder. Middlesex were led by the most talented captain of the day, Mike Brearley. Their spin attack revolved around John Emburey and Phil

Edmonds, the West Indian Wayne Daniel opened the bowling, and Mike Gatting, who succeeded Brearley as captain, was the leading run-getter. In a golden period in the late 1970s and 1980s, Middlesex won the County Championship seven times and gained seven one-day trophies. Essex won 11.

With counties fielding overseas players and with the movement of players between counties on the increase, the spread of trophies was greater than in the past. Aside from Essex and Middlesex, seven counties – Hampshire, Kent, Lancashire, Nottinghamshire,

Somerset, Warwickshire and Worcestershire – won at least five titles and, Durham apart, all the rest boasted at least one. Warwickshire, with the services of Brian Lara in 1994 and Allan Donald in 1995, won the championship both seasons and in 1994 also gained the Sunday League and Benson & Hedges titles. This was the season in which Lara recorded the first first-class innings of more than 500 – 501 not out against Durham at Edgbaston.

Sussex's Allan Wells is clean bowled by Warwickshire's Neil Smith in the 1993 NatWest Trophy final at Lord's.

A fundamental change took place in county cricket in the late 1990s. In 1999, the 40-over Sunday League was split into two nine-team divisions, with three up and three down. In 2000, the County Championship adopted the same format, with all matches being played over four days. For the Sunday League, the counties chose wacky nicknames and teams played two day-night fixtures in the league with batsmen being accompanied to the wicket by their own signature tunes, usually one of the latest chart-topping songs, wearing brightly-coloured clothing.

In 2001, Yorkshire recaptured the County Championship, which it had last won in 1968. In 2003, Sussex, which had competed in the County Championship since 1864, won the title for the first time. However, the decision to split the Championship into two sections did not have the desired effect of creating two "classes" of county, simply because promotion and relegation was based on three up, three down. In most seasons the margins between counties promoted or relegated and the others were very slight. In the five seasons 2001 to 2005, five different clubs headed Division One, a state of affairs that had happened just once in the previous century. The promotion system was changed from 2006, with two counties going up and two going down.

As far as the one-day competitions were concerned, the Benson & Hedges Cup was replaced after 2002 by a 20-overs-a-side competition – called Twenty/20 – and run on similar lines to the B&H, except that the two semi-finals and the final were staged on the same day at the same venue. Each innings lasted about one hour and a complete game two-and-a-half hours. Twenty/20 proved very popular with the public. The unpopular "Sunday League" 45-over format will be abandoned in 2006 and revert to 40 overs a side. The C&G Trophy for 2006 will become a competition based on mini-leagues followed by finals between the top sides, rather than the straight knock-

Lancashire's Andrew Flintoff (far left) and Andrew Symonds (standing) look on from the dugout during their side's Twenty/20 semi-final clash against Surrey at The Oval in 2005.

out formula which has reigned since its inception.

One rule which has crept into the county circuit in recent years, is the "borrowing" of players from their registered county to another county. Thus, for the first time since 1872, players can appear in competitive matches for more than one county in the same season. The use of "replacement" overseas stars when the main overseas player is unavailable has also become increasingly employed.

TWENTY/20

2003 at Trent Bridge
FINAL: SURREY 119-1 (10.5 OVERS)
BEAT WARWICKSHIRE 115
(18.5 OVERS) BY 9 WKTS

2004 at Edgbaston
FINAL: LEICESTERSHIRE 169-3
(19.1 OVERS) BEAT SURREY
168-6 (20 OVERS) BY 7 WKTS

2005 at The Oval
FINAL: SOMERSET 118-3 (14.1 OVERS)
BEAT LANCASHIRE 114-8
(16 OVERS) BY 7 WKTS

2006 at Trent Bridge
FINAL: LEICESTERSHIRE 177-2
(20 OVERS) BEAT
NOTTINGHAMSHIRE 173-8
(20 OVERS) BY 4 RUNS

2007 at Edgbaston
FINAL: KENT 147-6 (19.3 OVERS)
BEAT GLOUCESTERSHIRE 146-8
(20 OVERS) BY 4 WKTS

2008 at The Rose Bowl
FINAL: MIDDLESEX 187-6 (20 OVERS)
BEAT KENT 184-5 (20 OVERS)
BY 3 RUNS

2009 at Edgbaston
FINAL: SUSSEX 172-7 (20 OVERS)
BEAT SOMERSET 109
(17.2 OVERS) BY 63 RUNS

2010 at The Rose Bowl
FINAL: HAMPSHIRE 173-5 (20 OVERS)
BEAT SOMERSET 173-6 (20 OVERS)
LOSING LEAST WICKETS

COUNTY CHAMPIONS SINCE 1864

Year	County	Year	County	Year	County	Year	County
1864	SURREY	1895	SURREY	1936	DERBY	1977	KENT, MIDDLESEX
1865	NOTTINGHAMSHIRE	1896	YORKSHIRE	1937	YORKSHIRE	1978	KENT
1866	MIDDLESEX	1897	LANCASHIRE	1938	YORKSHIRE	1979	ESSEX
1867	YORKSHIRE	1898	YORKSHIRE	1939	YORKSHIRE	1980	MIDDLESEX
1868	NOTTINGHAMSHIRE	1899	SURREY	1946	YORKSHIRE	1981	NOTTINGHAMSHIRE
1869	NOTTINGHAMSHIRE, YORKSHIRE	1900	YORKSHIRE	1947	MIDDLESEX	1982	MIDDLESEX
1870	YORKSHIRE	1901	YORKSHIRE	1948	GLAMORGAN	1983	ESSEX
1871	NOTTINGHAMSHIRE	1902	YORKSHIRE	1949	MIDDLESEX, YORKSHIRE	1984	ESSEX
1872	NOTTINGHAMSHIRE	1903	MIDDLESEX	1950	LANCASHIRE, SURREY	1985	MIDDLESEX
1873	GLOUCESTERSHIRE, NOTTINGHAMSHIRE	1904	LANCASHIRE	1951	WARWICKSHIRE	1986	ESSEX
1874	GLOUCESTERSHIRE	1905	YORKSHIRE	1952	SURREY	1987	NOTTINGHAMSHIRE
1875	NOTTINGHAMSHIRE	1906	KENT	1953	SURREY	1988	WORCESTERSHIRE
1876	GLOUCESTERSHIRE	1907	NOTTINGHAMSHIRE	1954	SURREY	1989	WORCESTERSHIRE
1877	GLOUCESTERSHIRE	1908	YORKSHIRE	1955	SURREY	1990	MIDDLESEX
1878	UNDECIDED	1909	KENT	1956	SURREY	1991	ESSEX
1879	NOTTINGHAMSHIRE, LANCASHIRE	1910	KENT	1957	SURREY	1992	ESSEX
1880	NOTTINGHAMSHIRE	1911	WARWICKSHIRE	1958	SURREY	1993	MIDDLESEX
1881	LANCASHIRE	1912	YORKSHIRE	1959	YORKSHIRE	1994	WARWICKSHIRE
1882	NOTTINGHAMSHIRE, LANCASHIRE	1913	KENT	1960	YORKSHIRE	1995	WARWICKSHIRE
1883	NOTTINGHAMSHIRE	1914	SURREY	1961	HAMPSHIRE	1996	LEICESTERSHIRE
1884	NOTTINGHAMSHIRE	1919	YORKSHIRE	1962	YORKSHIRE	1997	GLAMORGAN
1885	NOTTINGHAMSHIRE	1920	MIDDLESEX	1963	YORKSHIRE	1998	LEICESTERSHIRE
1886	SURREY	1921	MIDDLESEX	1964	WORCESTERSHIRE	1999	SURREY
1887	SURREY	1922	YORKSHIRE	1965	WORCESTERSHIRE	2000	SURREY
1888	SURREY	1923	YORKSHIRE	1966	YORKSHIRE	2001	YORKSHIRE
1889	SURREY, LANCASHIRE, NOTTINGHAMSHIRE	1924	YORKSHIRE	1967	YORKSHIRE	2002	SURREY
1890	SURREY	1925	YORKSHIRE	1968	YORKSHIRE	2003	SUSSEX
1891	SURREY	1926	LANCASHIRE	1969	GLAMORGAN	2004	WARWICKSHIRE
1892	SURREY	1927	LANCASHIRE	1970	KENT	2005	NOTTINGHAMSHIRE
1893	YORKSHIRE	1928	LANCASHIRE	1971	SURREY	2006	SUSSEX
1894	SURREY	1929	NOTTINGHAMSHIRE	1972	WARWICKSHIRE	2007	SUSSEX
		1930	LANCASHIRE	1973	HAMPSHIRE	2008	DURHAM
		1931	YORKSHIRE	1974	WORCESTERSHIRE	2009	DURHAM
		1932	YORKSHIRE	1975	LEICESTERSHIRE	2010	NOTTINGHAMSHIRE
		1933	YORKSHIRE	1976	MIDDLESEX		
		1934	LANCASHIRE				
		1935	YORKSHIRE				

GILLETTE/NATWEST/C&G/FRIENDS PROVIDENT TROPHY

1963 SUSSEX 168 (60.2 OVERS) BEAT WORCESTERSHIRE 154 (63.2 OVERS) BY 14 RUNS
1964 SUSSEX 131-2 (43 OVERS) BEAT WARWICKSHIRE 127 (48 OVERS) BY 8 WKTS
1965 YORKSHIRE 317-4 (60 OVERS) BEAT SURREY 142 (40.4 OVERS) BY 175 RUNS
1966 WARWICKSHIRE 159-5 (56.4 OVERS) BEAT WORCESTERSHIRE 155-8 (60 OVERS) BY 5 WKTS
1967 KENT 193 (59.4 OVERS) BEAT SOMERSET 161 (54.5 OVERS) BY 32 RUNS
1968 WARWICKSHIRE 215-6 (57 OVERS) BEAT SUSSEX 214-7 (60 OVERS) BY 4 WKTS
1969 YORKSHIRE 219-8 (60 OVERS) BEAT DERBYSHIRE 150 (54.4 OVERS) BY 69 RUNS
1970 LANCASHIRE 185-4 (55.1 OVERS) BEAT SUSSEX 184-9 (60 OVERS) BY 6 WKTS
1971 LANCASHIRE 224-7 (60 OVERS) BEAT KENT 200 (56.2 OVERS) BY 24 RUNS
1972 LANCASHIRE 235-6 (56.4 OVERS) BEAT WARWICKSHIRE 234-9 (60 OVERS) BY4 WKTS
1973 GLOUCESTERSHIRE 248-8 (60 OVERS) BEAT SUSSEX 208 (56.5 OVERS) BY 40 RUNS
1974 KENT 122-6 (56.4 OVERS) BEAT LANCASHIRE 118 (60 OVERS) BY 4 WKTS
1975 LANCASHIRE 182-3 (57 OVERS) BEAT MIDDLESEX 180-8 (60 OVERS) BY 7 WKTS
1976 NORTHAMPTONSHIRE 199-6 (58.1 OVERS) BEAT LANCASHIRE 195-7 (60 OVERS) BY 4 WKTS
1977 MIDDLESEX 178-5 (55.4 OVERS) BEAT GLAMORGAN 177-9 (60 OVERS) BY 5 WKTS
1978 SUSSEX 211-5 (53.1 OVERS) BEAT SOMERSET 207-7 (60 OVERS) BY 5 WKTS
1979 SOMERSET 269-8 (60 OVERS) BEAT NORTHAMPTONSHIRE 224 (56.3 OVERS) BY 45 RUNS
1980 MIDDLESEX 202-3 (53.5 OVERS) BEAT SURREY 201 (60 OVERS) BY 7 WKTS
1981 DERBYSHIRE 235-6 (60 OVERS) BEAT NORTHAMPTON 235-9 (60 OVERS) BY LOSING FEWER WKTS
1982 SURREY 159-1 (34.4 OVERS) BEAT WARWICKSHIRE 158 (57.2 OVERS) BY 9 WKTS
1983 SOMERSET 193-9 (50 OVERS) BEAT KENT 169 (47.1 OVERS) BY 24 RUNS
1984 MIDDLESEX 236-6 (60 OVERS) BEAT KENT 232-6 (60 OVERS) BY 4 WKTS
1985 ESSEX 280-2 (60 OVERS) BEAT NOTTINGHAMSHIRE 279-5 (60 OVERS) BY 1 RUN
1986 SUSSEX 243-3 (58.2 OVERS) BEAT LANCASHIRE 242-8 (60 OVERS) BY 7 WKTS

1987 NOTTINGHAMSHIRE 231-7 (49.3 OVERS) BEAT NORTHAMPTONSHIRE 228-3 (50 OVERS) BY 3 WKTS
1988 MIDDLESEX 162-7 (55.3 OVERS) BEAT WORCESTERSHIRE 161-9 (60 OVERS) BY 3 WKTS
1989 WARWICKSHIRE 211-6 (59.4 OVERS) BEAT MIDDLESEX 210-5 (60 OVERS) BY 4 WKTS
1990 LANCASHIRE 173-3 (45.4 OVERS) BEAT NORTHAMPTONSHIRE 171 (60 OVERS) BY 7 WKTS
1991 HAMPSHIRE 243-6 (59.4 OVERS) BEAT SURREY 240-5 (60 OVERS) BY 4 WKTS
1992 NORTHAMPTONSHIRE 211-2 (49.4 OVERS) BEAT LEICESTERSHIRE 208-7 (60 OVERS) BY 8 WKTS
1993 WARWICKSHIRE 322-5 (60 OVERS) BEAT SUSSEX 321-6 (60 OVERS) BY 5 WKTS
1994 WORCESTERSHIRE 227-2 (49.1 OVERS) BEAT WARWICKSHIRE 223-9 (60 OVERS) BY 8 WKTS
1995 WARWICKSHIRE 203-6 (58.5 OVERS) BEAT NORTHAMPTONSHIRE 200 (59.5 OVERS) BY 4 WKTS
1996 LANCASHIRE 186 (60 OVERS) BEAT ESSEX 57 (27.2 OVERS) BY 129 RUNS
1997 ESSEX 171-1 (26.3 OVERS) BEAT WARWICKSHIRE 170-8 (60 OVERS) BY 9 WKTS
1998 LANCASHIRE 109-3 (30.2 OVERS) BEAT DERBYSHIRE 108 (36.4 OVERS) BY 7 WKTS
1999 GLOUCESTERSHIRE 230-8 (50 OVERS) BEAT SOMERSET 180 (45.1 OVERS) BY 50 RUNS
2000 GLOUCESTERSHIRE 122-3 (29.4 OVERS) BEAT WARWICKSHIRE 205-7 (50 OVERS) BY 22 RUNS (D/L METHOD)
2001 SOMERSET 271-5 (50 OVERS) BEAT LEICESTERSHIRE 230 (45.4 OVERS) BY 41 RUNS
2002 YORKSHIRE 260-4 (48 OVERS) BEAT SOMERSET 256-8 (50 OVERS) BY 6 WKTS
2003 GLOUCESTERSHIRE 150-3 (20.3 OVERS) BEAT WORCESTERSHIRE 149 (46.3 OVERS) BY 7 WKTS
2004 GLOUCESTERSHIRE 237-2 (43.5 OVERS) BEAT WORCESTERSHIRE 236-9 (50 OVERS) BY 8 WKTS
2005 HAMPSHIRE 290 (50 OVERS) BEAT WARWICKSHIRE 272 (49.2 OVERS) BY 18 RUNS
2006 SUSSEX 172 (47.1 OVERS) BEAT LANCASHIRE 157 (47.2 OVERS) BY 15 RUNS
2007 DURHAM 312-5 (50 OVERS) BEAT HAMPSHIRE 187 (41 OVERS) BY 125 RUNS
2008 ESSEX 218-5 (48.5 OVERS) BEAT KENT 214-8 (50 OVERS) BY 5 WKTS
2009 HAMPSHIRE 221-4 (40.3 OVERS) BEAT SUSSEX 219-9 (50 OVERS) BY 6 WKTS

MINOR COUNTY CHAMPIONS

Year	Champion	Year	Champion	Year	Champion	Year	Champion	Year	Champion	Year	Champion
1895	NORFOLK/DURHAM/ WORCESTERSHIRE	1911	STAFFORDSHIRE	1935	MIDDLESEX II	1960	LANCASHIRE II	1979	SUFFOLK	1998	STAFFORDSHIRE
1896	WORCESTERSHIRE	1912	IN ABEYANCE	1936	HERTFORDSHIRE	1961	SOMERSET II	1980	DURHAM	1999	CUMBERLAND
1897	WORCESTERSHIRE	1913	NORFOLK	1937	LANCASHIRE II	1962	WARWICKSHIRE II	1981	DURHAM	2000	DORSET
1898	WORCESTERSHIRE	1914	STAFFORDSHIRE	1938	BUCKINGHAMSHIRE	1963	CAMBRIDGESHIRE	1982	OXFORDSHIRE	2001	CHESHIRE/ LINCOLNSHIRE
1899	NORTHAMPTONSHIRE/ BUCKINGHAMSHIRE	1920	STAFFORDSHIRE	1939	SURREY II	1964	LANCASHIRE II	1983	HERTFORDSHIRE	2002	HEREFORDSHIRE/ NORFOLK
1900	GLAMORGAN/DURHAM/ NORTHAMPTONSHIRE	1921	STAFFORDSHIRE	1946	SUFFOLK	1965	SOMERSET II	1984	DURHAM		
1901	DURHAM	1922	BUCKINGHAMSHIRE	1947	YORKSHIRE II	1966	LINCOLNSHIRE	1985	CHESHIRE	2003	LINCOLNSHIRE
1902	WILTSHIRE	1923	BUCKINGHAMSHIRE	1948	LANCASHIRE II	1967	CHESHIRE	1986	CUMBERLAND	2004	BEDFORDSHIRE/DEVON
1903	NORTHAMPTONSHIRE	1924	BERKSHIRE	1949	LANCASHIRE II	1968	YORKSHIRE II	1987	BUCKINGHAMSHIRE	2005	CHESHIRE/SUFFOLK
1904	NORTHAMPTONSHIRE	1925	BUCKINGHAMSHIRE	1950	SURREY II	1969	BUCKINGHAMSHIRE	1988	CHESHIRE	2006	DEVON
1905	NORFOLK	1926	DURHAM	1951	KENT II	1970	BEDFORDSHIRE	1989	OXFORDSHIRE	2007	SUFFOLK
1906	STAFFORDSHIRE	1927	STAFFORDSHIRE	1952	BUCKINGHAMSHIRE	1971	YORKSHIRE II	1990	HERTFORDSHIRE	2008	DEVON
1907	LANCASHIRE II	1928	BERKSHIRE	1953	BERKSHIRE	1972	BEDFORDSHIRE	1991	STAFFORDSHIRE	2009	BUCKINGHAMSHIRE
1908	STAFFORDSHIRE	1929	OXFORDSHIRE	1954	SURREY II	1973	SHROPSHIRE	1992	STAFFORDSHIRE	2010	DORSET
1909	WILTSHIRE	1930	DURHAM	1955	SURREY II	1974	OXFORDSHIRE	1993	STAFFORDSHIRE		
1910	NORFOLK	1931	LEICESTERSHIRE II	1956	KENT II	1975	HERTFORDSHIRE	1994	DEVON		
		1932	BUCKINGHAMSHIRE	1957	YORKSHIRE II	1976	DURHAM	1995	DEVON		
		1933	UNDECIDED	1958	YORKSHIRE II	1977	SUFFOLK	1996	DEVON		
		1934	LANCASHIRE II	1959	WARWICKSHIRE II	1978	DEVON	1997	DEVON		

BENSON AND HEDGES CUP

1972	LEICESTERSHIRE 140-5 (46.5 OVERS) BEAT YORKSHIRE 136-9 (55 OVERS) BY 5 WKTS
1973	KENT 225-7 (55 OVERS) BEAT WORCESTERSHIRE 186 (51.4 OVERS) BY 39 RUNS
1974	SURREY 170 (54.1 OVERS) BEAT LEICESTERSHIRE 143 (54 OVERS) BY 27 RUNS
1975	LEICESTERSHIRE 150-5 (51.2 OVERS) BEAT MIDDLESEX 146 (54.2 OVERS) BY 5 WKTS
1976	KENT 236-7 (55 OVERS) BEAT WORCESTERSHIRE 193 (52.4 OVERS) BY 43 RUNS
1977	GLOUCESTERSHIRE 237-6 (55 OVERS) BEAT KENT 173 (47.3 OVERS) BY 64 RUNS
1978	KENT 151-4 (41.4 OVERS) BEAT DERBYSHIRE 147 (54.5 OVERS) BY 6 WKTS
1979	ESSEX 290-6 (55 OVERS) BEAT SURREY 255 (51.4 OVERS) BY 35 RUNS
1980	NORTHAMPTONSHIRE 209 (54.5 OVERS) BEAT ESSEX 203-8 (55 OVERS) BY 6 RUNS
1981	SOMERSET 197-3 (44.3 OVERS) BEAT SURREY 194-8 (55 OVERS) BY 7 WKTS
1982	SOMERSET 132-1 (33.1 OVERS) BEAT NOTTINGHAMSHIRE 130 (50.1 OVERS) BY 9 WKTS
1983	MIDDLESEX 196-8 (55 OVERS) BEAT ESSEX 192 (54.1 OVERS) BY 4 RUNS
1984	LANCASHIRE 140-4 (42.4 OVERS) BEAT WARWICKSHIRE 139 (50.4 OVERS) BY 6 WKTS
1985	LEICESTERSHIRE 215-5 (52 OVERS) BEAT ESSEX 213-8 (55 OVERS) BY 5 WKTS
1986	MIDDLESEX 199-7 (55 OVERS) BEAT KENT 197-8 (55 OVERS) BY 2 RUNS
1987	YORKSHIRE 244-6 (55 OVERS) BEAT NORTHAMPTONSHIRE 244-7 (55 OVERS) BY LOSING FEWER WKTS
1988	HAMPSHIRE 118-3 (31.5 OVERS) BEAT DERBYSHIRE 117 (46.3 OVERS) BY 7 WKTS
1989	NOTTINGHAMSHIRE 244-7 (55 OVERS) BEAT ESSEX 243-7 (55 OVERS) BY 3 WKTS
1990	LANCASHIRE 241-8 (55 OVERS) BEAT WORCESTERSHIRE 172 (54 OVERS) BY 69 RUNS
1991	WORCESTERSHIRE 236-8 (55 OVERS) BEAT LANCASHIRE 171 (47.2 OVERS) BY 65 RUNS
1992	HAMPSHIRE 253-5 (55 OVERS) BEAT KENT 212 (52.3 OVERS) BY 41 RUNS
1993	DERBYSHIRE 252-6 (55 OVERS) BEAT LANCASHIRE 246-7 (55 OVERS) BY 6 RUNS
1994	WARWICKSHIRE 172-4 (44.2 OVERS) BEAT WORCESTERSHIRE 170 (55 OVERS) BY 6 WKTS
1995	LANCASHIRE 274-7 (55 OVERS) BEAT KENT 239 (52.1 OVERS) BY 35 RUNS
1996	LANCASHIRE 245-9 (50 OVERS) BEAT NORTHAMPTONSHIRE 214 (48.3 OVERS) BY 31 RUNS
1997	SURREY 215-2 (45 OVERS) BEAT KENT 212-9 (50 OVERS) BY 8 WKTS
1998	ESSEX 268-7 (50 OVERS) BEAT LEICESTERSHIRE 76 (27.4 OVERS) BY 192 RUNS
1999	GLOUCESTERSHIRE 291-9 (50 OVERS) BEAT YORKSHIRE 167 (40 OVERS) BY 124 RUNS
2000	GLAMORGAN 225 (49.3 OVERS) BEAT GLOUCESTERSHIRE 226-3 (46.5 OVERS) BY 7 WKTS
2001	SURREY 244 (49.4 OVERS) BEAT GLOUCESTERSHIRE 197 (45.5 OVERS) BY 47 RUNS
2002	WARWICKSHIRE 182-5 (36.2 OVERS) BEAT ESSEX 181-8 (50 OVERS) BY 5 WKTS

SUNDAY LEAGUE CHAMPIONS

Year	Champion	Year	Champion
1968	NORTHAMPTONSHIRE	1989	LANCASHIRE
1969	LANCASHIRE	1990	DERBYSHIRE
1970	LANCASHIRE	1991	NOTTINGHAMSHIRE
1971	WORCESTERSHIRE	1992	MIDDLESEX
1972	KENT	1993	GLAMORGAN
1973	KENT	1994	WARWICKSHIRE
1974	LEICESTERSHIRE	1995	KENT
1975	HAMPSHIRE	1996	SURREY
1976	KENT	1997	WARWICKSHIRE
1977	LEICESTERSHIRE	1998	LANCASHIRE
1978	HAMPSHIRE	1999	LANCASHIRE
1979	SOMERSET	2000	GLOUCESTERSHIRE
1980	WARWICKSHIRE	2001	KENT
1981	ESSEX	2002	GLAMORGAN
1982	SUSSEX	2003	ESSEX
1983	YORKSHIRE	2004	GLAMORGAN
1984	ESSEX	2005	ESSEX
1985	ESSEX	2006	ESSEX
1986	HAMPSHIRE	2007	WORCESTERSHIRE
1987	WORCESTERSHIRE	2008	SUSSEX
1988	WORCESTERSHIRE	2009	SUSSEX

SECOND XI ONE-DAY COMPETITION

Year	Champion	Year	Champion
1986	NORTHAMPTONSHIRE	1999	MIDDLESEX
1987	DERBYSHIRE	2000	MIDDLESEX
1988	YORKSHIRE	2001	HAMPSHIRE
1989	MIDDLESEX	2002	KENT
1990	LANCASHIRE	2003	HAMPSHIRE
1991	NOTTINGHAMSHIRE	2004	WORCESTERSHIRE
1992	SURREY	2005	SUSSEX
1993	LEICESTERSHIRE	2006	WARWICKSHIRE
1994	YORKSHIRE	2007	MIDDLESEX
1995	LEICESTERSHIRE	2008	HAMPSHIRE
1996	LEICESTERSHIRE	2009	YORKSHIRE
1997	LANCASHIRE	2010	ESSEX
1998	NORTHAMPTONSHIRE		

SECOND XI CHAMPIONS

Year	Champion	Year	Champion
1959	GLOUCESTERSHIRE	1985	NOTTINGHAMSHIRE
1960	NORTHAMPTONSHIRE	1986	LANCASHIRE
1961	KENT	1987	KENT, YORKSHIRE
1962	WORCESTERSHIRE	1988	SURREY
1963	WORCESTERSHIRE	1989	MIDDLESEX
1964	LANCASHIRE	1990	SUSSEX
1965	GLAMORGAN	1991	YORKSHIRE
1966	SURREY	1992	SURREY
1967	HAMPSHIRE	1993	MIDDLESEX
1968	SURREY	1994	SOMERSET
1969	KENT	1995	HAMPSHIRE
1970	KENT	1996	WARWICKSHIRE
1971	HAMPSHIRE	1997	LANCASHIRE
1972	NOTTINGHAMSHIRE	1998	NORTHAMPTONSHIRE
1973	ESSEX	1999	MIDDLESEX
1974	MIDDLESEX	2000	LEICESTERSHIRE
1975	SURREY	2001	SURREY
1976	KENT	2002	KENT
1977	YORKSHIRE	2003	YORKSHIRE
1978	SUSSEX	2004	SOMERSET
1979	WARWICKSHIRE	2005	KENT
1980	GLAMORGAN	2006	KENT
1981	HAMPSHIRE	2007	SUSSEX
1982	WORCESTERSHIRE	2008	DURHAM
1983	LEICESTERSHIRE	2009	SURREY
1984	YORKSHIRE	2010	SURREY

AUSTRALIA

The colonies of New South Wales and Victoria opposed each other in a first-class cricket match for the first time in 1855-56. Prior to that, the only major inter-colonial games had been between Tasmania and Victoria. In the period 1855-56 to 1871-72, Victoria generally got the better of their arch-enemy. The wickets were dreadful and, in the first ten years, it was unusual for an innings total to exceed 100. In 1862-63, when New South Wales won the annual match after losing five in succession, an umpiring dispute caused the game to be cancelled for the next two seasons.

The first individual hundred in the series, and indeed the first first-class hundred ever scored in Australia, came in 1867-68, when Dick Wardill hit 110 for Victoria. Wardill, a Liverpudlian, captained Victoria and was one of the main promoters behind the English team, led by W.G. Grace, which came out to Australia in 1873-74. Wardill, however, did not play against Grace's side. In the winter of 1873, it was found he had embezzled his employers out of £7,000. He eluded the police, but committed suicide.

While Wardill was the outstanding batsman of the era, Sam Cosstick was

Above: **Wicket-keeper/batsman Ryan Campbell hits out for the Retravision Warriors (Western Australia) in his side's match against the Queensland Bulls at the WACA in January 2006.**

Right: **It was back-to-back success for Western Australia in the Sheffield Shield in 1999. Inspired by a magical 115 from Simon Katich, WA romped to an innings-and-31-run final victory over Queensland at the Gabba.**

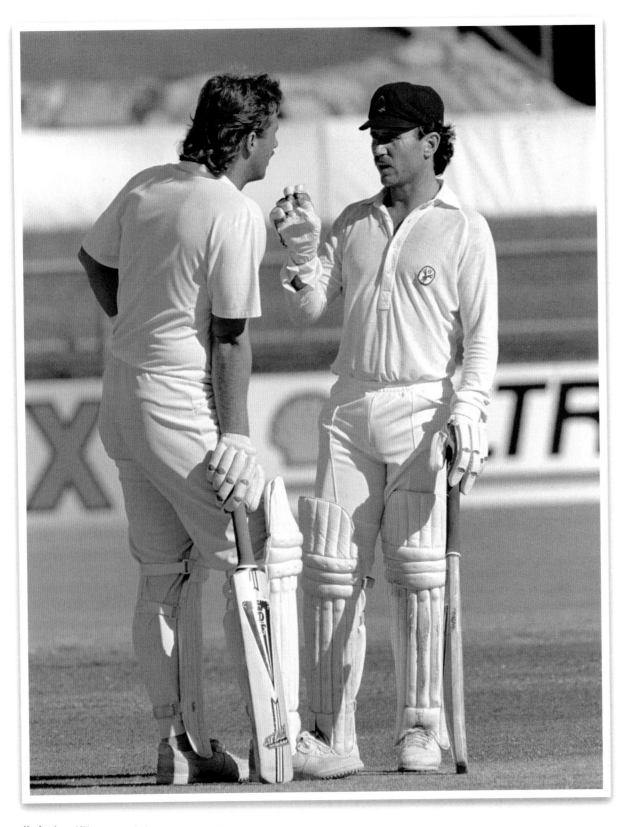

Victoria's greatest bowler – fast round-arm – and a slogging batsman.

Of the two established English players who were tempted to stay in Australia after touring with the English team, Charles Lawrence was employed by the Albert Club in Sydney, while William Caffyn was initially in Melbourne, but after one season also switched to Sydney.

With Victoria apparently too good for New South Wales, it was decided in 1872-73 that Victoria should not only play a combined New South Wales, Tasmania and South Australia team, but that the latter should be allowed 13 men! The odds were too great and Victoria lost by five wickets.

Two months later, Victoria opposed New South Wales in an 11-a-side game and, mainly thanks to Cosstick's 11 for 51, the former won.

From 1874-75 it was New South Wales' turn to dominate. Playing home and away each year, New South Wales won seven straight games – Charles Bannerman, who was to score the first Test hundred, was the batting star, while F.R. Spofforth (The Demon) developed into a unique bowler. He was quite lethal whatever the wicket. In the 1880s, the two sides were evenly matched; frequently one victory in the first fixture was reversed in the second. Billy Murdoch scored the first triple hundred for New South Wales in 1881-82. Fast-medium bowler Charles Turner (The Terror) also belonged to New South Wales.

South Australia opposed Victoria in a first-class match for the first time in 1880-81 (the former had previously played Tasmania). The Adelaide side found an outstanding all-rounder, George Giffen. His figures were quite formidable: in one game against Victoria he hit 271 and took 16 wickets; other combinations were 237 and 12, 135 and 13, 166 and 14. He was considered Australia's answer to W.G. Grace.

Having been bitter opponents for many years, Allan Border (right) and Ian Botham found themselves on the same side during the 1989 season, as the legendary England all-rounder played a season for Queensland in the Sheffield Shield.

THE SHEFFIELD SHIELD

Lord Sheffield, the leading patron of Sussex cricket, agreed to finance an English team to Australia for the 1891-92 season. Soon after his arrival in Australia, in November 1891, Lord Sheffield offered to pay for a trophy which could be competed for by the three main cricketing colonies. By the end of this tour, the cricketing authorities in Australia had set up the Australasian Cricket Council, one of whose tasks was to purchase a suitable trophy, with money which Lord Sheffield donated. The three colonies each played home and away matches with the other two in 1892-93. Matches were timeless and Victoria won all their four contests, thus being the first winners of the Sheffield Shield.

This three-way contest continued until 1925-26. Of the 30 seasons played (it was suspended from 1915-16 to 1918-19), New South Wales won 17 times, Victoria ten and South Australia three.

The best sequence of wins came between 1901-02 and 1906-07 when New South Wales recorded six successive titles. Victor Trumper, the outstanding batsman of his generation, was New South Wales's great run-getter in this period. Albert Cotter, the fastest bowler of the day, also represented New South Wales.

A major change came for the 1926-27 season. Queensland were admitted to the Sheffield Shield and simultaneously timeless matches for the Shield were abandoned, with four-and-a-half day matches introduced. Queensland had taken part in first-

class matches since 1892-93. This season was also unusual as South Australia claimed the title for the first time since 1912-13. South Australia relied on the brilliant leg breaks of Clarrie Grimmett.

Don Bradman arrived and dominated Australian domestic cricket, just as he did Test cricket. Initially he played for New South Wales, but the season he switched to South Australia, the latter immediately won the title again. Queensland remained the minnows, winning only 12 times in their first 83 matches up to the Second World War.

Western Australia took their first title in their first Shield season of 1947-48. However, they played only four matches, while the rest played seven. This system remained in place until 1956-57 - with the exception of 1954-55, when a bizarre arrangement was

Queensland's Shane Watson scored an unbeaten 200, out of his side's massive total of 900 for 6, in their victory over Victoria in the 2006 Sheffield Shield final.

tried whereby Western Australia played only two games and the rest four.

New South Wales had a run of nine consecutive Shield titles from 1953-54 to 1961-62. They had two great all-rounders in Richie Benaud and Alan Davidson, as well as the batting of Norman O'Neill. Ray Lindwall, the fearsome fast bowler, switched from New South Wales to Queensland for the 1954-55 season.

In 1961-62, three West Indian Test players, Gary Sobers, Rohan Kanhai and Wesley Hall, were imported for the Sheffield Shield. Hall took 43 wickets for Queensland, Kanhai made 533 runs for Western Australia

and Sobers topped both batting and bowling for South Australia. More importantly, the crowds flocked to see them - South Australia's gate receipts rose by two-and-a-half times.

The 1970s saw Western Australia out in front - six titles in nine seasons to 1980-81. The period also saw seasons when the Australian Packer players were banned from the Shield and the increase of international games meant that the top players missed many matches. Attendances at Shield games dropped to new lows.

Tasmania rose to Shield status for the 1977-78 season. In their first five seasons, they played one match against each opponent, while the rest played home and away. To avoid a percentage system, the points gained by Tasmania were multiplied by nine and divided by five.

A one-day knock-out competition began in 1969-70. Tasmania participated from the start, as did New Zealand - in fact the Kiwis won the first title. An innings was limited to 40 eight-ball overs until 1978-79 and since then 50 six-ball overs. In 1978-79 Tasmania won the competition. In the same year, they won their first Shield match. Much of the team's success was due to the skills of Jack Simmons, the Lancashire all-rounder. Queensland finally won the Sheffield Shield in 1994-95.

It took until the autumn of 1999 for a sponsor to be be found for the Sheffield Shield. National Foods Ltd paid A$22 million per annum for four years and the competition was renamed the Pura Milk Cup.

THE CRICKET ACADEMY

In 1987-88, the Australian Cricket Board appointed Jack Potter to head the Australian Cricket Institute of Sport's Youth Squad - 16 of Australia's most promising young players were brought together in Adelaide for special training, seminars and coaching. This was the start of the Australian Cricket Academy. The idea was based on the enormous success of East Germany's training programme of athletes for the Olympics.

The New South Wales players celebrate after they managed to hang on for a dramatic one-run win over South Australia in Adelaide to secure the 2006 ING Cup.

Six years later, the Academy's "graduates" included Shane Warne, Michael Bevan, Michael Slater and Glenn McGrath. The Academy led to schools of sporting excellence being set up in every state. They pick up potential players at a very young age, with the best transferring to the Academy at age 19. This system has meant that, from the mid-1990s, Australia became the world's top cricketing nation.

On the domestic front, the unremitting international schedule has meant that top players are rarely seen. The authorities tried day-night first-class matches, but these totally failed to attract spectators and have been generally abandoned. So poor were attendances that Melbourne Cricket Ground, the traditional home of cricket, deliberately staged football matches on the same dates as Victoria had arranged cricket matches - hitherto unheard of, but TV now controls everything.

A new team was introduced into the major one-day domestic competition - Australian Capital Territory - but they dropped out in 2000 after three seasons. Domestic first-class cricket is now almost totally ignored by the media - both broadcast and written.

Pura Milk Cup crowds are pitiful - 166 people watched Victoria play Queensland in 2003-04.

Also in 2003-04, the Australian Cricket Board re-branded itself as "Cricket Australia".

SHEFFIELD SHIELD

1892-93	VICTORIA	1914-15	VICTORIA	1947-48	WESTERN AUSTRALIA	1969-70	VICTORIA	1992-93	NEW SOUTH WALES
1893-94	SOUTH AUSTRALIA	1919-20	NEW SOUTH WALES	1948-49	NEW SOUTH WALES	1970-71	SOUTH AUSTRALIA	1993-94	NEW SOUTH WALES
1894-95	VICTORIA	1921-22	VICTORIA	1949-50	NEW SOUTH WALES	1971-72	WESTERN AUSTRALIA	1994-95	QUEENSLAND
1895-96	NEW SOUTH WALES	1922-23	NEW SOUTH WALES	1950-51	VICTORIA	1972-73	WESTERN AUSTRALIA	1995-96	SOUTH AUSTRALIA
1896-97	NEW SOUTH WALES	1923-24	VICTORIA	1951-52	NEW SOUTH WALES	1973-74	VICTORIA	1996-97	QUEENSLAND
1897-98	VICTORIA	1924-25	VICTORIA	1952-53	SOUTH AUSTRALIA	1974-75	WESTERN AUSTRALIAN	1997-98	WESTERN AUSTRALIA
1898-99	VICTORIA	1925-26	NEW SOUTH WALES	1953-54	NEW SOUTH WALES	1975-76	SOUTH AUSTRALIA	1998-99	WESTERN AUSTRALIA
1899-00	NEW SOUTH WALES	1926-27	SOUTH AUSTRALIA	1954-55	NEW SOUTH WALES	1976-77	WESTERN AUSTRALIA		
1900-01	VICTORIA	1927-28	VICTORIA	1955-56	NEW SOUTH WALES	1977-78	WESTERN AUSTRALIA		
1901-02	NEW SOUTH WALES	1928-29	NEW SOUTH WALES	1956-57	NEW SOUTH WALES	1978-79	VICTORIA	**PURA MILK CUP**	
1902-03	NEW SOUTH WALES	1929-30	VICTORIA	1957-58	NEW SOUTH WALES	1979-80	VICTORIA		
1903-04	NEW SOUTH WALES	1930-31	VICTORIA	1958-59	NEW SOUTH WALES	1980-81	WESTERN AUSTRALIA	1999-00	QUEENSLAND
1904-05	NEW SOUTH WALES	1931-32	NEW SOUTH WALES	1959-60	NEW SOUTH WALES	1981-82	SOUTH AUSTRALIA	2000-01	QUEENSLAND
1905-06	NEW SOUTH WALES	1932-33	NEW SOUTH WALES	1960-61	NEW SOUTH WALES	1982-83	NEW SOUTH WALES	2001-02	QUEENSLAND
1906-07	NEW SOUTH WALES	1933-34	VICTORIA	1961-62	NEW SOUTH WALES	1983-84	WESTERN AUSTRALIA	2002-03	NEW SOUTH WALES
1907-08	VICTORIA	1934-35	VICTORIA	1962-63	VICTORIA	1984-85	NEW SOUTH WALES	2003-04	VICTORIA
1908-09	NEW SOUTH WALES	1935-36	SOUTH AUSTRALIA	1963-64	SOUTH AUSTRALIA	1986-87	WESTERN AUSTRALIA	2004-05	NEW SOUTH WALES
1909-10	SOUTH AUSTRALIA	1936-37	VICTORIA	1964-65	NEW SOUTH WALES	1987-88	WESTERN AUSTRALIA	2005-06	QUEENSLAND
1910-11	NEW SOUTH WALES	1937-38	NEW SOUTH WALES	1965-66	NEW SOUTH WALES	1988-89	WESTERN AUSTRALIA	2006-07	NEW SOUTH WALES
1911-12	NEW SOUTH WALES	1938-39	SOUTH AUSTRALIA	1966-67	VICTORIA	1989-90	NEW SOUTH WALES	2007-08	QUEENSLAND
1912-13	SOUTH AUSTRALIA	1939-40	NEW SOUTH WALES	1967-68	WESTERN AUSTRALIA	1990-91	VICTORIA	2008-09	VICTORIA
1913-14	NEW SOUTH WALES	1946-47	VICTORIA	1968-69	SOUTH AUSTRALIA	1991-92	WESTERN AUSTRALIA	2009-10	VICTORIA

LIMITED-OVERS COMPETITION

V&G AUSTRALASIAN COLA-COLACOMPETITION

1969-70	NEW ZEALAND
1972-73	WESTERN AUSTRALIA

AUSTRALASIAN COCA-COLA COMPETITION

1969-70	VICTORIA
1972-73	NEW ZEALAND

GILLETTE CUP

1973-74	WESTERN AUSTRALIA
1974-75	NEW ZEALAND
1975-76	QUEENSLAND
1976-77	WESTERN AUSTRALIA
1977-78	WESTERN AUSTRALIA
1978-79	TASMANIA

MCDONALD'S CUP

1979-80	VICTORIA 199-6 (47.4 OVERS) BEAT NEW SOUTH WALES 198-8 (50 OVERS) 4 WKTS
1980-81	QUEENSLAND 188-9 (48 OVERS) BEAT WESTERN AUSTRALIA 116 (32.5 OVERS) BY 72 RUNS
1981-82	QUEENSLAND 224-8 (47 OVERS) BEAT NEW SOUTH WALES 197 (44.4 OVERS) BY 27 RUNS
1982-83	WESTERN AUSTRALIA 198-6 (49.1 OVERS) BEAT NEW SOUTH WALES 195-6 (50 OVERS) BY 4 WKTS
1983-84	SOUTH AUSTRALIA 256-6 (49 OVERS) BEAT WESTERN AUSTRALIA 248-9 (49 OVERS) BY 8 RUNS

1984-85	NEW SOUTH WALES278-7 (50 OVERS) BEAT SOUTH AUSTRALIA 190 (45.5 OVERS) BY 88 RUNS
1985-86	WESTERN AUSTRALIA 167 (38 OVERS) BEAT VICTORIA 148 (36.5 OVERS) BY 19 RUNS
1986-87	SOUTH AUSTRALIA 325-6 (50 OVERS) BEAT TASMANIA 239-9 (50 OVERS) BY 86 RUNS
1987-88	NEW SOUTH WALES 219-7 (50 OVERS) BEAT SOUTH AUSTRALIA 196-6 (50 OVERS) BY 23 RUNS

FEDERATED AUTOMOBILE INSURANCE

1988-89	QUEENSLAND 253-4 (50 OVERS)BEAT VICTORIA 90 (32.4 OVERS) BY 163 RUNS
1989-90	WESTERN AUSTRALIA 88-3 (19.1 OVERS) BEAT SOUTH AUSTRALIA 87 (34.5 OVERS) BY 7 WKTS
1990-91	WESTERN AUSTRALIA 236-3 (44.5 OVERS) BEAT NEW SOUTH WALES 235-7 (50 OVERS) BY 7 WKTS
1991-92	NEW SOUTH WALES 199-9 (50 OVERS) BEAT WESTERN AUSTRALIA 130 (40.1 OVERS) BY 69 RUNS

MERCANTILE MUTUAL CUP

1992-93	NEW SOUTH WALES 187-6 (49.4 OVERS) BEAT VICTORIA 186 (50 OVERS) BY 4 WKTS
1993-94	NEW SOUTH WALES 264-4 (50 OVERS) BEAT WESTERN AUSTRALIA 218-9 (49 OVERS) ON FASTER SCORING RATE
1994-95	VICTORIA 170-6 (44.5 OVERS) BEAT SOUTH AUSTRALIA 169 (46.4 OVERS) BY 4 WKTS
1995-96	QUEENSLAND 167-6 (44.5 OVERS) BEAT WESTERN AUSTRALIA 166 (49.1 OVERS) BY 4 WKTS
1996-97	WESTERN AUSTRALIA 149-2 (35 OVERS) BEAT QUEENSLAND 148 (40.1 OVERS) BY 8 WKTS
1997-98	QUEENSLAND 167-8 (47.5 OVERS) BEAT NEW SOUTH WALES 166 (49.3 OVERS) BY 2 WKTS

1998-99	VICTORIA 231 (50 OVERS) BEAT NEW SOUTH WALES 192 (45.3 OVERS) BY 39 RUNS
1999-00	WESTERN AUSTRALIA 301-6 (50 OVERS) BEAT QUEENSLAND 256 (45.2 OVERS) BY 45 RUNS
2000-01	NEW SOUTH WALES 273-4 (48.2 OVERS) BEAT WESTERN AUSTRALIA 272-7 (50 OVERS) BY 6 WKTS
2001-02	NEW SOUTH WALES 204 (50 OVERS) BEAT QUEENSLAND 185 (48.5 OVERS) BY 19 RUNS

ING CUP

2002-03	NEW SOUTH WALES 208-3 (26.5 OVERS) BEAT WESTERN AUSTRALIA 207 (49.5 OVERS) BY 7 WKTS
2003-04	WESTERN AUSTRALIA 248-6 (49.4 OVERS) BEAT QUEENSLAND 244 (49.1 OVERS) BY 4 WKTS
2004-05	TASMANIA 247-3 (47.1 OVERS) BEAT QUEENSLAND 246-7 (50 OVERS) BY 7 WKTS
2005-06	NEW SOUTH WALES 155-9 (40.4 OVERS) BEAT SOUTH AUSTRALIA 154 (43.5 OVERS) BY 1 WKT

FORD RANGER CUP

2006-07	QUEENSLAND 274-5 (50 OVERS) BEAT VICTORIA 253-9 (50 OVERS) BY 21 RUNS
2007-08	TASMANIA 131-9 (30.1 OVERS) BEAT VICTORIA 158 (37.3 OVERS) BY 1 WKT (D/L)
2008-09	QUEENSLAND 187-8 (50 OVERS) BEAT VICTORIA 175 (48 OVERS) BY 12 RUNS
2009-10	TASMANIA 304-6 (50 OVERS) BEAT VICTORIA 194 (42.1 OVERS) BY 110 RUNS

RYOBI CUP

2010-11	VICTORIA 194 (36.4 OVERS) BEAT TASMANIA 109 (31.1 OVERS) BY 84 RUNS

SOUTH AFRICA

The first competition organized for major teams in South Africa was instituted in 1876. The silver inscription on the competition trophy – a cricket bat – reads: "Presented to the cricketers of the Colony of Good Hope by the municipality of Port Elizabeth." Named the Champion Bat Competition, the trophy was won twice by King William's Town, and once each by Kimberley, Port Elizabeth and Western Province. The final competition took place in 1890.

The Champion Bat Competition, which was only granted first-class status in 1890, was put in abeyance when the Currie Cup was established. Sir Donald Currie, the founder of the Castle Shipping Line, which carried passengers and goods between the United Kingdom and South Africa, donated a cup to be presented to the South African team which performed best against the 1888-89 England tourists.

Kimberley were awarded the Cup and from 1889-90 onwards the Currie Cup was competed for by the major sides in the country. In the first year, just one Currie Cup game took place, Transvaal challenging and beating Kimberley. The second season was a repeat of the first, except that Kimberley won the cup back. There was no competition in 1891-92 because of the tour of an England side – this was indeed to be the pattern for many years to come. If a first-class touring side visited South Africa, the Currie Cup was abandoned for the season.

Frank Hearne, the Kent allrounder, emigrated to South Africa and was engaged as coach to

Trevor Goddard (left) and Jackie McGlew played an integral part in Natal's domination of the South African domestic scene in the late 1950s and early '60s.

Western Province from 1889. He also played for them, making a material difference to the strength of that side. They won the Currie Cup in 1892-93 and took the title in three out of the next four competitions.

The Boer War caused a gap from 1898-99 to 1901-02, then Transvaal won the title, all the matches being staged in Port Elizabeth.

It is amusing now to note the career of P.H. de Villiers. He had played for Western Province, but moved to Transvaal and fought on the Boer side. According to legend, he was wearing his cricketing gear when captured by the British, shipped out as a P.O.W. to Ceylon, where he organized what he called the Curry Cup, among fellow prisoners, then a P.O.W. team against Ceylon match, which the Governor of Ceylon attended.

The Edwardian era saw the emergence of some quite brilliant googly bowlers: Aubrey Faulkner of Transvaal; A.E.E. Vogler, who played for three different provinces; and Gordon White of Transvaal. A fourth notable spin bowler was Reggie Schwarz. When he toured England with the 1907 South Africans, he topped the first-class bowling table with 137 wickets at 11.79 each. Curiously, while at Cambridge University, Schwarz had not only failed to gain a blue, but he never played in a first-class game for the University. He played for Transvaal from 1902-03 to 1909-10.

The great batsman of this era was Dave Nourse, whose career began with Natal in 1896-97 and ended with Western Province in 1935-36. Long before his final game, he was known as the Grand Old Man of South African cricket.

Virtually all cricket in South Africa had been played on matting wickets, but this changed and by the time Wally Hammond's England side toured in 1938-39, all the principal grounds had turf wickets. The only

matting wickets encountered by the tourists were in Rhodesia.

A major change in the Currie Cup competition occurred in 1951-'52 when the provincial sides were divided into two sections. Section A comprised Eastern Province, Natal, Transvaal and Western Province; Section B comprised Orange Free State, Rhodesia, Border, North-Eastern Transvaal and Griqualand West. The authorities reverted to a single division in 1960-61,

but in 1962-63 went back to two divisions.

Natal were, by and large, the strongest team from the 1930s right through to the late 1960s and had three notable players in the 1950s and early 60s: Roy McLean, Jackie McGlew and Trevor Goddard.

Transvaal wrested the cup from Natal in 1968-69. They were to dominate the competition for the next 20 years during which, because of the political situation, South

Shaun Pollock is the latest member of his country's most famous sporting dynasty. His father Peter and uncle Graeme both played with distinction for South Africa.

Africa was excluded from the Test arena.

In 1982-83, Transvaal played in all the competition's 22 matches and lost just one. The team was led by Clive Rice; the leading scorer was Jimmy Cook; the bowling was opened by Vincent van der Bijl; and

Alan Kourie, slow left arm, was the principal wicket-taker.

The major domestic limited-overs competition began in 1969-70 on an unofficial basis - sponsored by Gillette - but, in the second year, it was recognized and ran on a knock-out basis until 1979-80, after which the semi-finals were played over two legs (home and away). From 1986-87, the teams were divided into two pools with the top two sides going into the semi-finals.

In 1981-82, a new competition, played under lights and sponsored by Benson & Hedges, was introduced. This, using coloured clothing and other novelties, took the public interest away from the original competition, so much so that 1992-93 saw the end of the daytime limited-overs competition.

Currie becomes Castle

The beginning of the 1990s saw the political situation in South Africa change. The two governing bodies of cricket in the country - the South African Cricket Union and the South African Cricket Board - joined to form

Captain Dale Benkenstein's second-innings 259 (out of 754) was enough to secure the Natal Dolphins Supersport Series success against Northerns in the 2002 final.

the United Cricket Board of South Africa. One of the consequences of the amalgamation was a restructuring of the Currie Cup. The name was changed to the Castle Cup.

Eastern Province wrested the top place in domestic cricket from Rice's Transvaal during this period – in 1991-92 Eastern won the Castle Cup for the third time in four years. Another side to flourish was Orange Free State, managed by Eddie Barlow, whose stars were the West Indian Franklyn Stephenson and the fast bowler Allan Donald. Below the top level, further changes took place in that the lower division of the first-class scene was divided into two sections, the UCB Bowl and the President's Competition. The efforts made by Barlow in the Free State paid off as the side won the Castle Cup for the first time in 1992-93 then, the following year, performed the double by retaining the title and taking the Benson & Hedges Night Competition as well.

The Castle Cup was replaced by the Super Sports Series in 1996-97, and there were several name changes: Transvaal became Gauteng; Western Transvaal became North West and Northern Transvaal became Northerns.

Cricket in South Africa is proving ever more popular and its base is growing as the talents of the black and coloured cricketers are being discovered and utilized, notably in Soweto. In order to reflect the racial mix of the country, in 1999 it was made compulsory for first-class provincial sides to include at least one coloured player in any XI.

Also in that year the Super Sports Series rules were altered. Instead of a single league, the teams were divided into two pools. The top four in each pool then went on to a Super Eight Final League.

The defeat of South Africa by Australia in 2000-01 and the apparent decline of cricket standards in provincial matches, prompted the United Cricket Board to appoint a firm of independent consultants to review cricket overall and make recommendations. The result was that six professional teams were created from the existing principal provincial sides, for example Gauteng and North West were reformed as the "Lions"; Free State became the "Eagles". In 2003-04, these new teams played in a new competition based on the English Twenty/20 concept. It was enormously successful with 153,000 spectators watching the 17 matches.

In 2004-05, the same six teams competed in the first-class competition. The 11 old clubs were formed into an amateur league, while a third tier of clubs had a similar competition at a still lower level.

While the reduction in teams at the top level improved the standards, it meant fewer opportunities for full-time professionals, which resulted in some promising young players seeking employment overseas - most notably Kevin Pietersen.

CASTLE CUP

1889-90	TRANSVAAL	1934-35	TRANSVAAL	1973-74	NATAL
1890-91	KIMBERLEY	1936-37	NATAL	1974-75	WESTERN PROVINCE
1892-93	WESTERN PROVINCE	1937-38	NATAL, TRANSVAAL	1975-76	NATAL
1893-94	WESTERN PROVINCE	1946-47	NATAL	1976-77	NATAL
1894-95	TRANSVAAL	1947-48	NATAL	1977-78	WESTERN PROVINCE
1896-97	WESTERN PROVINCE	1950-51	TRANSVAAL	1978-79	TRANSVAAL
1897-98	WESTERN PROVINCE	1951-52	NATAL	1979-80	TRANSVAAL
1902-03	TRANSVAAL	1952-53	WESTERN PROVINCE	1980-81	NATAL
1903-04	TRANSVAAL	1954-55	NATAL	1981-82	WESTERN PROVINCE
1904-05	TRANSVAAL	1955-56	WESTERN PROVINCE	1982-83	TRANSVAAL
1906-07	TRANSVAAL	1958-59	TRANSVAAL	1983-84	TRANSVAAL
1908-09	WESTERN PROVINCE	1959-60	NATAL	1984-85	TRANSVAAL
1910-11	NATAL	1960-61	NATAL	1985-86	WESTERN PROVINCE
1912-13	NATAL	1962-63	NATAL	1986-87	TRANSVAAL
1920-21	WESTERN PROVINCE	1963-64	NATAL	1987-88	TRANSVAAL
1921-22	NATAL,	1965-66	NATAL, TRANSVAAL	1988-89	EASTERN PROVINCE
	TRANSVAAL,	1966-67	NATAL	1989-90	EASTERN PROVINCE,
	WESTERN PROVINCE	1967-68	NATAL		WESTERN PROVINCE
1923-24	TRANSVAAL	1968-69	TRANSVAAL	1990-91	WESTERN PROVINCE
1925-26	TRANSVAAL	1969-70	TRANSVAAL,	1991-92	EASTERN PROVINCE
1926-27	TRANSVAAL		WESTERN PROVINCE	1992-93	ORANGE FREE STATE
1929-30	TRANSVAAL	1970-71	TRANSVAAL	1993-94	ORANGE FREE STATE
1931-32	WESTERN PROVINCE	1971-72	TRANSVAAL	1994-95	NATAL
1933-34	NATAL	1972-73	TRANSVAAL	1995-96	WESTERN PROVINCE

SUPERSPORT SERIES

1996-97	NATAL	2001-02	KWAZULU-NATAL	2005-06	DOLPHINS
1997-98	FREE STATE	2002-03	EASTERNS	2006-07	TITANS
1998-99	WESTERN PROVINCE	2003-04	WESTERN PROVINCE	2007-08	EAGLES
1999-00	GAUTENG	2004-05	EAGLES,	2008-09	TITANS
2000-01	WESTERN PROVINCE		DOLPHINS	2009-10	CAPE COBRAS

BENSON AND HEDGES NIGHT SERIES

1981-82 TRANSVAAL 265-7 (47.3 OVERS) BEAT NATAL 263 (49.3 OVERS) BY 3 WKTS	BEAT WESTERN PROVINCE 244-2 (45 OVERS) BY 6 WKTS
1982-83 TRANSVAAL 277-4 (42.0 OVERS) BEAT WESTERN PROVINCE 275-9 (45 OVERS) BY 6 WKTS	**1992-93** TRANSVAAL 193-7 (45 OVERS) BEAT NATAL 192-8 (45 OVERS) BY 1 RUN
1983-84 NATAL 125-3 (29.2 OVERS) BEAT EASTERN PROVINCE 124 (37.3 OVERS) BY 7 WKTS	**1993-94** ORANGE FREE STATE 108-3 (28.1 OVERS) BEAT NATAL 103 (36.2 OVERS) BY 7 WKTS
1984-85 TRANSVAAL 179-3 (36.2 OVERS) BEAT NORTHERN TRANSVAAL 176 (43.1 OVERS) BY 7 WKTS	**1994-95** ORANGE FREE STATE 291-8 (50 OVERS) BEAT EASTERN PROVINCE 177-8 (50 OVERS) BY 113 RUNS
1985-86 WESTERN PROVINCE 265-4 (45 OVERS) BEAT NORTHERN TRANSVAAL 253-9 (45 OVERS) BY 12 RUNS	**1995-96** ORANGE FREE STATE 290-6 (45 OVERS) BEAT TRANSVAAL 148 (37.4 OVERS) BY 142 RUNS
1986-87 WESTERN PROVINCE 205-6 (45 OVERS) BEAT TRANSVAAL 164 (41.4 OVERS) BY 41 RUNS	**1996-97** NATAL BEAT WESTERN PROVINCE WINNING TWO OUT OF THREE FINALS
1987-88 WESTERN PROVINCE 190-5 (44 OVERS) BEAT TRANSVAAL 189 (44.3 OVERS) BY 5 WKTS	**1997-98** GAUTENG 193-7 (43.2 OVERS) BEAT NORTH ERNS 192 (40.5 OVERS) BY 3 WKTS
1988-89 ORANGE FREE STATE 213 (45 OVERS) BEAT WESTERN PROVINCE 152 (39.4 OVERS) BY 61 RUNS	**1998-99** GRIQUALAND WEST 199-4 (45 OVERS) BEAT BORDER 198-6 (45 OVERS) BY 6 WKTS
1989-90 EASTERN PROVINCE 205-9 (45 OVERS) BEAT NATAL 202 (44.5 OVERS) BY 1 WKT	**1999-00** BOLAND 209-6 (45 OVERS) BEAT EASTERN PROVINCE 173-8 (45 OVERS) BY 36 RUNS
1990-91 WESTERN PROVINCE 168-4 (39.3 OVERS) BEAT NATAL 164-8 (45 OVERS) BY 6 WKTS	**2000-01** KWAZULU-NATAL 217-7 (44 OVERS) BEAT NORTHERNS 214 (45 OVERS) BY 3 WKTS
1991-92 EASTERN PROVINCE 246-4 (44.1 OVERS)	**2001-02** KWAZULU-NATAL 223-6 (45 OVERS) BEAT WESTERN PROVINCE 195-9 (45 OVERS) BY 28 RUNS

UCB BOWL

1977-78	NORTHERN TRANSVAAL	1991-92	EASTERN TRANSVAAL
1978-79	NORTHERN TRANSVAAL	1992-93	BOLAND
1979-80	NATAL B	1993-94	TRANSVAAL B,
1980-81	WESTERN PROVINCE B		WESTERN PROVINCE B
1981-82	BOLAND	1994-95	NATAL B
1982-83	WESTERN PROVINCE B	1995-96	GRIQUALAND WEST
1983-84	WESTERN PROVINCE B	1996-97	EASTERN PROVINCE B
1984-85	TRANSVAAL B	1997-98	NORTH WEST
1985-86	BOLAND	1998-99	NORTH WEST
1986-87	TRANSVAAL B	1999-00	WESTERN PROVINCE B
1987-88	BOLAND	2000-01	WESTERN PROVINCE B
1988-89	BORDER		
1989-90	BORDER, WESTERN PROVINCE B		
1990-91	BORDER, WESTERN PROVINCE B		

STANDARD BANK CUP

2002-03 WESTERN PROVINCE 129-1 (12.5 OVERS) BEAT GRIQUALAND WEST 125 (38.2 OVERS) BY 9 WKTS
2003-04 GAUTENG 146-3 (33.3 OVERS) BEAT EASTERNS 144 (43.3 OVERS) BY 7 WKTS
2004-05 EAGLES 259-3 (43.4 OVERS) BEAT TITANS 258-5 (45 OVERS) BY 7 WKTS
2005-06 EAGLES 143-8 (39.2 OVERS) BEAT TITANS 142 (42.3 OVERS) BY 2 WKTS

PRO 20 SERIES

2006-07 LIONS 148-4 (17.4 OVERS) BEAT CAPE COBRAS 147-9 (20 OVERS) BY 6 WKTS
2007-08 EAGLES 158-7 (20 OVERS) BEAT CAPE COBRAS 152-6 (20 OVERS) BY 6 RUNS
2008-09 CAPE COBRAS 147-6 (20 OVERS) BEAT EAGLES 125-8 (20 OVERS) BY 22 RUNS
2009-10 WARRIORS 186-2 (20 OVERS) BEAT LIONS 104 (17.5 OVERS) BY 82 RUNS

NEW ZEALAND

The first three-day game between two New Zealand provinces – Otago v Canterbury – at Dunedin in January 1864 is considered as the starting point of first-class cricket in the country. They met annually in the single New Zealand first-class game until 1873-74, when Auckland, Nelson and Wellington joined the sides designated as first-class. Taranki acquired first-class status in 1882-83 and Hawkes Bay in 1883-84.

The provinces were presented with a trophy by Lord Plunkett, the Governor-General, in 1906-07. The New Zealand Cricket Council awarded it to Canterbury on the grounds that the province had given the best performance against the MCC side which had just toured.

The trophy – a shield – was to be competed for on a challenge basis. Auckland, in December 1907, were the first successful challengers and they managed to retain it for more than three years.

In 1921, the New Zealand Cricket

Above: **Having made his Test debut at the age of 18, Daniel Vettori went on to captain New Zealand and become one of the world's leading spin bowlers.**

Right: **Under Stephen Fleming's astute leadership, the Black Caps developed into one of the world's major cricketing forces – particularly in the one-day arena.**

A brilliant Man of the Match-winning all-round performance from Chris Cairns (4 for 53 followed by an unbeaten 41) was the difference between the two sides as Canterbury beat Central Districts by five wickets in the 2006 Shell Cup final.

Council decided to set up a league. Despite the fact that various New Zealand sides had imported professionals from England to improve the standard, it cannot be said that the quality prior to the First World War was high. There was no question of New Zealand warranting Test-match status and touring sides to the country were not up to Sheffield Shield rank.

The four major associations which comprised the initial Plunkett league were Auckland, Canterbury, Otago and Wellington. Hawkes Bay was designated a minor association. The Hawke Cup was the trophy for the minor associations and continued to be run on a challenge basis.

After the Second World War, two more sides were promoted to first-class status and joined the Plunkett Shield, Central Districts, in 1950-51, and Northern Districts, in 1956-57. In general, the sides were fairly evenly matched and, apart from a four-season period in the 1930s - when Auckland won successive titles - no side has been champion for more than two consecutive summers. Notable Auckland players of that purple patch were batsmen Mervyn Wallace, Graham Vivian and Bill Carson and fast bowler Jack Cowie.

Directly after the Second World War, New Zealand produced a record-breaking batsman, Bert Sutcliffe. Initially he played for Auckland, but then switched to Otago, for whom he hit two triple-centuries, the highest being 385 against Canterbury in 1952-53. This remains the Plunkett Shield record.

After the appearance of Bert Sutcliffe, came the debut of John Reid, who played for Wellington from 1947-48 to 1964-65, apart from two seasons with Otago. The Hadlee family were the major force for Canterbury. Walter Hadlee's career commenced in the 1930s and continued until 1951-52. His three sons all represented the province

Mathew Sinclair averaged 47.42 with the bat as Central Districts collected the State Championship in the 2005-06 season.

and one, Richard Hadlee, was the greatest cricketer New Zealand has yet produced. Initially a tearaway fast bowler, he developed into not only the most accurate bowler of his generation, but also a very aggressive left-hand middle-order batsman. The brothers Martin and Jeff Crowe, first with Auckland until Martin moved to Central Districts, were major batsmen of the 1980s.

In 1975-76, Shell Oil took over sponsorship of the Plunkett Shield. At first there was a Shell Cup for the league winners and a Shell Trophy for a knock-out competition, but in the 1979-80 season the trophy was given to the league winners and the cup to the winners of a limited-overs competition which had commenced in 1971-72.

In 1997-98 "Conference Cricket" was introduced, with four teams, three from New Zealand and Bangladesh. The teams competed in both four-day and one-day matches. In 1998-99, the one-day matches were ditched and Pakistan A replaced Bangladesh. The whole plan was scrapped for 2000-01.

In 2002-03, the Cricket Players' Association, formed in 2001, saw how much money the Board was earning through TV deals and demanded a 60 per cent pay rise for their 128 members. When this was rejected, the players went on strike. The strike lasted six weeks. Stephen Fleming and Chris Cairns acted as negotiators on behalf of the players and, eventually, a four-year contract system was agreed together with a 15 per cent pay rise.

The first-class State Championship had a revised format in 2001-02, and yet another one for 2003-04.

NZ MOTOR CORPORATION TOURNAMENT

1971-72	CANTERBURY 129-3 (33.3 OVERS) BEAT WELLINGTON 127 (36.5 OVERS) BY 7 WKTS
1972-73	AUCKLAND 209-6 (40 OVERS) BEAT OTAGO 144 (34 OVERS) BY 65 RUNS
1973-74	WELLINGTON 212-9 (34 OVERS) BEAT AUCKLAND 209-7 (35 OVERS) BY 1 WKT
1974-75	WELLINGTON 181-7 (35 OVERS) BEAT NORTHERN DISTRICTS 165-8 (35 OVERS) BY 16 RUNS
1975-76	CANTERBURY 233-6 (35 OVERS) BEAT WELLINGTON 153-7 (35 OVERS) BY 80 RUNS
1976-77	CANTERBURY 178-7 (34.1 OVERS) BEAT NORTHERN DISTRICTS 176-7 (35 OVERS) BY 3 WKTS

GILLETTE CUP

| 1977-78 | CANTERBURY 211-9 (30 OVERS) BEAT NORTHERN DISTRICTS 154-9 (30 OVERS) BY 57 RUNS |
| 1978-79 | AUCKLAND 156 (34.6 OVERS) BEAT CANTERBURY 143-9 (35 OVERS) BY 13 RUNS |

NATIONAL KNOCK-OUT TOURNAMENT

| 1979-89 | NORTHERN DISTRICTS 183-8 (50 OVERS) BEAT OTAGO 182-8 (50 OVERS) BY 2 WKTS |

SHELL CUP KNOCK-OUT TOURNAMENT

1980-81	AUCKLAND 188-7 (49.1 OVERS) BEAT CANTERBURY 186 (49.3 OVERS) BY 3 WKTS
1981-82	WELLINGTON 205-2 (47.5 OVERS) BEAT CANTERBURY 204-7 (50 OVERS) BY 8 WKTS
1982-83	AUCKLAND 212-5 (49.1 OVERS) BEAT NORTHERN DISTRICTS 210 (49.2 OVERS) BY 5 WKTS
1983-84	AUCKLAND 130-5 (33.3 OVERS) BEAT WELLINGTON 129-6 (35 OVERS) BY 5 WKTS
1984-85	CENTRAL DISTRICTS 156-2 (43.2 OVERS) BEAT WELLINGTON 153 (48.2 OVERS) BY 8 WKTS
1985-86*	CANTERBURY
1986-87*	AUCKLAND
1987-88*	OTAGO
1988-89*	WELLINGTON

*THESE TEAMS WERE THE WINNERS WHEN THIS COMPETITION WAS RUN ON A LEAGUE BASIS DURING THESE SEASONS.

1989-90	AUCKLAND 198-8 (50 OVERS) BEAT CENTRAL DISTRICTS 176-9 (50 OVERS) BY 22 RUNS
1990-91	WELLINGTON 214-8 (50 OVERS) BEAT CENTRAL DISTRICTS 140 (42.4 OVERS) BY 74 RUNS
1991-92	CANTERBURY 252 (49.4 OVERS) BEAT WELLINGTON 249 (49.4 OVERS) BY 3 RUNS
1992-93	CANTERBURY 183-8 (50 OVERS) BEAT OTAGO 169-9 (50 OVERS) BY 14 RUNS
1993-94	CANTERBURY 240-7 (50 OVERS) BEAT CENTRAL DISTRICTS 215 (49 OVERS) BY 25 RUNS
1994-95	NORTHERN DISTRICTS 256-8 (50 OVERS) BEAT WELLINGTON 108(29.3 OVERS) BY 148 RUNS
1995-96	CANTERBURY 329-5 (50 OVERS) BEAT NORTHERN DISTRICTS 213 (44.4 OVERS) BY 116 RUNS
1996-97	CANTERBURY 204-7 (50 OVERS) BEAT WELLINGTON 81 (33.5 OVERS) BY 123 RUNS
1997-98	NORTHERN DISTRICTS 189-9 (50 OVERS) BEAT CANTERBURY 134 (33.1 OVERS) BY 55 RUNS
1998-99	CANTERBURY 217-7 (50 OVERS) BEAT WELLINGTON 168 (44 OVERS) BY 49 RUNS
1999-00	CANTERBURY 225-3 (41.5 OVERS) BEAT AUCKLAND 224-6 (50 OVERS) BY 7 WKTS
2000-01	CENTRAL DISTRICT BEAT CANTERBURY WINNING TWO OUT OF THREE FINALS.
2001-02	WELLINGTON 200-9 (50 OVERS) BEAT CANTERBURY 147 (44.3 OVERS) BY 53 RUNS
2002-03	NORTHERN DISTRICTS 234-7 (50 OVERS) BEAT AUCKLAND 217-7 (50 OVERS) BY 17 RUNS
2003-04	CENTRAL DISTRICTS 354-5 (50 OVERS) BEAT CANTERBURY 255 (41.2 OVERS) BY 99 RUNS
2004-05	NORTHERN DISTRICTS 190-9 (50 OVERS) BEAT CENTRAL DISTRICTS 170 (48.2 OVERS) BY 20 RUNS
2005-06	CANTERBURY 214-5 (35.2 OVERS) BEAT CENTRAL DISTRICTS 212-8 (50 OVERS) BY 5 WKTS
2006-07	AUCKLAND 120-5 (21.3 OVERS) BEAT OTAGO 119 (41.4 OVERS) BY 5 WKTS
2007-08	OTAGO 311-3 (50 OVERS) BEAT AUCKLAND 310-7 (50 OVERS) BY 3 WKTS
2008-09	NORTHERN DISTRICTS 238-9 (50 OVERS) BEAT OTAGO 189 (45.4 OVERS) BY 49 RUNS
2009-10	NORTHERN DISTRICTS 304-3 (50 OVERS) BEAT AUCKLAND 283-9 (50 OVERS) BY 21 RUNS
2010-11	AUCKLAND 335-6 (50 OVERS) BEAT CANTERBURY 329-9 (50 OVERS) BY 6 RUNS

PLUNKETT SHIELD

CANTERBURY	TO DEC 17, 1907
AUCKLAND	DEC 17, 1907 TO FEB 1, 1911
CANTERBURY	FEB 1, 1911 TO FEB 12, 1912
AUCKLAND	FEB 12, 1912 TO JAN 31, 1913
CANTERBURY	JAN 31,1913 TO DEC 27, 1918
WELLINGTON	DEC 27, 1918 TO JAN 24, 1919
CANTERBURY	JAN 24, 1919 TO JAN 4, 1920
AUCKLAND	JAN 4, 1920 TO JAN 10, 1921
WELLINGTON	FROM JAN 10, 1921

1921-22	AUCKLAND
1922-23	CANTERBURY
1923-24	WELLINGTON
1924-25	OTAGO
1925-26	WELLINGTON
1926-27	AUCKLAND

1927-28	WELLINGTON
1928-29	AUCKLAND
1929-30	WELLINGTON
1930-31	CANTERBURY
1931-32	WELLINGTON
1932-33	OTAGO
1933-34	AUCKLAND
1934-35	CANTERBURY
1935-36	WELLINGTON
1936-37	AUCKLAND
1937-38	AUCKLAND
1938-39	AUCKLAND
1939-40	AUCKLAND
1940-45	NO COMPETITION
1945-46	CANTERBURY
1946-47	AUCKLAND
1947-48	OTAGO
1948-49	CANTERBURY
1949-50	WELLINGTON
1950-51	OTAGO
1951-52	CANTERBURY
1952-53	OTAGO
1953-54	CENTRAL DISTRICTS

1954-55	WELLINGTON
1955-56	CANTERBURY
1956-57	WELLINGTON
1957-58	OTAGO
1958-59	AUCKLAND
1959-60	CANTERBURY
1960-61	WELLINGTON
1961-62	WELLINGTON
1962-63	NORTHERN DISTRICTS
1963-64	AUCKLAND
1964-65	CANTERBURY
1965-66	WELLINGTON
1966-67	CENTRAL DISTRICTS
1967-68	CENTRAL DISTRICTS
1968-69	AUCKLAND
1969-70	OTAGO
1970-71	CENTRAL DISTRICTS
1971-72	OTAGO
1972-73	WELLINGTON
1973-74	WELLINGTON
1974-75	OTAGO

SHELL TROPHY

1975-76	CANTERBURY (CUP), CANTERBURY (TROPHY)
1976-77	NORTHERN DISTRICTS (CUP), OTAGO (TROPHY)
1977-78	CANTERBURY (CUP), AUCKLAND (TROPHY)
1978-79	OTAGO (CUP), OTAGO (TROPHY)
1979-80	NORTHERN DISTRICTS
1980-81	AUCKLAND
1981-82	WELLINGTON
1982-83	WELLINGTON
1983-84	CANTERBURY
1984-85	WELLINGTON
1985-86	OTAGO
1986-87	CENTRAL DISTRICTS
1987-88	OTAGO
1988-89	AUCKLAND
1989-90	WELLINGTON
1990-91	AUCKLAND
1991-92	CENTRAL DISTRICTS, NORTHERN DISTRICTS
1992-93	NORTHERN DISTRICTS

1993-94	CANTERBURY
1994-95	AUCKLAND
1995-96	AUCKLAND
1996-97	CANTERBURY
1997-98	CANTERBURY
1998-99	CENTRAL DISTRICTS
1999-00	NORTHERN DISTRICTS
2000-01	WELLINGTON
2001-02	AUCKLAND
2002-03	AUCKLAND

STATE CHAMPIONSHIP

2003-04	WELLINGTON
2004-05	AUCKLAND
2005-06	CENTRAL DISTRICTS
2004-05	AUCKLAND
2006-07	NORTHERN DISTRICTS
2007-08	CANTERBURY
2008-09	AUCKLAND
2009-10	NORTHERN DISTRICTS (PLUNKETT SHIELD)

WEST INDIES

The match between Barbados and Demerara played in Bridgetown on 15 and 16 February 1865 is considered as the start of first-class cricket in the West Indies. In 1868-69, Trinidad played Demerara in two matches, both in Port of Spain, and are considered "first-class" from those matches. Matches between the three colonies continued intermittently for 20 years or more, but attempts to organize some sort of proper competition between the colonies came to nothing – despite the fact that, in 1886, G.N. Wyatt of British Guiana had managed to pick a fairly representative West Indian side to tour the United States.

In September 1891, Trinidad agreed to play in a triangular inter-colonial tournament in Bridgetown. Barbados won it, mainly thanks to brothers Clifford and Percy Goodman, the former a fast-medium bowler and the latter a batsman.

Jamaica was too far away to compete in this tournament and they had to wait for overseas touring sides before it could field a representative XI. Jamaica's first first-class game was against R.S. Lucas's English touring team in 1894-95.

Between 1911-12 and 1921-22 the Intercolonial Tournament was not staged. The next competition, in Georgetown, saw Barbados win by an innings in the final. In 1924-25, Jamaica opposed Barbados for the first time in Bridgetown, having played another island in first-class matches

Left: **Trinidad's Learie Constantine – the first true star of West Indies cricket. It is said of him that no man played cricket for a living with greater gusto.**

Right: **After his retirement from the game, Constantine was called to the bar in 1954. He served as an MP in Trinidad's first democratic parliament and was knighted in 1962.**

only once before, when Trinidad visited Kingston in 1905-06. All three games in 1924-25 ended as draws, the pitches being perfect for batting.

In the 1920s, Trinidad gradually overtook Barbados as the major force in the Caribbean. British Guiana were also building up their strength and, in 1929-30, won the Intercolonial Trophy for the first time since 1895-96 - throughout the 1930s, the trophy was in the hands of either Guiana or Trinidad and the once-all-powerful Barbados team was out in the cold.

Trinidad's outstanding cricketer from the First World War was Learie Constantine, an all-rounder who could change the course of any match. In the mid-1930s, however, he more or less emigrated to England. George Headley was the second great international West Indian star; his career batting record gave an average just a shade under 70. Unfortunately, he lived in Jamaica and thus took no part in the Intercolonial Trophy matches.

THE SHELL SHIELD

The 1938-39 season saw the end of the old trophy and a proper competition did not re-emerge until 1965-66, when Shell Oil sponsored a trophy. At first the competition involved Barbados, British Guiana, Jamaica, Trinidad and Combined Islands (Leewards and Windwards). In the second season, the Leewards and Windwards played as separate sides but, from 1969 to 1981, the two groups united again. From 1981-82, the Leewards and Windwards have participated as individual competitors. In 1987-88, the Shell Shield was replaced by the Red Stripe Cup.

Barbados were the major force in the days of the Shell Shield, winning the trophy 12 times out of the 21 occasions on which it was held.

In the 1960s, Barbados had Gary Sobers, the most talented

Chasing Barbados' total of 249, Sewnarine Chattergoon hit a majestic 119 as Guyana clinched the KFC Cup for the second time in three seasons in 2005-06. Later in the season, Chattergoon confirmed his promise with a century for West Indies A against England A in the second Test.

cricketer of his time. Conrad Hunte and Seymour Nurse were the main batsmen and Charlie Griffith led the bowling attack. In the late 1970s, Barbados won five titles in a row, with a fast bowling attack of Wayne Daniel, Joel Garner and Vanburn Holder, and opening batsmen

Gordon Greenidge and Desmond Haynes. The Leeward Islands found two quite outstanding cricketers, Viv Richards and Andy Roberts, and took the title in 1980-81.

The principal limited-overs competition began as the Gillette Cup in 1975-76.

Two countries in the West Indies have also had their own internal first-class competition. In British Guiana (Guyana since 1966), the Jones Cup - later the Guystae Trophy and Sookram Trophy - was originally contested by the three counties, Demerara, Berbice and

Essequibo, from 1954 to 1991. And in Trinidad and Tobago, the Beaumont Cup was competed for from 1926 to 1979-80.

In 1996-97, it was decided that the first-class teams should play each other home and away, thus doubling the number of games. This proved financially disastrous. The following season the competition reverted to five matches per side; Red Stripe transferred their sponsorship to the one-day competition and the first-class competition was renamed the President's Cup. In 1998-99, a new sponsor was found and the first-class competition was for the Busta Cup.

Serious financial losses by the West Indies Cricket Board, plus the on-going controversy over the Test leadership, led to much unrest among the first-class West Indian cricketers in the late 1990s. The doubling of Red Stripe Cup fixtures in 1996-97 had cost the Board dearly.

There was further embarrassment for the Board when it was discovered that seven of the players they had picked for the Under-19 World Cup squad were ineligible, being over age.

A disastrous tour of South Africa in 1998-99, which began with an infamous row at Heathrow Airport, did nothing to enhance West Indies' most famous cricketer, Brian Lara. Politicians and academics became involved in West Indies cricket in 1999-2000 in an effort to discover what was wrong with the game in the islands. The result was a severe criticism of the standard of the first-class competition. Pat Rousseau, the long-serving Board president, was succeeded by Wes Hall.

In Grenada, a cricket academy was opened, under the control of Rudi Webster, but financial problems reduced the options open to the Board. One idea that was implemented was the introduction of an overseas team into the domestic tournament. England A took part in 2000-01 and Bangladesh A in 2001-02, but this proved too expensive, as was the plan to invite Bermuda and the USA to take part in the major one-day competition.

In 2002-03, the Board actually showed a surplus of $1 million, having lost $15 million in the previous three years. The spectre of rows between the Board and the players, plus the financial position, continues to dog progress in the West Indies. In 2006, the Board concentrated most of its efforts on upgrading the 12 cricket stadia in preparation for the 2007 World Cup.

GILLETTE CUP

| 1975-76 | BARBADOS 191 (49.3 OVERS) BEAT TRINIDAD & TOBAGO 148 (39.5 OVERS) BY 43 RUNS |
| 1976-77 | BARBADOS 97-2 (27 OVERS) BEAT TRINIDAD & TOBAGO 95 (33.3 OVERS) BY 8 WKTS |

GEDDES GRANT- HARRISON LINE TROPHY

1977-78	JAMAICA AND LEEWARD ISLANDS SHARED THE TROPHY AS THE FINAL WAS ABANDONED
1978-79	TRINIDAD & TOBAGO 214-9 (50 OVERS) BEAT BARBADOS 158 (47.1 OVERS) BY 56 RUNS
1979-80	GUYANA 327-7 (50 OVERS) BEAT LEEWARD ISLANDS 224 (41.1 OVERS) BY 103 RUNS
1980-81	TRINIDAD & TOBAGO 128-6 (42 OVERS) BEAT BARBADOS 127 (49 OVERS) BY 4 WKTS
1981-82	LEEWARD ISLANDS 95-5 (29.3 OVERS) BEAT BARBADOS 94 (37.5 OVERS) BY 5 WKTS
1982-83	GUYANA 211-8 (41 OVERS) BEAT JAMAICA 83 (25 OVERS) BY 128 RUNS
1983-84	JAMAICA 213-7 (41 OVERS) BEAT LEEWARD ISLANDS 212-9 (42 OVERS) BY 2 WKTS
1984-85	GUYANA 140-5 (41 OVERS) BEAT JAMAICA 139 (46.1 OVERS) BY 5 WKTS
1985-86	JAMAICA 173-4 (34.3 OVERS) BEAT LEEWARD ISLANDS 169-8 (39 OVERS) BY 6 WKTS
1986-87	JAMAICA 252-6 (46 OVERS) BEAT BARBADOS 249-3 (49 OVERS) BY 4 WKTS
1987-88	BARBADOS 219-9 (46 OVERS) BEAT JAMAICA 218-8 (46 OVERS) BY 1 WKT

GEDDES GRANT SHIELD

1988-89	WINDWARD ISLANDS 155-9 (49.3 OVERS) BEAT GUYANA 154-9 (50 OVERS) BY 1 WKT
1989-90	TRINIDAD & TOBAGO 180-5 (44.2 OVERS) BEAT BARBADOS 178-9 (47 OVERS) BY 5 WKTS
1990-91	JAMAICA 232-6 (49.5 OVERS) BEAT LEEWARD ISLANDS 228-8 (50 OVERS) BY 4 WKTS
1991-92	TRINIDAD & TOBAGO 167-2(37.3 OVERS) BEAT BARBADOS 163 (49.3 OVERS) BY 8 WKTS
1992-93	GUYANA AND LEEWARD ISLANDS SHARED THE SHIELD AS THE FINAL WAS ABANDONED
1993-94	LEEWARD ISLANDS 289-6 (50 OVERS) BEAT BARBADOS 255 (46.1 OVERS) BY 34 RUNS

SHELL-SANDALS TROPHY

1994-95	LEEWARD ISLANDS188 (49 OVERS) BEAT BARBADOS 110 (31 OVERS) BY 78 RUNS
1995-96	TRINIDAD & TOBAGO AND GUYANA JOINT WINNERS AFTER RAIN PREVENTED THE FINAL BEING COMPLETED
1996-97	TRINIDAD & TOBAGO AND TOBAGO 236-4 (50 OVERS) BEAT GUYANA 227 (49.3 OVERS) BY 9 RUNS

RED STRIPE BOWL

1997-98	LEEWARD ISLANDS 245 (49.4 OVERS) BEAT GUYANA 215-9 (50 OVERS) BY 30 RUNS
1998-99	GUYANA 226-7 (50 OVERS) BEAT LEEWARD ISLANDS 174 (45.5 OVERS) BY 52 RUNS
1999-00	LEEWARD ISLANDS 228-7 (50 OVERS) LOST TO JAMAICA 177-6 (38 OVERS) - D/L METHOD
2000-01	WINDWARD ISLANDS 164 (42.5 OVERS) BEAT LEEWARD ISLANDS 163-8 (50 OVERS) BY 5 WKTS
2001-02	GUYANA 223-4 (46.5 OVERS) BEAT BARBADOS 221-5 (50 OVERS) BY SIX WKTS
2002-03	BARBADOS 241-8 (50 OVERS) BEAT JAMAICA 208 (46.2 OVERS) BY 33 RUNS
2003-04	GUYANA 212-9 (50 OVERS) BEAT BARBADOS 156 (36 OVERS) BY 27 RUNS (D/L METHOD)
2004-05	TRINIDAD & TOBAGO 161-6 (39.2 OVERS) BEAT GUYANA 160 (43.4 OVERS) BY 4 WKTS

KFC CUP

2005-06	GUYANA 247-7 (49 OVERS) BEAT BARBADOS 249-8 (50 OVERS) ON SCORING RATE
2006-07	TRINIDAD & TOBAGO 210-8 (50 OVERS) BEAT WINDWARD ISLANDS 205 (49.4 OVERS) BY 5 RUNS
2007-08	JAMAICA 230 (50 OVERS) BEAT TRINIDAD & TOBAGO 202 (49.3 OVERS) BY 28 RUNS

WEST INDIES BOARD CUP

2008-09	TRINIDAD & TOBAGO 143-3 (27 OVERS) BEAT BARBADOS 142 (45.5 OVERS) BY 7 WKTS
2009-10	TRINIDAD & TOBAGO 286-6 (50 OVERS) BEAT GUYANA 205 (45.3 OVERS) BY 81 RUNS
2010-11	LEEWARD ISLANDS 139 (32.7 OVERS) TIED WITH BARBADOS 139 (38 OVERS)

SHELL SHIELD

1965-66	BARBADOS
1966-67	BARBADOS
1967-68	NO COMPETITION
1968-69	JAMAICA
1969-70	TRINIDAD & TOBAGO
1970-71	TRINIDAD & TOBAGO
1971-72	BARBADOS
1972-73	GUYANA
1973-74	BARBADOS
1974-75	GUYANA
1975-76	BARBADOS, TRINIDAD & TOBAGO
1976-77	BARBADOS
1977-78	BARBADOS
1978-79	BARBADOS
1979-80	BARBADOS
1980-81	COMBINED ISLANDS
1981-82	BARBADOS
1982-83	GUYANA
1983-84	BARBADOS
1984-85	TRINIDAD & TOBAGO
1985-86	BARBADOS
1986-87	GUYANA

RED STRIPE CUP

1987-88	JAMAICA
1988-89	JAMAICA
1989-90	LEEWARD ISLANDS
1990-91	BARBADOS
1991-92	JAMAICA
1992-93	GUYANA
1993-94	LEEWARD ISLANDS
1994-95	BARBADOS
1995-96	LEEWARD ISLANDS
1996-97	BARBADOS

PRESIDENT'S CUP

| 1997-98 | LEEWARD ISLANDS, GUYANA |

BUSTA CUP

1998-99	BARBADOS
1999-00	JAMAICA
2000-01	BARBADOS
2001-02	JAMAICA

CARIB BEER CUP

2002-03	BARBADOS
2003-04	BARBADOS
2004-05	JAMAICA
2005-06	TRINIDAD & TOBAGO
2006-07	TRINIDAD & TOBAGO
2007-08	JAMAICA
2008-09	JAMAICA
2009-10	JAMAICA

CHAMPIONS TEAMS

1891-92	BARBADOS
1893-94	BARBADOS
1895-96	DEMERARA
1897-98	BARBADOS
1890-00	BARBADOS
1901-02	TRINIDAD
1903-04	TRINIDAD
1905-06	BARBADOS
1907-08	TRINIDAD
1908-09	BARBADOS
1909-10	TRINIDAD
1910-11	BARBADOS
1911-12	BARBADOS
1921-22	NO RESULT
1922-23	BARBADOS
1923-24	BARBADOS
1924-25	TRINIDAD
1925-26	TRINIDAD
1926-27	BARBADOS
1928-29	TRINIDAD
1929-30	BRITISH GUIANA
1931-32	TRINIDAD
1933-34	TRINIDAD
1934-35	BRITISH GUIANA
1935-36	BRITISH GUIANA
1936-37	TRINIDAD
1937-38	BRITISH GUIANA
1938-39	TRINIDAD

INDIA

At first it appears odd that the first major cricket club in India should be established in Calcutta and through the 19th and much of the 20th century be regarded as the premier club in India, when the most important competition in the sub-continent until the 1930s was centred 1,000 miles away in Bombay.

The origins of the Calcutta Cricket Club are obscure. What is known is that, in 1792, the club was established at Eden Gardens and, in 1804, Robert Vansittart, an Old Etonian, hit the first recorded century on the Eden Gardens ground. The Calcutta Club, however, was exclusively European and as such gave no encouragement to the Indians to learn or participate in cricket. It was aloof and remained so well into the 20th century.

In contrast, the Parsees of Bombay took readily to cricket. Their first organized club was set up in 1848 and, in 1877, the Parsees opposed the Europeans for the first time – the Indians lost. Undeterred by their defeat, the number of Parsees playing cricket multiplied as did their clubs and, in 1886, they were able to finance a team to tour England. A programme of 28 matches was arranged against modest opposition – as the organizers pointed out, this was a tour on which to learn. Socially the matches were a great success

Chosen as the Wisden Cricketer of the Year in 1937 and with a first-class average of 71, Vijay Merchant (left) was one of the early stars of Indian cricket.

and, at Queen Victoria's behest, the Parsees played at Windsor against Prince Christian Victor's Team. A second such tour took place in 1888. On this visit was M.E. Pavri, who was to become the greatest Parsee cricketer of his day. He played for

Middlesex in 1895 while he was in England qualifying as a doctor.

First-class cricket in India began in 1892-93 when the Parsees opposed the Europeans of Bombay Presidency in two matches arranged for three days each. This fixture then became the major annual contest in India. In that first season, an English team toured the sub-continent, playing four first-class games.

In 1905-06, the Hindus joined in the European-Parsee contest, which therefore became a triangular series. In 1912-13, with the advent of a Muslim side, the contest became quadrangular, but it remained confined to Bombay and Poona. Similar communal tournaments were later arranged in Nagpur (Central Provinces Quadrangular), Lahore (Northern India Tournament) and Karachi (Sind Tournament). Apart from the Bombay Tournament, the status of the matches in these communal contests is very complicated and readers interested in the subject are advised to consult the *Guide to First-Class Cricket Matches Played in India* published in 1986.

It was not until the MCC toured India in 1926-27 that any substantial moves were made to create an Indian Cricket Board of Control. A board was duly formed and encouraged the formation of cricket associations based on the various Indian provinces.

Apart from the Ranji Trophy and the various communal tournaments between the wars, the most notable competition was the Moin-ud-Dowlah Gold Cup. This was originally staged at Secunderabad in 1927-28. Run by the Nawab Behram-ud-Dowlah, it was strictly for invited teams and the various Indian rulers gathered together notable players in order to build a strong XI and win the trophy. The tournament lapsed when the founder died in 1938. It was revived in 1948-49, but ended in 1978-79.

Centuries from Vinayak Mane (106), Wasim Jaffer (133) and Amol Muzumdar (146) were enough to secure victory for Mumbai in the 2006 Ranji Trophy final against Tamil Nadu. It was the second successive season that Mumbai had walked away with the main prize in India's premier first-class competition.

No look at Indian first-class cricket would be complete without a mention of the Maharajkumar of Vizianagram. A major patron of Indian cricket between the wars he vied with the Maharajah of Patiala for having the last word on cricketing affairs. In 1930-31, the MCC cancelled their proposed tour of India owing to the civil unrest created by Gandhi's independence movement. Vizianagram chose a picked team of Indian players and engaged the leading England batsmen, Hobbs and Sutcliffe. He then tried to fulfil the fixtures left vacant by the MCC. A fixture list of 16 matches was arranged plus entry into the Nawab's Gold Cup.

Indian independence in 1947 saw the end of the communal tournaments, though the Cricket Club of India staged a zonal tournament in Bombay for three seasons, the last being 1948-49.

THE RANJI TROPHY

In a meeting held in Simla in July 1934, the Board arranged a Cricket Championship of India which became known as the Ranji Trophy, when H.H. Sir Bhupindra Singh Mahinder Bahadur, Maharaja of Patiala, presented a trophy for the new competition in memory of K.S. Ranjitsinhji who had recently died. India is divided into five zones, North, South, East, West and Central, and each runs a league competition. The winners then went into a national semi-final and then a final to decide the ultimate winners.

The Ranji Trophy is India's equivalent of the County Championship in England. Zones disappeared in 2003 and a promotion-relegation system now exists between the Elite and Plate sections, each divided into two sections. For 2005-06 the teams were (with Ranji One-Day Trophy zones):

Bombay (now Mumbai) has dominated throughout the 70-odd

Elite A: Karnataka (S)
Bengal (E)
Gujarat (W)
Delhi (N)
Mumbai (W)
Railways (C)
Maharashtra (W)
Tamil Nadu (S)

Elite B: Services (N)
Haryana (N)
Andhra (S)
Punjab (N)
Baroda (W)
Hyderabad (S)
Uttar Pradesh (C)

Plate A: Saurashtra (W)
Tripura (E)
Orissa (E)
Goa (S)
Vidarbha (C)
Himachal Pradesh (N)

Plate B: Assam (E)
Jharkhand (E)
Madhya Pradesh (C)
Rajasthan (C)
Jammu & Kashmir (N)
Kerala (S)

years of the competiton, winning 34 times; no other side has claimed the title more than six times. Over the past decade the standard of cricket in the lesser-known outposts of Indian cricket has improved quite markedly. For example, in 2000-01, Baroda, Railways, Orissa and Punjab - teams that in the past were usually on the fringes of the competition - were the semi-finalists in the Ranji Trophy.

The outstanding feature of the Ranji Trophy has been the high scores achieved. More than 60 batsmen have averaged more than 100 and three have exceeded 200, with Rusi Modi in 1944 hitting 1,008 at an average of 201.60. He played for Bombay, as did such noted batsmen as Sunil Gavaskar, Vijay Merchant, Ajit Wadekar and Polly Umrigar. Among the bowlers, the Haryana left-arm spinner Rajinder Goel took 640 Ranji Trophy wickets - 100 more than the second on the list - but never played Test cricket.

In 1961-62, the Board of Control established a new competition which aimed to give a higher standard of cricket than the Ranji Trophy. It was named the "Zonal Tournament" for the Duleepsinhji Trophy - but was more usually known as the "Duleep Trophy". Duleepsinhji was a nephew of Ranjitsinhji and both played Test cricket for England.

The two major limited-overs competitions of the present day are the Deodhar Trophy and the Wills Trophy. The former, established in 1973-74, involves teams on the same basis as the Duleep Trophy. The Wills Trophy is competed for by the five zonal winners of the Ranji Trophy, plus two representative sides which draw their players from the Ranji Trophy teams not involved. This competition began in 1977-78.

In March 2000, a betting scandal unfolded and with such personalties as Kapil Dev, the national coach, and Mohammad Azharuddin being the centre of accusations, the press almost ignored domestic cricket for the next year.

However, like all Test-playing nations, India saw fewer and fewer international stars appearing in domestic first-class cricket, especially when, in 2002-03, central contracts for 20 top players were introduced.

The Duleep Trophy also saw a major change with three "Elite" XIs and two "Plate" XIs competing. The limited-overs Deodhar Trophy saw another basic change. England A were invited to take part, while each of the Indian sides co-opted an overseas fast bowler so their batsmen could

Below: **Wasim Jaffer took the batting plaudits in the 2006 Duleep Trophy, amassing 309 runs at an average of 61.80.**

improve standards against seamers.

An unusual scandal emerged in November 2003 when Abhijit Kale was suspended for allegedly offering bribes to selectors in exchange for selection on India's tour to Australia.

There were problems for Ranji Trophy teams in 2007-08 because the rebel Indian Cricket League clash with Trophy matches and Ranji teams lost their best players. The wealthy Board of Control, however, was able to pay Ranji Trophy players a million rupees per season, so clubs could afford to employ professional support staff.

DULEEP TROPHY

This competition is run between the five zones formerly used in the Ranji Trophy and an overseas guest team. Originally a knockout competition, it is now played on a two-group system with a final for the group winners.

1961-62	WEST ZONE
1962-63	WEST ZONE
1963-64	WEST ZONE
1964-65	WEST ZONE
1965-66	SOUTH ZONE
1966-67	SOUTH ZONE
1967-68	SOUTH ZONE
1968-69	WEST ZONE
1969-70	WEST ZONE
1970-71	SOUTH ZONE
1971-72	CENTRAL ZONE
1972-73	WEST ZONE
1973-74	NORTH ZONE
1974-75	SOUTH ZONE
1975-76	SOUTH ZONE
1976-77	WEST ZONE
1977-78	WEST ZONE
1978-79	NORTH ZONE
1979-80	NORTH ZONE
1980-81	WEST ZONE
1981-82	WEST ZONE
1982-83	NORTH ZONE
1983-84	NORTH ZONE
1984-85	SOUTH ZONE
1985-86	WEST ZONE
1986-87	SOUTH ZONE
1987-88	SOUTH ZONE
1988-89	NORTH ZONE, WEST ZONE
1989-90	SOUTH ZONE
1990-91	NORTH ZONE
1991-92	NORTH ZONE
1992-93	NORTH ZONE
1993-94	NORTH ZONE
1994-95	NORTH ZONE
1995-96	SOUTH ZONE
1996-97	CENTRAL ZONE, WEST ZONE
1998-99	CENTRAL ZONE
1999-00	NORTH ZONE
2000-01	NORTH ZONE
2001-02	WEST ZONE
2002-03	ELITE C
2003-04	NORTH ZONE
2004-05	CENTRAL ZONE
2005-06	WEST ZONE
2006-07	NORTH ZONE
2007-08	NORTH ZONE
2008-09	WEST ZONE
2009-10	WEST ZONE
2010-11	SOUTH ZONE

RANJI TROPHY

1934-35	BOMBAY
1935-36	BOMBAY
1936-37	NAWANGAR
1937-38	HYDERABAD
1938-39	BENGAL
1939-40	MAHARASHTRA
1940-41	MAHARASHTRA
1941-42	BOMBAY
1942-43	BARODA
1943-44	WESTERN INDIA
1944-45	BOMBAY
1945-46	HOLKAR
1946-47	BARODA
1947-48	HOLKAR
1948-49	BOMBAY
1949-50	BARODA
1950-51	HOLKAR
1951-52	BOMBAY
1952-53	HOLKAR
1953-54	BOMBAY
1954-55	MADRAS
1955-56	BOMBAY
1956-57	BOMBAY
1957-58	BARODA
1958-59	BOMBAY
1959-60	BOMBAY
1960-61	BOMBAY
1961-62	BOMBAY
1962-63	BOMBAY
1963-64	BOMBAY
1964-65	BOMBAY
1965-66	BOMBAY
1966-67	BOMBAY
1967-68	BOMBAY
1968-69	BOMBAY
1969-70	BOMBAY
1970-71	BOMBAY
1971-72	BOMBAY
1972-73	BOMBAY
1973-74	KARNATAKA
1974-75	BOMBAY
1975-76	BOMBAY
1976-77	BOMBAY
1977-78	KARNATAKA
1978-79	DELHI
1979-80	DELHI
1980-81	BOMBAY
1981-82	DELHI
1982-83	KARNATAKA
1983-84	BOMBAY
1984-85	BOMBAY
1985-86	DELHI
1986-87	HYDERABAD
1987-88	TAMIL NADU
1988-89	DELHI
1989-90	BENGAL
1990-91	HARYANA
1991-92	DELHI
1992-93	PUNJAB
1993-94	BOMBAY
1994-95	BOMBAY
1995-96	KARNATAKA
1996-97	BOMBAY
1997-98	KARNATAKA
1998-99	KARNATAKA
1999-00	MUMBAI (FORMERLY BOMBAY)
2000-01	BARODA
2001-02	RAILWAYS
2002-03	MUMBAI
2003-04	MUMBAI
2004-05	RAILWAYS
2005-06	UTTAR PRADESH
2006-07	MUMBAI
2007-08	DELHI
2008-09	MUMBAI
2009-10	MUMBAI

DEODHAR TROPHY

This competition is played between the five zonal teams. Originally played on a knockout basis, it was changed to a league from 1993-94. The competition has been held in a single zone over two weeks with two matches played on each of five days. The overs limit was 60 until 1979-80 and thereafter has been 50.

1973-74	SOUTH ZONE 185 (52.1 OVERS) BEAT WEST ZONE 101 (38 OVERS) BY 84 RUNS
1974-75	SOUTH ZONE 263-5 (60 OVERS) BEAT WEST ZONE 255-9 (60 OVERS) BY 8 RUNS
1975-76	WEST ZONE 185 (55.2 OVERS) BEAT SOUTH ZONE 161 (49 OVERS) BY 24 RUNS
1976-77	CENTRAL ZONE 207-7 (56 OVERS) BEAT SOUTH ZONE 206-9 (60 OVERS) BY 3 WKTS
1977-78	NORTH ZONE 177-0 (38.5 OVERS) BEAT WEST ZONE 174 (53 OVERS) BY 10 WKTS
1978-79	SOUTH ZONE 247 (59.4 OVERS) BEAT NORTH ZONE 218 (56.1 OVERS) BY 29 RUNS
1979-80	WEST ZONE 246-6 (48 OVERS) BEAT NORTH ZONE 245-9 (50 OVERS) BY 4 WKTS
1980-81	SOUTH ZONE 275-5 (50 OVERS) BEAT WEST ZONE 189-7 (50 OVERS) BY 86 RUNS
1981-82	SOUTH ZONE 260-5 (50 OVERS) BEAT CENTRAL ZONE 147 (50 OVERS) BY 113 RUNS
1982-83	WEST ZONE 198-9 (46 OVERS) BEAT NORTH ZONE 185-9 (46 OVERS) BY 13 RUNS
1983-84	WEST ZONE 309 (48.4 OVERS) BEAT NORTH ZONE 266 (47.2 OVERS) BY 43 RUNS
1984-85	WEST ZONE 218-4 (37.5 OVERS) BEAT NORTH ZONE 214-8 (45 OVERS) BY 6 WKTS
1985-86	WEST ZONE 227-9 (47 OVERS) BEAT NORTH ZONE 196 (44.5 OVERS) BY 31 RUNS
1986-87	NORTH ZONE 207-1 (39.5 OVERS) BEAT WEST ZONE 206-9 (48 OVERS) BY 9 WKTS
1987-88	NORTH ZONE 223-3 (45.2 OVERS) BEAT WEST ZONE 221-7 (50 OVERS) BY 7 WKTS
1988-89	NORTH ZONE 243-6 (45 OVERS) BEAT SOUTH ZONE 239-8 (46 OVERS) BY 4 WKTS
1989-90	NORTH ZONE 319-6 (50 OVERS) BEAT SOUTH ZONE 263-8 (50 OVERS) BY 56 RUNS
1990-91	WEST ZONE 304-3 (44 OVERS) BEAT EAST ZONE 260 (41.4 OVERS) BY 44 RUNS
1991-92	SOUTH ZONE 158-7 (35 OVERS) BEAT CENTRAL ZONE 122 (33.2 OVERS) BY 36 RUNS
1992-93	EAST ZONE
1993-94	EAST ZONE
1994-95	CENTRAL ZONE
1995-96	NORTH ZONE
1996-97	EAST ZONE
1997-98	NORTH ZONE
1998-99	CENTRAL ZONE
1999-00	NORTH ZONE
2000-01	NORTH ZONE
2001-02	SOUTH ZONE
2002-03	NORTH ZONE
2003-04	EAST ZONE
2004-05	NORTH ZONE
2005-06	NORTH ZONE
2006-07	WEST ZONE
2007-08	CENTRAL ZONE
2008-09	WEST ZONE
2009-10	WEST ZONE
2010-11	SOUTH ZONE

WILLS TROPHY

This competition is played on a knockout basis between the five zonal winners of the previous seasons's Ranji Trophy plus two representative sides, who choose their players from the other Ranji Trophy teams. The overs limit is 50 per side, although in the first two seasons 60 overs per side were played. In 1993-94, Ranji Trophy one-day matches were introduced as qualification for the following season's Wills Trophy.

1977-78	WILLS XI 214-3 (52.3 OVERS) BEAT PRESIDENT'S XI 213-4 (60 OVERS) BY 7 WKTS
1978-79	DELHI 253-7 (60 OVERS) BEAT BOMBAY 253 (56.1 OVERS) BY LOSING FEWER WKTS
1979-80	NO COMPETITION
1980-81	WILLS XI 218-7 (49.3 OVERS) BEAT PRESIDENT'S XI 216-8 (50 OVERS) BY 3 WKTS
1981-82	BOMBAY 225-7 (50 OVERS) BEAT PRESIDENT'S XI 210-8 (50 OVERS) BY 15 RUNS
1982-83	BOMBAY 158 (47.1 OVERS) BEAT DELHI 99 (42.1 OVERS) BY 59 RUNS
1983-84	PRESIDENT'S XI 269-6 (42 OVERS) BEAT KARNATAKA 242-9 (42 OVERS) BY 27 RUNS
1984-85	WILLS XI 252-4 (46.1 OVERS) BEAT PRESIDENT'S XI 249 (49.4) BY 6 WKTS
1985-86	BOMBAY 228-9 (46.2 OVERS) BEAT DELHI 226-5 (47 OVERS) BY 1 WKT
1986-87	DELHI 258-8 (50 OVERS) BEAT MAHARASHTRA 159 (37.4 OVERS) BY 99 RUNS
1987-88	PRESIDENT'S XI 244-5 (47 OVERS) BEAT KARNATAKA 184 (45.5 OVERS) BY 60 RUNS
1988-89	DELHI 205-2 (44.1 OVERS) BEAT RAILWAYS 200 (48.2 OVERS) BY 8 WKTS
1989-90	WILLS XI 265-4 (47.3 OVERS) BEAT DELHI 261-9 (49 OVERS) BY 6 WKTS
1990-91	BOMBAY 257-3 (46.5 OVERS) BEAT WILLS XI 254-9 (49 OVERS) BY 7 WKTS
1991-92	PRESIDENT'S XI 234-8 (50 OVERS) BEAT WILLS XI 206-8 (50 OVERS) BY 28 RUNS
1992-93	PRESIDENT'S XI 128 (43.2 OVERS) BEAT DELHI 128 (44.4 OVERS) ON SCORING RATE
1993-94	NO COMPETITION
1994-95	BOMBAY
1995-96	WILLS XI
1996-97	BOMBAY
1997-98	MUMBAI (FORMERLY BOMBAY)
1998-99	MUMBAI
1999-00	MUMBAI
2000-01	BOARD PRESIDENT'S XI
2001-02	INDIA 'A'

BCCI TROPHY

2002-03	TAMIL NADU

RANJI TROPHY ONE DAY

2003-04	MUMBAI
2004-05	TAMIL NADU, UTTAR PRADESH
2001-02	WEST ZONE
2002-03	ELITE C
2003-04	NORTH ZONE
2004-05	CENTRAL ZONE
2005-06	RAILWAYS
2006-07	RAILWAYS

HAZARE TROPHY

2007-08	SAURASHTRA
2008-09	TAMIL NADU
2009-10	TAMIL NADU
2010-11	JHARKHAND

PAKISTAN

The Dominion of Pakistan was created on 18 July 1947. It was formed from two separate parts of the former Indian Empire: in the West, there was Baluchistan, Sind, North West Frontier Province and West Punjab; Eastern Pakistan was made up of East Bengal and the Sylhot district of Assam. The three main cricketing centres in Pakistan were all in the west – at Lahore, Karachi and Peshawar. (In March 1971, East Pakistan became Bangladesh.)

The only first-class matches involving a Pakistan side staged in 1947–48 were Sind v Bombay, in Bombay, and Punjab University v Punjab Governor's XI. In 1948–49, the West Indian side touring India

played two first-class matches in Pakistan and, a few months later, a Pakistan team toured Ceylon.

Pakistan was admitted as a member of the ICC in July 1952 and played its first Test, against India, in the 1952–53 season. The first domestic first-class competition in Pakistan was arranged for the following season. The competition was called the Qaid-i-Azam ("The Great Leader") Trophy, a reference to Mohammad Ali Jinnah, who founded the Pakistan State.

Seven teams competed in the first competition: Punjab, Karachi, Sind, North West Frontier Province, Bahawalpur, Services and Railways. Two other sides were entered,

East Pakistan and Baluchistan, but both withdrew. They did, however, compete in the second season, 1954–55. It was soon clear that the sides were ill-matched and it was agreed that, in 1956–57, Karachi and Punjab should enter three teams each. There have been numerous changes since both in the teams taking part and in the way the competition has been run.

In 1960–61, the Board of Control instituted the President Ayub Trophy, donated by Field-Marshal Ayub Khan. In 1970–71, this was replaced by the BCCP Trophy, which lasted two seasons, to be replaced by the Patron's Trophy.

The Patron's Trophy was

downgraded to non-first-class – with matches of two-day duration – in 1999–2000, but reinstated as first class for 2000–01. In 2002–03, it was merged with the Qaid-i-Azam Trophy.

From the late 1950s, a number of other competitions were granted first-class status for a few seasons.

The principle limited-overs competition is for the Wills Cup. This began in 1980–81 as a 45-overs-a-side contest, the teams being divided into two leagues with the top two

Two legends of Pakistani cricket. Javed Miandad (below) scored 8,832 runs in 124 Tests and Imran Khan (right), with more than 3,500 runs and 362 wickets in 88 Tests, led Pakistan to World Cup glory in 1992.

Above: **The future's bright: Pakistan Under-19s celebrate their 2006 World Cup win.**

Left: **Taufeeq Omar scored a fine 88 in the 2005-06 Patrons Cup final.**

teams in each league meeting in a knock-out semi-final round.

The Pakistan Board of Control has tinkered with the game's domestic structure almost annually over the last decade. In 2002-03, for example, the regional and departmental teams had competed alongside each other for the Q-i-A Trophy, then, in 2003-04, they were once again split, while the Patron's Trophy was revived after having lapsed for one season. Teams' identities change quite frequently. Faisalabad absorbed Sargodha, Bahawalpur became Multan and Sialkot was a merger of Gujranwala and Sheikhupura.

In 2004-05, the first-class competition was regionally based, but extended to 11 teams, with Karachi and Lahore fielding two teams each. The Patron's Trophy was altered to include new teams - Defence Housing Authority (DHA), Karachi Port Trust (KPT) and Pakistan Telecom Company Limited (PTCL). Agricultural Development Bank of Pakistan changed its name to Zarai Taraquiati Bank Limited.

Due to terrorist attacks and ongoing security issues, international matches have not been played in Pakistan since 2009.

QUAID-E-AZAM TROPHY

1953-54	BAHAWALPUR	1975-76	NATIONAL BANK	1992-93	KARACHI
1954-55	KARACHI	1976-77	BANK	1993-94	LAHORE
1956-57	PUNJAB	1977-78	HABIB BANK	1994-95	KARACHI BLUES
1957-58	BAHAWALPUR	1978-79	NATIONAL BANK	1995-96	KARACHI BLUES
1958-59	KARACHI	1979-80	PIA	1996-97	LAHORE CITY
1959-60	KARACHI	1980-81	UNITED BANK	1997-98	KARACHI BLUES
1961-62	KARACHI BLUES	1981-82	NATIONAL BANK	1998-99	PESHAWAR
1962-63	KARACHI A	1982-83	UNITED BANK	1999-00	PIA
1963-64	KARACHI BLUES	1983-84	NATIONAL BANK	2000-01	LAHORE BLUES
1964-65	KARACHI BLUES	1984-85	UNITED BANK	2001-02	KARACHI WHITES
1966-67	KARACHI	1985-86	KARACHI	2002-03	PIA
1968-69	LAHORE	1986-87	NATIONAL BANK	2003-04	FAISALABAD
1969-70	PIA	1987-88	PIA	2004-05	PESHAWAR
1970-71	KARACHI BLUES	1988-89	ADBP	2005-06	SIALKOT
1972-73	RAILWAYS	1989-90	PIA	2006-07	KARACHI URBAN
1973-74	RAILWAYS	1990-91	KARACHI WHITES	2007-08	SUI NORTHERN GAS
1974-75	PUNJAB A	1991-92	KARACHI WHITES	2008-09	SIALKOT
				2009-10	KARACHI BLUES

PATRON'S TROPHY

1970-71	PIA	1982-83	PACO	1994-95	ALLIED BANK
1971-72	PIA	1983-84	KARACHI BLUES	1996-97	UNITED BANK
1972-73	KARACHI BLUES	1984-85	KARACHI WHITES	1997-98	HABIB BANK
1973-74	RAILWAYS	1985-86	KARACHI WHITES	1998-99	HABIB BANK
1974-75	NATIONAL BANK	1986-87	NATIONAL BANK	1999-00	LAHORE CITY BLUES
1975-76	NATIONAL BANK	1987-88	HABIB BANK	2000-01	CUSTOMS
1976-77	HABIB BANK	1988-89	KARACHI	2001-02	NATIONAL BANK
1977-78	HABIB BANK	1989-90	KARACHI WHITES	2002-03	NO COMPETITION
1978-79	NATIONAL BANK	1990-91	ADBP	2003-04	ZT BANK LTD
1979-80	IDBP	1991-92	HABIB BANK	2004-05	HABIB BANK, PIA
1980-81	RAWALPINDI	1992-93	HABIB BANK	2005-06	NATIONAL BANK
1981-82	ALLIED BANK	1993-94	ADBP	2006-07	HABIB BANK

WILLS CUP/TISSOT CUP

1980-81	PIA 230 (45 OVERS) BEAT UNITED BANK 225 (44.1 OVERS) BY 5 RUNS
1981-82	PIA 132-3 (32.5 OVERS) BEAT LAHORE 131 (42.3 OVERS) BY 7 WKTS
1982-83	PIA 206-9 (45 OVERS) BEAT HABIB BANK 173 (43.2 OVERS) BY 33 RUNS
1983-84	HABIB BANK 182-3 (41 OVERS) BEAT PIA 181 (39.4 OVERS) BY 7 WKTS
1984-85	NO COMPETITION
1985-86	PIA 257-3 (45 OVERS) BEAT UNITED BANK 254-9 (45 OVERS) BY 3 RUNS
1986-87	HABIB BANK 155-7 (49.2 OVERS) BEAT UNITED BANK 154 (48.1 OVERS) BY 3 WKTS
1987-88	PIA 212-8 (47.4 OVERS) BEAT UNITED BANK 206-8 (49 OVERS) BY 2 WKTS
1988-89	UNITED BANK 228-6 (45 OVERS) BEAT PIA 228 (45 OVERS) BY LOSING FEWER WKTS
1989-90	HABIB BANK 178-2 (42.4 OVERS) BEAT PIA 177 (46.3 OVERS) BY 8 WKTS
1990-91	HABIB BANK 241-4 (45 OVERS) BEAT UNITED BANK 185-9 (45 OVERS) BY 6 WKTS
1991-92	HABIB BANK 254-5 (39 OVERS) BEAT PIA 234-4 (43 OVERS) BY 5 WKTS
1992-93	NATIONAL BANK 272-5 (48 OVERS) BEAT HABIB BANK 269-6 (50 OVERS) BY 5 WKTS
1993-94	HABIB BANK 249-5 (50 OVERS) BEAT RAWALPINDI 203-8 (50 OVERS) BY 46 RUNS
1994-95	NATIONAL BANK 215-2 (43.2 OVERS) BEAT PIA 211 (44.4 OVERS) BY 8 WKTS
1995-96	PIA 125-3 (30.5 OVERS) BEAT RAWALPINDI 124 (42.4 OVERS) BY 7 WKTS
1996-97	ALLIED BANK 252-4 (42.1 OVERS) BEAT NAT. BANK 251-9 (50 OVERS) BY 6 WKTS
1997-98	ALLIED BANK 248 (48 OVERS) BEAT PIA 216 (48.3 OVERS) BY 32 RUNS
1998-99	ALLIED BANK 260-6 (47.4) BEAT PAKISTAN CUSTOMS 259-9 (50 OVERS) BY 4 WKTS
1999-00	PIA 310-4 (50 OVERS) BEAT REDCO 272-9 (50 OVERS) BY 38 RUNS
2000-01	KARACHI WHITES 278-5 (50 OVERS) BEAT SHEIKHUPURA 199 BY 79 RUNS
2001-02	PIA 236-9 (50 OVERS) BEAT HABIB BANK 230 (49.5 OVERS) BY 6 RUNS
2002-03	PIA 273-7 (50 OVERS) BEAT WAPDA 218-9 (50 OVERS) BY 55 RUNS
2003-04	HABIB BANK 266-7 (50 OVERS) BEAT PIA 135 (39.1 OVERS) BY 131 RUNS
2004-05	WAPDA 288-9 (50 OVERS) BEAT PIA 252 (49.2 OVERS) BY 36 RUNS

ABN CUP

2005-06	FAISALABAD 248-3 (44.1 OVERS) BEAT LAHORE 244 (49.4 OVERS) BY 7 WKTS
2006-07	PESHAWAR 138-2 (35.5 OVERS) BEAT SIALKOT 137 (27.4 OVERS) BY 8 WKTS
2007-08	SUI NORTHERN GAS 128-3 (27.1 OVERS) BEAT HABIB BANK 127 (33.1 OVERS) BY 7 WKTS

RBS CUP

2008-09	PIA 315-6 (50 OVERS) BEAT NATIONAL BANK 256 (45.5 OVERS) BY 59 RUNS
2009-10	SNGP 284-7 (50 OVERS) BEAT SIALKOT 152 (39.5 OVERS) BY 132 RUNS

SRI LANKA

The Europeans v Ceylonese match was contested from 1887 to 1933. In the early 20th century, it was the biggest match on the island. A representative Ceylon Cricket Association was formed in 1922 and from 1924 organized a club championship.

There were 15 first-class teams in 1924, but most "first-class" matches were scheduled for one day only. In 1937, the championship became the Daily News Trophy, but was renamed the P. Saravanamuttu Trophy in 1950. It only gained first-class designation from 1988-89, and it was known as the Lakspray Trophy. Ceylon's best-known cricketers of this era were Dr C.H. Gunasekara and F.C. de Saram.

So far as recognized first-class matches are concerned, it was confined to matches played by representative teams overseas or games against visiting touring sides. Until the 1970s, most England and Australia Test teams sailing between the two countries refuelled at Colombo and, when at all possible, a match was arranged between the tourists and a team from the island.

The first game against the tourists took place in October 1882, when England opposed 18 of Colombo. Eight years later, the Australians played in Colombo. Between these two visits England first toured India and commenced their matches in Colombo. They played two games, a three-day fixture against All-Ceylon and a two-day match against Colombo CC, both of which were won by an innings. In 1924, England were bowled out for 73 in Colombo.

Sri Lanka – Ceylon's name from 1972 – was raised to full membership of the ICC in 1981 and gained Test-match status.

In 1990-91, the Lakspray Trophy was renamed the Sara Trophy after the new sponsors. In addition to the Sara Trophy, an Inter-Provincial tournament started to be ranked as first-class from 1989-90, the sides competing for the Singer Trophy.

A list of current first-class domestic sides is difficult to compile, because clubs compete in a non-first-class section before being entered into the first-class part of the Sara Trophy.

In June 1990, an Inter-Provincial competition, sponsored by Singer and based on the Duleep Trophy was launched. Four teams competed, Southern, Central, Western and North-Western. Two other innovations at this time were an Under-23 limited-overs competition for the Brown's Trophy and the Delmege Trophy. The Sara Trophy had no fewer than 30 teams competing in 1990-91, with the top 12 clubs playing three-day first-class matches. The other 18, having been eliminated, played for the Delmege Trophy. Only the final was first-class. Another innovation was the Pure Beverages Under-19 Championship, for schools and colleges. The star in 1990-91 was Muttiah Muralitharan, who took a record 127 wickets for St Anthony's College.

In 1991-92, a new floodlit competition was launched – the R. Premadasa Challenge Trophy.

Fourteen clubs were entered into the 1992-93 Sara Trophy first-class section, but in the following summer, the number was reduced to eight. A "Super Tournament" was also tried with six teams competing in four-day matches, but the idea was ditched after just one season.

The R. Premadasa Trophy was replaced by the Hatton National Bank Trophy in 1994-95, won by Bloomfield, while the Under-23 Trophy was renamed the GTE Yellow Pages Trophy and was won by Nondescripts.

Sri Lanka's great, unexpected success, in the 1996 World Cup caused a cricket boom on the island, though the Inter-Provincial Trophy was cancelled owing to international commitments. However, the Sara Trophy was revamped with the number of matches virtually doubled to 104. In 1996-97, the Trophy was divided into two equal leagues with a knock-out final section. Colombo C.C. ended as winners. The following year they were suspended due to irregularities.

Internal rows in 1998-99 led to a court suspending the Cricket Board

Avishka Gunawardene led the way for the Sinhalese Sports Club in their 2006 Premier League Trophy final with a scintillating knock of 103.

executive committee. The Sports Minister appointed an interim committee. This put major domestic matches in abeyance for a month. The Premier Trophy superseded the Sara Trophy, though in 1999-2000 a new format was introduced with a final "super-league".

The cricket board was again dissolved by the Sports Minister in 2000-01. The historic Gopalan Trophy was revived, having been in abeyance since 1982-83. Yet more alterations were made to the Premier Trophy and another new Invitation Trophy was brought in. The President of the Board announced plans to revamp the game and create "Sri Lanka Cricket", based on the Australian model but, in January 2004, he was arrested for alleged passport offences.

In December 2004, the tsunami put a temporary stop to internal bickering and over the last few years the major talking point has been the bowling of Muralitharan, especially his "doosra".

Aravinda de Silva stood tall for Sri Lanka for 18 years, playing in 93 Tests and scoring 6,361 runs at an average of 42.97 for his country. His tally included 20 centuries.

STAR TROPHY		PREMIER TROPHY	
1988-89	NONDESCRIPTS, SINHALESE SC	1998-99	BLOOMFIELD
1889-90	SINHALESE SC	1999-00	COLTS
1990-91	SINHALESE SC	2000-01	NONDESCRIPTS
1991-92	COLTS	2001-02	COLTS
1992-93	SINHALESE SC	2002-03	MOORS
1993-94	NONDESCRIPTS	2003-04	BLOOMFIELD
1994-95	BLOOMFIELD, SINHALESE SC	2004-05	COLTS
1995-96	COLOMBO	2005-06	SINHALESE SC
1996-97	BLOOMFIELD	2006-07	COLOMBO
1997-98	SINHALESE SC	2007-08	SINHALESE SC
		2008-09	COLTS
		2009-10	KANDURATA

ZIMBABWE

Andy Flower, a veteran of 63 Tests for Zimbabwe (4,794 runs at an average of 51.54), announced his retirement from international cricket in 2003. He cited "the death of democracy" in Zimbabwe as his reason. In 2009 he was appointed cricket coach to England.

It is believed that the first cricket match took place in Zimbabwe (formerly Rhodesia) as early as August 1890 near Fort Victoria. The first English cricket side to visit was Lord Hawke's Team of 1898-99.

J.D. Logan, a well-known South African cricket patron, asked Lord Hawke to purchase a cup which could be used as a trophy competed for by the principal clubs in Rhodesia. It was not, however, until 1903-04 that a suitable competition was organized, with Matabeleland as the first winners.

Before Zimbabwe's independence in 1981, Rhodesia had played as a first-class team in the South African Currie Cup, albeit sporadically until 1946-47 and regularly thereafter.

The country was granted Test-match status in July 1992 and for the 1993-94 season organized a programme of domestic first-class games for the Logan Cup. However, in 1995-96, the cricket Board reduced the number of first-class sides to two, Mashonaland and Matabeleland, and they played three matches to decide the title.

Zimbabwe's most successful players since gaining Test status include David Houghton, Eddo Brandes, brothers Andrew and Grant Flower, and Heath Streak – plus John Traicos, the only cricketer to play Tests for both South Africa and Zimbabwe.

In 1996-97, with Alistair Campbell as captain, Zimbabwe had the better of England in two drawn Tests; then Sri Lanka, the World Cup holders, were beaten in Sharjah. They swept a triangular series with Kenya and Bangladesh in October

1998, showing evidence of the gap between the countries.

But, just as Zimbabwe cricket seemed to be on the rise, two prob-lems emerged. First, government funding for development was reduced, then Test players began to distrust the way the governing body was running the game.

During 2000-01, players alleged that there was political interference with the selection of the national side and resented the idea of a quota system promoting black players into the squad. Black players of Test standard were gradually emerging – Hamilton Masakadza was the first black Zimbabwean player to hit a century in domestic first-class cricket and for his country.

Australia's cancellation of their tour to Zimbabwe in 2001-02 badly affected the Board's finances. The question of whether they should co-host the 2003 World Cup dominated the preceding summer. Things went further downhill when Andy Flower and bowler Henry Olonga wore black armbands to mark the death of democracy in the country. They went into exile, substantially weakening the national team. Several other players also quit. Then Test captain Heath Streak was sacked after he confronted the Board with his team's grievances.

The ICC sent a delegation to Zimbabwe to see if racism was dominating the country's cricket, but failed to find any evidence. Sadly, with so many of the players leaving the country, the team representing Zimbabwe five years into the new century is now only – in terms of a decade earlier – a "third XI".

At the time of writing, matters have not improved for Zimbabwe; the ICC have suspended them from Test cricket.

BANGLADESH

After the partition of India, the country now known as Bangladesh formed the eastern section of Pakistan. Four first-class teams from East Pakistan took part in competitions. Bangladesh became an independent nation in 1973, by which time cricket there was in a poor state. However, the MCC were persuaded to visit the country in 1976-77. A second tour took place in 1980-81.

Bangladesh have taken part in six ICC Trophy tournaments, winning in 1997 and reaching the semi-finals in 1982 and 1990. In 1988-89, they held their first official one-day international tournament, hosting India, Pakistan and Sri Lanka, but were outplayed by their visitors. In 1999, Bangladesh beat Pakistan in a World Cup match, but this landmark was dwarfed on 26 June 2000, when the ICC granted Bangladesh Test-match status. The country played its first Test against India in November 2000 in Dhaka. In May and June 2000, they staged the Asian Cup.

A major domestic "National League" competition was established in 1999-2000 comprising six teams: Dhaka, Chittagong, Khulna, Rajshadi, Barisaal and Sylhet. In 2000-01, the league increased to eight teams. Chittagong were the unexpected winners of the first year, but the Board did not grant the competition first-class status.

In 2001-02 the National League (sponsored by Ispahani Mirzapore Tea) was regarded as first class, and won by Dhaka. Khulma were champions in 2002-03, but Dhaka claimed the title in both 2003-04 and 2004-05.

In 2001-02, Bangladesh struggled to compete at Test level and by July 2002, 12 of their 13 Tests had been lost, rain causing a draw in the other one. The country also lost 20 consecutive one-day internationals. Annual changes in the head coach did not help the Test squad's chances; Trevor Chappell was the third coach in three years in 2002.

Another 13 Test defeats were suffered in 2002-03, plus 25 one-day losses. A number of critics suggested that Bangladesh should lose its Test status, especially after their very poor showing in the 2003 World Cup.

The fact that the head of the Cricket Board was a government appointee came in for adverse comment.

When Dav Whatmore was given the coach's job, the team did seem to improve and a first Test victory was achieved, though at the expense of a depleted Zimbabwe. Bangladesh toured West Indies and certainly the squad looked a more robust outfit, even if they failed to win. No less than 14 major players signed for the rebel ICL, causing more problems for domestic cricket.

The Under-19 World Cup was held in Bangladesh in 2004, when nearly every match was played in front of a capacity crowd – this demonstrates the enthusiasm for cricket in the country and, in time, there is no doubt that enthusiasm will translate itself into a viable Test team.

Javed Omar, one of a number of Bangladesh's young guns who is struggling to find his feet in the Test arena. He got off to a good start, though, becoming the first player in the history of Test cricket to carry his bat on debut (v Zimbabwe at Bulawayo in 2001).

SCOTLAND

There are odd references to cricket in Scotland in the 18th century, but the game did not become established in the country outside the military and landed gentry until the middle of the 19th century and the first match by a so-called Scotland team took place in 1865. The Scottish Cricket Union was formed in 1879, dissolved in 1883 and re-established in 1908. Much confusion was caused to cricket statisticians by the fact that Scotland apparently played two matches simultaneously in 1878, one against Yorkshire, the other against England. Closer inspection reveals, however, that Yorkshire played the "Gents of Edinburgh".

The first first-class match involving Scotland took place in 1905, when the opponents were the Australian tourists. The West Indies were played in 1906 and South Africa in 1907.

The first recorded inter-county game was in 1851, East Lothian playing Stirling. The Scottish County Championship was established in 1902 and continued, with gaps for the two World Wars, until 1995. Aberdeen, Forfar, Perthshire and Stirlingshire played every year. Apart from those counties, others which at one time were champions were Clackmannan, Ayrshire and West Lothian.

In 1996, there was a drastic reorganization of major club cricket in Scotland. A new National Scottish League was created, of two divisions, with ten clubs in each and with promotion and relegation. Division One comprises Aberdeenshire, Arbroath Utd, Carlton, Freuchie, Grange, Heriots FP, Prestwick, Strathmore, Watsonians and West Lothian. The authorities have, however, established a knockout competition for the old Scottish counties.

Scotland entered the English Benson & Hedges competition in

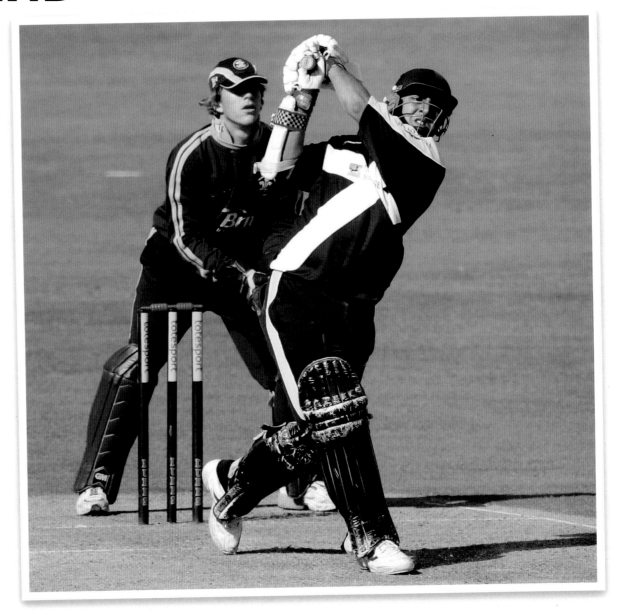

1980 and the NatWest Trophy in 1981. Their success was limited, with only two wins in the former and none in the latter. In 2003 - as the Scottish Saltires - they began a three-year spell in Division Two of the 45-over National (Sunday) League.

Scotland entered the ICC Trophy competition for the first time in 1997 and finished in third place. They gained a place in the 1999 World Cup, but failed to win a single match.

In 2001, taking part in the ICC Trophy in Canada, Scotland won four out of five matches in the initial league stage, then qualified for the play-off for third place. They lost to Canada and therefore did not qualify for the 2003 World Cup. They were consigned to the tension of a play-off after a dramatic collapse against Namibia in their final Super League match when, needing ten runs to win off two overs with three wickets in hand, they lost.

Jawad Hussain goes on the attack for Scotland in their National Cricket League Division Two encounter v Surrey in 2005.

Scotland beat Canada in the Inter-continental Cup final in 2004 and continued their good form in the 2005 ICC Trophy in Ireland, where they defeated the hosts in the final.

They took part in the 2007 World Cup, but once again failed to win a match.

IRELAND

Although there is a reference to cricket supposedly being banned in Ireland by Cromwell's Commissioners in 1656, it is very probable that hurling rather than cricket was the subject. Hurling goes back to 1200 BC according to the standard works of reference; cricket in Ireland does not appear until AD 1792. The match in question, played in Phoenix Park, Dublin, was arranged by Colonel Lennox, later the Duke of Richmond, and involved the Dublin Garrison against "All-Ireland". The Phoenix Club in Dublin was founded in about 1830 and, at about the same time, cricket was introduced into Dublin University.

The original Irish Cricket Union was formed in 1884–85, though the present governing body did not come into being until 1923. The most important matches by representative Irish teams in the 19th century were against the MCC, I Zingari and Scotland, and the first recognized first-class games by Ireland came in May 1902 when an Irish side came to England. Prior to this, Dublin University had played four first-class matches in 1895.

The status of matches by Ireland up to 1947 is very complex and readers are advised to study the *Guide to First-Class Matches in the British Isles*, published by the Association of Cricket Statisticians, if they wish to know the full details.

At present, only Ireland's match against Scotland is given first-class status. In 1980, Ireland was admitted into England's Gillette Cup competition and has been a regular competitor since, but the side has yet to win a game. They also entered the Benson & Hedges Cup from 1991.

In 1994, Ireland competed in the ICC Trophy for the first time, winning four games out of seven. In 1997, they had a successful run and reached the quarter-finals. Ireland had high hopes in the 2001 ICC Trophy. They qualified for the Super League, but ended bottom of the eight-nation league. The Irish were hosts for the 2005 ICC Trophy and went all the way to the final before losing to Scotland.

Ireland enjoyed a very successful Cricket World Cup in 2007, beating Pakistan in their Group match and qualifying for the Super Eights.

By winning the 2007-08 Inter-Continental Cup, Ireland confirmed their position as the leading non-Test match cricketing country.

Kyle McCallan celebrates the fall of Dwayne Smith during Ireland's surprising six-wicket victory against the West Indies played at Stormont, Belfast, in 2004.

EUROPE

CORFU

The single ground for cricket is in fact the main square in Corfu Town, part of the playing area being the tarmac of the car parking area round the square.

The Ionian Islands were a British Protectorate from 1815 to 1863 and inter-regimental games were played by the troops stationed there. The Greeks continued to play cricket after the islands reverted to Greece and two Greek clubs were established, playing either against each other or against visiting British sides. Sir Percy Kahn kept cricket going there between the wars, but the Second World War saw the end of matches. A revival took place following an appeal in the *Cricketer* magazine in 1952. Since that date, the popularity of Corfu with British tourists has meant that cricket is played there on a regular basis.

DENMARK

Cricket was introduced to Denmark in the 1860s by the British engineers involved in laying out the country's railway system. It was not until after the First World War that teams from England began to make fairly regular visits to Denmark and not until the 1950s that Denmark began to play the Netherlands in "Test" matches.

In the ICC Trophy in both 1979 and 1986, they came third, losing in 1979 to Sri Lanka in the semi-finals and to the Netherlands in 1986. In 1997, Denmark made it as far as the quarter-finals.

The European Championship was inaugurated in 1996 and the initial tournament was staged in Denmark. The home side finished in third place, beating an England side in a play-off.

Denmark initially performed well in the 2001 ICC Trophy, topping the Division One, Group B table, but then failed to make much of a mark in the Super League which followed. The lack of turf pitches in the country is holding back its progress towards first-class status.

FRANCE

Considering the proximity of France to the Kentish heartland of cricket, it is surprising that the game has never really established itself among the French. A visit by English cricketers to Paris was arranged for 1789, but it was hastily cancelled – just before the team was to cross the Channel – because the Revolution had started.

In the 1820s and onward, cricket was played extensively in the Pas de Calais among the Nottingham lace workers who had emigrated there, but few French names are found in the extant scores. In the 1860s, fashionable Paris toyed with cricket and again one or two English touring sides were organized – this time they actually arrived! However, most of the "French" players were English residents in the capital.

This enthusiasm for cricket among English residents continued through to the 20th century. In 1930, there was a French Cricket Federation and two leagues, one in Paris and the other in the north. The Standard Athletic Club of Paris sent a team to England annually, but no French players were among the sides. The only time cricket was part of the Olympic Games was in 1900 when the Devon County Wanderers, representing England, came up against "France". The former won by 158 runs.

After the Second World War ,various British army sides played cricket in France and made up so-called French teams to oppose Belgium and the Netherlands.

Denmark's Ole Mortensen was the best of the continental players to have made their mark in the County Championship. In an 11-year spell for Derbyshire he took 434 wickets.

In the last ten years or so, the number of French-born cricketers has grown and, in 1995, the MCC toured France, playing seven matches. The country takes part in the European Nations Cup. Nottinghamshire also sent a team to play France in 1995. An application to join the ICC as an associate member was made, but was turned down. A fresh application was made in 1998 and the Federation Française de Baseball, Softball et Cricket became associate members of the ICC.

GERMANY

There are many reports of cricket matches in Germany in the 19th century. A club was formed in Berlin in 1858 and Hamburg played Frankfurt in 1863. A cricket festival in Hamburg in 1865 included a match billed as France v Germany, but virtually all the players were English. A book of cricket instructions was published in Stuttgart in 1893; although the written part is fairly accurate, the illustrations were clearly created by someone with no cricket knowledge. The bowlers were wearing pads and gloves, the bats resemble Indian clubs and the wicket is the same width as its height!

The Berlin Cricket League was founded in 1898 and even continued in the First World War. In 1927, a correspondent from Berlin wrote to *The Cricketer* suggesting that a German side should tour England. The tour eventually took place in 1930 and the German team – which significantly comprised German-born players – played four matches. In 1937, the Gentlemen of Worcestershire paid a visit to Germany.

With many British troops stationed in Germany after the Second World War, there were frequent tours to Germany by English club sides, but their matches were, almost without exception, against British regimental sides rather than German-born cricketers. The resumption of cricket by German players has been a fairly recent development, but there are now around 50 clubs.

In 1992, the German team was undefeated in the European Cricketer Cup held in England and went on to play the MCC at Lord's for the first time. It has to be admitted that not one of the German XI who played at Lord's was German-born. Nevertheless, Germany's cricket association became an affiliated member of the ICC in 1991 and, in the last few seasons, German cricket has begun to make progress beyond the British expatriate community. New leagues are springing up and matches are being played against other European nations.

Now an associate member of the ICC, Germany performed well in the 2000 European Championship held in Scotland and, in 2001, travelled to Canada to participate, for the first time in the ICC Trophy. As debutants they made an immediate impression, managing to win three matches out of the five that they played, overcoming Italy, West Africa and Gibraltar. However, defeats at the hands of eventual group winners and tournament runners-up Namibia and Nepal – the latter by only two runs – saw them narrowly miss out on a place in the final Super League.

GIBRALTAR

The first recorded match in the colony took place in 1822. Most of the cricket on the Rock has involved the military stationed there.

Gibraltar Cricket Club was founded in 1883. The Gibraltar Cricket Association was formed in 1960 and, nine years later, joined the ICC as an associate member.

The Cryptics visited Gibraltar in 1927 and the Yorkshire Gents toured in 1935. Teams from Gibraltar have made some trips to Portugal. The principal team is Gibraltar Cricket Club – a reduction of British Forces in recent years has meant that this club dominates the domestic scene.

Gibraltar had to withdraw from the 1979 ICC Competition, but have taken part, not with much success, in the five subsequent tournaments. In Canada in 2001, Gibraltar won two out of their five matches.

ITALY

Although there had been occasional cricket matches in Italy from the late 18th century, cricket on an organized basis and involving Italians did not really take off until the 1980s.

Italy became an associate member of the ICC in 1995 and played in the ICC Trophy for the first time in 1997, but with little success. At club level, however, more has been achieved. The Cesena Club won the European Club Championship in 1996, and brought the title to Italy for the second year running.

THE NETHERLANDS

Cricket in the Netherlands goes back to 1855, when some South African students at Utrecht University introduced the game, but it failed to take root and the first proper Dutch club was not formed until 1875.

In the 1880s, it is believed, there were some hundred or so clubs. In 1883, the Nederlandse Cricket-Bond was founded and, in 1892, the first

Holland's Bas Zuiderent, who made his international debut in 1996, was part of the Sussex squad that won the County Championship for the first time in 2003.

Dutch side visited Britain. Prior to the First World War, the best-known Dutch cricketer was C.J. Posthuma, who appeared in some first-class matches in England.

Between the wars the major British club to visit the Netherlands, the Free Foresters, scarcely missed a single season without going across the North Sea. Despite the obvious difficulties, cricket continued to be played every season between 1940 and 1945, though owing to travel restrictions matches were played on a regional basis.

The Free Foresters resumed their annual tour in 1946. In 1964, the Australians, who went to the Netherlands briefly while on tour to England, were beaten in a one-day game. In the first two ICC Trophy contests, the Netherlands did not shine but, in 1986, they reached the final before being defeated by Zimbabwe. The 1990 final was a repeat of 1986, with the same outcome. Four years later, the Netherlands finished in third place, beating Bermuda in the play-off. In the 1997 ICC Trophy, the Dutch team were unfortunate to come up against Bangladesh after having achieved a place in the last eight.

Owing to their success in the 1994 ICC Trophy, the Netherlands qualified for the 1996 World Cup on the Indian sub-continent. However, they failed to win any of their five matches, their best performance being against England, when they lost by 49 runs.

In 2000, the Dutch team won the European Championship and came second to Kenya in the Emerging Nations Tournament. In 2001, they were losing finalists in the ICC Trophy Competition.

Taking part in the 2003 World Cup, they won one match – against Namibia. The Netherlands took part in the Inter-continental Cup in 2004 and in the 2005 ICC Trophy, where they finished a disappointing fifth.

PORTUGAL

The British played some cricket in Portugal in the 18th century and there are references to informal games during the Peninsular Wars. A club was established in Oporto in 1855 and, when a second club came into being in Lisbon, an annual fixture began between the two sides, both of whom were entirely composed of British residents. Cricket teams from England, notably the Cryptics, have made regular trips to Portugal since the 1920s.

In the 19th century, Tom Westray took a side out to Portugal once or twice. Pelham Warner gives an interesting account of his visit with Westray's side, when matches were played against Oporto and All-Portugal.

For many years Portugal and its cricketers remained aloof from competitive matches, but in 1995 it joined the European Nations Cup and, to the surprise of most rivals, took the title, but the majority of players were of English descent.

In the 1999 European Nations Cup, Portugal proved this was no flash in the pan by again reaching the final, but this time they finished as runners-up, losing to Greece.

SPAIN

Occasional cricket matches were played in Spain from the second half of the 19th century, but it cannot be said that any serious matches were staged until the British began to take up residence there after the Second World War. Spain joined the ICC in 1992 as an affiliated member and, in 1995, played against both Italy and Portugal for the first time in matches arranged for two days. Barcelona and Javea are two of the main cricketing centres.

In June 1989, the first Spanish cricket tournament took place in the capital, Madrid, involving four teams: Madrid, Malaga, Balearic XI and Barcelona. The home team were the winners.

ASIA

BURMA

Some kind of cricket was played in Burma in 1824 when British troops took Rangoon. Through the 19th century cricket was regularly played among the various regiments stationed in the country. King Thebaw seemed quite keen on the game in the 1870s, but refused to field and "was in the habit of using very injurious language to anyone who bowled him".

Burma opposed the MCC in a first-class match in 1926-27, at a time when Hubert Ashton, the Essex cricketer, was working for the Burmah Oil Company. After the Japanese occupation during the Second World War, there was limited cricket among the British residents but, in recent years, it has all but died out as little or no cricket has been played there.

CHINA

In the 19th century the main centre of cricket in China was Shanghai. The annual match between Shanghai and Hong Kong commenced in 1866 and Shanghai sent a team to Japan in 1893.

In 1929 there was a Shanghai Cricket League comprising six teams. Another centre of cricket at this time was Wei-Hai-Wei, with most of the players there being from the Royal Navy.

The development of the game in Peking was spasmodic – when Peking Civilians opposed British Legation Guard in 1931, it was noted that this was the first game in the city for several years. The Mission Boys' School in Chungking also had an established cricket ground in the 1930s.

So far as the Chinese themselves were concerned, very few attempted to play the game, though B. Oeitiongham, from China, came close to obtaining a place in the Eton XI in 1926 and appeared for Eton 2nd XI. Later, the post-war period saw cricket disappear from China, but in the 1990s the Beijing International Sixes Tournament was founded and in the third such tournament, in 1996, an all-Chinese team competed for the first time. It is to be hoped that cricket will grow in popularity.

HONG KONG

Britain acquired Hong Kong as a result of the Opium Wars of the 1840s and cricket is reported to have been played there as early as 1840. The Hong Kong Cricket Club was formed in 1851 and its series of matches against Shanghai commenced in 1866. In 1882, the Hong Kong side under Captain J. Dunn was travelling homeward from Shanghai when their ship was sunk in a typhoon, with all lives lost. In all, 37 matches were played between the two sides, the final game taking place in 1948.

In 1890, Hong Kong began its series against Singapore, and the colony has also played matches in more recent times against Malaysia. The Hong Kong teams have been predominantly British, with the Chinese taking little interest, but in recent years there has been a growing number of Chinese playing at junior level. The Hong Kong Sixes competition has brought world-class players to the colony and the competition has drawn the cricket world's attention to the territory for the first time.

Hong Kong took part in the ICC Trophy for the first time in 1982 and have played in four subsequent competitions. In 1994 and 1997, they did well enough to reach the second round, but both times were outplayed by the top ICC Trophy sides and ended up in eighth place.

In 2001, even though Hong Kong were seeded sixth for the tournament, the side performed poorly, winning just a single game, and failed to qualify for the second round in the ICC Trophy played in Toronto, Canada. As a result of this poor showing, Hong Kong were not invited to the 2005 competition.

ISRAEL

Part of the Ottoman Empire until 1917, the country became a British Mandate in 1920. Within a few years cricket was being played on a regular basis by the British Forces and civil administration in what was then Palestine. In 1935, Lord Melchett took a team to Palestine and five matches were played.

Israel gained independence in 1948. Its national side took part in the first ICC Trophy Tournament in 1979 and has continued to play in the subsequent competitions. Its results, however, have been disappointing – after the first three tournaments, Israel had won only one out of 19 matches. Israel took part in the European Championships in 1996, but failed to win a single game.

The structure of cricket in the country is being revamped and proper coaching schemes and cricket at youth level are now operating. These should improve the standard of the game considerably, especially after the appointment of a national coach.

The first all-weather practice facility was officially opened in 2000 by the ICC chief executive David Richards, who paid a three-day visit to the country. Unfortunately, Israel did not compete in the ICC 2001 Competition.

An arena fit for Test cricket in the UAE. Built at a cost of $US30 million, and with a capacity of 20,000, the Abu Dhabi stadium hosted the Tsunami Relief Tournament in 2005.

JAPAN

Probably the first game in Japan took place in 1863 when British residents in Yokohama opposed visitors from the Royal Navy. According to reports, because of unrest in the city, the players were armed!

The one regular fixture before and after the First World War was Yokohama v Kobe. It commenced in 1884 and in the 1930s was a three-day match. In 1919, a team from Shanghai visited Japan and played in both Kobe and Yokohama, but such visits seem to have been rare.

In more recent years, cricket has had a slightly higher profile and a cup competition has been established since 1993. Some native Japanese are taking up the game, which in the past was exclusively played by expatriates. A hopeful sign is the emergence of five university sides, but there is a scarcity of suitable grounds.

MALAYSIA

The present Malaysia Cricket Association was formed in 1963 and includes Sarawak and Sabah (formerly North Borneo). Cricket began there in the second half of the 19th century, when the Malay States came under the protection of the British government.

The major match between the wars was Federated Malay States (i.e. Perak, Selangor and Negri Sembilan) against Straits Settlements (Singapore, Penang and Malacca). At this time, the Singapore Cricket Club acted as the unofficial controlling body.

In 1927, a strong Australian touring side was defeated in Kuala Lumpur and the All Malaya team of this period was probably about first-class standard, although their matches are not generally recognized as first-class.

In the first two ICC Trophy competitions, Malaysia failed to win a match but, in 1986, they gained

Omani batsman Adnan Ilyas hammers a boundary on his way to scoring 168 not out against Hong Kong during the Youth Asia Cup tournament played in Karachi in 2003.

three victories. The country only had moderate success in 1990 and 1994. The highly successful 1997 ICC competition was staged in Malaysia and, although the home side did not reach the final eight, cricket in the country as a whole is on the increase and the main domestic tournaments are flourishing.

Malaysia did not fare as well as expected in the 2001 ICC Trophy, failing to gain a place in the final Super League. They also took part in the Inter-continental Cup in 2004.

SINGAPORE

Singapore was founded in 1819 and from 1826 formed part of the Straits Settlements. The first reported cricket took place in 1852 and Singapore was from then considered the centre of cricket in the Settlements.

In 1890-91, a triangular tournament was staged in Singapore between Hong Kong, Ceylon and the Settlements, the home side being victorious. Three years afterwards, a team was sent to Ceylon. Matches between the Federated Malay States and the Straits Settlements were played on a regular basis between the wars. In May 1927, a strong Australian side, including Bill Woodfull and Charles Macartney, played two games against Singapore, both of which the tourists won by an innings.

After the Japanese occupation, the Singapore Cricket Club was flourishing again in 1947; Hong Kong made several visits to both Singapore and Malaya. Singapore became an independent state in 1965 and its team has taken part in the ICC Trophy since 1979.

At present, there is a flourishing league with 19 teams split into two divisions. In April 1996, Singapore staged the Singer Tournament – limited-over matches between India, Pakistan and Sri Lanka.

UNITED ARAB EMIRATES

On 13 April 1984, some four years after starting his project to build an international cricket stadium in Sharjah, Abdul Rehman Bukhatir saw his ambitions realized when the Asian Cup – involving India, Pakistan and Sri Lanka – was staged there. Some 15,000 spectators watched India beat Pakistan in the final

Since that momentous day, more one-day internationals have been played in Sharjah than at any other venue and in the 1995-96 season the total reached 100. Domestic cricket in the seven Emirates has flourished on the back of the international stadium and both leagues and knock-out competitions are operating.

In 1994, the United Arab Emirates entered the ICC Trophy for the first time. They outplayed all their rivals, winning all nine matches, and beating Kenya in the final by two wickets. This success qualified the team for the 1996 World Cup. However, they failed to make much impression on the Test-playing opponents and the Emirates' only victory was at the expense of the Netherlands.

In the ICC Trophy of 2001, the Emirates failed to get into the Super League stage of the competition.

The Emirates lost to Canada in the semi-final of the Inter-continental Cup in 2004 and finished sixth in the 2005 ICC Trophy in Ireland.

AFRICA

KENYA

The British East Africa Company secured what was to become Kenya Colony in 1888; the first cricket match of note took place in 1899 and, in 1910, the annual fixture Officials v Settlers was established.

By 1933, the Asian community had developed their cricket to the extent that a match against Europeans was arranged. This fixture vied with Officials v Settlers as the major game of the season, and both continued after the Second World War. The first "international" took place in 1951 when Kenya met Tanganyika and in 1953 came the formation of the Kenya Cricket Association.

The MCC toured East Africa, including Kenya, in 1957-58 under the leadership of former England Test captain Freddie Brown. Basil D'Oliveira led a South African non-European side to Kenya in 1958.

In the first ICC Trophy contest of 1979, Kenya played as part of East Africa, but in 1982 they broke away, playing as a separate country. The standard of cricket has improved over the years and in the 1997 ICC Trophy, Kenya reached the final.

The most important series of matches played in Kenya took place in Nairobi in September and October 1996, when Kenya, South Africa, Pakistan and Sri Lanka met. The competition, sponsored by the Sameer Group, was won by South Africa. Kenya had taken part in the World Cup of 1996 and caused a major upset by beating the West Indies, but it proved their only victory in their five matches.

In August 2001, West Indies made the first full tour by a Test-playing nation to Kenya and they won all three one-day matches. The ICC ruled that from 1997-98 Kenya would be granted first-class status.

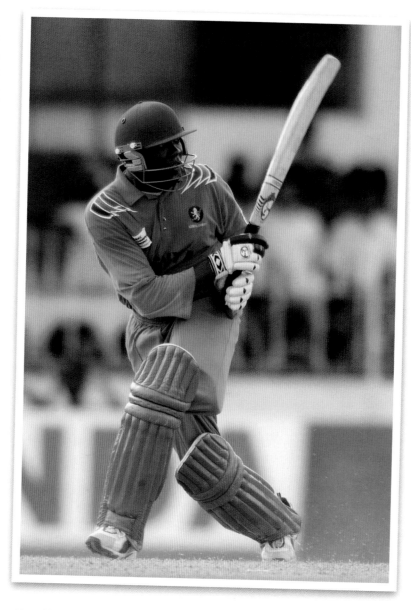

Steve Tikolo has been Kenya's leading player for over a decade. A veteran of more than 110 one-day internationals, he has also played first-class cricket for Border in South Africa.

Kenya were the surprise team in the 2003 World Cup, winning four pool matches and qualifying for the Super Six play-offs. They took part in West Indies first-class cricket in 2003-04, but did not win a match. They lost to Scotland in the semi-final of the 2004 Inter-continental Cup.

NAMIBIA

This sparsely populated country was a German colony from 1890 until 1915. From 1920 the League of Nations gave a mandate to South Africa to administer the country. Namibia became an independent nation in 1990. Namibia took part in the ICC Trophy competitions of 1994 and 1997, but with little success. From 1996, South Africa allowed Namibia to compete in the UCB Bowl. In April 1996, a South African Country Districts side visited Windhoek and played three one-day matches against local sides.

Namibia, who play regularly in South Africa, gained experience in the 2003 World Cup, but failed to win a match. Namibia also played in the Inter-continental Cup in 2004.

NIGERIA

The British presence in Nigeria commenced with the annexation of Lagos island in 1861, but it was not until 1914 that the colony of Nigeria was established. The neighbouring Gold Coast had played for the first time in 1904. Matches between Gold Coast and Nigeria started in 1926 and continued through to recent times. In the mid-1930s, two Cricket Associations were formed, one for Europeans and one for Africans. The two organizations merged in 1956.

Nigeria is part of West Africa insofar as the ICC Trophy competition is concerned. West Africa first participated in 1982, when they failed to win a match. The side did not take part in the 1986 and 1990 tournaments, but returned in 1994 when, after again failing to win a match in the main competition, West Africa played in the Wooden Spoon Deluxe Group and won all three games. However, the 1997 tournament saw the side improving very little.

Nigeria won the 1988 triangular tournament against Ghana and Gambia in emphatic style, beating Gambia by 10 wickets and Ghana by an innings and 15 runs.

In the 2001 ICC Trophy, Nigeria remained part of the West African team, which failed to win a single

match. In 2002, Nigeria – with around 1,000 players in a population of 150 million – were elected associate members of the ICC.

TANZANIA

Until the First World War Tanganyika was a German colony, while the second element of Tanzania was the British Protectorate of Zanzibar, ruled by the Sultan. There was some cricket in Zanzibar in the 19th century, but cricket in Tanganyika did not become established until the 1920s and it was not until after the Second World War that, with the formation of the Twigas CC in 1951, international games commenced. The Twigas opposed the Kenya Kongonis and also toured England. The MCC visited Dar-es-Salaam for the first time in 1957–58 and the South African Non-European side also visited the country in the same season.

Tanzania came into being in 1964 and, in January 1974, under the captaincy of J.M. Brearley, the MCC toured the country. In the game against Tanzania at Dar-es-Salaam the home country had the better of a high-scoring draw, gaining a lead on first innings.

Namibian opening batsman A.J. Burger, also known as Jan-Berrie Burger, provided England with a few moments of concern in their 2003 World Cup encounter when he smashed a run-a-ball 85.

Tanzania participates in the ICC Trophy as part of East & Central Africa, a combination of countries which had been admitted to the ICC in 1966.

AMERICAS/OCEANIA

ARGENTINA

The first cricket club was not established in the Argentine until 1831. The continuing influx of Britons led to more clubs and more cricket, and, in 1868, an Argentine side went to Montevideo in Uruguay.

The major match of the Argentine season, North v South, was founded in 1891, the principal cricketers of the day being the Leach family, several of whom had played for Lancashire. The Argentine Cricket Association was formed in 1913, by which time the first first-class matches had been played. These were the three games between the 1911-12 MCC side and a representative Argentine XI.

Between the two World Wars three sides from England – MCC in 1926-27, Sir Julien Cahn's in 1929-30 and Sir Theodore Brinckman's in 1937-38 – toured the country playing first-class matches. Argentina also opposed both Brazil and Chile during the same period. In 1932, a South American side, comprising mainly Argentine players, toured the British Isles and played a number of first-class matches. After the Second World War, the MCC sent a side to Argentina in 1958-59, but the major games were not considered first-class.

As an associate member of ICC, Argentina have taken part in the ICC Trophy, but with little success.

Argentina took part in the first ever Americas' Cup in Toronto in 2000, but finished bottom. In domestic cricket, the four leading clubs now each field a professional and this is improving standards.

The second Americas' Cup was staged in Argentina in 2002 and was won by the United States of America; Argentina failed to win any of their four matches.

BERMUDA

Although a British garrison was stationed in Bermuda fron 1701 until the 1950s, the first records of cricket come in 1844.. The following year, Bermuda Cricket Club was formed. With the colony's close proximity to the United States, it is hardly surprising that the first team to tour Bermuda came from the States – Philadephia Zingari opposed the Garrison in three matches in 1891. The early years of the 20th century saw regular tours between Bermuda and Philadelphia. The principal Bermudan cricketers of the period were the brothers J.R. and G.C. Conyers. The former was a fine batsman, while the latter bowled slow right arm. The 1912 Australian tourists to England played a game against Bermuda on their way home and had difficulty in winning.

In the inter-war period, the most important event was the 1933 tour by Sir Julien Cahn's English team. Five matches were played and a general holiday was proclaimed for the major fixture against Somerset CC.

After the Second World War, various West Indian sides visited Bermuda. The first tour by Bermuda to England took place in 1960, at which time W.F. Hayward was the driving force behind the team. Further tours took place, both to England and to Canada.

The major domestic match in Bermuda is the cup match between the two clubs, Somerset and St Georges. Alma Hunt is considered the best cricketer Bermuda has produced and he came close to being selected for the West Indies. Bermuda joined the ICC in 1966 and competed in the first ICC Trophy in 1979. The West Indies are continuing to encourage cricket in Bermuda and the country was invited to take part in the Shell-Sandals Limited-Overs competition, which involves the first-class West Indian sides, in October 1996. Though they failed to win a match, Bermuda impressed the West Indies Board and it is hoped that Bermuda will, at some date in the near future, compete in the first-class Red Stripe competition.

Bermuda took part in the West Indies Red Stripe One-Day Competition in 1998-99, but lost all their matches; they did not repeat the experiment the following season. The suggestion that Bermuda take part in the first-class West Indian competition was not taken up.

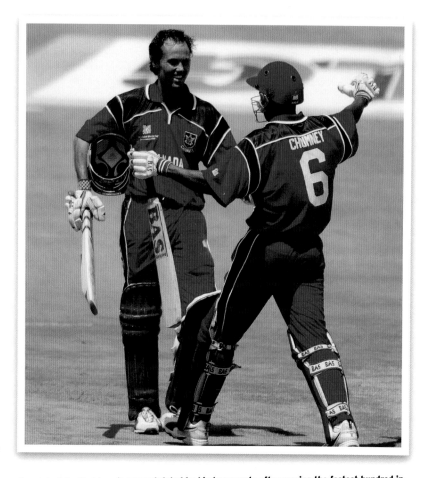

Canada's John Davidson is congratulated by his team-mate after scoring the fastest hundred in World Cup history (off just 67 balls) against the West Indies in the 2003 World Cup.

CANADA

Although there are stray references to cricket in Canada in the 18th century, it was during the 1820s that the game really became established. Toronto Cricket Club was founded in 1827 by George A. Barber, a master at Upper Canada College, who also encouraged cricket there. In 1859, George Parr's England side, sponsored by the Montreal Club, toured Canada and United States. By 1864, a club had been formed in Winnipeg and in the next decade cricket reached the West Coast. In 1844, came the first Canada v USA match, attended by 5,000 spectators and at which it is reported that $100,000 changed hands in the betting fraternity.

The Marquis of Lansdowne, Governor-General in the 1880s, was a very keen cricketer and gave much encouragement to the sport, helping to sponsor the 1887 Canadian tour to England: there had been an earlier one in 1880, but this had collapsed when it was discovered that the Canadian captain was in fact a deserter from the British Army.

England teams made a number of visits to Canada through the late 19th century and the first half of the 20th century, but Canadian cricket was weak.

The most famous inter-war event in Canadian cricket was the 1932 tour by the Australians – the visitors included Bradman in their side.

Although Canada toured England in 1954 and played some first-class matches, the game was not making great strides in Canada itself, as many of the players were British exiles. In the 1960s, though, with immigrants from the West Indies and the Indian sub-continent, the number of active cricketers increased.

In 1968, the Canadian Cricket Association was incorporated. The country entered the ICC Trophy in 1979 and has competed in all the subsequent contests. In 1996, a series of one-day internationals between India and Pakistan were staged at the Toronto Cricket Club – the first matches of such standing to be played in Canada. Two difficulties face cricketers in Canada today: one is that most grounds are also public parks and the second is that government funding has been substantially reduced. There are at present about 10,000 adult players.

The Canadian cricket authorities are striving for status as a top-class one-day international country. The inaugural Americas' Cup was staged in Canada in 2000, but there have been problems in the staging of what had become the annual India

v Pakistan one-day international in Toronto. Ten new turf squares have been recently laid and it is hoped that this will improve standards and encourage more cricket. Twenty-two teams competed in the ICC Trophy in Canada in June and July 2001. Canada came third in the competition, qualifying them for the 2003 World Cup, where they won just one match. Canada lost to Scotland in the Inter-continental Cup final in 2004.

FIJI

The first cricket in Fiji took place in about 1874. The founding father of cricket's rapid development was the Attorney-General, J.S. Udal. The islanders took to the game, so much so that in 1894-95 a Fijian team toured New Zealand and played the major provinces. The team comprised six Europeans and six Fijians. These games were recognized as first-class. In 1908, one of the smallest islands in the Fijian group actually sent a touring team to Australia.

The major problem in the colony was the lack of touring sides visiting the islands for any but the briefest of stays. In the late 1930s, Philip Snow came to Fiji. He made every effort to promote the game and two further tours were organized to New Zealand, in 1947-48 and 1953-54.

Fiji was elected an associate member of the ICC in 1965; in the 1970s, various Indian teams toured. The country has taken part in the ICC Trophy competitions, but the game is battling for popularity against rugby and is certainly not as strong as it was in the 1940s.

PAPUA NEW GUINEA

Until 1918, the country was divided into two halves, the northern half being a German colony, the southern a British colony. Cricket was taught at missionary stations in the British colony before the First World War, but the other half did not see cricket until about 1921, when it became a

League of Nations Mandate.

In the 1930s, two mission stations, at Samarai and Kwato, played cricket against each other every Saturday – there was no time limit, but as soon as one match was complete the next commenced. In Port Moresby a competition was established in 1937 for sides in the capital.

A Board of Control was founded in 1972 and the country joined the ICC in 1973, two years before becoming independent. In the 1982 ICC Trophy, Papua finished third, beating Bangladesh in the play-off. The country reached the second round in 1990, but has not been so successful in the last three contests. In July 2003, Papua New Guinea won the South Pacific Games.

UNITED STATES OF AMERICA

The first report of a match in New York was published in 1751. Between then and 1780 cricket flourished, but the War of Independence seems to have brought cricket to a standstill. The game revived, though, and the creation of the St George's Club in 1839 had a great influence on cricket's popularity. The club sent a team to Toronto in 1840 and from this stemmed the first United States v Canada match of 1844.

By this time cricket was well-established in Philadelphia and, in the 1850s, there were regular matches between various clubs from the two great cities. The first English touring side of 1859 played in both New York and Philadelphia.

The American Civil War had a disastrous effect on American cricket and did much to encourage cricket's rival, baseball.

By the 1870s, Philadelphia had become the cricketing centre of the States. When an international tournament was arranged in Halifax, Nova Scotia, in 1874, the United States were represented by the Philadelphians who duly won both the

tournament and the Halifax Cup. This cup was taken back to Philadelphia and used as the trophy for what was probably the first cricket league in the world. It ran until 1926.

Although the Philadelphians toured England, playing county teams, from 1883 to 1908 and were granted first-class status for three of their five tours, first-class domestic cricket in the United States was a very occasional affair being mostly games between Philadelphia and the English or Australian tourists.

After the First World War, cricket of any serious nature almost died out, though a league kept going in the Chicago area, and English residents in Hollywood, under the leadership of the film star and former England Test cricketer C. Aubrey Smith, played friendly games.

The post-war revival of cricket was engineered by John Marder, who established the United States Cricket Association in 1961 and, in 1968, organized a team to tour Britain, playing a series of 21 games. They joined the ICC in 1965 and have been regular entrants in the ICC Trophy since it started in 1979.

In 1996, a rival United States Cricket Federation was created.

In October 2000, the United States beat Barbados in the Red Stripe, one-day cup competition. Earlier the same summer, the United States toured England and gained victories both against MCC and Yorkshire 2nd XI. In the 2001 ICC Trophy, the side qualified for the Super League, but had disappointing results and therefore did not qualify for the World Cup in 2003. Off the field of play matters are fraught, with much bickering between officials, though the United States won the Americas' Cup in 2002.

The first first-class match in the USA since 1912 was staged at Fort Lauderdale, Florida, in May 2004, but the United States lost to Canada. And there was a disappointing tenth-place finish in the 2005 ICC Trophy.

WORLD TWENTY20 2010

England surprisingly won the World Twenty20 cup in 2010, held in the West Indies during May. Captained by Paul Collingwood, they comfortably beat Australia in the final in Barbados. Chasing 146 for 7, the Australian 20-over total, England made 148 for 3 in 17 overs, with their South African imports, Craig Kieswetter and Kevin Pietersen scoring 63 and 47 respectively. England had beaten Sri Lanka, for whom Mahela Jayawardene top-scored in the tournament with 302 runs, in the semi-final, while Australia beat Pakistan.

The inaugural World Twenty 20 cup took place in South Africa in September 2007, when India beat Pakistan in the final. The New Zealand and Australia teams were the losing semi-finalists.

The second event was held in England in June 2009. Pakistan beat India in the final, with the losing semi-finalists being South Africa and the West Indies.

Above: **Captain Paul Collingwood lifts the cup and celebrates with the rest of the England team.**

Above: **Part of the appeal of Twenty20 cricket is its carnival atmosphere.**

Right: **Kevin Pietersen's contribution to England's success was immense.**

Below right: **England pose for the photograhers after their win.**

WORLD TWENTY20 FINALS

2007 (SOUTH AFRICA):
INDIA 157 FOR 5
    (GAMBHIR 75, SHARMA 30, UMAR GUL 3-28)
PAKISTAN 152
    (MISBAH-UL-HAQ 43, IMRAN NAZIR 33, PATHAN 3-16, SINGH 3-26)

2009 (ENGLAND):
SRI LANKA 138 FOR 6
    (SANGAKARRA 64 NOT OUT, ABDUL RAZZAQ 3-20)
PAKISTAN 139 FOR 2
    (SHAHID ALFRIDI 54 NOT OUT, KAMRAN AKMAL 57)

2010 (WEST INDIES):
AUSTRALIA 147 FOR 6
    (D HUSSEY 59, WHITE 30, SIDEBOTHAM 2-26)
ENGLAND 148 FOR 3
    (KIESWETTER 63, PIETERSEN 47)

3 TEST CRICKET

The first plans for international cricket were made in 1789, when the Duke of Dorset, a patron of Kent cricket and at the time the British Ambassador in Paris, arranged for a side captained by William Yalden, the Surrey wicket-keeper, to play matches in France.

Sachin Tendulkar celebrates his 50th Test century, in 2010. He was the inspiration behind India's No. 1 ICC ranking in 2011.

However, when the side reached Dover to board the ferry, they were met by the Duke coming the other way. He was fleeing from the French Revolution... and that was the end of that idea. The world had to wait until 1844 before the first international cricket match took place, and this match nowadays sounds as unlikely as that abortive tour of France. It was a match between the United States and Canada, played in New York. In those days, North America was considered the strongest cricketing area outside England, and this was reflected in the calibre of the English side sent on the first cricketing tour. It went to Canada and the USA in 1859 under the captaincy of George Parr, captain of Nottinghamshire, and included the leading players of the day. The team won all five matches played (against 22 on the opposition side) and staged three exhibition matches.

Two years later, in 1861-62, a team toured Australia. Many of the 1859 tourists couldn't agree terms, but two went: H.H. Stephenson, the captain, and William Caffyn, both of Surrey, who had five Surrey colleagues with them. Again, most

of the 12 matches were against 22 players, and two were lost. There were also two exhibitions, in one of which the World beat Surrey by six wickets.

There followed two more tours to Australia, during the second of which, in 1873-74, W.G. Grace led the side, and two more to America, one by an amateur team in which W.G. was merely the leading batsman, before the first important tour of Australia in 1876-77. The team for this tour was led by James Lillywhite (Jr) of Sussex, the nephew of Fred and cousin of James (Sr) and John, all of Sussex. They mostly played against sides of 15, 18 or 22 players, but on this tour, for the first time, three matches were played which are considered now to be "first-class". The first was against New South Wales, who followed on but held on for a draw when an innings defeat was the likeliest outcome. The other two first-class games were against Australia and have come to be regarded as the first two Test matches.

Not that they were known as Test matches then, although the term "Test match" in relation to cricket

had been used as early as the first English tour to Australia in 1861-62. This sentence regarding the tourists appeared in Hammersley's *Victorian Cricketer's Guide*, published in Melbourne in 1862: "Of the 13 matches played, five only can be termed 'Test matches'; the three played at Melbourne and the two at Sydney." It wasn't until the 1880s that the term "Test match" to describe the England-Australia matches gradually became more widespread. Even then, which matches qualified for the description was disputed until the beginning of the 20th century. It was then that the list in *Australian Cricket and Cricketers* by C.P. Moody, published in Melbourne in 1894, came to be regarded as the official list.

The series of matches which a Rest of the World team played in the 1970s, and the Australia v ICC World XI Super-Test of 2005, although officially designated Test matches, are not included in this section.

Right: **Graeme Swann of England celebrates after taking a wicket during day five of the second Ashes Test at the Adelaide Oval on 7 December 2010.**

ENGLAND v AUSTRALIA

The first ball in the first Tests was bowled by Alfred Shaw of Nottinghamshire and was received by Charles Bannerman of New South Wales, who scored the first Test century, 165, before retiring hurt with a split finger. Australia, 245 and 104, beat England, 196 and 108, by 45 runs. A second Test was arranged two weeks later for the benefit of the touring professionals, which England won by four wickets to square the rubber.

In 1880, an Australian team toured England and Charles Alcock (who had arranged the first soccer international match), arranged a Test at The Oval for 6-8 September. W.G. Grace played and scored 152, England forced the follow-on and won by five wickets.

Australia really established their credentials in the 1881-82 season, when they beat a strong English touring side 2-0 with two draws. They then caused a big shock in 1882 at The Oval. Unusually, both teams were at something like full strength. England needed a mere 85 in the fourth innings to win. Openers Hornby and Barlow were out at 15, but Grace and Ullyett took the score past 50 and all seemed over. Yet

The first Australian side to tour England. Charles Bannerman, the first player to receive a ball in Test cricket, is seated front left.

F.R. Spofforth, the "Demon Bowler", gradually ate through the remaining England wickets until the last one fell at 77 - Australia won by seven runs. Spofforth took seven wickets in each innings.

English cricket followers could

hardly believe this result – the masters, at full strength, had been beaten. *The Sporting Times* published its famous obituary notice, framed in a black border, which read: "In affectionate remembrance of English cricket which died at The Oval on 29 August 1882, deeply lamented by a large circle of sorrowing friends and acquaintances. R.I.P. N.B. – The body will be cremated, and the ashes taken to Australia."

The Ashes

In the English winter after this defeat, the Honourable Ivo Bligh took a party to Australia at the invitation of the Melbourne Cricket Club. Bligh, before the departure for Australia, said at a dinner that he would be bringing "the ashes of English cricket" back.

England won a well-fought third Test decider at Sydney by 69 runs. At this juncture, according to legend, some Melbourne ladies burned a bail, placed the ashes in a small urn and presented them to Bligh as the "ashes of England cricket" which he had won back. The urn was labelled "The Ashes" and carried a short type-written poem. It was given to Bligh in an embroidered velvet bag, and urn and bag are now kept in the Memorial Gallery at Lord's. However, after this a fourth Test was arranged and finished in a four-wicket win for Australia.

In 1887-88, two rival teams went to Australia: that of Shrewsbury, Shaw and Lillywhite and G.F. Vernon's team captained by Lord Hawke. The two teams combined to play one Test at Sydney, with England winning after dismissing Australia for 42 and 82, George Lohmann and Bobby Peel taking ten and nine wickets respectively.

The first Test of 1894-95 at Sydney was sensational. Australia made 586, with Syd Gregory scoring 201. England, out for 325, followed on and, thanks to solid all-down-the-order contributions, made 437,

setting Australia 177 to win. Bobby Peel (6 for 67) and Johnny Briggs then took advantage of a sticky sixth-day wicket to dismiss Australia for 166 and a ten-run victory. The aggregate runs scored, 1,514, was at the time a record for all first-class cricket.

Dawn of the Golden Age

The "Golden Age" of cricket was dawning, with great players and great deeds abounding. In the second Test of 1896, K.S. Ranjitsinhji of Sussex became the first Indian to play Test cricket and made a century (154 not out) on his debut, the second English batsman to do so after Grace. In the same matc,h Australia's George Giffen, in his 30th Test, became the first player to complete 1,000 runs and 100 wickets in Tests.

In the first Test of 1899 at Trent Bridge, which was drawn, W.G. Grace played his last Test, captaining England at the age of nearly 51. Making his debut (with a duck) was Victor Trumper, a batsman whom many Australians compared with the later Bradman. In the second Test, he made 135 not out to help win the only match to be decided.

In 1901-02, Syd Barnes took six wickets in the first Test, which England won by an innings and 124, and 13 wickets in the second Test, which Australia won. Then Barnes injured his knee, and Australia won the series 4-1 with one of their greatest sides.

When the party came to England in 1902, England too had one of its best sides. In the first Test at Edgbaston, England made 376 for 9 declared (Tyldesley 138) and dismissed Australia for 36, still their lowest score in Tests (Rhodes 7 for 17). Australia were 46 for 2 following-on when rain intervened. Clem Hill made 119 in the only Test ever to be played at Sheffield (Bramall Lane) and Australia won by 143 runs.

Australia won the series at Old

Trafford. Trumper and Duff had 100 up in 57 minutes, and by lunch, at 173 for 1, Trumper had completed his century. But Jackson scored a century for England, Australia were shot out for 86 and England needed only 124 to win. At 92 for 3 and 107 for 5, it seemed a doddle, but Australia won by three runs.

The last Test at The Oval, although "dead", was even closer, and one of the most exciting on record. Australia left England a target of 263, which looked hopeless when Jessop went in at 48 for 5. Jessop then played one of the most famous of all innings, 104 in 75 minutes (then the fastest-ever Test century), Hirst stuck for 58 not out and, when Rhodes came in as last man, 15 were still required, but they got them to record a famous one-wicket victory.

Enter the MCC

England regained the Ashes in 1903-04, when R.E. Foster, of the famous Worcestershire family of cricketers, made 287 on his debut in the first Test, putting on 130 for the last wicket with Rhodes. This was the first tour sponsored by the MCC rather than by private sponsors. Such teams were always known as MCC until 1977-78 when, henceforth, they were called England.

The 1907-08 series was notable for the debut of Jack Hobbs in the second Test at Melbourne. He made 83 and 28, and England won by one wicket, thanks to a last-wicket stand of 39. An eighth-wicket partnership turned the series Australia's way in the third, setting up a 4-1 win. Roger Hartigan of Queensland, batting at No. 8 in his Test debut, scored 116 at Adelaide, helping Clem Hill (160), who came in at No. 9, add 243 in the second innings.

The 1911-12 series in Australia was the last for Clem Hill, who led Australia, and Victor Trumper, who were the only batsmen at the time

to have passed 3,000 Test runs. Trumper made 113 as Australia won the first Test, but England won the rest, with Jack Hobbs in the form that made him the best batsman of his day. He made 662 runs, average 82.75, including 178 at Melbourne out of 323 for the first wicket with Wilfred Rhodes (179).

The First World War interrupted Test cricket, and Australia dominated on resumption in 1920-21 winning the series 5-0. Less than two months after the last Test they were beginning the first in England, and Australia continued their run by winning the first three Tests. The final two were drawn. In the next series, in 1924-25, Herbert Sutcliffe established the best-known of all opening partnerships with Hobbs. Their first three opening stands against Australia were 157, 110 and 283. It was a series in which 14 centuries were scored, and half of them were scored by Hobbs (3) and Sutcliffe (4).

The famous Ashes urn.

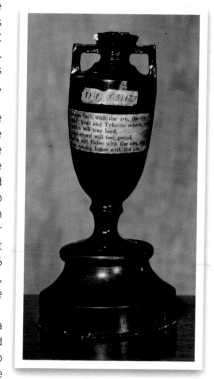

England at last regained the Ashes in 1926. After four draws in a rain-affected season, England began their second innings at The Oval 22 in arrears. On a sticky wicket on the third day, Hobbs (100) and Sutcliffe (161) opened with a legendary stand of 172. England won the match by 289 runs.

The majestic Walter Hammond was the star of the 1928-29 series. England won the first Test by 675 runs and won the second at Sydney by eight wickets. England scored 636, with Hammond getting 251. Hammond made 200 in the next Test and 119 not out and 177 in the fourth. He ended the series with what is still an Ashes record for England of 905 runs (average 113.12). A 19-year-old New South Wales batsman Archie Jackson, making his debut in the fourth Test, played one of the great innings of the series in his first knock, 164. Sadly ill-health cut short his career.

Bradman and bodyline

The 1930 series was the last for Hobbs, and the one in which Don Bradman established his reputation as the greatest batsman the world had ever seen. England won the first Test, despite Bradman's 131 in the second innings. The series was levelled at Lord's with Bradman getting 254 in a brilliant innings. With skipper W.M. Woodfull getting 155, Australia totalled 729 for 6 declared. The third and fourth Tests were drawn, but Bradman established a new Test record with an innings of 334 at Headingley, including 309 on the first day, still a Test record. Australia won the match by an innings and the series at The Oval, with Bradman getting 232 and W.H. Ponsford 110. Bradman's 974 runs in the series (average 139.14) is still a Test record.

In order to combat the new superbatsman, Douglas Jardine, the England captain for the 1932-33 tour to Australia, employed a tactic which he called "leg-theory" and which the Australians called "bodyline". It produced the most bitter tour of all, with the Australian Board calling the English unsporting, questions being raised in parliament and much diplomatic activity aimed at preventing a secession of Australia from the Empire. The method involved packing the leg side with fielders and bowling short, with Harold Larwood being the main weapon. England won the series 4-1.

The bodyline argument came to its head in the third Test at Adelaide, when Aussie captain Woodfull and wicket-keeper Bill Oldfield were both badly injured. Larwood did most to win the series with 33 wickets at 19.51, but such was the bitterness that he became a scapegoat and did not play for England again.

The 1934 series belonged to Bradman again, as Australia won 2-1. Australia won the first Test, but England won by an innings at Lord's when, on a sticky wicket, Yorkshire's Hedley Verity took 14 wickets for 80 on one day - the most taken in a day in an Ashes Test. Bradman made 304 in the drawn fourth Test at Headingley and with Bill Ponsford (181) added 388 for the fourth wicket. Australia won the series at The Oval, where Bradman (244) and Ponsford (266) did even better, adding 451 for the second wicket.

When England returned to Australia for the first series after the bodyline controversy, in 1936-37, they won the first two Tests overwhelmingly. However, Bradman turned the tide in the third Test with clever captaincy. On a Melbourne sticky wicket, after England declared at 76 for 9, 124 behind, Bradman sent in his tailenders while the wicket eased. He came in at No. 7 with the score on 97 for 5. He scored 270, and shared a stand of 346 with Jack Fingleton (136). A second-innings

212 at Adelaide after England led on first innings and 169 in the last Test at Melbourne were Bradman's further contributions as Australia came back to win 3-2.

In the first Test of the 1938 series, Len Hutton and Denis Compton each got a century in their Ashes debuts, but Lancashire left-hander Eddie Paynter topped them all with 216 not out. Stan McCabe made 232 in reply in a drawn match. Hammond scored 240 and W.A. Brown 206 not out (carrying his bat) in a drawn second Test. Australia finally forced a result in the fourth at Headingley, thanks to the bowling of Bill O'Reilly, who took five wickets in each innings. With the series undecided, the fifth Test at The Oval was played to a finish and records tumbled. Len Hutton scored 364 in 13 hours 17 minutes, then the highest score in Tests and still the highest in Ashes matches. In a total of 903 for 7, L.O.B. Fleetwood-Smith conceded the most runs in a Test innings - 298 (he got one wicket). England won by an innings and 579 runs.

After the war, the two batting giants of the 1930s, Hammond and Bradman, led the two sides in the 1946-47 series but, as after the First World War, England took a long time to regain form, and Australia won 3-0.

Records fell in the second Test at Sydney, when Bradman and Sidney Barnes each scored 234 and made a fifth-wicket partnership of 405, then a record for all first-class cricket.

The Australian side which toured England in 1948 was possibly the strongest ever, winning the Tests 4-0. Australia won at Headingley after N.W.D. Yardley's declaration at 365 for 8 set Australia 404 to win in 344 minutes on the last day. Arthur Morris (182) and Don Bradman (173 not out) put on 301 for the second wicket in 217 minutes and Australia won at 404 for 3.

Bradman's last appearance in Tests came at The Oval and he was cheered all the way to the wicket, given three cheers by the players, and then bowled second ball by Eric Hollies for 0 - a mere four runs would have given him a Test match career average of 100.

Hutton hits back

The Aussies won the first four Tests in 1950-51 and England at last won the final match. In the first Test at Melbourne, Trevor Bailey and Alec Bedser did well to bowl Australia out for 228 on a good pitch. On an unplayable sticky pitch, 20 wickets then fell on the third day. England declared at 68 for 7, Australia declared at 32 for 7, and England were reduced to 30 for 6. On the last morning Hutton, who was held back to No. 8, scored 62 not out of the last 92 runs, but England were 70 short. There were remarkable innings at Adelaide: Morris 206 for Australia out of 371, Hutton 156 not

The Indian prince K.S. Ranjitsinghji made a century for England on his debut.

out, carrying his bat out of 272. At Melbourne, England won by eight wickets. Hutton was easily the outstanding batsman, his average of 88.83 being more than twice that of anybody else on either side.

The Ashes returned to England in 1953, by virtue of an eight-wicket win at The Oval after four closely fought draws. Perhaps the best match was at Lord's, where at the close on the fourth day, England were 20 for 3, needing 343. Willie Watson, in his first Ashes match, played a masterly defensive innings of 109 in 346 minutes and, with the help of Trevor Bailey (71 in 257 minutes), saved the day, England being 282 for 7 at the close.

By 1954-55 England had some fast bowlers in Frank Tyson and Brian Statham to challenge the dominance that Lindwall and Miller had established over England. At Sydney and Melbourne, Tyson bowled brilliantly in the fourth innings to win matches after Australia had led on first innings, and England recorded a 3-1 series victory.

England again came from behind in 1956 to win the series 2-1. At Old Trafford, Jim Laker produced the Test bowling performance of all time with 9 for 37 in the first innings and 10 for 53 in the second. His 19 wickets in the match is a record for all first-class cricket, let alone Tests, the next highest being 17. Laker's 46 wickets (at 9.60) in the series is also an Ashes record.

Bowled over by Benaud

Australia, led by Richie Benaud, regained the Ashes in 1958-59 emphatically, 4-0, but the tour was marred by bitterness over the bowling styles of the Australian bowlers, most of whom were eventually called for "throwing".

Australia's retention of the Ashes in 1961 was more satisfactory. The series was won by Benaud's inspired

bowling at Old Trafford. England were set 256 to win. At 150 for 1, with Ted Dexter a dazzling 76 in 84 minutes, England were coasting, but Benaud had Dexter caught behind, May bowled round his legs for a duck, and England subsided to a 54-run defeat, with Benaud completing a spell of 5 for 12.

In a series mostly dominated by batsmen, the 1962-63 series was drawn 1-1. It was the last series for the Australian stalwarts Neil Harvey and Alan Davidson.

Australia won the only match to be decided in 1964 at Headingley, with Peter Burge of Queensland scoring 160. At Old Trafford, Australia's 656 for 8 declared (new captain Bobby Simpson 311, Bill Lawrey 106) was replied to with 611 (Ken Barrington 256, skipper Ted Dexter 174). At The Oval, Fred Trueman became the first bowler to claim 300 wickets in Tests.

In 1965-66 the sides drew 1-1. Doug Walters made his Test debut at Brisbane with 155. England won at Sydney and Australia at Adelaide with Simpson (225) and Lawry (119) opening with a stand of 244. Ken Barrington played his last match at Adelaide by scoring 60 and 102, thus completing ten consecutive innings there of over 50. In the fifth Test at Melbourne, Bob Cowper made 307 for Australia.

There was another 1-1 in 1968. England squared the series at The Oval with five minutes left. With Australia needing 352 to win and being 86 for 5 at lunch, a freak storm flooded the ground. Spectators helped in mopping up and England grabbed the last five wickets for 15 runs, mainly through Derek Underwood (7 for 50).

Six Tests were arranged for 1970-71, but the third, due to be played at Melbourne, was abandoned without a ball bowled, and was rearranged. Greg Chappell made his debut at

Perth and made 108 in a draw. England won at Sydney by 299 runs with John Snow of Sussex taking 7 for 20 as Australia were out for 116. Dennis Lillee made his Test debut at Adelaide and took five wickets in his first innings. England won again at Sydney in the last Test. In Australia's first innings a bouncer from Snow hit Terry Jenner on the head. When Snow went to field on the boundary a drunk grabbed his shirt, and beer cans were thrown. The players left the field. Australia, set 223 to win, were bowled out for 160. England took the series 2-0.

The 1972 series was closely fought. After England won the first Test by 89 runs, Bob Massie made an astonishing debut at Lord's, taking eight wickets in each innings, and Australia levelled the series. England won the fourth Test at Headingley when freak weather conditions caused the outbreak of a fungus on the wicket, and Underwood took ten wickets in the match. Australia drew the series by winning the last Test at The Oval by five wickets. Ian Chappell (118) and Greg Chappell (113) provided the first instance of brothers each scoring centuries in the same innings of a Test.

"Lilian Thomson"

Australia won decisively in 1974-75 by 4-1, thanks mainly to "Lilian Thomson", otherwise Jeff Thomson and Dennis Lillee, the opening fast bowlers. They took 57 wickets between them in the first five Tests, with England winning the last when Thomson was unfit and Lillee bowled only six overs.

In 1975, a win in the first Test at Edgbaston was enough to give Australia the series. At Headingley, the match was abandoned as vandals, protesting against the conviction of a man they claimed was innocent, wrecked the pitch with oil and knives.

Jack Hobbs, "The Master", had an outstanding record against Australia.

A one-off Centenary Test was played in March 1977 at Melbourne and coincidentally was won by Australia by the same margin as the first-ever Test - 45 runs. The heroes were Dennis Lillee, with 11 wickets, and Derek Randall who, in his first England-Australia Test, scored 174 as England reached 417, the highest fourth-innings score between the countries.

The Packer series

The Centenary Test was used to finalize plans for Kerry Packer's World Series Cricket in which Packer bought up Test players for his own series of matches. The 1977 Ashes series was therefore deprived of the England captain, a ringleader in the project. Mike Brearley took over; England won 3-0. In the third Test, Ian Botham made his debut, taking five first-innings wickets.

By the time England toured Australia in 1978-79, the whole group of Packer players had been named and were not considered for the Tests. England won the series easily by 5–1. Allan Border made his debut in the third Test at Melbourne, and fast bowler Rodney Hogg topped the averages and took 41 wickets. England also toured the following season, when WSC had been disbanded. Australia won all three matches in a series dominated by bowlers.

A second Centenary Test was played at Lord's in 1980, on the anniversary of the first Test played in England (though that was at The Oval). It was completely spoiled by rain and ended in a draw.

The 1981 series was one of the most remarkable of all. Australia (with Kim Hughes as captain and Terry Alderman marking his debut by taking nine wickets) won a low-scoring first Test by four wickets. At Lord's, where the match was drawn, England captain Ian Botham made a pair and was replaced at Headingley by Brearley, but remained in the team.

Botham bounces back

The third Test at Headingley saw a change in the fortunes of both England and Botham that came straight out of schoolboy fiction. Australia made 401 (Botham 6 for 49) and dismissed England for 174 (Botham 50). England followed on, and when Botham arrived at the wicket they were 105 for 5. Soon they were 135 for 7 – still 92 behind. Botham then proceeded to add 117 with Graham Dilley (56), 67 with Chris Old (29) and 37 with Bob Willis (2). He finished on 149 not out. It looked a magnificent but probably futile gesture, as Australia still needed a mere 130 runs to win. But Botham quickly got a wicket in Australia's second innings and so inspired Bob Willis that Willis grabbed 8 for 43 and at 111 all out Australia had been beaten by 18 runs. It was only the second time in

Ian Botham bowls during the third Ashes Test match against Australia at Headingley, Leeds. His heroics led England to an unlikely victory, winning the match by 18 runs.

905 Tests that a team had won after following on.

Botham played a quiet role at Edgbaston until Australia, needing 151 to win, reached 105 for 4. He then took five wickets for one run in 28 balls and England had won by 29 runs. At Old Trafford he began his second innings at 104 for 5 and scored 118, reaching his century in 86 balls. England totalled 404, won by 103 runs and retained the Ashes. The sixth Test was drawn. Amid all this, Terry Alderman took 42 wickets, still the most in an Ashes series by an Australian.

Australia got back the Ashes 2–1 in 1982–83. England were weakened by the absence of players who had gone on a "rebel" tour to South Africa and who had been given a three-year ban. In a drawn match at Perth, some hooligans invaded the pitch and, in making a rugby tackle on one of them, Alderman dislocated

his shoulder and took no further part in the series. England's win was very close, all four innings being between 284 and 294. Australia required 292, and were 218 when last man Jeff Thomson joined Allan Border. In a partnership of over two hours they refused 29 singles in order to manipulate the strike, but Thomson was out at 288 for 21, leaving Border 62 not out. The last wicket belonged to Botham, who completed 1,000 runs and 100 wickets against Australia.

Allan Border and David Gower were the new captains for the 1985 series which, by winning the last two Tests by an innings, England took 3–1. England went ahead 3–1 at Edgbaston, where Australia, at 335 for 8 at the end of the second day, were apparently safe from defeat, but England were inspired on the third day, grabbing the last two wickets and scoring 355 for 1 by the

close. Gower (215) and Robinson (148) added 315 for the second wicket and England declared at 595 for 5 for an easy win. England won as clearly at The Oval, with Gooch getting 196 and Gower 157.

England kept the Ashes in 1986–87 under the captaincy of Mike Gatting. They won the first and fourth Tests comfortably and Australia's victory in the last was academic. Chris Broad made centuries in three successive Tests and topped the batting averages at 69.57, but his 487 runs was topped by Australia's Dean Jones, who scored 511.

Broad stumps up

Australia celebrated the bicentenary of British colonization in 1988 with a one-off Test match at Sydney. Chris Broad, out for 133, his fourth century in six Tests in Australia, smashed a stump out of the ground and was fined £500 by his manager. Australia followed on, but 184 not out by David Boon saved the game.

An under-rated Australian party in 1989 soon changed their opponents' estimation of them. At Headingley, they made 601 for 7 declared to win by 210 runs. Australia then made it 2–0, winning by six wickets at Lord's. The next Test was spoiled by rain, but Steve Waugh, by scoring 43, took his total runs for the series to 393 before being out, a record in Ashes matches. A fourth Test win by nine wickets, Australia's 100th victory over England in 267 contests, sealed the Ashes for Australia. At Trent Bridge, Mark Taylor and Geoff Marsh batted throughout the first day, scoring 301 runs. Next day they took their stand to 329, beating the Hobbs and Rhodes stand of 323 in 1911–12. Australia won by an innings and 180 runs. The sixth Test was drawn. Waugh topped the averages at 126.50, but Taylor's aggregate of 839 remains the third-highest in a Test series. With 41 wickets at 17.37,

Geoff Boycott on his way to scoring his 100th first-class century, during the fourth Test match against Australia at Headingley in 1977.

Terry Alderman became the first to achieve the feat of taking 40 or more wickets in a Test series twice.

The most notable occurrence in the 1990-91 series was the debut of Mark Waugh at Adelaide, making him and Steve the first twins to play Test cricket. Mark Waugh began his Test career with 138. Australia wrapped up the series 3-0 at Perth.

Allan Border captained Australia for the last time in Ashes matches on the tour of 1993. Shane Warne made an explosive entry into Ashes Tests by bowling Mike Gatting with a fizzing leg break with his first ball – the fifth bowler to take a wicket with his first ball in Ashes matches. Warne took eight wickets in the match and Australia won by 179 runs. Gooch, the England captain, was out "handled the ball" in the second innings for 133, having punched it away as it bounced up after a defensive shot. At Lord's and Headingley, Australia won by an innings and Graham Gooch resigned the England captaincy. Mike Atherton took over for the last two Tests. Australia

won by eight wickets at Edgbaston, but England at last managed a win at The Oval by 161 runs, their first against Australia in 19 Tests.

Taylor's men dominate

Mike Atherton took his first side to Australia in 1994-95. Warne got the first hat-trick in Ashes Tests for 91 years as Australia went two up. England had much the best of a drawn third Test and won the fourth Test comfortably by 106 runs. But in the last Test, at Perth, they collapsed badly in the fourth innings and lost by 329 runs.

Mark Taylor's side to England in 1997 won a six-Test series 3-2. At Old Trafford, Steve Waugh made a century in each innings, the first to do so in Ashes Tests for 50 years.

In 1998-99, victories in the second and third Tests saw Australia retain the Ashes with two Tests remaining. England won an exciting fourth Test at Melbourne by 12 runs. In the final Test, Darren Gough registered the only England hat-trick in Ashes Tests in the 20th century, and Michael Slater

played a remarkable innings of 123 out of 184, thus making 66.8 per cent of the runs, the highest proportion since Charles Bannerman's 67.3 per cent in the very first Test match of all. Australia eventually won by 98 runs.

Steve Waugh captained Australia on the tour to England in 2001. At Edgbaston, Australia made 576, England could muster only 164 and lost by an innings. At Lord's, where Australia won by eight wickets, Mark Waugh established a world record with his 158th Test catch. Australia retained the Ashes (thus holding them for the seventh successive series) at Trent Bridge, achieving a target of 158 for the loss of three wickets. At Headingley, England were set 315 to win in 110 overs, of

which 17.3 were immediately lost. On the last day, a magnificent innings of 173 not out by Mark Butcher steered England to a six-wicket victory. At The Oval, Australia won by an innings. Steve and Mark Waugh became the second brothers, after Ian and Greg Chappell, to each score a century in an Ashes Test.

England avoided a whitewash in their 2002-03 tour of Australia ,where attendances were the highest for years, by winning the final Test. Australia won the first four Tests easily. The scene was set at Brisbane, where crowds were the biggest for 70 years. Nasser Hussain put Steve Waugh's Aussies in and saw the score reach 339 before the second wicket fell. Australia won by 384 after bowling out England for a paltry 79 in the fourth innings.

The margin was an innings and 51 runs at Adelaide, where there were again record crowds. Michael Vaughan scored 177 of England's 342, but Ricky Ponting got a second series ton. Another innings victory at Perth was followed by a five-wicket win at Melbourne, where Justin Langer scored 250 and Vaughan got a second hundred. At last England managed a victory at Sydney, by 225 runs, helped by 183 from Vaughan.

Vaughan's 633 runs (av. 63.30) was the outstanding batting performance of the tour, while three Aussies topped 400: Matthew Hayden (496, av. 62), Justin Langer (423, av. 52.87) and Ricky Ponting (417, av. 52.12). Jason Gillespie took 20 wickets at 24.60, as did Andy Caddick at 34.50, while Glenn McGrath had 19 wickets at 20.

ENGLAND v AUSTRALIA

	MATCHES	ENG	AUS	DRAW	SERIES	ENG	AUS	DRAW
IN AUSTRALIA	170	57	86	27	39	13	21	5
IN ENGLAND	156	45	47	64	36	17	15	4
TOTALS	326	102	133	91	75	30	36	9

THE ASHES 2005

Kevin Pietersen, with three fifties and a century in the final Test, shone in the Ashes. He scored 473 runs, the best aggregate on either side.

The 2005 series in England was possibly the most memorable of all, with close finishes and four exciting last days. The exception was the Lord's first Test, where Glenn McGrath took nine wickets for 82, including his 500th in Test cricket and Australia won by 139 runs.

McGrath was injured by stepping on a ball in the warm-up at Edgbaston, and England raced to 407 on the first day. But with a first-innings lead of 99 they were reduced by Shane Warne to 131 for 9 in the second knock, and only a last wicket stand of 51 between Andrew Flintoff (whose nine sixes were an Ashes record) allowed them to set Australia 282 to win. At 137 for 7, it looked as if England would win on the fourth day, but Australia held out and a large crowd turned up to watch the formality of England getting the last two wickets on the fifth day. But coming together at 220, Brett Lee and Michael Kasprowicz added 59 and amid unbearable tension took the score to within three of victory before Kasprowicz gloved Steve Harmison to the wicket-keeper. England's 2-run win was the narrowest in Ashes Tests.

McGrath returned at Old Trafford. England had the upper hand throughout, with Michael Vaughan (166) and Andrew Strauss (106) making centuries. Warne took his 600th Test wicket, then a Test record. Rain on the third day cost 76 overs, delaying England's declaration, which nevertheless set Australia 413 to win. Ricky Ponting's 175 set up another tense last-wicket finish with McGrath and Lee having to withstand the last four overs to earn a draw at 371` for 9.

With the series level at Trent Bridge, England again took the iniative, with Flintoff scoring 102 out of 477. Australia were made to follow 259 behind, and scored 387 setting England only 129 to win, but with Warne getting three quick wickets and Simon Jones injured, England were still anxious at 116 for 7, but Ashley Giles and Matthew Hoggard added 13 for England to win.

With England needing a draw at the Oval to regain the Ashes, Warne again grabbed four quick wickets as England batted first, but again Flintoff (72) came to the rescue, joining Strauss (129) and England reached 373. This seemed inadequate when Justin Langer (105) and Matthew Hayden (138) opened with a stand of 185. The score reached 261 for 1 before Flintoff got Hayden and Ponting and then, with the help of Hoggard, polished off the last five wickets for 11, giving England a lead of 6. It was still not over and on the last day England were 126 for 5, with defeat on the cards. But Kevin Pietersen (158, including seven 6s,) and Giles (59) put on 109, England reached 335, Australia's token innings lasted only four balls before bad light intervened and the Ashes were won.

Each side had a giant, and they were named joint Players of the Series. Flintoff made 402 runs (av 40.20), at the fastest rate of the series, and was England's top wicket-taker with 24 wickets, usually taken at vital times. Warne, who could also claim to be an all-rounder, took 40 wickets (only Laker with 48 had more in an Ashes series) at 19.92 and scored 249 runs (av 27.66).

THE ASHES 2006/2007

Aussie skipper Ricky Ponting was determined to get the Ashes back in 2006-07, and began by winning the toss at Brisbane and scoring 196. Glenn McGrath (6 for 50) was instrumental in shooting out England, now captained by 2005 hero Andrew Flintoff, for 157. The follow-on was not enforced, Ponting declaring at 202 for 1 (Justin Langer 100 not out), setting England 648 to win. By getting 370, the highest fourth innings in a Gabba Test, they regained some respectability.

When Paul Collingwood scored 206 and Kevin Pietersen 158 at Adelaide, allowing England to declare at 551 for 6 (McGrath and Shane Warne between them taking one wicket for 274) it appeared the defence of the Ashes was to be a serious one, but Ponting and Michael Clarke scored centuries in reply to England's strong opening and Australia's deficit was only 38. England then collapsed abysmally to Warne (4 for 49) for 129, leaving Australia only 168 to get to win. England's first-innings declaration was too early, as Australia had plenty of time to knock off the runs for the loss of four wickets.

England could not now afford to lose another Test and, having brought Monty Panesar into the side, did well to dismiss Australia for 244 at Perth (Panesar 5 for 92). But the batting collapsed again and they were all out for 215. Second time round Mike Hussey (103), Michael Clarke (135 not out) and Adam Gilchrist (102 not out) allowed a declaration at 527 for 5 and, despite Alastair Cook's 116, England could reach only 350 and lost by 206. The Ashes were gone.

England appeared demoralised at Melbourne. The Boxing Day crowd

Shane Warne (top) celebrates taking his 700th wicket, during day one of the fourth Ashes Test in Melbourne. Andrew Strauss is the victim.

of 89,155 (the 45-year-old record of 90,000 was not quite surpassed) had come to see Shane Warne be first to 700 Test wickets. They had not long to wait. With his 20th ball he bowled Strauss, England's top scorer with 50, and ended with 5 for 39 in a total of 159. Matthew Hayden and Andrew Symonds each got 150,

Australia reached 419, and England were bundled out again for 161.

Humbled captain Flintoff, who had carried an injury throughout the series, managed to top score in the final Test at Sydney with 89. This was the first Ashes test for 37 years without a century or a bowler getting four wickets in an innings.

The result was a familiar one for the series: an easy win (by 10 wickets) for Australia. It was the first Ashes whitewash since 1920-21. Captain Ricky Ponting was Player of the Series with 576 runs (av 82.28). Stuart Clarke, surprisingly, was easily the outstanding bowler, with 26 wickets at 17.03 each.

THE ASHES 2009

The excitement of the last-minute finishes in 2005 was repeated in the first Test of 2009 at the new Test ground at Cardiff where, just like at Old Trafford in 2005, the last pair were attempting to bat their way to a draw. England, under Andrew Strauss, scored 435 in an even batting display (top score only 69). Australia, once again led by Ricky Ponting, declared at 674 for 6, with four century makers: Simon Katich (122), Ponting (150), Marcus North (125 not out) and Brad Haddin (121). Australia's lead: 239. When last man Monty Panesar joined Jimmy Anderson at the wicket, England were 233 for 9. The first task was to earn the six runs needed to make Australia bat again and the second task was to bat until there was no time for Australia to bat again. Both tasks were achieved and the match ended with England 252 for 9.

England were rejuvenated at Lord's, where the openers Strauss (161) and Alastair Cook (95) began with a stand of 196. England reached 425 and Strauss did not enforce the follow-on when Australia were dismissed for 215, and declared at 311 for 6, setting Australia 522 to win. Australia batted better than the first time, especially down the order, with Haddin and Mitchell Johnson supporting Michael Clarke's 136, but Andrew Flintoff found some of his old fire to get 5 for 92 and England won by 115.

Andrew Strauss celebrates his century during day one of the second Ashes Test at Lord's on 16 July 2009. Strauss went on to make 161. His partnership with Alastair Cook, who fell only five runs short of making his own century, helped put England in a dominant position. They went on to win the match.

Rain interrupted play too much at Edgbaston for a result, although England, batting second, got a lead of 113 and had hopes of an Australian second-innings collapse, but Australia had no problems in batting out time. Ponting became Australia's highest run-scorer, passing Allan Border, and trailing only Tendulkar and Lara overall.

Flintoff was controversially dropped for the Headingley Test on fitness grounds, despite having made 74 at Edgbaston. England were shot out for 102 (Peter Siddle 5 for 21). Australia piled up 445 and won by an innings and 80.

In the deciding Test at the Oval, England's 332 was about par for the course, but Australia, having reached 73 before a wicket fell, collapsed before Stuart Broad, who came on as England's fifth bowler, and took 5 for 37 as Australia lost 8 wickets for 71 in one session. They were all out for 160. Jonathan Trott, making his England debut, scored 119 as England declared at 373 for 9, setting Australia two whole days and 21 overs (in which they reached 80 for no wicket) to get 546 to win. Mike Hussey scored a century but Flintoff, who had been recalled for his farewell Test (he was to undergo knee surgery) brilliantly ran out Ponting when the score was 217 for 2, and from then on Australia subsided to 348. England had regained the Ashes, 2-1.

Strauss scored most runs in the series (474, av 52.66) and Ben Hilfenhaus was the best bowler with 22 wickets (av 27.45), but an oddity of the series was that the losers, Australia, scored eight centuries to England's two, and claimed 81 wickets to England's 69.

THE ASHES 2010/2011

England switched everything round again in the fourth Test at Melbourne. How different was Boxing Day 2011 to Boxing Day 2007, when a full ground saw Warne take his 700th Test wicket. Australia suffered perhaps their worst Ashes day ever. Jimmy Anderson, Tremlett, and Tim Bresnan shot out Australia by tea for 98, and then Strauss and Cook slammed 157 without loss by stumps. In Australia's innings, all the batsmen were caught, six behind the wicket by Prior, equalling the Ashes record, and the other four in the arc between keeper and gully. On the second day Trott began an eight-hour innings of 168 not out which ended when he ran out of partners at 513. Bresnan's four second-innings wickets in Australia's 258 brought victory by an innings and 157 runs.

With the Ashes retained, England rubbed it in at Sydney, dismissing Australia for 280 and then amassing 644 (Cook 189, Ian Bell 155, Prior 118). Australia were dismissed again for 281 for defeat by an innings and 83 runs. England won 3-1, each win being by an innings and had twice scored over 600 and twice more over 500.

The statistics were extraordinary, England averaging 51.14 runs per wicket, their highest in an Ashes series, and Australia 29.23. Cook was Player of the Series, his 766 runs being fifth-highest in Ashes series. His average was 127.67. Hussey scored 570 runs (av 63.33). Jonathan Trott, with 445 runs, averaged 89.00. Anderson had most wickets with 24 (at 26.04 each), but Tremlett had 17 at 23.35 in only three Tests and Bresnan 11 at 19.04 in two Tests.

Above: **Alastair Cook bats during day five of the first Ashes Test at The Gabba in Brisbane. He went on to make 235 not out.**

Ricky Pointing was captain of Australia for a fourth Ashes. His record of won one, lost two was a statistic he wanted to put right. But England knew they had the better team.

It started badly for England with captain Strauss out third ball for 0 at Brisbane. It worsened when, at 197 for 4, Peter Siddle dismissed Alastair Cook, Matt Prior and Stuart Broad in a hat-trick, finishing with 6 for 54 in England's 260. Mike Hussey (195) and Brad Haddin (136) put on 307 for Australia's sixth wicket, and they reached 481. However this stand was passed when England batted. Strauss scored 110 out of a first-wicket stand of 188, then Cook (235 not out) and Jonathan Trott (133 not out) added 329 before England declared at 517

for 1, and the game was drawn. Cook's innings was the third highest by an Englishman in Australia.

At Adelaide, Australia batted and were soon 2 for 3 wickets but, thanks to Hussey (93), managed to reach 245. England's batting continued roughly where it left off at Perth. With Cook getting 148 and Kevin Pietersen 227, England declared at 620 for 5, having scored 1,137 for 6 wickets in two innings. Only rain threatened England's overwhelming victory, but the last six wickets fell for 66 runs as Australia were all out 304, two and a half hours before the deluge began. Australia's stubborn opener, Simon Katich, and England's most economical bowler, Stuart Broad, were forced out of the series through injury.

Remarkably, with Australia at their lowest ebb for years, things turned around at Perth. Mitchell Johnson, who had been dropped for the second Test after 0 for 170 and a duck at Brisbane, returned. He top-scored with 62 in Australia's total of 268, then took three top wickets for 4 runs on the second morning. England were shot out for 187 and despite Chris Tremlett, flown over to replace Broad, taking 5 for 87 in Australia's 308, England crashed to 123, with Ryan Harris taking six wickets. He and Man of the Match Johnson each took 9 wickets in the match as Australia won by 267 runs. Mike Hussey's second-innings 116 made him the first batsman to register six successive Ashes scores of 50 or more.

ENGLAND v SOUTH AFRICA

Herschelle Gibbs enjoyed himself against England during their five-match series against South Africa in 2003, scoring 478 runs (including two centuries) at an average of 53.11.

The third country to play Test matches was South Africa. The first touring party from England came in 1889. After playing sides of 15, 18 and 22 players, they played two matches against 11 South Africans. These two matches have become recognized as the first two Tests in South African cricket. England were overwhelmingly superior, and remained so for some years.

It was not till 1905-06 that the South Africans won their first match and their first series, 4-1.

South Africa played their first Tests overseas in 1907, when they lost 1-0 in England.

Sydney Barnes tormented South Africa in 1913-14 when England won 4-0. Barnes set a record for all Tests, which still stands, by taking 49 wickets in the series, and he played in only the first four Tests. He took 17 for 159 at Johannesburg, a record which has been passed only once since, by Jim Laker in 1956.

The 1930s were better for South Africa. They won 1-0 in 1930-31 by winning the first Test by 28 runs and drawing the rest. The fourth Test was the last played in South Africa on matting wickets. In 1935, they won their first Test in England and with it the series.

"Timeless Test"

The 1938-39 series in South Africa featured the famous "timeless Test" at Durban. England had taken a 1-0 lead in a batsman-dominated series, so the last Test, as it could decide the rubber, was played to a finish. South Africa made 530 and England 316. Then South Africa made 481, setting England 696 to win. Bill Edrich got 219, but at tea on the tenth day, with England still 42 short at 654 for 5, rain caused the match to be abandoned, as England had to leave on a two-day rail journey to catch their ship at Cape Town. It is the longest first-class match.

In the first series after the war, there was a run-feast for Compton, Edrich, Nourse, Melville and Mitchell. Compton made 753 in the Tests, at an average of 94.12, but Edrich had a higher average, 110.40, with 552 runs. Melville (189 and 104 not out) made a century in each innings in the first Test, and Mitchell (120 and 189 not out) did it in the fifth. Melville's 117 at Lord's was his fourth century in successive Test innings, dating back to before the war, all against England. England won 3-0.

England won 3-1 in 1951, when South Africa's captain Dudley Nourse made 208 at Trent Bridge, batting in great pain from a fractured thumb. At The Oval, Len Hutton played a ball from Athol Rowan into the air and played it again as it was about to land on the stumps. However, Russell Endean was moving to catch it, and Hutton became the only batsman in Test cricket to be given out "obstructing the field".

In 1956-57 at Cape Town, Russell Endean himself prevented a ball rebounding on to his stumps with his hand, and became the first player to be given out "handled the ball" in Tests. At Durban, Tayfield delivered a record 137 balls without conceding a run in the first innings. He was easily the best bowler of the series with 37 wickets, the most by a South African in a Test series.

Apartheid and after

Series planned for South Africa in 1968-69 and England in 1970 were cancelled because of apartheid and the "D'Oliveira affair" when Basil D'Oliveira, a Cape-Coloured domiciled in England, was banned by the South African prime minister from touring with the England side. Unfortunately for South Africa, they were building at that time their strongest-ever side.

Cricket relations did not resume until 1994 when South Africa toured England and played a three-match series. At Lord's, South Africa won convincingly by 356 runs. Following a high-scoring draw at Headingley, South Africa appeared in command at The Oval until Devon Malcolm took 9 for 57 to skittle South Africa for 172. England hit 205 for 2 for an eight-wicket win.

England returned to South Africa in 1996-97 after 32 years. At Johannesburg, wicket-keeper Jack

Russell took 11 catches in the match, a record number of dismissals for all Test cricket. After four draws, South Africa won the last Test and the series at Cape Town by ten wickets.

South Africa visited England in 1998 captained by Hansie Cronje. After a rain-spoilt first Test, South Africa won the second and nearly the third. England followed on and on the last day Robert Croft batted for three hours (37 not out) to save the match. The scores finished level with England on 369 for 9. England won the series 2-1.

Nasser Hussain led England to South Africa in 1999-2000. The first Test at Johannesburg started sensationally on a damp pitch in poor light, England being reduced to 2 for 4, three of them to Allan Donald. They never recovered and South Africa won by nine wickets, then took the series 2-1.

South Africa's new captain, 22-year-old Graeme Smith, was the star of the 2003 series back in England, beginning with innings of 277, 85 and 259. In all he made 713 runs, average 79.33. Marcus Trescothick, with 219 and 69 not out at The Oval, did most to help England level the series 2-2.

Strauss waltz

Michael Vaughan captained England to South Africa in 2004-05. In the first Test at Port Elizabeth, South Africa lost captain Graeme Smith without a run on the board, but totalled 337. England got a lead of 88 and then bowled out South Africa for 229 and won by seven wickets, thanks to Andrew Strauss, who added 94 not out to a first-innings 126. It was England's eighth successive Test win, a national record. Rain prevented this being improved in the second Test at Durban. Although South Africa, with Kallis scoring 162, led by 193 on first innings, England made 570 for 7 declared, with Trescothick, Strauss

Graeme Smith was outstanding on his tours to England in 2003 and 2008.

and Thorpe getting hundreds, and South Africa were 290 for 8 when the rain came. England's 13-match unbeaten run then ended at Cape Town. Another Kallis century and an England first-innings collapse meant a 196-run South African win.

England's 411 for 8 declared (Strauss 147) at Johannesburg was surpassed by South Africa's 419 (Gibbs 161). Trescothick (180) then helped England to 332 for 9 declared and Matthew Hoggard's 7 for 61 removed South Africa for 247 and a 77-run win for England. This was

enough to win the series 2-1 as the fifth Test at Centurion was drawn. Strauss was Player of the Series with 656 runs at 77.88.

In England in 2008, a high-scoring draw at Lord's was followed by a resounding ten-wicket win for

South Africa at Headingley, with A.B. de Villiers scoring 174 and Ashwell Prince 149. South Africa then took a series-winning 2-0 lead by reaching 283 for 5 in the fourth innings at Edgbaston, after being 93 for 4. Captain Graeme Smith carried his bat for 154. The England captain Michael Vaughan tearfully resigned in the aftermath and Kevin Pietersen was named as the new captain for the final Test at The Oval. Pietersen's first-innings 100 was the basis for England's six-wicket victory.

The first Test in South Africa at Centurion in 2009-10 had an exciting finish. England were set 314 to win, and the match was subsiding peacefully at 205 for 4 when five wickets tumbled quickly, and the last-wicket pair, Paul Collingwood and Graham Onions, had to survive 19 balls to secure the draw, at 218 for 9. Nine wickets from Graeme Swann and centuries from Alastair Cook and Ian Bell earned England an easy innings win in the second Test, but in the third Test they had to repeat their escapology act. After an absorbing match, England's No. 11, Graham Onions, again came to the wicket, this time with 17 balls remaining. He survived a pulsating last over for the draw. South Africa would claim justice was finally done when they won the fourth Test by an innings to tie the series. Captain Graeme Smith scored the only century, and was the series top run-scorer with 427 (av 61.00). England's Graeme Swann had most wickets (21 at 31.38) but South Africa's fast bowlers Morne Morkel (19 at 21.47) and Dale Steyn (15 at 23.80) swung the balance.

ENGLAND v SOUTH AFRICA

	MATCHES	ENG	SA	DRAW	SERIES	ENG	SA	DRAW
IN SOUTH AFRICA	77	29	18	30	18	10	5	3
IN ENGLAND	61	27	11	23	14	9	3	2
TOTALS	138	56	29	53	32	19	8	5

AUSTRALIA v SOUTH AFRICA

In 1902 the Australians, on their way home from England, played three Tests in South Africa. They won the last two, despite South Africa's J.H. Sinclair scoring 100 in 80 minutes.

The South Africans visited Australia in 1910-11 and lost 4-1. Although Trumper topped the batting averages, Aubrey Faulkner scored most runs – 732, a South African record for a series. South Africa failed to beat Australia in a Test after this until 1952-53, 25 Tests later. Bradman dominated the batting in Australia in 1931-32, making 806 runs and averaging 201.50. At Adelaide he made 299 not out, running out the No. 11 batsman when going for a quick single.

In 1952-53, South Africa won their second match ever against Australia at Melbourne, thanks largely to 162 not out from Russell Endean and 13 for 165 by Hugh Tayfield. South Africa then drew the series in the last Test at Melbourne. Australia, with Neil Harvey making 205, totalled 520. South Africa made 435 and needed 295 in the fourth innings, and won by six wickets. Harvey made 834 runs in the series to average 92.66. Tayfield took 30 wickets.

Australia continued to win until Trevor Goddard led a team to Australia in 1963-64. Australia won the first Test. Graeme Pollock made 122 at Sydney and, while still not 20 years old, 175 at Adelaide. He and Eddie Barlow (201) added 341 for South Africa's third wicket. This levelled the series and the last Test was drawn.

There were to be no more close shaves. In 1966-67 in South Africa the home team won 3-1 for their first series win over Australia. Nobody would have guessed this outcome on the second day of the series, Christmas Eve, when Australia

Shane Warne has excelled against all countries, but particularly against South Africa. In 24 Tests against them he took 130 wickets (at 24.16).

passed South Africa's total of 199 with only one wicket down. But South Africa made 620 in the second innings (Denis Lindsay 182) and won by 233 runs, their first victory over Australia at home. After Australia won the second Test, South Africa won the third and the fifth for their

historic win.

Even this performance was nothing to 1969-70, when South Africa won all four of the Tests played. Barry Richards made his debut in the first Test, and scored 140 in the second at Durban, where Graeme Pollock made 274, then the

highest score for South Africa in Tests. South Africa made 622 for 9 declared, won by an innings and 129, and won the last two Tests by over 300 runs. Lindsay conceded no byes in any Test. Pollock and Richards topped the batting. It was Richards' only Test series before South Africa were ejected from the Test arena. His average for Tests is therefore 72.57. Pollock ended his Test career with 2,256 runs (average 60.97).

The contests between the countries were revived in 1993–94 when the two series ended 1–1 with one draw. In the second, Allan Border made his final Test appearance with a record number of appearances (156) and runs (11,174). Australia won the next series in 1996–97 by 2–1 in South Africa. Steve Waugh was the outstanding player of the series with 313 runs, average 78.25.

The teams met again in Australia in 1997–98, when Australia won 1–0. The first Test was drawn. Australia decisively won the second, and South Africa had the better of the draw in the third. Mark Taylor carried his bat in Australia's first innings for 169 not out from a total of 350. The series top scorers on each side made 279, Mark Waugh (average 69.75) and Gary Kirsten (55.80). Shane Warne took 20 wickets at 20.85.

The series in Australia in 2001-02 was billed as a world championship. Australia won by a knock-out, taking all three Tests by big margins: 246 runs, nine wickets and ten wickets. Matthew Hayden made a century in each match, aggregate 430 (av. 107.5). His first four innings took his Test aggregate for the year (2001) to 1,391, bettered only by Viv Richards in 1976 and Sunny Gavaskar in 1979.

A disappointed South Africa promised revenge at home some two months later, but Australia made 652 for 7 declared at Johannesburg and won by an innings and 360. South Africa fought back from 92 for 6 at Cape Town to lose eventually by only four wickets and beat Australia by five wickets in the final Test at Durban. Australia's Adam Gilchrist made 473 runs (av. 157.6) and claimed 15 victims behind the stumps. His 204 not out in the first Test was the fastest Test double century (212 balls) – but only for two weeks.

Australia won a three-Test home series 2–0 in 2005–06, with captain Ricky Ponting scoring three centuries, two in the final Test, to total 515 runs at an average of 103.00. Australia then won 3–0 in South Africa later that season, with newcomer Stuart Clark named as Man of the Series after taking 20 wickets.

South Africa won their first series in Australia in 2008–09 by 2–1. In the first Test at Perth they achieved the second highest fourth-innings winning total in Tests with 414 for 4, with captain Graeme Smith getting 108, A.B. de Villiers 106 not out and Jean-Paul Duminy 50 not out on his debut. South Africa won the second Test by nine wickets, with Duminy getting 166. With Paul Harris (39) and Dale Steyn (76) he helped take South Africa's first-innings score from 184 for 7 past Australia's 394 to 431 for 9. Steyn also took ten wickets in the match. Australia won the final Test, in which Smith retired hurt in the first innings. He was nevertheless voted Player of the Series.

By losing the final Test in Australia in 2008-09, South Africa failed to end Australia's reign as unofficial world champions, but they had a further chance to do so later in the season in South Africa. Unfortunately for them, the series was the opposite of the previous one, with Australia winning the first two Tests and South Africa the third. Marcus North became the eighteenth Australian to score a century on debut at Johannesburg in a 162-run victory. At Durban, Phillip Hughes, at 20, became the youngest player to score a century in each innings of a Test (it was his second Test) as the Aussies won by 175 runs. South Africa won the dead match by an innings, with Ashwell Prince, Jacques Kallis and A.B. de Villiers each scoring hundreds in a total of 651. Australia's Mitchell Johnson was Man of the Series with 16 wickets and a maiden Test century in the final Test.

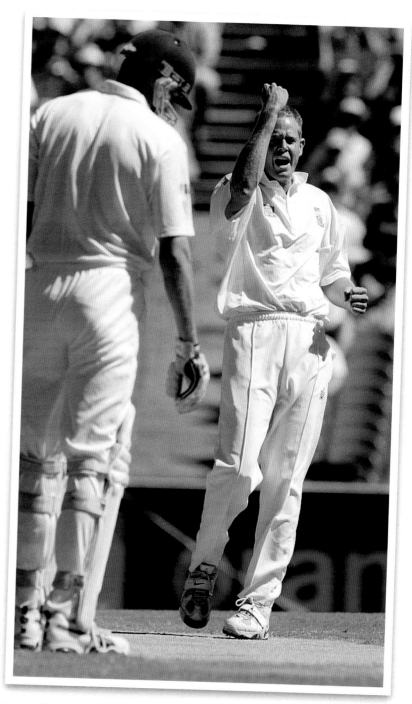

Shaun Pollock recorded his best Test figures (7 for 87) against Australia, at Adelaide in 1997-98.

AUSTRALIA v SOUTH AFRICA

	MATCHES	AUS	SA	DRAW	SERIES	AUS	SA	DRAW
IN SOUTH AFRICA	45	23	11	9	12	9	2	1
IN AUSTRALIA	35	20	7	8	9	5	1	3
IN ENGLAND	3	2	0	1	1	1	0	0
TOTALS	83	47	18	18	22	15	3	4

ENGLAND v WEST INDIES

Success for Matthew Hoggard as he takes the wicket of West Indies' Ryan Hinds in the third Test at Barbados in 2004 to complete his hat-trick.

An all-amateur English side toured the West Indies in 1894-95, and tours were made regularly after this from 1910. The first West Indian party toured England in 1900. It was during the fourth tour to England, in 1928, that three Tests were played in the 41-match programme. England won all three by an innings. In 1929-30, however, the series was shared 1-1 with two draws. George Headley, aged 20, on his debut, made 176 in the first Test and ended with four centuries,

703 runs and an average of 87.87.

In 1933 in England, West Indies fast bowlers Learie Constantine and Manny Martindale bowled bodyline at Old Trafford, but Jardine scored a century. England won 2-0. In 1934-35, the West Indies won 2-1 and Headley averaged 97.00. In the last Test series before the war, in 1939, England won at Lord's and drew the other two Tests. Headley scored a century in each innings at Lord's. After two draws, on resumption in 1947-48, the

West Indies won the last two Tests.

Calypso classic

West Indian cricket really came of age in 1950. Alf Valentine must have wondered what it was all about as he took the first eight wickets to fall in his first Test at Old Trafford. Nevertheless, England won. It all turned round at Lord's in the second Test when Ramadhin took 11 wickets to add to Valentine's seven and the West Indies won by 322. The West Indian

steel bands were telling everybody that it was "at Lord's where they done it ... with those little pals of mine, Ramadhin and Valentine". The West Indies slaughtered England both at Trent Bridge and The Oval, and won 3-1.

Wisden Trophy

The Wisden Trophy was a new prize on offer in 1963. The West Indies won it 3-1, their first series win for 13 years, and defended it under Garfield Sobers in 1966, winning 3-1.

England, under Colin Cowdrey, won the series 1-0 in 1967-68, but lost the Wisden Trophy in 1973 when the West Indies won 2-0. A drawn five-Test series in 1973-74 saw Dennis Amiss score 262 not out in the second Test and Lawrence Rowe 302. The West Indies, under Clive Lloyd, were beginning their long mastery of all countries in 1976, when they won the series 3-0. Vivian Richards scored 232 in his first innings against England and 291 at The Oval while Gordon Greenidge made a century in each innings at Old Trafford.

Blackwashed

In 1984 and 1985-86 the West Indies won all ten Tests in what were called "blackwashes". All the margins were big. In both series it was the West Indian fast bowlers Malcolm Marshall and Joel Garner who did the most damage. In 1984, in the second Test at Lord's, England got a first-innings lead, and David Gower was able to declare on the last morning and set the West Indies 342 to win. Greenidge made 214 not out and the West Indies won by nine wickets. Greenidge made another double-century at Old Trafford. In the 1985-86 series, Viv Richards made 110 not out in the fifth Test, his century coming in 56 balls, the fastest hundred in terms of balls

The West Indies' series-winning captain Chris Gayle launches a six off Monty Panesar in Jamaica.

received in Test cricket.

England's run of defeats ended with a rain-interrupted Test in 1988, but the West Indies won the next four. It took until 1991 before England drew a series, 2-2. The 1993-94 series was the series of Brian Lara. The West Indies won 4-1 and, in the last Test in Antigua, he scored 375 runs, a record Test innings. His aggregate for the series was 798, average 99.75.

In 1995, Dominic Cork made an impressive debut for England at Lord's, with 7 for 43 and his hat-trick at Old Trafford helped England share the series 2-2. The first Test in 1997-98 was one of the most extraordinary in Test history, lasting only 62 balls. The batsmen were constantly hit and England made it to 17 for 3, when the umpires decided the pitch was unfit and the match was abandoned, a unique occasion in Test cricket. West Indies registered a 3-1 series win.

West Indies began with an emphatic win in 2000, but England levelled the series in a remarkable turnaround at Lord's. West Indies made 267 for 9 on the first day, then for the first time in Test history, part of all four innings took place on the second day. West Indies' last wicket fell, England were dismissed for 134, West Indies for 54, their lowest total against England, thanks mainly to Andy Caddick's 5 for 16, and England were nought for nought overnight. On the third day, England reached 191 for 8 to win. After a drawn third Test, England won by an innings at Headingley and by 158 runs at Lord's to clinch a 3-1 series win.

A superb series followed in 2003-04. With Brian Lara and Michael Vaughan captains, England impressively won the first three Tests. At Kingston, Steve Harmison destroyed the West Indies with 7 for 12 in a second innings of 47 all out, their lowest in Tests. Harmison and Simon Jones were the heroes of a seven-wicket win in Trinidad, with Jones and father Jeff becoming the only England father-and-son to get five wickets in an innings. At Bridgetown, Matthew Hoggard took a hat-trick and Andrew Flintoff seven wickets in all as England won by eight wickets. Graham Thorpe scored 119 not out in England's first innings of 226, with extras (20) being the next-highest scorer. But the performance of the series came in the fourth and final Test in Antigua, with Lara regaining the world record Test score with 400 not out in a West Indies total of 751 for 5 declared, the highest total made against England. He and Ridley Jacobs (107 not out) added a West Indian sixth-wicket record of 282. England followed on, but easily saved the match.

Twenty years after "blackwash", England "whitewashed" the West Indies in 2004. It started at Lord's with a century in each innings by captain Michael Vaughan, another from Andrew Strauss and a double century from Robert Key. Shivnarine Chanderpaul made 128 and 97 in a losing cause. At Edgbaston, Marcus Trescothick scored a century in each innings, Andrew Flintoff made 167 and Ashley Giles had his second nine-wicket haul in Tests. Ramnaresh Sarwan made 139 for the West Indies. At Old Trafford West Indies had a first-innings lead of 65, but were skittled for 165 in the second innings. England completed the whitewash at The Oval, after forcing West Indies to follow on. Flintoff and Chanderpaul were joint Players of the Series, with Flintoff heading both England's batting and bowling averages with 387 (average 64.50) and 14 wickets at 21.21. Giles took 22 wickets. Chanderpaul scored 437 runs (av. 72.83), and Chris Gayle 400 in a losing cause.

In the West Indies in 2008-09, the home side won the first Test in Jamaica by an innings after England, captained by Andrew Strauss, collapsed for 51 in the second innings, having been 26 for 7. Jerome Taylor took eight wickets (5-11 in the second innings). The second Test was abandoned after ten balls because of an appalling pitch. A fifth Test was added to the sries, but the remaining Tests were drawn, although England could have won them with earlier declarations, West Indies hanging on with one and two wickets left, respectively. Ramnaresh Sarwan was the most successful batsman with 626 runs (av. 104.33), while Graeme Swann took 19 wickets for England in three Tests.

The series resumed in England in May 2009, the West Indies touring for two Tests. In horrid weather, the visitors followed on twice and lost heavily in both Tests. New England No. 3 Ravi Bopara scored two centuries.

ENGLAND v WEST INDIES

	MATCHES	ENG	WI	DRAW	SERIES	ENG	WI	DRAW
IN ENGLAND	76	27	29	20	18	8	8	2
IN WEST INDIES	65	13	24	28	14	3	5	6
TOTALS	141	40	53	48	32	11	13	8

ENGLAND v NEW ZEALAND

New Zealand entered the Test fold in 1929-30 when England toured. The first Test was at Christchurch, and England won by eight wickets. C.S. Dempster proved the best New Zealand batsman, scoring his country's first century (136) at Wellington, and incidentally putting on 276 with John Mills (117) for the first wicket.

For the first 40 years or so of their meetings, England had much the better of the matches between the countries. In the second of the two-match 1932-33 series, Walter Hammond made 336 not out, the highest Test score at the time. Since he was only once out, his average of 563.00 for the series remains, unsurprisingly, a record for all Tests.

In 1949 at Lord's, Martin Donnelly scored 206, the first double-century by a New Zealander against England. In 1954-55 at Auckland, New Zealand were dismissed for 26, the lowest score by any country in Tests. New Zealand were nevertheless given their only five-Test tour to date in 1958, managing only one draw, in a rain-ruined match at The Oval. In 1965, John Edrich scored 310 not out for England at Headingley. In another defeat for New Zealand in 1969, Glenn Turner carried his bat at Lord's for 43 not out in a total of 131.

Although New Zealand lost 2-0 in a three-match series in 1973, there was evidence that better things were coming. Set 479 to win at Trent Bridge, they passed 400 with only five out, but were all out for 440. At Lord's, New Zealand made 551 for 9 declared. Captain Bev Congdon made 176 and 175 in these innings.

The next series, in 1974-75, was

An exuberant appeal from Ian Botham as Jeff Crowe is lbw for the Englishman's record 356th Test wicket, at The Oval in 1986.

overshadowed by the accident to New Zealand debutant Ewen Chatfield, whose heart stopped after a hair-line fracture of the skull caused by a ball from Peter Lever. Fortunately, MCC physio Bernard Thomas resuscitated him and he made a full recovery.

Arise, Sir Richard

England toured New Zealand in 1977-78. New Zealand won at Wellington, where Richard Hadlee took 6 for 26 (ten in the match) to dismiss England for 64 in the second innings. It was New Zealand's first win over England in their 48th Test. The series, holn 1983, New Zealand won their first Test in England, by five wickets at Headingley, although lost the series 3-1. The 1983-84 series saw New Zealand's big breakthrough. Dismissing England for 82 and 93 at Christchurch, they won by an innings and 132. Richard Hadlee was the star, taking eight wickets and top-scoring with 99 in 81 balls. Two draws gave New Zealand their first series win against England.

On their next trip to England in 1986, New Zealand repeated the formula, winning the middle one of the three Tests for another 1-0 win.

Thanks to an innings win at Trent Bridge, England won the 1994 series 1-0, and then won the 1996-97 series 2-0, after New Zealand had saved the first Test at Auckland with a last-wicket stand lasting 166 minutes between Nathan Astle (102 not out) and Danny Morrison (14 not out).

New Zealand, under Stephen Fleming, visited England in 1999 and won a four-match series by 2-1.

In 2001-02, a remarkable first Test at Christchurch saw England, with Graham Thorpe scoring 200 not out and Andrew Flintoff 137 in a 281 sixth-wicket stand set New Zealand 550 to win. Amazingly, they threatened to do it, getting 451, the second-highest fourth-innings total

in Tests. Astle cracked 222 from 168 balls, his 200 coming from 153 balls. New Zealand squared the series with a 78-run victory at Auckland.

At Lord's in 2004, Andrew Strauss made his England debut and scored 112 and 83 (run out). The run-out came courtesy of Nasser Hussain when England were chasing 282 to win on the last afternoon. At 143 for 3 the match remained even, but Hussain made 103 not out and England won by seven wickets. Shortly after the game, Hussain announced his retirement from Test cricket.

At Headingley, England's victory was more clear-cut, by nine wickets, with Marcus Trescothick and Geraint Jones both century-makers. A four-wicket win at Trent Bridge, led by Thorpe's hundred, completed a whitewash, though Stephen Fleming and Scott Styris both made centuries for the visitors.

New Zealand won the first Test of a home three-match series in 2007-08 by 189 runs, with Ross Taylor making his first Test century, but England came back strongly to win the second Test by 126 runs. In the decider at Napier, England were 4 for three wickets on the first morning, but recovered to win the match by 121 runs and the series 2-1. The Player of the Match, and also the Player of the Series, was Ryan Sidebottom, whose 24 wickets in a three-match series had not been bettered since 1895-96.

After a washout at Lord's in 2008, England won the remaining Tests for a convincing 2-0 series win. At Old Trafford they turned a first-innings defecit of 179 into a six-wicket win, before winning the third Test by an innings and nine runs.

Nathan Astle salutes the crowd after reaching his double-century (off just 155 balls) against England at Christchurch in 2002. It was the fastest Test double-hundred ever recorded.

ENGLAND v NEW ZEALAND

	MATCHES	ENG	NZ	DRAW	SERIES	ENG	NZ	DRAW
IN NEW ZEALAND	44	18	4	22	17	10	1	6
IN ENGLAND	50	27	4	19	15	12	2	1
TOTALS	94	45	8	41	32	22	3	7

AUSTRALIA v WEST INDIES

The West Indies played their first Tests against Australia when touring in 1930-31. They lost the first four Tests, but won the last. The same 4-1 result was recorded in the West Indies' next tour in 1951-52, but the matches were more closely fought.

Ian Johnson led the first Australian Test tour to the West Indies in 1954-55 and won 3-0 in a series remarkable for heavy scoring, with 21 centuries being scored. Clyde Walcott's series aggregate of 827, with five centuries, is sixth in the all-time list. Neil Harvey, however, topped the averages at 108.33.

Frank Worrell Trophy

The series in Australia in 1960-61 is one of the great series, and led to the presentation of the Frank Worrell Trophy, named after the West Indian captain, to the winners. It got off to a superb start at Brisbane with the first of only two tied Tests. Australia required 233 to win and recovered from 92 for 6 to require six with three wickets left when the last over began, bowled by Wes Hall. A leg-bye was followed by Benaud caught behind for 52. A bye to the keeper came from the fourth ball and a single from the fifth. Grant was run out going for a third and winning run off the sixth – 232 for 9, level. On the seventh ball another winning run was tried, but Solomon threw down the wicket from sideways on for another run out and the match was tied. Alan Davidson became the first player to complete 100 runs and ten wickets in a Test. Australia won the second Test, the West Indies the third, and Australia won the deciding fifth Test by two wickets.

Australia beat an ageing West Indian touring side 3-1 in 1968-69 with Doug Walters making four centuries in four matches, including

The Waugh twins (Mark on left) added 271 together to win 1994-95 series in the West Indies.

242 and 103 in the fifth Test at Sydney. He averaged 116.50. Two wins kept Australia on top in the West Indies in 1972-73.

After, the West Indies, with a new resurgent team led by Clive Lloyd, had won the first World Cup, the series in Australia in 1975-76 was billed as the "world championship". After Australia won the first Test and the West Indies the second, the West Indies disappointed and Australia won the last four Tests.

World Series Cricket meant the teams in the West Indies in 1977-78 weren't representative. However,

the West Indies' 3-1 win gave them the Frank Worrell Trophy, which they were to hold for 17 years. Back with full-strength sides in Australia in 1979-80, the West Indies confirmed their new superiority. Their fast-bowling battery of Andy Roberts, Michael Holding, Joel Garner and Colin Croft were the masters. While the 1981-82 series was drawn 1-1, the West Indies won 3-0 at home in 1983-84 in a series remarkable for the fact that they did not lose a second-innings wicket all series.

The West Indies won a very bad-tempered series in 1984-85.

Australian captain Kim Hughes resigned in tears after the second Test and Allan Border took over. Australia's draw in the fourth Test ended a run of 11 successive wins by West Indies. Australia then won the fifth Test at Sydney.

Under Viv Richards, the West Indies won 3-1 in Australia in 1988-89. The West Indies won the first three Tests to ensure retention of the Frank Worrell Trophy. Courtney Walsh surprised himself with a hat-trick in the first Test, spread over both innings. In a brave 13-wicket performance at Perth, Merv Hughes bettered this with a unique Test hat-trick with wickets in three separate overs. In the West Indies' first innings he took the ninth wicket with the last ball of one over and the tenth with the first ball of the next. He completed the hat-trick with his first ball of the West Indies' second innings. In the third Test, at Melbourne, Malcolm Marshall took his 300th Test wicket. Australia won the fourth Test and drew the last.

The West Indies maintained their superiority 2-1 in 1990-91, but it was another bad-tempered series, remarkable for the dismissal of Dean Jones in the second Test at Georgetown. Thinking he was bowled (not hearing a no-ball call), he was returning to the pavilion when Carl Hooper, who fielded the ball, pulled a stump from the ground. Jones was given run out, which eventually turned out to be an umpiring mistake.

The same 2-1 score for the West Indies was repeated in 1992-93 in Australia, but they had to win the last two Tests. Brian Lara announced his arrival in the top flight with an innings of 277 in the drawn third Test. The West Indies won the fourth Test by one run. Australia were set 186 to win, and seemed out of it at 74 for 7, but the last-wicket pair put on 40 and just failed to clinch the series. Having escaped, the West Indies won the last Test in three days by an innings. Curtley Ambrose, with 33 wickets was named the Man of the Series.

Australia, under Mark Taylor, at last beat the West Indies in 1994-95, West Indies' first series defeat in 15 years and the first on their own soil for 22 years. In fact, they had won 20 and drawn nine of their 29 previous series. After three Tests, in which Australia won the first, rain the second and the West Indies the third, the final, decisive Test was fought at Kingston, Jamaica. Australia won decisively by an innings and 53 runs, with outstanding contributions from the Waugh twins, Steve (200) and Mark (126), who put on 271 together, more than half of Australia's total and more than either of the West Indies' innings.

The West Indies went to Australia in 1996-97 to try to reassert their mastery, but lost the first two Tests by 123 and 124 runs. They came back to win the third Test by six wickets, but Australia clinched the Frank Worrell Trophy in the fourth by an emphatic margin of an innings and 83 runs. An easy ten-wicket win for the West Indies in the final Test only narrowed the defeat to 3-2. Wicketkeeper Ian Healey topped the series' batting averages for Australia with 356 runs at 59.33, while Glenn McGrath topped the bowling with 26 wickets at 17.42.

A series in West Indies in 1998-99 was drawn 2-2. A big win by 312 runs was registered by Australia in the first Test when West Indies were shot out for 51 in their second innings (Glenn McGrath 5 for 28, Jason Gillespie 4 for 18), but the West Indies fought back from this disaster in the second Test to win by ten wickets, after Brian Lara scored 231. West Indies won a very

Brian Lara's highest score against Australia (277) came at Sydney in the 1992-93 series.

exciting third Test at Bridgetown. With Steve Waugh getting 199, Australia led on first innings by 161, but were dismissed for 146 in their second knock. Needing 308, West Indies were 105 for 5, and 248 for 8, but Lara was playing a magnificent innings, and with the last man in he reached 153 not out and squeezed a one-wicket win. Australia came back in the fourth and final Test to win by 176 runs, tie the series 2-2 and retain the Frank Worrell Trophy. Lara topped the series batting with 546 runs, average 91.00. Steve Waugh, with 409, average 58.42 was best for the Aussies. McGrath, with 30

wickets at 16.93 was best bowler and Courtney Walsh, 26 at 20.88, was West Indies' best.

When West Indies went to Australia in 2000-01, Australia were established as the strongest side in the world, while West Indies were in the dumps. By winning the first

two Tests by an innings, Australia established a record by winning 12 Tests in succession (beating West Indies' record). Australia went on to complete a 5-0 whitewash in the series. It was a team performance.

Australia, under the captaincy of Steve Waugh, won a four-Test series 3-1 in the West Indies in 2002-03. The West Indies won the final Test with a fourth-innings total of 418 for 7, but Australia's bowlers were in control with Stuart McGill (20 wickets), Jason Gillespie and Brett Lee (17 each) the best. Jermaine Lawson took 14 wickets for West Indies. Ricky Ponting (523 runs, av. 130.75) and Brian Lara (533 runs, av. 66.62) were the leading batsmen.

Australia, led by Ricky Ponting, who made a century in each innings of the fourth Test, won a home series 3-0 in 2005-06. Michael Hussey averaged 120.33 (with 361 runs).

Australia won a three-match series 2-0 in the West Indies in 2007-08. All three games went into the fifth day. The Aussie captain, Ricky Ponting, passed 10,000 runs in Tests in Antigua, but the Player of the Series was Shivnarine Chanderpaul, who scored 442 runs at an average of 147.33.

After Australia won the first Test by an innings at home in 2009-10, West Indies put up a fight in a drawn second Test and a narrow defeat in the third. Captain Chris Gayle was the inspiration, carrying his bat for 165 not out in a total of 317 in the second innings at Adelaide, and racing to a century in 70 balls at Perth, but it was 2-0 to Australia.

AUSTRALIA v WEST INDIES

	MATCHES	AUS	WI	DRAW	SERIES	AUS	WI	DRAW
IN AUSTRALIA	63	35	18	10*	14	9	4	1
IN WEST INDIES	45	17	14	14	10	5	4	1
TOTALS	108	52	32	24*	24	14	8	2

* INCLUDES ONE TIE

SOUTH AFRICA v NEW ZEALAND

The first Test series not to involve either England or Australia began in 1931-32 when the South African tourists played two Tests in New Zealand, winning both easily. Twenty-one years later, South Africa won a repeat two-match tour 1-0.

In 1953-54, New Zealand toured South Africa for a five-match series. Although South Africa won 4-0, the series is remembered for the magnificent innings of 80 not out by Bert Sutcliffe in Johannesburg in a match which spanned Christmas. On Christmas Day, the New Zealand party was devastated as news came through of a train smash at home which had killed 151 people, including the fiancée of tourist Bob Blair, who was playing. New Zealand had to go in to bat. The pitch was very fiery and South African fast bowler Neil Adcock, in his second Test, bowled Chapple and Poore off their chests and sent Sutcliffe and Miller to hospital. Sutcliffe, going in at 9 for 2, was immediately hit on the head (no helmets then) and sank to the turf. After five minutes, he was helped from the field and rushed to hospital, where he fainted under treatment. However, at 81 for 6, with New Zealand still needing 41 to avoid the follow-on, he returned to the wicket, face pale and head swathed in bandage. Inspired, he was 55 not out when New Zealand reached 154 for 9, having had his bandages readjusted after they had been disturbed by his onslaught. And then the crowd stood in silence as 22-year-old Blair, who had been left in the hotel, came out to bat, to be met by Sutcliffe. They added 33 for the last wicket in ten minutes, during which time Sutcliffe hit Tayfield for three sixes in an over and took a single to keep the strike, only to see Blair himself hit a six. It was Blair's only scoring stroke – he was soon stumped and walked off with Sutcliffe's arm around him.

In 1961-62, New Zealand won their first Tests overseas and drew the series 2-2. In 1963-64 in New Zealand, with anti-apartheid demonstrators in evidence, all three Tests were drawn.

The countries resumed acquaintances with a three-match series in South Africa in 1994-95. New Zealand won the first Test, but South Africa took the last two to become the first side to come from behind in the 20th century to win a three-Test series. South Africa were then guests at Auckland for New Zealand's centenary match and spoiled the party by overturning a first-innings deficit to win by 93 runs.

South Africa won a three-match series in New Zealand by 1-0 in 1998-99. In the first Test they made 621 for 5 declared (Daryll Cullinan 275 not out, a South African record), but failed to win, partly because Geoff Allott, batting at No. 11, set his own world record in batting for 101 minutes for 0. South Africa won the third Test by eight wickets. In the series, Cullinan scored 427 for once out.

In 2000-01, South Africa won a three-match series 2-0. Young South African fast bowler Makhaya Ntini was named Man of the Series.

A closely fought three-match series was drawn 1-1 in New Zealand in 2003-04. New Zealand's victory in the second Test was their first at home against South Africa. Scott Styris made 170 and Chris Cairns 158 in that match, while Gary Kirten's 78 in his final Test helped South Africa level the series.

South Africa won a home three-match series 2-0 in 2005-06 with Makhaya Ntini getting 20 wickets and the Player of the Series award, and easily won both matches of a home two-match series in 2007-08, when New Zealand were afflicted by numerous injuries and illnesses. Jacques Kallis and Hashim Amla shared partnerships of 330 and 220 runs, but the Player of the Series was Dale Steyn, who took ten wickets in each match at an overall average of 9.20.

New Zealand's Scott Styris hits out on his way to a century during the second Test against South Africa played at Eden Park, Auckland, in March 2004.

SOUTH AFRICA v NEW ZEALAND

	MATCHES	SA	NZ	DRAW	SERIES	SA	NZ	DRAW
IN NEW ZEALAND	14	6	1	7	6	4	0	2
IN SOUTH AFRICA	21	14	3	4	10	8	0	2
TOTALS	35	20	4	11	16	12	0	4

ENGLAND v INDIA

Sunil Gavaskar averaged 28.20 against England, well below his career average of 51.12.

India's inaugural Test took place at Lord's. England beat a side led by C.K. Nayudu by 158 runs. In 1933-34 England toured India, who played their first three home Tests. England won 2-0. "Lala" Amarnath made his country's first Test century.

England remained dominant until they sent a not-quite-representative side to India in 1961-62. After three draws, India won the last two Tests for their first series win over England.

India won the next two series. After two draws, India came from behind to win the third and last Test at The Oval, when Chandrasekhar's 6 for 38 shot England out in the second innings for 101. It was England's first defeat in 27 Tests.

Captain Tony Greig led England to a 3-1 win in India in 1976-77, their first there for 43 years. England then beat India by 10 wickets in India's Golden Jubilee Test at Bombay in 1979. There were six Tests in India in 1981-82. India won the first; there then followed five long draws.

The series in 1984-85 was marked by tragedy. The Indian prime minister, Mrs Indira Gandhi, was assassinated and the British Deputy High Commissioner to Western India was murdered, having entertained the tourists the day before. England won the series 2-1, despite losing the first Test when 18-year-old spinner Laxman Sivaramakrishnan took six wickets in each innings, and despite Mohammad Azharuddin becoming the first Test cricketer to make centuries in each of his first three Tests. He averaged 109.75 in his first series. At Madras, Mike Gatting and Graeme Fowler each made double centuries in England's 652 for 7 declared.

India, led by Kapil Dev, had their revenge in 1986 in England, winning 2-0 with one drawn. England's 1-0 win in three Tests in 1990 was notable for the match at Lord's, when Graham Gooch made 333 and 123 – his total of 456 being the highest aggregate in a Test. He is the only batsman in first-class cricket to score 300 and 100 in the same match. For India, Azharuddin made a century in 87 balls; Kapil Dev, partnering the No. 11, hit a Test-record four successive sixes in an over, the last saving the follow-on; and 17-year-old Sachin Tendulkar took a breathtaking catch in the deep. At Old Trafford, Tendulkar, at 17 years 122 days, became the second-youngest Test century-maker, and at The Oval, India made their highest score against England: 606 for 9 declared. Gooch's aggregate of 752 runs (average 125.33) is a record for a three-match series.

India's revenge in 1992-93 was complete, as they won all three matches, two by an innings and the other by eight wickets. Newcomer Vinod Kambli made 224 in his third Test match. In 1996 in England, the home side won a well-fought series 1-0. Saurav Ganguly became only the third batsman in history to score a century in his first two Test innings.

Ganguly was captain when England toured in 2001-02. India's spinners Anil Kumble and Harbhajan Singh dominated in India's 1-0 win. A few months later, in England, the home side won the opening Test at Lord's by 170 runs. India held on for a high-scoring draw at Trent Bridge, and then won by an innings at Headingley, when Rahul Dravid (148), Sachin Tendulkar (193) and Ganguly (128) all made centuries. Both teams topped 500 in another draw at The Oval. Michael Vaughan (616 runs, average 102.6) and Dravid (602, average 100.3) both achieved century averages. Injuries forced Andrew Flintoff to captain England in a 1-1 drawn series in India in 2005-06. Alastair Cook made a century on debut for England.

Rain caused both sides to collapse in the first innings when a three-match series got under way at Lord's in 2007. India's last pair held out on the last afternoon, with Mahendra Dhoni on 76 not out, when gloom and rain gave India a draw. A seven-wicket win at Trent Bridge proved enough for India to win the series, as they ensured a draw at The Oval with their highest innings in England, 664. Zaheer Khan with 18 wickets was top bowler of the series, and Kevin Pietersen the best batsman.

Pietersen was captain when England visited India in 2008-09. The terrorist attack on Mumbai caused the team to return home before the Test series began, but they returned for a two-match series. Andrew Strauss made centuries in each innings at Chennai, and Pietersen declared setting India 287 to win. Good batting, especially by Virender Sehwag and Sachin Tendulkar, enabled India to reach the target for a six-wicket win. The second Test was drawn, with persistent early morning fog causing loss of play.

ENGLAND v INDIA

	MATCHES	ENG	INDIA	DRAW	SERIES	ENG	INDIA	DRAW
IN ENGLAND	44	22	4	18	14	11	3	0
IN INDIA	48	11	13	24	12	4	5	3
TOTALS	92	33	17	42	26	15	8	3

AUSTRALIA v NEW ZEALAND

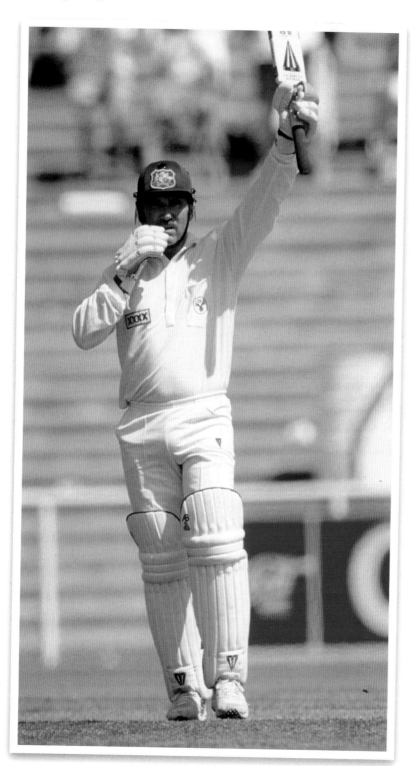

Allan Border salutes the crowd after passing Sunil Gavaskar's record for the most runs scored in Tests during Australia's game against New Zealand at Christchurch in February 1993.

Surprisingly, Australia and New Zealand did not meet each other in Test cricket until a match played at Wellington on 29 and 30 March 1946 was retrospectively granted Test status. New Zealand were dismissed for 42 and 54 and Australia won by an innings and 103 runs.

Although each country toured the other in the 1960s, Tests were not resumed until 1973-74 in Australia with a three-Test tour in each country. Australia won 2-0 at home and drew 1-1 away, when New Zealand recorded the first victory over their neighbours at Christchurch, with Glenn Turner (101 and 110 not out) becoming the first New Zealander to get a 100 in each innings of a Test. At Wellington, both Chappell brothers performed the feat for Australia: Ian 145 and 121 and Greg 247 not out and 133. Australia won the series in 1976-77 and 1980-81 before New Zealand again won a match to tie the series in 1981-82.

In 1985-86, New Zealand went to Australia and won 2-1, thanks largely to Richard Hadlee, who took 33 wickets at 12.50. New Zealand proved it was no fluke by winning 1-0 in the same season in New Zealand.

Australia won 1-0 in Australia in 1987-88, but only after their last pair held out for four overs to draw the last Test. In 1989-90, there was one Test in each country, with New Zealand recording the only win at Wellington.

In New Zealand in 1992-93, Allan Border passed Sunil Gavaskar's Test aggregate of 10,122 runs. New Zealand won the third Test to square the series. In 1993-94, Australia won 2-0 at home. At Brisbane, Allan Border played his 150th Test and held his 150th catch.

A three-match series in 1997-98 in Australia was won 2-0 by the hosts, with Australia winning the first Test by 186 runs and the second by an innings and 70. The third was drawn when New Zealand's last pair held out to thwart the Aussies.

In 1999-2000 New Zealand were hosts. Australia won the series 3-0, thus extending their winning sequence in Tests to ten. In the third, wicket-keeper Adam Gilchrist took five catches in each innings, beating Gil Langley's Australian record of nine in a Test.

New Zealand visited Australia in 2001-02 and gave the all-conquering Aussies a fright in a series of three draws. At 274 for 6, New Zealand fell ten runs short of victory in the first Test and, in the second, Australia were hanging on with three wickets left at stumps.

Australia won both Tests by large margins in Australia in 2004-05, the highlights being Justin Langer's 215 in Adelaide and Glenn McGrath's 61 batting at No. 11 in Brisbane. Later in the season, in New Zealand, they won 2-0 with one draw.

Australia won two-match series 2-0 in Australia in 2008-09 and in New Zealand in 2009-10. Michael Clarke excelled in each series.

AUSTRALIA v NEW ZEALAND

	MATCHES	AUS	NZ	DRAW	SERIES	AUS	NZ	DRAW
IN NEW ZEALAND	24	12	5	7	10	5	2	3
IN AUSTRALIA	26	14	2	10	10	7	1	2
TOTALS	50	26	7	17	20	12	3	5

AUSTRALIA v INDIA

India's first Test series against Australia was played in 1947–48 and Australia won 4–0. It was not until 1979–80 that India won their first series against Australia, by 2–0, led by Kapil Dev's 28 wickets.

The three-match series in India in 2000–01 was one of the greatest. Australia won by ten wickets in the first Test. In the second, they made 445 (Harbhajan Singh's 7 for 123 included India's first Test hat-trick) and then bowled out India for 171. Following-on, and at 232 for 4, Rahul Dravid (180) joined V.V.S. Laxman (281) and the pair put on 376 to help India declare at 657 for 7, setting Australia 384 to win. Six for 73 by Harbhajan got them out for 212 and a win for India by 171 runs. It was the third time in Test history that a team won after following on, and the victory ended Australia's sequence of 16 consecutive victories. The third Test lived up to the second and also provided a tense finish. India needed 155 to win. Laxman's 66 got them home with two wickets to spare. Harbhajan, the Man of the Series, scored the winning run. In the series, he took 32 of the 50 Australia wickets to fall, for 545 runs, average 17.03.

A magnificent four-match series in Australia in 2003–04 was drawn 1–1. Despite Ricky Ponting's 242, India came from behind for a four-wicket win at Adelaide, with Dravid making 233 and Laxman 138. Australia's nine-wicket win came at Melbourne, despite 195 from Virender Sehwag, with Ponting making 257 and Matthew Hayden 136. At Sydney, India made 705 for 7 (Sachin Tendulkar 241 not out), but in captain Steve Waugh's last Test, Australia held on for the draw with Waugh getting 80 in his last innings. Ponting scored 706 runs (average 100.85), Dravid 633 (av. 123.80). Amid the batting heroics, Anil Kumble's 24 wickets at 29.58 was outstanding.

A four-Test return in India in 2004–05 was won decisively by Australia. Led by Adam Gilchrist, it was Australia's first series win in India for 35 years. The highlights included Michael Clarke's century on his debut in the first Test, Anil Kumble's 13 wickets in the drawn second Test, Damien Martyn's run of

V.V.S. Laxman's 281 for India against Australia in the second Test at Calcutta in 2000–01 inspired his side to a famous 171-run victory, despite the home side being forced to follow-on.

104, 114 and 97 in successive innings, and Clarke's 6 for 9 in the fourth Test, which India won.

There was an acrimonious start to the 2007–08 series in Australia, which Australia won 2–1. Brett Lee was the Player of the Series.

India won a four-match series 2–0 in India in 2008–09, winning at Mohali by 320 runs and at Nagpur by 172. In a high-scoring draw at Delhi both Gautam Gambhir and V.V.S. Laxman scored double centuries in India's total of 613 for seven declared. Sachin Tendulkar reached 12,000 runs in Tests in Mohali and scored his 40th Test hundred in Nagpur.

Australia lost a two-match series 2–0 in India in 2010–11. At Mohali, Australia's two top-scorers, Shane Watson (126) and Tim Paine (92) were both dropped on 0, allowing Australia to get a lead of 23, and eventually set India 216 to win. At 124 for 8, this looked very unlikely. But V.V.S. Laxman, batting with a runner at 7 after being heavily injected for back spasms, was joined by Ishant Sharma (31) and they added 81 before last man Pragyan Ojha helped Laxman (73 not out) get the last 11 runs for victory. At Bangalore, Sachin Tendulkar scored 214, putting on 308 for the third wicket with Murali Vijay (139), but although India passed Australia's 478 with only five wickets down, their eventual lead was only 17. However, set 207 to win, they won by seven wickets with Tendulkar (403 in the series, average 134.33) still there.

AUSTRALIA v INDIA

	MATCHES	AUS	IND	DRAW	SERIES	AUS	IND	DRAW
IN AUSTRALIA	36	22	5	9	9	6	0	3
IN INDIA	42	12	15	15*	12	4	6	2
TOTALS	78	34	20	24*	21	10	6	5

* INCLUDES ONE TIE

WEST INDIES v INDIA

Tests between the two started with a five-Test series in India in 1948-49. Everton Weekes, having made a century in his last Test innings against England, scored centuries in his first four in India and was then run out for 90 when attempting a sixth in succession. The West Indies won the only match decided, the fourth Test. In the last, India, chasing 361 to win, were 355 for 8 at the close. Weekes made 779 runs, average 111.28.

The West Indies maintained their supremacy in four series in the 1950s and 1960s, winning 11 matches to none. In India in 1958-59, there were complaints about the use of bouncers by the West Indians and Roy Gilchrist was sent home for bowling beamers. In 1961-62, the West Indies achieved a 5-0 whitewash. At Bridgetown, the Indian captain, N.J. Contractor, suffered a fractured skull when hit by a ball from C.C. Griffith, which ended his Test career.

India's first victory against the West Indies in 1970-71 was enough to win the series. Sunil Gavaskar made his Test debut at Port-of-Spain and scored 65 and 67 not out. Dilip Sardesai made 112 as India won by seven wickets. Jack Noriega, whose four Tests all came in this series, took 9 for 95, the best analysis recorded by a West Indian. In the fifth Test (his fourth), Gavaskar became only the second batsman (after K.D. Walters) to score a century and a double-century in the same Test. He scored 774 runs in the series, average 154.80.

With Clive Lloyd as captain, the West Indies won excitingly in 1974-75 in India by 3-2. The West Indies won the final deciding Test by 201 runs, with Lloyd making 242 not out, and topping the batting, while Andy Roberts' 32 wickets was then a series record for the West Indies.

The 1975-76 series in the West

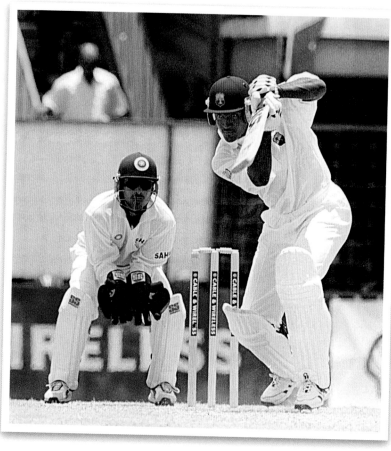

Carl Hooper hits out on his way to scoring 233 against India at Georgetown in 2001-02.

Indies was a sour affair. After the West Indies won the first Test, India levelled in the third with a magnificent win. They were set 403 to win in the fourth innings and, with Gavaskar getting 102 and Viswanath 112, won by six wickets. Their score of 406 for 4 was the highest fourth-innings total made to win a Test match. The West Indies won the fourth and final Test with what the Indians regarded as intimidatory bowling on a variable pitch. In protest, Bedi declared India's first innings total at 306 for 6, with two players injured. India were all out for 97 in the second innings with five players absent hurt. The West Indies needed only 13 to win.

India took their revenge in 1978-79 with their first series win over the West Indies in India, 1-0, in a high-scoring, six-Test series. India won by three wickets in a match which became a bouncer war. Gavaskar led the series batting with 732 runs, average 91.50.

In 1982-83, the West Indies won a Test remarkably by taking four Indian wickets and scoring 173 for 6

in the final session of play, with four balls of their allotted 26 overs left. In 1983-84 at Ahmedabad, Gavaskar scored the runs that took his Test aggregate past the previous record of 8,114 set by Geoffrey Boycott.

In the tied series in India in 1987-88 there was a remarkable Test debut by Narendra Hirwani, a little-known, bespectacled leg-spinner who took 8 for 61 and 8 for 75 in India's victory at Madras. His 16 for 136 are the best match figures by a debutant in a Test match.

In 1994-95, the West Indies tied the series in the last Test to maintain their 15-year unbeaten record.

With the batting geniuses Brian Lara and Sachin Tendulkar captaining the sides, the West Indies won the series of 1996-97 by virtue of a single win at Bridgetown. On an increasingly difficult wicket they were bowled out for 140 in the third innings but dismissed India, who needed only 120 runs in the fourth, for just 81.

In the first Test in the West Indies in 2001-02, home captain Carl Hooper made 233 and 144 not out, but India drew, then won the second Test by 37 runs. West Indies took two of the last three Tests, however, to win 2-1. Hooper (579 runs at an average of 82.71) and Shivnarine Chanderpaul (562 runs, average 140.50) were the stars.

In India, in 2002-03, India won 2-0 with one drawn. This time the outstanding player was a bowler, Harbhajan Singh, with 20 wickets at 16.75 each.

WEST INDIES v INDIA

	MATCHES	WI	IND	DRAW	SERIES	WI	IND	DRAW
IN INDIA	40	14	7	19	9	5	2	2
IN WEST INDIES	38	16	3	19	8	7	1	0
TOTALS	78	30	10	38	17	12	3	2

WEST INDIES v NEW ZEALAND

field after tea on the third day as a protest against an umpire, but did so eventually and saved the match.

The West Indies got their revenge 2-0 in the Caribbean in 1984-85 amid a flurry of bouncers from Marshall and Garner. After a draw in 1986-87, the West Indies won two two-Test series in the 1990s 1-0, before New Zealand reversed the trend with a 2-0 home victory in 1999-2000. Chris Cairns was outstanding and Mathew Sinclair, making his Test debut, scored 214. New Zealand at last won a two-match series in the West Indies in 2002-03. Captain Stephen Fleming made 130 as the Kiwis won by 204 runs in Bridgetown, while the second Test was drawn.

Two matches were won by New Zealand in a home series in 2005-06, with the third match washed out. Chasing 291 at Auckland, West Indies were 148 before the first wicket fell, but collapsed and lost by 27, thanks to the bowling of Shane Bond, who got Lara out with the first ball he bowled to him in each innings. Chris Gayle, with 213 runs, was the leading run scorer.

In the 2008-09 series in New Zealand a new referral system was tried whereby either side could appeal to the third umpire if they disagreed with an umpire's decision. The general view was that the system was not a success. Both matches were drawn, with Chris Gayle's 197 at Napier the highlight.

J.D.C. Goddard's strong West Indian side played two Tests in New Zealand in 1951-52 and won 1-0.

New Zealand won a match in the West Indies' next visit in 1955-56, but lost the series 3-1. The third series in New Zealand, 1968-69, was drawn. Seymour Nurse played innings for the West Indies of 168 and 258, averaging 111.60 for the series. All five Tests were drawn in New Zealand's first tour to the West Indies in 1971-72, but in 1979-80, back in New Zealand, they won the three-Test series 1-0. The West Indians behaved badly after New Zealand's one-wicket win (from a leg-bye) in the first Test, and only Desmond Haynes attended the presentation. In the second Test, the West Indies refused to take the

Chris Gayle smashed seven sixes and 20 fours in his 197 at Napier in December 2008.

WEST INDIES v NEW ZEALAND

	MATCHES	WI	NZ	DRAW	SERIES	WI	NZ	DRAW
IN NEW ZEALAND	24	7	8	9	9	3	3	3
IN WEST INDIES	13	3	1	9	4	2	1	2
TOTALS	37	10	9	18	13	5	4	5

INDIA v PAKISTAN

The bitter, often interrupted rivalry between India and Pakistan began in 1952-53, when India were the hosts for Pakistan's first Test series. India won the first match, Pakistan the second, in a match where Nazar Mohammad of Pakistan carried his bat for 124 not out in a score of 331 and became the first player to be on the field for an entire completed Test match. India took the series 2-1. A run of 13 consecutive draws followed. The 1954-55 series in Pakistan was the first five-Test series not to produce a result and in India, in 1960-61, there were again five draws.

Tests resumed in 1978-79, when Pakistan won 2-0. India reversed the result in India the following season by winning 2-0. In 1982-83, it was Pakistan's turn. They won 3-0 and captain Imran Khan's 40 wickets remains the best series haul for any Pakistani in Tests. At Hyderabad, Mudassar Nazar (231) and Javed Miandad (280 not out) put on 451 for the third wicket, equalling the then highest stand in Test cricket. And at Lahore, Mudassar became the second Pakistani to carry his bat in a Test innings, the first having been his father, Nazar Mohammad.

The only series of four succeeding ones to produce a result was in 1986-87 in India when, after four dull draws, Pakistan won an exciting final Test by 16 runs having set India 221.

A series in 1989-90 in Pakistan produced four draws. The teams did not meet again for nine years when, in 1998-99, a two-match series in India resulted in a win for each side. Anil Kumble took all ten (for 74 runs) wickets in Pakistan's second innings in Delhi, only the second time a bowler had taken all ten in a Test.

Because of political troubles, it was 2003-04 before the next series. India won for the first time in Pakistan when, at Multan, Virender Sehwag (309) became India's first triple centurion. India scored 675 for 5 declared and won by an innings and 52 runs. A solid all-round performance in the second Test saw Pakistan draw level with a nine-wicket win, but India took the decider when Rahul Dravid made 270 out of a total of 600 at Rawalpindi. The return three-Test series in India was drawn 1-1.

After two high-scoring draws in 2005-06, Pakistan took the third Test to win a home series. Eleven batsmen averaged over 50, the best being Younis Khan of Pakistan with 110.60 (553 runs). There were 13 centuries in three games, the highest being Virender Sehwag's 254 for India.

After three years out of Test cricket, Saurav Ganguly returned to the India side for a home series in 2007-08 and was voted Player of the Series, scoring 239 at Bangalore and 102 at Kolkata, matches in which India scored over 600 in the first innings to draw. As they had won the first Test in Delhi by six wickets, they thus won the series. Anil Kumble was captain.

Shoaib Akhtar celebrates as Pakistan near victory and a series win over India in 2006.

INDIA v PAKISTAN

	MATCHES	IND	PAK	DRAW	SERIES	IND	PAK	DRAW
IN INDIA	33	7	5	21	8	3	1	4
IN PAKISTAN	26	2	7	17	7	1	3	3
TOTALS	59	9	12	38	15	4	4	7

ENGLAND v PAKISTAN

Umpires Doctrove and Hair (right) show Pakistan captain Inzamam-ul-Haq (in cap) what they believed to be ball-tampering in The Oval Test of 2006.

Pakistan toured England in 1954 to play four Tests. England won the second Test at Trent Bridge by an innings, and in the draws at Lord's and Old Trafford dismissed Pakistan for 87 and 90 respectively. So it was a shock when Pakistan tied the series at The Oval with a 24-run win.

Pakistan eventually won their second match against England at Lord's in 1982, when Mohsin Khan scored the first Test double-century there for 33 years, and Pakistan won by ten wickets. England, however, won the series 2-1. But at home in 1983-84, Pakistan won their first series against England 1-0, by virtue of winning the first Test at Karachi. When set to score

65 in the fourth innings, they lost seven wickets getting them.

Pakistan then won the next six series including that in 1987-88 when the England captain Mike Gatting famously rowed with umpire Shakoor Rana and a whole day's play was lost waiting for apologies.

Controversy and sometimes bad feeling has been a feature of many of the matches between the two countries. In 2000-01 in Pakistan England won 1-0 in dramatic fashion. Needing 176 in a minimum 44 overs in the final Test, England found Pakistan bowling at such a slow over rate that captain Moin Khan was reminded of the

spirit of the game by the referee. The umpires refused to stop the game and England won by six wickets, even though it was almost dark when the game was over.

The 2006 series ended in great controversy when umpire D.B. Hair judged England to be winners of the final match at The Oval because Pakistan allegedly refused to continue the match following a

ball-tampering incident. England won the series 3-0.

A four-match series in England in 2010 ended in controversy when during the last Test three Pakistan players were accused by a newspaper of deliberately bowling no-balls at certain times for betting purposes. They were later suspended. So far as the cricket was concerned, England won the opening Test by 354 runs with James Anderson getting 11 wickets. In the second Test, Pakistan were dismissed in the first innings for 72 and England eventually won by nine wickets. Fortunes turned at the Oval, where England were 94 for 7 before Matt Prior (84) and Stuart Broad (48) put on 119 for the eighth wicket. Pakistan got a lead, and when England collapsed again before Pakistan's quick bowlers in the second innings from 194 for 3 to 222 all out, Pakistan needed only 146 to win and, though nervously, won by four wickets. Pakistan's quickies again had England in trouble in the final Test at Lord's but, with the score 102 for 7, Stuart Broad (169) joined Jonathan Trott (184) in a stand of 332, the highest-ever eighth wicket stand in Test history. A demoralised Pakistan were dismissed for 74 and lost by an innings and 225 runs. England thus took the series 3-1. Trott was the outstanding batsman with 404 runs (av 67.33), while Anderson took 23 wickets at 13.73 and Graeme Swann took 22 at 12.22.

ENGLAND v PAKISTAN

	MATCHES	ENG	PAK	DRAW	SERIES	ENG	PAK	DRAW
IN ENGLAND	47	20	9	18	13	7	3	3
IN PAKISTAN	24	2	4	18	8	2	3	3
TOTALS	71	22	13	36	21	9	6	6

NEW ZEALAND v PAKISTAN

151 for the last wicket, the highest score in Tests.

Pakistan's batsmen were on top in the 1970s and '80s. In 1996-97, a two-match series in Pakistan ended 1-1, with Pakistan's debutant Mohammad Zahid taking 11 for 130 in the second Test at Rawalpindi, the best by a Pakistani on Test debut. In New Zealand, in 2000-01, the highlight was an over from Younis Khan which Craig McMillan hit for a Test record 26 runs: 4, 4, 4, 4, 6, 4.

A scheduled two-match series in Pakistan in 2002-03 was called off after the first Test when a bomb exploded outside the New Zealanders' hotel. Pakistan had won the Test by an innings and 324 runs with Inzamam-ul-Haq scoring 329.

In a two-match series in New Zealand, in 2003-04, Pakistan won 1-0. At Wellington, they trailed by 170, but Shoaib Akhtar (6 for 30) dismissed New Zealand for 103 and Pakistan made 277 for 3 to win.

The 2009-10 series in New Zealand ended 1-1, but New Zealand, chasing 208 to win the decider, were 90 for 0 wicket when rain ended play, so might have just had the edge. The all-round performance of captain Daniel Vettori was the highlight. However Vettori announced he would be standing down as skipper after Pakistan won a two-match series 1-0 in New Zealand in 2010-11, despite making the only hundred of the series. New Pakistan captain Misbah-ul-Haq scored 62, 99 and 70 not out in his three innings.

New Zealand's Craig McMillan salutes the crowd after smashing a Test record 26 runs off an over from Younis Khan in the third Test against Pakistan in Hamilton in March 2001. He was finally out, caught, for 98.

New Zealand first toured Pakistan in 1955-56. Pakistan won the first two matches of a three-Test series.

New Zealand's first series win came in 1969-70 in Pakistan, when they won by five wickets in Lahore. It was New Zealand's first series win against any opposition, 40 years after their first Test.

The great Richard Hadlee made his Test debut against Pakistan in 1972-73. In a drawn Test at Auckland, New Zealand's Brian Hastings and Richard Collinge added

NEW ZEALAND v PAKISTAN

	MATCHES	NZ	PAK	DRAW	SERIES	NZ	PAK	DRAW
IN PAKISTAN	21	2	13	6	8	1	6	1
IN NEW ZEALAND	29	5	10	14	12	1	8	3
TOTALS	50	7	23	20	20	2	14	4

NEW ZEALAND v INDIA

Less than a week after completing their first Test series in Pakistan in 1955-56, New Zealand began their first series in India, and were easily beaten 2-0 in the five Test series.

India won the two series in the 1960s, 1-0 at home in 1964-65 and 3-1 away in 1967-68 – their first Test win away from home – thanks to excellent spin bowling. Graham Dowling made 239 at Christchurch. New Zealand were deprived of their first series win over India in 1969-70 when rain ruined the deciding Test.

They had to wait until 1980-81 for that first success, winning by 62 runs at Wellington and the series 1-0. Each side won at home in series in the late 1980s. A one-off Test in Hamilton in 1993-94 was drawn, and India recorded a 1-0 win in 1995-96, a victory at Bangalore being enough.

The first Test in New Zealand in 1998-99 was abandoned at Dunedin without a ball being bowled. New Zealand won the second, and the series when the third was drawn, despite Rahul Dravid compiling a century in each innings.

India won the middle one of three Tests in India in 1999-2000. Sachin Tendulkar was the outstanding batsman with 435 runs, average 108.75, and Anil Kumble was the best bowler with 20 wickets at 18.20.

India's batsmen fared miserably in New Zealand in 2002-03, failing to reach 200 in four innings. Daryl Tuffey (13 wickets at 8.69), Shane Bond (12 at 16.33) and Jacob Oram (11 at 11.09) ensured a 2-0 win.

Batsmen were on top when both Tests were drawn in India in 2003-

04. Nine players made hundreds, four in New Zealand's 630 for 6 declared in the second Test. In the first, Rahul Dravid made 222 for India.

In 2008-09 India won a three-Test series 1-0 in New Zealand, by winning the first Test by ten wickets. Gautan Gambhir top-scored with 445 (average 89.00) and Harbhajan Singh took 16 wickets at 21.37.

In India in 2010-11, the first two Tests were evenly drawn, with Harbhajan Singh making a century

Anil Kumble (with 20 wickets) proved the difference between the two sides in 1999-2000.

in each for India and Brendon McCullum getting 225 at Hyderabad for New Zealand. But in the final Test at Nagpur, New Zealand were skittled for 193 and 175, and India won by an innings and 198, with Dravid scoring 191. Virender Zehwag had 398 runs (av 99.50) but the series award went to Harbhajan Singh with 315 runs (av 105.00) and 10 wickets (av 42.00).

NEW ZEALAND v INDIA

	MATCHES	NZ	IND	DRAW	SERIES	NZ	IND	DRAW
IN INDIA	29	2	11	16	9	0	7	2
IN NEW ZEALAND	21	7	5	9	8	4	3	1
TOTALS	50	9	16	25	17	4	10	3

AUSTRALIA v PAKISTAN

The first Test between the two countries came in 1956. The first day at Karachi, on a matting wicket, produced 95 runs, still the lowest for a full day's play in Tests: Australia 80, Pakistan 15 for 2. Pakistan eventually won by nine wickets.

Australia gained revenge 2-0 during a second visit in 1959-60. Single Tests in each country were played in 1964-65; both were drawn.

Pakistan made their first three-match tour in 1972-73, and Australia won 3-0. Mushtaq Mohammad led Pakistan on tours in 1976-77 and 1978-79 and both tours ended 1-1. In the first, Imran Khan's hauls of six wickets in each innings at Sydney sealed Pakistan's first victory in Australia.

Pakistan's first rubber victory followed in 1979-80 in Pakistan. A seven-wicket win in Karachi was followed by two draws. At Lahore, Allan Border scored 150 and 153, the first player to reach 150 in each innings of a Test. Under Imran Khan, Pakistan won 3-0 in 1982-83, all easy wins. Leg-spinner Abdul Qadir's 22 wickets in the series were crucial.

The first five-Test series between the countries was won 2-0 by Australia at home in 1983-84. At the end of the series, three great Australians announced their retirements: Greg Chappell, Dennis Lillee and Rodney Marsh.

Pakistan won 1-0 in Pakistan in 1988-89, thanks partly to captain Javed Miandad's batting, but the Australians objected officially to the umpiring at Karachi. Australia won 1-0 in 1989-90, Pakistan 1-0 in 1994-95 and Australia 2-1 in 1995-96, all in their own countries. This last series began in a bitter atmosphere after Australian players had made allegations of attempted bribery – by at least one Pakistan player – to lose in Pakistan the previous season.

Australia won a high-scoring series in Pakistan in 1998-99, 1-0, with two drawn. The Aussie captain, Mark Taylor, batted the first two days at Peshawar to make 334 not out from a total of 599 for 4, thus equalling Donald Bradman's record Test score for Australia. Unselfishly he declared overnight, without attempting to better the record. Australia scored a 3-0 whitewash at home in 1999-2000 with an outstanding team performance.

The sides played a three-match series in Sri Lanka and Sharjah in 2002-03. The temperature at Colombo touched 48°C in the first Test, which Australia narrowly won, but they won both of the Sharjah Tests by an innings, Pakistan scoring 59 and 53 in the first. Shane Warne was the dominant player, taking 27 wickets.

In Australia in 2004-05, the Australians won all three Tests easily. Damien Martyn and Ricky Ponting both averaged over 100, and Glenn McGrath topped the bowling with 18 wickets at 14.44 each. Adam Gilchrist played his 65th consecutive Test since his debut, an Australian record. Australia pulled out of a tour of Pakistan in 2007-08 after the assassination of Benazir Bhutto, the former prime minister.

Pakistan visited Australia in 2009-10 and lost all three Tests, although they contributed massively to their own defeat in the second Test. At the start of the fourth day Australia were only 80 ahead with two wickets remaining, but Mike Hussey (134 not out) and Peter Siddle added 123 for the ninth wicket and Australia won by 36

Glenn McGrath and Justin Langer celebrate victory over Pakistan in Perth in 2004.

runs. Hussey was dropped three times by wicket-keeper Kamran Akmal.

Because Tests were banned in Pakistan following the terrorist attack on the Sri Lankan team in 2009, the countries played two matches in England in July 2010. Australia won by 150 runs at Lord's but Pakistan won by three wickets at Headingley, where they bowled Australia out for 88 in the first innings. Their fast bowlers Mohammad Amir, Mohammad Asif and Umar Gul were particularly effective.

AUSTRALIA v PAKISTAN

	Matches	Aus	Pak	Draw	Series	Aus	Pak	Draw
IN PAKISTAN	20	3	7	10	8	2	5	1
IN AUSTRALIA	32	21	4	7	11	18	0	3
IN SHARJAH	3	3	0	0	1	1	0	0
IN ENGLAND	2	1	1	0	1	0	0	1
TOTALS	57	28	12	17	21	21	5	5

WEST INDIES v PAKISTAN

In 1957-58, A.H. Kardar took a Pakistan team on a five-match tour of the West Indies. It proved to be record-breaking. In the first Test at Bridgetown, Nasim-ul-Ghani of Pakistan became the youngest Test player (since beaten) at 16 years 248 days and, when Pakistan followed on 473 behind, Hanif Mohammad scored 337, the second-highest Test score (since beaten), in 16 hours te minutes, then the longest innings in first-class cricket.

In the third Test at Kingston, Gary Sobers, aged 21, scored 365 not out, the highest score in Tests until 1993-94. With Hunte (260), he put on 446 for the second wicket. The West Indies made 790 for 3 declared. In the fourth Test, Sobers made a century in each innings. Pakistan won the last Test, the West Indies taking the series 3-1.

The following season, Pakistan won 2-1 at home with captain Fazal Mahmood getting 21 wickets in the three Tests. There was a gap of 15 years before the countries met again.

In 1974-75 at Karachi both sides made their highest scores in Pakistan. Pakistan made 406 for 8 declared, and West Indies replied with 493.

The final Test of 1976-77 in the West Indies was reached with the sides 1-1, West Indies winning the decider. In 1980-81 in the Tests in Pakistan, West Indies won the only match decided.

There was a particularly fine performance by Abdul Qadir at Faisalabad in 1986-87 when he took 6 for 16 in helping rout the West Indies for 53. At Bridgetown in 1987-88, Pakistan had a great opportunity to win their first series in the West Indies when, in the last Test, the West Indies, set 266 to win - and so draw the series

– were 207 for 8. Jeffrey Dujon (29) and Winston Benjamin (40) provided the runs. In this match, a spectator struck by Abdul Qadir after abusing him was paid not to press charges.

There was more trouble on Pakistan's next tour of the West Indies in 1992-93. Four Pakistan players were arrested on a beach in Grenada for "constructive possession" of marijuana. The Pakistanis, who protested their innocence, threatened to call off the tour, which was locally billed as the "world championship". The charges were dropped, but the first Test was delayed by one day. The West Indies' eventual 2-0 win was the biggest since the first series in 1957-58. Richie Richardson was the winning captain.

However, at home in 1997-98, Pakistan whitewashed West Indies 3-0, beating them by an innings twice and ten wickets. Inzamam-ul-Haq and Aamir Sohail each averaged over a hundred. By contrast, the 1999-2000 series in the West Indies could not have been closer, with the West Indies winning the third Test by one wicket after two draws.

The first-ever Test series at Sharjah was played in 2001-02, between Pakistan and the West Indies. Pakistan won both of the Tests easily.

A poorly attended two-match series in the West Indies in 2004-05 was drawn 1-1. Brian Lara was Player of the Series with 331 runs.

In the 2006-07 series, Mohammed Yousuf scored 665 runs (av. 133.00) and reached a new Test record of 1,788 runs in a calendar year. Pakistan won the series 2-0.

Danish Kaneria celebrates the wicket of Brian Lara at Sabina Park, Jamaica, in 2005.

WEST INDIES v PAKISTAN

	MATCHES	WI	PAK	DRAW	SERIES	WI	PAK	DRAW
IN WEST INDIES	21	10	4	7	6	4	0	2
IN PAKISTAN	21	4	9	8	7	1	3	3
IN SHARJAH	2	0	2	0	1	0	1	0
TOTALS	44	14	15	15	14	5	4	5

ENGLAND v SRI LANKA

Muttiah Muralitharan celebrates the downfall of yet another England batsman. In 16 Tests against England, the Sri Lankan spin wizard has taken 112 wickets at an average of only 20.06.

Sri Lanka were the eighth country to achieve Test status when, in 1981-82, England played a Test in Colombo after touring India. England won by seven wickets. Not until 1992-93 did Sri Lanka register their first victory, at Colombo, by five wickets.

Sri Lanka won their first Test in England at The Oval in 1998 and their first series 1-0 at home in 2003-04, winning the third Test by an innings. Spinner Muttiah Muralitharan starred with 26 wickets, at the miserly average of just 12.30.

Unexpectedly, after a poor start, Sri Lanka won the third and last Test of the 2006 series, which was tied. Muralitharan's 8 for 70 was a Trent Bridge Test record.

Sri Lanka's win by 88 runs, after being behind in the first innings, in the first Test in Kandy in 2007-08 was enough to win the series. Kumar Sangakkara scored 92 and 152. Sanath Jayasuriya retired from Test cricket after the match as Sri Lanka's leading run-scorer. Mahela Jayawardene passed his aggregate in the next match and, with 195 and 213 not out in the drawn second and third Tests was elected Player of the Series.

ENGLAND v SRI LANKA

	MATCHES	ENG	SL	DRAW	SERIES	ENG	SL	DRAW
IN SRI LANKA	11	3	4	4	3	1	2	0
IN ENGLAND	10	5	2	3	2	1	0	1
TOTALS	21	8	6	7	5	2	2	1

PAKISTAN v SRI LANKA

Sri Lanka visited Pakistan for a three-Test series in 1981-82 and Pakistan won 2-0. In 1995-96, however, Sri Lanka won the series in Pakistan 2-1.

Sri Lanka won a series 2-1 in Pakistan in 1999-2000, winning the first Test by two wickets; Arjuna Ranatunga returned with a broken thumb when Sri Lanka needed 43 with eight wickets down to squeeze out the win. In a return in Sri Lanka, Pakistan reversed the result 2-0. Four Pakistan batsmen scored centuries in the same innings, and their bowler, Abdul Razzaq, became (at 20) the youngest player to get a Test hat-trick.

The teams met in the final of the Asian Test Championship in Lahore in 2001-02, Sri Lanka winning by eight wickets. The highlight was 230 from keeper Kumar Sangakkara. A well-fought two-match series in Pakistan in 2004-05 was drawn 1-1. Sanath Jayasuriya was Player of the Series, his 424 runs averaging 106.00.

Pakistan won a two-match series 1-0 in Sri Lanka in 2005-06 by overturning a first-innings deficit of 109 at Kandy by dismissing Sri Lanka for 73 and scoring 183 for 2 to win. Mohammad Asif was the Man of the Series with 17 wickets.

Sri Lanka toured Pakistan in 2008-09 after India had pulled out following the terrorist attack in Mumbai in December 2008. Sadly the tour was curtailed when the Sri Lankan team was itself attacked by terrorists during the second Test at Lahore, with several players injured and six policemen killed. Both Tests were drawn with 1553 runs scored in the first for the loss of just 18 wickets. Highest innings in the series were: Younis Khan (Pakistan) 313, Thilan Samaraweera (Sri Lanka) 231 and 214, and Mahela Jayawardene (Sri Lanka) 240. Samaraweera was the worst injured of the Sri Lankan players.

Test cricket resumed between the countries in Sri Lanka in July 2009. Pakistan's batting failed to cope with the spin bowling of Nuwan Kulasekara and debutant Ranguna Herath and they lost 2-0 in a three-match series. Sri Lanka were captained for the first time by Kumar Sangakkara.

PAKISTAN v SRI LANKA

	MATCHES	PAK	SL	DRAW	SERIES	PAK	SL	DRAW
IN PAKISTAN	21	8	6	7	7	3	2	2
IN SRI LANKA	13	5	3	5	5	2	1	2
IN BANGLADESH	1	1	0	0	–	–	–	–
TOTALS	35	14	9	12	12	5	3	4

INDIA v SRI LANKA

Sri Lanka played a Test in Madras in 1982-83 which ended in a draw. In their first three-Test series, in Sri Lanka in 1985-86, Sri Lanka won 1-0, gaining their first Test win in their 14th Test.

At Chandigarh in 1990-91, India's 21-year-old slow left-armer Venkatapathy Raju, after 6 for 12 in the first innings, ended the match with the astonishing analysis of 53.5-38-37-8.

In 1997-98 Sri Lanka beat the 39-year-old record for the highest Test score by making 952 for 6 declared. Sanath Jayasuriya (340) and Roshan Mahanama (225) established a new record Test partnership of 576.

Sri Lanka won 2-1 in a home series in 2001-02. The star performer was Muttiah Muralitharan, who captured 23 wickets at 19.30. India won 2-0 at home in 2005-06, with Anil Kumble's 20 wickets proving the difference between the two sides.

Sri Lanka won an exciting series at home in 2008-09. There were four centuries as they made 600 for six declared to win the first Test by an innings, but Virender Sehwag carried his bat for 201 not out as India levelled in the second. Kumar Sangakkara made a decisive 144 to help win the decider. The Player of the Series was the Sri Lankan spinner, Ajantha Mendis, with 26 wickets (8, 10 and 8) in his debut series.

By winning a three-match home series 2-0 in 2009-10, India reached No.1 in the ICC Test rankings for the first time. In a high-scoring series, India averaged over 550 an innings, with Man of the Series Virender Sehwag scoring 491 runs (av 122.75). Rahul Dravid, Gautum Gambhir and Mahendra Dhoni also scored two centuries each for India, while Sri Lanka made the highest Test score made in India (760 for 7

declared) in Ahmedabad, with Mahela Jayawardene making 275 and P. Jayawardene 154 not out.

When the home side, Sri Lanka, scored 520 for 8 declared and dismissed India for 276 and 338, winning by 10 wickets at Galle in 2010-11, and then declared at 642 for 4 at Colombo, it seemed that India's supremacy in Test cricket might be about to disappear, but India replied with 707 and the match was drawn. In the third match, also at Colombo, Sri Lanka's 425 was matched by India's 436, and when Sri Lanka were then 125 for 8 it seemed all over. But a ninth wicket stand of

118 by Thilan Samaraweera and Ajantha Mendis set India 257 to win. V.V.S. Laxman's stylish 103 not out saw them home by five wickets to tie the series. Overall batsmen ruled, especially the Sir Lankan skipper, Kumar Sangakkara, with 467 runs (av 116.75), Sachin Tendulkar 390 (78.00), Virender Sehwag 342 (68.40) and Thilan Samaraweera 306 (153.00). But one bowler deserves mention: Muttiah Muralitharan, who bowed out of Test cricket after the first Test, when his eight wickets took his total to a world record 800, the last one being taken with his last ball.

INDIA v SRI LANKA

	MATCHES	IND	SL	DRAW	SERIES	IND	SL	DRAW
IN INDIA	17	10	0	7	7	5	0	2
IN SRI LANKA	18	4	6	8	6	1	3	2
TOTALS	35	14	6	15	13	6	3	4

NEW ZEALAND v SRI LANKA

Sri Lanka visited New Zealand and Australia in 1982-83 with a weak side and lost both Tests by a wide margin.

New Zealand won 2-0 in Sri Lanka in 1983-84. In 1986-87 in Sri Lanka, only one drawn Test was played, the other two being cancelled after a bomb killed 150 near the

tourists' hotel. There was another series without a result in 1990-91, but there were records in the first Test at Wellington. Sri Lanka made their then highest score, 497 for 9 declared, with Aravinda de Silva getting 267. Facing a deficit of 323, New Zealand then made 671 for 4, with Martin Crowe scoring 299.

Sri Lanka won 1-0 in 1992-93 at home, but again there was a bomb before the Tests started, and six New Zealanders voted to return home. The first Test was drawn, but Sri Lanka won the second of a two-match series. The win was repeated in New Zealand in 1994-95. At least New Zealand had the consolation of wicket-keeper Adam Parore setting a new Test record of not conceding a bye while 2,323 runs were scored. New Zealand comfortably won a home series 2-0 in 1996-97.

Sri Lanka came back from losing the first Test to beat New Zealand 2-1 in Sri Lanka 1997-98.

Both matches were drawn in Sri Lanka in 2002-03. New Zealand captain Stephen Fleming made 274 and 69, both not out, in the first Test at Colombo. The 2004-05 series saw heavy scoring and success for New Zealand, but in 2006-07, the series was tied, with Muralitharan taking the starring role with a sensational 17 wickets in the two games.

Sri Lanka's batting was too strong for New Zealand in a home series in 2009-10. They won both Tests, by 202 and 96, having declared in both second innings. Man of the Series was Thilan Samaraweera with a century in each match.

NEW ZEALAND v SRI LANKA

	MATCHES	NZ	SL	DRAW	SERIES	NZ	SL	DRAW
IN NEW ZEALAND	13	6	2	5	6	3	1	2
IN SRI LANKA	13	3	5	5	6	1	3	2
TOTALS	26	9	7	10	12	4	4	4

AUSTRALIA v SRI LANKA

Australia won one Test in Kandy in 1982-83 and another in Australia in 1987-88, both by an innings. Then for 12 years Sri Lanka did no better than draw, although in 1992-93 only a brilliant catch by Allan Border saved the Australians in Colombo, when Sri Lanka lost their last eight wickets for 37 runs to lose by 16 as spinners Shane Warne and Greg Matthews ran riot.

Sri Lanka's win by four wickets in Kandy in 1999-2000 ended the rot,

bringing them their first defeat of Australia, and their first series win.

In Sri Lanka in 2003-04, both Shane Warne and Muttiah Muralitharan were approaching 500 Test wickets. Warne won the race, reaching 500 in the first Test, Murali in the second. Australia batted first and trailed on first innings each time, but recovered to win all three times. Warne took 26 wickets, Murali 31.

In 2004-05, Australia won a two-

Test series 1-0 at home. The most notable performance was Matthew Hayden's century in each innings in the drawn match. Murali - who didn't

tour - and Warne ended the series with 527 wickets each. Australia lost only 11 wickets in winning both Tests at home in 2007-08.

AUSTRALIA v SRI LANKA

	MATCHES	AUS	SL	DRAW	SERIES	AUS	SL	DRAW
IN SRI LANKA	10	5	1	4	4	3	1	0
IN AUSTRALIA	10	8	0	2	5	5	0	0
TOTALS	20	13	1	6	9	8	1	0

SOUTH AFRICA v WEST INDIES

Ramnaresh Sarwan on the attack in the third Test against South Africa at Newlands in 2004.

South Africa's re-admittance to Test cricket after the apartheid ban which lasted 22 years was marked by their first meeting with the West Indies in a one-off Test at Bridgetown, Barbados, in 1991-92. Andrew Hudson became the first South African to make a century on Test debut, but the West Indies won.

West Indies toured South Africa in 1998-99 and were whitewashed 5-0, Jacques Kallis (485 runs), Shaun Pollock (29 wickets) and Allan Donald (23) shining for the home side. South Africa won again, when Courtney Walsh became the first bowler in Test history to reach 500 wickets.

South Africa easily won a four-match series 3-0 at home in 2003-04. Kallis batted superbly, scoring

712 runs at an average of 178.00. The bowling stars were Makhaya Ntini, with 29 wickets at 21.37, and Andre Nel, 22 at 23.18.

In a four-match series dominated by batsmen in the West Indies in 2004-05, South Africa won 2-0. In the fourth Test, Chris Gayle scored 317, while in the first, both Wavell Hinds and Shivnarine Chanderpaul hit double-centuries. South Africa won 2-1 at home in 2007-08 after losing the first Test. Shaun Pollock retired with 421 Test wickets at 23.11.

In the West Indies in 2009-10 South Africa won two Tests with one drawn. Graeme Smith, AB de Villiers and Shivnarine Chanderpaul were the most successful batsmen, Jacques Kallis the best all-rounder, but Man of the Series was Dale Steyn, with 15 wickets.

SOUTH AFRICA v WEST INDIES

	MATCHES	WI	SA	DRAW	SERIES	WI	SA	DRAW
IN WEST INDIES	13	2	6	5	3	0	3	0
IN SOUTH AFRICA	12	1	10	1	3	0	3	0
TOTALS	25	3	16	6	6	0	6	0

INDIA v ZIMBABWE

India in 2000-01, with India winning 1-0, despite Andy Flower scoring 540 runs in four innings, twice out. Rahul Dravid made 432 in three innings for once out and Sachin Tendulkar 362 in three innings, twice out. A return in Zimbabwe in June 2001 was drawn 1-1. India won 2-0 at home in 2001-02, with spinners Anil Kumble (16 wickets at 18.12) and Harbajan Singh (12 at 19.66) in control.

India won a two-match series in Zimbabwe in 2005-06 at a canter. They won the first Test by an innings and 90 runs and the second by ten wickets, with Irfan Pathan India's chief destroyer, recording match figures of 12 for 126.

A moment of history in Zimbabwe cricket as captain Dave Houghton greets India captain Mohammed Azharuddin at the toss before his country's first ever Test match. Houghton went on to score a century in the game.

Zimbabwe became the ninth Test-playing country in 1992-93 when they drew with India in Harare. Their captain, David Houghton, scored 121 and became the first player to make a century in his country's inaugural Test since Charles Bannerman in the very first Test of all, 116 years earlier. In Delhi later the same season, India won easily. Zimbabwe beat India for the first time in Zimbabwe in 1998-99 winning by 61 runs. The first series of two Tests, between the countries took place in

INDIA v ZIMBABWE

	MATCHES	IND	ZIM	DRAW	SERIES	IND	ZIM	DRAW
IN ZIMBABWE	6	3	2	1	2	1	0	1
IN INDIA	5	4	0	1	2	2	0	0
TOTALS	11	7	2	2	4	3	0	1

NEW ZEALAND v ZIMBABWE

Ten days after their first-ever Test against India, Zimbabwe played New Zealand at Bulawayo, but rain prevented a result, which meant that Zimbabwe became the only Test country to avoid defeat in each of their first two Tests. In the second Test, New Zealand won convincingly. Two Tests in New Zealand in 1995-96 were drawn. Both Tests of a series in Zimbabwe in 1997-98 were drawn, with Grant Flower making a century in each innings in the first, and with New Zealand needing 11 with two wickets left at the end of the second. New Zealand won both Tests of a series at home later in the season.

It was tighter, but still 2-0 for New Zealand in Zimbabwe in 2000-01, but Zimbabwe drew a one-off Test in New Zealand later that season. New Zealand easily won both matches of a series in Zimbabwe in 2005-06.

NEW ZEALAND v ZIMBABWE

	MATCHES	NZ	ZIM	DRAW	SERIES	NZ	ZIM	DRAW
IN ZIMBABWE	8	5	0	3	4	3	0	1
IN NEW ZEALAND	5	2	0	3	2	1	0	1
TOTALS	13	7	0	6	6	4	0	2

SOUTH AFRICA v INDIA

South Africa entertained India in 1992-93 in their first home series since being banned from Test cricket. South Africa's Jimmy Cook immediately made history as the first debutant to be out first ball of a Test. The South African captain Kepler Wessels scored 118 and became the first player to score Test centuries for two different countries, having made four centuries for Australia. When India batted, Sachin Tendulkar became the first player to be given out (run out) by the third umpire watching the television slow-motion replay, this being the first series of "trial by television". South Africa won their first Test and series (with three draws) since their re-admission. Solid batting all through and 20 wickets from fast bowler Allan Donald made the difference between the sides.

A series in India in 1996-97 resulted in a 2-1 win for India. Gary Kirsten made a century in each innings for South Africa in Calcutta, but Mohammed Azharuddin was the series' best batsman. A return series in South Africa, however, ended 2-0 in favour of South Africa, as did the series in India in 1999-2000 and South Africa in 2001-02. In the last, a third Test, which South Africa also won, was declared unofficial after India refused to accept a one-match ban on Virender Sehwag for intimidatory appealing.

India deservedly won a two-match series 1-0 in India in 2004-05. The series in South Africa in 2006-07 began with South Africa being bowled out for 84 and losing the first match, but the home side fought back in great style, winning the next two games and the series.

Virender Sehwag on his way to 164 against South Africa at Kanpur in 2004.

In India in 2007-08, the two highest-ranking teams after Australia drew 1-1. Highlights were Virender Sehwag's 319 from 304 balls at Chennai and Harbhajan Singh's seven wickets which helped India tie the series at Kanpur.

With India now ranked No. 1 and South Africa challenging, the two-match Series in 2009-10 was remarkable in that both matches were won by an innings. At Nagpur, South Africa declared at 558 for 6, with Hashim Amla getting 253 not out and Jacques Kallis 173, the pair adding 340 for the third wicket. Dale Steyn took ten wickets as India were dismissed twice, still six runs short of making South Africa bat again. At Kolkata, Amla (114) was again in a big stand, this time of 209 for the second wicket with Alviro Petersen (114) but South Africa collapsed to 296. With Virender Sehweg (165) and Sachin Tendulkar (106) each making their second centuries of the series, and V.V.S. Laxman (143 not out) and captain Mahendra Dhoni (132 not out) adding an unbeaten 259 for the seventh wicket, India reached 643 for 6 declared. India managed to dismiss South Africa again for 290 with nine balls remaining.

South Africa then played India again, this time at home. They began well, dismissing India at Centurion for 136. Amla beat that score with his fourth successive century against India (140) but was overshadowed by Kallis (201 not out). With AB de Villiers scoring 129, South Africa declared at 620 for 4 and won by an innings and 25. In Durban, however, India won by 87, thanks to V.V.S. Laxman's masterly 96. In a tense decider at Cape Town, Kallis made a century in each innings (161 and 109 not out). Nevertheless India earned a first-innings lead of 2 and with South Africa 98 for 5 looked favourites to win. But South Africa reached 341 and India were happy to bat through the last day to 166 for 3 to draw and retain their No. 1 spot.

SOUTH AFRICA v INDIA

	MATCHES	SA	IND	DRAW	SERIES	SA	IND	DRAW
IN SOUTH AFRICA	15	7	2	6	5	4	0	1
IN INDIA	12	5	5	2	5	1	2	2
TOTALS	27	12	7	8	10	5	2	3

SOUTH AFRICA v SRI LANKA

The series of Tests began in 1993-94 when South Africa won a three-match series in Sri Lanka, 1-0. After two more losses Sri Lanka finally drew a three-match series in 1999-2000, after winning the first Test by an innings. Since then each series has been won by the home side, Sri Lanka excelling in 2006-07 with two wins, by an innings and by one wicket. In the first, Mahela Jayawardene made 374, and with Kumar Sangakkara (287) put on 624 for the third wicket, the highest partnership in first-class cricket. Muralitharan took 22 wickets in the two Tests at 18.00 each.

SOUTH AFRICA v SRI LANKA

	MATCHES	SA	SL	DRAW	SERIES	SA	SL	DRAW
IN SRI LANKA	10	2	4	4	4	1	2	1
IN SOUTH AFRICA	7	6	0	1	3	3	0	0
TOTALS	17	8	4	5	7	4	2	1

PAKISTAN v ZIMBABWE

Zimbabwe lost their first series in Pakistan 2-0 in 1993-94 but, next season, in Zimbabwe recorded their first Test win, by an innings and 64. Grant Flower scored 201 not out for Zimbabwe, adding 269 for the fourth wicket with his brother Andy (156). Pakistan won the series 2-1. In 1996-97 and 1997-98 Pakistan won 1-0. In the former, Wasim Akram made 257 not out for Pakistan, the highest score by a No. 8. His stand of 313 with Saqlain Mushtaq (79) was a Test record. In a rain-affected 1998-99 series, Zimbabwe won 1-0, but lost 2-0 in back at home in 2002-03.

PAKISTAN v ZIMBABWE

	MATCHES	PAK	ZIM	DRAW	SERIES	PAK	ZIM	DRAW
IN PAKISTAN	7	3	1	3	3	2	1	0
IN ZIMBABWE	7	5	1	1	3	3	0	0
TOTALS	14	8	2	4	6	5	1	0

WEST INDIES v SRI LANKA

Kumar Sangakkara in action during the first day of the second Test match against the West Indies in Colombo. He went on to score 150 runs.

Since rain spoiled their first Test at Moratuwa in 1993-94, the home side has dominated, with some outstanding performances. Muttiah Muralitharan took 17 wickets in each series in 2001-02 and 2005-06, ably supported by Chaminda Vass. Brian Lara scored 688 runs in the former series, but his side lost 3-0. In 2010-11, when the monsoon ruined all three Tests in Sri Lanka, Chris Gayle smashed 333 at Galle out of a total of 580 for 9, and Sri Lanka's Kumar Sangakkara scored 150 at Colombo.

WEST INDIES v SRI LANKA

	MATCHES	WI	SL	DRAW	SERIES	WI	SL	DRAW
IN SRI LANKA	9	0	5	4	4	0	2	2
IN WEST INDIES	6	3	1	2	3	2	0	1
TOTALS	15	3	6	6	7	2	2	3

SOUTH AFRICA v PAKISTAN

Because Pakistan were banned from hosting Tests after the terrorist attack on the Sri Lankan team bus in 2009, the two countries met in a two-match series on neutral ground, the first Test matches to be held at Dubai and Abu Dhabi. Both new Test pitches were flat and lifeless, producing an average of over 50 runs a wicket, ending in two score-bores. In both matches, Pakistan, set a large fourth-innings target, were able to save the games for the loss of three wickets in each case. In Abu Dhabi, AB de Villiers set a new South African Test record score with 278 not out. In the series Jacques Kallis scored two centuries, Graeme Smith and Hashim Amla one each, while Younis Khan scored one for Pakistan. No bowler managed more then six wickets.

Graeme Smith hits out on his way to scoring 151 against Pakistan at Cape Town in 2002-03.

Pakistan visited Johannesburg for a single Test in 1994-95, which South Africa won by 324 runs.

South Africa have generally had the better of it since. They easily won two home Tests in 2002-03. Outstanding was an opening stand of 368 at Cape Town between Hershelle Gibbs (228) and Graeme Smith (151). Pakistan then won 1-0 at home in 2003-04.

But South Africa won a close series 2-1 in 2006-07 and won a two-match series 1-0 in 2007-08, with Jacques Kallis making 421 runs at an average of 210.50.

SOUTH AFRICA v PAKISTAN

	MATCHES	SA	PAK	DRAW	SERIES	SA	PAK	DRAW
IN SOUTH AFRICA	11	7	2	2	4	3	0	1
IN PAKISTAN	5	1	1	3	2	1	1	0
IN DUBAI AND ABU DHABI	2	0	0	2	1	0	0	1
TOTALS	18	8	3	7	7	4	1	2S

SRI LANKA v ZIMBABWE

Test cricket's then youngest nations met in Zimbabwe in 1994-95, and drew three times. David Houghton's 266 remains Zimbabwe's highest Test innings. Sri Lanka won both home series 2-0 in 1996-97 and 1997-98 and won a three-Test series 1-0 in Zimbabwe in 1999-2000, though Andy Flower topped the batting with 388 for Zimbabwe. Sri Lanka won 3-0 at home in 2001-02 and in 2003-04 destroyed a dispute-ridden Zimbabwe with two innings defeats, Marvin Atapattu getting 249 and Kumar Sangakkara 270 in an innings of 713 for 3 in Bulawayo.

SRI LANKA v ZIMBABWE

	MATCHES	SL	ZIM	DRAW	SERIES	SL	ZIM	DRAW
IN ZIMBABWE	8	3	0	5	3	2	0	1
IN SRI LANKA	7	7	0	0	3	3	0	0
TOTALS	15	10	0	5	6	5	0	1

ENGLAND v BANGLADESH

England were the last of the Test-playing countries to take on Bangladesh. They played a two-match series in Bangladesh in 2003-04 and won both matches, but needed to bat twice in each. England's total of 295 in the first Test was the lowest Test score by a touring side in Bangladesh.

England lost only three wickets per match in beating Bangladesh twice by an innings in a home series in early summer 2005. Marcus Trescothick scored 194 and 151, and Michael Vaughan and Ian Bell scored hundreds, while Matthew Hoggard took 14 wickets.

Alastair Cook captained the England side which played two Tests in Bangladesh in 2009-10. He top-scored with 173 as England made 599 for 6 declared at the Chittagong. With a lead of 303, England did not enforce the follow-on and eventually won by 181 runs, with Graeme Swann getting 10 wickets in a Test for the first time, five in each innings. After Bangladesh scored 419 at Dhaka, England got a lead of 77, thanks to Ian Bell's 138, and scored 209 for 1 (Cook 109 not out) to win by 9 wickets. The Bangladesh skipper Shakib Al Hasan was Man of the Match with 49, 96 and four wickets.

In a two-match Series in England in 2010, Jonathan Trott scored 226 and 36 not out at Lord's as England won by eight wickets, but Man of the Match was Steven Finn with 9 wickets on his Test debut. Ian Bell took this honour at Old Trafford for his 138 as England won by an innings. Finn, who took six more wickets, shared Man of the Series with the exciting Bangladesh opener Tamim Iqbal who, after a century at Lord's, made 108 at Old Trafford, exactly half his side's total of 216.

Tamim Iqbal celebrates his century for Bangladesh during day four of the first Test at Lords on 30 May 2010. This was not his only success of the series as he proved himself to be an opening batsman of considerable talent with another century in the next Test at Old Trafford.

ENGLAND v BANGLADESH

	MATCHES	ENG	BAN	DRAW	SERIES	ENG	BAN	DRAW
IN BANGLADESH	4	4	0	0	2	2	0	0
IN ENGLAND	4	4	0	0	2	2	0	0
TOTALS	8	8	0	0	4	4	0	0

SOUTH AFRICA v ZIMBABWE

South Africa won a single Test match against Zimbabwe in Harare in 1995-96 season. Allan Donald took 8 for 71, his best in Tests. They also won both matches played in 1999-2000, one in each country, by an innings in each case. South Africa won 1-0 in Zimbabwe in 2001-02. In the defeat ,Zimbabwe's Andy Flower scored 142 and 199 not out.

Zimbabwe travelled to South Africa in 2004-05 and suffered two innings defeats. In the first Test, at Cape Town, they were dismissed for 54 in their first innings - their lowest Test score - and fell to defeat inside two days in what was the 11th shortest Test in the history of the game. They made a better fist of things in the second Test at Centurion, but an unbeaten century from Ashwell Prince and six wickets for Monde Zondeki condemned them to a second defeat.

SOUTH AFRICA v ZIMBABWE

	MATCHES	SA	ZIM	DRAW	SERIES	SA	ZIM	DRAW
IN ZIMBABWE	4	3	0	1	1	1	0	0
IN SOUTH AFRICA	3	3	0	1	1	1	0	0
TOTALS	7	6	0	1	2	2	0	0

ENGLAND v ZIMBABWE

England played a two-match Test series in Zimbabwe in 1996-97. In the first Test, at Bulawayo, England gained a first-innings lead of 30 and, when Zimbabwe were dismissed for 234 in their second knock, needed 205 to win in a minimum 37 overs.

A second-wicket partnership of 137 between Nick Knight and Alec Stewart took the score to 154, but

England failed to press home the advantage and finished on 204 for 6, managing only a draw with the scores level, the first such instance in Test cricket. The second Test was spoiled by rain and ended in a draw.

Zimbabwe toured England in 2000 and 2003, losing three of the four Tests by an innings, with rain spoiling the other (in 2000).

Andy Flower and Heath Streak were the respective captains, while Murray Goodwin scored 148 not out at Trent Bridge in 2000.

ENGLAND v ZIMBABWE

	MATCHES	ENG	ZIM	DRAW	SERIES	ENG	ZIM	DRAW
IN ZIMBABWE	2	0	0	2	1	0	0	1
IN ENGLAND	4	3	0	1	2	2	0	0
TOTALS	6	3	0	3	3	2	0	1

AUSTRALIA v ZIMBABWE

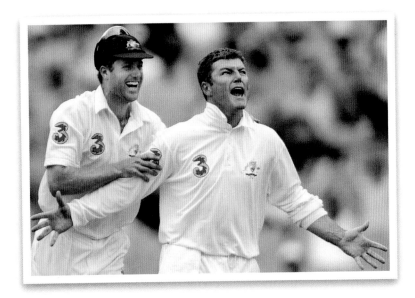

Australia visited Zimbabwe in 1999-2000 and played a single Test, winning by ten wickets. Zimbabwe made 194 and 232 (Murray Goodwin was top-scorer for the hosts with 91), while Steve Waugh made the only century of the match, 151 not out, in Australia's 422 all out.

In 2003-04, Australia won both Tests. Matthew Hayden dominated, making a record Test score (since surpassed) of 380 at Perth. At Sydney he made 20 and 101 not out, to average 250.50 for the series.

AUSTRALIA v ZIMBABWE

	MATCHES	AUS	ZIM	DRAW	SERIES	AUS	ZIM	DRAW
IN ZIMBABWE	1	1	0	0	0	0	0	0
IN AUSTRALIA	2	2	0	0	1	1	0	0
TOTALS	3	3	0	0	1	1	0	0

Australian leg-spinner Stuart MacGill made himself unavailable for his country's games against Zimbabwe in 2004 on moral grounds.

WEST INDIES v ZIMBABWE

Zimbabwe toured the West Indies in 1999-2000. In the first Test, they dismissed West Indies for 187 then 147 after making 236 in their first innings (Andy Flower 113 not out). Zimbabwe needed only 99 to win, but were out for 63. West Indies were captained by Jimmy Adams for the first time. They won the second Test by ten wickets, a match notable for Courtney Walsh passing Kapil Dev's world record of 434 Test wickets in front of his home crowd at Sabina Park. West Indies won 1-0 in Zimbabwe in July 2000. Back in Harare in November 2003, Zimbabwe batted impressively in the first Test, racking up a mighty 507 in their first innings, with captain Heath Streak batting for nearly six hours for an unbeaten 127. However, the hosts were frustrated in their bid for victory by the West Indies' last-wicket pair, who hung on for 31 minutes to save the game. They would regret it, as they went on to lose the second Test to a Brian Lara-inspired West Indies by 129 runs.

Courtney Walsh celebrates taking the wicket of Henry Olonga at Sabina Park, Jamaica, in March 2000. It was his 435th Test wicket and took him past Kapil Dev's record.

WEST INDIES v ZIMBABWE

	MATCHES	WI	ZIM	DRAW	SERIES	WI	ZIM	DRAW
IN WEST INDIES	2	2	0	0	1	1	0	0
IN ZIMBABWE	4	2	0	2	2	2	0	0
TOTALS	6	4	0	2	3	3	0	0

INDIA v BANGLADESH

On 10 November 2000, Bangladesh became the tenth Test-playing country, losing to India by ten wickets in a one-off match in Dhaka. India toured Bangladesh in 2004-05 when Sachin Tendulkar scored 248 not out in the first Test and Anil Kumble passed Kapil Dev's national record of 434 Test wickets. India have had much the better of the exchanges, but Bangladesh put up a good show at home in 2009-10 when their opener Tamim Iqbal made 151 in the first Test.

INDIA v BANGLADESH

	MATCHES	IND	BAN	DRAW	SERIES	IND	BAN	DRAW
IN BANGLADESH	7	6	0	1	3	3	0	0
TOTALS	7	6	0	1	3	3	0	0

ZIMBABWE v BANGLADESH

The two newest Test nations met in Zimbabwe in 2000-01. Zimbabwe won 2-0. Bangladesh's Javed Omar (85 not out) became the second man to carry his bat on his Test debut. Andy Flower equalled the record of Everton Weekes in scoring seven Test fifties in a row.

Zimbabwe won two rain-spoiled series 1-0 away in 2001-02 and at home in 2003-04.

Bangladesh won their first Test - at the 35th attempt - and first series 1-0 against Zimbabwe at home in 2004-05. Enamul Haque Jr, with 18 wickets, was Player of the Series.

ZIMBABWE v BANGLADESH

	MATCHES	ZIM	BAN	DRAW	SERIES	ZIM	BAN	DRAW
IN ZIMBABWE	4	3	0	1	2	2	0	0
IN BANGLADESH	4	1	1	2	2	1	1	0
TOTALS	8	4	1	3	4	3	1	0

PAKISTAN v BANGLADESH

Pakistan played Bangladesh in the Asian Test Championship in August 2000 in Multan and lost only three wickets in winning by an innings and 264 runs. Pakistan's next two Tests were in January, also against Bangladesh – but on tour – and were both won by an innings.

Three Tests in Pakistan in 2003- 04 were all won by the home team. In the first Test, Yasir Hameed made a century in each innings for Pakistan (170 and 105). After two easy victories, Pakistan were made to work a little harder in the final Test at Multan, with local hero Inzamam- ul-Haq scoring 138 not out to inspire his side to a one-wicket victory.

PAKISTAN v BANGLADESH

	MATCHES	PAK	BAN	DRAW	SERIES	PAK	BAN	DRAW
IN PAKISTAN	4	4	0	0	1	1	0	0
IN BANGLADESH	2	2	0	0	1	1	0	0
TOTALS	6	6	0	0	2	2	0	0

SRI LANKA v BANGLADESH

Sri Lanka have beaten Bangladesh in all 12 Tests played, beginning with an innings and 137 runs win in the Asian Test Championship in Colombo in September 2001. Outstanding performances include Pinnaduwage De Silva's 206 in 2002-03, and Muralitharan's 14 wickets for 135, average 9.64, in a two-Test series in 2005-06. Sri Lanka won all three Tests at home in 2007-08 by an innings, with Kumar Sangakarra scoring two not-out double centuries and Muralitharan capturing 26 wickets. In Bangladesh in 2008-09 Tillekeratne Dilshan scored 162 and 143 and took four wickets for 10 in the second Test.

Although they have lost all 12 Tests against Sri Lanka, Bangladesh have celebrated both a Test match and a series victory – cause for celebration at Chittagong against Zimbabwe in 2004-05.

SRI LANKA v BANGLADESH

	MATCHES	SL	BAN	DRAW	SERIES	SL	BAN	DRAW
IN SRI LANKA	8	8	0	0	3	3	0	0
IN BANGLADESH	4	4	0	0	2	2	0	0
TOTALS	12	12	0	0	5	5	0	0

NEW ZEALAND v BANGLADESH

The two-Test series in New Zealand in 2001-02 and in Bangladesh in 2004- 05 both resulted in 2-0 victories for New Zealand, with four innings wins. Stephen Hemming's double century, James Franklin's hat-trick and Daniel Vettori's 20 wickets, all in the second series, were highlights. It was 2-0 again for New Zealand in 2007-08, but closer in 2008-09 when Bangladesh earned a draw (plus a defeat). New Zealand won a Test at home in 2009- 10 by 121 runs, with Martin Guptill (189) and Brendon McCullum (180) putting on 339 for the sixth wicket in New Zealand's first innings.

NEW ZEALAND v BANGLADESH

	MATCHES	NZ	BAN	DRAW	SERIES	NZ	BAN	DRAW
IN NEW ZEALAND	5	5	0	0	2	2	0	0
IN BANGLADESH	4	3	0	1	2	2	0	0
TOTALS	9	8	0	1	4	4	0	0

SOUTH AFRICA v BANGLADESH

South Africa first played a two-Test series at home to Bangladesh in 2001-02, which they won 2-0. They have won all matches between the countries since. In 2002-03, Jacques Rudolph made 222 not out on debut for South Africa – in a 429-run third-wicket partnership with Boeta Dippenaar (177 not out). South Africa won 2-0 both away in 2007-08 and at home in 2008-09. At Chittagong, Neil McKenzie (226) and Graeme Smith (232) put on 415 for the first wicket.

SOUTH AFRICA v BANGLADESH

	MATCHES	SA	BAN	DRAW	SERIES	SA	BAN	DRAW
IN SOUTH AFRICA	4	4	0	0	2	2	0	0
IN BANGLADESH	4	4	0	0	2	2	0	0
TOTALS	8	8	0	0	4	4	0	0

WEST INDIES v BANGLADESH

Bangladesh hosted the West Indies in a two-match series in 2002-03, losing them both.

In the West Indies in 2003-04, Bangladesh led on first innings and drew the first Test, but they lost the second – and the series– by an innings, with Ramnaresh Sarwan scoring 261 not out, with further centuries from Brian Lara and Shivnarine Chanderpaul.

Bangladesh, with one Test win in their first 59 Tests, went to West Indies in July 2009 and won both Tests in the series, by 95 runs and four wickets, largely because of strike action by West Indies first choice players.

A moment of joy for Bangladesh as Tareq Khan runs out Devon Smith in the first Test in St Lucia in May 2004. The match ended in a draw.

WEST INDIES v BANGLADESH

	MATCHES	WI	BAN	DRAW	SERIES	WI	BAN	DRAW
IN BANGLADESH	2	2	0	0	1	1	0	0
IN WEST INDIES	4	1	2	1	2	1	1	0
TOTALS	6	3	2	1	3	2	1	0

AUSTRALIA v BANGLADESH

Australia beat Bangladesh in Australia in June/July 2003 twice by an innings. Australian skipper Steve Waugh became the captain with the most wins (38) and the first to score 150 against each of the other nine Test countries. The matches were played in Darwin and Cairns. Australia won 2-0 in Bangladesh in 2005-06, although 158 behind on first innings in the first Test, while Jason Gillespie scored 201 not out in the second.

AUSTRALIA v BANGLADESH

	MATCHES	AUS	BAN	DRAW	SERIES	AUS	BAN	DRAW
IN AUSTRALIA	2	2	0	0	1	1	0	0
IN BANGLADESH	2	2	0	0	1	1	0	0
TOTALS	4	4	0	0	2	2	0	0

TOTAL TEST RESULTS 1876-77 to 2011

	PLAYED	WON	LOST	DRAWN	TIED	WIN:LOSS RATIO		PLAYED	WON	LOST	DRAWN	TIED	WIN:LOSS RATIO
AUSTRALIA	729	340	192	195	2	1.771	ENGLAND	897	317	259	321	0	1.224
PAKISTAN	354	106	99	149	0	1.107	WEST INDIES	470	152	150	167	1	1.033
SOUTH AFRICA	358	125	124	109	0	1.008	SRI LANKA	196	61	69	66	0	0.871
INDIA	437	106	138	192	1	0.768	NEW ZEALAND	364	68	147	149	0	0.463
ZIMBABWE	83	8	49	26	0	0.163	BANGLADESH	68	3	59	6	0	0.051

4 THE CRICKET WORLD CUP

For many years the pinnacle of the soccer world has been the World Cup. Although cricket's rules and regulations pre-date soccer's by over one hundred years, it was not until 1975 that the cricket authorities managed to organize a similar event. Even then, instead of being Test cricket, it was confined to one-day matches.

Opposite: **Victory for Australia in the 2003 World Cup in South Africa.**
Below: **The Sri Lankans shocked the Australians in the 1995 World Cup final.**

The World Cup, held every four years, has proved a popular success and nothing was more appropriate than that the 1996 World Cup should be won by Sri Lanka, until then considered by many to be inferior to the senior Test-playing sides.

The first attempt in England to organize an international competition which involved more than one other country was staged in 1912. England invited Australia and South Africa to come and play a Triangular Tournament of Test matches. Unfortunately, to quote a contemporary source "we had one of the most appalling summers ever known, even in England". It rained and rained. The cricket press forecast that it was an idea which would probably not be repeated for a generation. And so it proved.

In 1975, for the first World Cup, the *Wisden Almanack* commenced its report with "The First World Cup cricket tournament proved an outstanding success. Blessed by perfect weather, ideal conditions prevailed." Unlike the 1912 Triangular tournament, the authorities did not have to wait a generation to repeat the experiment.

WORLD CUP 1975

VENUE: ENGLAND

FIRST BLOOD TO WEST INDIES

The first World Cup was staged in England in June 1975. The trophy at stake was the Prudential Cup - Prudential having sponsored the competition to the tune of £100,000. There were eight countries competing: the six current Test-playing nations plus East Africa and Sri Lanka. It was noted with regret that South Africa were omitted. The teams were divided into two groups of four and the top two in each group would then meet in a knock-out semi-final round. Each match would consist of 60 overs per side − the number used in the English Gillette Cup competition.

The first four matches commenced on 7 June at Lord's, Headingley, Old Trafford and Edgbaston. The most popular game was Australia v Pakistan at Headingley, where the ground sold out. Australia, batting first, reached 278 for 7, with Ross Edwards making a hard-hit 80. Pakistan lost Sadiq, Zaheer and Mushtaq cheaply and the game seemed all over, but Majid Khan was joined by Asif Iqbal and the score rose to 181 for 4 off 41 overs. Dennis Lillee returned to demolish the tail and bring Australia an easy win.

At Lord's, England completely outplayed India, after Dennis Amiss hit 137 − India's style was utterly cramped as they could only score 132 for 3 off their 60 overs and England won by 202 runs. The minnows, Sri Lanka and East Africa, fell to the West Indies and New Zealand, with Glenn Turner making 171 not out for the latter.

A swashbuckling 102 from captain Clive Lloyd (off just 85 balls) turned the first World Cup final on its head. The West Indies went on to beat Australia by 17 runs at Lord's.

West Indies' Alvin Kallicharan eases the ball through the midwicket area. In a group match, he hit an electric 35 off just ten balls.

The second batch of games saw England beat New Zealand, Keith Fletcher making 131. Australia beat Sri Lanka, though only by 52 runs, a margin which would have been less if Jeff Thomson had not forced Wettimuny and Mendis to retire hurt when both were well established. India walked over East Africa —winning by ten wickets with 30.1 overs to spare. The most exciting game was at Edgbaston, where an incredible tenth-wicket stand of 64 by Deryck Murray and Andy Roberts produced a one-wicket victory for the West Indies over Pakistan. Sarfraz Nawaz had blown away the top West Indian batsmen.

The third batch of games saw England outplay East Africa, while Pakistan, put in to bat, dealt convincingly with Sri Lanka. The most exciting game was West Indies v Australia at The Oval. Clive Lloyd put Australia in and the fast attack led by Andy Roberts kept the Australia total below 200.

For Australia everything now depended on Lillee and Thomson, but the former was out of sorts and a brilliant batting display by Alvin Kallicharran, who hit 35 off ten deliveries from Lillee, saw the West Indies win with 14 overs to spare.

In the other game, an unbeaten century by Glenn Turner saw New Zealand home against India at Old Trafford.

The first semi-final produced bitter criticism of the Headingley pitch, which was green and damp. Australia put England in and none of the home batsmen could master the conditions. England were bowled out for 93, with Gary Gilmour, the left-arm seamer, returning figures of 6 for 16. Australia's batsmen also found the pitch difficult, but Gilmour hit an unbeaten 28 and his team won by four wickets.

In the second semi-final, the winner of the toss, Clive Lloyd, also put the opposition in. New Zealand fared better on The Oval pitch than England had done at Headingley, but they could only make a modest 158 and Kallicharran again starred as the outstanding Caribbean batsman.

The final was staged at Lord's between Australia and the West Indies before a capacity crowd of 26,000. The West Indies were put in and lost their first three wickets for 50. Clive Lloyd joined Rohan Kanhai in a partnership which changed the game. Lloyd was on his best form, as was demonstrated when he hooked Lillee for six. With the latter batsmen all making useful contributions, the West Indian total reached a very respectable 291 for 8.

Australia were not daunted by the target set. Ian Chappell batted very competently for 62, opener Alan Turner made 40, but some brilliant fielding, allied to a casual approach to running, meant that no fewer than four Australians were run out, including, most importantly, both Greg and Ian Chappell. Despite these errors, Australia lost only by the narrow margin of 17 runs, the game not ending until nearly quarter to nine. Prince Philip presented the trophy to Clive Lloyd amid great cheers from the large contingent of West Indian supporters in the crowd. Clive Lloyd was also given the Man of the Match award.

FINAL QUALIFYING TABLES

Group A

	P	W	L	PTS
ENGLAND	3	3	0	12
NEW ZEALAND	3	2	1	8
INDIA	3	1	2	4
EAST AFRICA	3	0	3	0

Group B

	P	W	L	PTS
WEST INDIES	3	3	0	12
AUSTRALIA	2	2	1	8
PAKISTAN	3	1	2	4
SRI LANKA	3	0	3	0

Semi-finals

ENGLAND 93 (36.2 OVERS)
AUSTRALIA 94-6 (28.4 OVERS)
AUSTRALIA WON BY FOUR WICKETS
MAN OF THE MATCH: G.J. GILMOUR

NEW ZEALAND 158 (52.2 OVERS)
WEST INDIES 159-5 (40.1 OVERS)
WEST INDIES WON BY FIVE WICKETS
MAN OF THE MATCH:
A.I. KALLICHARRAN

Final

WEST INDIES 291-8 (60 OVERS)
AUSTRALIA 274 (58.4 OVERS)
WEST INDIES WON BY 17 RUNS
MAN OF THE MATCH: C.H. LLOYD

WORLD CUP 1979

VENUE: **ENGLAND**

ENGLISH WEATHER CAN'T KEEP THE CARIBS DOWN

In 1975, the World Cup had been played in a flaming English June; four years later, June was not quite so kind, though only one match was totally washed out. However ,the Prudential Assurance Company upped their sponsorship to £250,000 and, because of increased prices, the receipts for matches were nearly double those of 1975, though the spectator numbers dropped by 28,000. The format was the same as for the first World Cup and there was only one team change, Canada replacing East Africa. Each side was allowed 60 overs, but the umpires were now instructed to deal more harshly with wides and bouncers.

The first batch of matches took place on 9 June at Edgbaston, Lord's, Headingley and Trent Bridge, the match of the round being that at headquarters between England and Australia. All tickets were sold prior to the day, and Mike Brearley, viewing a dull grey morning, put the opposition in. Runs came very slowly – only 14 off the first ten overs – and by the time the first wicket fell the scoreboard read 56 off 21 overs. Brearley amazed everyone by putting Geoff Boycott on to bowl, but his tactic proved correct as Boycott removed both Andrew Hilditch and Kim Hughes. This was followed by a rash of run outs - four in all - and England were set just 160 to win. Graham Gooch made 53, Brearley 44 and England won by six wickets. In the three other games, the West Indies crushed India: 75 from Viswanath enabled the Indians to make 190 all out before Gordon Greenidge and Desmond Haynes opened for the West Indies with a stand of 138. The former went on to a century and, in partnership with

Collis King scored a brilliant 86 in the final, outscoring Viv Richards in a partnership of 139 in only 21 overs.

West Indies supporters celebrated with noisy vigour as their players again won the World Cup with exciting cricket.

John Wright batting well, New Zealand kept in touch with the target and required 14 from the final over – they couldn't manage it, England winning by nine runs. In the other semi, the West Indies scored a rapid 293 for 6, Gordon Greenidge being the top run-getter with 73.

For Pakistan, Majid Khan and Zaheer added 166 for the second wicket in 36 overs, before Colin Croft took three wickets in 12 balls and seized the initiative.

A full house at Lord's saw an outstanding batting display by Viv Richards, 138 not out, and, though Mike Brearley and Geoff Boycott opened England's reply with a stand of 129, the scoring rate was too low. Viv Richards was Man of the Match as the West Indies won by 92 runs.

Viv Richards, brought a nine-wicket victory. The Pakistan v Canada match saw a very similar result, Pakistan cruising home by eight wickets, with Sadiq making a top score of 57 not out.

The same scenario occurred at Trent Bridge, where New Zealand won by nine wickets against Sri Lanka, Glenn Turner being the star batsman with 83 not out.

The weather affected the second batch of matches – all three days of the West Indies v Sri Lanka game saw the players sitting in the Leeds pavilion. At Old Trafford, the first day of England v Canada was washed out. The match began an hour late on day two in very poor conditions. Canada were bowled out for 45, Chris Old taking 4 for 8. It

took England 13.5 overs to knock off the runs.

At Trent Bridge play was possible on the first day of Australia v Pakistan. Australia were without Rodney Hogg and Pakistan scored freely to reach 286 for 7 on a rain-interrupted day. On the second day, the Australian batting never looked like scoring the runs required and Pakistan sailed home. New Zealand's batsmen found no difficulty in scoring the 183 required off India's attack – Bruce Edgar hit 84 and with John Wright added 100 before the first wicket fell.

In the third batch of games, Sri Lanka took centre stage, being the first non-Test-playing country to win a game in the World Cup. Playing India at Old Trafford, they

were without their captain, Anura Tennekoon, but still hit 238 for 5, with three players making fifties. The Indian innings did not begin until the second day. India seemed confident while Sunil Gavaskar and A.D. Gaekwad put on 60 for the first wicket, but the leg breaks of Somachandra de Silva caused the middle order problems and Sri Lanka dismissed their opponents for 191.

Brilliant sunshine greeted the semi-finals. There was a very exciting game at Old Trafford. New Zealand put England in and, though both Mike Brearley and Graham Gooch made fifties, Richard Hadlee caused all the early batsmen problems. Derek Randall came in at No. 7 to make the tail wag and pushed the total over 200. With

FINAL QUALIFYING TABLES

Group A

	P	W	L	PTS
ENGLAND	3	3	0	12
PAKISTAN	3	2	1	8
AUSTRALIA	3	1	2	4
CANADA	3	0	3	0

Group B

	P	W	L	NR	PTS
WEST INDIES	3	2	0	1	10
NEW ZEALAND	3	2	1	0	8
SRI LANKA	3	1	1	1	6
INDIA	3	0	3	0	0

Semi-finals

ENGLAND	221-8 (60 OVERS)
NEW ZEALAND	212-9 (60 OVERS)
	ENGLAND WON BY NINE RUNS
	MAN OF THE MATCH: G.A. GOOCH
WEST INDIES	293-6 (60 OVERS)
PAKISTAN	250 (56.2 OVERS)
	WEST INDIES WON BY 43 RUNS
	MAN OF THE MATCH: C.G. GREENIDGE

Final

WEST INDIES	286-9 (60 OVERS)
ENGLAND	194 (51 OVERS)
	WEST INDIES WON BY 92 RUNS
	MAN OF THE MATCH: I.V.A. RICHARDS

WORLD CUP 1983

VENUE: **ENGLAND**

UNDERDOGS INDIA BEAT THE ODDS

The third World Cup, again sponsored by Prudential, saw the company put £500,000 into the kitty. The total attendance rose to 232,081, but the number of matches was substantially increased, each team in the group playing six games instead of three. Again the competition was staged in England, with one team change from the previous tournament: Zimbabwe replaced Canada. The weather was much kinder than in 1979, though England suffered a very wet May.

The sensation of the first batch of matches came at Trent Bridge where Zimbabwe beat Australia by 13 runs. The Zimbabwean captain, Duncan Fletcher, rescued his side from a poor start with an innings of 69 and the total was 239 for 6. Fletcher then took 4 for 42 as Australia struggled against some accurate bowling and good fielding.

India also caused an upset by beating the West Indies at Old Trafford. For once, the Caribbean batting was not up to the mark, Andy Roberts and last man Joel Garner being their highest scorers as India won by 34 runs.

In the second batch of games, the West Indies recovered their poise with a 101-run win over Australia, Winston Davis returning figures of 7 for 51. England always looked like beating Sri Lanka, David Gower scoring 130, and for New Zealand

India captain Kapil Dev made major contributions with both bat and ball as his team shocked everyone to win the trophy.

Richard Hadlee bowled brilliantly as Pakistan crashed to three down before a run was on the board. New Zealand won by 52 runs.

Australia won at last in the third batch of games, trouncing India by 162 runs; Trevor Chappell made 110 and Ken MacLeay took 6 for 39. Zimbabwe were brushed aside by the West Indies at Worcester, Gordon Greenidge making 105 not out.

Round four saw a nail-biting finish at Edgbaston, where New Zealand beat England with one delivery unbowled and two wickets in hand. David Gower was again in splendid form for the home country, making 92 not out, but few of his compatriots could master Richard Hadlee. John Bracewell hit the penultimate ball for four to seal England's fate.

Australia managed to put Zimbabwe in their place when they played the return fixture at Southampton, while all England's batsmen – Fowler, Tavare, Gower and Lamb – flourished at the expense of Pakistan. On the same day, however, at Derby, Sri Lanka gained their single victory of the tournament, beating New Zealand by three wickets; Ashantha de Mel took 5 for 32 as the Kiwis were dismissed for 181, then Roy Dias hit 64 not out to bring Sri Lanka victory by three wickets. Zimbabwe nearly pulled off a sensation against India at Tunbridge Wells: India were five down for 17 and seven for 78, but Kapil Dev, coming in at No. 6 hit 175 and, with Kirmani, added 126 for the ninth wicket. Even so, Zimbabwe batted well in reply, losing by just 31 runs. India went on to beat Australia by 118 runs at Chelmsford, Madan Lal taking 4 for 20 as Australia collapsed in their effort to get 248, being 129 all out. This gave India a place in the semi-finals, against all the bookmakers' odds.

In the first semi-final, India met England at Old Trafford. To everyone's surprise, the England

Big smiles from captain Kapil Dev and Man of the Match Mohinder Amarnath as they enjoy possession of the World Cup after the surprise win for India that ended the West Indies' domination.

batting failed to score with any authority against a modest Indian attack and India had no trouble in reaching their target of 214, with Yashpal Sharma hitting 61. In the other semi-final, Pakistan had the more difficult task of scoring from the formidable West Indian attack. Mohsin Khan made 70, but no one stayed with him and the West Indies

were left needing 185. Viv Richards was in top form, making 80 not out as the Caribs won with 11.2 overs and eight wickets in hand.

The underdogs India therefore came to Lord's to meet Clive Lloyd's West Indians. Lloyd duly won the toss and, naturally, put India in. Facing Roberts, Garner, Marshall and Holding, the Indian batsmen

were dismissed for 183, only Srikkanth managing to top 30. For the crowd it seemed as if the West Indies merely had an afternoon's stroll in order to win the £20,000 prize. Gordon Greenidge, that most prolific of one-day batsmen, was out for a single – a minor disappointment. Desmond Haynes and Viv Richards took the total to 50 in an easy manner, then Madan Lal, bowling medium-pace seamers, struck. He dismissed Haynes, Richards and Gomes. Clive Lloyd fell to Binny and the score was suddenly 66 for 5, then 76 for 6. Malcolm Marshall came to partner wicket-keeper Dujon. Three figures were on the board. Gradually the two seemed to be turning the game the West Indies' way, but Mohinder Amarnath dismissed both and India won by 43 runs.

FINAL QUALIFYING TABLES

Group A

	P	W	L	PTS
ENGLAND	6	5	1	20
PAKISTAN	6	3	3	12
NEW ZEALAND	6	3	3	12
SRI LANKA	6	1	5	4

Group B

	P	W	L	PTS
WEST INDIES	6	5	1	20
INDIA	6	4	2	16
AUSTRALIA	6	2	4	8
ZIMBABWE	6	1	5	4

Semi-finals

ENGLAND	213 (60 OVERS)
INDIA	217-4 (54.4 OVERS)
	INDIA WON BY SIX WICKETS
	MAN OF THE MATCH: M. AMARNATH

PAKISTAN	184-8 (60 OVERS)
WEST INDIES	188-2 (48.4 OVERS)
	WEST INDIES WON BY EIGHT WICKETS
	MAN OF THE MATCH: I.V.A. RICHARDS

Final

INDIA	183 (54.4 OVERS)
WEST INDIES	140 (52 OVERS)
	INDIA WON BY 43 RUNS
	MAN OF THE MATCH: M. AMARNATH

WORLD CUP 1987

VENUE: **INDIA AND PAKISTAN**

AUSSIES BATTLE THROUGH

The fourth World Cup, sponsored by Reliance, was staged in India and Pakistan. The same eight sides as played in 1983 were assembled and, as in the third cup, each team played six matches to settle positions in two group tables. The number of overs per side was reduced from 60 to 50. The Group A matches were played in India and Group B in Pakistan. Each country staged a semi-final, with the final held in Calcutta.

The competition got off to an exciting start in Madras. Geoff Marsh hit 110 as Australia began the game by making 270 for 7. India made a confident reply, Gavaskar, Srikkanth and Sidhu all in good form, so that the total rose to 207 for 2. Craig McDermott, however, removed India's middle order and Australia won off the penultimate ball by one run. The next day in Hyderabad saw a match of almost equal excitement, when New Zealand beat Zimbabwe by three runs.

The Kiwis made 242. Zimbabwe seemed a one-man band as David Houghton batted totally unsupported and the score slumped to 104 for 7.

Then Butchart arrived at No. 9, the total doubled before the next wicket went down and New Zealand only won by dint of two run outs, when Zimbabwe required six from the final over.

Heavy rain at Indore meant that the first Australia v New Zealand game was put off to the second day and reduced to 30 overs per side. Through David Boon and Dean Jones, Australia made 199 for 4. New Zealand made good progress and were 133 for 2. They needed seven from the final over, but lost three wickets and made only three runs.

For the rest of the matches in Group A, the advantage remained

Allan Border, captain of Australia, and Mike Gatting, the England captain, shake hands before the World Cup final, which Australia went on to win by seven runs.

with Australia and India, who both won five of six matches. In the final four games, India beat Zimbabwe by seven wickets and New Zealand by nine wickets, Sunil Gavaskar hitting a marvellous, unbeaten 103 in the second game. Australia beat New Zealand by 17 runs, with Geoff Marsh scoring 126 not out, and Zimbabwe by 70 runs, with Boon making 93.

Over in Pakistan, the host country had a tight match against Sri Lanka,

Bill Athey took the England score to 66 for 1; Mike Gatting and Allan Lamb made useful contributions, but England were gradually slipping behind the run-rate. They needed 46 runs off the last five overs, but it was only narrowed to 17 off the final McDermott over, a task beyond Foster and Small. Australia, therefore, took the fourth World Cup by seven runs.

The main difference between this cup on the Indian sub-continent and those held in England was that the spin bowlers had much more opportunity – Hemmings and Emburey, for example, bowled 20 overs in the final – which was bound to add to the interest and break the dreadful monotony of pace.

The West Indies missed out on the semi-finals in 1987, but Viv Richards set a then World Cup record when he scored 181 in a group match.

only winning by 15 runs, in spite of 103 by Javed Miandad. A well-fought battle in Gujranwala, gave England a two-wicket win over the West Indies – who would go on to lose to Pakistan by the slender margin of one wicket – with Allan Lamb scoring 67, but England then came unstuck against Abdul Qadir whose spin brought Pakistan victory by 18 runs at Rawalpindi.

On the same day in Karachi, Viv Richards broke the World Cup record with an innings of 181 off 125 balls; Desmond Haynes also hit a century in the same game as Sri Lanka conceded 360 runs and lost by 191 runs. In the return fixture, Sri

Lanka did much better but, needing 37 off the final four overs, Sri Lanka couldn't score off Patterson and Benjamin, so the West Indies won by 25. England, though, did manage to beat the West Indies in Jaipur and thus qualify for the semi-finals. Graham Gooch made 92.

In the first semi in Lahore, Australia batted well to make 267 for 8 – for once Qadir failed to take a wicket. Javed Miandad and Imran Khan added 112 for the fourth Pakistani wicket after the first three batsmen fell cheaply, but Craig McDermott bowled accurately, taking 5 for 44 as the latter home batsmen contributed little.

India put England in in Bombay. Gooch mastered the slow pitch and scored 115, giving England a total of 254. India looked on target so long as Azharuddin was attacking but, once Eddie Hemmings had him leg before, the English bowler took command. About 70,000 spectators came to watch the final in Calcutta. Australia decided to bat first. David Boon and Geoff Marsh took full advantage of some erratic opening overs by DeFreitas and Small and this, in the end, proved the vital concession of the match. Allan Border and Mike Veletta kept Australia's runs flowing, so that England required 254. Gooch and

FINAL QUALIFYING TABLES

Group A

	P	W	L	PTS
INDIA	6	5	1	20
AUSTRALIA	6	5	1	20
NEW ZEALAND	6	2	4	8
ZIMBABWE	6	0	6	0

Group B

	P	W	L	PTS
PAKISTAN	6	5	1	20
ENGLAND	6	4	2	16
WEST INDIES	6	3	3	12
SRI LANKA	6	0	6	0

Semi-finals

AUSTRALIA	267-8 (50 OVERS)
PAKISTAN	249 (49 OVERS)
	AUSTRALIA WON BY 18 RUNS
	MAN OF THE MATCH:
	C.J. MCDERMOTT

ENGLAND	254-6 (50 OVERS)
INDIA	219 (45.3 OVERS)
	ENGLAND WON BY 35 RUNS
	MAN OF THE MATCH: G.A. GOOCH

Final

AUSTRALIA	253-5
ENGLAND	246-8 (50 OVERS)
	AUSTRALIA WON BY SEVEN RUNS
	MAN OF THE MATCH: D.C. BOON

WORLD CUP 1992

VENUE: **AUSTRALIA, NEW ZEALAND**

IMRAN HAS THE LAST LAUGH

There was a sensible format for the fifth World Cup in Australia and New Zealand in 1992. With South Africa recently returned to the fold of international cricket and Zimbabwe joining the Test match countries for the first time, there were nine entrants who played each other on a league basis with the top four qualifying for the semi-finals and final. So every country played at least eight matches. However, in the event, neither finalist could claim to have got there without luck or controversy – Pakistan by virtue of a point awarded for a "no-result" in a match they would almost certainly have lost, and England with the help of a "wet weather" rule,

which guaranteed them a semi-final win when the match was still in the balance.

The tournament was sold with the maximum amount of aggressive hype by Australian television, but the home country's expected easy ride to the knock-out stages received a jolt in the first match, when joint hosts New Zealand beat them by 37 runs. The New Zealand captain Martin Crowe made 100 not out in a

Pakistan captain Imran Khan celebrates capturing the wicket of Richard Illingworth to secure the World Cup as his side beat England by 22 runs in the 1992 final.

total of 248 for 6, and then, despite 100 from David Boon, Australia were bowled out for 211.

It was the start of a spectacular run by the New Zealanders, who won their first seven matches and lost only to Pakistan in their last, by which time they had long qualified for the semi-finals. Martin Crowe, with 456 runs, was the highest scorer of the tournament, his average of 114 being 45 higher than the next best.

Australia also lost their second match, comprehensively beaten by nine wickets by South Africa, who made 171 for 1 wicket in reply to 170 for 9. Kepler Wessels, the South African captain, who had played Tests for Australia, made 81 not out. "This is the greatest moment in South African cricket," said Ali Bacher.

Apart from New Zealand, the only other team to march impressively on and clinch an early place in the semi-finals were England. A thrilling opening match with India was won by nine runs, and after six matches they had won five and drawn unluckily with Pakistan. After bowling Pakistan out for 74 (Pringle 3 for 8) England were 24 for 1 when persistent rain ended it. England finally lost to New Zealand and Zimbabwe when it didn't matter, giving Zimbabwe their only points.

South Africa became the third team to book a semi-final place by beating India in their last match, but the fourth semi-final place rested on the matches on the last day of the league section. The West Indies could have it by beating Australia, Australia could have it by beating the West Indies, but only if Pakistan lost, and Pakistan, who had started disastrously, could have it by beating New Zealand, provided Australia beat the West Indies. This last was what happened, thanks to Wasim Akram taking 4 for 32 and an innings of 119 not out by opener Ramiz Raja.

As it happened, Pakistan had to play New Zealand again in the semi-final in Auckland. New Zealand made an excellent 262 for 7, with Martin Crowe run out for 91, but Pakistan achieved the runs thanks to a patient 57 not out by Javed Miandad, who anchored the innings, and a spectacular knock by Man of the Match Inzamam-Ul-Haq, who came in at 140 for 4 and scored 60 in 37 balls.

In the other semi-final, South Africa put England in and bowled only 45 overs in their allotted time, from which England made 252 for 6. With 10.10 p.m. fixed for the end of the day-night match, South Africa had reached 231 for 6 with 13 balls remaining when a downpour stopped play. When the players returned, the umpires decreed there was time for only seven balls but, as under the rules the lowest-scoring over of England's innings was discarded, the target was not reduced. However, before play could begin, there was another stoppage, reducing the time allowed to only one ball. This time the target was reduced by one run to 21, and that was that.

Pakistan started slowly in the final, but scraped 249 for 6. England batted disappointingly and were all out in the last over for 227, with Wasim Akram – who not only took three wickets but also scored a vital 33 in 18 balls at the end of the Pakistan innings, becoming Man of the Match. Martin Crowe was "Champion Player" of the tournament, winning cash and a Nissan motor car. Javed Miandad and South Africa's Peter Kirsten were the other batsmen to top 400 runs, while David Boon of Australia and Ramiz Raja each made two centuries. Wasim Akram took the most wickets, 18, at the best average, 18.78, while Chris Harris (New Zealand), Ian Botham (England) and Mushtaq Ahmed (Pakistan) all captured 16 wickets.

The Pakistan skipper Imran Khan accepted the biggest prize, however, and couldn't help beaming at the way fortune had smiled for his team at halfway, after winning only one of their first five matches, had won all five thereafter.

New Zealand's Martin Crowe finished as the tournament's leading scorer, with 456 runs at the impressive average of 114.00. His side fell at the semi-final stage to Pakistan.

FINAL QUALIFYING TABLES

Group A

	P	W	L	NR	Pts	NRR
NEW ZEALAND	8	7	1	0	14	0.59
ENGLAND	8	5	2	1	11	0.47
SOUTH AFRICA	8	5	3	0	10	0.14
PAKISTAN	8	4	3	1	9	0.16
AUSTRALIA	8	4	4	0	8	0.2
WEST INDIES	8	4	4	0	8	0.07
INDIA	8	2	5	1	5	0.14
SRI LANKA	8	2	5	1	5	-0.68
ZIMBABWE	8	1	7	0	2	-1.14

NRR = Net Run Rate, calculated by subtracting runs per over conceded from runs per over scored, to be used in the event of a tie on points.

Semi-finals

NEW ZEALAND	262-7 (50 OVERS) (M.D. CROWE 91)
PAKISTAN	264-6 (49 OVERS) (INZAMAM-UL-HAQ 60, JAVED MIANDAD 57 NOT OUT) *PAKISTAN WON BY FOUR WICKETS* MAN OF THE MATCH: INZAMAM-UL-HAQ
ENGLAND	252-6 (45 OVERS) (HICK 83)
SOUTH AFRICA	(REVISED TARGET 252 IN 43 OVERS) 232-6 (43 OVERS) *ENGLAND WON BY 19 RUNS* MAN OF THE MATCH: G.A. HICK

Final

PAKISTAN	249-6 (50 OVERS) (IMRAN KHAN 72, JAVED MIANDAD 58, PRINGLE 3-22)
ENGLAND	227 (49.2 OVERS) (FAIRBROTHER 62, WASIM AKRAM 3-49, MUSHTAQ AHMED 3-41) *PAKISTAN WON BY 22 RUNS* MAN OF THE MATCH: WASIM AKRAM

WORLD CUP 1996

SRI LANKA CONQUERS THE WORLD

There were 12 participants in the 1996 World Cup – the nine from 1992 (Zimbabwe were now a Test-playing country) plus Kenya, the Netherlands and the United Arab Emirates. The teams were split into two groups of six, with each team to play the five others in their group, the top four in each group to play in the quarter-finals of the knock-out stage. The whole tournament lasted 33 days in which 35 matches were played. The schedule consisted of 37 matches, but both Australia and the West Indies forfeited their games against Sri Lanka, refusing to travel there after a terrorist bomb had killed 80 people in Colombo.

Sri Lanka, who were given the points for a win, were therefore more or less guaranteed a quarter-final place, but they nevertheless earned it by beating their other three opponents, Zimbabwe, India (in Delhi) and Kenya, against whom they made a world record for a one-day international of 398 for 5.

The group produced one of cricket's biggest shocks when Kenya defeated the West Indies. With only one professional in their side, Kenya made 166 and dismissed the West Indies for 93. The result caused a crisis meeting of the West Indian Board, and Richie Richardson was lucky to retain the captaincy. However, 93 not out in the West Indies' final match, helping them beat Australia and qualify for the quarter-finals, proved his character. In Group B, South Africa were impressive in winning all five matches, but there were no real surprises.

In the first quarter-final, Sri Lanka confirmed their form with an exciting victory over England. Sri Lanka were responsible in this tournament for a tactical innovation in limited-overs cricket by launching a batting assault from the first ball, the philosophy being to score fast while the fielding restrictions are in force, rather than build a foundation for a late assault. Coming together at 12, Jayasuriya and Gurusinha added 100 in 65 balls. Jayasuriya made 82 in 44 balls, including 22 in one over from DeFreitas.

The sub-continent would have liked to see India play Pakistan in the final, but the two met at Bangalore in the quarters. With Pakistan's skipper, Wasim Akram, unfit, India won by 39 runs, after Pakistan had forfeited an over of their innings for a slow over-rate.

The new favourites, South Africa, were beaten by 19 runs by a rejuvenated West Indies, for whom Brian Lara made 111, while Australia beat New Zealand, despite a fine New Zealand total of 286 for 9, of which Chris Harris made 130 and Lee Germon 89. Mark Waugh's 110 helped Australia to a comfortable win in the end by six wickets. Thus all four sides from Group A qualified for the semi-finals. Both of these were extraordinary matches, one in cricketing terms, the other because of crowd disturbances.

At Calcutta, India put in Sri Lanka. Both openers were out in the first over, caught at third man. In fact,

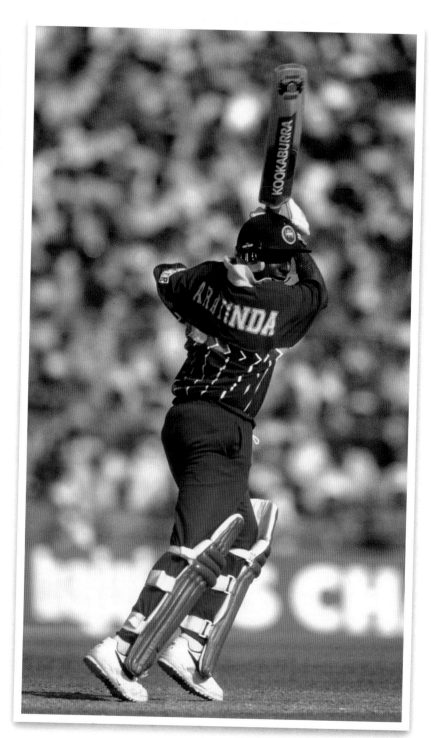

Aravinda de Silva, the Man of the Match in the final, with a sparkling 107 not out.

the first three batsmen contributed just two runs, but Aravinda de Silva continued attacking, reaching 53 in 32 balls, and Sri Lanka recovered to 251 for 8. India reached 98 for 1, but Sanath Jayasuriya then dismissed both Tendulkar (65) and Manjrekar (25) and India collapsed in disarray. At 120 for 8 after 34.1 overs, the 110,000 crowd began throwing bottles on the pitch, and referee Clive Lloyd took the teams off for a 20-minute cooling-off period. However, when the players returned, the bottle-throwing resumed, and Lloyd awarded the match to Sri Lanka by default.

In the other semi-final, Australia began disastrously, and were 15 for 4 before Stuart Law (72) and Michael Bevan (69) squeezed the total to 207 for 8. At 165 for two, with Chanderpaul (80) and Richie Richardson established, the West Indies needed 43 in seven overs to win, but Shane Warne (4 for 36) inspired a panic. The last eight wickets went for 37 in 50 balls, leaving Richardson stranded on 49 not out and the West Indies five runs short of Australia.

Australia started well in the final, had 82 up in the first 15 overs and reached 137 before the second wicket fell, but Sri Lanka's bowlers then bowled very well and kept the final total down to a manageable 241 for 7. When Sri Lanka batted, a brilliant innings of 107 by Aravinda de Silva took his country to a convincing victory with runs and wickets in hand. Among the individual performances, Sachin Tendulkar made most runs, 523, while Australia's Mark Waugh and Aravinda de Silva of Sri Lanka also topped 400. Arjuna Ranatunga, the winning captain, averaged 120 by virtue of four not-outs.

Security men in the stands as India's match with Sri Lanka was ended by crowd trouble.

FINAL QUALIFYING TABLES

Group A

	P	W	L	PTS
SRI LANKA	5	5	0	10
AUSTRALIA	5	3	2	6
INDIA	5	3	2	6
WEST INDIES	5	2	3	4
ZIMBABWE	5	1	4	2
KENYA	5	1	4	2

Group B

	P	W	L	PTS
SOUTH AFRICA	5	5	0	10
PAKISTAN	5	4	1	8
NEW ZEALAND	5	3	2	6
ENGLAND	5	2	3	4
UNITED ARAB EMIRATES	5	1	4	2
THE NETHERLANDS	5	0	5	0

Quarter-finals

ENGLAND	235-8
SRI LANKA	236-5 (40.4 OVERS)
INDIA	287-8
PAKISTAN	248-9
WEST INDIES	264-8
SOUTH AFRICA	245
NEW ZEALAND	286-9
AUSTRALIA	289-4 (47.5 OVERS)

Semi-finals

SRI LANKA	251-8
INDIA	120-8 (34.1 OVERS) *(PLAY ENDED BECAUSE OF CROWD ENCROACHMENT -MATCH AWARDED TO SRI LANKA)* MAN OF THE MATCH: P. A. DE SILVA
AUSTRALIA	207-8
WEST INDIES	202 *AUSTRALIA WON BY FIVE RUNS* MAN OF THE MATCH: S. K. WARNE

Final

AUSTRALIA	241-7 (TAYLOR 75, DE SILVA 3-42)
SRI LANKA	245-3 (46.2 OVERS) (GURUSINHA 65, DE SILVA 107 NOT OUT) *SRI LANKA WON BY SEVEN WICKETS* MAN OF THE MATCH: P. A. DE SILVA

WORLD CUP 1999

VENUE: ENGLAND, WALES, SCOTLAND, IRELAND, NETHERLANDS

RUN OUT MIX-UP HELPS THE AUSSIES

Twelve teams competed in 1999, Scotland and Bangladesh replacing the Netherlands and the United Arab Emirates from 1996. From two initial groups of six, the top three went forward to the second stage, called the Super Six. Each team played three matches against the three teams from the opposite group, so that all six teams had then played each other once. The top four in the league table produced by these results provided the semi-finalists.

While most matches were played in England, two (involving Scotland) took place in Edinburgh, and one each in Cardiff, Dublin and Amstelveen in Holland.

In the opening match at Lord's, England beat the holders, Sri Lanka, who went on to lose twice more in Group A and were eliminated at the earliest stage. South Africa, India and Zimbabwe led the group, with England (on net run-rate) and Kenya also being eliminated. The surprise team was Zimbabwe who, after beating Kenya, beat India by three runs. India, chasing 253, lost their last three wickets to Henry Olonga in one over. In their last match Zimbabwe beat South Africa by 48 runs. Neil Johnson opened both batting and bowling for Zimbabwe, scoring 76 and taking 3 for 27.

Lance Klusener (running) and Allan Donald are caught at the same end as the South Africans lose a dramatic semi-final encounter.

India's batsmen provided the record-breaking in this group. Against Kenya, Sachin Tendulkar (140) and Rahul Dravid (104) put on 237 unbroken for the third wicket against Kenya, a record World Cup partnership which lasted only until India's next match, when Dravid again (145) and Saurav Ganguly (183) added 318 for the second wicket against Sri Lanka.

In Group B Australia, after beating Scotland, lost their next two matches. New Zealand beat them by five wickets, with Roger Twose getting 80 not out, after Geoff Allott had four Aussie wickets for 37. Then in a thrilling game at Headingley, Pakistan beat Australia by ten runs. The Aussies, set 276, needed 13 in the last over, but skipper Wasim Akram grabbed the last two wickets. Pakistan, Australia and New Zealand progressed. Bangladesh, who also beat Scotland, provided the shock of the tournament by beating Pakistan by 62 runs. A sell-out 7,000 crowd at Northampton went ballistic.

In the Super Six, Australia won all their three matches, but Zimbabwe caused momentary anxiety at Lord's. Chasing 304, they stood at 153 for 1 after 28 overs, but couldn't maintain the pace, and ended at 259 for 6. Neil Johnson scored 132 not out from 144 balls.

Pakistan were beaten by India and South Africa. South Africa were set 221 to win, and were 58 for 5. But Lance Klusener, the batsman who most excited the World Cup audiences, cracked 46 off 41 balls to win it by three wickets with an over to spare.

New Zealand made 241 for 7 in the first semi-final at a sold-out Old Trafford. Shoaib Akhtar was the main destroyer. Pakistan began with a World Cup record opening stand of 194 between Saeed Anwar (113 not out) and Wajahatullah Wasti (94) and a 12-minute pitch invasion was all that delayed Pakistan thereafter.

Australia's Adam Gilchrist soon settled the final, reaching 50 in 33 balls batting at No. 1.

At Edgbaston, another sell-out, Australia made 213 (Shaun Pollock 5-36). With six down for 175 Klusener (31 not out) came in. He faced the last over from Fleming with nine wanted and the last pair together. He hit two fours, and off the fourth ball charged down the pitch for the winning run after a push past the bowler. He made his ground, but Allan Donald, his partner, was slow to respond, the ball was rolled back from bowler to keeper and Donald was run out halfway down the pitch. A great match was tied, but Australia went to the final on a better net run-rate in the Super Six.

At Lord's, 30,000 saw a disappointing final. Pakistan failed to perform and were out for 132 (Warne 4 for 33). Australia knocked off the runs in the 21st over for an eight-wicket win.

Dravid was top batsman of the tournament with 461 runs, followed by Steve Waugh, Saurav Ganguly, Mark Waugh, Saeed Anwar and Neil Johnson (all 367 plus). Geoff Allott and Shane Warne (20) had most wickets, followed by Glenn McGrath, Lance Klusener and Saqlain Mushtaq.

FINAL QUALIFYING TABLES

Group A

	P	W	L	NR	PTS	NRR
SOUTH AFRICA	5	4	1	0	8	0.85
INDIA	5	3	2	0	6	1.28
ZIMBABWE	5	3	2	0	6	0.01
ENGLAND	5	3	2	0	6	-0.33
SRI LANKA	5	2	3	0	4	-0.80
KENYA	5	0	5	0	0	-1.19

Group B

	P	W	L	NR	PTS	NRR
PAKISTAN	5	4	1	0	8	0.50
AUSTRALIA	5	3	2	0	6	0.73
NEW ZEALAND	5	3	2	0	6	0.57
WEST INDIES	5	3	2	0	6	0.49
BANGLADESH	5	2	3	0	4	-0.52
SCOTLAND	5	0	5	0	0	-1.92

Super Six

	P	W	L	NR	PTS	NRR
PAKISTAN	5	3	2	0	6	0.65
AUSTRALIA	5	3	2	0	6	0.36
SOUTH AFRICA	5	3	2	0	6	0.17
NEW ZEALAND	5	2	2	1	5	-0.52
ZIMBABWE	5	2	2	1	5	-0.79
INDIA	5	1	4	0	2	-0.15

Semi-finals

NEW ZEALAND	241-7
PAKISTAN	242-1
	MAN OF THE MATCH: SHOAIB AKHTAR

AUSTRALIA	213
SOUTH AFRICA	213
	MAN OF THE MATCH: SHANE WARNE (AUSTRALIA GO THROUGH ON NET RUN RATE IN SUPER SIX)

Final

PAKISTAN	132
AUSTRALIA	133-2
	MAN OF THE MATCH: SHANE WARNE

WORLD CUP 2003

VENUE: **SOUTH AFRICA, ZIMBABWE, KENYA**

UNBEATEN AUSTRALIA NEVER THREATENED

The format for the 2003 World Cup played on the African continent was the same as that for the 1999 renewal, except that 14 teams competed instead of 12. Scotland was the only country missing from the 1999 competitors, with the Netherlands, Namibia and Canada coming in. All Zimbabwe's six Pool matches were scheduled for Harare or Bulawayo, while two of Kenya's were to be played in Nairobi. All other games took place at 12 venues in South Africa. Nine of the 54 matches were timed for 2.30 starts, with floodlit finishes, which, as the tournament progressed, seemed to give the side batting first a slight advantage.

Prolonged controversy surrounded the ICC's decision to play matches in Zimbabwe, with there being strong political objections from many sides because of the oppressive Zimbabwe regime. In the end, after bitter debates in the countries due to play there, only England refused, a decision largely taken by the players themselves in opposition to the England and Wales Cricket Board. New Zealand, meanwhile, declined to play in Nairobi on safety grounds. England, therefore, forfeited their match to Zimbabwe and New Zealand likewise to Kenya. The decisions proved crucial to England's chance of reaching the Super Six stage, but New Zealand overcame the loss of points by beating the West Indies and

South Africa in a dramatic match in which captain Stephen Fleming was inspirational.

There was sensation even before the matches began. Shane Warne, who announced before leaving for the World Cup that it would be his farewell to one-day internationals, was sent home from South Africa before a ball was bowled, having been tested positive for taking a banned substance, in this instance some diuretics, allegedly on the advice of his mother. He was banned by the Australian Cricket Board for a year.

The matches themselves started with a shock, when the main hosts, South Africa, anxious to make up for their disappointing semi-final exit in 1999, lost the opening match to the West Indies by three runs. A scintillating 116 by Brian Lara turned the match. South Africa were then beaten by New Zealand, when rain reduced the Kiwis' target and they galloped to a nine-wicket win. Despite this, South Africa might have saved themselves by beating Sri Lanka in their last match, but miscalculated the Duckworth-Lewis figures and tied a match they could have won. Sri Lanka, New Zealand and Kenya (who beat Sri Lanka and took the points from the cancelled game with New Zealand) qualified from Pool B.

In Pool A, the Zimbabwe players Andy Flower and Henry Olonga issued a statement before their opening match "mourning the death of democracy in our beloved Zimbabwe" and wore black

Ricky Ponting took over from Steve Waugh as captain and, with an average of over 50, helped Australia to their third win.

411 (av. 51.37), Adam Gilchrist 408 (av. 40.80) and Marvan Atapattu 368 (av. 61.33). Best bowlers were Chaminda Vaas (20 wickets at 14.85), Glenn McGrath (19 at 18.68), Andy Bichel (18 at 10.66, the best all-rounder of the tournament) and Shoaib Akhtar (17 at 17.05, and who reached 100 mph).

FINAL QUALIFYING TABLES

Pool A

	P	W	L	T	NR	PTS	SS BONUS*
AUSTRALIA	6	6	0	0	0	24	4
INDIA	6	5	1	0	0	20	4
ZIMBABWE	6	3	2	0	1	14	3.5
ENGLAND	6	3	3	0	0	12	-
PAKISTAN	6	2	3	0	1	10	-
HOLLAND	6	1	5	0	0	4	-
NAMIBIA	6	0	6	0	0	0	-

Pool B

	P	W	L	T	NR	PTS	SS BONUS*
SRI LANKA	6	4	1	1	0	18	3.5
KENYA	6	4	2	0	0	16	2
NEW ZEALAND	6	4	2	0	0	16	4
WEST INDIES	6	3	2	0	1	14	-
SOUTH AFRICA	6	3	2	1	0	14	-
CANADA	6	1	5	0	0	4	-
BANGLADESH	6	0	5	0	1	2	-

*QUALIFIERS CARRIED FORWARD 1 BONUS POINT TO THE SUPER SIX FOR A WIN AGAINST A NON-QUALIFIER (0.5 POINT FOR A TIE OR NO RESULT).

Super Six

	P	W	L	T	NR	PTS*
AUSTRALIA	5	5	0	0	0	24
INDIA	5	4	1	0	0	20
KENYA	5	3	2	0	0	14
SRI LANKA	5	2	3	0	0	11.5
NEW ZEALAND	5	1	4	0	0	8
ZIMBABWE	5	0	5	0	0	3.5

*INCLUDING BONUS POINTS CARRIED FORWARD

Semi-finals

AUSTRALIA	212-7 (50 OVERS)
SRI LANKA	123-7 (38.1 OVERS)
	MAN OF THE MATCH: ANDREW SYMONDS

INDIA	240-7 (50 OVERS)
KENYA	179 (46.2 OVERS)
	MAN OF THE MATCH: SAURAV GANGULY

Final

AUSTRALIA	359-2 (50 OVERS)
INDIA	234 (39.2 OVERS)
	MAN OF THE MATCH: RICKY PONTING

The Australians, despite losing Shane Warne, who was sent home for a drug offence, never really looked in trouble, and remained unbeaten throughout the tournament; a comfortable win over India in the final merely emphasized their superiority.

armbands during the game. Olonga was dropped from subsequent matches, but a players' revolt saved Flower when the selectors later wished to drop him, too. Having lost to India and Australia, who were to head Pool A, England's last hope of the Super Six disappeared when Zimbabwe received two points for a "no result" against Pakistan, and took third place.

The Super Six provided no real shocks, but Kenya's place as third in the table, and thus in the semi-finals, would have been a major surprise before the event. Their forfeited match against New Zealand meant they carried forward ten points to the Super Six, and defeating Zimbabwe was enough to get them through.

In the semis, Australia's batting was saved at 144 for 5 by Andrew Symonds, and Sri Lanka never got going. When rain sent the result to Duckworth-Lewis, Australia were in the driving seat. Kenya's dream predictably came to an end with defeat by India.

Australia won the final, in style, making a big score and dismissing Tendulkar for 4. From then on, there was no doubting the winner.

The best batsman in the series was Sachin Tendulkar, with 673 runs (av. 61.18). Saurav Ganguly scored 465 (av. 58.12), Ricky Ponting

WORLD CUP 2007

VENUE: **WEST INDIES**

AUSTRALIA ROMP TO WORLD CUP HAT-TRICK

Sixteen countries competed in the 2007 World Cup compared to 14 in 2003 and 12 in 1999. The teams were initially divided into four groups of four. The top two in each group would progress to the Super Eights, when each team would play six matches and have one result carried forward from the group stage. The top four teams in the Super Eights then moved on to play in the knockout semi-finals. The whole competition was arranged over seven weeks. A time considered too long by many of the tournament's critics.

Australia were 9-4 favourites, South Africa second at 9-2 and Sri Lanka third at 7-1 at the start of the tournament.

The fourth day of the group matches saw two major upsets. Bangladesh beat India by five wickets with Mushfiqur Rahim hitting an unbeaten 56 for the winners; even more surprising was Ireland's – who had tied with Zimbabwe earlier in the week – three-wicket victory over Pakistan, with Niall O'Brien's 72 the backbone of their success. Pakistan had already lost to the West Indies and their shock defeat to Ireland knocked them out of the tournament. Two days later, the Pakistan coach Bob Woolmer was found dead in his bathroom at the team's hotel in Jamaica. Speculation as to the cause of death clouded the remainder of the competition.

At the same time reports of misbehaviour by England's Andrew Flintoff resulted in him being sacked as England vice-captain and omitted from the next England match (fortunately this was against the very moderate Canadian side).

India's defeat by Bangladesh meant that they had to beat Sri Lanka to have any hope of progressing to the Super Eights. Sri Lanka through their two unorthodox bowlers, Surappulige Malinga and Muttiah Muralitharan and the inspirational batting of Mahela Jayawardene and Sanath Jayasuriya, were showing exceptional form. They duly demolished India and the latter were on their way home.

So into Super Eights went Ireland and Bangladesh.

Australia, New Zealand, Sri Lanka and West Indies began the Super Eights with a two-point advantage over the rest of the teams following their group successes. Australia beat West Indies by 103 runs in their first Super Eights game, with Matthew Hayden hitting 158 and Glenn McGrath taking 3-31. From then on Australia never faltered, winning all their Super Eight matches with quite devastating ease. Sri Lanka lost to South Africa by one wicket in the second Super Eights game and were later beaten by Australia, but were otherwise successful. Bangladesh were beaten by New Zealand by nine wickets and by Australia by ten wickets, but upset the form guide when they bowled out South Africa for 184 and won that game by 67 runs.

In the closing stages of the Super

Adam Gilchrist put in a Man of the Match-winning performance in the final, hammering 149 off just 104 balls, with eight sixes, as Australia put Sri Lanka to the sword.

It's all smiles for Ricky Ponting and Adam Gilchrist as Australia become the first team in World Cup history to win three successive finals. The brutal truth for the rest of the cricket world was that nobody came close to challenging them.

FINAL QUALIFYING TABLES

Group A

	P	W	L	NR	PTS	RR
AUSTRALIA	3	3	0	0	6	3.43
SOUTH AFRICA	3	2	1	0	4	2.40
HOLLAND	3	1	2	0	2	-2.53
SCOTLAND	3	0	3	0	0	-3.88

Group B

	P	W	L	NR	PTS	RR
SRI LANKA	3	3	0	0	6	3.33
BANGLADESH	3	2	1	0	4	-1.52
INDIA	3	1	2	0	2	1.21
BERMUDA	3	0	3	0	0	-4.34

Group C

	P	W	L	NR	PTS	RR
NEW ZEALAND	3	3	0	0	6	2.14
ENGLAND	3	2	1	0	4	0.42
KENYA	3	1	2	0	2	-1.19
CANADA	3	0	3	0	0	-1.39

Group D

	P	W	L	NR	PTS	RR
WEST INDIES	3	3	0	0	6	0.80
IRELAND	3	1	1	1	3	-0.10
PAKISTAN	3	1	2	0	2	0.09
ZIMBABWE	3	0	2	1	1	-0.88

Super Eights

	P	W	L	NR	PTS	RR
AUSTRALIA	7	7	0	0	14	2.40
SRI LANKA	7	5	2	0	10	1.48
NEW ZEALAND	7	5	2	0	10	0.25
SOUTH AFRICA	7	4	3	0	8	0.31
ENGLAND	7	3	4	0	6	-0.39
WEST INDIES	7	2	5	0	4	-0.57
BANGLADESH	7	1	6	0	2	-1.51
IRELAND	7	1	6	0	2	-1.73

Semi-Finals

SRI LANKA	289-5 (50 OVERS)
NEW ZEALAND	208 (41.4 OVERS)
	MAN OF THE MATCH: MAHELA JAYAWARDENE

SOUTH AFRICA	149 (43.5 OVERS)
AUSTRALIA	153-3 (31.3 OVERS)
	MAN OF THE MATCH: GLENN MCGRATH

Final

AUSTRALIA	281-4 (38 OVERS)
SRI LANKA	215-8 (38 OVERS)
	MAN OF THE MATCH: ADAM GILCHRIST

Eights the last place in the semi-finals depended on the outcome of the England v. South Africa match. In the event Andrew Hall took 5-18 to dismiss England for 154. England's batting throughout the competition depended almost entirely on Kevin Pietersen. This time he failed. Then Graeme Smith, the South African captain, hit 89 not out, as South Africa won by nine wickets. Two days later, England's coach, Duncan Fletcher, resigned.

In the semi-finals, a brilliant innings by Jayawardene gave Sri Lanka an easy win over New Zealand. Glenn McGrath bowled exceptionally well to give Australia a seven-wicket win at the expense of South Africa. Rain delayed the start of the final between Australia and Sri Lanka in Bridgetown. Adam Gilchrist hit the fastest hundred in any final and reached 149 with Australia making 281 for 4 off 38 overs. Sri Lanka never appeared likely to top this score, but the latter part of their innings was played in appalling light, which did little to enhance the game of cricket. However, the winners, Australia, completely justified their status as the world's top cricketing country.

WORLD CUP 2011

MS Dhoni puts some more runs on the board as his India side moved towards victory. Dhoni's contribution was immense both with with the bat and in his role as captain.

VENUE: **BANGLADESH, INDIA AND SRI LANKA**

INDIA TRIUMPH IN MUMBAI

Yet another change of format. The number of teams competing was reduced by two to 14 and the teams were in two groups rather than four for the preliminary stages. Pakistand and South Africa topped the two group tables, but the final was played out between the two teams who came second in the tables - India and Sri Lanka.

The Final was billed as the last battle of the veterans - Tendulkar and Muralitharan. Tendulkar required one hundred to bring his International total to 100 100s, Muralitharan had announced his intention of retiring after the match. In the event, the Sri Lankan spinner failed to take a wicket, whilst Tendulkar scored just 18.

Sri Lanka, batting first, scored a respectable 274-6 due to an unbeaten 103 by Jayawardene. In response, India lost their two most prized batsmen, Sehwag and Tendulkar, to Malinga with only 31 on the board. Gambhir stood firm then at 114 for 3 was joined by captain Dhoni. The pair added 109 with Dhoni going on to 91 not out, bringing India victory by 6 wickets. Dhoni received the Man of the Match Award both for his batting and captaincy. Yuvraj Singh, who was batting with Dhoni when victory came, was awarded the Player of the Series Trophy.

In the semi-final, India had beaten Pakistan, a match happily played without any major non-cricketing incidents; Tendulkar was India's highest scorer with a lucky 85. The other semi-final saw New Zealand beaten by Sri Lanka - the sixth time the Black Caps have lost a semi-final on the world stage. Set a target of 218, Sri Lanka cruised to 160 for one, but lost four wickets for 25, giving New Zealand some hope, before Sri Lanka recovered.

Australia, England, South Africa and West Indies were the losing quarter-finalists. England were utterly humiliated by Sri Lanka in Colombo, suffering the worst possible defeat - by ten wickets as the two Sri Lankan openers, Tharanga (102*) and Dishan (108*) toyed with the modest England attack, even though England's sole class spinner, Swann, opened the bowling. Australia's much criticized captain, Ponting, after a lacklustre series of innings, hit a commanding 104 to enable his side to reach 260-6, but fifties from Tendulkar, Gambhir and Yuvraj Singh saw India home with 14 balls and five wickets to spare.

New Zealand appeared in a losing position against South Africa, the former were 221-8 and South Africa 108 for two, but were then bowled out for 172 off 43.2 overs, six players failing to reach double figures. West Indies' departure in the quarter-final echoed England's. The Caribbean side were beaten by 10 wickets by Pakistan, when their batting, apart from Chanderpaul, was routed - all out for 112.

In the Group stage of the competition, England's progress

was the most bizarre. In the very first match England had a lucky escape against the Netherlands. Ten Doeschate hit a century for the Dutch and England scraped home with just eight balls unbowled. Then came the dramatic tie – the only one of the competition – against India. Tendulkar hit 120, as India made 338, then Strauss played the innings of his life (158) to bring England a vital point. England then suffered the indignity of defeat at the hands of Ireland, Kevin O'Brien hitting perhaps the greatest innings of the tournament, as Ireland won in the last over by three wickets. A low scoring game with South Africa was won by just six runs, followed by defeat by Bangladesh in Chittagong by two wickets. In the end England had to await results from other matches to see if they would progress to the quarter-finals.

The main complaints from the press centred on the length of the tournament and the amount of travelling involved. The games were carefully spread out to allow maximum TV coverage and income. The crowds for the home countries were tremendous, but other games were poorly attended. England and Australia had played an Ashes Test series prior to the competition, plus seven One Day Internationals and injuries to among others, Pietersen and Broad, certainly had an strong adverse effect on England's overall chances in the competition.

The victory by India was greeted with great enthusiasm not only in India, but in the Indian communities overseas. It is true indicator of where cricket's beating heart now really lies.

Indian cricketers, including veteran Sachin Tendulkar (second left), celebrate with the trophy after victory in the 2011 Cricket World Cup final over Sri Lanka at the Wankhede Stadium in Mumbai on 2 April 2011. India beat Sri Lanka by six wickets.

FINAL QUALIFYING TABLES

Group A

	P	W	L	D	NR	PTS	NRR
PAKISTAN	6	5	1	0	0	10	0.76
SRI LANKA	6	4	1	0	1	9	2.58
AUSTRALIA	6	4	1	0	1	9	1.12
NEW ZEALAND	6	4	2	0	0	8	1.14
ZIMBABWE	6	2	4	0	0	4	0.03
CANADA	6	1	5	0	0	2	-1.99
KENYA	6	0	6	0	0	0	-3.04

Group B

	P	W	L	D	NR	PTS	NRR
SOUTH AFRICA	6	5	1	0	0	10	2.03
INDIA	6	4	1	1	0	9	0.90
ENGLAND	6	3	2	1	0	7	0.07
WEST INDIES	6	3	3	0	0	6	1.07
BANGLADESH	6	3	3	0	0	6	-1.36
IRELAND	6	2	4	0	0	4	-0.70
NETHERLANDS	6	0	6	0	0	0	-2.05

Quarter-Finals

WEST INDIES 112 (43.3 OVERS)
PAKISTAN 113-0 (20.5 OVERS)
MAN OF THE MATCH: MOHAMMAD HAFEEZ

AUSTRALIA 260-6 (50 OVERS)
INDIA 261-5 (47.4 OVERS)
MAN OF THE MATCH: YUVRAJ SINGH

NEW ZEALAND 221-8 (50 OVERS)
SOUTH AFRICA 172 (43.2 OVERS)
MAN OF THE MATCH: J.D.P. ORAM

ENGLAND 229-6(50 OVERS)
SRI LANKA 231-0(39.3 OVERS)
MAN OF THE MATCH: T.M. DILSHAN

Semi-Finals

NEW ZEALAND 217 (48.5 OVERS)
SRI LANKA 220-5 (47.5 OVERS)
MAN OF THE MATCH: T.M. DILSHAN

INDIA 260-9 (50 OVERS)
PAKISTAN 231 (49.5 OVERS)
MAN OF THE MATCH: S.R. TENDULKAR

Final

SRI LANKA 274-6 (50 OVERS)
INDIA 277-4 (48.2 OVERS)
MAN OF THE MATCH: M.S. DHONI

5 THE GREAT CRICKETERS

Cricket is a statisticians delight, but the greatest players are not necessarily those whose figures dwarf everyone else's; they are the cricketers who impress by their personality, style, the excitement they generate and the mark which they leave on the game.

In this section are included 236 such masters of the game, from W.G. Grace onwards. Of course, no two cricket lovers would chose exactly the same players as each other, so any omissions of particular players are apologised for in advance. They take in over 140 years of cricket (W.G. Grace made his first-class debut in 1865). They come from nine Test-playing countries (nobody from Bangladesh has really had the time to make their mark in the Test arena) and are masters of all the arts of the game: batting, bowling, fielding, wicket-keeping

and captaincy. There has been a bias towards modern players in our choice as it is thought that readers might prefer information about the players reaching stardom today, such as Alastair Cook and Dale Steyn, and other great players of current or recent eminence, such as Sachin Tendulkar or Shane Warne, rather than those who are dead or who have long since retired from the game.

Of the 236 players featured, 27 of them have been given full-page treatment, and again there has been a leaning towards the modern. Of the 27, there are 13 who are predominantly batsmen, seven who are all-rounders (of which the last 20 or so years has seen a glut of outstanding ones), six bowlers and a wicket-keeper who is also an outstanding batsman. Eight Test-playing countries are represented.

Also included are the scorers of the most Test runs, the takers of the most Test wickets and the all-rounders with the most impressive figures. This, in itself, leads to a bias towards modern players, as more and more Test cricket is played as each year passes. However, irrespective of the figures, all of the 236 players featured in this section have contributed richly to the great game.

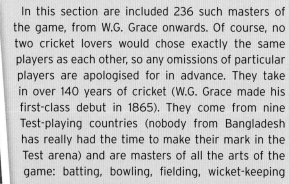

Top left: **Considered by many to be the complete bowler, Dennis Lillee took 355 wickets in his 70 Test matches and formed a fearsome new-ball partnership with Jeff Thomson.**

Left: **Andrew Strauss is one of a rare breed of Test cricketers who has thrived on the responsibility of captaining his country. He was England's go-to man following the resignation of Kevin Pieterson in early 2009.**

Right: **The cricketer that England has been waiting for since Ian Botham bowed out of the Test arena in the early nineties, Andrew "Freddie" Flintoff announced his arrival as a world-class performer in 2005.**

ABDUL QADIR

Born: 15 SEPTEMBER 1955, LAHORE, PAKISTAN
Teams: PUNJAB (1975-76); LAHORE (1975-76 TO 1984-85); HABIB BANK (1975-76 TO 1995-96)
First-class: 208 MATCHES; 3,740 RUNS, AVERAGE 18.33; 960 WICKETS, AVERAGE 23.22
Tests (1977-78 to 1990-91): 67 MATCHES; 1,029 RUNS, AVERAGE 15.59; 236 WICKETS, AVERAGE 32.80

It was Abdul Qadir who announced the renaissance of leg-break and googly bowlers in Test cricket when he played three Tests against England in Pakistan in 1977-78. He disappointed in England the following summer when he was troubled by injury, but by the time he returned in 1982 he was a potent force and his six wickets at Lord's played a significant part in Pakistan's victory.

In 1982-83, he took 22 wickets in three tests as Pakistan had a clean sweep against Australia, and he became the first bowler to take 100 wickets in a Pakistan season. The following season, he took 19 wickets in three Tests as Pakistan beat England in a rubber for the first time, and ten wickets at The Oval in August 1987 ensured Pakistan's series victory in England. Three months later, Qadir produced an outstanding display of leg-spin and googly bowling when he took 9 for 56 and 4 for 45 to bring Pakistan an innings victory over England at Lahore. His first-innings figures are a record for Pakistan in Test cricket, and he became only the second Pakistani bowler to take 200 Test wickets.

His bouncy run to the wicket, unquenchable enthusiasm and passionate appeals established his character with the crowd. Often in disagreement with authority, he was a spin bowler with a fast bowler's attitude and temperament.

BOBBY ABEL

Born: 30 NOVEMBER 1857, ROTHERHITHE, SURREY
Died: 10 DECEMBER 1936, STOCKWELL, LONDON
Teams: SURREY (1881-1904)
First-class: 627 MATCHES; 33,124 RUNS, AVERAGE 35.46; 236 WICKETS, AVERAGE 24.00
Tests (1888-1902): 13 MATCHES; 744 RUNS, AVERAGE 37.20

A diminutive opening batsman, Bobby Abel became one of the great favourites at The Oval where he was dubbed "The Guv'nor". Surrey adopted a policy of recruiting young professionals in the late 1870s and engaged Abel as an off-break bowler. He was 23 before he made his first-class debut and it was some years before he established himself. He did not score a century until 1886, and it was an innings of 144 against the Australians that season which really set him on his way, when he scored 1,000 runs in a season for the first time. He was to repeat that feat on 13 other occasions.

He toured Australia and South Africa with England sides and, in Sydney, January 1892, he became the first England player to carry his bat through a completed Test innings. He was unbeaten for 132 out of 307. Three years earlier, he had hit 120 against South Africa in Cape Town.

In 1893, his career was threatened by an eye infection, but he recovered to exceed 2,000 runs every season between 1895 and 1902. In 1899, he made 357 not out against Somerset at The Oval, which remains the highest score ever made for Surrey. In the same season, he and Tom Hayward scored 448 for Surrey's fourth wicket against Yorkshire at The Oval, and this remained a world record for 50 years.

In 1901, he created another record when he scored 3,309 runs in first-class cricket. His team-mate Tom Hayward was to better this five years later.

Abel's eye problem came back, and his career ended abruptly in 1904. He coached Surrey in 1907. He also coached at Dulwich College and ran a sports shop.

JIMMY ADAMS

Born: 9 JANUARY 1968, PORT MARIA, JAMAICA
Teams: JAMAICA (1984-85 TO 2000-01); NOTTINGHAMSHIRE (1994); FREE STATE (2002-03)
First-class: 202 MATCHES; 11,234 RUNS, AVERAGE 39.69; 103 WICKETS, AVERAGE 40.39
Tests (1991-92 to 2000-01): 54 MATCHES; 3,010 RUNS, AVERAGE 41.23; 27 WICKETS, AVERAGE 49.48

Jimmy Adams is an all-round cricketer in every sense – a stylish left-handed batsman, a slow left-arm bowler and a player who has also played limited-over internationals as a wicket-keeper. He hit 79 and took four for 43 on his Test debut, against South Africa, and made his first Test century against England at Bouda, 1993-94. This was the second game of the series; in the first he had scored 95 not out and taken six catches to equal the Test record.

He played for several seasons in the Durham League, but assisted Nottinghamshire in 1994, and the following winter he hit two Test centuries against India. He toured England in 1995 and, at one time, was ranked number one batsman in the world, but he suffered a severe blow on the head at Taunton, from which it took him some time to recover.

He replaced Lara as captain of the West Indies, but was himself replaced following the West Indies defeat, 5-0 against Australia in 2000-01. He played Minor Counties cricket in England for Wiltshire in 2004.

NEIL ADCOCK

Born: 8 MARCH 1931, SEA POINT, CAPE TOWN, SOUTH AFRICA
Teams: TRANSVAAL (1952-53 TO 1959-60); NATAL (1960-61 TO 1962-63)
First-class: 99 MATCHES, 451 RUNS, AVERAGE 5.50; 405 WICKETS, AVERAGE 17.25
Tests (1953-54 to 1961-62): 26 MATCHES, 146 RUNS, AVERAGE 5.40; 104 WICKETS, AVERAGE 21.10

A tall fast bowler, Neil Adcock found his way into the South African side after only nine first-class matches. He was an immediate success, taking three wickets in the second innings as South Africa beat New Zealand in Durban and followed this with 8 for 87 in the match as the Springboks triumphed in Johannesburg. He finished his first Test series with 24 wickets. He was a hostile bowler, full of passion, but he was troubled by various injuries, and it was not until his second tour of England in 1960 that he showed himself at his best. In five Tests, he took 26 wickets at 22.57 runs each, and his total for the tour was a record 108. These achievements were all the more remarkable when one considers that his new-ball partner was no-balled out of Test cricket on this tour for his illegal action. Adcock is one of only

Abdul Qadir: Pakistan's great spinner.

five South African bowlers to have taken 100 wickets in Test cricket.

Following his retirement, he became a radio commentator.

TERRY ALDERMAN

Born: 12 JUNE 1956, SUBIACO, PERTH, WESTERN AUSTRALIA
Teams: WESTERN AUSTRALIA (1974-75 TO 1992-93); KENT (1984-86); GLOUCESTERSHIRE (1988)
First-class: 245 MATCHES; 1,307 RUNS, AVERAGE 8.32; 956 WICKETS, AVERAGE 23.74
Tests (1981 to 1990-91): 41 MATCHES; 203 RUNS, AVERAGE 6.54; 170 WICKETS, AVERAGE 27.15

Terry Alderman was a right-arm fast medium-pace bowler whose control and late movement proved too much for most English batsmen. He had not played Test cricket until he came to England in 1981, and nine wickets in the first match at Trent Bridge, when he bowled unchanged through the second innings, gave an early indication of his worth. He finished the series, in which Australia were beaten, with a record 42 wickets in six Tests.

In 1982-83, Alderman's career suffered a severe setback when he dislocated a shoulder while tackling a pitch-invader during the first Test. The injury ended his season. He was due to tour England in 1985, but was withdrawn from the party when he revealed that he had signed to go to South Africa. He had enjoyed a good season for Kent in 1984 and was to have an outstanding one in 1986. He later assisted Gloucestershire with great success. He complemented his bowling with excellent slip fielding.

A key member of the overwhelmingly successful Australian side in 1989, he took 41 wickets in the series, five times capturing a wicket in his opening over. A modest and courteous man, fiercely competitive, he coached Western Australia in 1992-93.

GUBBY ALLEN

Born: 31 JULY 1902, BELLEVUE HILL, SYDNEY, AUSTRALIA
Died: 29 NOVEMBER 1989, ST JOHN'S WOOD, LONDON
Teams: MIDDLESEX (1921-1950); CAMBRIDGE UNIVERSITY (1922-23)
First-class: 265 MATCHES; 9,232 RUNS, AVERAGE 28.67; 788 WICKETS, AVERAGE 22.32
Tests (1930 to 1947-48): 25 MATCHES; 750 RUNS, AVERAGE 24.19; 81 WICKETS, AVERAGE 29.37

In 1929, he became the only man to take all ten wickets in an innings of a county match at Lord's, Lancashire being the opponents, and the following year he made his debut for England against Australia. His selection was opposed in some quarters as he had been born in Australia, and his uncle had been an Australian Test cricketer. He toured Australia with Jardine's side, 1932-33, and took 21 wickets in the "bodyline" series, although he himself refused to bowl leg-theory.

He captained England against India in 1936 and was appointed to lead the side to Australia in 1936-37.

Allen was not a county captain, and many believed his appointment was due to his Australian connections and had been made in an attempt to heal the wounds that existed following the "bodyline" tour. England won the first two Tests but lost the next three.

Allen played no more Test cricket before the Second World War but, astonishingly, was recalled to lead England in the West Indies in 1947-48, at the age of 45. He pulled a calf muscle on the boat on the way out, could not play in the first Test and, for the first time in history, the MCC went through a tour without a win to their credit.

Very close to his mentor Sir Pelham Warner, Allen succeeded him as the most influential administrator in the game, holding all the high offices. He was knighted for services to cricket in 1986.

LALA AMARNATH

Born: 11 SEPTEMBER 1911, LAHORE, INDIA
Died: 5 AUGUST 2000 NEW DELHI, INDIA
Teams: HINDUS (1929-30 TO 1939-40); SOUTHERN PUNJAB (1933-34 TO 1951-52); PATIALA (1953-54 TO 1957-58); UTTAR PRADESH (1956-57); RAILWAYS (1958-59 TO 1960-61)
First-class: 186 MATCHES; 10,426 RUNS, AVERAGE 41.38; 463 WICKETS, AVERAGE 22.98
Tests (1933-34 to 1952-53): 24 MATCHES; 878 RUNS, AVERAGE 24.38; 45 WICKETS, AVERAGE 32.91

Although his given name was Nanik, Amarnath, the father of two Test cricketers, was always known as "Lala". By the time the MCC toured India in 1933-34, he was recognized as an accomplished batsman and was selected for the first Test match. He hit a century in the second innings, the first to be scored for India in a Test. It was during this season that his medium-pace bowling developed – for he had originally been a wicket-keeper – and he arrived in England in 1936 as an all-rounder of international standing, which was confirmed by 32 wickets and three centuries in the early part of the tour. His anger at the way in which the tour was being managed caused this instinctive and impetuous cricketer to erupt, and he was sent home for disciplinary proceedings. Later enquiries found him "not guilty".

He played in the Lancashire League, toured England in 1946 and took eight wickets at Old Trafford. He captained India in Australia in 1947-48 and was the leading wicket-taker in the series. He retained the captaincy for the home series against West Indies in 1948-49, and kept wicket in the fifth Test when Sen was injured, holding five catches.

Demanding more money and better travelling conditions, he was suspended from domestic cricket at the end of that series and was omitted from the side that toured England in 1952. The tour was a disaster, and he was reinstated as captain for the inaugural series against Pakistan in 1952-53, leading India to their first victory in a Test rubber. He enjoyed a fine series, but learned that he was to be replaced for the trip to the West Indies. He left the game an embittered man.

He found consolation in the achievements of his sons. Mohinder scored more than 4,000 Test runs and was Man of the Match in the World Cup final in 1983.

Terry Alderman: tormented the English batsmen.

CURTLY AMBROSE

SEE PAGE 165

LESLIE AMES

Born: 3 DECEMBER 1905, ELHAM, KENT
Died: 27 FEBRUARY 1990, CANTERBURY, KENT
Teams: KENT (1926-51)
First-class: 593 MATCHES; 37,248 RUNS, AVERAGE
43.51; 24 WICKETS, AVERAGE 33.37;
CAUGHT 704, STUMPED 417
Tests (1929 To 1938-39): 47 MATCHES;
2,434 RUNS, AVERAGE 40.56; CAUGHT 74,
STUMPED 23

Les Ames was the outstanding wicket-keeper-batsman of the inter-war period and he remains the only wicket-keeper to have scored a hundred hundreds in first-class cricket; eight of them came in Test matches. He joined Kent as a batsman in 1923, took up wicket-keeping and gained a regular place in the county side in 1927. This was the first of 17 seasons in which he scored 1,000 runs. In 1933, he made 3,058 runs. In 1928, he created a new wicket-keeping record with 122 dismissals, but he beat this the following season with 128 dismissals. It is a record which is not likely to be beaten, nor is his record of 64 stumpings in 1932 when he claimed a hundred victims for the third time.

He holds another wicket-keeping record in that he made 417 stumpings in his career. Many of these came off "Tich" Freeman, the leg-spinner, with whom Ames had an almost supernatural understanding.

By 1938, he had begun to suffer from back trouble and he did not keep wicket after the Second World War, although he remained a prolific scorer. He was the first professional to become a selector, and was both secretary and manager of Kent during a very successful period for the county.

Leslie Ames: England's first great wicket-keeper.

JAMES ANDERSON

Born: 30 JULY 1982, BURNLEY, LANCASHIRE
Teams: LANCASHIRE (2002-10); AUCKLAND (2007-08)
First-class: 118 MATCHES; 818 RUNS, AVERAGE 9.73; 493
WICKETS, AVERAGE 27.64
Tests (2003 to 2010-11): 57 MATCHES; 524 RUNS,
AVERAGE 11.64; 212 WICKETS, AVERAGE 31.10

Jimmy Anderson is a tall (6ft 2in) right-arm opening fast-medium bowler. He made his first-class debut in 2002, and his Test debut, aged not quite 21, against Zimbabwe in 2003 at Lord's. He took five wickets in the first innings. His problem was inconsistency, with unplayable spells being mixed with expensive ones. Injury ruined 2006 for him, and when he went to Australia and played in the first two and last Tests, he did little. He began to regain his top form in 2007. On his day he can swing the ball alarmingly both ways, and by concentrating on containment rather than attempting to bowl the perfect ball each delivery he proved more consistent. He produced his best Test figures at Trent Bridge in 2008 (7 for 43) against New Zealand but bowled only moderately (12 wickets at 45.16), although playing in all five Tests of the successful 2009 Ashes series. In 2010 he really came into his own, getting his best match figures (11 for 71) against Pakistan, again at Trent Bridge. He bowled wonderfully in the Ashes win in Australia in 2010-11, being the leading wicket-taker with 24 at 26.04. He is an excellent fielder and good tail-end batsman, who batted for 69 minutes at No. 10 to save the first Ashes Test at Cardiff in 2009.

WARWICK ARMSTRONG

Born: 22 MAY 1879, KYNETON, VICTORIA, AUSTRALIA
Died: 13 JULY 1947, DARLING POINT, SYDNEY,
NEW SOUTH WALES, AUSTRALIA
Teams: VICTORIA (1898-99 TO 1921-22)
First-class: 269 MATCHES; 16,158 RUNS,
AVERAGE 46.83; 832 WICKETS,
AVERAGE 19.71
Tests (1901-02 to 1921): 50 MATCHES; 2,863 RUNS,
AVERAGE 38.69; 87 WICKETS, AVERAGE 33.59

Warwick Armstrong was totally professional in his approach to the game. He was born to be a winner, and he showed no mercy to his opponents. He was a giant of a man who became known as "The Big Ship". He was a fine right-handed batsman and a medium-pace bowler who had turned to leg-breaks by 1905. His standing as an all-rounder can be seen from the fact that in three of his four tours of England – 1905, 1909 and 1921 – he completed the "double". In 1905, he scored 1,902 runs and took 122 wickets. His first visit to England had been three years earlier.

He was a mighty force in the Australian side of the Edwardian period, a good stroke-player and a relentlessly accurate bowler, but his relationship with the Australian Board was always strained. He was one of six players who refused to take part in the Triangular Tournament of 1912.

He became captain of Australia when cricket resumed after the First World War and scored three centuries in the 1920-21 series which Australia won 5-0. They followed England back to England and won the first three Tests of the 1921 series at the end of which Armstrong retired.

There were those in authority who had not wanted Armstrong to lead the great 1921 side, but his players never wavered in their loyalty to him. His captaincy was shrewd, forthright, calculating, persistent and even ruthless, and in many ways he bridged the gap between the Golden Age and the ultra-professional approach of today. Ten Tests as captain, eight wins and two draws is a record to be envied.

CURTLY AMBROSE
Late starter, but fast

FIRST-CLASS CAREER
(1985-86 to 2000, 239 matches)
Batting: RUNS 3,448, AVERAGE 13.95;
  HIGHEST SCORE 78, CENTURIES 0
Bowling: WICKETS 941; RUNS 19,048, AVERAGE 20.24;
  BEST 8-45
Catches: 88

TESTS
(1987-88 to 2000, 98 matches)
Batting: RUNS 1,439, AVERAGE 12.40;
  HIGHEST SCORE 53, CENTURIES 0
Bowling: WICKETS 405; RUNS 8,501, AVERAGE 20.99;
  BEST 8-45
Catches: 18

Curtly Ambrose, 6ft 7in tall, was a natural basketball player. It was not until he was 17 that he paid much attention to cricket and then it was only on the beach. In 1985, aged 21, he played for his village team. His performances were such that he graduated almost at once to the Antiguan side and created something of a sensation by taking 7 for 67 in his first game – against St Kitts. That was enough to win a place in the Leewards team and thus make his first-class debut in 1986. In 1987-88, he took 35 wickets, average 15.51 in five matches – a new record. From those statistics it was straight into the West Indies side for the Tests against the touring Pakistan team – he made his debut in April 1988 and played in all three Tests, plus the one-days, being the leading bowler in the latter series. The next leap forward was a place in the West Indies side to England. The trip was a great success. The press noted:

Curtley Ambrose: fast bowler supreme.

"The height of his delivery, the bounce he could generate and his direct method made him a constant menace and earned him 22 Test wickets."

Northants gave Ambrose a contract for 1989 and he was to stay with that county until 1996. On his second trip with the West Indies to England, in 1991, Ambrose topped both Test and first-class bowling tables. Wisden picked him as one of the "Players of the Year".

When Ambrose made his third tour to England in 1995, the constant treadmill of Test cricket was beginning to take its toll. He had missed the November tour to India because of a shoulder injury, but still not fully fit had toured New Zealand in the following January, then came back to the West Indies for a home series v Australia. Tempers were now beginning to fray, but Ambrose topped the bowling table, though the West Indies lost the series. Straight from that defeat the West Indies landed in England. This was not a happy tour: one player was ordered home for disciplinary reasons and others, including Ambrose, were reprimanded. It seemed as if his Test career was ending.

Ambrose, however, thought otherwise – he came back to England for a fourth time in 2000. This he announced would be his finale – it would also be Walsh's last trip to England. It would be appropriate to record that this was a triumphant tour. Ambrose and Walsh topped the Test bowling figures, but the rest of the attack was very feeble and England won the series 3-1. In the final Test at The Oval, the England team formed guards of honour as the pair came on the field. An emotional occasion, but England, who had already clinched the series, strode to another victory.

1963	1986	1988	1989	1997	2000
Born Curtly Elconn Lynwall Ambrose on 21 September 1963, Swetes Village, Antigua	First-class debut on 12 February, in Shell Shield for Leeward Islands v Guyana at Bourda	Test debut 2 April, West Indies v Pakistan at Bourda	Debut for Northamptonshire 20 May, at Swansea	Completes "Double" of 1,000 Test runs and 100 Test wickets, 8 April	Final Test appearance 31 August –4 September, West Indies v England at The Oval

ASIF IQBAL

Born: 6 JUNE 1943, HYDERABAD, INDIA
Teams: HYDERABAD (1959-60); KARACHI (1961-62 TO 1968-69); PIA (1964-65 TO 1979-80); NATIONAL BANK (1976-77); KENT (1968-82)
First-class: 440 MATCHES; 23,329 RUNS, AVERAGE 37.26; 291 WICKETS, AVERAGE 30.15
Tests (1964-65 to 1979-80): 58 MATCHES; 3,575 RUNS, AVERAGE 38.85; 53 WICKETS, AVERAGE 28.33

Asif Iqbal began his career in India, but emigrated to Pakistan in 1961. He made his Test debut three years later, batting at No. 10 and opening the bowling with his medium pace. An exciting batsman, who could adapt his style according to the needs of the moment, he made his first Test century against England at The Oval in 1967, when he went in at No. 9 and scored 146 in 170 minutes, sharing a record stand of 190 with Intikhab Alam.

Asif was a dynamic cricketer with Kent, whom he captained in 1968, and he played a major part in one of the most successful periods in that county's history. Between 1964 and 1977, he appeared in a record 45 consecutive Tests for Pakistan. He then announced his retirement from Test cricket and, a month later, joined Kerry Packer's World Series. He had long pressed for better financial rewards for Pakistani players.

When the differences between Packer and the cricketing authorities were resolved, Asif returned to Test cricket and led Pakistan against India in 1979-80. It was the first time the two nations had met for almost 19 years, and this series marked the end of Asif's career. He has remained in the game, mainly as an entrepreneur involved with Sharjah and as Pakistan's representative on the ICC for a time.

WILLIAM ASTILL

Born: 1 MARCH 1888, RATBY, LEICESTERSHIRE
Died: 10 FEBRUARY 1948, STONEYGATE, LEICESTERSHIRE
Teams: LEICESTERSHIRE (1906-39)
First-class: 733 MATCHES; 22,731 RUNS, AVERAGE 22.55; 2,431 WICKETS, AVERAGE 23.76
Tests (1927-28 to 1929-30): 9 MATCHES; 190 RUNS, AVERAGE 12.66; 25 WICKETS, AVERAGE 34.24

Ewart Astill was one of those great county professionals of the inter-war period whose achievements and abilities were never rewarded to the extent that they deserved. He made his debut in 1906, and he was ever-present in the next two seasons. As the First World War approached he lost form, but when he was demobilized after the war he was better than ever. A reliable middle-order batsman and a slow to medium-pace bowler who could turn the ball either way, he completed the all-rounder's "double" every season from 1921 until 1930 with the exception of 1927.

His consistency was finally rewarded when he was chosen to tour South Africa in 1927-28, and he made his Test debut at the age of 39. Two years later, he went to the West Indies and played in all four Test matches there.

He was a fine slip fielder and had a good cricket brain, and when he became the first professional to captain Leicestershire in 1935, the county enjoyed one of the most successful periods of their history.

Astill was a very good billiards player, an excellent pianist and vocalist and a good ukulele player. He was an accomplished coach and did some fine work in this field.

MIKE ATHERTON

Born: 23 MARCH 1968, MANCHESTER, LANCASHIRE
Teams: CAMBRIDGE UNIVERSITY (1987-89); LANCASHIRE (1987-01)
First-class: 336 MATCHES; 21,929 RUNS, AVERAGE 40.03; 108 WICKETS, AVERAGE 43.82
Tests (1989-01): 115 MATCHES; 7,728 RUNS, AVERAGE 37.69; 2 WICKETS, AVERAGE 151.00

Mike Atherton: nobody has captained England on more occasions.

Michael Atherton was a solid, dependable opening batsman who enjoyed the longest of reigns as England captain. He made his Test debut in the Ashes series of 1989 and proved his worth a year later with Test centuries against India and New Zealand. A back operation and a loss of form against the West Indies and India brought one of the troughs of his career, but he returned in strength for the Ashes series of 1993. He had forged a good opening partnership with Gooch, and he made 80 and 99 in the Lord's Test and 55 and 63 at Headingley. Gooch stood down as captain when the Ashes were lost, and Atherton, 25 years old, succeeded him as captain. England won the last game in the series, their first success for 11 matches.

Although he did well in the Caribbean the following winter, England lost the series 3-1 and were bowled out for 46 in Trinidad. There was victory over New Zealand, but there were problems against South Africa when television cameras spotted him ball-tampering, for which he was censured and fined. There was no success in Australia and his body language did not inspire confidence or optimism, but he led England to victory over India in 1996, only to lose to Pakistan in the second half of the summer.

Attitude and performance in Zimbabwe brought heavy criticism of the England side, but redemption came in New Zealand where Atherton batted well and he was reappointed England captain for the whole of the 1997 summer. He is currently the cricket correspondent of *The Times* as as well as commentating on matches.

Atherton captained England to the West Indies in 1997-98, but resigned after losing the series. He had led England in 52 Tests. He continued as a member of the England team until the close of 2001, when he announced his retirement from top-class cricket. He is now a well-known broadcaster.

MOHAMMAD AZHARUDDIN

Born: 8 FEBRUARY 1963, HYDERABAD, INDIA
Teams: HYDERABAD (1981-82 TO 1999-00); DERBYSHIRE (1991 AND 1994)
First-class: 229 MATCHES; 15,855 RUNS AVERAGE 51.98; 17 WICKETS, AVERAGE 46.23
Tests (1984-85 to 1999-00): 99 MATCHES; 6,215 RUNS, AVERAGE 45.03; NO WICKETS FOR 12 RUNS

Mohammad Azharuddin created a record when he began his Test career with three centuries in successive matches against England in 1984-85. He proved that this was no temporary glory by being the leading run-scorer in England in 1986, as India took the series.

His form lapsed a little, but he reasserted himself with an innings of 199 against Sri Lanka at Kanpur in December 1986. He was named as captain of the side to tour New Zealand in 1989-90, and to England in 1990. He hit hundreds at Lord's and Old Trafford.

Azharuddin became the most successful captain in Indian Test history, but a loss of form and poor results in South Africa, failure in the World Cup and eventually the loss of the series in England in 1996, cost him the leadership. He continued to hold his place in the side, but defeat in the Caribbean, coupled with indisciplined batting and a tumultuous private life, led to his being dropped from the side.

Azharuddin's final Test saw him make the only century in the 1999-2000 series v South Africa. He also led Hyderabad to the Ranji Trophy final. These feats were soon forgotten when the Indian Board of Control banned him from cricket for life in December 2000 for taking money from bookies to fix cricket matches. Thus the career of one of India's greatest batsmen came to an end – he had captained his country in 47 of his 99 Tests.

TREVOR BAILEY

Born: 3 DECEMBER 1923, WESTCLIFF-ON-SEA, ESSEX
Died: 10 FEBRUARY 2011, WESTCLIFF-ON-SEA
Teams: ESSEX (1946-67); CAMBRIDGE UNIVERSITY (1947-48); PRIME MINISTER'S XI, INDIA (1963-64)
First-class: 682 MATCHES; 28,641 RUNS, AVERAGE 33.42; 2,082 WICKETS, AVERAGE 23.13
Tests (1949 to 1958-59): 61 MATCHES; 2,290 RUNS, AVERAGE 29.74; 132 WICKETS, AVERAGE 29.21

The best all-round cricketer to represent England in the post-war period until the arrival of Ian Botham, Trevor Bailey played a mighty role in England's rise from the depths to the recapturing of the Ashes in 1953 and their subsequent eminence in world cricket.

Educated at Dulwich College, he became known to audiences at Lord's during the war before joining the Royal Marines as soon as he left school. He served in Europe, but he was demobilized in time to play for Essex in 1946. He went up to Cambridge the following year and, by 1949, was recognized as a bowler of genuine pace, a most reliable batsman and a brilliant close-to-the-wicket fielder. He was also a talented soccer player who got his blue and won an FA Amateur Cup medal with Walthamstow Avenue.

He had an excellent debut Test series against New Zealand in 1949, and when Hutton took over the captaincy of the England side Bailey was seen as an integral part of the plan to recapture the Ashes. At Lord's in 1953, he batted 257 minutes for 71 and added 163 with Willie Watson. This was one of the great rearguard actions of Test cricket. The partnership saved the match, and Bailey was a national hero. He bowled and batted well to help save the Headingley Test, and in the final victorious Test at The Oval, he hit 64 to complete a memorable series.

He went to the West Indies as Hutton's vice-captain in 1953-54, and had the remarkable bowling figures of 7 for 34 in the first innings in Jamaica, where Hutton made a double-century. Bailey's outstanding Test career continued until 1959, and even after that he continued to give fine service for Essex until 1967, captaining the county from 1955 until 1966. He performed the "double" eight times and is the only man to have scored 2,000 runs and taken 100 wickets in a post-war season, 1959.

Nicknamed "Barnacle" for his adhesive batting qualities in Test cricket, he could score quickly when needed. Since retirement, he became a noted journalist, author and broadcaster. He was a man with a zest for life and a great generosity of spirit.

WARREN BARDSLEY

Born: 6 DECEMBER 1882, NEVERTIRE, WARREN, NEW SOUTH WALES, AUSTRALIA
Died: 20 JANUARY 1954, COLLAROY PLATEAU, BONDI, SYDNEY, NEW SOUTH WALES
Teams: NEW SOUTH WALES (1903-04 TO 1925-26)
First-class: 250 MATCHES; 17,025 RUNS, AVERAGE 49.92; NO WICKETS FOR 41 RUNS
Tests (1909-1926): 41 MATCHES; 2,469 RUNS, AVERAGE 40.47

Warren Bardsley was a stylish left-handed opening batsman of impeccable technique. He toured England four times and reached 2,000 runs on three of those trips.

He made his Test debut in 1909 and, in the fifth test, at The Oval, he scored 136 and 130, so becoming the first batsman to score a century in each innings of a Test match.

He made three hundreds against South Africa, but he was to wait until 1926 for his third and final century against England. He made 193 not out at Lord's which, at the time, was the highest score that had been made in a Lord's Test.

He captained Australia in the next two Tests, at Headingley and Old Trafford, when Herbie Collins was ill.

EDDIE BARLOW

Born: 12 AUGUST 1940, PRETORIA, SOUTH AFRICA
Died: 30 DECEMBER 2005, ST HELIER, JERSEY
Teams: TRANSVAAL (1959-60 TO 1967-68); EASTERN PROVINCE (1964-65 TO 1965-66); WESTERN PROVINCE (1968-69 TO 1980-81); DERBYSHIRE (1976-78); BOLAND (1981-82 TO 1982-83)
First-class: 283 MATCHES; 18,212 RUNS, AVERAGE 39.16; 571 WICKETS, AVERAGE 24.14
Tests (1961-62 to 1969-70): 30 MATCHES; 2,516 RUNS, AVERAGE 45.74; 40 WICKETS, AVERAGE 34.05

Eddie Barlow was a tenacious all-rounder, a right-handed batsman and right-arm medium-pace bowler of strength and determination. He was an integral part of a powerful South African side in the 1960s, but his Test career was cut short as a result of his country's expulsion from international cricket. He had six Test centuries to his credit, including 201 against Australia at Adelaide in 1963-64.

He spent three seasons with Derbyshire, taking over the captaincy midway through the first year. A modest and warm man, he proved a belligerent leader who drove the county to new levels of fitness and attainment.

Barlow became a fine ambassador for his country and for the game. He coached Gloucestershire in 1990 and 1991 before his death in 2005.

Mohammad Azharuddin: made an outstanding start to his Test career.

SYD BARNES

Born: 19 APRIL 1873, SMETHWICK, STAFFORDSHIRE
Died: 26 DECEMBER 1967, CHADSMOOR, STAFFORDSHIRE
Teams: WARWICKSHIRE (1894-96); LANCASHIRE (1899-1903); WALES (1927-30)
First-class: 133 MATCHES; 1,573 RUNS, AVERAGE 12.78; 719 WICKETS, AVERAGE 17.09
Tests (1901-02 to 1913-14): 27 MATCHES; 242 RUNS, AVERAGE 8.06; 189 WICKETS, AVERAGE 16.43

Sydney Barnes played four games for Warwickshire and 46 for Lancashire, but he preferred league cricket to the county game. In spite of this fact, those who saw him and those who played against him considered him the greatest bowler of his time and, in the opinion of many, he remains the greatest bowler the game has known. He bowled at medium pace, was a master of length and of variations in flight and could turn the ball either way. He was able to adapt his bowling to any conditions. Barnes was not an easy man. Gaunt, dark and brooding, he did not suffer fools gladly, and he needed handling carefully. He was virtually unknown when A.C. MacLaren invited him to tour Australia in 1901-02. He took 5 for 65 and 1 for 74 in the first Test and had match figures of 13 for 163 in the second, after which injury hampered his tour. He played one Test against Australia in 1902 taking seven wickets, and thereafter spent most of his time in the leagues, issuing forth only to tour with England when invited.

In Australia in 1911-12, he took 34 wickets, average 22.38, in five Tests. In the Triangular Tournament of 1912, he took 39 wickets, average 10.3, and in South Africa, 1913-14, he took 49 wickets, average 10.93, in four Tests, which remains a world record. That marked the end of his Test career. After the First World War he confined himself to the leagues and to the Minor Counties with Staffordshire, for whom he played until 1935 when he was 62 years old. He is said to have taken all ten wickets in an innings seven times and to have taken 6,229 wickets, average 8.33, in competitive matches in his long career.

KEN BARRINGTON

Born: 24 NOVEMBER 1930, READING, BERKSHIRE
Died: 14 MARCH 1981, NEEDHAM'S POINT, BARBADOS
Teams: SURREY (1953-68)
First-class: 533 MATCHES; 31,714 RUNS, AVERAGE 45.63; 273 WICKETS, AVERAGE 32.62
Tests (1955-68): 82 MATCHES; 6,806 RUNS, AVERAGE 58.67; 29 WICKETS, AVERAGE 44.82

Stocky, with a pronounced nose and chin which suggested defiance, Ken Barrington was a very sound middle-order batsman, a rock on which England so often depended. He had to fight his way into a strong Surrey side, but in two years he was in the England side – 1955, the same year in which he was capped. He made 0 against South Africa on his debut, but he was to make amends for this with 20 Test centuries, the first nine of them abroad. His first in England was his highest, 256 against Australia at Old Trafford in 1964, when he and Dexter put on 246 for the third wicket.

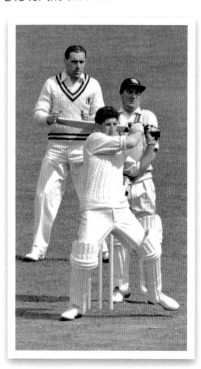

Ken Barrington: a rock for England.

Barrington was a very difficult batsman to dislodge, and he proved the bane of Pakistan in 1967 when he hit centuries in three successive Tests. He played his last Test against Australia at Headingly in 1968.

The following winter, playing in a double-wicket tournament in Australia, he suffered a mild heart attack and was forced to retire. He became a selector and managed England touring sides. He was assistant manager and coach to the England side in the Caribbean in 1981, when he died suddenly of a heart attack in the middle of a Test match. A most popular man, he is much missed.

BISHEN BEDI

Born: 25 SEPTEMBER 1946, AMRITSAR, INDIA
Teams: NORTHERN PUNJAB (1961-62 TO 1966-67); DELHI (1968-69 TO 1980-81); NORTHAMPTONSHIRE (1972-77)
First-class: 370 MATCHES; 3,584 RUNS, AVERAGE 11.37; 1,560 WICKETS, AVERAGE 21.69
Tests (1966-67 to 1979): 67 MATCHES; 656 RUNS, AVERAGE 8.98; 266 WICKETS, AVERAGE 28.71

A slow left-arm bowler whose action was an aesthetic delight, Bishen Bedi was a most popular cricketer whose brightly coloured patkas became a feature of Test cricket and of the English county scene for several years. He was only 15 when he first played in the Ranji Trophy, and his Test debut came against the West Indies in Calcutta, December 1966. His Test career ended with the last match in the 1979 series in England.

Surprisingly, he was not very successful in Tests in England although he enjoyed triumphs with Northamptonshire, whom he captained with flair. He also led India in 22 Tests, but he was outspoken and never far from controversy, being banned once for giving an unauthorized television interview and leading a move for improved payments.

He twice took 25 wickets in a series against England in India and took 21 wickets in Australia in 1969-70. Since his retirement he has managed Indian sides.

ALEC BEDSER

Born: 4 JULY 1918, READING, BERKSHIRE
Died: 4 APRIL 2010, WOKING
Teams: SURREY (1939-60)
First-class: 485 MATCHES; 5,735 RUNS, AVERAGE 14.51; 1,924 WICKETS, AVERAGE 20.41
Tests (1946-55): 51 matches; 714 runs, AVERAGE 12.75; 236 WICKETS, AVERAGE 24.89

Alec Bedser played a handful of matches for Surrey in 1939, and then saw the early years of his career consumed by the war. He and his identical twin brother Eric were on the beaches at Dunkirk but, in the closing year of the war, Alec Bedser came into prominence in matches at Lord's. He was a truly great right-arm medium-fast bowler with a model action and an economic run to the wicket. A very strong man, he gave the impression that he could bowl all day and sometimes did. In the years immediately after the Second World War, he carried the England attack on his broad shoulders. He began his Test career with 7 for 49 and 4 for 96 against India at Lord's in 1946, and followed with another 11 wickets at Old Trafford. In Australia, the following winter, he gained the respect of Bradman's men, but he was forced to plough a lonely furrow.

It was in 1953 that he finally gained the reward for his years of endeavour. When England regained the Ashes, Bedser was one of the heroes of the hour, claiming a record 39 wickets in five Tests. That outstanding achievement was almost the end of his Test career, for when he went to Australia with Hutton's side in 1954-55, he had an attack of shingles and lost his place in the side after the first Test. He played his last Test against South Africa at Old Trafford in 1955. He took four wickets which brought his total to 236, at the time a record for Test cricket.

He was a major force in Surrey's run of seven consecutive championships, and he led the side on occasions. He was an England selector for over 20 years and was first awarded the OBE and then knighted for his services to cricket.

IAN BELL

Born: 11 APRIL 1982, WALSGRAVE, COVENTRY, WARWICKSHIRE
Teams: WARWICKSHIRE (1999-2010)
First-class: 180 MATCHES, 12,277, AVERAGE 45.13; 47 WICKETS, AVERAGE 33.27
Tests (2004 to 2010-11): 62 MATCHES, 4,192 RUNS, AVERAGE 44.12; 1 WICKET, AVERAGE 76.00S

Bell was an elegant and outstanding batsman in his days at Princethorpe College, Rugby, making his first-class debut in 1999 and soon captaining the England Under-19 team. He averaged 64.30 in scoring 836 runs for Warwickshire in 2001, while still not yet 20 years old. That winter he joined the England party in New Zealand when Mark Butcher was injured. He impressed Rod Marsh, then coaching for the England academy, as a future Test batsman. He made his Test debut in the final Test against the West Indies in 2004, when he scored 70 in his only innings at The Oval. A maiden Test century came against Bangladesh at Chester-le-Street the following season, when through not-outs his Test average briefly reached 279.

He failed against Australia, but then hit three centuries in successive Tests in Pakistan. However, he developed a worrying habit of scoring 40 or 50 masterly runs then getting out, as if his elegance had become casualness. A Test century in New Zealand, and 199 against South Africa at Lord's in 2008 (the first English player to be out for 199 in a Test) did not altogether erase this impression, however he played a major part in the 2010-11 Ashes success, averaging 65.80.

RICHIE BENAUD

Born: 6 OCTOBER 1930, PENRITH, NEW SOUTH WALES, AUSTRALIA
Teams: NEW SOUTH WALES (1948-49 TO 1963-64)
First-class: 259 MATCHES, 11,719, AVERAGE 36.50; 945 WICKETS, AVERAGE 24.73
Tests (1951-52 to 1963-64): 63 MATCHES, 2,201 RUNS, AVERAGE 24.45; 248 WICKETS, AVERAGE 27.03

Richie Benaud has argued that he would not have won a place in the Australian side had he not learned how to bat. He was an exciting batsman, but he was an even greater leg-break bowler, and he was a captain who must rank alongside Bradman and Armstrong as Australia's greatest. He, more than any other man, lifted Australian cricket from a period of tedium and gloom to a position of supremacy.

He made his Test debut against the West Indies in 1951-52, and played four Tests against South Africa the following season. He toured England in 1953 and made little impact, but he was an astute cricketer and learned much. He was in the side that was shattered by Tyson and Statham in 1954-55, but he played a major part in Australia's revival weeks later when they won three Tests in the Caribbean. In the fifth match, at Sabina Park, he reached a maiden Test century in 78 minutes.

In 1956, he hit 97 at Lord's and when Australia went to India he took 7 for 72 in Madras to set up his side's victory. He followed this with 11 wickets in the win in Calcutta. A year later, he dominated the series in South Africa with two centuries and 30 wickets.

He succeeded Craig as captain of Australia and immediately won back the Ashes (1958-59), found success in India and was victorious in a thrilling series against Worrell's West Indians.

In 1961, he was troubled by an injured shoulder, yet his Australian side retained the Ashes when, at Old Trafford, Benaud himself put in a remarkable spell of bowling on the last afternoon to take 6 for 70 and win the match. When he departed from Test cricket, he could claim that he had led Australia in six Test series of which five were won and one drawn. His contribution as both player and captain had been incalculable.

He worked to establish Kerry Packer's World Series and became a journalist and commentator. His wit, charm, lucidity and deep knowledge of the game have made him an outstanding personality.

COLIN BLYTHE

Born: 30 MAY 1879, DEPTFORD, KENT
Died: 8 NOVEMBER 1917, PASSCHENDAELE, BELGIUM
Teams: KENT (1899-1914)
First-class: 439 MATCHES; 4,443 RUNS, AVERAGE 9.87; 2,503 WICKETS, AVERAGE 16.81
Tests (1901-02 TO 1909-10): 19 MATCHES; 183 RUNS, AVERAGE 9.63; 100 WICKETS, AVERAGE 18.63

"Charlie" Blythe was one of the two great left-arm spinners of the Edwardian period, the other being Wilfred Rhodes. Blythe was rhythmic and graceful, a master of flight. He was a most intelligent bowler who made full use of his height. In 14 of his 15 full seasons in first-class cricket, he captured 100 wickets, and it is likely that he would have played more for England had he not been subject to epileptic fits.

Artistic (he played the violin) and highly strung, he had match figures of 7 for 56 on his Test debut against Australia in 1901-02, and he was second only to Barnes among England bowlers for the series. He enjoyed a fine tour of South Africa in 1905-06, taking 11 for 118 in Cape Town when England won their only match of the rubber. He had even greater success in 1907, when he took 8 for 59 and 7 for 40 against South Africa at Headingley, so becoming the only bowler to take 15 South African wickets in a Test in England.

He was at the height of his powers in 1914 and had played in four championship-winning sides, when war broke out and he enlisted. He was killed in action in 1917.

DAVID BOON

Born: 29 DECEMBER 1960, LAUNCESTON, TASMANIA
Teams: TASMANIA (1978-79 TO 1998-99), DURHAM (1997-99)
First-class: 350 MATCHES; 23,473, AVERAGE 44.00; 14 WICKETS, AVERAGE 49.71
Tests (1984-85 to 1995-96): 107 MATCHES; 7,422 RUNS, AVERAGE 43,65; NO WICKETS FOR 14 RUNS

Short, compact and strong, David Boon possessed a rock-like defence, but he also had a wide range of shots, specializing in a vicious square-cut. He played three Tests against the West Indies in 1984-85, and three on the tour of England a few months later, but it was not until he moved up to open the innings against India, in 1985-86, that he recorded his first Test century. His partnership with Geoff Marsh became renowned, but when Mark Taylor came into the side Boon reverted to No. 3 with equal success.

At first a slip fielder, he became a most capable short-leg, brave, reliable and most agile for a heavy man. He hit 200 against New Zealand at Perth in 1989-90, and runs flowed from him in every series. He was a foundation on which Australia built their success in the late 1980s and early 1990s. He announced his retirement from Test cricket before the World Cup in 1996, and scored a century against Sri Lanka in his penultimate appearance. It was his 21st Test hundred.

Boon captained Durham for three seasons 1997 to 1999, and Tasmania from 1992-93 to 1998-99, retiring from first-class cricket at the end of 1999. He was awarded an MBE for his services to cricket.

ALLAN BORDER

SEE PAGE 171

BERNARD BOSANQUET

Born: 13 OCTOBER 1877, BULLS CROSS, ENFIELD, MIDDLESEX
Died: 12 OCTOBER 1936, WYKEHURST, EWHURST, SURREY
Teams: OXFORD UNIVERSITY (1898-1900); MIDDLESEX (1898-1919)
First-class: 235 MATCHES; 11,696 RUNS, AVERAGE 33.41; 629 WICKETS, AVERAGE 23.80
Tests (1903-04 to 1905): 7 MATCHES; 147 RUNS, AVERAGE 13.36; 25 WICKETS, AVERAGE 24.16

A tall, upstanding right-handed batsman who won his blue all three years at Oxford, Bosanquet was originally a medium-pace bowler. He played four Tests in Australia in 1903-04 and three against Australia in England in 1905. It was in the first of these Tests in England, at Trent Bridge, that Bosanquet took 8 for 107 in the second innings and won the match. It is not as a player, however, that Bosanquet is best remembered, but as the perfecter of the googly, the off-break with the leg-break action – a delivery that is still known as the "Bosie" in Australia after its inventor.

Bosanquet developed the googly by playing billiards fives or "twisty grab". In the early part of the 20th century, it was feared that the googly would ruin the game, but it simply brought more mystery and vitality to it.

Bosanquet declined as a bowler after 1905, but advanced as a batsman and headed the national averages in 1908 when he hit 214 in 195 minutes for the Rest of England against the Champion County. He was an accomplished billiards player, ice hockey player and hammer thrower. He was father of the late Reginald Bosanquet, the television news reader.

IAN BOTHAM

SEE PAGE 172

GEOFF BOYCOTT

SEE PAGE 175

DONALD BRADMAN

SEE PAGE 176

JOHNNY BRIGGS

Born: 3 OCTOBER 1862, SUTTON-IN-ASHFIELD, NOTTINGHAMSHIRE
Died: 11 JANUARY 1902, HEALD GREEN, CHEADLE, CHESHIRE
Teams: LANCASHIRE (1879-1900)
First-class: 535 MATCHES; 14,092 RUNS, AVERAGE 18.27; 2,221 WICKETS, AVERAGE 15.95
Tests (1884-85 to 1899): 33 MATCHES; 815 RUNS, AVERAGE 18.11; 118 WICKETS, AVERAGE 17.75

Short, cheerful and immensely popular, Johnny Briggs made his first-class debut at the age of 16. He was a right-handed batsman and a fine fielder, but he developed into a slow left-arm bowler, although it was not until 1886 that he was truly recognized in that capacity.

In 1888-89, in South Africa, he took 21 wickets in two Tests, and his 15 for 28 at Cape Town constituted a record for one day in Test cricket as did his 8 for 11, all bowled, in the second innings.

He had both a century and a hat-trick for England against Australia and was wonderfully consistent. At Headingley in 1899, he took 3 for 53 on the first day against Australia. That evening he had a violent epileptic fit and played no more cricket until the next season when he seems to have been as good as ever. He suffered another violent attack, however, and was confined to Cheadle Asylum, where he died at the age of 39.

STUART BROAD

Born: 24 JUNE 1986, NOTTINGHAM
Teams: LEICESTERSHIRE (2005-07); NOTTINGHAMSHIRE (2008-10)
First-class: 77 MATCHES; 1,959 RUNS, AVERAGE 25.11; 261 WICKETS, AVERAGE 29.32
Tests (2007-08 to 2010-11): 34 MATCHES; 1,096 RUNS, AVERAGE 27.40; 99 WICKETS, AVERAGE 35.24

The son of former England Test opener Chris Broad, Stuart Broad's reputation grew as quickly as his height – he is 6ft 5in. Beginning as an opening batsman, his height helped him become a very good right-arm fast-medium Test bowler, and with his batting skills he is considered now an all-rounder. He made his first-class debut for Leicestershire while still a teenager, and was immediately sent out as a replacement to the England A team in the West Indies, making his debut for England A in 2006. Injury delayed his full Test debut, which came in December 2007 against Sri Lanka at Colombo. He then performed well in New Zealand, and in the Ashes-recovering series in 2009 topped the England bowlers with 18 wickets at 30.22, and also contributed 234 runs (av 29.25). He did well in South Africa, his 4 for 43 in the second innings at Durban helping England win in a tied series. His batting was to the fore against Pakistan in 2010, where at Lord's he joined Trott with the score 102 for 7, and hit 169 while they added 332 runs, a record eighth-wicket Test stand, while his 169 was the second highest in Tests by a No. 9 batsman. Injury forced him home after two Tests in Australia in 2010-11, and again after he'd impressed in the World Cup 2011.

SHIV CHANDERPAUL

Born: 16 AUGUST 1974, UNITY VILLAGE, GUYANA
Teams: GUYANA (1991-92 TO 2009-10), DURHAM (2007-09, LANCASHIRE 2010)
First-class: 264 MATCHES; 19,101 RUNS, AVERAGE 54.26; 56 WICKETS, AVERAGE 43.80
Tests (1993-94 to 2010-11): 129 MATCHES; 9,063 RUNS, AVERAGE 48.98; 8 WICKETS, AVERAGE 105.62

A left-hand batsman, Chanderpaul is in style a total contrast to his predecessor as West Indian captain, Brian Lara. Not for Chanderpaul the panache of the great record breaker; he is much more circumspect, scoring his runs methodically. Although he made his Test debut in Test matches v England on his home patch in Georgetown in March 1994, he was picked more for his leg-breaks than his batting – in fact he hit a competent 62 and failed to take a wicket and retained his place for

Shivnarine Chanderpaul: serial run-getter.

the rest of the series, ending with an average of 57.60.

In 1995-96, Chanderpaul hit 303 for Guyana v Jamaica – the first triple-hundred in West Indian regional cricket for nearly 50 years. He had serious problems with a floating bone in his foot, but after this was taken out in 2000, his run-getting resumed and, in 2001-02, he scored three hundreds in the four Tests v India. His tours to Australia and South Africa were also successes, though he fared poorly against England in 2003-04. Owing to disputes over players' contracts, he found himself appointed West Indies captain, but resigned from the post after about a year in April 2006. He played for Durham in 2007-09, joining the county after averaging 148.66 against England in the 2007 series.

ALLAN BORDER
Reluctant captain

FIRST-CLASS CAREER
(1976-77 to 1995-96, 385 matches)
Batting: RUNS 27,131, AVERAGE 51.38;
HIGHEST SCORE 205; CENTURIES 70
Bowling: WICKETS 106; RUNS 4,161; AVERAGE 39.25;
BEST 7-46
Catches: 379

TESTS
(1978-79 to 1993-94, 156 matches)
Batting: RUNS 11,174, AVERAGE 50.56;
HIGHEST SCORE 200 NOT OUT; CENTURIES 27
Bowling: WICKETS 39; RUNS 1,525; AVERAGE 39.10;
BEST 7-46
Catches: 156

Allan Border: the great Sir Len Hutton tipped him for greatness.

Described by no less a person than Sir Len Hutton as the best left-hand batsman in the world, Allan Border had then, in 1987, scored a mere 2,593 Test match runs. Hutton was not a bad judge. A decade or so later, Border ended his international career with a record 11,174 runs to his name and had created another record by captaining Australia in 93 consecutive matches.

Brought up in a harbourside suburb of Sydney, Border was educated at North Sydney Boys' High, which had a reputation for producing Test cricketers. Coached by the former England all-rounder Barry Knight, he got his first opportunity in the Sheffield Shield side for New South Wales in January 1977 when several senior players were on Test duty. Paying his own air fare to England in 1977, he was fortunate to be asked to play for Gloucestershire Second XI, which stood him in good stead for the 1977-78 Australia season. The

fact that Kerry Packer siphoned off the cream of Australia for his World Series matches, left an opening for Border in the depleted Australian Test side of 1978-79. Border grabbed his chance, topping the Test batting averages for the series v England and thus making certain of a place in the Australian 1979 team to England for the World Cup.

After the Packer episode ended, he retained his place in the Test side and came to England for the 1981 Ashes series – Australia lost 3-1, but Border,

quick on his feet and possessed of a sound technique added to great determination, finished the series with 533 runs, at an average of 59.22 - the best by a long distance in terms of average and run aggregate.

Border had also secured his financial future in the game by accepting a lucrative deal to move from Sydney to Brisbane, his stint with Queensland beginning in 1980-81 – it continued until he retired. When Australia toured the West Indies in 1983-84, Border was vice-

captain to Kim Hughes. Facing the formidable West Indies fast attack, the Australians, save for Border, were humiliated. In 1984-85, the West Indies visited Australia. After the first two Tests, Hughes was to resign and Border, rather reluctantly, took on the leadership.

It was not a post he appeared to relish, but he studied the problems, literally grew into the job and became as successful a captain as he was a batsman. He was thus in charge when Australia toured England in 1985 – he batted quite brilliantly, but even his qualities could not hide the inadequacies of his colleagues and England won the series 3-1. Australia's strengths were not helped by the fact that an Australian "rebel" side had toured South Africa and its members were banned from "official" Tests. When England went Down Under in 1986-87, England once more came out on top, this time 2-1.

Border's record as captain was not impressive but, in 1989, on the next Ashes rubber – up to then his Australians had won only one series out of eight - the tide turned. Australia won four Tests, England none. This success was just the beginning and Border beat England again in 1990-91 and again in 1993, both times by emphatic margins. He finally retired after the Australia v South Africa series of 1993-94 in South Africa.

1955	1977	1978	1984	1989	1994
Born Allan Robert Border on 27 July, Cremorne, New South Wales	First-class debut on 13 January for New South Wales v Queensland at Brisbane	Test debut on 29 December for Australia v England at Melbourne	First Test as Australia's captain, on 7 December, Australia v West Indies at Adelaide	Captained Australia when the Ashes regained at Old Trafford the first captain to win back the trophy in England	Played in his final Test for Australia v South Africa in Durban ending on 29 March

IAN BOTHAM
Beefy to the Rescue

FIRST-CLASS CAREER
(1974 to 1993, 402 matches)
Batting: RUNS 19,399, AVERAGE 33.97;
HIGHEST SCORE 228; CENTURIES 38
Bowling: WICKETS 1,172; RUNS 31,902; AVERAGE 27.22;
BEST 8-34
Catches: 354

TESTS
(1977 to 1992, 102 matches)
Batting: RUNS 5,200, AVERAGE 33.54;
HIGHEST SCORE 208; CENTURIES 14
Bowling: WICKETS 383; RUNS 10,878;
AVERAGE 28.40; BEST 8-34
Catches: 120

After making his debut for Somerset in 1974, it wasn't long before Botham was England's best all-rounder – an aggressive batsman, a fine swing bowler and a brilliant and charismatic fielder. He made his Test debut against the Australians at Trent Bridge in 1977 and claimed five wickets in the Australian first innings.

In the winter, he scored his first Test century, against New Zealand (and also took eight wickets in the match). By the following summer he was England's star when he hit two centuries against Pakistan and achieved his best-ever bowling performance, 8 for 34.

Over a quarter of Botham's first-class matches were Tests, well over a quarter of his total runs were made in Tests, and practically a third of his total wickets were taken in Tests. The Test match arena became his natural habitat. In 1979, he passed 1,000 Test runs and 100 Test wickets in his 21st Test, two fewer than the previous quickest (Mankad), and in 1979–80, in India's Golden Jubilee Test in Bombay, he became the first to score a century and take ten wickets in a Test (114 and 13 for 106).

Botham became captain of England in 1980, but this proved the only area in which he failed. His form suffered and, after the second Test against Australia in 1981, he resigned the captaincy.

In answer, at Headingley in the next match, Botham produced one of the greatest all-round performances ever.

Ian Botham: a player who could make things happen

Having taken 6 for 95 and scored 50 in the first innings, he went out to bat with England, following on, 105 for 5 in the second innings. Later, at 135 for 7 England still required 92 to avoid an innings defeat, with bookmakers quoting a victory at 500-1. In a heroic display of hitting, Botham smashed 149 not out and, with Bob Willis inspired to his best-ever bowling, helped dismiss Australia for 111 and give England an 18-run victory.

At Edgbaston in the next Test, Botham claimed 5 for 1 to finish off the Aussies and give England a 29-run win, and then a magnificent 118 at Old Trafford gave England a third consecutive win. He went on to become the third, and youngest, to reach 2,000 Test runs and 200 Test wickets. Then, in 1984, he became the first-ever Test player to reach 3,000 runs and 300 wickets. In 1986, Botham became the leading wicket-taker in Test history when he passed Dennis Lillee's 355.

Throughout his career, Botham made his own rules and was the centre of much controversy.

In retirement, there have been well-publicized walks for charity, and much successful television work. In 2007 Botham received a knighthood.

1955
Born Ian Terence Botham, 24 November at Oldfield, Heswell, Cheshire

1974
Made career-defining debut for Somerset, hitting winning boundary after having four teeth knocked out in Benson & Hedges quarter-final at Taunton on 12 June

1977
Made Test debut v Australia, Trent Bridge, 28 July to 2 August. First victim Greg Chappell in first-innings 5 for 74

1979
Reached 1,000 runs and 100 wickets in a record 21 Tests, v India at The Oval, 30 August to 4 September

1980
Took 13 wickets and scored 114 in India's Golden Jubilee Test at Bombay on 15-19 February, the first to score a century and take ten wickets in a Test

1981
Scored 50 and 149 not out and took seven wickets to win Ashes Test after England had been 500-1 against, 16-21 July, at Headingley

1986
Overtook Dennis Lillee's total of 355 to become the leading wicket-taker in Test matches, v New Zealand at The Oval, 21-26 August

1992
Plays last Test for England, v Pakistan at Lord's, 18-21 June

1993
Retires from first-class cricket and starts media career

BHAGWAT CHANDRASEKHAR

Born: 17 MAY 1945, MYSORE, INDIA
Teams: KARNATAKA (1963-64 TO 1979-80)
First-class: 246 MATCHES; 600 RUNS, AVERAGE 4.61; 1,063 WICKETS, AVERAGE 24.03
Tests (1963-64 TO 1979): 58 MATCHES; 167 RUNS, AVERAGE 4.07; 242 WICKETS, AVERAGE 29.74

Chandrasekhar bowled his leg-breaks at a brisk pace and he proved a match-winner in Test cricket when leg-break bowling seemed to be a dying art. He made an immediate impression when he made his Test debut against England in 1963-64, and he bowled India to victory over Australia in Bombay a year later. By 1966-67, he was one of a trio of spinners who began to make India a formidable force in world cricket, and he took 18 wickets in three Tests against the West Indies. He bowled well in England in 1967, but the home side won the series. Four years later, he took 6 for 38 in the second innings at The Oval, and India beat England in England for the first time. His 8 for 72 in the first innings at Delhi in 1972-73, was still unable to prevent

England winning by six wickets, but he ended the rubber with a record 35 wickets and India took the series. He also bowled India to victory over Australia in Australia for the first time in 1977-78, taking 12 for 104 in the match and claiming his 200th Test wicket in the process. Thereafter he was handicapped by injury and lost form. He played his last Test in England in 1979 and retired the following year.

GREG CHAPPELL

Born: 7 AUGUST 1948, UNLEY, ADELAIDE, SOUTH AUSTRALIA
Teams: SOUTH AUSTRALIA (1966-67 TO 1972-73); SOMERSET (1968-69); QUEENSLAND (1973-74 TO 1983-84)
First-class: 321 MATCHES; 24,535 RUNS, AVERAGE 52.20; 291 WICKETS, AVERAGE 29.95
Tests (1970-71 TO 1983-84): 87 MATCHES; 7,110 RUNS, AVERAGE 53.86; 47 WICKETS, AVERAGE 40.70

Grandson of one Test captain, Victor Richardson, and brother of another, Ian, Greg Chappell was a tall, slim, elegant batsman who sharpened his technique with Somerset, hit the first century in the Sunday League and 18 months later, scored a hundred

on his Test debut against England in Perth. Now an integral part of the Australian side and of his brother's plans to revive Australian cricket, he hit centuries at Lord's and The Oval in the 1972 Ashes series and made 247 not out against New Zealand at Wellington in 1973-74. He also made 133 in the second innings.

His brother groomed him to take over as captain of Australia, and in his first Test as captain, against the West Indies at Brisbane in 1975-76, he created a record by scoring a century in each innings. In 1972, he and Ian had provided the first instance of brothers scoring centuries in the same innings of a Test, against England at The Oval.

The Packer affair sapped the strength of the Australian side in 1977 but, when it was resolved, Greg Chappell was reinstated as captain, leading Australia for the last time against Sri Lanka in 1983. He seemed to select when he would play and this attitude, and his notorious tactics in a one-day international against New Zealand – when he told his brother Trevor to bowl under-arm, brought him much criticism, but he had a

dignified air and a desire to win, and he was a fine cricketer.

IAN CHAPPELL

Born: 26 SEPTEMBER 1943, UNLEY, ADELAIDE, SOUTH AUSTRALIA
Teams: SOUTH AUSTRALIA (1961-62 TO 1979-80); LANCASHIRE (1963)
First-class: 262 MATCHES; 19,680 RUNS, AVERAGE 48.35; 176 WICKETS, AVERAGE 37.57
Tests (1964-65 TO 1979-80): 75 MATCHES; 5,345 RUNS, AVERAGE 42.42; 20 WICKETS, AVERAGE 65.80

The eldest of three brothers, all of whom played for Australia, Ian Chappell was a determined, gritty batsman, a brilliant slip fielder and an occasional leg-break bowler. Greg, too, turned to leg-breaks with some success after beginning as a medium-pacer. Ian made his Test debut against Pakistan in 1964, but he did not win a regular place in the Australian side until three years later. His first Test hundred came against India in 1967-68, and he did well in England the following summer. This was a low period in Australian cricket history, however, and when Illingworth's side got the upper hand in Australia in 1970-71, Lawry was dropped for the last Test and Ian Chappell appointed as captain.

He immediately set about reshaping the Australian side, and they became a formidable, ruthless team. In 1972, he and his brother Greg scored centuries in the last Test at The Oval to win the match and draw the series against England. Wins over Pakistan, the West Indies and, in 1975, England followed. Ian Chappell then handed over the captaincy to Greg, while he himself set about establishing Packer's World Series, and in all that followed he proved a very tough negotiator.

His success as a batsman and captain are undeniable, but he was abrasive to opponents and authority. His colourful language and tendency to run his side as a self-contained unit answerable to no one did cause controversy.

Greg Chappell: from a family of Australian captains and a very stylish batsman.

MICHAEL CLARKE

Born: 2 APRIL 1981, LIVERPOOL, NEW SOUTH WALES
Teams: NEW SOUTH WALES (1999 TO 2010-11); HAMPSHIRE (2004)
First-class: 129 MATCHES; 8,922 RUNS, AVERAGE 44.61; 32 WICKETS, AVERAGE 47.18
Tests (2004-05 to 2010-11): 69 MATCHES; 4,742 RUNS, AVERAGE 46.49; 21 WICKETS, AVERAGE 39.14

Michael Clarke, batting at No. 6, hit an astonishing 151 on his Australian Test debut v India in Bangalore in October 2004. That was the first Test of the series; in the third game at Nagpur he hit 91 and 73. Pretty impressive for the 23-year-old, but then in the final Test, when Shane Warne was injured on the eve of the game, Clarke's slow left-arm spin was called in and he captured six wickets for only nine runs, India plunging from 153 for 3 to 205 all out. Clarke, the debutant, topped both Australia's batting and bowling averages for the Test series. It can also be added that his catching and fielding throughout were of the highest order. His attacking batsmanship made an immediate impact in one-day internationals, since he hit 208 runs before being dismissed for the first time at that level.

Clarke's best innings of the 2005 Ashes series was 91 at Lord's, the highest innings by anyone in the game. In the 2006-07 Ashes series he hit 389 runs, average 77.80, including centuries at both Adelaide and Perth. When Ricky Ponting has been absent injured or rested, Clarke has taken over as captain of Australia. He had a poor return in the 2010-11 Ashes, averaging 21.44.

BRIAN CLOSE

Born: 24 FEBRUARY 1931, RAWDON, LEEDS, YORKSHIRE
Teams: YORKSHIRE (1949-70); SOMERSET (1971-77)
First-class: 786 MATCHES; 34,994 RUNS, AVERAGE 33.26; 1,171 WICKETS, AVERAGE 26.42
Tests (1949-76): 22 MATCHES; 887 RUNS, AVERAGE 25.34; 18 WICKETS, AVERAGE 29.55

Brian Close did the "double" in his first season in first-class cricket and played for England against New Zealand. He was a left-handed batsman who suited his mood to the occasion, a medium-pace or off-break bowler and a brave and brilliant close-to-the-wicket fielder. He was the youngest to gain a Yorkshire cap, but never quite lived up to that early promise, and his 22 Test caps were spread over a period of 27 years.

He was something of a cricketing eccentric, who was very popular with his players, and he captained Yorkshire from 1963 to 1970. With England outplayed by the West Indies, Close was appointed captain for the last Test in 1966, and England won. Honest, brave and an astute tactician, he led England to more successes over India and Pakistan, but the tactics he adopted in a county match against Warwickshire caused an outcry, and his invitation to lead England in the Caribbean was withdrawn. At Tony Greig's insistence, he was recalled to the England side in 1976 at the age of 45 because he was such a tough fighter.

A brush with the Yorkshire committee caused him to move to Somerset whom he captained from 1972 until his retirement. He led England seven times, and won six and drew one of the matches in which he was captain.

DENIS COMPTON

Born: 23 MAY 1918, HENDON, MIDDLESEX
Died: 23 APRIL 1997, WINDSOR, BERKSHIRE
Teams: MIDDLESEX (1936-58); HOLKAR (1944-45); EUROPEANS (1944-45 TO 1945-46)
First-class: 515 MATCHES; 38,942 RUNS, AVERAGE 51.85; 622 WICKETS, AVERAGE 32.27
Tests (1937 TO 1956-57): 78 MATCHES; 5,807 RUNS, AVERAGE 50.06; 25 WICKETS, AVERAGE 56.40

In the entire history of cricket, no player gave more pleasure or entertained a crowd more fully than Denis Compton. By any standards he was a pure genius, and his delight in what he was doing, his passion for the game, was as transparent as it was infectious. The sun always seemed to shine when he played cricket. He was first picked for Middlesex as a slow left-arm bowler and was effective, if eccentric, in this area to the end of his career. He batted No. 11 in his first match, but within weeks he was No. 4, and he completed 1,000 runs by the end of the season, a feat he accomplished 14 times in England and three times overseas. The following season, he was in the England side against New Zealand at The Oval (run out 65), and he scored a century in his first Test against Australia in 1938. He was unable to tour at this time, because he was under contract to Arsenal FC, winning an FA Cup-winners' medal in 1950, a League Championship medal in 1948 and being capped for England in wartime internationals.

He went to Australia in 1946-47, and scored a century in each innings of the Adelaide Test. The following summer he broke all records. He made 3,816 runs, average 90.85, and hit 18 centuries. It seems likely that these records will never be beaten.

In five Tests against the South Africans, he hit 753 runs, average 94.12. That season he also took 73 wickets in all first-class matches.

In 1948, against the might of Bradman's Australians, he hit 184 at Trent Bridge and an unbeaten 145 at Old Trafford, after he had been forced to retire hurt early in his innings. In South Africa in 1948-49, he hit 300 in 181 minutes for MCC against NE Transvaal. It remains the fastest triple-century ever recorded. By now, he was being troubled by an old knee injury sustained while playing football. It was to prove a severe handicap and was to shorten his career. He had a kneecap removed, scored 278 against Pakistan in 1954 and, two years later, hit 94 in his last Test against Australia at The Oval.

He worked as a PR consultant and as a journalist and continued to charm all who met him. His one piece of advice to young cricketers was: "Enjoy it. It is over all too soon."

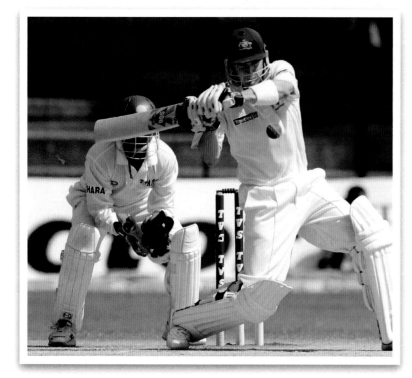

Michael Clarke, an outstanding all-rounder.

GEOFFREY BOYCOTT
Dedicated run-gatherer

FIRST-CLASS CAREER
(1962 to 1986, 609 matches)
Batting: RUNS 48,426; AVERAGE 56.83;
HIGHEST SCORE 261 NOT OUT;
CENTURIES 151
Bowling: WICKETS 45; RUNS 1,459;
AVERAGE 32.42; BEST 4-14
Catches: 264

TESTS
(1964 to 1981-82, 108 matches)
Batting: RUNS 8,114; AVERAGE 47.72;
HIGHEST SCORE 246 NOT OUT;
CENTURIES 22
Bowling: WICKETS 7; RUNS 382;
AVERAGE 54.57; BEST 3-47
Catches: 33

Geoffrey Boycott was one of the greatest opening batsmen that the game has known. He dedicated his life to the art of batting, practising assiduously and eschewing any shot that might even hint at threatening the loss of his wicket. Boycott demonstrated outstanding ability from his earliest years and joined Ackworth C.C. at the age of ten. In 1961, he had a regular place in the Yorkshire team – he topped that season's batting table. His first-class debut for Yorkshire came v Pakistan in 1962. After a century in the 1963 Whitsun Roses match, he had become a permanent member of the side.

His success that year was quite astonishing – he ended second in the national first-class batting averages, 1,628 runs, average 45.22. Boycott's Test debut came in the initial match of the 1964 Ashes series. Once more he was quite remarkable; only Ken Barrington had a better Test batting average that summer and Boycott was picked as one of Wisden's Cricketers of the Year. There was a blip in 1965 and he was dropped from the England side for the final Test of the year – almost as a reaction, he hit a totally uncharacteristic fast hundred in the Gillette Cup final v Surrey - Yorkshire won by a wide margin.

The highlight of his 1967 season was his 246 not out, made without a blemish, v India, but so painfully slow was his innings, that the selectors decided to omit him from the next game! He was gaining a reputation for playing for himself rather than his team.

During the 1970-71 tour to Australia, the press voted him the best batsman in the world – his record that series was 657 runs, average 93.85. 1971 saw him appointed as captain of Yorkshire – embarrassingly the county had its worst Championship year to date, while Boycott broke sundry batting records with 2,503 runs, average 100.12. He was the first Englishman to average above 100 in a first-class season.

In 1974, he decided that following the Old Trafford Test, he was no longer available for England. Three years of self-imposed Test exile began.

On his return to Tests in 1977, he immediately scored 107 and 80 not out v Australia at Trent Bridge and then a further hundred in the Headingly Test. It was his 100th hundred in first-class cricket.

The winter of 1977-78 saw him unexpectedly England captain, when the current leader, Mike Brearley, was forced to abandon the tour through injury. On the 1981-82 England tour to India he broke two records, overtaking the most runs in Test cricket of Gary Sobers and reaching 40,000 first-class runs. Later in the same winter he went with the "rebel" England squad to South Africa and this action ended his official Test career.

At the end of the 1982 summer, Yorkshire decided not to renew Boycott's playing contract, but had to change their policy when a pro-Boycott lobby group was formed.

In 1984 he stood for the Yorkshire Committee and won the seat for Wakefield. This did not make relations between Boycott and his supporters and the rest of the Yorkshire members very easy. Boycott finally retired as a player in 1986 and from the Yorkshire Committee in 1993. He is now a well-known cricket commentator.

Geoffrey Boycott: at the end of his career he was Test cricket's leading run-scorer.

1940	1962	1964	1971	1978	1986
Born Geoffrey Boycott on 21 October, at Fitzwilliam, Yorks	First-class debut at Bradford on 16 June, Yorks v Pakistan	Test debut at Trent Bridge on 4 June, England v Australia	First match as Yorkshire captain v Warwickshire on 8-11 May, scoring 61 and 110	Captained England for first time v Pakistan in Karachi on 18 January	Final first-class match, Yorkshire v Northants at Scarborough, 10-12 September

DONALD BRADMAN
The Don of Batting

Donald Bradman: the best the game has seen.

There can be no other choice than Sir Donald George Bradman as the best batsman the world has ever seen. Because of the increase nowadays in the number of matches, especially Test matches, many have surpassed him in aggregates, but his career average stands on its own, 24 above the next player's, and his Test average is nearly 40 above anybody else's. A measure of his stature is that his worth as a Test run-getter practically equalled that of Allan Border and Viv Richards added together!

Bradman spent his boyhood in Bowral, 80 miles from Sydney, and developed his hand and eye co-ordination by hitting golf balls against a wall with a stump. In his first Sheffield Shield match aged 19 he scored 118, and throughout his career he continued to score a century for every three innings he played. And not only single centuries – 37 times he went past 200, six times past 300, both still records. His highest score is 452 not out. And he scored his runs quickly, only 12 times in his career batting for longer than six hours. His runs came all round the wicket, from a great variety of shots, with the pull shot being particularly associated with him.

He came to England in 1930 with a huge reputation, and scored 236 in the first match at Worcester (he repeated the double-century on his next two visits). In the Headingley Test, he came in at No. 3 and was 309 not out at close, eventually going on to 334, an Ashes record at the time (he repeated the triple-century on his next Test at Headingley). Many consider his innings in the Lord's Test his finest. Coming to the wicket in mid-afternoon, he was not out 155 at the close, and went on to 254. He himself picked this innings as his greatest because "every ball went where I wanted it to go". Never, at Test level, had an innings been so dominating. In that series, Bradman scored 974 runs, still a record for a single series, and averaged 139.14.

Bradman's dominance was such that "bodyline" was used to counter him in 1932-33, and it worked, as his average was "only" 56.57 – still the best on either side. He was dominant again in 1934 and was captain on his tour of England in 1938. The Second World War took six years out of Bradman's career and his health wasn't perfect when cricket resumed. Nevertheless, he carried on at only slightly below his peak and led an Australian side to England in 1948 that remained unbeaten and is generally considered the best side to have toured England. When he went out to bat in his last Test at The Oval, he needed only four runs to make sure of a Test average of 100, but he was bowled for a duck, some said because he still had a tear in his eye from his reception. If so, it would have been untypical of Bradman, who had the self-sufficiency of a genius.

Apart from his batting, Bradman was a brilliant fielder at cover-point and a very shrewd and thoughtful captain. He was knighted in 1949 and, on his retirement, became an influential figure in Australian cricket as an administrator. He was awarded Australia's highest honour, the companion of the Order of Australia, in 1981.

FIRST-CLASS CAREER
(1927-28 to 1948-49, 234 matches)
Batting: RUNS 28,067; AVERAGE 95.14; HIGHEST SCORE 452 NOT OUT; CENTURIES 117
Bowling: WICKETS 36; RUNS 1,367; AVERAGE 37.97; BEST 3-35
Catches: 131 (plus 1 stumped)

TESTS
(1928-29 to 1948, 52 matches)
Batting: RUNS 6,996; AVERAGE 99.94; HIGHEST SCORE 334; CENTURIES 19
Bowling: WICKETS 2; RUNS 72; AV. 36.00; BEST 1-8
Catches: 32

1908
Born Donald George Bradman on 27 August at Cootamundra, New South Wales, Australia

1927-28
Marks his first-class debut for New South Wales with a century (118) at the age of 18

1928
Made Test debut v England at Brisbane on 30 November. Scored 18 and 1 and was dropped for the second Test, but made 449 runs at an average of 89.80 in the last three Tests of the series

1930
Plays his finest innings on his first appearance at Lord's v England on 28 June. Ended up scoring 254

1930
Made the then Test record score of 334 v England at Headingley, 11 and 12 July. He scored 309, a Test record, on the first day, batting at No. 3

1932-33
English bowlers, led by Harold Larwood, resort to "bodyline" tactics in an attempt to stop him from scoring – he averages 56.57 for the series

1948
Made last Test appearance v England at The Oval, 14-18 August and was out for a duck

2001
Died amid national mourning in Adelaide, South Australia, on 25 February

LEARIE CONSTANTINE

Born: 21 SEPTEMBER 1901, PETIT VALLEY, DIEGO MARTIN, TRINIDAD
Died: 1 JULY 1971, BRONDESBURY, HAMPSTEAD, LONDON
Teams: TRINIDAD (1921-22 TO 1934-35); FREELOOTERS, INDIA (1934-5); BARBADOS (1938-39)
First-class: 119 MATCHES; 4,475 RUNS, AVERAGE 24.05; 439 WICKETS, AVERAGE 20.48
Tests (1928-39): 18 MATCHES; 635 RUNS, AVERAGE 19.24; 58 WICKETS, AVERAGE 30.10

Learie Constantine was an outstandingly dynamic cricketer: a violent batsman, a fast bowler and a spectacular fielder. He toured with the West Indies to England four times between 1923 and 1939 and to Australia in 1930-31. During the 1930s he played in the Lancashire League. He did much work, even taking legal action, successfully, to improve the status of black people in England. His greatest joy came at the end of the war when England met the Dominions at Lord's. Constantine was the only black man in the side, but the rest of the team insisted that he should captain them. It was his last first-class match.

A barrister, a writer and an MP in the Trinidad parliament, he came back to London as High Commissioner for Trinidad and Tobago. He was awarded the MBE, knighted and finally created a Life Peer, Baron of Maraval and Nelson. He was posthumously awarded Trinidad's highest honour, the Trinity Cross.

ALASTAIR COOK

Born: 25 DECEMBER 1984, GLOUCESTER
Teams: ESSEX (2003-10)
First-class: 142 MATCHES; 10,722 RUNS, AVERAGE 46.41; 6 WICKETS, AVERAGE 34.16
TESTS (2005-06 TO 2010-11): 65 MATCHES; 5,130 RUNS, AVERAGE 47.50; 0 WICKETS FOR 1 RUN

A tall, stylish hard-hitting left-hand opening batsman, Alastair Cook was marked for stardom after a brilliant school career. He made his first-class debut aged 18, and captained England in the Under-19 World Cup. He made his Test debut in India in 2006, scoring a century in the second innings, the first of many which quickly followed. He captained England in Bangladesh when Strauss declined to tour, and scored centuries in each Test. He lost form in 2010, but kept his place for the Ashes tour of Australia in 2010-11. He had an outstanding tour, scoring 766 runs (av 127.67), and was the Man of the Series. In doing so, he passed 5,000 Test runs, the second-youngest player, after Sachin Tendulkar, to achieve this feat.

COLIN COWDREY

Born: 24 DECEMBER 1932, BANGALORE, INDIA
Died: 4 DECEMBER 2000, LITTLEHAMPTON, SUSSEX
Teams: KENT (1950-76); OXFORD UNIVERSITY (1952-54)
First-class: 692 MATCHES; 42,719 RUNS, AVERAGE 42.89; 65 WICKETS, AVERAGE 51.21
Tests (1954-55 to 1974-75): 114 MATCHES; 7,624 RUNS, AVERAGE 44.06; NO WICKETS FOR 104 RUNS

One of the very finest and most accomplished of post-war batsmen, Cowdrey was a prolific scorer who hit 107 centuries in first-class cricket and created a record by playing 114 times for England, whom he captained on 27 occasions. He was a brilliant slip fielder and, as a batsman, was a stylist who sought perfection.

He made his Test debut on Hutton's 1954-55 tour of Australia. He had been a surprise choice, but was an instant success and his innings of 102 out of 191 in the third Test at Melbourne saved England from disaster in a match that they went on to win.

In 1957, at Edgbaston, he and Peter May shared a record partnership of 411 for the fourth wicket against the West Indies. In 1963 at Lord's, again against the West indies, he had his left arm broken by a ball from Wes Hall, but he went out to bat with his arm in plaster to save the day. Fortunately, he did not have to face a delivery. He gained the England captaincy, later than some thought he deserved, in 1966, then lost and regained it, taking England to the Caribbean in 1967-68, and winning the series against expectations. Then, unluckily, he lost the captaincy again after injury in a Sunday League game. In 1974-75, he was called to Australia at the age of 42. It was an emergency, and he was needed to help combat the fast bowlers. It was his sixth tour of the country where he was very popular.

He was a revolutionary president of the MCC and an active chairman of the ICC. He was knighted for his services to cricket in the New Year's Honours List in 1992.

MARTIN CROWE

Born: 22 SEPTEMBER 1962, HENDERSON, AUCKLAND, NEW ZEALAND
Teams: AUCKLAND (1979-80 TO 1982-83); CENTRAL DISTRICTS (1983-84 TO 1989-90); SOMERSET (1984-88); WELLINGTON (1990-91 TO 1994-95)
First-class: 247 MATCHES; 19,608 RUNS, AVERAGE 56.02; 119 WICKETS, AVERAGE 33.70
Tests (1981-82 to 1995-96): 77 MATCHES; 5,444 RUNS, AVERAGE 45.36; 14 WICKETS, AVERAGE 48.28

Not only one of the greatest batsmen of his generation, but one of the finest of all New Zealand batsmen, Martin Crowe made his Test debut in the rain-ruined match against Australia at Wellington in February 1982, when he was still seven months short of his 20th birthday. Tall, orthodox in style, elegant and powerful in execution, sound in temperament, he made his first Test century against England at Wellington in 1983-84, saving a match which had looked lost. By the end of his Test career, he had 17 hundreds to his credit and had scored more Test runs than any other New Zealand batsman.

Initially, he bowled at a brisk medium pace, but a back injury, one of several which marred his career, effectively brought an end to his capacity as a bowler.

He made a great impact in his years with Somerset, encouraging young uncapped players and doing much for team spirit, but there was also controversy in that by offering him

Martin Crowe: a prolific run-scorer for New Zealand.

a new contract in 1987, Somerset brought to an end their association with Viv Richards and Joel Garner.

There was a reluctance to burden him with the captaincy of New Zealand too early in his career, but the decline in form of his elder brother Jeff and John Wright's unwillingness to do the job led to Martin Crowe being asked to take a young and inexperienced side to Pakistan in 1990-91. He battled bravely against the odds and when he led New Zealand in New Zealand for the first time, he hit 299 against Sri Lanka at Wellington. This is the highest score ever made by a New Zealander in Test history and he and Andrew Jones established a world record when they added 467 for the third wicket. Crowe scored centuries against all Test-playing nations with the exception of South Africa.

He developed a knee problem which necessitated an operation and caused him to play with a splint. He scored runs even though he was in pain, but following the tour of India in 1995-96, when he was in obvious trouble, he was asked to prove his fitness. Reluctantly, he was forced to retire and a great player passed from the game.

JOSEPH DARLING

Born: 21 NOVEMBER 1870, GLEN OSMOND, ADELAIDE,
SOUTH AUSTRALIA
Died: 2 JANUARY 1946, HOBART, TASMANIA
Teams: SOUTH AUSTRALIA (1893-94 TO 1907-08)
First-class: 202 MATCHES; 10,635 RUNS,
AVERAGE 34.52; 1 WICKET, AVERAGE 55.00
Tests (1894-95 to 1905): 34 MATCHES; 1,657
RUNS, AVERAGE 28.56

Son of a member of the Legislative Council who was responsible for introducing the bill which granted the lease on land that became Adelaide Oval, Joe Darling excelled as a left-handed batsman at college. First he worked in banking and then in wheat farming, so that it seemed he was lost to sport. But, in 1893-94, he returned to Adelaide to open

a sports store and, a year later, thickset with face burned by the sun, he was in the Australian side. He first toured England in 1896 and became an opening batsman. On his next three tours – 1899, 1902, and 1905 – he captained the side.

Against MacLaren's side in 1897-98, he became the first batsman to hit three centuries in a Test rubber and the first to aggregate 500 runs in a series. In the third Test, at Adelaide, he made 178 and reached his century with the first six ever hit in Test cricket. To score six a batsman had to hit the ball out of the ground at that time. In the final Test, he hit 160 in 175 minutes.

A man of the utmost integrity, Darling was elected to the captaincy by his fellow players, who revered him, and he worked hard on their behalf while maintaining strict discipline. He retired to help his wife raise their 15 children. He settled in Tasmania, reared merino sheep and became a successful politician.

ALAN DAVIDSON

Born: 14 JUNE 1929, LISAROW, GOSFORD,
NEW SOUTH WALES
Teams: NEW SOUTH WALES (1949-50 TO 1962-63)
First-class: 193 MATCHES; 6,804 RUNS, AVERAGE 32.86;
672 WICKETS, AVERAGE 20.90
Tests (1953 to 1962-63): 44 MATCHES; 1,328
RUNS, AVERAGE 24.59; 186 WICKETS, AVERAGE 20.53

A left-handed fast bowler and a left-handed batsman who could hit the ball very hard, Alan Davidson made his Test debut in 1953, playing in all five matches. In 1958-59, he took 24 wickets against England and, two years later, he took 33 wickets and scored 212 runs against the West Indies. In the first match of that series, at Brisbane, he became the first player to score 100 runs and take ten wickets in a Test.

In 25 Tests against England, he made 750 runs and took 84 wickets. He also held 23 catches to complete a fine record.

He was president of the New

South Wales Cricket Association for many years and was also director of Rothman's National Sports Foundation.

ARAVINDA DE SILVA

Born: 17 OCTOBER 1965, COLOMBO, CEYLON
Teams: NONDESCRIPTS (1988-89 TO 2002); KENT (1995)
First-class: 220 MATCHES; 15,000 RUNS, AVERAGE
48.38; 129 WICKETS, AVERAGE 29.17
Tests (1984 to 2002): 93 MATCHES; 6,361 RUNS,
AVERAGE 42.97; 29 WICKETS, AVERAGE 41.65

Right-handed, wristy, quick-footed, Aravinda de Silva might even have scored more Test runs had he not been so eager to score so quickly. As it is, he has a host of records to his credit. His 267 against New Zealand at Wellington in 1990-91, is a national record. Twice he has reached a Test century with a six, and he became the first batsman to score an unbeaten century in each innings of a Test match, against Pakistan in 1997.

A useful off-break bowler, he played for Kent in 1995, scoring 1,781 runs, average 59.36, and in the Benson & Hedges Cup final made 112 against Lancashire, one of the most thrilling and greatest innings ever seen at Lord's.

When Sri Lanka won the World Cup in 1996, de Silva took the Man of the Match award in both the semi-final and the final, in which he scored an unbeaten century.

He is Sri Lanka's leading run-scorer in Test cricket. In 2002-03, he appeared only in one-day matches.

Aravinda de Silva: an inspired shot-maker who hit a rich seam of form in the 1996 World Cup and carried his country all the way to the final and victory over Australia.

TED DEXTER

Born: 15 MAY 1935, MILAN, ITALY
Teams: CAMBRIDGE UNIVERSITY (1956-58); SUSSEX (1957-68)
First-class: 327 MATCHES, 21,150 RUNS, AVERAGE 40.75; 419 WICKETS, AVERAGE 29.92
Tests (1958-68): 62 MATCHES; 4,502 RUNS, AVERAGE 47.89; 66 WICKETS, AVERAGE 34.93

An exciting attacking batsman, classical in style, and a most capable medium-pace bowler, Ted Dexter made an immediate impact at Cambridge and played for England against New Zealand at Old Trafford in 1958. The following winter he was flown to Australia to boost a sagging England side. He was a right-handed batsman of regal splendour, authority and immense power. Imperious of manner, he earned the nickname of "Lord Ted". He captained Sussex from 1960 to 1965, and he first led England in Pakistan and India in 1961-62, scoring 205, the highest innings of his career, against Pakistan in Karachi. He continued as England captain until the end of 1964, giving way to Cowdrey for just one "trial" Test in 1962.

For such an enterprising cricketer, he was a rather disappointing captain, being a great theorist and seemingly prone to lose interest. He was not the best handler of men, probably because he was so multi-talented. He was also a very fine golfer.

He missed the tour of India in 1963-64, and stood as Conservative candidate against the future Labour prime minister, James Callaghan, in the autumn of 1964. He was unsuccessful and joined the England side in South Africa where he played under M.J.K. Smith. In 1965, he broke a leg and retired, but he continued to make infrequent appearances for Sussex and last played for England in 1968.

He was appointed chairman of the England committee in 1989 and held the job for four years. He did much good, intelligent work behind the scenes, but England's lack of success brought him unfair criticism. His contribution to the re-ordering of the game has never been fully appreciated.

ALLAN DONALD

Born: 20 OCTOBER 1966, BLOEMFONTEIN, SOUTH AFRICA
Teams: ORANGE FREE STATE (1985-86 TO 2003-04); WARWICKSHIRE (1987-2000); WORCESTERSHIRE (2002)
First-class: 316 MATCHES; 2,785 RUNS, AVERAGE 12.05; 1,216 WICKETS, AVERAGE 22.76
Tests (1991-92 to 2001-02): 72 MATCHES; 652 RUNS, AVERAGE 10.68; 330 WICKETS, AVERAGE 22.25

A fast bowler of genuine pace, Allan Donald had proved his quality before South Africa's re-admission to Test cricket. His arrival at Warwickshire brought about a revival in the county's fortunes. He claimed 86 wickets in 1989, 83 in 1991 and 89 in 1995. Although his entry into Test cricket was late, he quickly became the fourth South African to take 100 Test wickets, but his eventual total of 330 has since been overtaken by Shaun Pollock.

He bowled with dedication and passion at all times, but he kept a fuller length than most fast bowlers of his generation. He demolished Zimbabwe with 8 for 71 and 3 for 42 at Harare, 1995-96, and his best bowling in domestic cricket is his 8 for 37 for Free State against Transvaal at Johannesburg in 1986-87. Donald became the first South African to reach 300 Test wickets. He was his country's outstanding bowler in the two series against England in 1998 and in 1999-2000.

MARTIN DONNELLY

Born: 17 OCTOBER 1917, NGARUAWAHIA, AUCKLAND, NEW ZEALAND
Died: 22 OCTOBER 1999, SYDNEY, NSW, AUSTRALIA
Teams: WELLINGTON (1936-37 TO 1940-41) CANTERBURY (1938-39 TO 1939-40); MIDDLESEX (1946); OXFORD UNIVERSITY (1946-1947); WARWICKSHIRE (1948-1950)
First-class: 131 MATCHES; 9,250 RUNS, AVERAGE 47.43; 43 WICKETS, AVERAGE 39.13
Tests (1937-1949): 7 MATCHES; 582 RUNS, AVERAGE 52.90; NO WICKETS FOR 20 RUNS

A left-handed batsman of immense power and grace, Martin Donnelly was a natural athlete who represented Oxford University and England at rugby. His Test matches

Allan Donald: a bowler of genuine pace with over 300 Test wickets to his name.

were for New Zealand against England, in England and, when he made his debut at Lord's in 1937, he was the second youngest cricketer ever to represent New Zealand. He scored 1,414 runs on the tour.

He lost valuable years to the war, in which he served as major in the Egyptian and Italian campaigns.

A graduate of University College, Canterbury, he went up to Oxford in 1946 and captained the XI in 1947. He was a prolific run-scorer and hit 162 not out in three hours for the Gentlemen against the Players.

He played for Middlesex against the Indian tourists in 1946, but he went into business when he came down from Oxford and appeared for Warwickshire in 20 matches during the next three seasons.

In 1949, when New Zealand toured England, he excelled with 2,287 runs, average 61.81, which included 462 runs, average 77.00, in the Tests. At Lord's, he made 206, the first double-century in Test cricket by a New Zealand batsman.

His work took him to Australia and he settled in Sydney, leaving lovers of the game with a memory of charm and graciousness.

RAHUL DRAVID

SEE PAGE 181

JEFFREY DUJON

Born: 28 MAY 1956, KINGSTON, JAMAICA
Teams: JAMAICA (1974-75 TO 1991-92)
First-class: 194 MATCHES; 9,308 RUNS, AVERAGE 38.14;
1 WICKET, AVERAGE 45.00; CAUGHT 434,
STUMPED 19;
Tests (1981-82 to 1991): 81 MATCHES; 3,322 RUNS,
AVERAGE 31.94; CAUGHT 267, STUMPED 5

An elegant right-handed batsman and graceful, acrobatic wicket-keeper, Jeff Dujon established himself in the West Indian side on the tour of Australia in 1982-83, and the following season in the Caribbean hit his first Test century, against India in Antigua. He and Clive Lloyd put on 207 for the sixth wicket, and the West Indies won the series. Indeed, Dujon never played in a Test side which lost a series, and he was a member of the West Indian team which won a record 11 Tests in succession in 1984-85. He hit hundreds against England and Australia and claimed five Test centuries in all, a fine feat considering that he was invariably batting at No. 7.

He had no serious rival for the position of West Indian keeper, and there was an outcry when he was finally omitted after an indifferent display against England in 1991.

Jeffrey Dujon: a fine wicket-keeper and batsman.

JOHN EDRICH

Born: 21 JUNE 1937, BLOFIELD, NORFOLK
Teams: SURREY (1958-78)
First-class: 564 MATCHES; 39,790 RUNS, AVERAGE
45.47; NO WICKETS FOR 53 RUNS
Tests (1963-76): 77 MATCHES; 5,138 RUNS AVERAGE
43.54; NO WICKETS FOR 23 RUNS

A member of a famous Norfolk cricketing family, John Edrich was a solid, chunky, tough and dependable left-hand opening batsman who reached 1,000 runs in a season 21 times, including twice overseas. On six of those occasions he reached 2,000. He captained Surrey from 1973 to 1977, and led England in Sydney in 1974-75, when Denness dropped himself through lack of form. He had his ribs broken by the first ball he received from Lillee in the second innings and was forced to retire. Typically of Edrich, he returned to bat for two-and-a-half hours for an unbeaten 33.

He was one of that select group of batsmen who have scored a hundred hundreds, the highest of which was 310 not out against New Zealand at Headingley in 1965. He hit five sixes and 52 fours, the most boundaries ever hit in a Test innings.

BILL EDRICH

Born: 26 MARCH 1916, LINGWOOD, NORFOLK
Died: 24 APRIL 1986, WHITEHILL COURT, CHESHAM,
BUCKINGHAMSHIRE
Teams: MIDDLESEX (1937-58)
First-class: 571 MATCHES; 36,965 RUNS, AVERAGE
42.39; 479 WICKETS, AVERAGE 33.31
Tests (1938 TO 54-55): 39 MATCHES; 2,440 RUNS,
AVERAGE 40.00; 41 WICKETS, AVERAGE 41.29

Bill Edrich had three brothers and a cousin (John) who played county cricket, and there was a time when the Edriches could have fielded a full XI. Bill Edrich played for Norfolk from 1932 to 1936 when he should have made his debut for Middlesex, but his registration was delayed and he had to wait another year. He hit 2,154 runs in 1937, and the following season he scored 1,000 runs before the end of May and played for England against Australia. His first eight Tests were disastrous for him, but the ninth, against South Africa at Durban in 1938-39, saw him score 219.

A determined and aggressive batsman who finally settled at No. 3, and a quick bowler off a shortish run who opened the England attack immediately after the Second World War, Edrich lived life to the full. He served in the RAF and was awarded the DFC and, pre-war, he played soccer for Tottenham Hotspur. He was a late selection for the England tour of Australia in 1946-47, but was named as senior professional. He turned amateur the following summer, probably hoping for the England captaincy, but his lust for living was not always in accord with the ideals of England selectors – which perhaps explains why he was often omitted from sides that he should have been in.

In 1947, he and his great friend Denis Compton rewrote the record books. The Middlesex "twins" excited a nation with their exploits as Edrich scored 3,539 runs, an aggregate beaten only by Compton that same summer, and hit 12 centuries, including his career-best 267 not out against Northamptonshire.

The following season, he and Compton shared a Middlesex third-wicket record stand of 424 undefeated against Somerset. He captained Middlesex and, on retirement, returned to play for Norfolk. He was a man of intelligence and charm, and was always good company.

Dogged by personal tragedies, he served as a Test selector and, more recently, as England batting coach.

RAHUL DRAVID
Impassable wall

FIRST-CLASS CAREER
(1990-91 to 2010-11, 282 matches)
Batting: RUNS 22,446; AVERAGE 55.69;
HIGHEST SCORE 270; CENTURIES 62
Bowling: WICKETS 5; RUNS 273; AVERAGE 54.60;
BEST 2-16
Catches: 341

TESTS
(1996 TO 2010-11, 149 MATCHES)
Batting: RUNS 12,040; AVERAGE 52.80;
HIGHEST SCORE 270; CENTURIES 31
Bowling: WICKETS 1; RUNS 39; AVERAGE 39.00;
BEST 1-18
Catches: 199

Rahul Dravid: unrivalled powers of concentration.

During the 2005-06 Test series between India and England, Rahul Dravid, nicknamed 'The Wall', was the one batsman most feared by the English bowlers. In spite of the extra burden of the captaincy, Dravid's concentration remains his strongest point. It is an ability that he has developed since he was a youngster. His mind is simply focused on the ball about to be delivered and never distracted. Undoubtedly he is the greatest Indian batsman to occupy the first wicket down post and has placed himself in terms of Test batting average even above the great Tendulkar. That said, Dravid does not interest himself in mundane statistics, he looks at the value of his runs in each specific situation. He bats with style and has clearly absorbed the classic textbook strokes that have been passed down through generations.

The son of a food scientist, Dravid was encouraged to continue his education through to university level,

rather than, as a teenager, devote all his time to cricket – he has a degree in commerce from Bangalore University. His initial appearances in first-class cricket were in the knock-out stages of the 1990-91 Ranji Trophy, playing for Karnataka. He made an immediate impression, scoring 82 in his first game against Maharashtra at Pune and then in his

second 134 against Bengal at Eden Gardens, Calcutta. The following season saw him picked for the South Zone in the Duleep Trophy matches and he averaged 48.22. In 1992-93 produced two brilliant innings of 200 and 56 – both not out – v Andhra in Bangalore, as a result of which he was selected for the Board President's

XI and then Indian Under-25s against the England touring side. In both 1993-94 and 1994-95, Dravid averaged over 50 during the season. These statistics, however, were dwarfed the next year, when he hit 968 runs at an average of 80.66.

He made his debut in the third Test of 1996, at Lord's. Dravid scored 95 and the press noted his "soundness of temperament and technique". He returned to England for the 1999 World Cup. India did not obtain a place in the semi-finals, but this did not prevent Dravid scoring more runs in the Cup than any other batsman, regardless of his country. In the match at Taunton v Sri Lanka, Ganguly and Dravid added a world one-day record partnership of 318 for the second wicket. A few months later, Dravid, this time in conjunction with Tendulkar, smashed that record with a stand worth 331 – against New Zealand at Hyderabad. In the 2000-01 India v Australia Test series, Dravid's batting played a major role in India's victories in both Kolkata and Chennai. In Kolkata, Dravid hit 180 and in Chennai he made 81. It was perhaps the most illustrious moment in India's Test history.

For Dravid these innings were the start of an incredible sequence of innings – he hit four double-centuries in 15 Tests. At the beginning of 2005-06, he assumed captaincy of the Indian one-day side and then graduated to the leadership of the Test team.

1973
Born Rahul Dravid on 11 January at Indore, India

1991
First-class debut Karnataka v Maharashtra at Pune, 2 February

1996
One-day international debut India v Sri Lanka in Singapore, 3 April. Test debut, India v England at Lord's, 20 June

1999
May-June, highest run-getter in the World Cup

2004
13-15 April, he hit 270 for India v Pakistan, batting for 12 hours and 20 minutes

2005
During October he captained India to a six wins to one versus Sri Lanka

GODFREY EVANS

Born: 18 AUGUST 1920, FINCHLEY, MIDDLESEX
Died: 3 MAY 1999, NORTHAMPTON
Teams: KENT (1939-67)
First-class: 465 MATCHES; 14,882 RUNS, AVERAGE 21.22; 2 WICKETS, AVERAGE 122.50; CAUGHT 816, STUMPED 250
Tests (1946-59): 91 MATCHES; 2,439 RUNS, AVERAGE 20.49; CAUGHT 173, STUMPED 46

One of the very greatest of wicket-keepers and an entertainer much loved by the crowd, Godfrey Evans appeared for Kent in a handful of matches in 1939 before succeeding Les Ames in 1946. Within a year he was England's first-choice keeper. He was an extrovert and he was spectacular, but he was eminently dependable, and his keeping standing up to Alec Bedser became one of the features of immediate post-war cricket. He was also a capable batsman who reached 1,000 runs in a season four times, and he hit seven centuries, two of them in Tests. Against India at Lord's in 1952, he made 105, and 98 of these runs came before lunch, yet in Adelaide in 1946-47, he created a world record when he batted for 97 minutes before scoring his first run in the second innings. He could bat as the occasion demanded, but perhaps he never treated batting quite seriously enough in county matches.

He made four tours to Australia and two to South Africa and the West Indies, and he was popular everywhere. On his retirement, he was employed by Ladbrokes.

FAZAL MAHMOOD

Born: 18 FEBRUARY 1927, LAHORE, INDIA
Died: 30 MAY 2005, LAHORE, PAKISTAN
Teams: NORTHERN INDIA (1943-44 TO 1946-47); PUNJAB (1951-52 TO 1956-57); LAHORE (1958-59)
First-class: 111 MATCHES; 2,602 RUNS, AVERAGE 23.02; 460 WICKETS, AVERAGE 19.11
Tests (1952-53 to 1962): 34 MATCHES; 620 RUNS, AVERAGE 14.09; 139 WICKETS, AVERAGE 24.70

Fazal Mahmood was a right-arm fast-medium pace bowler whose style was akin to Alec Bedser's. He was selected for India's tour of Australia in 1947-48, but stood down on the announcement of the Partition and waited for his international debut until 1952-53 when Pakistan entered Test cricket. In his country's second Test, against India at Lucknow, he took 5 for 52 and 7 for 42 to bring Pakistan an historic victory. He had proved himself particularly devastating on matting, but he was equally effective in England in 1954. He captured four wickets at Lord's and Old Trafford, and at The Oval he took 6 for 53 and 6 for 46 to take Pakistan to victory over England.

A national hero, happy and popular, he was chosen to lead Pakistan when Kardar stepped down, but Fazal did not have Kardar's social status. With the added responsibility of being the main strike bowler, his captaincy suffered. It had begun sensationally when he put the West Indies in at Karachi and took seven wickets to bowl his side to a ten-wicket victory. Thereafter, his bowling declined and his captaincy was criticized as factions developed. When he left Test cricket, he had a Pakistan record of 139 wickets to his credit.

ANDREW FLINTOFF

SEE PAGE 184

TICH FREEMAN

Born: 17 MAY 1888, LEWISHAM, LONDON
Died: 28 JANUARY 1965, BEARSTED, KENT
Teams: KENT (1914-36)
First-class: 592 MATCHES; 4,961 RUNS, AVERAGE 9.50; 3,776 WICKETS, AVERAGE 18.42
Tests (1924-25 to 1929): 12 MATCHES; 154 RUNS, AVERAGE 14.00; 66 WICKETS, AVERAGE 25.86

His height earning him the nickname "Tich", Freeman took more wickets in county cricket than any other bowler in the history of the game, and only Wilfred Rhodes took more wickets in all first-class cricket. In 1928, he became the only bowler to

Fazal Mahmood: triumphed at The Oval in 1954 to bring Pakistan their first win in England.

capture 300 wickets in a season, 304 at 18.05 runs each, and in the seven seasons that followed he took more than 200 wickets each season, so that between 1928 and 1935 he took 2,090 wickets. In 1936, he captured "only" 108 wickets for Kent and was not re-engaged.

Standing 5ft 2in, "Tich" Freeman was a leg-break and googly bowler who had immaculate control and posed difficulties with his flight which, because of his height, often had a low trajectory. That he played only 12 times for England and never against Australia in England is one of the unsolved mysteries of the game. In 1928, he took 22 wickets in three Tests against the West Indies, but he did not appear in a single Test on the tour of Australia that followed. Against South Africa in 1929, he captured 22 wickets in two matches, yet he did not play for England after that series.

He became a record wicket-taker in the Birmingham League after he left first-class cricket.

CHARLES FRY

Born: 25 APRIL 1872, WEST CROYDON, SURREY
Died: 7 SEPTEMBER 1956, CHILD'S HILL, HAMPSTEAD, LONDON
Teams: OXFORD UNIVERSITY (1892-95); SUSSEX (1894-1908); LONDON COUNTY (1900-1902); HAMPSHIRE (1909-1921); EUROPEANS (1921-22)
First-class: 394 MATCHES; 30,886 RUNS, AVERAGE 50.22; 166 WICKETS, AVERAGE 29.34
Tests (1895-96 to 1912): 26 MATCHES; 1,223 RUNS, AVERAGE 32.18; NO WICKETS FOR 3 RUNS

Charles Fry made only one tour abroad with an England side, to South Africa in 1895-96, shortly after coming down from Oxford. He played in the first two Tests of the series, and his remaining 24 Test matches were all played in England. He would have been a regular choice for his country had he been able to spare the time.

A first-class honours graduate in Classical Moderations, he won his blue in all four years at Oxford and also won blues for soccer and athletics. He would also have won a blue for rugby, but for injury. In 1893, he equalled the world long-jump record. He was capped for England against Ireland at soccer in 1901 and played for Southampton in the FA Cup final the following year. He was an author, journalist, broadcaster, fought three unsuccessful campaigns as a Liberal candidate, represented India at the League of Nations, captained Sussex from 1904 to 1908, edited a magazine and founded and directed the training ship *Mercury*. After the First World War, it was alleged that he was offered and declined the throne of Albania.

A correct batsman and great thinker on the game, he hit six centuries in succession in 1901 and made 3,147 runs, average 78.67, in the season. His list of activities and achievements gives ample reason as to why he did not play more for England. He captained England in the 1912 Triangular Tournament, winning four and drawing two of the six matches, but he was frequently the "kingmaker". He maintained that he was asked to replace Douglas as England captain in 1921, but could not spare the time and suggested Tennyson.

SOURAV GANGULY

Born: 8 JULY 1972, CALCUTTA (KOLKATA), BENGAL, INDIA
Teams: BENGAL (1988-89 TO 2010-11); LANCASHIRE (2000); GLAMORGAN (2005); NORTHAMPTONSHIRE (2006); KOLKATA KNIGHT RIDERS (2008-09)
First-class: 248 MATCHES; 15,263 RUNS, AVERAGE 43.98; 164 WICKETS, AVERAGE 37.04
Tests (1996 TO 2008-09): 113 MATCHES; 7,212 RUNS, AVERAGE 42.17; 32 WICKETS, AVERAGE 52.53

Sourav Ganguly courted controversy throughout his career: how good was he, should he captain India, could he galvanize a side, or was he aloof, arrogant and a disruptive influence - the same questions stalked him.

He did not make his first-class debut until he was 27 years old. He was a scintillating, quick-scoring batsman, particularly on the offside, although he could be unsettled by fast bowling and looked languid in the field. Nevertheless, he made his debut for India at Lord's against England in 1996 and scored a brilliant 131, going on to become only the third player ever to score centuries in his first two Test innings when he made 136 at Trent Bridge. His series average was 105.00.

Ganguly first captained India in a one-day match against South Africa in 2000, when the match-fixing scandal surrounding Hansie Cronje was coming to a peak. He proved one of the most successful of India's captains, in particular leading the side to its amazing comeback against Australia in the fantastic series of 2000-01, and drawing in Australia in 2003-04. He lost the captaincy in 2004-05 after differences with coach Greg Chappell, but made a spirited return to Test cricket in 2006-07. He announced before the first Test that he would retire at the end of the series against Australia at home in 2008-09, and he did, his last Test innings being a first-ball duck, but India won 2-0 and he averaged 54.00.

JOEL GARNER

Born: 16 DECEMBER 1952, ENTERPRISE, CHRIST CHURCH, BARBADOS
Teams: BARBADOS (1975-76 TO 1987-88); SOMERSET (1977-86)
First-class: 214 MATCHES; 2,964 RUNS, AVERAGE 16.74; 881 WICKETS, AVERAGE 18.53
Tests (1976-77 TO 1986-87): 58 MATCHES; 672 RUNS, AVERAGE 12.44; 259 WICKETS, AVERAGE 20.97

At 6ft 8in tall, Joel Garner, "Big Bird", was a giant of a fast bowler. He used his height to the full, generated considerable pace off a comparatively short run and swung and cut the ball both ways. His first Test series was against Pakistan in 1976-77, and he took 25 wickets in five matches. He took 13 wickets in the first two Tests against Australia the following season, but missed the rest of the series because of his association with World Series Cricket. In the World Cup final at Lord's in 1979, he took 5 for 38 to ensure the West Indies' victory over England, and he was a major factor in Somerset winning both the Sunday League and the NatWest Trophy the same year. The county had won no trophies before this time.

A shoulder injury handicapped him for a while, but he played a significant part in the West Indies' record 11 consecutive Test victories. He was not the least of a formidable quartet of fast bowlers. He was captain of Barbados when they won the Shell Shield, and, amid controversy, was released by Somerset after the 1986 season. A genial man, he was popular wherever he went.

MIKE GATTING

Born: 6 JUNE 1957, KINGSBURY, MIDDLESEX
Teams: MIDDLESEX (1975-98)
First-class: 551 MATCHES, 36,549 RUNS, AVERAGE 49.52; 158 WICKETS, AVERAGE 29.76
Tests (1977-78 TO 1994-95): 79 MATCHES, 4,409 RUNS, AVERAGE 35.55; 4 WICKETS, AVERAGE 79.25

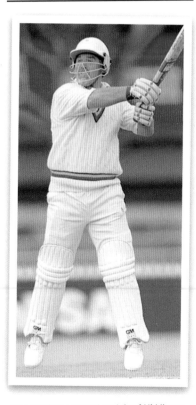

Mike Gatting: a rugged captain of Middlesex and England.

A batsman capable of taking apart any attack and a medium-pace bowler, Mike Gatting was a dedicated professional who succeeded Mike Brearley as captain of Middlesex in 1983 and led them to every honour before standing down in 1997. A prolific scorer in county cricket, he made his Test debut in Pakistan in 1977-78, but did not score a Test hundred until his 54th innings at Bombay in 1984-85. He hit a double-century later in the same series.

When Gower fell out of favour after losing the first Test to India in 1986, Gatting was named as England captain. He could not reverse the trend against India and lost to New Zealand the same summer, but he led a harmonious side to victory in Australia the following winter. There was unease about his captaincy when Pakistan won in England in 1987, although Gatting himself hit two centuries in the series. A dreadful reverse sweep cost him his wicket in the World Cup final later the same year and, according to some critics, also lost England the match. When the team went to Pakistan he had a notorious confrontation with umpire Shakoor Rana, and the following summer he was the subject of allegations in a newspaper regarding his social life. He was relieved of the captaincy and stood down after the third Test.

Gatting played against Australia in 1989, but it was revealed that he was to lead a side to South Africa, and he was automatically banned from Test cricket. He resumed his Test career in India in 1992-93, and was a controversial choice to tour Australia in 1994-95, but he did not enjoy a successful tour. Tough, rugged and honest, he retired in 1998 having hit 1,000 runs in a season for the 19th time. In 2000, he retired as director of coaching with Middlesex.

SUNIL GAVASKAR

SEE PAGE 185

ANDREW FLINTOFF
Fearless Freddie

FIRST-CLASS CAREER
(1995 to 2009, 183 matches)
Batting: RUNS 9,027; AVERAGE 33.80;
HIGHEST SCORE 167; CENTURIES 15
Bowling: WICKETS 350; RUNS 11,059; AVERAGE 31.59;
BEST 5-24
Catches: 180

TESTS
(1996 TO 2009, 78 MATCHES)
Batting: RUNS 3,795; AVERAGE 31.89;
HIGHEST SCORE 167; CENTURIES 5
Bowling: WICKETS 219; RUNS 7,303; AVERAGE 33.34;
BEST 5-58
Catches: 52

"Freddie" Flintoff became England's successor to Ian Botham as the powerful, fast-bowling, six-hitting, boy's superhero of his day. His feats in the exciting Ashes-winning series of 2005 have already passed into legend.

He made his debut for Lancashire in 1995 when the then slender 17-year-old scored 7 and 0, took no wickets and dropped five catches against Hampshire. However, he impressed on an England Under-19 tour in 1996-97 and showed his hitting power in 1998 with 34 runs from the first seven balls of an over containing two no-balls from Surrey's Alex Tudor, missing out on a world record by failing to score from the eighth. He made an inauspicious Test debut in 1998, which lasted one game, had a disappointing World

Andrew Flintoff: immensely powerful middle-order batsman and a fast, aggressive bowler.

Cup in 1999 and, suffering from back problems was warned by the England management to improve his fitness and reduce his weight. He was perceived as not taking the game seriously enough.

Freddie gradually pulled himself clear of physical frailty and his improved fitness brought more devil to his bowling. At 6ft 4in and immensely strong he could bowl at over 90mph and mastered reverse-swing. He was sent for to join the England party touring India in 2001-02, where he knuckled down with enthusiasm. A first Test century against New Zealand in 2002 was followed by outstanding all-round performances against South Africa in 2003 and in the emphatic series win the following winter in the Caribbean. A whitewash of West Indies followed in 2004, when he hit 167 at Edgbaston, and his 23 wickets helped England win in South Africa in 2004-05.

And then came his heroic exploits in the 2005 Ashes. He made crucial efforts with bat and ball. Innings of 68 and 73 at vital times, plus seven wickets were instrumental in a two-run win to level the series in the second Test, a brilliant century in the fourth led to another win to give England the series lead.

Injuries to the touring party to India in 2005-06 led him to becoming an inspiring captain as England fought back to level the series 1-1. Called upon to lead England in the 2006-07 Ashes series, he saw his country defeated 5-0.

He continued to be dogged by injury and announced his retirement in September 2010.

1977	**1995**	**1998**	**1999**	**2002**
Born Andrew Flintoff on December 6 at Preston, Lancashire	Made debut for Lancashire v Hampshire at Portsmouth. Scored 7 and 0 and took 0 wickets for 39 runs. He also dropped five catches in the match	Awarded his county cap, was elected Young Cricketer of the Year by the Cricket Writers' Club and made his Test debut, v South Africa at Trent Bridge	Has a disappointing World Cup and is accused of being unfit and overweight	Scores his first century for England against New Zealand at Christchurch

2004	**2005**	**2005**	**2006**	**2006-07**
Made his highest Test score of 167 from 191 balls with 17 fours and seven sixes v West Indies in second Test at Edgbaston	Hit nine sixes in innings of 68 and 73, an Ashes record (beating Ian Botham's six) v Australia in the second Test at Edgbaston	Inspires England to victory in the Ashes series	Captains England to a drawn series in India in Michael Vaughan's absence through injury	In Michael Vaughan's absence, captains England in their Ashes defence, but lose the series 5-0.

SUNIL GAVASKAR
The Little Master

FIRST-CLASS CAREER
(1967-68 to 1986-87, 348 matches)
Batting: RUNS 25,834; AVERAGE 51.46;
HIGHEST SCORE 340; CENTURIES 81
Bowling: WICKETS 22; RUNS 1,240; AVERAGE 56.36;
BEST 3-43
Catches: 293

TESTS
(1970-71 TO 1986-87, 125 MATCHES)
Batting: RUNS 10,122; AVERAGE 51.12;
HIGHEST SCORE 236 NOT OUT;
CENTURIES 34
Bowling: WICKETS 1; RUNS 206; AV. 206; BEST 1-34
Catches: 108

Sunny Gavaskar, less than 5ft 5in tall, had a perfect batting technique. Thoroughly reliable, he became the best opening batsman in the world. He was the first batsman to score 10,000 runs in Tests and the first to reach 30 Test centuries – his eventual totals at the end of his career of 10,122 runs and 34 centuries being records.

Gavaskar made his first-class debut aged 17 in 1966-67, and his debut for India in 1970-71 as a 21-year-old on a tour of West Indies. He made 65 and 67 not out as India won their first Test match against the West Indies in their 25th attempt. In the remaining three Tests he scored centuries in each, including two in the final Test, 124 and 220. India won their first series against the West Indies, and

Sunil Gavaskar: technique personified.

Gavaskar's aggregate of 774 (average 154.80) was the highest for an Indian batsman or any player on debut.

In 1976, he became the first Indian batsman to score 1,000 Test runs in a calendar year, a feat he repeated in 1978 and 1979. He replaced Bedi for the first of 47 appearances as India's captain for the visit of the West Indies in 1978-79 and celebrated with 205 in the first Test. In the third he became the first batsman to score a century in each innings on three occasions.

In England, in 1979, a magnificent 221 on the last day of the series earned a draw, but just failed to save the series for India.

Gavaskar's series of firsts continued in 1982-83 when he was the first Indian to carry his bat in a Test with 127 not out against Pakistan. In 1983-84, with the West Indies the visitors, he passed Boycott's record aggregate of Test runs in the second Test and passed Bradman's record of 29 Test centuries in the sixth Test, when he made his highest Test score of 236 not out.

Gavaskar scored 188 for the Rest of the World in MCC's bicentenary match at Lord's in 1987 and retired after the 1987-88 World Cup, which was held in India and Pakistan.

1949	**1966-67**	**1970-71**	**1971**
Born Sunil Manohar Gavaskar on 10 July, Bombay, India	Makes first-class debut for Bombay at the age of 17	Made Test debut in West Indies and scored 774 runs in the series, average 154.80: had innings of 65, 67 not out, 116, 64 not out, 1, 117 not out, 124 and 220 not out	Famously knocked over by John Snow when attempting a quick run at Lord's; Snow received a one-match ban

1976	**1978-79**	**1979**	**1986-87**
Becomes the first Indian cricketer to score 1,000 runs in a calendar year	Captained India for the first time and celebrated with 205 not against West Indies	Made 1,000 runs in a calendar year for the third time in four years. His 1,555 was second highest aggregate ever	Retired from Test cricket holding the record for the most number of runs scored (10,122) and the most number of centuries (34)

HERSCHELLE GIBBS

Born: 23 FEBRUARY 1974, GREEN POINT, CAPE TOWN, SOUTH AFRICA
Teams: WESTERN PROVINCE (1990-91 TO 2006-07), CAPE COBRAS (2005-06 TO 2008-09), GLAMORGAN (2008-09)
First-class: 193 MATCHES; 13,425 RUNS, AVERAGE 42.21; 3 WICKETS, AVERAGE 26.00
Tests (1996-97 to 2007-08): 90 MATCHES; 6,167 RUNS, AVERAGE 41.95; 0 WICKETS

An outstanding athlete at school, Herschelle Gibbs excelled at almost every sporting activity. He played soccer for South Africa at Under-15 level, represented South African Schools at both rugby and cricket and held the school 100-metre sprint record. He made his first-class debut for Western Province in 1990-91, when he was still only 16. In this match he scored an excellent 77 for the B side and was then upgraded to the senior Province team.

A natural batsman, he seemed to possess all the shots in the book, almost from day one – his best stroke being the extra-cover drive. He was also a brilliant fielder in the gully and some authorities placed him almost in the Jonty Rhodes standard.

Gibbs' introduction into international cricket came against Kenya in Nairobi in October 1996 and in the following month he made his Test debut against India in Kolkata. In the 2002-03 season his flamboyant batting really began to make the headlines beyond South Africa. Touring England with the 2003 South Africans he averaged 53.11 in the five Tests, and in the final Test at The Oval hit 183. The one blot on his career to date was being entangled in the Cronje match-fixing scandal. Gibbs received a six-month ban and also a fine. Fortunately, he managed to regain his Test place after the ban and still has some years' cricket ahead of him. He caused a stir in the 2007 World Cup when he hit six sixes off a Daan van Bunge over in South Africa's match against Holland.

Herschelle Gibbs: possesses all the shots in the book.

LANCE GIBBS

Born: 29 SEPTEMBER 1934, QUEENSTOWN, GEORGETOWN, BRITISH GUIANA
Teams: BRITISH GUIANA/GUYANA (1953-54 TO 1974-75); WARWICKSHIRE (1967-73); SOUTH AUSTRALIA (1969-70)
First-class: 330 MATCHES; 1,729 RUNS, AVERAGE 8.55; 1,024 WICKETS, AVERAGE 22.72
Tests (1957-58 to 1975-76): 79 MATCHES; 488 RUNS, AVERAGE 6.97; 309 WICKETS, AVERAGE 29.09

With his long fingers, Lance Gibbs was one of the greatest of off-spin bowlers and a very fine fielder in the gully. In his first Test series, against Pakistan in 1957-58, he took 17 wickets in four Tests, and in Australia he took 19 wickets in three Tests. At Sydney, he took three wickets in four balls, and in the next Test, at Adelaide, he performed the hat-trick. A year later, in Barbados, he bowled the West Indies to victory over India with 8 for 38 in the second innings. In fact, he took 8 for 6 in 15.3 overs, 14 of which were maidens. His success continued unabated and, when he retired, his 309 Test wickets was a record.

He enjoyed much success with Warwickshire and captured 131 wickets in first-class matches in 1971. He settled in the United States, played for the USA against Canada in 1983, and managed the West Indies in England in 1991.

ADAM GILCHRIST

SEE PAGE 187

ASHLEY GILES

Born: 19 MARCH 1973, CHERTSEY, SURREY.
Teams: WARWICKSHIRE (1995-2006)
First-class: 178 MATCHES; 5,346 RUNS, AVERAGE 26.33; 539 WICKETS, AVERAGE 29.60
Tests (1998 to 2006-07): 54 MATCHES; 1,421 RUNS, AVERAGE 20.89; 143 WICKETS, AVERAGE 40.60

For the third Test against South Africa at Old Trafford in 1998, the England selectors decided to increase the spin attack by adding Giles to the incumbent Croft – between them they conceded 209 runs but managed just a single wicket as South Africa hit 552 for 5. The experiment was discontinued!

In 2000-01, Giles went with England to the sub-continent and played in all six Tests. His left-arm spin captured 17 wickets against Pakistan, heading the Test bowling table. His command of line and length, as well as his demeanour, received critical praise. When the West Indies toured England in 2004, he captured 22 wickets in the four-match series and because of his bowling England won all four games. Now established as England's principal spinner, he played through the 2005 Ashes series – surprisingly, Giles began as a seam bowler, until back trouble forced him to try spin. Unlike many left armers, he usually bowls over the wicket and pitches the ball in line with the leg stump.

After injury caused him to miss the 2006 domestic season, he recovered his fitness to take part in the 2006-07 Ashes series, but lost his place in the side to Monty Panesar. His hip problem led to his retirement in 2007.

ADAM GILCHRIST
Attacking keeper

FIRST-CLASS CAREER
(1992-93 TO 2007-08, 190 MATCHES)

Batting:	RUNS 10,334; AVERAGE 44.16; HIGHEST SCORE 204 NOT OUT; CENTURIES 30
Bowling:	WICKETS 0
Catches:	756
Stumpings:	55

TESTS
(1999-00 TO 2007-08, 96 MATCHES)

Batting:	RUNS 5,570; AVERAGE 47.60; HIGHEST SCORE 204 NOT OUT; CENTURIES 17
Bowling:	WICKETS 0
Catches:	379
Stumpings:	37

Adam Gilchrist: the most successful wicket-keeper-batsmen ever, the speed at which he scored runs turned many matches Australia's way, best illustrated by his 59-ball 102 at Perth in January. 2007.

Gilchrist was one of the best wicket-keeper-batsman in the world. The fact that he also had to captain Australia in a number of matches – owing to the absence of first Steve Waugh, then Ricky Ponting – added to his versatility.

Born in Bellingen in New South Wales, Adam Gilchrist was the son of a teacher who was also a keen cricketer. Adam, educated at Kadina High School, opted at the age of 17 to accept a cricket scholarship, rather than to go to university. This took him to England where he played club cricket for Richmond in the Middlesex League. In 1991, aged 20, he returned as a member of the Australian Under-19 squad. Gilchrist was the main run-getter on the trip, hitting 1,122 runs, average 80.14. In 1991-92, he went with the Australia Academy side to South Africa.

His first-class debut came for New South Wales in 1992-93, purely as a batsman. In 1993-94, he made just three first-class appearances and decided to move to Western Australia, where he had effectively been offered the wicket-keeping job in the state side. This caused a slight rumpus, since the present incumbent, Zoehrer, who had played Tests for Australia, had no wish to retire. Clearly Gilchrist's batting ability swayed the Perth authorities. In his first season with his new side, Gilchrist created a new state record by obtaining 51 dismissals. In 1995-96, he went one better by having 54 dismissals, a new Sheffield Shield record. His batting was also developing rapidly – in the Shield final v South Australia he hit an astonishing 189 not out, including five sixes. He finished the year in the top ten in the Australian first-class batting table and was now being spoken of as the obvious successor to Ian Healy, the Test keeper. His international debut came in October 1996 in a one-day game and he was picked as reserve to Healy on the 1997 Ashes tour to England. With Healy still in place, Gilchrist played in one first-class game on the trip and two one-day internationals, just as a batsman.

1997-98 saw him chosen in front of Healy as batsman-wicket-keeper for one-day internationals in New Zealand – he had opened the innings in the final of the Carlton & United Series Cup, hitting 100 off 104 balls. During the 1999 World Cup Gilchrist broke into the Test arena – he scored 81 off 88 balls and had six dismissals. This confounded critics who thought him a one-day man. In his second Test appearance, at the Bellerive Oval, he hit 149 and drew compliments from Steve Waugh.

When the 2001 Ashes tour of England came round, Gilchrist was the man in possession – he also captained Australia in the fourth Test when Waugh was absent through injury. In 2001-02, he hit the fastest recorded Test double-hundred – v South Africa in Johannesburg and was on top of the official world batting rankings.

He retired from Test cricket during the 2007-08 season. In 2010 he played in a number of One Day matches for Middlesex.

1971
Born Adam Craig Gilchrist on 14 November 1971 at Bellingen, New South Wales

1993
First-class debut for New South Wales v Tasmania at Sydney on 28 January

1996
One-day international debut for Australia v South Africa in Faridabad on 25 October

1999
Test debut for Australia v Pakistan in Brisbane on 5 November

2001
Captained Australia in a Test match for first time, v England

2006-07
Hits a World Cup final best 149 off 104 balls as Australia win third successive World Cup

GRAHAM GOOCH

Born: 23 JULY 1953, WHIPPS CROSS, LEYTONSTONE, ESSEX
Teams: ESSEX (1973-97): WESTERN PROVINCE (1982-83 TO 1983-84)
First-class: 581 MATCHES; 44,846 RUNS, AVERAGE 49.01; 246 WICKETS, AVERAGE 34.37
Tests (1975 to 1994-95): 118 MATCHES; 8,900 RUNS, AVERAGE 42.58; 23 WICKETS, AVERAGE 46.47

By the end of 1993, Graham Gooch stood surveying the game of cricket like an Alexander with no more worlds to conquer. He had scored more than a hundred hundreds, scored more runs in Test cricket than any other English batsman, and more centuries for Essex than any other cricketer. He had played in more than 100 Tests, had captained England in victory and defeat, had made 333, the highest score by an England captain, and 123 against India at Lord's in 1990. He had scored more runs in the Sunday League, Benson & Hedges Cup and 60-over competition than any other batsman, more runs in a season and more runs in a career than any other Essex batsman, and had captained his county to success in the championship as well as being an integral part of the side who had enjoyed a golden period winning every honour in the game.

His career, though, has not been without its share of upsets and controversy. His Test career had begun with a "pair" against Australia in 1975, and he would have played more for England had he not excommunicated himself by joining a rebel tour in South Africa. He stood at the wicket suggesting a brooding melancholy, but he was a batsman of tremendous power, and he was the scourge of attacks all over the world, as 20 Test hundreds would testify. He was also a medium-pace bowler and a very fine slip fielder.

A fitness fanatic, he captained England in 34 Tests and went to Australia in 1994-95, under Mike Atherton, for his last Test series.

He retired from county cricket at the close of the 1997 season, but reappeared in one first-class match in 2000.

DAVID GOWER

Born: 1 APRIL 1957, TUNBRIDGE WELLS, KENT
Teams: LEICESTERSHIRE (1975-89); HAMPSHIRE (1990-93)
First-class: 448 MATCHES; 26,339 RUNS, AVERAGE 40.08; 4 WICKETS, AVERAGE 56.75
Tests (1978-92): 117 MATCHES; 8,231 RUNS, AVERAGE 44.25; 1 WICKET, AVERAGE 20.00

An effortless left-hander who timed the ball with a sweetness that few have been able to match, David Gower made his Test debut against Pakistan at Edgbaston in 1978. The first ball he received in Test cricket he hit for four, and by the time his Test career finished 14 years later he had scored more runs in Test cricket than any other batsman. Tall and blond, he had a languid eloquence with the bat and so delicate was his timing that his batting always had a suggestion of human frailty, which just added to its attraction.

He had the style of the carefree amateur of the Golden Age, and with his looks and grace, he might have been better playing in that age, as the mood took him and expenses allowed. He would have graced the Golden Age as he would have any era in which he batted. He abandoned his degree studies at London University to become a cricketer with Leicestershire in 1975, and if he took some time to prove himself statistically, his class was ever apparent. His first Test hundred came at The Oval in the second half of the 1978 summer. It was made against New Zealand and was followed by a century in Australia and 200 not out against India in 1979. Gower first captained England against Pakistan in 1982-83, when he hit two centuries. He was unfortunate in being handed the poisoned chalice of captaining England against the powerful West Indies side in 1984, and England lost 5-0. The following winter, in India, he led with tact, shrewdness and calm, and England won the series, which was played against the most tragic of backgrounds.

In 1985, his side regained the Ashes from a weakened Australian team and he hit three centuries in the series, including 215 at Edgbaston. Then, in the winter, England lost 5-0 to the West Indies for the second time and he took much blame for what many saw as his diffident approach. He was replaced when England lost to India, restored when England entertained Australia in 1989 and were soundly beaten, and was not selected in the party to tour the West Indies the following winter. Back in the side in 1990 and chosen for the trip to Australia, he made two centuries, but he upset skipper Gooch and the management when he and John Morris "buzzed" their team-mates with a pair of Tiger Moth aircraft while they were in the middle of a match against Queensland. When he was not selected for the tour of India in 1992-93, members of the MCC forced a special General Meeting to voice dissatisfaction at the way in which the game was being run.

Gower decided to retire and he became successful on television as a presenter and commentator.

Graham Gooch: no England player has scored more runs in Test cricket.

W.G. GRACE

Born: 18 JULY 1848, DOWNEND, BRISTOL
Died: 23 OCTOBER 1915, MOTTINGHAM, KENT
Teams: GLOUCESTERSHIRE (1870-99); LONDON COUNTY (1900-04)
First-class: 869 MATCHES; 54,211 RUNS; AVERAGE 39.45; 2,809 WICKETS, AVERAGE 18.14
Tests (1880 to 1889): 1,090 RUNS, AVERAGE 32.29; WICKETS 9, AVERAGE 26.22

William Gilbert Grace was not only the most famous cricketer of all time, but in his day was the best-known Englishman. With his big beard and burly frame, he was instantly recognizable. His brothers E.M., G.F. and Henry all played first-class cricket for Gloucestershire, the first two also for England (all three played together in one Test).

When he was 18, he scored 224 not out for England against Surrey at The Oval. He dominated the Gentlemen (i.e. amateurs) v Players match – one of the showpieces of the season for 156 years.

When 23, Grace had one of his best seasons, establishing a record aggregate of runs, 2,739, and the highest average, 78.25, more than double the second highest. He also became the first to score ten centuries in a season. In 1874, he was the first person to perform the double of 1,000 runs and 100 wickets – although some record books claim he did it in 1873. His stature in the game led to stories of his grandeur, such as the occasion when, given out early, he refused to go, saying that the crowd had come to see him bat, not to see the umpire giving him out.

As a batsman, Grace was a master. Although he scored 344 for the MCC against Kent in 1876, his career batting average of just under 40 would not be remarkable today. But one has to consider the pitches, extremely dangerous by today's standards. Grace was the first player to score 20,000 runs and the first to each target up to 50,000. He was the first to score 100 centuries.

As a bowler, he established yet another first – he was the first player

to take 2,000 first-class wickets.

At his peak he was called "the champion". He had already reached his peak before Test match cricket began. He toured North America in 1872 and took a team to Australia in 1873-74, but there were no first-class matches. Although he played his first Test in 1880, and captained England from 1888 to 1899, he played only 22 Tests. He hit the first England Test hundred in his first innings in Tests, 152 at The Oval, the first Test played in England. Although his powers began to wane in the 1890s, he had a magnificent season in 1895, when he became the first batsman to score 1,000 runs in May. That season he completed his 100th hundred. No wonder a "shilling testimonial" for him realized £9,000.

TOM GRAVENEY

Born: 16 JUNE 1927, RIDING MILL, NORTHUMBERLAND
Teams: GLOUCESTERSHIRE (1948-60); WORCESTERSHIRE (1961-70); QUEENSLAND (1969-70 TO 1971-72)
First-class: 732 MATCHES; 47,793 RUNS, AVERAGE 44.91; 80 WICKETS, AVERAGE 37.96
Tests (1951 TO 69): 79 MATCHES; 4,882 RUNS, AVERAGE 44.38; 1 WICKET, AVERAGE 167.00

Tom Graveney scored 122 first-class centuries and reached 1,000 runs in an English season 20 times. He was one of the most attractive batsmen to have appeared since the war, full of grace and elegance.

He first played for England against South Africa in 1951, and the following winter he hit the first of his 11 Test centuries, 175 against India at Bombay. His highest Test score was 258 against the West Indies at Trent Bridge in 1957. Graveney had an outstanding record against the West Indies and played a major part in the series victory in the Caribbean in 1967-68, hitting 118 in Trinidad. He made 75 against the West Indies at Old Trafford in 1969, but was banned for appearing in a benefit game on a Sunday and never played Test cricket again.

He was president of the MCC for 2004-05.

GORDON GREENIDGE

Born: 1 MAY 1951, BLACK BESS, ST PETER, BARBADOS
Teams: HAMPSHIRE (1970-87); BARBADOS (1972-73 TO 1990-91)
First-class: 523 MATCHES; 37,354 RUNS, AVERAGE 45.88; 18 WICKETS, AVERAGE 26.61
Tests (1974-75 to 1990-91): 108 MATCHES; 7,558 RUNS, AVERAGE 44.72; NO WICKET FOR 4 RUNS

A brilliantly aggressive right-handed opening batsman, Gordon Greenidge was brought to England at the age of 12 and lived and was educated in Reading. He could have played for England, but chose the West Indies instead, and with Desmond Haynes formed one of the most successful opening partnerships Test cricket has known. They shared 16 century partnerships in 89 Tests together. In county cricket, he had another

formidable opening partnership with the South African Barry Richards. Greenidge was prolific in all forms of cricket, and at one time he held the record for the highest score in all three one-day competitions in England.

He hit double-centuries against England, Australia and New Zealand and made 19 Test centuries in all. Perhaps his most memorable innings came at Lord's in 1984 when the West Indies were set 342 runs to win in just over five hours. Greenidge made 214 not out off 241 balls with two sixes and 29 fours, and the West Indies won by nine wickets.

Greenidge captained the West Indies on one occasion when Viv Richards was unfit.

Gordon Greenidge: chose to play for West Indies rather than England and became a Caribbean legend.

SYD GREGORY

Born: 14 APRIL 1870, MOORE PARK, RANDWICK, SYDNEY, NEW SOUTH WALES, AUSTRALIA
Died: 1 AUGUST 1929, MOORE PARK, RANDWICK, SYDNEY, NEW SOUTH WALES, AUSTRALIA
Teams: NEW SOUTH WALES (1889-90 TO 1911-12)
First-class: 369 MATCHES; 15,190 RUNS, AVERAGE 28.25; 2 WICKETS, AVERAGE 195.00
Tests (1890-1912): 58 MATCHES; 2,282 RUNS, AVERAGE 24.53; NO WICKETS FOR 33 RUNS

Known as "Little Tich" because he was only 5ft 4in tall, Syd Gregory was a quick-scoring, middle-order, right-handed batsman whose consistency and, above all, brilliant fielding at cover kept him in the Australian side for 22 years. He made the first of his eight tours to England in 1890, and on four of his tours he exceeded 1,000 runs. The first of his four Test hundreds came at Sydney in December 1894, when he hit 201 in 244 minutes. This was the first double-century to be scored in a Test in Australia. He made a century at Lord's in 1896, and at The Oval three years later.

When Clem Hill and five other leading players refused to play in the Triangular Tournament in England in 1912, Syd Gregory was recalled to captain the side after an absence of three years from Test cricket. The side was woefully weak and ill-disciplined and, at 42, Gregory was past his best.

TONY GREIG

Born: 6 OCTOBER 1946, QUEENSTOWN, SOUTH AFRICA
Teams: BORDER (1965-66 TO 1969-70); SUSSEX (1966-78); EASTERN PROVINCE (1970-71 TO 1971-72)
First-class: 350 MATCHES; 16,660 RUNS, AVERAGE 31.19; 856 WICKETS, AVERAGE 28.85
Tests (1972-77): 58 MATCHES; 3,599 RUNS, AVERAGE 40.43; 141 WICKETS, AVERAGE 32.20

The son of a Scottish RAF officer with a distinguished war record who was posted to South Africa at the end of the war, Tony Greig excites the same conflicting passions as Jardine. Standing 6ft 7in tall, with blond hair and an engaging smile, he was a brave, attacking batsman and

Tony Greig: an England captain who spent years trying to shake off his South African tag.

a right-arm medium-pace bowler who also bowled off-breaks to good effect. A dominant and attractive personality, he qualified for Sussex and made an impact with 156 against Lancashire in his first championship match in 1967. He played for England against Rest of the World in 1970, and two years later made his Test debut, hitting 57 and 62 and taking 1 for 21 and 4 for 53 against Australia at Old Trafford. It was the first of an unbroken sequence of 58 Tests.

The first of his eight Test centuries came against India the following winter, and a year later, as vice-captain on the tour of the Caribbean, he hit a century in the third Test and bowled England to a sensational victory and a draw in the series in the last Test when he took 8 for 86 and 5 for 70 with his off-breaks. His outstanding match analysis in this game remains a record for England against the West Indies.

He was also involved in a contro-versial incident with Kallicharran in this series and was deprived of the vice-captaincy in Australia. Having

led Sussex since 1973, when Denness was sacked in 1975 he became captain of England. Immensely popular, he instilled self-belief and a fighting spirit into a flagging England side. He would smile even when beaten, but there were always those ready to remind him he was South African.

He inspired England to a memorable series victory in England in 1976-77, and English cricket was respectful and joyful, but in the Centenary Test in Melbourne, it was learned that he had been recruiting players for Packer's World Series. Regarded by some as a traitor, he was sacked as captain and did not play Test cricket after 1977. He had been the first man to score 3,000 runs and to take 100 Test wickets for England, and his record stands comparison with anyone's.

He settled in Australia and worked as a commentator and in insurance. His actions brought sponsorship and more money into cricket and he shook the establishment out of complacency. It would be difficult to find a professional cricketer who has

anything but praise and affection for him. It was also revealed that he suffered from a mild form of epilepsy.

CLARRIE GRIMMETT

Born: 25 DECEMBER 1891, CAVERSHAM, DUNEDIN, NEW ZEALAND
Died: 2 MAY 1980, KENSINGTON PARK, ADELAIDE, SOUTH AUSTRALIA
Teams: WELLINGTON (1911-12 TO 1913-14); VICTORIA (1918-19 TO 1923-24); SOUTH AUSTRALIA (1924-25 TO 1940-41)
First-class: 248 MATCHES; 4,720 RUNS, AVERAGE 17.67; 1,424 WICKETS, AVERAGE 22.28
Tests (1924-25 to 1935-36): 37 MATCHES; 557 RUNS, AVERAGE 13.92; 216 WICKETS, AVERAGE 24.21

Clarrie Grimmett was the first bowler to take 200 Test wickets. He was a leg-break and googly bowler who was born in New Zealand and moved to Australia at the start of the First World War. A sign-writer by trade, he worked hard at his bowling and became a prolific wicket-taker in the Sheffield Shield, but he was 33 before he made his Test debut against England at Sydney in 1924-25. He took 5 for 45 and 6 for 37. On the tour of England in 1926, he took over 100 wickets, and he and fellow leg-spinner Arthur Mailey were the main Test wicket-takers.

Mailey had departed by 1928-29, and Grimmett bore the burden of the Australian attack, capturing 23 wickets but sending down nearly 400 overs in the Tests. In 1930, when he again captured more than 100 wickets in England, including all 10 for 37 in an innings against Yorkshire, he took 29 Test wickets, and the following winter he mesmerized the West Indies in Australia, claiming 33 wickets in the series. He repeated this feat in only four Tests against South Africa the following season. He was again successful in England in 1934, and in South Africa in 1935-36, he broke all records with 44 wickets, average 14.59, in five Tests. Astonishingly, he never played Test cricket again, although many thought he should have come to England in 1938, even at the age of 46.

GEORGE GUNN

Born: 13 JUNE 1879, HUCKNALL TORKARD, NOTTINGHAMSHIRE
Died: 29 JUNE 1958, TYLERS GREEN, CUCKFIELD, SUSSEX
Teams: NOTTINGHAMSHIRE (1902-32)
First-class: 643 MATCHES; 35,208 RUNS, AVERAGE 35.96; 66 WICKETS, AVERAGE 35.68
Tests (1907-08 to 1929-30): 15 MATCHES; 1,120 RUNS, AVERAGE 40.00; NO WICKETS FOR 8 RUNS

A small, slim right-handed opening batsman, George Gunn was one of a cricketing family and, for a period, he and his son played alongside each other in the Nottinghamshire side. George Gunn was a batsman in the classical mould, but he was an eccentric and played as the mood took him, which is probably why his only Test in England was against Australia at Lord's in 1909. The previous series, 1907-08, he had been in Australia and was called into the England side in an emergency. He made 119 and 74 in his first Test, hit another century in the last Test and headed the batting averages for the series. He reached 1,000 runs in a season 20 times and had a fine opening partnership with W.W. Whysall. His last Test was against the West Indies in Jamaica, in April 1930. He scored 85 and 47 run out. He was just short of his 51st birthday.

RICHARD HADLEE

SEE PAGE 192

WES HALL

Born: 12 SEPTEMBER 1937, ST MICHAEL, BARBADOS, WEST INDIES
Teams: BARBADOS (1955-56 TO 1970-71); TRINIDAD (1966-67 TO 1969-70); QUEENSLAND 1961-62 TO 1962-63)
First-class: 170 MATCHES; 2,673 RUNS, AVERAGE 15.10; 546 WICKETS, AVERAGE 26.14
Tests (1958-59 to 1968-69): 48 MATCHES; 818 RUNS, AVERAGE 15.73; 192 WICKETS, AVERAGE 26.38

After beginning his career as a wicket-keeper-batsman, the 6ft 2in Wes Hall developed into one of the great fast bowlers of the early 1960s.

He took a very long run and brought the ball down from a great height, his smooth run-up foreshadowing that of Michael Holding in its athleticism and grace. He made his Test debut for the West Indies on a tour of India and Pakistan in 1958-59, taking 46 wickets in the eight Tests at a cost of less than 18 runs. He took 22 wickets against the English tourists the following year, and 21 in the great tour of Australia in 1960-61, nine of them in the famous tied Test.

With Charlie Griffith as his partner, he was formidable when the West Indies beat England 3-1 in 1963 and bowled throughout the 200 minutes of the last day at Lord's, including the last over when England drew needing six to win with the last pair together and Cowdrey batting with a broken arm in plaster. He was a slogging tailender, although at Trinidad in 1967-68 he batted throughout the last two hours with Sobers to save the match against England. On retiring he went into politics and became Sports Minister in Barbados.

WALTER HAMMOND

Born: 19 JUNE 1903, DOVER, KENT
Died: 1 JULY 1965, KLOOF, SOUTH AFRICA
Teams: GLOUCESTERSHIRE (1920-51); SOUTH AFRICAN AIR FORCE (1942-43)
First-class: 634 MATCHES; 50,551 RUNS, AVERAGE 56.10; 732 WICKETS, AVERAGE 30.58
Tests (1927-28 to 1946-47): 85 MATCHES; 7,249 RUNS, AVERAGE 58.45; 83 WICKETS, AVERAGE 37.80

Hammond was the outstanding English cricketer of the 1930s, topping the batting averages for each of the eight seasons between 1933 and 1946. No English batsman has beaten his total of 36 double-centuries, and his highest score of 336 not out, made for England against New Zealand in 1932-33, was at the time a Test match record. His average for the two-match series was 563. His County Championship debut was delayed because of objections about his qualification and he returned from a tour of the West Indies in 1925-26 with a mystery illness which made him miss the 1926 season altogether. He came back so well in 1927 that he made his Test debut in South Africa the following winter.

He was a majestic batsman, whose off-drive was regarded as one of the classic shots of cricket, a more than useful fast-medium bowler and a brilliant fielder at slip, where for Gloucestershire against Surrey in 1928 he held a world record ten catches. Against Australia, in the 1928-29 series, he made 905 runs, then a record, averaging 113.12.

Hammond turned amateur in 1938 and was immediately given the England captaincy, which he retained until the first tour after the war, in 1946-47, when his powers at last began to decline. He was a strange, aloof man, not popular as a captain, and played rarely after his Test career ended, finally going to live in South Africa. Of his many records, his total of 7,249 runs in Tests stood for nearly 25 years.

STEVE HARMISON

Born: 23 OCTOBER 1978, ASHINGTON, NORTHUMBERLAND
Teams: DURHAM (1996-2010)
First-class: 199 MATCHES; 1,810 RUNS, AVERAGE 9.84; 713 WICKETS, AVERAGE 27.94
Tests (2002 to 2009): 62 MATCHES; 742 RUNS, AVERAGE 12.16; 222 WICKETS, AVERAGE 31.94

A right-arm fast bowler who formed a principal part of the England seam attack during the 2005 Ashes series, Harmison first came to the public's attention during England's 2003-04 visit to the West Indies. In the first Test in Kingston, Jamaica, he captured seven wickets for just 12 runs in the home side's second innings as they lurched to 47 all out. In the second Test he grabbed a further 6 for 61 and in the whole series topped England's bowling averages with 23 wickets at 14.86 runs each. The West Indies came to England for the 2004 summer; Harmison picked up another 17 wickets against them, having already taken 21 against New Zealand, the country which immediately preceded the visit from the Caribbean.

Steve Harmison had made his debut for Durham at the age of 17, then he joined the England Under-19 side in Pakistan. Things went awry. The sub-continent did not suit him; he was homesick, injured and came home early. A spate of niggling injuries disrupted his career in 1997 and the critics began to suggest that another "bright prospect" had withered on the vine. The England selectors, however, had not given up. He made his Test debut in 2002 – fast, dangerous, but at times erratic. In 2003-04 everything clicked. In 2005-06, Harmison played in the three Tests v Pakistan and two against India.

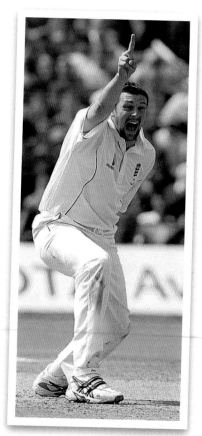

Steve Harmison: tall, fast and aggressive.

RICHARD HADLEE
The Lionheart

FIRST-CLASS CAREER
(1971-72 to 1990, 342 matches)
Batting: RUNS 12,052; AVERAGE 31.71; HIGHEST
SCORE 210 NOT OUT; CENTURIES 47
Bowling: WICKETS 1,490; RUNS 26,998;
AVERAGE 18.11; BEST 9-52
Catches: 198

TESTS
(1972-73 TO 1990, 86 MATCHES)
Batting: RUNS 3,124; AVERAGE 27.16; HIGHEST
SCORE 151 NOT OUT; CENTURIES 2
Bowling: WICKETS 431; RUNS 9,611; AVERAGE 22.29;
BEST 9-52
Catches: 39

Richard John Hadlee comes from a cricketing family. His father, W.A., captained New Zealand, and of his four cricketing brothers, D.R. played for New Zealand, and B.G. for Canterbury.

Tall and wiry rather than muscular, he began playing for Canterbury in 1971-72 and, a year later, made his Test debut against Pakistan. He really came to the fore in 1975-76 against India when, in the third Test, he took 4 for 35 and 7 for 23 to help win the match by an innings and square the series. These were the best match figures produced by a New Zealander at the time. In 1977-78 at Wellington, he was instrumental in New Zealand beating England for the first time, in the 48th match between them.

He took ten wickets, his 6 for 26 in the second innings skittling England for 64 when they were chasing 137. In 1979-80, he scored his first Test hundred, and his 11 wickets in the first Test against the West Indies set up the one-wicket win which gave New Zealand their first Test rubber at home after 50 years of trying.

Hadlee then began an astonishing revival in the fortunes of Nottinghamshire. In 1981, he took 100 wickets, the only bowler to do so, and Nottinghamshire won the championship for the first time for 62 years. From 1980 to 1987 at Nottinghamshire, he achieved complete domination over county batsmen, finishing top of the bowling averages five times.

Meanwhile he revived New Zealand. Their win at Headingley in 1983 caused such euphoria that back home the demands on Hadlee led him to suffer a breakdown. But a quick course in motivation by a psychologist soon had him back on form, and in England in 1984 he performed the double of 1,000 runs and 100 wickets. He also hit his highest score, 210 not out, against Middlesex.

In Australia in 1985-86, he achieved his best analysis, 9 for

Richard Hadlee: helped change the fortunes of both New Zealand and Nottinghamshire cricket.

52, and his 33 wickets in the three-match series gave New Zealand their first series victory over Australia.

Hadlee said farewell to Nottinghamshire in 1987 by helping them to win the championship again. His Test wicket-taking continued: in 1988-89 he passed Ian Botham's world record by capturing his 374th wicket in India; he passed 400 in 1989-90 on his home ground of Christchurch and finished in 1990 with 431. It had

taken only 86 Tests, a remarkable strike rate of five wickets per match. In nine of those Tests he had taken ten wickets; 36 times he took five wickets in an innings. He was awarded an MBE in 1980 and a knighthood in 1990 on his final tour to England.

In retirement, he took on the running of a plant nursery in Christchurch with his wife, and travels the world, being frequently seen at Trent Bridge.

1951	**1971-72**	**1973**	**1978**
Born Richard John Hadlee on 3 July at St Albans, Christchurch, New Zealand	Makes his first-class debut for Christchurch and forms new-ball partnership with his elder brother, Dayle	Made his Test debut v Pakistan at Wellington on 2-5 February. Scored 46 runs and ended with match figures of 2 for 112	Took ten wickets, including 6 for 26 in England's innings of 64 in New Zealand's first-ever victory over England, Wellington, 10-15 February

1980	**1981**	**1984**	**1990**
Took 11 wickets in a match to set up New Zealand's first-ever series win at home after 50 years, v West Indies, Dunedin, 8-13 February	Was the only bowler in the country to take 100 wickets as he inspired Notthinghamshire to their first County Championship in 62 years	Achieves double of 1,000 runs and 100 wickets in County Championship for Nottinghamshire	Became the first player to take 400 Test wickets when bowling Sanjay Manjrekar, v India at Christchurch, 2-5 February

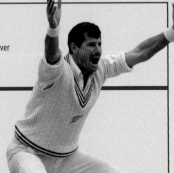

HANIF MOHAMMAD

Born: 21 DECEMBER 1934, JUNAGADH, INDIA
Teams: BAHAWALPUR (1953-54); KARACHI (1954-55 TO 1968-69); PIA (1960-61 TO 1975-76)
First-class: 238 MATCHES; 17,059 RUNS, AVERAGE 52.32; 53 WICKETS, AVERAGE 28.47
Tests (1952-53 TO 1969-70): 55 MATCHES; 3,915 RUNS, AVERAGE 43.98; 1 WICKET, AVERAGE 95.00

Hanif Mohammad, nicknamed "The Little Master", was a small batsman with an immaculate defence and limitless concentration. He made his first-class debut for Karachi and Bahawalpur in 1951-52 when only 16 years old, and after the partition of India made his Test debut for Pakistan against India in 1952-53, in Pakistan's first-ever Test. At 17 years 300 days, he was the world's youngest Test wicket-keeper. He also opened the batting, scoring 51 in his first innings, and he soon dropped wicket-keeping to become a specialist batsman.

His Test career comprised 55 of Pakistan's first 57 Tests. In the first Test against the West Indies in Bridgetown in 1957-58, when Pakistan followed on 473 behind, he made the then second-highest Test score of 337 to save the match, batting for 16 hours, ten minutes, the longest Test innings. In 1958-59, batting for Karachi against Bahawalpur at Karachi, he was run out off the last ball of the day for 499, the highest score in first-class cricket until Brian Lara beat it in 1994. He captained Pakistan in 11 Tests. He is the brother of Wazir, Mushtaq and Sadiq, and the father of Shoaib, all Pakistani Test players.

HARBHAJAN SINGH

Born: 3 JULY 1980, JULIUNDUR (JALANDHAR), PUNJAB, INDIA
Teams: PUNJAB (1997-2009), SURREY (2005-07); MUMBAI INDIANS (2008-09)
First-class: 157 MATCHES; 3,416 RUNS, AVERAGE 19.56; 670 WICKETS, AVERAGE 28.41
Tests (1997-98 TO 2010-11): 93 MATCHES; 2,008 RUNS, AVERAGE 18.59; 393 WICKETS, AVERAGE 31.85

Bowling right-arm off-breaks, Harbhajan Singh is a very aggressive player whose enthusiasm has at times brought him problems with the authorities. He took over from Kumble as India's leading spinner.

Making his first-class debut in the 1997-98 season, he forced his way into the final Test against Australia that season. Initially, his Test performances were disappointing and, when his action was queried, he needed the old England off-spinner Fred Titmus to iron it out for him. Since then, he has reserved some of his best performances for Tests against Australia, and excelled in their 2000-01 series in India, being voted the Man of the Series. Having lost the first Test, India followed on in the second, despite Harbhajan's 7 for 123, including India's first-ever Test hat-trick. Brilliant Indian batting in the follow-on allowed them to set Australia a target of 384, and Harbhajan's 6 for 73 won the match. India won the final Test and the series, with Harbhajan taking 32 of the 50 Aussie wickets to fall.

Harbhajan's aggression went too far in 2007-08, when there were words between him and the Australian Andrew Symonds during the one-day matches in India, which continued into the next Test series. In Sydney in January 2008 Harbhajan was charged with racially abusing Symonds, and initially was given a three-Test ban, reduced to a fine when the racist angle was dismissed. Three months later Harbhajan was banned for 11 IPL matches for slapping his team-mate Sreesanth.

NEIL HARVEY

Born: 8 OCTOBER 1928, FITZROY, MELBOURNE, VICTORIA, AUSTRALIA
Teams: VICTORIA (1946-47 TO 1956-57); NEW SOUTH WALES (1958-59 TO 1962-63)
First-class: 306 MATCHES; 21,699 RUNS, AVERAGE 50.93; 30 WICKETS, AVERAGE 36.86
Tests (1947-48 TO 1962-63): 79 MATCHES; 6,149 RUNS, AVERAGE 48.41; 3 WICKETS, AVERAGE 40.00

Neil Harvey was a brilliant left-handed middle-order batsman, an occasional off-break bowler and an outstanding fielder. He had just turned 18 when he first played for Victoria and a year later made his Test debut against India. In his second Test he became the youngest Australian to score a century, at 19 years 121 days. He came to England with Bradman's great side in 1948, and became the first Aussie left-hander to make 100 on his debut against England. He was at the wicket in the second innings with Bradman as Australia scored 404 for 3 on the last day to win. For the next 15 years, Harvey was Australia's leading batsman.

In 1949-50 in South Africa, he hit four centuries and averaged 132.00, including a magnificent 152 not out to win on a crumbling pitch after Australia had made 75 in the first innings. He made four centuries against South Africa in 1952-53 (average 92.66) and three in the West Indies in 1954-55 (average 108.33). He captained Australia once, at Lord's in 1961, and Australia won. Twenty-one of his 67 centuries were in Tests, the highest, 205, against South Africa in Melbourne in 1952-53, and his Test aggregate was at the time second only to Bradman for Australia.

LINDSAY HASSETT

Born: 28 AUGUST 1913, GEELONG, VICTORIA, AUSTRALIA
Died: 16 JUNE 1993, BATEMAN'S BAY, NEW SOUTH WALES, AUSTRALIA
Teams: VICTORIA (1932-33 TO 1952-53)
First-class: 216 MATCHES; 16,890 RUNS, AVERAGE 58.24; 18 WICKETS, AVERAGE 39.05
Tests (1938-53): 43 MATCHES; 3,073 RUNS, AVERAGE 46.56; NO WICKET FOR 78

The 17-year-old Lindsay Hassett made 147 not out against the touring West Indians two years before he made his first-class debut for Victoria. Only 5ft 6in, he was a neat, quick-footed batsman with all the strokes, and a polished fielder.

In 1938 he toured England, making his debut in the first Test. After the war, he captained the Australian Services team in the unofficial Victory Tests in England and India. Vice-captain to Bradman on the 1948 tour of England, he took over the Australian captaincy for the 1949-50 tour of South Africa. He was an excellent captain with a well-known sense of humour – perhaps his most public joke coming after he had twice dropped Washbrook on the boundary in a Test at Old Trafford, when he borrowed a policeman's helmet in preparation for the next one. He retired in 1953.

MATTHEW HAYDEN

Born: 29 OCTOBER 1971, KINGAROY, QUEENSLAND, AUSTRALIA
Teams: QUEENSLAND (1991-92 TO 2007-08); HAMPSHIRE (1997); NORTHANTS (1999-2001)
First-class: 295 MATCHES; 24,603 RUNS, AVERAGE 52.57; 17 WICKETS, AVERAGE 39.47
Tests (1993-94 to 2008-09): 103 MATCHES; 8,625 RUNS, AVERAGE 50.73; 0 WICKETS

Matthew Hayden was a run-maker from childhood, but was perceived to have a faulty technique.

Matthew Hayden: for a while, the tall left-hander held the record for Test cricket's highest score.

Nevertheless on his debut for Queensland he made 149 in an all-out aggressive display. His first Test came in 1993-94 in South Africa but, by March 2000, when recalled against New Zealand, he had made only seven appearances. He blossomed spectacularly in India in 2000-01, finishing the calendar year 2001 with 1,391 Test runs, then third highest of all time. From February 2001 to January 2003 he scored 2,560 in 25 Tests, with 11 centuries, and an average of 67.36. He changed the style of Test opening batsmen by attacking from the first ball, and against Zimbabwe in Perth in 2003-04 played the then highest Test innings of 380.

DESMOND HAYNES

Born: 15 FEBRUARY 1956, ST JAMES, BARBADOS, WEST INDIES
Teams: BARBADOS (1976-77 TO 1994-95); MIDDLESEX (1989-94)
First-class: 360 MATCHES; 25,027 RUNS, AVERAGE 46.17; 7 WICKETS, AVERAGE 28.71
Tests (1977-78 to 1993-94): 116 MATCHES; 7,487 RUNS, AVERAGE 42.29; 1 WICKET, AVERAGE 8.00

Desmond Haynes was a sound but aggressive opening batsman who made over 100 Test appearances for the West Indies, 89 of them in a prolific partnership with Gordon Greenidge, with whom he shared a record 16 century opening partnerships. Including World Cups, he made seven tours to England and eight to Australia, as well as tours to Pakistan, India, New Zealand and Zimbabwe. His first tour to England as a Test player, in 1980, was his most successful, when he averaged 51.33 in the Tests. In 1984, his 125 at The Oval in the fifth Test guaranteed the West Indies' "blackwash" – the first side to win all five in a rubber in England. A hamstring injury in 1988 ended a run of 78 consecutive Tests. He captained the West Indies in four Tests in 1990.

He played county cricket for Middlesex from 1989 and, in 1990,

Desmond Haynes: formed part of a formidable opening pair along with Gordon Greenidge. Together they put on a Test record 16 century partnerships for West Indies.

he hit 2,346 runs, average 69.00, including his career highest of 255 not out against Sussex at Lord's. His highest in Tests also came at Lord's, 184 against England in 1980. He was immensely successful in international one-day cricket, with a record number of runs, 8,649 (average 41.38), and centuries, 17.

TOM HAYWARD

Born: 29 MARCH 1871, CAMBRIDGE
Died: 19 JULY 1939, CAMBRIDGE
Teams: SURREY (1893-1914)
First-class: 712 MATCHES; 43,551 RUNS, AVERAGE 41.79; 481 WICKETS, AVERAGE 22.95
Tests (1895-96 to 1909): 35 MATCHES; 1,999 RUNS, AVERAGE 34.46; 14 WICKETS, AVERAGE 38.64

One of a famous cricketing family, Tom Hayward was a most reliable right-handed opening batsman, who, in 1906, scored 3,518 runs in an English

season, which stood as a record until 1947. In 1913, he became the first professional to score 100 hundreds in first-class cricket, and he reached 1,000 or more runs in a season for 20 consecutive seasons beginning in 1895. In 1900, he scored 1,000 runs before the end of May. He was also a useful medium-pace bowler, and in 1897 he completed the "double". The following year, he scored an unbeaten 315 against Lancashire at The Oval.

His Test debut came against South Africa in 1895-96, and he hit 122 at Johannesburg in his second match. He was a tremendous influence on Jack Hobbs, who followed him from Cambridge to The Oval, and he was Hobbs's first great opening partner, the pair sharing 40 partnerships of 100 or more. Hayward was also involved in six century first-wicket stands for England.

He was coach at Oxford after his retirement.

VIJAY HAZARE

Born: 11 MARCH 1915, SANGLI, MAHARASHTRA, INDIA
Died: 12 DECEMBER 2004, BARODA, INDIA
Teams: MAHARASHTRA (1934-35 TO 1940-41); CENTRAL INDIA (1935-36 TO 1938-39); BARODA (1941-42)
First-class: 238 MATCHES; 18,740 RUNS, AVERAGE 58.38; 595 WICKETS, AVERAGE 24.61
Tests (1946 to 1952-53): 30 MATCHES; 2,192 RUNS, AVERAGE 47.65; 20 WICKETS, AVERAGE 61.00

A small, right-handed batsman with the full complement of wristy strokes and a medium-pace bowler, Vijay Hazare made two scores of over 300 in his career, and he and Gul Mahomed created a world record when they put on 577 for Baroda's fourth wicket against Holkar in 1946-47. In 1939-40, he had established himself with 316 not out for Maharashtra against Baroda and had hit another triple-century the same season. Duleepsinhji apart, who played his cricket in England, Hazare was the first Indian to hit a triple-century and certainly the first to hit two. Coached by Clarrie Grimmett, he made his Test debut in England in 1946 and, at Adelaide in 1947-48, he became the first batsman to score a century in each innings of a Test for India. He was to go on to score centuries against each of the four countries against whom he played.

He was named captain of the side to tour England in 1952. His team was weak and, despite his consistent batting, the tour was a disaster.

He was deposed as captain for the inaugural series against Pakistan, but he still managed a century in Bombay. He was reinstated for the tour of the West Indies in 1952-53, but India lost and that marked the end of his international career. Nevertheless, he can proudly boast that he scored two centuries against England in 1951-52, and captained his country to their first-ever Test victory in the same series.

GEORGE HEADLEY

Born: 30 MAY 1909, COLON, PANAMA
Died: 30 NOVEMBER 1983, MEADOWBRIDGE, KINGSTON, JAMAICA
Teams: JAMAICA (1927-28 TO 1953-54)
First-class: 103 MATCHES; 9,921 RUNS, AVERAGE 69.86; 51 WICKETS, AVERAGE 36.11
Tests (1929-30 TO 1953-54): 22 MATCHES; 2,190 RUNS, AVERAGE 60.83; NO WICKETS FOR 230 RUNS

In the 1930s, George Headley was nicknamed the "Black Bradman", and his Test record still shows him to have been one of the greatest batsmen in the history of the game. He announced his quality in his first Test match, hitting 176 against England in the second innings at Bridgetown. In the third Test, in Georgetown, he became the first West Indian to score a century in each innings, and this feat was followed by 223 in the fourth and final Test in Kingston. He remains the only batsman to score four Test hundreds before the age of 21

and, until the record was beaten by Javed Miandad, he was the youngest batsman to score a double-century in Test cricket.

The West Indies toured Australia in 1930-31, and lost the Test series 4-1, but Headley hit two centuries. He scored 169 against England at Old Trafford in 1933, and headed the first-class averages, and he took an unbeaten 270 off the England bowlers at Kingston in 1935. In 1939, he became the first man to score a century in each innings in a Test match at Lord's.

Headley had a fine cricket brain, but was denied the West Indian captaincy until 1948, and then led the side for only one Test. He was the first black man to captain them.

He was a professional in the Lancashire League and both his son and grandson became Test cricketers, his grandson, Dean, for England.

PATSY HENDREN

Born: 5 FEBRUARY 1889, TURNHAM GREEN, MIDDLESEX
Died: 4 OCTOBER 1962, TOOTING BEC, LONDON
Teams: MIDDLESEX (1907-37)
First-class: 833 MATCHES; 57,611 RUNS, AVERAGE 50.80; 47 WICKETS, AVERAGE 54.76
Tests (1920-21 to 1934-35): 51 MATCHES; 3,525 RUNS, AVERAGE 47.63; 1 WICKET, AVERAGE 31.00

"Patsy" Hendren, a great entertainer and one of the best loved characters the game has known, hit 170 first-class hundreds in his career. For a decade after the First World War, he was an integral part of England's middle order, and he was a fine outfielder.

He did not have the easiest of Test baptisms against Armstrong's Australians, and it was not until Headingley in 1924, that he scored the first of his seven Test centuries, 132 against South Africa. He hit his second in the same series. He was part of Chapman's side which regained the Ashes in 1926, and he thrived in the West Indies in 1929-30, when he hit four double-centuries during the tour. His aggregate for the tour was 1,765 runs, average 135.76, which remains a record, and it included his highest Test innings, 205 not out in Trinidad. He hit 301 not out for Middlesex against Worcestershire in 1933, and three times he exceeded 3,000 runs in a season.

He coached Sussex and at Harrow following his retirement, and he was the Middlesex scorer between 1953 and 59.

GRAEME HICK

Born: 23 MAY 1966, SALISBURY, RHODESIA
Teams: ZIMBABWE (1983-84 TO 1985-86); WORCESTERSHIRE (1984-2008); NORTHERN DISTRICTS (1987-88 TO 1988-89); QUEENSLAND (1990-91)
First-class: 526 MATCHES; 41,112 RUNS, AVERAGE 52.23; 232 WICKETS, AVERAGE 44.43
Tests (1991-2001): 65 MATCHES; 3,383, AVERAGE 31.32; 23 WICKETS, AVERAGE 56.78

Before they attained Test status, Zimbabwe invested much money and hope in Graeme Hick, a right-

handed batsman of phenomenal potential and great power. He is also a capable off-break bowler and fine slip fielder. Hick decided to play league cricket, to qualify for Worcestershire and, ultimately, for England.

Tall and confident, Hick appeared to be realizing the potential all had recognized during the seven years of county cricket he played prior to qualifying for England. He was the youngest cricketer to score 2,000 runs in a season; in 1986, he scored 1,000 runs before the end of May 1988, and became the youngest player to reach 50 first-class centuries. While reaching his thousand before the end of May, he hit an astonishing 405 against Somerset. He was equally effective in New Zealand and, after a slow start, scored well for Queensland, although the Australians were never so enthusiastic about him as the English press.

Able to play Test cricket in 1991, he was looked upon as England's saviour, but he found international cricket a tough proposition. In his 22nd Test innings, he scored 178 against India in Bombay, and there was a century against South Africa at Leeds in 1994, but in 1996 he was vulnerable to both the guile of Mushtaq and the speed of Waqar.

Since then, Hick was in and out of the England Test side. He was given yet another opportunity on the winter tour of 2000-01 to Pakistan and Sri Lanka, but failed to produce any worthwhile innings. He was therefore excluded for the Tests of 2001. In contrast, his overall form in one-day Internationals has been quite acceptable and he played a big part in helping England to the World Cup final in 1992.

In 1998 he became the second youngest player ever to score 100 centuries in first-class matches. He was captain of Worcestershire from 2000 to 2002. Hick retired at the end of the 2008 season.

Graeme Hick: although he destroyed county bowling, and hit 404 off Somerset at Taunton, he never quite convinced in the Test arena.

CLEM HILL

Born: 18 MARCH 1877, HINDMARSH, ADELAIDE, SOUTH AUSTRALIA
Died: 5 SEPTEMBER 1945, PARKVILLE, MELBOURNE, VICTORIA, AUSTRALIA
Teams: SOUTH AUSTRALIA (1892-93 TO 1922-23)
First-class: 252 MATCHES; 17,213 RUNS, AVERAGE 43.57; 10 WICKETS, AVERAGE 32.30
Tests (1896 to 1911-12): 49 MATCHES; 3,412 RUNS, AVERAGE 39.21

A short, powerful left-handed batsman with a crouched stance, Clem Hill delighted crowds with his sound defence and explosive attack. He had the right temperament for the big occasion and rarely failed, although he was always at his best on the hard wickets in Australia. He was a magnificent fielder in the deep where he took some memorable catches, notably one to dismiss Lilley in the Old Trafford Test of 1902 which Australia won by three runs.

Not included in the side to tour England in 1896, he scored a double-century against New South Wales, and a public outcry caused him to be added to the party. His first Test century came at Melbourne in 1897-98, when he hit 188, the highest score made by an Under-21 in an Ashes Test. In 1900-01, he made an unbeaten 365 for South Australia against New South Wales. In three successive Test innings the following season he scored 99, 98 and 97. In 1899 he hit a magnificent 135 at Lord's and followed it up in his next tour of Engand, in 1902, by hitting 119 in the only Test match ever to be played at Bramall Lane, Sheffield - it was by far the highest innings of the match.

His relations with the Australian Board were uneasy, and he twice refused to tour England. He captained Australia to success against South Africa in 1910-11, but lost heavily to Douglas's side the following season, and that defeat by England ended his Test career. It was alleged that he was involved in a fight with a selector.

GEORGE HIRST

Born: 7 SEPTEMBER 1871, KIRKHEATON, YORKSHIRE
Died: 10 MAY 1954, LINDLEY, HUDDERSFIELD, YORKSHIRE
Teams: YORKSHIRE (1891-1929); EUROPEANS (1921-22)
First-class: 826 MATCHES; 36,356 RUNS, AVERAGE 34.13; 2,742 WICKETS, AVERAGE 18.73
Tests (1897-98 to 1909): 24 MATCHES; 790 RUNS, AVERAGE 22.57; 59 WICKETS, AVERAGE 30.00

In the years before the First World War, there were those who believed that if you needed a man to die for you on the cricket field, you would choose George Hirst. He was loyal, tough and kind, and he lived and breathed Yorkshire and cricket. He bowled medium-fast left-arm, and he batted right-handed with skill and aggression. He performed the "double" 14 times, and he is the only man in the history of the game to have taken 200 wickets and scored 2,000 runs in the same season – 2,385 runs and 208 wickets in 1906. Hirst's achievements for his native county are legion, yet his Test record was surprisingly moderate. Perhaps his most famous exploit was when he and Rhodes brought England victory over Australia at The Oval in 1902 by scoring the 15 runs needed in a tense last-wicket stand. Hirst, who had match figures of 6 for 84, was unbeaten on 58. He coached at Eton for many years on his retirement.

JACK HOBBS

SEE PAGE 197

MATTHEW HOGGARD

Born: 31 DECEMBER 1976, LEEDS, YORKSHIRE
Teams: YORKSHIRE (1996-2009); FREE STATE (1998-99 TO 1999-00); LEICESTERSHIRE (2010)
First-class: 210 MATCHES; 1,684 RUNS, AVERAGE 9.05; 718 WICKETS, AVERAGE 27.17
Tests (2000 to 2007-08): 67 MATCHES; 473 RUNS, AVERAGE 7.27, 248 WICKETS, AVERAGE 30.50

An integral part of the 2005 England Ashes squad, Hoggard opened the bowling partnering Steve Harmison in all five Tests and while not as charismatic as the other three seamers who demolished Australia, did perform a very sound role and finished with 16 wickets at 29.56 runs each. Prior to these games Hoggard topped the Test bowling table in the series v Bangladesh.

His early cricket was with Pudsey Congs and the Yorkshire Academy. In 1995-96, Hoggard was drafted into the England Under-19 side touring Zimbabwe; he replaced Alex Tudor. Then, in 1996, Hoggard represented England Under-19s in the Tests v New Zealand. In the same season came his first-class debut for Yorkshire. He was not an immediate success, but over the next two seasons he increased his pace and at the same time his accuracy. Towards the end of the 1998 summer he found a regular place in the Yorkshire side. Tall and well-built, he has the ideal physique for a fast bowler. There was a temporary set-back in 1999 due to a knee injury, but in 2000 came his Test debut v West Indies at Lord's. The following winter he toured Pakistan and Sri Lanka with the England side – in Pakistan he topped the first-class bowling figures, but did not feature in the Test side, nor was he seen in the England team during the 2001 Ashes series. In 2001-02 he did establish himself in the Test side, playing in all six Tests and taking the most wickets. After a poor performance in New Zealand in 2007-08, the England selectors lost confidence in him.

MICHAEL HOLDING

Born: 16 FEBRUARY 1954, HALF WAY TREE, KINGSTON, JAMAICA
Teams: JAMAICA (1972-73 TO 1988-89); LANCASHIRE (1981); TASMANIA (1982-83); DERBYSHIRE (1983-89); CANTERBURY (1987-88);
First-class: 222 MATCHES; 3,600 RUNS, AVERAGE 15.00; 778 WICKETS, AVERAGE 23.43
Tests (1975-76 TO 1986-87): 60 MATCHES; 910 RUNS, AVERAGE 13.78; 249 WICKETS, AVERAGE 23.68

A right-arm fast bowler, Michael Holding made the art look easy, and it is not hard to understand why batsmen referred to him as "Whispering Death". Initially, he lacked control, but soon his considerable pace was allied with accuracy and remarkable stamina, and, by 1976, he was the most formidable of the West Indies' pace quartet. At Old Trafford that year, he took 5 for 17 as England were hurried out for 71. In the final Test, at The Oval, he produced an astonishing display of fast bowling. On a benign pitch on which Amiss made a double-century and England scored 435, he took 8 for 92, the best figures by a West Indian bowler against England, and when he took 6 for 57 in the second innings to win the game, he became the first West Indian to take more than 200 Test wickets.

A man of education and charm, he fell from grace when he reacted angrily against an umpire's decision in New Zealand by kicking over the stumps. This was not characteristic. He performed well for both Derbyshire and for Tasmania and is now a popular commentator.

Whispering Death's stealth-like approach to the popping crease was one of Test cricket's most fearsome sights in the 1970s and '80s.

JACK HOBBS
The Master

Jack Hobbs's first-class debut came in a match in which the opposing captain was W.G. Grace, and his last Test series was Don Bradman's second, so the three great figures of pre-Second World War cricket succeeded each other almost seamlessly. Hobbs ended his career with a record number of runs and a record number of centuries, neither of which have ever been beaten – and which in all probability never will. While most would agree Bradman stands supreme as the best batsman of all time, Hobbs has his champions, who point to his mastery in all conditions, including on the notorious English sticky wickets that occurred frequently in the days when pitches weren't covered. Hobbs himself would not have worried about his place in the pantheon of the game's greats, as he played with a modesty that did not seek big scores.

Jack Hobbs: his career aggregate of 61,670 runs is still a record.

Hobbs played for Cambridgeshire at 18, and four years later made his Surrey debut, beginning a long partnership with fellow Cambridge opening bat Tom Hayward. He was lucky in his career to have three great opening partners – after Hayward was Andy Sandham, for Surrey, and Herbert Sutcliffe, for England. In all, Hobbs was to make a world record 168 opening century partnerships, mostly with these players. Fifteen times Hobbs and Sutcliffe posted century opening partnerships in Tests and 26 times altogether. Their most famous partnership was in 1926 at The Oval when, after an hour's batting the night before, their second-innings partnership was interrupted by overnight rain that threatened to see England all out by lunchtime. Instead the score was 161 without loss. Hobbs made 100, Sutcliffe 161 and a first-innings deficit was transformed into a 289-run victory to regain the Ashes.

It was a golden time for Hobbs. In 1925 he closed in on W.G. Grace's record number of centuries (then held to be 126). At Taunton in August, against Somerset, he equalled the record in the first innings and beat it in the second, scoring his 14th century of the season, a new record. He ended with 15, a record finally beaten by Denis Compton in 1947. It is remarkable that his two aggregate records, runs and centuries, still stand after over 70 years.

Hobbs was a brilliant cover field and a useful swing bowler – he actually opened the batting and the bowling in three Tests – but, above all, it was his style and effortless grace that earned him his soubriquet, "The Master".

1882	1905	1907-08	1925	1934	1953	1963
Born John Berry Hobbs on 16 December at Cambridge	Makes his first-class debut for Surrey	Made his Test debut in the second Test on the tour of Australia, making 83 and 20 as England win by one wicket	Passed W.G. Grace's record number of centuries, passed 100 a record 15 times during the season, and made his highest aggregate, 3,024 runs	Retired with a record first-class career aggregate of 61,760 runs, and record number of centuries, 199, records that still stand today	Awarded a knighthood for services to cricket	Died aged 81 on 21 December at Hove, in Sussex

CONRAD HUNTE

Born: 9 MAY 1932, SHOREY'S VILLAGE, ST ANDREW,
BARBADOS
Died: 3 DECEMBER 1999, SYDNEY, AUSTRALIA
Teams: BARBADOS (1950-51 TO 1966-67)
First-class: 132 MATCHES; 8,916 RUNS, AVERAGE 43.92;
17 WICKETS, AVERAGE 37.88
Tests (1957-58 to 1966-67): 44 MATCHES; 3,245
RUNS, AVERAGE 45.06; 2 WICKETS, AVERAGE 55.00

Conrad Hunte was a most reliable and sound opening batsman and an excellent fielder. He scored 142 on his Test debut against Pakistan in 1957-58 and, in the third Test of the same series, he made 260, sharing a second-wicket stand of 446 with Sobers. A third century came in the fourth Test, and he had a different kind of record in the last when he became the first West Indian to be out to the first ball of a Test match. In England in 1966, he began the series with a flourishing 135, but three years earlier he had done even better with 182 followed by an unbeaten 108 in the final Test.

Hunte was a natural batsman who liked to attack, but who played to the needs of his side, and consistency was his trade mark. Following his retirement, he worked for the Moral Rearmament movement and coached in South African townships.

NASSER HUSSAIN

Born: 28 MARCH 1968, MADRAS, INDIA
Teams: ESSEX (1987-2004)
First-class: 334 MATCHES; 20,698 RUNS,
AVERAGE 42.06; 2 WICKETS, AVERAGE 161.50
Tests (1989-90 to 2004): 96 MATCHES;
5,764 RUNS, AVERAGE 37.18; NO WICKETS

Although born in India, Hussain was educated in England. His father had played in Madras and was determined that Nasser would have a successful career in cricket. As a batsman he flourished at county level, and performed well for England because he was aware of his own limitations.

He took over the captaincy of England from Alec Stewart in 1999, with his first tour in charge coming against South Africa the following winter. England failed in both Tests and one days, though Hussain topped the batting table by a large margin and won praise for his handling of the media. Both his campaigns against Australia ended with defeat by four matches to one and, after the second in 2002-03 there were cries for his head. In 2003, England struggled in the World Cup and Hussain resigned as one-day captain. Not long afterwards, he also quit the Test captaincy, but continued as a player. In May 2004, Hussain hit 103 not out as England beat New Zealand at Lord's – two days later, Hussain announced his retirement from both Test and county cricket. Thus he missed the triumph of the 2005 Ashes series, though he was part of all the changes that had made it possible.

MICHAEL HUSSEY

Born: 27 MAY 1975, MORLEY, WESTERN AUSTRALIA
Teams: WESTERN AUSTRALIA (1994-2011);
NORTHAMPTONSHIRE (2001-03); GLOUCESTERSHIRE
(2004); DURHAM (2005); CHENNAI SUPER KINGS
(2008-09)
First-class: 245 MATCHES; 20,726 RUNS,
AVERAGE 52.47; 22 WICKETS, AVERAGE 39.86
Tests (2005-06 to 2010-11): 59 MATCHES;
4,650 RUNS, AVERAGE 51.09; 2 WICKETS

Michael Hussey made his first-class debut in 1994-95 as a left-hand opening batsman and occasional right-arm medium bowler but, despite some prolific scoring feats, it took him 11 years to break into the powerful Australian Test side. He had scored 15,313 runs, a record for an Aussie debutant, before he got his chance when Justin Langer fractured a rib. A debut innings of a single against the West Indies at Brisbane was soon forgotten as he added centuries in the second and third Tests to top the series averages with 361 runs at 120.33. Later in the season he dropped down the

Michael Hussey: 11 years' perseverance paid off when he made his debut for Australia in November 2005.

order after Langer's recovery, and made 122 against South Africa at Melbourne, adding 107 for the last wicket with McGrath (11). Hussey went on to complete his first 1,000 Test runs in only 166 days, a record.

Hussey made his mark in English cricket, turning out for Northamptonshire, Gloucestershire and Durham, averaging over 70 in four out of five seasons between 2001 and 2005, becoming only the third player after Hammond and Hick to score three triple-hundreds in county cricket. A decline in form meant Hussey took no part in Australia losing the Ashes in 2005, but his 458 (average 91.66) were vital in their reclaiming them in 2006-07. Now a middle-order batsman, he continues to have ups and downs. A disastrous series in Australia against South Africa in 2008-09 brought his Test average, which was 84 after 20 Tests, down to a "mere" 55.29.

LEN HUTTON

Born: 23 JUNE 1916, FULNECK, PUDSEY, YORKSHIRE
Died: 6 SEPTEMBER 1990, NORBITON,
KINGSTON-UPON-THAMES, SURREY
Teams: YORKSHIRE (1934-55)
First-class: 513 MATCHES; 40,140 RUNS, AVERAGE 55.51;
170 WICKETS, AVERAGE 29.51
Tests (1937 to 1954-55): 79 MATCHES; 6,971 RUNS,
AVERAGE 56.67; 3 WICKETS, AVERAGE 77.33

Len Hutton was one of the greatest opening batsmen that cricket has seen and, in the opinion of many, England has never had a better captain. He batted in the classical mould. There was time to spare and he had the mastery of every shot without resorting to brutality. In the years before the war, he was also a useful leg-break bowler. He was reared in the hard and eminently successful Yorkshire side of the 1930s and gained early guidance from his opening partner Herbert Sutcliffe.

Chosen for England against New Zealand in 1937, he was out for 0 and 1 on his Test debut, but he made the first of his 19 Test hundreds in the next match. The following season, he scored a century in his first Test against Australia and, at The Oval, he made history by batting 13 hours 17 minutes to score 364, which was to remain the highest score in Test cricket for nearly 20 years. He was 22 years old. Against the West Indies in 1939, he played innings of 196 and 165 not out to bring his aggregate to 1,109 runs in his last eight Tests before the outbreak of war.

An injury sustained in an accident early in the war led to him being invalided out of the army in 1942, and his left arm was now two inches shorter than his right. If, in the post-war years, he was not quite the batsman he had been in 1939, he was still as good as anyone in the world.

Despite bad periods, when England faced a crisis of captaincy, they turned to Hutton. When he led England against India at Leeds in 1952 he was the first professional to captain England in England. He scored two centuries in the series, which England won resoundingly. Traditionalists were still opposed to his appointment, but he regained the Ashes in 1953, led England to a draw in the Caribbean after they had been two Tests down and retained the Ashes in Australia in 1954-55.

His own form did not falter, but a back problem and, one feels, weariness, caused him to retire. He was, and remains, a national hero, who was knighted in 1956 for his services to cricket. He had led England out of the wilderness.

RAYMOND ILLINGWORTH

Born: 8 JUNE 1932, PUDSEY, YORKSHIRE
Teams: YORKSHIRE (1951-83); LEICESTERSHIRE (1969-78)
First-class: 787 MATCHES; 24,134 RUNS, AVERAGE 28.06; 2,072 WICKETS, AVERAGE 20.28
Tests (1958-73): 61 MATCHES; 1,836 RUNS, AVERAGE 23.24; 122 WICKETS, AVERAGE 31.20

Ray Illingworth had a most eventful career, both during and after his playing days. A right-handed, solid middle-order batsman and off-break bowler, he completed the "double" six times and won a place in the England side between 1958 and 1969, experiencing modest success. He had been a vital member of the Yorkshire side, but a contractual dispute led him to leave his native county and become captain of Leicestershire. His success with his new county was phenomenal, for they won all the domestic competitions bar the Gillette Cup during the period when he was their captain. But he had led the side in only eight first-class matches when he was called upon to lead England in place of the injured Colin Cowdrey in 1969. There was immediate success over the West Indies, and he both regained and defended the Ashes. He did not suffer

Ray Illingworth: a shrewd leader.

defeat in a Test match until his 20th game in charge, and there are those who say that he was the best captain they ever played under. The defeat by India, followed by heavy defeats at the hands of the West Indies in 1973, ended his Test career.

In 1979, he retired from first-class cricket and became manager of Yorkshire, but problems at the club forced him to assume the captaincy in 1982 at the age of 50. He finally stood down in 1983.

In 1993, he became chairman of selectors, but his three years in charge were neither happy nor good for the game.

IMRAN KHAN

SEE PAGE 200

INZAMAN-UL-HAQ

SEE PAGE 201

ARCHIE JACKSON

Born: 5 SEPTEMBER 1909, RUTHERGLEN, LANARK, SCOTLAND
Died: 16 FEBRUARY 1933, CLAYFIELDS, BRISBANE, QUEENSLAND, AUSTRALIA
Teams: NEW SOUTH WALES (1926-27 TO 1930-31)
First-class: 70 MATCHES; 4,383 RUNS, AVERAGE 45.65
Tests (1928-29 to 1930-31): 8 MATCHES; 474 RUNS, AVERAGE 47.40

Archie Jackson was a right-handed batsman of grace and beauty who seemed destined for greatness, but who was the stuff of tragedy. He played his first Test match against England at Adelaide in February, 1929, and made 164, becoming the youngest player to score a century in an Ashes series. He arrived in England in 1930 with a reputation higher than Bradman's. He scored a thousand runs, but he appeared in only two Tests. He played four times against the West Indies the following winter, but his health was failing. He moved to Brisbane to be near his girlfriend

and in the hope that a better climate would improve matters, but he died at the age of 23.

F. S. JACKSON

Born: 21 NOVEMBER 1870, ALLERTON HALL, CHAPEL ALLERTON, LEEDS, YORKSHIRE
Died: 9 MARCH 1947, KNIGHTSBRIDGE, LONDON
Teams: CAMBRIDGE UNIVERSITY (1890-93); YORKSHIRE (1890-1907)
First-class: 309 MATCHES; 15,901 RUNS, AVERAGE 33.83; 774 WICKETS, AVERAGE 20.37
Tests (1893-1905): 20 MATCHES; 1,415 RUNS, AVERAGE 48.79; 24 WICKETS, AVERAGE 33.29

Educated at Harrow and Cambridge, where he won his blue all four years and was captain for two seasons, Sir Stanley Jackson was rarely able to play regularly although he was an all-rounder of outstanding ability, a right-handed stylish batsman and fast-medium pace bowler, who did the "double" in 1898. He had made his Test debut at Lord's in 1893, scoring 91 and 5. At The Oval, he made 103, but he was unable to play in the third and final Test. All his Test matches were in England against Australia.

He served in the Boer War, was invalided home with enteric fever and was persuaded to play for the Gentlemen against the Players at Scarborough while convalescing. He hit 13 and 42 against an attack which included Hirst and Rhodes, and then he went back to the Boer War. He was an MP for 11 years, was Financial Secretary to the War Office and Party Chairman, but as soon as Baldwin became Prime Minister, Jackson was sent to India as Governor of Bengal where he narrowly escaped assassination.

Jackson was chosen for England whenever available and captained the side in 1905 when two Tests were won and three drawn. Jackson topped both the England batting and bowling averages for the series.

He was president of the MCC, a Test selector and president of Yorkshire CCC from 1939 until his death.

IMRAN KHAN
Captain Marvel

Imran Khan: inspirational leader for Pakistan.

Imran Khan Niazi had a strange cricket career. A fierce critic of the structure of the first-class game in Pakistan, he did not play domestic cricket in his own country after 1980-81. Although he played county cricket in England from 1971 to 1988, his appearances were limited, as they were when he played five times for New South Wales. By the end of his career, he was only playing international cricket.

While still at school, he made his first-class debut, aged 16-and-a-half, for Lahore as a medium-fast bowler and opening bat. The chairman of selectors was his uncle, the captain his cousin. He was picked for the tour of England in 1971, making his Test debut at Edgbaston. He failed to take a wicket, but had already agreed to play for Worcestershire while studying at Worcester Royal Grammar School. He went to Oxford University and won blues in 1973-75. In 1974, he played in three Tests for the Pakistani touring side, taking just five wickets. After leaving Oxford he played for Pakistan International Airways for six years. At the same time he played in England, moving from Worcestershire to Sussex in 1977.

He was given a third chance to establish himself in the Pakistan Test side in 1976-77 and seized it. With a yard or two of pace added, he was a genuine fast bowler. In three series that season, against New Zealand, Australia and the West Indies, he took 57 wickets. Twelve in the third Test at Sydney against Australia helped Pakistan win in Australia for the first time.

By 1981-82 he had become his country's leading wicket-taker, but internal strife in Pakistan's cricket politics led to eight players, including Imran, being omitted from the first two Tests against Sri Lanka. Restored in the third Test, Imran achieved his best Test bowling, 8 for 58, at Lahore (and 6 for 58 in the second innings).

After the turmoil, Imran was chosen as captain for the tour of England in 1982. Captaincy inspired him and, although the three-match series was lost 2-1, he took 21 wickets and scored 212 runs. Back in Pakistan, his side won all three Tests against Australia and then beat India 3-0 in a six-Test series.

In Australia in 1983-84, he played in the last two Tests as captain and batsman only – a tribute to his genuine all-round qualities. He averaged 56.66.

In 1986-87, he took 18 wickets at only 11.05 each against the West Indies. In 1987, he led Pakistan to their first series victory in England, topping the bowling averages and scoring an imperious 118 at The Oval. In the West Indies the following winter, he took 23 wickets at 18.31, but Pakistan narrowly lost the final Test when they could have made themselves cricket's unofficial world champions. However, Imran achieved this in another way when he led Pakistan to win the World Cup in Australia in 1991-92. He retired from cricket after this.

He remains one of the handful of all-rounders (including Ian Botham, Richard Hadlee, Kapil Dev and Shaun Pollock) who have scored 3,000 runs and taken 300 wickets in Tests.

After raising funds for a cancer hospital following his mother's death in 1985, he became a prominent figure in politics while at the same time, by marrying (then separating from) a society heiress, retaining the fascination that he is held in by the popular press.

FIRST-CLASS CAREER
(1969-70 to 1991-92, 382 matches)
Batting: RUNS 17,771; AVERAGE 36.79; HIGHEST SCORE 170; CENTURIES 30
Bowling: WICKETS 1,287; RUNS 28,726; AVERAGE 22.32; BEST 8-34
Catches: 117

TESTS
(1971 TO 1999-92, 88 MATCHES)
Batting: RUNS 3,807; AVERAGE 37.69; HIGHEST SCORE 136; CENTURIES 6
Bowling: WICKETS 362; RUNS 8,258; AVERAGE 22.81; BEST 8-58
Catches: 28

1952
Born Imran Khan Niazi on 25 November at Lahore, Pakistan

1971
Made Test debut on tour of England at Edgbaston, 3-8 June. He was run out for 5 and did not take a wicket

1977
Took six wickets in each innings (12 for 165 in the match) as Pakistan won first-ever Test victory in Australia, Sydney, 14-18 January

1981-82
Internal politics see him left out of first two Tests v Sri Lanka. He is reinstated for the third Test

1982
Appointed Pakistan captain for tour to England – ends three-match series with 21 wickets and 212 runs

1982-83
Captained Pakistan to 3-0 Test series victories over India and Australia, taking 53 for 729 (average 13.75). He also scored a century.

1987-88
Takes 23 wickets at 18.31 in losing " world championship" series against the West Indies

1992
Led Pakistan to victory in the World Cup in Australia and New Zealand. After winning only one of their first five matches, they beat England in the final.

2002
Became a Member of Parliament for Mianwali in the October elections

INZAMAN-UL-HAQ
Pakistan's Mr Reliable

FIRST-CLASS CAREER
(1985-86 to 2007-08, 245 matches)
Batting: RUNS 16,785; AVERAGE 50.10; HIGHEST
SCORE 329; CENTURIES 45
Bowling: WICKETS 39; RUNS 1,295;
AVERAGE 33.20; BEST 5-80
Catches: 172

TESTS
(1992 to 2007-08, 119 MATCHES)
Batting: RUNS 8,829; AVERAGE 50.16;
HIGHEST SCORE 329;
CENTURIES 25
Bowling: WICKETS 0; RUNS 8
Catches: 81

The outstanding Pakistani batsman of his generation, Inzamam combined bulk and strength with surprising subtlety. The delicacy of his touch when batting was combined with an aggressive instinct that made the accumulation of runs seem inevitable. He was particularly strong off his legs and was an outstanding player of pace bowling.

He first played for Pakistan when picked for a one-day international against the West Indies in 1991-92, and first captured world attention with his performances in Pakistan's triumph in the 1992 World Cup in Australia. He did not do well in his first Test series in England in 1992, but made his first Test hundred in the tour of West Indies the following winter. By 1993-94, when he topped

Inzamam-ul-Haq: Pakistan's leading Test run-scorer.

the Pakistan Test averages on the tour to New Zealand with 75.33 he was beginning to establish himself as one of the world's leading batsmen.

An undefeated 58 decided a close match with Australia in Karachi in 1994-95, but it was New Zealand who suffered when he made his highest Test score, 329 at Lahore in 2001-02. Another great innings came in his home town of Multan in 2003, when Pakistan seemed certain to he humbled by Bangladesh. His 138 not out saved the day.

An innings of 184 helped win the final Test (Inzamam's 100th) against India in 2004-05 and tie the series, and, in 2005-06, he scored heavily, including a century in each innings in Faisalabad, when Pakistan beat the Ashes-winning England 2-0. He was the outstanding batsman of the series with 431 runs, average 107.75, on the way passing Javed Miandad's Pakistan record of 23 Test centuries, and joining him as the only Pakistan batsmen with over 8,000 Test runs. In fact the calendar year of 2005 was superb for Inzamam, as he scored 999 runs in only seven Tests (average 99.90). He retired after the 2007-08 season.

1970	**1991-92**	**1992**	**1992**	**1992-93**
Born Inzamam-ul-Haq on 3 March 1970 in Multan, Punjab	Makes his first appearance for Pakistan in a one-day international v West Indies at Lahore and scored 20	Helped Pakistan win World Cup final with Man of the Match-winning 60 in 37 balls in the semi-final and a crucial 42 in the final	Made his Test debut for Pakistan against England at Edgbaston	Scores first Test century for Pakistan (123) v West Indies at Antigua, 1-6 May

2002	**2003**	**2004-05**	**2006-07**
Made his highest Test score (then the tenth highest of all time) of 329 against New Zealand at Lahore, 1-2 May	Made captain of Pakistan in September, and captained his first match in the second Test v South Africa at Faisalabad in October	Scores 184 v India at Bangalore in his 100th appearance for Pakistan	Steps down as captain of the Paksitan side after their early elimination from the World Cup

DOUGLAS JARDINE

Born: 23 OCTOBER 1900, MALABAR HILL, BOMBAY, INDIA
Died: JUNE 18, 1958, MONTREUX, SWITZERLAND
Teams: OXFORD UNIVERSITY (1920-23); SURREY (1921-33)
First-class: 262 MATCHES; 14,848 RUNS, AVERAGE 46.83; 48 WICKETS, AVERAGE 31.10
Tests (1928 to 1933-34): 22 MATCHES; 1,296 RUNS, AVERAGE 48.00; NO WICKETS FOR 10 RUNS

Few captains of England have excited as much passion and controversy as Douglas Jardine; none has been more successful.

He played for Surrey while still at Oxford and won his first Test caps against the West Indies in 1928. He went with Chapman's side to Australia in 1928-29, played in all five Tests and averaged 46.62. He also raised the passions of the Australian crowd, who saw him as aloof. He batted in a brightly coloured Harlequin cap and was regarded as part of the Establishment.

Jardine led England against New Zealand in 1931 and against India in 1932, and was the obvious choice to take the side to Australia in 1932-33.

He asserted that, all things being equal, he would select a Northerner over a Southerner. He discussed tactics with Arthur Carr, the Nottinghamshire and former England skipper, and he evolved leg-theory, fast bowling on the leg side to a leg-side field. It was later dubbed "bodyline". In Larwood, and to a lesser extent Voce, he had the bowlers to make the theory effective. England won the series 4-1. He was the subject of fierce criticism, but he was worshipped by his men.

In 1933, he captained England against the West Indies – who employed leg-theory at Jardine. He countered it with a century. He took the side to India the following winter, but announced that he would not play against Australia in 1934. There were those who believed that he had been let down by the administration. He was only 33 years old when he retired from cricket. In 15 Tests as captain, he won nine and lost only once. He averaged 50 with the bat.

JAVED MIANDAD

Born: 12 JUNE 1957, KARACHI, PAKISTAN
Teams: KARACHI (1973-74 TO 1975-76); SIND (1973-74 TO 1975-76); SUSSEX (1976-79); HABIB BANK (1976-77 TO 1995-96); GLAMORGAN (1980-85)
First-class: 402 MATCHES; 28,647 RUNS, AVERAGE 53.44; 191 WICKETS, AVERAGE 33.48
Tests (1976-77 to 1994-95): 124 MATCHES; 8,832 RUNS, AVERAGE 52.57; 17 WICKETS, AVERAGE 40.11

One of the most exciting batsman of his day, Javed Miandad towered over other Pakistani batsman in his achievements. He has 23 Test centuries to his credit, and he was the first Pakistani to reach 8,000 runs in Tests. His three centuries over 250 are: 280 not out against India at Hyderabad in 1982-83, then second only to Hanif Mohammad's triple-century in the Caribbean, then 271 against New Zealand at Auckland in 1988-89, and 260 against England at The Oval in 1987.

A strong aggressive, right-handed batsman with every shot at his command, Javed has captained Pakistan with distinction, although he has never been far from controversy.

Certainly his exploits helped to take Pakistan to eminence in world cricket, and he played a major part in the winning of the World Cup in 1992. On retirement, he was Pakistan's most capped player.

SANATH JAYASURIYA

Born: 30 JUNE 1969, MATARA, CEYLON
Teams: COLOMBO (1988-89 TO 1996-97); BLOOMFIELD (1996-97 TO 2010-11); SOMERSET (2005); LANCASHIRE (2007); MUMBAI INDIANS (2008-09)
First-class: 263 MATCHES; 14,782 RUNS, AVERAGE 38.49; 205 WICKETS, AVERAGE 32.77
Tests (1990-91 to 2007-08): 110 MATCHES; 6,973 RUNS, AVERAGE 40.07; 98 WICKETS, AVERAGE 34.34

Jayasuriya won his first Test cap for Sri Lanka in New Zealand in 1990-91. A forceful left-handed batsman and left-arm spin bowler, he was slow to establish himself in the Sri Lankan side. It was in the 1996 World Cup

that he sprang to prominence.

Used as an opener and in his all-round capacity, he was voted the most valuable man of the tournament, and he devastated England in the quarter-final with 82 off 44 balls, a brilliant innings. In August 1997 he made the fourth highest Test score when making 340 against India at Colombo, sharing in a record Test stand for any wicket of 576 with Roshan Mahanama.

He retired from Test Cricket in 2007-08, but continued to play in One Day Internationals, becoming the oldest batsman to score in such matches in 2009.

MAHELA JAYAWARDENE

Born: 27 MAY 1977, COLOMBO, SRI LANKA
Teams: SINHALESE SPORTS CLUB (1995-96 TO 2009-10); KINGS XI PUNJAB (2008-09)
First-class: 198 MATCHES; 15,296 RUNS, AVERAGE 52.56; 52 WICKETS, AVERAGE 30.98
Tests (1997 to 2010-11): 116 MATCHES; 9,527 RUNS, AVERAGE 53.82; 6 WICKETS, AVERAGE 48.66

Making his first-class debut in 1995-96, Jayawardene was selected for his first Test in August 1997. Against India at Colombo, he made 66 in a total of 952 for 6 declared, including 340 from Sanath Jayasuriya, a Sri Lankan record that Jayawardene would eventually go on to beat. He scored 167 on a difficult pitch against New

Javed Miandad: when he retired he was Pakistan's most-capped player and their highest run-scorer.

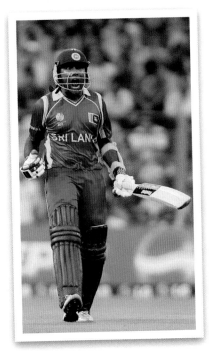

Mahela Jayawardene: successful captain.

Zealand at Galle in his fourth Test, and 242 against India at Colombo in his seventh. However, a loss of form ending in a poor 2003 World Cup led to his being dropped. Undaunted, he soon established himself again to prove one of the best batsmen Sri Lanka has produced, going on to 100 Test matches.

A right-hand batsman and useful right-arm medium bowler, he took over the captaincy of Sri Lanka for the tour of England in 2006 and scored 61 and 119 at Lord's to help save the match, before Sri Lanka went on to tie the series. Back in Sri Lanka they then beat South Africa 2-0 in a home series. In the first Test, Jayawardene scored his Sri Lankan Test record 374, and with Kumar Sangakarra established a world record first-class stand for any wicket by adding 624 for the third. He took Sri Lanka to the final of the World Cup in 2007 and to victory in the Asia Cup and in a home series against India in 2008. After leading Sri Lanka to victory against Bangladesh in 2008-09, Jayawardene announced he would retire as captain.

GILBERT JESSOP

Born: 19 MAY 1874, CHELTENHAM, GLOUCESTERSHIRE
Died: 11 MAY 1955, FORDINGTON, DORSET
Teams: GLOUCESTERSHIRE (1894-1914); CAMBRIDGE UNIVERSITY (1896-99); LONDON COUNTY (1900-03)
First-class: 493 MATCHES; 26,698 RUNS, AVERAGE 32.63; 873 WICKETS, AVERAGE 22.79
Tests (1899-1912): 18 matches; 569 RUNS, AVERAGE 21.88; 10 WICKETS, AVERAGE 35.40

Gilbert Jessop was the stuff of legend. Known as "The Croucher" because of his stance at the wicket, he was the most consistent fast scorer the game has known, capable of hitting all round the wicket, and a most exciting figure. He batted right-handed and was a fast right-arm bowler who opened the attack on his Test debut against Australia, Lord's, 1899. He went to Australia, 1901-02, but he was too adventurous a player to be a total success in Test cricket.

One of his 53 centuries came in 40 minutes, another in 42. He twice performed the "double", and he scored 1,000 runs in a season on 14 occasions, twice going on to 2,000. He captained both Cambridge University and Gloucestershire, and he was a secretary of that county for five years.

His name is most remembered for his 104 for England against Australia at The Oval in 1902. Going in at 48 for five, he reached his century in 75 minutes, the fastest century in Test history at that time, and England went on to win by one wicket.

IAN JOHNSON

Born: 8 DECEMBER 1917, NORTH MELBOURNE, VICTORIA, AUSTRALIA
Died: OCTOBER 9, 1998, MELBOURNE, AUSTRALIA
Teams: VICTORIA (1935-36 TO 1955-56)
First-class: 189 MATCHES; 4,905 RUNS, AVERAGE 22.92; 619 WICKETS, AVERAGE 23.30
Tests (1945-46 to 1956-57): 45 MATCHES; 1,000 RUNS, AVERAGE 18.51; 109 WICKETS, AVERAGE 29.19

Ian Johnson was a rare product for Australia, an off-break bowler. He relied more on variations in flight than in vicious turn, and he was a good lower-order batsman. He first played Test cricket in New Zealand in 1945-46, but he did not bowl. Indeed, he did not bowl until his third Test match, against England at Sydney in 1946-47, when he took 6 for 42 and 2 for 92. He did well against India in 1947-48, and he had a good tour of England in 1948, but had little effect in the Tests. He was not selected for the 1953 tour, so it was very surprising when he was named as captain of Australia in succession to Hassett in 1954-55.

Victory in the first Test was followed by destruction at the hands of Tyson and Statham. There was surprising success in the West Indies where Johnson took 7 for 44 to bring victory in Georgetown. In England in 1956, on pitches which aided spin, Johnson failed. When Laker took 19 wickets at Old Trafford Johnson had 4 for 151, which disappointed him bitterly. He took the side to India, but it was the magic of Benaud which won the series. In his last match, Johnson completed the "double" in Test cricket.

He later became secretary of Melbourne CC.

MITCHELL JOHNSON

Born: 2 NOVEMBER 1981, TOWNSVILLE, QUEENSLAND, AUSTRALIA
Teams: QUEENSLAND (2001-02 TO 2009-10), WESTERN AUSTRALIA (2010-11)
First-class: 73 MATCHES; 1,959 RUNS, AVERAGE 23.89; 278 WICKETS, AVERAGE 30.50
Tests (1947-48 to 1954-55): 42 MATCHES; 1,152 RUNS, AVERAGE 22.15; 181 WICKETS, AVERAGE 29.71

Mitchell Johnson is a fast left-arm strike bowler who can swing the ball alarmingly but who, frustratingly, can veer from sheer brilliance to ineffectiveness. Stress fractures to his back hindered his progress, delaying his Test debut for Australia till 2007. He made a big impact in two Test series against South Africa in 2008-09, twice breaking Graeme Smith's hand with his 95mph thunderbolts. In the first series he took 17 wickets and in the second, in which he took 16 and scored a century, he was the Man of the Series. His hard-hitting batting gives him aspirations to be an all-rounder. He did not shine in England in 2005, however, and his inconsistency was highlighted in the Ashes series of 2010-11, when he was so poor in the first Test (0 for 170 and a duck) that he was dropped for the second but, returning for the third, he was devastating, with 9 wickets for 82, a vital 61 and a Man of the Match award. In the fourth Test, he scored 6 and took 2 for 134. An enigma.

BILL JOHNSTON

Born: 26 FEBRUARY 1922, BEEAC, VICTORIA, AUSTRALIA
Died: 25 MAY 2007, MOSMAN, NSW, AUSTRALIA
Teams: VICTORIA (1945-46 TO 1954-55)
First-class: 142 MATCHES; 1,129 RUNS, AVERAGE 12.68; 554 WICKETS, AVERAGE 23.35
Tests (1947-48 to 1954-55): 40 MATCHES; 273 RUNS, AVERAGE 11.37

Bill Johnston was a tall, strongly built, left-arm fast-medium pace bowler who swung and cut the ball appreciably. He was quietly effective against India in 1947-48, but he took England by storm a few months later. He took 9 for 183 in the first Test, and he shared the new ball with Lindwall when Miller was injured. He finished the series with 27 wickets in the five Tests, and he took 102 on the tour. His first Test against South Africa in 1949-50, brought his best figures, 6 for 44, in the second innings. His took 23 wickets in the series as Australia won four of the five Tests, drawing in Johannesburg.

In successive home series, he scourged England with 22 wickets and the West Indies with 23. At the time, he had reached 100 Test wickets faster than any other bowler in history. In 1952-53, he took 21 wickets against South Africa, but there were signs of wear and tear, and he had a persistent knee injury which hampered him on the 1953 tour of England when, being dismissed only once, he had the experience of averaging 102 with the bat, top score 28. He did well in four Tests against England in 1954-55, while all about him fell, but that marked the end of his career. His son played for South Australia.

ALVIN KALLICHARRAN

Born: 21 MARCH 1949, PAIDAMA, BRITISH GUIANA
Teams: GUYANA (1966-67 TO 1980-81); WARWICKSHIRE (1971-90); QUEENSLAND (1977-78); TRANSVAAL (1981-82 TO 1983-84); ORANGE FREE STATE (1984-85 TO 1987-88)
First-class: 505 MATCHES; 32,650 RUNS, AVERAGE 43.64; 84 WICKETS, AVERAGE 47.97
Tests (1971-72 to 1980-81): 66 MATCHES; 4,399 RUNS, AVERAGE 44.43; 4 WICKETS, AVERAGE 39.50

A most attractive left-handed batsman and a useful right-arm leg-break bowler, Alvin Kallicharran graced county cricket for several seasons, eventually being registered as an English-qualified player. He hit 1,000 runs in an English season 12 times, and he scored 100 not out on his Test debut for the West Indies against New Zealand in Georgetown. This was followed by 101 in his next match in Trinidad. He was the second West Indian to accomplish this feat. He batted consistently against Australia and on his first tour of England in 1973, and in the Caribbean in 1973-74, he scored 158, 21, 93, and 119 in the first three Tests against England. He was equally successful in India the following year.

With the rest of the West Indian side, he signed to join Packer's World Series, but withdrew when he found he was in breach of contract with a Queensland radio station. Left as senior player, he captained the West Indies against Australia and India, making centuries in both series, but this was not a happy time for him. When Clive Lloyd returned, Kallicharran's form declined and he elected to play in South Africa, so exiling himself from Test cricket.

JACQUES KALLIS

SEE PAGE 205

ROHAN KANHAI

Born: 26 DECEMBER 1935, PORT MOURANT, BRITISH GUIANA
Teams: BRITISH GUIANA/GUYANA (1954-55 TO 1973-74); WESTERN AUSTRALIA (1961-62); TRINIDAD (1964-65); WARWICKSHIRE (1968-77); TASMANIA (1969-70)
First-class: 416 MATCHES; 28,774 RUNS, AVERAGE 49.01; 18 WICKETS, AVERAGE 56.05
Tests (1957 to 1973-74): 79 MATCHES; 6,227 RUNS, AVERAGE 47.53; NO WICKETS FOR 85 RUNS

Rohan Kanhai believed in the power of bat over ball, and he would have been at home in the Golden Age, for he was a master in all he did. One of the most thrilling sights of the 1960s was that of Kanhai on his backside as the ball thundered over the boundary at square-leg after a pull so vicious that it had swept the batsman off his feet.

He made his Test debut in the first Test of the West Indies' tour of England in 1957. Unwisely, he was asked to keep wicket in the first three Tests, but thereafter he was allowed to concentrate on his batting. His maiden Test hundred came against India, at Calcutta in 1958-59, when he scored 256. He was to make 15 more Test centuries.

Kanhai played in many parts of the globe and his contribution to Warwickshire cricket was immense. In 1974, at Edgbaston, he and John Jameson shared an unbroken second-wicket stand of 465 against Gloucestershire, which was, at the time, a world record.

In 1972-73, with Sobers recovering from an operation, Kanhai captained the West Indies against Australia. He was then 37 years old. He led them in two series against England, both of which were tinged with controversy. In 1973, at Edgbaston, umpire Fagg refused to take the field at the start of the third day because of Kanhai's

reaction to one of his decisions. The following winter, in Port-of-Spain, he was captain when Tony Greig ran out Kallicharran "after the close of play". Kallicharran was reinstated. In spite of these incidents, Kanhai was respected for having brought a sense of discipline to a West Indies side which had become very lax in the last years of Sobers' captaincy.

KAPIL DEV

SEE PAGE 206

ALAN KNOTT

Born: 9 APRIL 1946, BELVEDERE, KENT
Teams: KENT (1964-85)
First-class: 511 MATCHES; 18,105 RUNS, AVERAGE 29.63; 2 WICKETS, AVERAGE 43.50; CAUGHT 1,211, STUMPED 133
Tests (1967-81): 95 matches; 4,389 RUNS, AVERAGE 32.75; CAUGHT 250, STUMPED 19

A truly great wicket-keeper, Alan Knott was recognized as outstanding from

the moment he first played for Kent and forced his way into the England side within three years. In his first two Tests, against Pakistan, he held 12 catches and made a stumping, and an illustrious career was launched. Meticulous and fastidious to the point of eccentricity, he maintained a strict diet and a disciplined programme of exercise. Through constant application, he made himself into a batsman capable of scoring five Test centuries and defying any attack. His batting was unorthodox, but it was a style he evolved to suit his needs and abilities.

In both Test and county cricket, he fashioned a wonderful partnership with the left-arm spinner Derek Underwood, and they became a telling combination.

Knott's involvement with World Series Cricket and a tour of South Africa curtailed his Test career. He has aided England's coaching and selection, and his son James played occasionally for Surrey from 1995 to 1998, as a reserve wicket-keeper.

Alan Knott: possibly the best wicket-keeper England has ever produced.

JACQUES KALLIS
The Quiet All-Rounder

FIRST-CLASS CAREER
(1993-94 to 2010-11, 235 matches)
Batting: RUNS 18,299; AVERAGE 55.28; HIGHEST
SCORE 201; CENTURIES 57
Bowling: WICKETS 405; RUNS 12,607;
AVERAGE 31.12; BEST 6-54
Catches: 229

TESTS
(1995-96 to 2009-10, 144 MATCHES)
Batting: RUNS 11,864; AVERAGE 57.31; HIGHEST
SCORE 201; CENTURIES 40
Bowling: WICKETS 269; RUNS 8,605; AVERAGE 31.98;
BEST 6-54
Catches: 162

Jacques Kallis has few frills to his game. He bats for his side, takes vital wickets when necessary and is rarely thought of as being a cricketing legend. In fact, he most resembles the self-effacing professional of days gone by. Yet, in 2006, Jacques Kallis achieved a remarkable statistic. He joined the great Garfield Sobers, generally regarded as the best all-rounder who ever lived, as one of only two players to have scored 8,000 runs and taken 200 wickets in Test cricket. Furthermore, his averages are on a par with those of Sobers. He can claim to be the most under-rated player of his day.

Born in Cape Town in 1975, Kallis made his first-class debut in 1993-94. He is a right-hand batsman and a right-arm fast-medium bowler

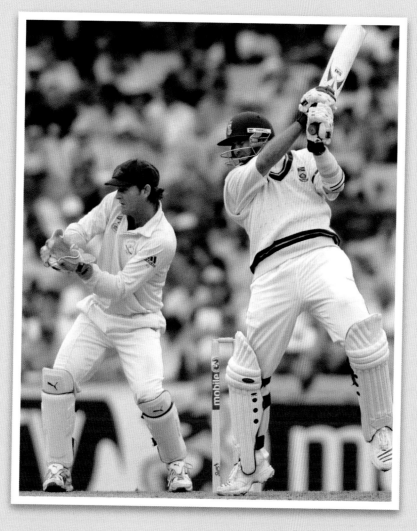

Jacques Kallis: his all-round credentials are on a par with those of Garfield Sobers.

who on occasion has been said to deliver the ball as quickly as his countryman Allan Donald. He made steady progress and came into the Test team just before Christmas in 1995 against England at Durban. He played in the third and fifth Tests and made a typically quiet start with 1 and 7 (in 96 minutes) and no wickets from his four overs. He followed up with some undistinguished appearances in the 1996 World Cup. His next Test appearance was delayed till the Boxing Day match in Australia in 1998, when he saved the match with his first Test century, his 101 making him Man of the Match. In this innings he showed his mature temperament by not reacting to Australian sledging. Gradually Kallis established himself as the No. 3 in the South African line-up.

Solid in defence, he has the strength and ability to hit the ball hard, but prefers ruthless efficiency. In 2003, he overtook Gary Kirsten as South Africa's leading run-maker and his performances in 2005 brought him the ICC awards as Test and overall Player of the Year. He is a fine slip fielder and young enough to add considerably to his already impressive career figures.

1975	**1993-94**	**1995**	**1998**	**2001**
Born Jacques Henry Kallis on 16 October at Pinelands, Cape Town, Cape Province, South Africa	Makes his first-class debut for Western Province	Made his Test debut at Durban in December in a drawn game with England. Made one run and was wicketless	Made his first Test century in Melbourne in December, his fourth-innings 101 against Australia, allowing South Africa to achieve a draw	Takes his 100th Test wicket, v India at Bloemfontein and becomes eighth player to take 100 wickets and score 3,000 Test runs

2002	**2003**	**2005**	**2006**	**2010**
Passes 4,000 Test runs with an unbeaten 75 v Bangladesh at Buffalo Park, East London	Passes 5,000 runs in Tests in match v West Indies at Durban (177)	Consistent performances against England (149 in third Test) and West Indies (109 not out, 78, 147) earned him ICC Player of the Year award	Became the second player after Garfield Sobers to achieve 8,000 runs and 200 wickets in Tests	Currently the leading all-rounder in Test Cricket with 11,864 runs, 269 wickets and 162 catches

KAPIL DEV
The Haryana Hurricane

FIRST-CLASS CAREER
(1975-76 to 1994-95, 275 matches)
Batting: RUNS 11,356; AVERAGE 32.91; HIGHEST
SCORE 193; CENTURIES 18
Bowling: WICKETS 835; RUNS 22,626;
AVERAGE 27.09; BEST 9-83
Catches: 192

TESTS
(1978-79 to 1993-94, 131 MATCHES)
Batting: RUNS 5,248; AVERAGE 31.05; HIGHEST
SCORE 163; CENTURIES 8
Bowling: WICKETS 434; RUNS 12,867;
AVERAGE 29.64; BEST 9-83
Catches: 64

Kapil Dev was one of a group of four outstanding all-rounders whose careers overlapped, the others being Ian Botham, Imran Khan and Richard Hadlee.

A strong charismatic man of over six foot, he made his first-class debut for Haryana in the Ranji Trophy of 1975-76, and took 6 for 19 in the first innings. He made his Test debut, aged 18, in 1978-79 against Pakistan in Faisalabad. Later that season, against the West Indies, he took seven wickets in a Test and in the following Test hit 126 not out.

In 1979-80, in India he excelled with 22 wickets against Australia and 32 against Pakistan, India winning both series 2-0. In the last of these Tests (his 25th) he became the youngest player to 100 Test wickets

Kapil Dev: the best all-rounder India has ever produced.

(and the fastest), the youngest to 1,000 Test runs and, of course, the youngest to complete the double. He was 21 years 27 days old.

In the first Test against England in 1981-82 he took six wickets and was top Indian scorer as India won and held on to win the series (Kapil Dev 22 wickets and 318 runs, average 53). In England the following summer the home side reversed the 1-0 result, but Kapil top-scored for India with 292 (average 73).

Kapil Dev captained India for the first time against the West Indies in 1982-83 and in England led his country to a surprise World Cup win. During this tournament he played a remarkable innings, coming in at No. 6 against Zimbabwe with India 10 for 4 (later 17 for 5 and 78 for 7) and smashing 175 not out.

He lost, regained, and lost again the Indian captaincy, but continued to score runs quickly and entertainingly and to take wickets. In 1993-94, in his final Test season, he overtook Richard Hadlee's record haul of 431 Test wickets, and he ended with 434. He is the only player to take 400 wickets and score 5,000 runs in Tests.

1959	**1975-76**	**1978**	**1980**	**1983**
Born Kapildev Ramlal Nikhanj on 6 January in Chandigarh, India	Makes his first-class debut for Haryana and takes 6 for 19 in first innings	Made Test debut v Pakistan at Faisalabad on October 16, aged 18 years 283 days	Completed the double of 1,000 Test runs and 100 Test wickets in record time (one year 105 days) and was the youngest to do so (21 years 27 days), February 3, Calcutta, v Pakistan	Captains India to victory in the World Cup final played at Lord's on June 25

1987	**1992**	**1994**	**1994**
Passes 300 Test-wicket mark in the game against Sri Lanka in Cuttack, 4-7 January, takes five wickets in the match	Takes his 400th Test wicket in the match against Australia at Perth, although India lose the match	Passes Richard Hadlee's record of 431 Test wickets with the wicket of H.P. Tillekaratne of Sri Lanka (caught Manjrekar), February 8, at Ahmedabad	Retired from Test cricket as the only player in the history of the game to have scored over 5,000 runs and to have taken 400 wickets in Test cricket

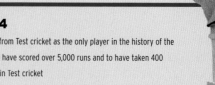

C.J. KORTRIGHT

Born: 9 JANUARY 1871, FURZE HALL, FRYERNING, INGATESTONE, ESSEX
Died: 12 DECEMBER 1952, BROOK STREET, SOUTH WEALD, ESSEX
Teams: ESSEX (1894-1907)
First-class: 170 MATCHES; 4,404 RUNS, AVERAGE 17.61; 489 WICKETS, AVERAGE 21.05

Although he never appeared in Test cricket, Kortright is regarded by many as the fastest bowler ever to have played county cricket. He first played for Essex before the county attained first-class status and his best season came in 1895, when he claimed 76 wickets at under 16 runs each. He was an amateur with a good private income and he captained Essex in 1903, but by then his bowling had declined and he played as a batsman.

ANIL KUMBLE

Born: 17 OCTOBER 1970, BANGALORE, INDIA
Teams: KARNATAKA (1989-90 TO 2006-07); NORTHAMPTONSHIRE (1995); LEICESTERSHIRE (2000); SURREY (2006), BANGALORE ROYAL CHALLENGERS (2008-09)
First-class: 244 MATCHES; 5,572 RUNS, AVERAGE 21.68; 1,136 WICKETS, AVERAGE 25.83
Tests (1990 to 2008-09): 132 MATCHES; 2,506 RUNS, AVERAGE 17.77; 619 WICKETS, AVERAGE 29.65

A leg-break bowler, Anil Kumble was one of the three spinners who destroyed England in India in 1992-93. He had made little impact when he toured England in 1990, playing in one Test and capturing three expensive wickets, but as he matured, he became a potent force in any attack. He bowled at a brisker pace than most spinners with relentless accuracy. Bespectacled and gentle, he was a most effective bowler in limited-over internationals as well as Test cricket.

He played for Northamptonshire in 1995 and, with 105 wickets in 17 games, he came close to taking them to the championship. In 1996, he failed to find form on India's tour of England, but he remains a vital part of India's attack.

In February 1999, he became the second man in Test history to capture all ten wickets in a single innings. The feat was for India v Pakistan in Delhi. His first eight overs cost 37 runs without a wicket; his next 19 overs again cost 37 runs, but included all ten wickets. Another record fell to Kumble in December 2004, when he passed Kapil Dev as India's all-time leading wicket-taker in Tests, reaching 500 in 2005-06 and 600 in 2008-09. Kumble retired from Test cricket in November 2008.

Anil Kumble: record wicket-taker for India.

JIM LAKER

Born: 9 FEBRUARY 1922, FRIZINGHALL, BRADFORD, YORKSHIRE
Died: 23 APRIL 1986, PUTNEY, LONDON
Teams: SURREY (1946-59); ESSEX (1962-64); AUCKLAND (1951-52)
First-class: 450 MATCHES; 7,304 RUNS, AVERAGE 16.60; 1,944 WICKETS, AVERAGE 18.41
Tests (1947-48 to 1958-59): 46 MATCHES; 676 RUNS, AVERAGE 14.08; 193 WICKETS, AVERAGE 21.24

The world of cricket has not seen a better off-spinner than Jim Laker, and his achievements stand as testimony to his greatness. A Yorkshireman who came south to follow his career with Surrey, for whom he made his debut shortly after the Second World War, he toured the West Indies in 1947-48, and was a success in a series that was mostly disastrous for England. Indeed, on his Test debut, he took 7 for 103 and 2 for 95. He took four wickets in his first Test against Australia a few months later, but it was some time before he could claim a regular place in the England side.

He was a vital member of the Surrey side which won the County Championship seven years in succession, and when Australia toured England in 1956 he took all ten of their wickets for 88 runs at The Oval. More sensational events were to follow. He took 11 for 113 in the Headingley Test, and in the next encounter, at Old Trafford, he performed the greatest bowling feat in cricket by taking 9 for 37 and 10 for 53. He finished the rubber with a record 46 wickets to his credit. His last Test was on the tour of Australia in 1958-59, when a great England side finally began to disintegrate. He wrote a book which caused him to part from Surrey in acrimony, although the wounds later healed and he served on the cricket committee. He played for Essex as an amateur, helping to bring on young bowlers and he earned fame as a commentator and journalist.

ALLAN LAMB

Born: 20 JUNE 1954, LANGEBAANWEG, CAPE PROVINCE, SOUTH AFRICA
Teams: WESTERN PROVINCE (1972-73 TO 1982-82); NORTHAMPTONSHIRE (1978-1995); ORANGE FREE STATE (1987-88)
First-class: 467 MATCHES; 32,502 RUNS, AVERAGE 48.94; 8 WICKETS, AVERAGE 24.87
Tests (1982-92): 79 matches; 4,656 RUNS, AVERAGE 36.09; 1 WICKET, AVERAGE 23.0

Allan Lamb learned his cricket in South Africa and played for Western Province before coming to England to assist Northamptonshire. His English parentage and residence allowed him to qualify for England in 1982, and he was immediately selected to play against India. He scored the first of his 14 Test hundreds in his third match.

A stocky, belligerent batsman, he took three centuries off the West Indian attack in 1984, and he played 45 successive Tests for England before being dropped after failures against India in 1986. He bounced back with a brave century against the West Indies in 1988, and he scored heavily for Northamptonshire, whom he captained from 1989 until 1995, taking them to success in the NatWest Trophy in 1992, and coming close to claiming the championship three years later.

A witty man and a joyful companion, he was an excellent batsman in limited-overs matches, and he and his friend Ian Botham toured venues with their "Lamb and Beef" show.

JUSTIN LANGER

Born: 21 NOVEMBER 1970, PERTH, WESTERN AUSTRALIA
Teams: WESTERN AUSTRALIA (1991-92 TO 2006-07); MIDDLESEX (1998-00); SOMERSET (2006-09)
First-Class: 360 MATCHES; 28,382 RUNS, AVERAGE 50.23; 5 WICKETS, AVERAGE 42.00
Tests (1992-93 to 2006-07): 105 MATCHES; 7,696 RUNS, AVERAGE 45.27; NO WICKETS

Langer was brought up in a cricket-crazy family; his father laid out a pitch in the backyard, then employed a coach to teach his son the batting basics. Left-handed, of medium height with nimble feet, his ambition was to play for Australia. In his first season of state cricket, he hit a brilliant 149 in the Sheffield Shield final and the following summer made his Test debut v West Indies in Adelaide. Progress at international level was, however, slow – even in 1997, when he was part of the Australian squad touring England, he failed to gain a place in any of the Tests.

Justin Langer: solid opening batsman who excelled for Australia.

During the 1998-99 Ashes series Langer was more fortunate and held the first wicket down place; in the previous few months he had joined Middlesex and was the first batsman in England to reach 1,000 runs. He returned to the county for the two summers that followed, being captain in 2000.

Continuing his Test career, he appeared in the 16 consecutive Tests, all of which ended in victory for Australia. Langer was now an opening bat. In 2005, he topped the Aussie averages during the famous Ashes battle. The one peculiarity of his career is that, though he played in 100 Tests, he has only eight one-day internationals to his name.

He retired from Test cricket following Australia's successful 2006-07 Ashes campaign.

BRIAN LARA

SEE PAGE 209

HAROLD LARWOOD

Born: 14 NOVEMBER 1904, NUNCARGATE, NOTTINGHAMSHIRE
Died: 22 JULY 1995, SYDNEY, AUSTRALIA
Teams: NOTTINGHAMSHIRE (1924-38); EUROPEANS (1936-37)
First-class: 361 MATCHES; 7,289 RUNS, AVERAGE 19.91; 1,427 WICKETS, AVERAGE 17.51
Tests (1926 to 1932-33): 21 MATCHES; 485 RUNS, AVERAGE 19.40; 78 WICKETS, AVERAGE 28.35

Harold Larwood's name will for ever be linked with the term "bodyline", and for all too brief a period he was regarded as the fastest and the best bowler in the world. He was right-arm, bowled off an 18-yard run and, although of only medium height, leapt into a high, classical, explosive delivery. He made his England debut during his first full season, 1926, toured Australia in 1928-29 and played against them in 1930, but it was the tour of Australia in 1932-33, that is best remembered. Bowling very fast and with unerring accuracy, he often attacked the line of the leg stump to a packed leg-side field. He took 33 wickets in the series, which England won 4-0, but he and Jardine were accused of intimidation and deliberately attacking the batsman's body.

Larwood never played Test cricket again, and he retired from county cricket owing to injury in 1938. He emigrated to Australia in 1949.

BILL LAWRY

Born: 11 FEBRUARY 1937, THORNBURY, MELBOURNE, VICTORIA, AUSTRALIA
Teams: VICTORIA (1955-56 TO 1971-72)
First-class: 249 MATCHES; 18,734 RUNS, AVERAGE 50.90; 5 WICKETS, AVERAGE 37.60
Tests (1961 to 1970-71): 67 MATCHES; 5,234 RUNS, AVERAGE 47.15; NO WICKETS FOR 6 RUNS

A tall, lean, left-handed opening batsman with immense powers of concentration and infinite patience, Bill Lawry enjoyed an excellent first Test series in England in 1961, when he hit two centuries and topped the batting averages in both the Test series and all first-class matches.

His was not the style, however, to win over spectators at a time when cricket was in crisis and accused of dullness. He was not well treated by the press, who continued to hound him when, as senior player, he automatically succeeded Simpson as captain in 1967-68. He won a series against India, drew with England and won a crushing victory in the West Indies after losing the first Test.

In the second, he and Ian Chappell added 298 in 310 minutes for the second wicket, and Lawry made 205. He also hit 151 in the last Test.

He led Australia to victory over India, but they were crushed in South Africa and, when things began to go wrong against Illingworth's side in 1970-71, he was relieved of the captaincy and dropped for the final Test. He has since worked as a commentator.

BRIAN LARA
The Seventh Son

FIRST-CLASS CAREER
(1987-88 to 2006-07, 261 matches)
Batting: RUNS 22,156; AVERAGE 51.88; HIGHEST
SCORE 501 NOT OUT; CENTURIES 65
Bowling: WICKETS 4; RUNS 416;
AVERAGE 104.00; BEST 1-1
Catches: 320

TESTS
(1990-91 to 2006-07, 131 MATCHES)
Batting: RUNS 11,953; AVERAGE 52.88;
HIGHEST SCORE 400 NOT OUT;
CENTURIES 34
Bowling: WICKETS 0
Catches: 164

Brian Lara: the record-breaking batsman acknowledges the crowd's applause.

To break one of cricket's greatest records would ensure a batsman a place in the record books forever. To break another, seemingly even more impregnable, only seven weeks later, sounds like something out of fiction. Yet Lara did it, and his place among the all-time greats was already secure at the age of 25.

Lara, the seventh son of 11 children, was taken to the Harvard Club by an older sister for cricket coaching aged seven. He made his Trinidad debut in 1987-88 and showed his class with 92 against Barbados fast bowlers Garner and Marshall.

His Test debut came in 1990-91, and his second appearance was in the historic first Test with South Africa after their return to Test cricket in 1991-92.

The following season he went to Australia, and in the third Test announced his class to the world by making 277. Later that season he helped the West Indies beat Pakistan in the three-match so-called "World Championship of Test Cricket" 1-0, averaging 43.20.

In 1993-94, England visited the West Indies. England had just reduced their deficit to 2-1 when the fifth Test began. Lara went out to bat at 11 for 1, which soon became 12 for 2. In a rain-interrupted innings he passed 300. Could he beat Sobers' 365? At 347 he was stuck for 18 minutes and was nearly yorked, but at 361 a four through the covers equalled the record, and next over another to square-leg beat it. He accepted six minutes of congratulations but was out through tiredness for 375 after 13 hours' batting. Sobers was one of the first to congratulate him.

Seven weeks after his great feat he went out to bat for Warwickshire against Durham at Edgbaston. Durham had declared at 556 for 8; Lara came in at 8 for 1. When 12, he was "bowled" from a no-ball, and he was dropped by the wicket-keeper at 18. But then he went on remorselessly. He was dropped at 238 and again at 413. When possibly the last over of the match began he was on 497 – Hanif Mohammad's world-record score was 499. He ended on 501 not out.

Since then Lara has played several outstanding innings amid periods of apparent loss of motivation. When, after ten years, his Test record score was beaten by Matthew Hayden's 380 against Zimbabwe in 2003-04, Lara reclaimed it within six months with 400 not out against England at St Johns, Antigua. In November 2005, with 226 and 17 against Australia at Adelaide, he became the leading run-scorer in Tests, beating Allan Border's record.

Lara replaced Courtney Walsh as West Indies captain in 1997-98, but has been an unsuccessful skipper, discarding or losing the role from time to time, as his batting brilliance was unable to halt the West Indies' decline as a force in recent years.

1969	1987-88	1990	1993	1994	1994
Born Brian Charles Lara on 2 May at Cantaro, Santa Cruz, Trinidad	Makes his first-class debut for Trinidad	Made Test debut at Lahore v Pakistan on 6-11 December. He scored a mature 44, but Pakistan held on to draw the game	Captures the attention of the cricket world with a masterful 277 (run out) for West Indies against Australia at Sydney, 2-6 January	Broke Test record with 375 v England at St John's, Antigua, 16-21 April	Broke world best-ever score with 501 not out for Warwickshire v Durham, Edgbaston, 2-6 June

1995	1997	2004	2006	2006-07
Passes 2,000 runs in Test cricket in his 22nd Test for West Indies in game v Australia at Bridgetown, Barbados	Reaches the 4,000-run landmark in his 45th Test match, v Sri Lanka at St Vincent	Regained world Test record (from Matthew Hayden) with 400 not out (43 fours, 4 sixes) v England at Antigua, April 10-14	Passes Allan Border's total to become the leading run-scorer in the history of Test cricket, v India at St Lucia	Retires from international cricket following the 2007 World Cup as the leading scorer in the history of Test cricket

V.V.S. LAXMAN

Born: 1 NOVEMBER 1974, HYDERABAD, INDIA
Teams: HYDERABAD (1992-93 TO 2009-10), LANCASHIRE (2007-09), DECCAN CHARGERS (2008-09)
First-class: 251 MATCHES; 18,642 RUNS, AVERAGE 52.51; 22 WICKETS, AVERAGE 34.27
Tests (1996-97 to 2008-09): 120 MATCHES; 7,903 RUNS, AVERAGE 47.32; 2 WICKETS, AVERAGE 63.00

One major landmark which will always be part of Laxman's c.v. occurred in the second Test between India and Australia at Eden Gardens, Calcutta in March 2001. Australia had been unbeaten in 16 successive Tests; India, batting second, made 171 in response to Australia's 445. The follow-on was enforced. Four second innings wickets went down for 232 – India still hadn't avoided an innings defeat. Laxman came in. With Dravid he added 376 for the fifth wicket and went on to make 281 – the highest innings ever by an Indian against Australia. Australia were bowled out

for 212 and India, thanks to Laxman, had broken Australia's record run of victories.

As a teenager, Laxman had a choice of a place in medical school – both of his parents were doctors – or a place with Indian Under-19s. He chose the latter. After a promising Test debut he struggled a little at the highest level, but on the domestic front in 1999-2000 he scored 353 for Hyderabad v Karnataka and made a record 1,415 runs in the Ranji Trophy. With a current batting average well over 50 in first-class cricket and over 45 in Tests, he is one of the major figures in Indian cricket.

MAURICE LEYLAND

Born: 20 JULY 1900, NEW PARK, HARROGATE, YORKSHIRE
Died: 1 JANUARY 1967, SCOTTON BANKS, HARROGATE, YORKSHIRE
Teams: YORKSHIRE (1920-1947); PATIALA (1926-27)
First-class: 686 MATCHES; 33,660 RUNS, AVERAGE 40.50; 466 WICKETS, AVERAGE 29.31
Tests (1928-1938): 41 MATCHES; 2,764 RUNS, AVERAGE 46.06; 6 WICKETS, AVERAGE 97.50

V.V.S. Laxman: hit a match-winning 281 v Australia in 2001 at Calcutta.

A tough left-hander whose fighting qualities epitomized Yorkshire cricket during the county's period of dominance in the 1930s, Leyland was also a fine outfielder and a very useful left-arm bowler who specialized in "Chinamen", the slow left-armer's off-break.

He was in the Yorkshire side for eight seasons before winning his first Test cap, against the West Indies in 1928. He failed to score, but he was a controversial choice ahead of Woolley for the tour of Australia the following winter. He only played in the last Test, scoring 137 and 53 not out. He was now a virtual regular in the England side and was invaluable to Jardine on the "bodyline" tour, providing what the captain wanted, "concrete" in the middle of the order.

His last Test was at The Oval against Australia in 1938 when he and Hutton put on a record 382 for the second wicket and Leyland made his highest Test score, 187.

He was 46 when cricket resumed after the war, but he played for two seasons and later coached Yorkshire.

DENNIS LILLEE

SEE PAGE 212

RAY LINDWALL

Born: 3 OCTOBER 1921, MASCOT, SYDNEY, NEW SOUTH WALES, AUSTRALIA
Died: 23 JUNE 1996, BRISBANE, AUSTRALIA
Teams: NEW SOUTH WALES (1941-42 TO 1953-54); QUEENSLAND (1954-55 TO 1959-60)
First-class: 228 MATCHES; 5,042 RUNS, AVERAGE 21.82; 794 WICKETS, AVERAGE 21.35
Tests (1945-46 to 1959-60): 61 MATCHES; 1502 RUNS, AVERAGE 21.15; 228 WICKETS, AVERAGE 23.03

Ray Lindwall had a beautiful fast bowler's action and he had no peer in the decade immediately following the Second World War. His Test debut was against New Zealand in 1945-46, and in the last two Tests against England the following season, he

took 15 wickets. Against India, at Adelaide in 1947-48, he took 7 for 38 in the second innings, which were to remain his best figures in Test cricket, but it was in England weeks later that he was to prove most devastating, taking 27 wickets in the series, which included 6 for 20 at The Oval as England were bowled out for 52. He continued to dominate batsmen, and he played Test cricket until he was 38, finishing with what was then a record number of wickets for an Australian.

He was a very useful, hard-hitting lower-order batsman and hit centuries against both England and the West Indies. He captained Australia once when Ian Johnson was unfit against India in Bombay in 1956-57.

CLIVE LLOYD

Born: 31 AUGUST 1944, QUEENSTOWN, GEORGETOWN, BRITISH GUIANA
Teams: BRITISH GUIANA/GUYANA (1963-64 TO 1982-83); LANCASHIRE (1968-86)
First-class: 490 MATCHES; 31,232 RUNS, AVERAGE 49.26; 114 WICKETS, AVERAGE 36.00
Tests (1966-67 to 1984-85): 110 MATCHES; 7,515 RUNS, AVERAGE 46.67; 10 WICKETS, AVERAGE 62.20

A hard-hitting, left-handed batsman, fine fielder and medium-pace bowler, Clive Lloyd captained the West Indies in 74 Tests and won 36 of them; both figures are records. He moved with the silkiness of a cat and began his long Test career with innings of 82 and 78 not out in the West Indies victory over India in Bombay in 1966-67. In his next series, he hit two centuries against England.

In 1974-75, he took over as captain of the West Indies for the tour of India. In his first match in charge, he reached 100 off 85 balls and finished with 163. In the fifth Test, he hit a career-best 242 not out. As well as his successes in Test matches, he took the West Indies to World Cup triumphs in 1975 and 1979.

He was criticized in that he simply rotated his four fast bowlers, and there were times when his sides appeared to lack discipline, but he won a record 11 Tests in a row between 1984 and 1985, and when he lost his last match as captain, in Sydney, January 1985, it was his first defeat in 26 matches.

He gave magnificent support to Lancashire, particularly when they dominated the one-day game, and he was immensely popular. He settled there in retirement, although he still retains a great interest in West Indian cricket and has managed several West Indian touring parties.

CHARLES MACARTNEY

Born: 27 JUNE 1886, WEST MAITLAND, NEW SOUTH WALES, AUSTRALIA
Died: 9 SEPTEMBER 1958, LITTLE BAY, SYDNEY, NEW SOUTH WALES, AUSTRALIA
Teams: NEW SOUTH WALES (1905-06 TO 1926-27)
First-class: 249 MATCHES; 15,019 RUNS, AVERAGE 45.78; 419 WICKETS, AVERAGE 20.95
Tests (1907-08 to 1926): 35 MATCHES; 2,131 RUNS, AVERAGE 41.78; 45 WICKETS, AVERAGE 27.55

Known as the "Governor General", Charles Macartney was a dominant batsman, never afraid to improvise and ever on the lookout for runs. There was artistry in his right-handed batting, but when he first came to England in 1909 he was primarily a slow left-arm bowler. His 7 for 58 and 4 for 27 won the Headingley Test on that first tour, but against South Africa, 1910-11, it was his batting that flourished. In the fifth Test, he opened the innings for the first time and made 137 and 56. In the second innings, he reached 50 in 35 minutes.

In 1920-21, at Sydney, he scored 170, his highest Test score in 244 minutes against England, and when Australia came to England in 1921 he hit the only Australian century of the rubber. It happened to be his fourth century in consecutive innings and followed his 345 in a day against Nottinghamshire.

In 1926, in England, he scored three hundreds in successive Test innings, becoming the first man to score three hundreds in a rubber in England. He retired from Test cricket after this tour.

ARCHIE MacLAREN

Born: 1 DECEMBER 1871, WHALLEY RANGE, MANCHESTER
Died: 17 NOVEMBER 1944, WARFIELD PARK, BRACKNELL, BERKSHIRE
Teams: LANCASHIRE (1890-1914)
First-class: 424 MATCHES; 22,236 RUNS, AVERAGE 34.15; 1 WICKET, AVERAGE 267.00
Tests (1894-95 to 1909): 35 MATCHES; 1,931 RUNS, AVERAGE 33.87

As a batsman, Archie MacLaren was one of the brightest jewels of the Golden Age, but as captain of England in 22 Tests against Australia and of Lancashire for 12 seasons his credentials are less impressive. A majestic right-handed batsman, rich in classical strokes, he came into the Lancashire side in 1890 straight from Harrow and made 108 against Sussex at Hove in his first match.

He hit 424 against Somerset at Taunton in 1895, the highest score in first-class cricket in England

Stan McCabe: pictured here walking out to bat with the great Don Bradman, on his third and final tour to England in 1938. He hit 232 out of Australia's total of 300 at Trent Bridge.

until Brian Lara's 501 in 1994. He went to Australia in 1894-95, and scored 120 in the fifth Test; all of his Tests were against Australia. Four of his five Test hundreds were made in Australia where the warmer climate was kinder to his lumbago. In his second tour of Australia in 1897-98, he became the first English batsman to hit two centuries in a rubber. The five Test series in which he captained England all ended in defeat, but he was a reluctant skipper in 1909 when, at 37, he felt that he was no longer up to standard.

In 1921, he fielded an all-amateur side against the conquering Australians and beat them in a match which has passed into legend. He took a side to New Zealand in 1922-23, and hit 200 not out in his last first-class match. He was 53 years old.

STAN McCABE

Born: 16 JULY 1910, GRENFELL, NEW SOUTH WALES, AUSTRALIA
Died: 25 AUGUST 1968, BEAUTY POINT, MOSMAN, SYDNEY, NEW SOUTH WALES, AUSTRALIA
Teams: NEW SOUTH WALES (1928-29 TO 1941-42)
First-class: 182 MATCHES; 11,951 RUNS, AVERAGE 49.38; 159 WICKETS, AVERAGE 33.72
Tests (1930-38): 39 MATCHES; 2,748 RUNS, AVERAGE 48.21; 36 WICKETS, AVERAGE 42.86

Short, stocky and strongly built, Stan McCabe was an attacking middle-order batsman and medium-pace bowler who played one of Test cricket's great innings when he hit 232 out of 300 at Trent Bridge in 1938. He batted heroically against Larwood and Voce at Sydney in 1932-33, to make an unbeaten 187, and he was consistently successful on his three tours of England in 1930, 1934 and 1938.

He made his first-class debut at the age of 18 and was the "baby" of the side on his first tour of England. He did not return to cricket after the Second World War, but set up a successful sporting equipment business.

DENNIS LILLEE
The Menace

Dennis Lillee: express pace.

For a decade, Dennis Lillee was one of the most feared fast bowlers ever to play cricket. By the time he retired, he had taken more wickets than any Test bowler before him. He had done it with great technique and with courage, for he had to overcome severe back problems. He had also done it in the way of most fast bowlers: with a swagger and a belligerence.

He made his debut for Western Australia in 1969-70 and took 32 Sheffield Shield wickets. The following season he was in the Test team against England, taking eight wickets in the series. In 1971, he played for Haslingden in the Lancashire League, reaping the benefit when he toured England in 1972 and took 31 Test wickets at 17.87. It was the most wickets an Australian had taken in a series in England at the time.

However, his fine progress broke down in the West Indies in 1972-73 when he ended the first Test with stress fractures in the back, which kept him in plaster for six weeks. His return to Tests was in 1974-75 against England, when he was at his best. With new partner Jeff Thomson, he shattered the English batting. Australia regained the Ashes 4-1, and retained them with a single win in England in 1975. Lillee took 46 English wickets in the two series.

Lillee and Thomson demolished the strong West Indians in 1975-76 when Australia were the strongest team in the world, largely thanks to their new-ball bowlers. Lillee took 11 wickets as Australia won the Centenary Test against England in 1976-77, but then joined Kerry Packer's World Series Cricket.

He returned to Tests in 1979-80, when, although less fast, he took 23 English wickets in three Tests, and went out to bat with an aluminium bat, actually scoring three runs with it before Brearley objected and the umpires ordered him to change it. Later Brearley became his 100th English victim in Tests. In 1981, he took 39 wickets in a losing series in England, but did at least win a bet when backing England at 500-1 to win the Headingley Test from an "impossible" position which, thanks to Botham, they did. His worst behaviour came in 1981-82 when, after impeding Javed Miandad, a player he was pleased to dislike, he kicked him. This earned a suspension from two one-day matches.

That same season, against the West Indies, he returned his best innings analysis in Tests with 7 for 83. Australia won the match, but the series was drawn. When Lillee had Gomes caught, he passed Lance Gibbs' record of 309 Test wickets. By the end of the match, his 85 Test wickets in 1981 were a new record for a calendar year.

Lillee was by now battling against back problems once more, and played in only four more Test series, three of them disappointingly, but in his final series, in 1983-84, he took 20 Pakistan wickets in a winning series. He, Greg Chappell and Rodney Marsh then retired from Tests together. If Thomson had been a great partner for Lillee, Marsh was more so, though less conspicuous. Both ended with a record 355 Test victims (Lillee's since passed) and their 95 shared dismissals (c Marsh b Lillee) was also a record. Lillee's total of 167 Ashes wickets was the most by any player against one country.

Lillee signed for Northamptonshire in 1988, but an ankle injury restricted his appearances to seven matches and the popular warrior finally called it a day.

FIRST-CLASS CAREER
(1969-70 to 1988, 198 matches)
Batting: RUNS 2,377; AVERAGE 13.90; HIGHEST SCORE 73 NOT OUT; CENTURIES 0
Bowling: WICKETS 882; RUNS 20,695; AVERAGE 23.46; BEST 8-29
Catches: 67

TESTS
(1970-71 to 1983-84, 70 MATCHES)
Batting: RUNS 905; AVERAGE 13.71; HIGHEST SCORE 73 NOT OUT; CENTURIES 0
Bowling: WICKETS 355; RUNS 8,493; AVERAGE 23.92; BEST 7-83
Catches: 23

1949	1969-70	1971	1972	1972-73
Born Dennis Keith Lillee on July 18 at Subiaco, Perth, Western Australia	Makes his first-class debut for Western Australia	Made Test debut in sixth Test against England at Adelaide on January 29 to February 3, and took five for 84 in the first innings	Took 31 Test wickets on tour of England, a record for an Australian at that time, including ten in the final Test	Suffers a stress fracture of back on tour of West Indies. Spends six weeks in plaster

1979-80	1981	1981	1981-82
Returns to the Test fold after a three-year stint in World Series Cricket	Became leading wicket-taker in Ashes Tests when beating Hugh Trumble's total of 141 v England, Headingley, July 16-21	Set records for the most Test wickets in a career (breaking Lance Gibbs' 309) and in a calendar year (85), at Melbourne against West Indies, December 26-30	Records best Test analysis of 7 for 83, v West Indies at Melbourne, 26-30 December

CRAIG McDERMOTT

Born: 14 APRIL 1965, IPSWICH, QUEENSLAND, AUSTRALIA
Teams: QUEENSLAND (1983-84 TO 1995-96)
First-class: 174 MATCHES; 2,856 RUNS, AVERAGE 16.32; 677 WICKETS, AVERAGE 28.10
Tests (1984-85 to 1995-96): 71 MATCHES; 940 RUNS, AVERAGE 12.20; 291 WICKETS, AVERAGE 28.62

Craig McDermott was forced to retire in 1997 because of persistent injury problems, but he could point to the fact that only Dennis Lillee had taken more wickets in Test cricket for Australia than he had. A red-headed, right-arm fast bowler, he took ten wickets in his first two Tests, against the West Indies, and in England in 1985, he claimed 30 wickets in the series to give him a sensational start to his Test career.

Craig McDermott: Aussie speed merchant.

TED McDONALD

Born: 6 JANUARY 1891, LAUNCESTON, TASMANIA, AUSTRALIA
Died: 22 JULY 1937, BLACKROD, BOLTON, LANCASHIRE
Teams: TASMANIA (1909-10 TO 1910-11); VICTORIA (1911-12 TO 1921-22); LANCASHIRE (1924-31)
First-class: 281 MATCHES; 2,663 RUNS, AVERAGE 10.44; 1,395 WICKETS, AVERAGE 20.76
Tests (1920-21 to 1921-22): 11 MATCHES; 116 RUNS, AVERAGE 16.57; 43 WICKETS, AVERAGE 33.27

Tall and strong, "Ted" McDonald was a natural athlete whose bowling was rhythmical and graceful. He had exceptional pace and could move the ball either way. He played in the last three Tests against England in 1920-21, making little impact, but the following summer, he and Jack Gregory destroyed England. McDonald finished the series with 27 wickets in the three-Test rubber in South Africa in 1921-22. He then joined Nelson in the Lancashire League and qualified for the Red Rose county. He was a key reason for Lancashire winning the championship four times in five seasons, beginning in 1926. He took 205 wickets in 1925 and 190 in 1928. He had no standing as a batsman, but he made a century in 100 minutes against Middlesex at Old Trafford in 1926.

At Old Trafford, he took 8 for 141 to become the youngest Australian ever to take eight wickets in a Test innings.

There were troughs as well as peaks in his career, but he destroyed India in 1991-92, with 31 wickets, average 12.83, in five Tests. He had agreed to play for Yorkshire the following summer, but he was waiting for an operation and was forced to withdraw. His tour of England in 1993, was blighted by the need for an operation on an intestinal complaint. Despite this, he returned in 1994-95 to take 32 English wickets and be the major force in the Ashes series. His last Test matches were against Sri Lanka. Capable of hitting hard and often, he was sometimes sent in early in one-day internationals to help lift the scoring-rate.

He was killed in the aftermath of a road accident. Signalling for help, he was knocked down by another car.

JACKIE McGLEW

Born: 11 MARCH 1929, PIETERMARITZBURG, SOUTH AFRICA
Died: 9 JUNE 1998, PRETORIA, SOUTH AFRICA
Teams: NATAL (1947-48 TO 1966-67)
First-class: 190 MATCHES; 12,170 RUNS, AVERAGE 45.92; 35 WICKETS, AVERAGE 26.62
Tests (1951 to 1961-62): 34 MATCHES; 2,440 RUNS, AVERAGE 42.06; NO WICKETS FOR 23 RUNS

An obdurate opening batsman with infinite patience, Jackie McGlew was an outstanding cover fielder and a respected and successful captain of Natal for several seasons. He first toured England in 1951 and made his Test debut at Trent Bridge. He was dropped after the second Test and accomplished little in four Tests in Australia in 1952-53, but when the team moved on to New Zealand he hit 255 not out at Wellington. This was then the highest score for South Africa in Test cricket, and he became only the second player to be on the field for the whole of a Test match.

Vice-captain for the tour of England in 1955, he led the side in the third and fourth Tests when Cheetham was injured, scored centuries in both and took South Africa to two victories. Appointed captain for the home series against England in 1956-57, he was able to play only in the second Test because of a shoulder injury. His replacement, van Ryneveld, did well and kept the job for the tour of Australia. McGlew, captain in the first Test when van Ryneveld was unavailable, hit two centuries in the series and was reinstated as captain when van Ryneveld retired.

McGlew led South Africa to England in 1960, but the series was painfully dull and he drew much of the criticism. In 1961-62, New Zealand surprisingly drew the series in South Africa. McGlew's last match ended in defeat and he finished with a thumb in splints and a shoulder in plaster.

He continued to play for Natal, and he never lost the reputation or nickname of being "Sticky".

GLENN McGRATH

SEE PAGE 214

GRAHAM McKENZIE

Born: 24 JUNE 1941, COTTESLOE, PERTH, WESTERN AUSTRALIA
Teams: WESTERN AUSTRALIA (1959-60 TO 1973-74); LEICESTERSHIRE (1969-75)
First-class: 383 MATCHES; 5,662 RUNS, AVERAGE 15.64; 1,219 WICKETS, AVERAGE 26.96
Tests: (1961 to 1970-71): 60 MATCHES; 945 RUNS, AVERAGE 12.27; 246 WICKETS, AVERAGE 29.78

"Garth" McKenzie had a superb physique and bowled fast with a smoothness and economy of style that were a model for younger players. At the time, he was the youngest cricketer to reach 100, 150 and 200 wickets in Test cricket, and he was Australia's main strike bowler for a decade. His Test debut came at Lord's in 1961, and his 5 for 37 in the second innings set up Australia's victory. He captured 20 wickets when the Ashes were retained against Dexter's side in 1962-63, and he had 29 in England in 1964, which equalled Grimmett's record at that time. In the Old Trafford Test, he gave a remarkable performance, taking 7 for 153 as England scored 611. His final Test came at Sydney in 1970-71, when he took his 246th wicket, just two short of Benaud's record, and was forced to retire hurt when struck in the mouth by a ball from Snow.

He gave fine service to Leicestershire for seven seasons, and they won the championship for the first time in his last season with them.

GLENN McGRATH
Record-breaking fast bowler

FIRST-CLASS CAREER
(1992-93 to 2006-07, 189 matches)
Batting: RUNS 977; AVERAGE 7.66; HIGHEST SCORE 61; CENTURIES 0
Bowling: WICKETS 835; RUNS 17,414; AVERAGE 20.85; BEST 8-24
Catches: 54

TESTS
(1993-94 to 2006-07, 124 MATCHES)
Batting: RUNS 641; AVERAGE 7.36; HIGHEST SCORE 61; CENTURIES 0
Bowling: WICKETS 563; RUNS 12,186; AVERAGE 21.64; BEST 8-24
Catches: 38

In the Ashes series of 2005 in England, Glenn McGrath became the fourth bowler in Test history to pass 500 wickets and the second fast bowler (after Courtney Walsh) to do so. He could not have contemplated this when he was the spindly young son of a Narromine sheep farmer and preferred golf and basketball because he couldn't get into the local Under-16s cricket team. He didn't play in a representative game until he was 17, and played for his home town of Dubbo.

A year later he was seen by some visiting New South Wales players and Doug Walters recommended him to Steve Rixon, who played for a Sydney club, Sutherland. At 19, McGrath moved to Sydney to play second grade cricket for Sutherland.

Glenn McGrath: a fast bowler with almost metronomic accuaracy.

He was sent to the Australian Cricket Academy in Adelaide. In January 1993, made his first appearance for New South Wales.

He made his Test debut after only seven first-class matches for New South Wales. He has seldom been out of the Test side since and has accumulated wickets regularly.

His career has not been entirely smooth however and, although genial off the pitch, he has a reputation of occasionally going over the top with his sledging.

It is part of McGrath's technique to single out an opposition batsman and announce that he is targetting him and, coincidence or not, he seems to succeed in getting some batsmen more often than the law of averages would suggest – Michael Atherton being a case in point. Only illness (of his wife) and injury halted his march to 500 wickets.

This milestone came in the first Ashes Test of 2005 when he had Marcus Trescothick caught by Langer at Lord's. He took nine wickets in this match in a masterly display. He retired from Test cricket after the 2006-07 Ashes series.

1970	**1992-93**	**1993**	**1994**	**1998**
Born Glenn Donald McGrath on 9 February at Dubbo, New South Wales, Australia	Makes his first-class debut for New South Wales	Made Test debut against New Zealand at Perth on November 12. He took three for 142 in the match, his first wicket being that of Mark Greatbatch	Plays in his first Ashes series and takes just six wickets at 38.16 with best bowling of 3 for 40	He was elected one of Wisden's Five Cricketers of the Year

1998-99	**2004**	**2005**	**2006-07**
Enjoys a successful series against the West Indies in the Caribbean taking 30 wickets in Australia's victorious series	Became the first Australian fast bowler to play 100 Test matches, at Nagpur in October. Produced best Test bowling with eight for 24 v Pakistan at Perth in December	Became the fourth bowler in the game's history to pass 500 Test wickets when he dismissed Marcus Trescothick in the first Test v England at Lord's, July 21	Retires from international cricket following Australia's successful defence of the World Cup

ROY MCLEAN

Born: 9 JULY 1930, PIETERMARITZBURG, SOUTH AFRICA
Died: 26 APRIL 2007, JOHANNESBURG, SOUTH AFRICA
Teams: NATAL (1949-50 TO 1965-66)
First-class: 200 MATCHES; 10,969 RUNS, AVERAGE 36.88; 2 WICKETS, AVERAGE 61.00
Tests (1951 to 1964-65): 40 MATCHES; 2,120 RUNS, AVERAGE 30.28; NO WICKETS FOR 1 RUN

A delightfully aggressive right-handed stroke-maker, Roy McLean was also a brilliant outfielder. His eagerness to score and to entertain was not always to the liking of the South African selectors, and his 11 "ducks" in his Test career was a sign of his impetuosity. He first played Test cricket during the 1951 tour of England, making 67 run out at Headingley. He topped 1,000 runs in 1955 and 1960, and he scored 142 in the Lord's Test on the first of those tours, hitting a brisk 50 at Old Trafford as South Africa successfully chased a target of 145 in 135 minutes. Not unnaturally, he was an immense favourite with crowds, who warmed to his fielding.

MAJID KHAN

Born: 28 SEPTEMBER 1946, LUDHIANA, INDIA
Teams: LAHORE (1961-62 TO 1982-83); PUNJAB (1964-65 TO 1967-68); PIA (1968-69 TO 1980-81); GLAMORGAN (1968-76); CAMBRIDGE UNIVERSITY (1970-72)
First-class: 410 MATCHES; 27,444 RUNS, AVERAGE 43.01; 223 WICKETS, AVERAGE 32.14
Tests (1964-65 to 1982-83): 63 MATCHES; 3,931 RUNS, AVERAGE 38.92; 27 WICKETS, AVERAGE 53.92

Son of Jahangir Khan, who played cricket for India with distinction, Majid was born in the year before Partition, but his cricket has been played in Pakistan. A highly gifted all-rounder, Majid was an attacking right-handed batsman, confident, calm and cultured, and a medium-pace or off-break bowler. His Test debut came against Australia in Karachi when he was out for 0 and opened the Pakistan bowling, claiming Bill Lawry as his first Test victim. He toured England in 1967

and, although he did little in the series, he hit an astonishing 147 not out in 89 minutes against Glamorgan. His innings included five sixes in an over off Roger Davis, and Glamorgan were prompted to engage him. He was a fine acquisition for the county and captained them for three years before finally leaving in acrimony and discord. He was a highly successful captain of Cambridge University.

His highest score against England was 99, but he hit eight Test centuries, three of them against Australia and two, including his highest, 167, against the West Indies. He was something of an amateur spirit, not totally at home in the new commercialism that was sweeping the game and, as a captain, he was shabbily treated by authorities both in Pakistan and at Glamorgan. He was later involved in cricket administration in Pakistan.

VINOO MANKAD

Born: 12 APRIL 1917, JAMNAGAR, INDIA
Died: 21 AUGUST 1978, BOMBAY, INDIA
Teams: WESTERN INDIA (1935-36); NAWANAGAR (1936-37 TO 1941-42); HINDUS (1936-37 TO 104-46); MAHARASHTRA (1943-44); GUJARAT (1944-45 TO 1950-51); BENGAL (1948-49); BOMBAY (1951-52 TO 1955-56); RAJASTHAN (1956-57 TO 1961-62)
First-class: 233 MATCHES; 11,591 RUNS, AVERAGE 34.70; 782 WICKETS, AVERAGE 24.53
Tests (1946 to 1958-59): 44 MATCHES; 2,109 RUNS, AVERAGE 31.47; 162 WICKETS, AVERAGE 32.32

"Vinoo" Mankad began his career with aspirations of becoming a fast bowler, but under the tutelage of the Sussex all-rounder A.F. Wensley, he became a left-arm spinner and a tenacious right-handed batsman who often opened the innings. He was India's first great spin bowler and the best all-rounder of his generation. His Test debut did not come until 1946 when he performed admirably in all three Tests and completed the "double" in all matches. He hit two centuries against Australia in 1947-48, and remained an automatic choice for India for the next decade. His first great moment came against

England at Madras in 1951-52, when he took 8 for 55 and 4 for 53 to bowl India to an innings victory, their first win in Test cricket. He captured 34 wickets in the series, a record at that time.

He received an offer to play in the Lancashire League, but said that he would not accept if the Indian Board assured him he would be picked to tour England in 1952. Insanely, they refused to give that assurance, but the side was so overwhelmed that Haslingden, his club, released him to play in three of the four Tests. He responded heroically. At Lord's, he hit 72 and then bowled 73 overs to take 5 for 196 as England made 537. He then scored 184 out of 378 before sending down another 24 overs.

In 1952-53, India won their first rubber, beating Pakistan. Mankad was again the hero, with 25 wickets in four Tests. In all, he hit five Test centuries, his highest being 231 against New Zealand at Madras in 1955-56, when he and Pankaj Roy scored 413 for the first wicket, which remains a world Test record.

RODNEY MARSH

Born: 11 NOVEMBER 1947, ARMADALE, PERTH, WESTERN AUSTRALIA
Teams: WESTERN AUSTRALIA (1968-69 TO 1983-84)
First-class: 257 MATCHES; 11,067, AVERAGE 31.17; 1 WICKET, AVERAGE 84.00; CAUGHT 803, STUMPED 66
Tests (1970-71 TO 1983-84): 96 MATCHES; 3,633 RUNS, AVERAGE 26.51; NO WICKETS FOR 54 RUNS; CAUGHT 343, STUMPED 12

No wicket-keeper had accounted for more batsmen in Test cricket than Rodney Marsh, until Ian Healy took his record. Had he not spent a period with World Series cricket, Marsh's record would have been even greater for he had no rival during the time that he was Australia's keeper. He first appeared on the Test scene in 1970-71 when Illingworth's side regained the Ashes, and was treated with contempt by English critics who dubbed him "iron gloves", but

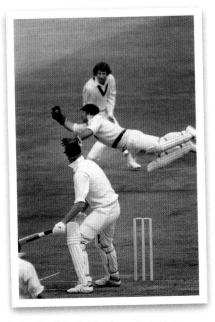

Rodney Marsh: behind the stumps for 96 Tests.

he made three stumpings during the series and scored an unbeaten 92 in his fourth match. His keeping improved dramatically and, when he hit 118 against Pakistan at Adelaide in 1972-73, he became the first Australian wicket-keeper to score a hundred in Test cricket. Two more were to follow before the end of his career, and he had made a century on his first-class debut.

Marsh became a folk hero, epitomizing the aggressive and determined cricket of the conquering Australians of the Chappell brothers' era and, off the field, he was a great favourite as he mingled warmly with people at social events. Having been director of the Australian Cricket Academy, he switched sides and held a similar post in English cricket. In 2005, he became ICC director of coaching.

MALCOLM MARSHALL

Born: 18 APRIL 1958, BRIDGETOWN, BARBADOS
Died: 4 NOVEMBER 1999, BRIDGETOWN, BARBADOS
Teams: BARBADOS (1977-78 TO 1990-91); HAMPSHIRE (1979-93); NATAL (1992-93 TO 1995-96)
First-class: 408 MATCHES; 11.004 RUNS, AVERAGE 24.83; 1,651 WICKETS, AVERAGE 19.10
Tests (1978-79 to 1991): 81 MATCHES; 1,810 RUNS, AVERAGE 18.85; 376 WICKETS, AVERAGE 20.94

Malcolm Marshall was possibly the greatest of a great battery of West Indian fast bowlers of the 1980s. Remarkably, he stood only 5ft 10in tall, but he made his lack of height an advantage. With his whippy action he could make his fastest deliveries skid off the wicket rather than dig in, making him a dangerous bowler to face in both senses. His assets were dedication, skill, ambition and fitness. He was in the Barbados side at 19, and in the Test side touring India at 20. The following summer he arrived at Hampshire as an overseas replacement for Andy Roberts and, beginning with nine wickets in his first match, he became one of the most successful of all imported cricketers. He played for Hampshire for 14 seasons, taking 100 wickets twice, including 134 (44 more than the next bowler) in 1982, when he recorded his best figures, 8 for 71 against Worcestershire.

In the 1984 Test at Headingley, he suffered a double fracture of his left thumb after only six overs, but came in to bat as last man with Gomes on 96, staying till Gomes got his hundred. Marshall then took 7 for 53 in England's second innings, his best Test figures at the time. He also took a catch. From then on he blossomed, becoming the leading strike bowler in the world. He loved bowling in England, and his best Test innings analysis was at Old Trafford in 1988 – 7 for 22. The following winter in Australia, he passed Lance Gibbs' total of 309 Test wickets to become the leading West Indian wicket-taker of all time.

When his Test career finished, he went to play for Natal in South Africa, where he improved his highest first-class score to 120 not out. He made seven first-class centuries in all. In 1996-97 he was appointed the West Indies coach. Although one of the world's most hostile and dangerous bowlers (he famously squashed England captain Mike Gatting's nose) he was a sunny and considerate man off the field, and liked by all. Sadly, he died of cancer when only 41.

PETER MAY

Born: 31 DECEMBER 1929, READING, BERKSHIRE
Died: 21 DECEMBER 1994, LIPHOOK, HAMPSHIRE
Teams: SURREY (1950-63); CAMBRIDGE UNIVERSITY (1950-52)
First-class: 388 MATCHES; 27,592 RUNS, AVERAGE 51.00; NO WICKETS FOR 49 RUNS
Tests (1951-61): 66 MATCHES; 4,537 RUNS, AVERAGE 46.77

The finest English batsman of the post-war era, Peter May first appeared for Surrey during his first year at Cambridge, and his England debut came the following season, against South Africa at Headingley. He made 158. He had a successful series against India in 1952, but a failure in the first Test of the Ashes series in 1953, led to his being dropped until the final Test when he returned to play a part in England's victory. From that point on, he was an automatic choice for England.

A tall, elegant batsman with the full range of classical stroke-play, he was immediately recognized as the natural successor to Hutton as England's captain. He learned the art of captaincy under the two outstanding leaders of his time, Hutton and Surridge, whom he succeeded as Surrey's captain during the period of that county's greatest glory. Gentle and well-mannered as he was, and greatly admired and respected by his men, May had a ruthless, professional streak which served him well in Test cricket. He became captain of England in 1955 and led the side on a record 41 occasions with a record 20 victories to his credit. In 1957, he ended the West Indian supremacy over England when he and Colin Cowdrey defied Ramadhin in a fourth-wicket stand of 411, a record. May made 285 not out in that innings.

The disappointment came in Australia in 1958-59, when a great England side broke up and was surprisingly and heavily defeated. A year later, May was forced home from the Caribbean for medical treatment and, although he returned briefly in 1961, he announced his retirement. Illness and pressure had taken their toll. He was still short of his 32nd birthday.

He later held every high office in the game, but his period as chairman of selectors was not a happy one. He was dealing with players who no longer spoke his language. Values had changed.

VIJAY MERCHANT

Born: 12 OCTOBER 1911, BOMBAY, INDIA
Died: 27 OCTOBER 1987, BOMBAY, INDIA
Teams: HINDUS (1929-30 TO 1945-46); BOMBAY (1933-34 TO 1950-51)
First-class: 150 MATCHES; 13,470 RUNS, AVERAGE 71.64; 65 WICKETS, AVERAGE 32.12
Tests (1933-34 to 1951-52): 10 MATCHES; 859 RUNS, AVERAGE 47.72; NO WICKETS FOR 40 RUNS

Merchant was small and compact, and there was a delicacy in his movement as he built an innings. A right-handed opener, he was India's first great batsman and he gave evidence of his greatness on his two tours to England, scoring 1,745 runs in 1936 and 2,385 runs in 1946. His Test career began against Jardine's side in 1933-34, when he batted in the middle order, but he opened on the 1936 tour and scored 114 in the second innings at Old Trafford when he and Mushtaq Ali put on 203 for the first wicket and saved the Test. In 1946, he scored 128 at The Oval. His third Test hundred was his highest, 154 against England in Delhi in 1951-52, when he and Hazare established an Indian record for the series by scoring 211 for the third wicket. This was Merchant's last Test, for he sustained a shoulder injury which ended his career. He held high office in the administration of Indian cricket after his retirement.

In domestic cricket, he bowled medium pace and hit 359 not out for Bombay against Maharashtra in 1933-34.

KEITH MILLER

Born: 28 NOVEMBER 1919, SUNSHINE, MELBOURNE, VICTORIA, AUSTRALIA
Died: 11 OCTOBER 2004, MORNINGTON, VICTORIA, AUSTRALIA.
Teams: VICTORIA (1937-38 TO 1946-47); NEW SOUTH WALES (1947-48 TO 1955-56); NOTTINGHAMSHIRE (1959)
First-class: 226 MATCHES; 14,183 RUNS, AVERAGE 48.90; 497 WICKETS, AVERAGE 22.30
Tests (1945-46 to 1956-57): 55 MATCHES; 2,958 RUNS, AVERAGE 36.97; 170 WICKETS, AVERAGE 22.97

Keith Miller was a glorious all-round cricketer. He was a tremendous hitter of the ball, powerful and brilliant in his stroke-play, and a magnificent fielder and a fast bowler whose partnership with Ray Lindwall became legendary. His lust for life was transmitted into his cricket, and he thrilled crowds with all that he did on the field.

He served in England during the war, played for the Australian Services, was outstanding in the Victory Tests and scored a memorable 185 in 165 minutes for the Dominions against England in 1945, an innings that was studded with gigantic sixes. He made his Test debut against New Zealand in 1945-46, and in his first Test against England a year later he took 7 for 60 in the first innings. In the fourth Test of the series he made 141 not out. In 1948, in England, he and Lindwall swept all before them initially, but injury prevented Miller from bowling for much of the time. His batting was still integral to Bradman's great side.

Tall and physically strong, Miller was a beautiful athlete, but he was a man of moods and he never found fun in destroying weak opposition. He relished a contest and, in the Caribbean in 1954-55, he hit three Test centuries and took 20 wickets

Keith Miller: thrilled an entire generation of cricket fans.

Lord's Test, where South Africa gained their famous victory.

He remained a dominant force, and when South Africa came to England in 1947, he hit 120 and 189 not out at The Oval and was on the field for the entire match bar eight minutes – 12 balls. There was a century and 99 against England in 1949-50 but, astonishingly, he was omitted when Australia went to South Africa a year later and so he retired.

MORNE MORKEL

Born: 6 OCTOBER 1984, VEREENIGING, TRANSVAAL, SOUTH AFRICA
Teams: EASTERNS (2003-04 TO 2006-07); TITANS (2004-05 TO 2010-11); KENT 2007; YORKSHIRE 2008
First-class: 64 MATCHES; 1,148 RUNS, AVERAGE 16.63; 238 WICKETS, AVERAGE 27.12
Tests (2006-07 to 2010-11): 31 MATCHES; 481 RUNS, AVERAGE 14.47; 113 WICKETS, AVERAGE 30.22

After a bright start, Morne Morkel's career stuttered a little through injury, but he re-established himself to partner Dale Steyn in providing South Africa with the most feared opening attack in Test cricket.

Bowling right-arm fast, he made his first-class debut in 2003-04 and his promise was spotted by Allan Donald, who coached him. A good performance against the Indian tourists in 2006-07 earned him his Test debut when Steyn pulled out of the second Test at Durban after India had won the first. An excellent performance with bat and ball helped South Africa to win. A stress fracture pegged him back but he performed well in South Africa's series win in Australia in 2008-09, and was South Africa's most successful bowler with 19 at 21.47 in the tied series with England in 2009-10. He could have had more than his 15 wickets in the three-match tied series with India in 2010-11.

ARTHUR MORRIS

Born: 19 JANUARY 1922, BONDI, NEW SOUTH WALES, AUSTRALIA
Teams: NEW SOUTH WALES (1940-41 TO 1954-55)
First-class: 162 MATCHES; 12,614 RUNS, AVERAGE 53.67; 12 WICKETS, AVERAGE 49.33
Tests (1946-47 to 1954-55): 46 MATCHES; 3,533 RUNS, AVERAGE 46.48; 2 WICKETS, AVERAGE 25.00

in the series. He never captained Australia, but he led New South Wales with a characteristic casual air that gave rise to many amusing stories. He retired in 1956, but he appeared for Nottinghamshire against Cambridge University in 1959 and scored 62 and 102 not out. He was also an author, journalist, commentator and general bon viveur who never lost his desire to live life to the full.

BRUCE MITCHELL

Born: 8 JANUARY 1909, FERRIERER DEEP GOLD MINE, JOHANNESBURG, SOUTH AFRICA
Died: 2 JULY 1995, JOHANNESBURG, SOUTH AFRICA
Teams: TRANSVAAL (1925-26 TO 1949-50)
First-class: 173 MATCHES; 11,395 RUNS, AVERAGE 45.39; 249 WICKETS, AVERAGE 25.63
Tests (1929 to 1948-49): 42 MATCHES; 3,471 RUNS, AVERAGE 48.88; 27 WICKETS, AVERAGE 51.11

Bruce Mitchell retains the record of having scored more runs in Test cricket than any other South African batsman. He was a stylish, right-handed opening batsman of infinite patience, a leg-break bowler and an outstanding slip fielder. He came to England in 1929, scored 88 and 61 not out on his Test debut at Edgbaston, and played in all five matches in the series. Against Chapman's team in 1930-31, he hit 123 at Cape Town and shared a record opening stand of 260 with Siedle. The following season, in New Zealand, he shared an opening partnership of 196 with Christy, which remains a record for the series. Mitchell made 113. When South Africa beat England in England for the first time in 1935, Mitchell hit two centuries, one of which was an unbeaten 164 in the

Morne Morkel (left): one of South Africa's most feared fast bowlers.

A century in each innings on the occasion of his first-class debut for New South Wales against Queensland heralded the career of Arthur Morris, one of the most graceful of left-handed opening batsman to have charmed the Test arena. In his first series against England in 1946-47, he scored three centuries in succession, including one in each innings at Adelaide.

In England in 1948, he had an outstanding tour and topped the Test matches' batting averages. His three centuries in the series included a match-winning 182 at Headingley where he and Bradman put on 301 in 217 minutes for the second wicket. He followed this with 196 (run out) at The Oval. He hit centuries in successive innings against South Africa in South Africa in 1949-50 and made 206 against Freddie Brown's side at Adelaide the following season.

He had a poor series in England in 1953, and his last series was against Hutton's side in 1954-55, when he hit 153 in the first Test. He captained Australia on two occasions.

MUTTIAH MURALITHARAN

SEE PAGE 219

DUDLEY NOURSE

Born: 12 NOVEMBER 1910, DURBAN, SOUTH AFRICA
Died: 14 AUGUST 1981, DURBAN, SOUTH AFRICA
Teams: NATAL (1931-32 TO 1952-53)
First-class: 175 MATCHES; 12,472 RUNS, AVERAGE 51.53; NO WICKETS FOR 124 RUNS
Tests (1935-1951): 34 MATCHES; 2,960 RUNS, AVERAGE 53.81; NO WICKETS FOR 9 RUNS

Son of "Dave" Nourse, a Test player of the Edwardian era, Dudley Nourse was a sound right-handed batsman who must rank among the most gifted produced by South Africa. In the years either side of the Second World War, he could lay claim to a place in a World XI. He came to England in 1935 and was in the side that won at Lord's – South Africa's first win in England – but it was against Australia the following winter that he truly revealed his international class. He hit 91 in the first Test and 231 in 289 minutes in the second at Johannesburg. Two centuries followed against England in 1938-39, and he was vice-captain to Melville on the 1947 tour when he hit centuries at Trent Bridge and Old Trafford. He succeeded Melville as South Africa's captain for the 1948-49 series against England, scoring 536 runs, average 76.57.

He captained the party to England in 1951 and, batting with a broken thumb and in considerable pain, he hit 208 in 550 minutes at Trent Bridge to equal the record of seven centuries against England. He was 40 years old.

MAKHAYA NTINI

Born: 6 JULY 1977, MDINGI, CAPE PROVINCE, SOUTH AFRICA
Teams: BORDER (1995-96 TO 2009); WARWICKSHIRE (2005); CHENNAI SUPER KINGS (2008 TO 2009)
First-class: 190 MATCHES; 1,284 RUNS, AVERAGE 9.44; 651 WICKETS; AVERAGE 28.98
Tests (1997-98 to 2009-10): 101 MATCHES; 699 RUNS, AVERAGE 9.84; 390 WICKETS; AVERAGE 28.82

A fast bowler with an action based on that of Malcolm Marshall, Ntini made his first-class debut in 1995-96, and two seasons later toured Australia before making his Test debut against Sri Lanka. The first black African to play for South Africa, his career was interrupted when, in 1999, he was initially convicted of rape, but was acquitted on appeal. He returned to the cricket scene to become a regular Test player, being Player of the Series against New Zealand in 2000-01. In 2003, he became the first South African to take ten wickets in a Test at Lord's (5-75 and 5-145, as South Africa won by an innings). In 2004-05 he took 13 West Indies wickets (6-95, 7-37) in Port-of-Spain, his best Test bowling figures. He took 45 Test wickets in the 2005-06 season, including 20 with some fiery bowling in a three-match home series against New Zealand, which South Africa won 2-0, with Ntini being voted Player of the Series. In 2006-07 he took 15 in a series against India and 19 against Pakistan, in the process passing 300 Test wickets. He had a dip in form after that and was dropped, but was back in the side for the wins in England in 2008 and Australia in 2008-09.

NORM O'NEILL

Born: 19 FEBRUARY 1937, CARLTON, NEW SOUTH WALES, SYDNEY, AUSTRALIA
Teams: NEW SOUTH WALES (1955-56 TO 1966-70)
First-class: 188 MATCHES; 13,859 RUNS, AVERAGE 50.95; 99 WICKETS, AVERAGE 41.01
Tests (1958-59 to 1964-65): 42 MATCHES; 2,779 RUNS, AVERAGE 45.55; 17 WICKETS, AVERAGE 39.23

Norman O'Neill was an unlucky cricketer in that he suffered from being dubbed "the new Bradman" when he first broke onto the scene. In spite of having only a moderate time in the Ashes series of 1958-59, he arrived in England two years later with an immense reputation. He had scored a century against Pakistan and two against India in 1959-60, and had made 181 against the West Indies in the famous tied Test of December 1960, but he found English conditions difficult in 1961 and did not score a century until the final Test, at The Oval. On the tour as a whole, though, he did well.

O'Neill was a highly entertaining right-handed batsman, rich in strokes, a useful leg-break bowler and a brilliant fielder. He was a warm and generous man, but he was a rather nervous starter and, although he hit six Test centuries, never quite accomplished all that had been expected of him. It should be said, though, that he was hampered by recurring knee trouble which eventually caused his retirement.

He appeared to become less enamoured of the game and, at the end of the series against the West Indies in the Caribbean in 1964-65, articles appeared under his name criticizing the action of Griffith, the West Indian fast bowler. His Test career was at an end, but he continued to score heavily in domestic cricket.

BILL O'REILLY

Born: 20 DECEMBER 1905, WHITE CLIFFS, NEW SOUTH WALES, AUSTRALIA
Died: 6 OCTOBER 1992, SUTHERLAND, SYDNEY, NEW SOUTH WALES
Teams: NEW SOUTH WALES (1927-28 TO 1945-46)
First-class: 135 MATCHES; 1,655 RUNS, AVERAGE 13.13; 774 WICKETS, AVERAGE 16.60
Tests (1931-32 to 1945-46): 27 MATCHES; 410 RUNS, AVERAGE 12.81; 144 WICKETS, AVERAGE 22.59

In the years immediately before the Second World War, "Tiger" O'Reilly was described as one of the greatest bowlers of all time. He bowled leg-breaks and googlies and had the ability to vary his pace and to make the ball rear awkwardly.

His Test debut came against South Africa in 1931-32. In the "bodyline" series a year later, he captured 27 wickets, including 10 for 129 at Melbourne where Australia gained their only victory of the rubber. In England in 1934, he was a huge success, heading the first-class averages and topping the Test averages with 28 wickets at 24.92 runs each. In his first Test in England, at Trent Bridge, he took 4 for 75 and 7 for 54, his best in Test cricket. He claimed 28 wickets in South Africa in 1935-36, and 25 against Allen's side the following year. In a full Test series, he never failed to take at least 20 wickets and, in four Tests in England in 1938, he captured 22 wickets at 27.72, a remarkable performance considering England's 903 for 7 at The Oval where he sent down 85 overs to take 3 for 178. At Headingley, he bowled Australia to victory with his third ten-wicket haul in Test cricket.

His last Test was in New Zealand shortly after the war, with match figures of 8 for 33. He became a well-respected cricket writer.

MUTTIAH MURALITHARAN
Spinning Genius

FIRST-CLASS CAREER
(1990 to 2010, 232 matches)
Batting: RUNS 2,192; AVERAGE 11.35; HIGHEST
SCORE 67; CENTURIES 0
Bowling: WICKETS 1,374; RUNS 26,997;
AVERAGE 19.64; BEST 9-51
Catches: 123

TESTS
(1992-93 to 2010, 132 MATCHES)
Batting: RUNS 1,259; AVERAGE 11.87; HIGHEST
SCORE 67; CENTURIES 0
Bowling: WICKETS 795; RUNS 18,023;
AVERAGE 22.67; BEST 9-51
Catches: 70

Muttiah Muralitharan is one of the greatest spinners the game has seen and the outstanding player in Sri Lanka's cricket history. He became the second player to reach 600 Test wickets. He is also the most controversial cricketer of modern times because of an elbow joint deformity that prevents him from fully straightening his right arm.

His main delivery is the off-break, but he varies this with a variety of top-spin and his "doosra", a leg-break.

He was too small to fulfil his ambition to be a fast bowler, so for hours he practised off-spin and developed the open-chested delivery he has today, with the flexible wrist action which imparts so much spin.

Aged 18 he went to Colombo to

Muttiah Muralitharan: wickets and controversy.

join the Tamil Union side and, after two first-class games, he was chosen to tour England in 1991. In 1992-93 he made his Test debut in Colombo against Australia, and took 4 for 56.

In 1998, his 16 for 220 was the best bowling in a Test match at The Oval as, for the first time, Sri Lanka beat England in England. There was a purple patch in the 2001-02 season. In August 2001, he took 23 wickets in a winning three-Test series against India. In November, against the West Indies, he took 21 in a two-match series, Sri Lanka winning both. In a three-match series against Zimbabwe beginning 27 December 2001, he tok 30 wickets at 9.80. At Kandy he took all nine wickets that fell on the first day. A dropped catch from the first ball next day prevented him taking all ten for 49 for a best-ever Test analysis.

He took 400 Test wickets in 72 matches, the youngest and quickest of those that achieved it. In 2004, he became the most prolific Test wicket-taker when overtaking Courtney Walsh's 519. With 795 Test wickets and 515 One-Day International wickets, he currently holds world records in both.

1972	**1992**	**1993**	**1995**	**1997**
Born Muttiah Muralitharan on 17 April in Kandy, Sri Lanka	Made Test debut on 28 August v Australia at Colombo taking 1 for 32 and two for 109 in a total of 51 overs	Made one-day international debut, v India on 12 August and took 1 for 38	Was no-balled by umpire Darrell Hair in the Test match starting 26 December v Australia in Melbourne	Takes his 100th Test wicket in the Test against New Zealand at Hamilton, 14-17 March. Takes six wickets in the match as Sri Lanka lose by 120 runs

1998	**1999**	**2004**	**2005**	**2007**
Took 16 for 220 in 113.5 overs as Sri Lanka won a Test in England for the first time. It was the most wickets and the most overs for a Test at The Oval, 27-28 August	One of Wisden's five Cricketers of the Year	Became leading wicket-taker in Tests when Mluckeki Nkala of Zimbabwe became his 520th victim at Harare in first Test, 6-8 May	Became the second player to reach 600 Test wickets and first with 50 Test five-fors, in 101st Test match	Retook Test bowling world record with wicket 709, bowling Paul Collingwood, Sri Lanka v England, Kandy, 2 December.

MONTY PANESAR

Born: 25 APRIL 1982, LUTON, BEDFORDSHIRE
Teams: NORTHAMPTONSHIRE (2001-09); SUSSEX 2010
First-class: 133 MATCHES; 1,034 RUNS, AVERAGE 8.91; 425 WICKETS, AVERAGE 32.49
Tests (2005-06 to 2009): 39 MATCHES; 187 RUNS, AVERAGE 5.50; WICKETS 126; AVERAGE 34.37

Mudhouden Singh Panesar, to give him his full name, established himself as one of England's must popular Test cricketers with his outstanding bowling against Pakistan in 2006. His patka, his beard, his exuberance at getting wickets and even his clumsiness in the field singled him out as a crowd-pleaser. A slow left-arm spin bowler, he played for England Under-19s before making his first-class debut against Leicestershire in 2001, when he took four wickets in each innings. He made his Test debut on the tour of India in 2005-06 at Nagpur, claiming Tendulkar as his first Test wicket. This was followed by his 17 wickets at 30.29 against Pakistan in England, which proved vital. He was outstanding again in England against the West Indies in 2007, when his 23 wickets at 18.69 helped win the series 3-0 and earned him the joint

Player of the Series award. However he was less successful against India and in Sri Lanka, and questions were asked about his lack of variety and an effective arm ball. He was dropped from the third Test in the West Indies in 2008-09 and needed to reaffirm his status.

EDDIE PAYNTER

Born: 5 NOVEMBER 1901, OSWALDTWISTLE, LANCASHIRE
Died: 5 FEBRUARY 1979, KEIGHLEY, YORKSHIRE
Teams: LANCASHIRE (1926-45)
First-class: 352 MATCHES; 20,075 RUNS, AVERAGE 42.46; 30 WICKETS, AVERAGE 45.70
Tests (1931-39): 20 MATCHES; 1,540 RUNS, AVERAGE 59.23

Eddie Paynter scored 322 for Lancashire in 1937 and was a most loyal servant to the Red Rose county. An attacking left-handed batsman and a brilliant fielder, he made his Test debut against New Zealand in 1931, and went to Australia with Jardine's team, 1932-33. He did not play until the third Test when he scored 77 and, in the next Test, became the stuff of legend when he rose from his sickbed to hit 83 at No.

8 with England in trouble. He scored a century in each innings of the first Test in South Africa in 1938-39, and made his highest Test score, 243, in the third match. He had not gained a regular place in the Lancashire side until 1931, and his career was effectively ended by the outbreak of the Second World War.

BOBBY PEEL

Born: 12 FEBRUARY 1857, CHURWELL, LEEDS, YORKSHIRE
Died: 12 AUGUST 1941, MORLEY, LEEDS, YORKSHIRE
Teams: YORKSHIRE (1882-98)
First-class: 436 MATCHES; 12,191 RUNS, AVERAGE 19.44; 1,775 WICKETS, AVERAGE 16.20
Tests (1884-85 to 1896): 20 MATCHES; 427 RUNS, AVERAGE 14.72; 101 WICKETS, AVERAGE 16.98

In the great Yorkshire tradition of slow left-arm bowlers, Bobby Peel maintained the principles of line and, especially, length. He was a most capable left-hand batsman who scored 210 not out against Warwickshire in 1896, the year he did the "double". He took 100 wickets in a season on seven other occasions. He was regarded as the best bowler of his type in England and made three trips to Australia. In his first Test in 1884-85, he took eight wickets at Sydney and finished the series with 21 to his credit. He was triumphant at Sydney again three years later when he had match figures of 10 for 58, and he and Lohmann bowled Australia out for 42 in the first innings.

Peel took 24 wickets in three Tests against Australia in 1888, including 7 for 31 and 4 for 37 in the final match at Old Trafford. Rarely, if ever, did he fail, and in his last Test, against Australia at The Oval in 1896, he took 2 for 30 and 6 for 23 to bowl England to victory.

The following year he took the field for Yorkshire in an inebriated state and, according to some reports, urinated against the sightscreen. As a result, Lord Hawke dismissed him immediately from the Yorkshire XI.

KEVIN PIETERSEN

SEE PAGE 221

GRAEME POLLOCK

Born: 27 FEBRUARY 1944, DURBAN, SOUTH AFRICA
Teams: EASTERN PROVINCE (1960-61 TO 1977-98); TRANSVAAL (1978-79 TO 1986-87)
First-class: 262 MATCHES; 20,940 RUNS, AVERAGE 54.67; 43 WICKETS, AVERAGE 47.65
Tests (1963-64 to 1969-70): 23 MATCHES; 2,256 RUNS, AVERAGE 60.97; 4 WICKETS, AVERAGE 51.00

Only Don Bradman ended a Test career with an average higher than Graeme Pollock's. One of the greatest of all batsmen, he was at his peak at a time when South Africa was banned from international cricket.

A schoolboy prodigy, when not quite 17 he became the youngest player to score a century in the Currie Cup. Less than two years later, he became the youngest South African to score a double-century and, when just past 20, he was made captain of Eastern Province. Although right-handed in all other things, Pollock batted left-handed.

He made his Test debut in Australia in 1963-64. An early century on that tour led Don Bradman to congratulate the 19-year-old on one of the best innings he'd seen. In the third Test he scored 175 in 283 minutes, becoming the third player to score two Test centuries before he was 20. Later, in a Test at Trent Bridge, he scored 125 from 145 balls, becoming the youngest ever to score 1,000 runs in Tests. In 1966-67 in South Africa, he averaged 76.51 against Australia, with South Africa winning the series 3-1, although before then they'd not beaten Australia in a match at home for 64 years. His last series was also against Australia, with South Africa winning 4-0 by huge margins, and Pollock topping the averages with 73.85, and playing South Africa's highest Test innings of 274. After that South Africa were banned because of the apartheid policy.

Monty Panesar's enthusiasm and exuberance appealed to the crowds.

KEVIN PIETERSEN
First-Class Career

Kevin Pietersen is a flamboyant cricketer. His outstanding batting skill, his switch-hitting style, the coloured hair at the beginning of his career, his inability to keep out of the news, have all contributed to his becoming one of the most exciting cricketers of his day.

Born in South Africa, he made his first-class debut for Natal aged 17. A right-hand batsman and right-arm off-break bowler, he quickly decided that his prospects of Test cricket would be greater in England than in South Africa and, having an English-born mother, chose to serve a four-year residential period to qualify for England. The former South African captain Clive Rice signed him for Nottinghamshire in 2000 and he made his debut in 2001. In each of his four seasons with Nottinghamshire he averaged over 50 with the bat.

He first played for England in the one-day internationals in Zimbabwe and South Africa in 2004-05. In

Kevin Pietersen: a destructive force in any form of the game.

South Africa, facing initially hostile crowds, he made three centuries in five innings. He made his Test debut against Australia in 2005. With 473 runs, average 52.55, he was top scorer of the series and his second innings of 158 at The Oval in the final Test secured the draw that won the Ashes.

When Pietersen made 226 against West Indies at Headingley in 2007, he achieved more runs in his first 25 Tests (2,553) than any batsman except Don Bradman. In 2008 he made 152 at Lord's in his first Test against the country of his birth, South Africa. On 7 August, after Vaughan had resigned

the England captaincy in a losing series, Pietersen became captain, and won the final Test. Naturally, he scored 100. However after a tour of India in 2008-09 he resigned the captaincy, finding he could not work with England coach Peter Moores, who also resigned. His form has dipped since then.

1980	**2003-04**	**2005**	**2007**	**2008**	**2009**
Born Kevin Peter Pietersen on 27 June 1980 at Pietermaritzburg, Natal, South Africa	Toured India with Engand A, making 104, 115, 32 and 94 in his four first-class innings, while other players floundered	After qualifying for England in September 2004, made his Test debut against Australia at Lord's on 21 July 2005, scoring 57 and 64 not out. Awarded MBE in New Year's honours list	Becomes only third England player in history to reach No.1 spot in the one-day international rankings	Captained England for the first time in fourth Test against South Africa on 7 August. He scored a century in a six-wicket win	Resigned the England captaincy after disagreements with coach Peter Moores became public

PETER POLLOCK

Born: 30 JUNE 1941, PIETERMARITZBURG, NATAL, SOUTH AFRICA
Teams: EASTERN PROVINCE (1958-59 TO 1971-72)
First-class: 127 MATCHES; 3,028 RUNS, AVERAGE 22.59; 485 WICKETS, AVERAGE 21.89
Tests (1961-62 to 1969-70): 28 MATCHES; 607 RUNS, AVERAGE 21.67; 116 WICKETS, AVERAGE 24.18

Tall, fair-haired and a bowler of genuine pace, Peter Pollock is Graeme Pollock's older brother. On his Test debut, aged 20, he took 3 for 61 and 6 for 38, his best Test figures, against New Zealand, and he finished the series with 17 wickets from three matches.

When South Africa drew the rubber in Australia in 1963-64, he confirmed his standing as a leading strike bowler with 25 wickets in the series. In 1965, in the three-match series in England, he claimed 20 wickets, and his 10 for 87 in 47.5 overs in the match at Trent Bridge brought South Africa victory and clinched the rubber.

In 1969-70, Australia were trounced in all four Tests in South Africa. The South African opening attack of Procter and Peter Pollock was lethal. Pollock had 15 wickets in the series, but he pulled a hamstring and could bowl only seven balls in the last innings of what was to be his final Test, for South Africa's exile from international cricket followed. When the exile ended in 1992, Pollock became chairman of selectors.

SHAUN POLLOCK

Born: 16 JULY 1973, PORT ELIZABETH, SOUTH AFRICA
Teams: NATAL (1991-92 TO 2006-07); WARWICKSHIRE (1996-2002), MUMBAI INDIANS (2008), DURHAM (2008)
First-class: 186 MATCHES; 7,023 RUNS, AVERAGE 33.12; 667 WICKETS, AVERAGE 23.25
Tests (1995-96 to 2007-08): 108 MATCHES; 3,781 RUNS, AVERAGE 32.31; 421 WICKETS, AVERAGE 23.11

The son of Peter Pollock and nephew of Graeme, Shaun is a genuinely fast right-arm bowler who swings the

Shaun Pollock: the son of a Test fast bowler and the nephew of South Africa's greatest batsman, he upheld the family tradition and became South Africa's captain in 1998.

ball both ways. He possesses a good bouncer and can produce a well-disguised slower ball. In addition he is no mean batsman – going in at No. 9 against the West Indies at Bridgetown in March 2001 he hit 106 not out.

His Test debut came in 1995-96 against England and he was even then the pick of his side's bowlers in a rain-affected game, then ended that series topping his country's bowling averages. He formed a most dangerous new-ball partnership with Allan Donald.

He appeared in county cricket only in 1996, when he effectively stood in for Donald in the Warwickshire

side. Pollock created a sensation in his first competitive game by capturing four wickets in four balls in the Benson & Hedges match v Leicestershire.

His first taste as South African captain came in the 1998 Commonwealth games in Malaysia; South Africa won the Gold Medal, but several countries failed to send their top players. In the famous tied semi-final, South Africa v Australia, in the World Cup in 1999, he returned the best bowling figures of 5 for 36, but unfortunately Australia went through to the final. He has been

consistently ranked in the top three in the Test bowling tables. He retired from Test cricket in February 2008.

BILL PONSFORD

Born: 19 OCTOBER 1900, NORTH FITZROY, MELBOURNE, VICTORIA, AUSTRALIA
Died: 6 APRIL 1991, KYNETON, VICTORIA, AUSTRALIA
Teams: VICTORIA (1920-21 TO 1933-34)
First-class: 162 MATCHES; 13,819 RUNS, AVERAGE 65.18; NO WICKETS FOR 41 RUNS
Tests (1924-25 to 1934): 29 MATCHES; 2,122 RUNS, AVERAGE 48.22

Before the arrival of Don Bradman, Bill Ponsford threatened to become the greatest run-accumulator the game had known. He made 429 against Tasmania at Melbourne in 1922-23, and five years later, on the same ground, he hit 437 against Queensland. He was a right-handed opening batsman whose defence looked impenetrable and who had a wide range of shots. He hit 110 on his Test debut, against England in 1924-25, and when he hit 128 at Melbourne, he became the first batsman to score centuries in his first two Tests. He became ill in England in 1926 and appeared only in the last two Tests. In Australia in 1928-29, he had his hand broken by a ball from Larwood in the second Test and did not play again in the series.

By 1930, his opening partnership with Woodfull was established, and the pair set up Australia's victory at The Oval with a stand of 159. Ponsford scored 110, and he followed this with two centuries against the West Indies a few months later. Two unsuccessful home series cast doubts on his ability at the top level but, at Headingley, 1934, he made 181, and in the next match, at The Oval, he and Bradman scored 451 in 316 minutes for a world-record partnership for the second wicket – Ponsford hit 266. His Test career ended following that Test.

RICKY PONTING

SEE PAGE 223

RICKY PONTING
Aggressive punter

FIRST-CLASS CAREER
(1992-93 to 2010-11, 255 matches)
Batting: RUNS 21,332; AVERAGE 55.98;
HIGHEST SCORE 257; CENTURIES 73
Bowling: WICKETS 14; RUNS 768;
AVERAGE 54.85; BEST 2-10
Catches: 270

TESTS
(1995-96 to 2010-11, 152 MATCHES)
Batting: RUNS 12,363; AVERAGE 53.51;
HIGHEST SCORE 257; CENTURIES 39
Bowling: WICKETS 5; RUNS 242;
AVERAGE 48.40; BEST 1-0
Catches: 178

Born in Tasmania (he is the first Tasmanian to captain Australia) he was outstanding as a youngster at Brooks Senior High School. Later Rod Marsh, coach at the Australian Academy, said he was the best teenage batsman he'd ever seen. He made his debut for Tasmania in 1992-93, scoring 56. Three years later, he made his debut for Australia at Perth against Sri Lanka and made 96.

Ponting is a very aggressive cricketer at home against all types of bowling, making his strokes with a full swing of the bat all round the wicket. He bowls a little right-arm medium or off-breaks and is a magnificent fielder.

There was a time in the late 1990s when his exuberant character threatened to hinder his career. He

Ricky Ponting: takes a bow for another Test century. To date he has scored 39 of them.

likes gambling (hence his nickname "Punter") and confessed to an alcohol problem after incidents in 1998 and 1999. He puts his reform down to meeting the girl who became his wife, Rianna. Beforehand, his Test batting average was 37 - five years later it was in the high 50s.

Despite his new-found maturity, it was a major surprise when the ACB chose the 27-year-old Ponting to replace Steve Waugh as captain of Australia's one-day side in 2002.

Ponting immediately had success as skipper by leading Australia to World Cup victory in 2003, scoring 140 not out from 121 balls in the final, when he was Man of the Match. The following winter, he excelled in a drawn Test series at home to India, averaging 100.85, with 242 in the second Test and 257, his highest Test score, in the third.

In 2004, he succeeded Steve Waugh as captain of the Test side, but suffered defeat in the 2005 Ashes series in England. He led Australia to a 2-0 win against South Africa and regained the Ashes brilliantly in 2006-07, but could not replicate that form in the 2009 or 2010-11 editions, losing both.

1974	**1992-93**	**1995**	**1997**	**2001**
Born Ricky Thomas Ponting, on 19 December in Launceston, Tasmania	Made first-class debut for Tasmania and scores 56	Made Test debut v Sri Lanka at Perth on 8 December and was unluckily dismissed on 96	Made 127 in his first Ashes Test as Australia won by an innings, 24-28 July, Headingley, Leeds	Passed 3,000 Test runs in his 49th Test, v New Zealand at Hobart, 22-26 November. Makes an unbeaten 157

2003	**2004**	**2005**	**2006**
Passes 5,000 runs in Test cricket in his 71st Test, v Zimbabwe at the SCG	Won Allan Border Medal as leading cricketer of the year, having won the World Cup and averaging over 100 in a series against India	Scored 207 v Pakistan on 2-5 January in Sydney to become the third Australian (after Don Bradman and Greg Chappell) to score four double centuries in Tests	Celebrated his 100th Test by scoring 120 and 143 not out in third Test v South Africa at Sydney, the first to score two centuries in his 100th Test

MIKE PROCTER

Born: 15 SEPTEMBER 1946, DURBAN, SOUTH AFRICA
Teams: GLOUCESTERSHIRE (1965-81); NATAL (1965-66 TO 1988-89); WESTERN PROVINCE (1969-70); RHODESIA (1970-71 TO 1975-76); ORANGE FREE STATE (1987-88)
First-class: 401 MATCHES; 21,936 RUNS, AVERAGE 36.01; 1,417 WICKETS, AVERAGE 19.53
Tests (1966-67 to 1969-70): 7 MATCHES; 226 RUNS, AVERAGE 25.11; 41 WICKETS, AVERAGE 15.02

One of the most dynamic performers the game of cricket has known, Mike Procter played only seven Test matches because his career only began to flower just as South Africa were excluded from international cricket.

Procter made his Test debut against Australia in South Africa during 1966-67, and took a total of 15 wickets in three matches. Three years later, against the very same opposition, he took 26 wickets in four Tests, finishing with his best, 6 for 73, at Port Elizabeth. In seven Test matches, he was never on a losing side, and South Africa won six of them.

His energies then had to be concentrated on domestic cricket. In 1970-71, he hit six hundreds in consecutive innings for Rhodesia, and he will always be remembered for his achievements with Gloucestershire and the influence he had on that county. He was a ferocious batsman, a fielder of brilliance and a fast bowler who occasionally turned to off-breaks. Gloucestershire won trophies when he was in the side, for he always seemed to be scoring runs, taking wickets or making a catch. He captained the county from 1977 to 1981. He hit 1,000 runs in a season nine times and took 100 wickets in a season twice.

He was cricket manager at Northamptonshire in 1990-91, and he held a similar position with the South African national side from 1992 to 1994. More recently, he has become a member of the International Cricket Council's elite panel of match referees.

Arjuna Ranatunga: World Cup-winning skipper.

SONNY RAMADHIN

Born: 1 MAY 1929, ESPERANCE VILLAGE, TRINIDAD
Teams: TRINIDAD (1949-50 TO 1952-53); LANCASHIRE (1964-65)
First-class: 184 MATCHES; 1,092 RUNS, AVERAGE 8.66; 758 WICKETS, AVERAGE 20.24
Tests (1950 to 1960-61): 43 MATCHES; 361 RUNS, AVERAGE 8.20; 158 WICKETS, AVERAGE 28.98

Sonny Ramadhin came to England in 1950 with a handful of first-class matches behind him and nothing known of him save that he was a spin bowler. Within months he had become the talk of the cricket world. Having been beaten in cold weather at Old Trafford, the West Indies won the remaining three Tests of the series and with Ramadhin took 26 wickets. He headed the first-class averages for the tour with 135 wickets, average 14.88. It was at Lord's that he and his spin partner Valentine bowled the West Indies to their first win in England. Ramadhin took 5 for 66 and 6 for 86. He had a perfect control of length, flighted the ball well, and bowled both off-breaks and leg-breaks – he truly was a "mystery" bowler. He was less successful in Australia, but he devastated the New Zealand batsmen.

He continued to trouble England in the Caribbean with 23 wickets in 1953-54, and when he arrived in England in 1957 and took a Test-best 7 for 49 in the first encounter at Edgbaston it seemed that England would again fall under his spell, but he was destroyed by May and Cowdrey in the second innings. He sent down 98 overs and took 2 for 179; he was never quite the same again.

He played Lancashire League cricket, but his venture into county cricket came late in his career and was not a success. He went on to become a publican.

ARJUNA RANATUNGA

Born: 1 DECEMBER 1963, COLOMBO, CEYLON
Teams: SINHALESE SC (1988-89 TO 1996-97)
First-class: 146 MATCHES; 7,941 RUNS, AVERAGE 42.33; 90 WICKETS, AVERAGE 32.65
Tests (1981-82 to 1996-97): 61 MATCHES; 3,471 RUNS, AVERAGE 35.41; 14 WICKETS, AVERAGE 67.28

A chunky, aggressive, left-handed batsman and a right-arm medium-pace bowler, Arjuna Ranatunga played in Sri Lanka's inaugural Test against England in February 1982. He was 18 years 78 days old and still attending Anada College. He hit 54, Sri Lanka's first 50 in Test cricket. A year later, he made 90 against Australia and, at Lord's in August 1984, hit a splendidly entertaining 84. He revealed himself as a joyous and enthusiastic cricketer, and his love of the game was infectious.

He hit centuries against India and Pakistan, and remained a consistent scorer. He first captained Sri Lanka in Australia in 1989-90 – it was not an easy time, but he battled on happily. Greatness awaited him, though. Sri Lanka became most adept at the one-day game and, in 1996, Ranatunga led them to victory in the World Cup. His own contribution was immense – he averaged 120.50 from the six matches and topped the batting averages for the competition.

K.S. RANJITSINHJI

Born: 10 SEPTEMBER 1872, SARODAR, KATHIAWAR, INDIA
Died: 2 APRIL 1933, JAMNAGAR, INDIA
Teams: CAMBRIDGE UNIVERSITY (1893-94); SUSSEX (1895-1920); LONDON COUNTY (1901-04)
First-class: 307 MATCHES; 24,692 RUNS, AVERAGE 56.37; 133 WICKETS, AVERAGE 34.59
Tests (1896-1902): 15 MATCHES; 989 RUNS, AVERAGE 44.95; 1 WICKET, AVERAGE 39.00

A batsman of feline grace and Eastern mystery, "Ranji" was a cricket legend. With exceptionally keen eyesight and supple and powerful wrists, he played shots that others could only imagine, and his leg-glance was breathtaking in audacity, beauty and execution. He had moderate success at Cambridge, but from 1899 to 1904 he was supreme among batsmen in England. He hit 3,159 runs in 1899, and followed this with 3,065 runs, average 87.57 in 1900. In three other seasons he reached 2,000 runs and in six more 1,000. He also reached 1,000 runs on a tour of Australia in 1897-98.

He was the first Indian to play Test cricket and the second batsman, after Grace, to hit a century on his Test debut. He was also the first batsman to score a hundred before lunch in a Test. He made 62 and 154 not out at Old Trafford in 1896, and he went from 41 to 154 in 130 minutes before lunch on the third day. In 1897-98, he hit 175 in his first Test in Australia.

Ranjitsinhji captained Sussex from 1899 to 1903 and then returned to India. He made infrequent appearances thereafter. As the Maharaja Jam Sahib of Nawanagar, he became involved in administration of his state and was a delegate to the League of Nations.

JOHN REID

Born: 3 JUNE 1928, AUCKLAND, NEW ZEALAND
Teams: WELLINGTON (1947-48 TO 1964-65); OTAGO (1956-57 TO 1957-58)
First-class: 246 MATCHES; 16,128 RUNS, AVERAGE 41.35; 466 WICKETS, AVERAGE 22.60
Tests (1949-1965): 58 MATCHES; 3,428 RUNS, AVERAGE 33.28; 85 WICKETS, AVERAGE 33.35

John Reid was a complete all-round cricketer, a hard-hitting middle-order batsman, a brisk bowler of off-cutters and a wicket-keeper of no mean ability. He made 50 and 25 on his Test debut at Old Trafford in 1949, and in his next match, at The Oval, he kept wicket and scored 93. He did not really blossom until the 1953-54 series in South Africa when, at Cape Town, he hit his maiden Test century.

New Zealand cricket had reached a low ebb by the mid-1950s and, following a crushing defeat by the West Indies at Dunedin in 1955-56, Reid was appointed captain. In the last match of the series, he top-scored with 84 and New Zealand won a famous victory. His side suffered badly in England in 1958, but in South Africa in 1961-62, against all expectations, New Zealand drew the series, each side winning two Tests. It was the first time New Zealand had won two Tests in a rubber and Reid topped the batting and bowling averages, hitting 142 in Johannesburg.

He led New Zealand in 34 consecutive Tests, but retired after the disappointing 1965 tour of England, feeling his side had made no real advance. In all, he hit six Test centuries.

WILFRED RHODES

Born: 29 OCTOBER 1877, KIRKHEATON, YORKSHIRE
Died: 8 JULY 1973, BRANKSOME PARK, DORSET
Teams: YORKSHIRE (1898-1930); PATIALA (1926-27); EUROPEANS (1921-22 TO 1922-23)
First-class: 1,110 MATCHES; 39,969 RUNS, AVERAGE 30.81; 4,204 WICKETS, AVERAGE 16.72
Tests (1899 to 1929-30): 58 MATCHES; 2,325 RUNS, AVERAGE 30.19; 127 WICKETS, AVERAGE 26.96

When Lord Hawke dismissed Robert Peel from the Yorkshire team in 1897 the county were left in need of a slow left-arm bowler. The vacancy was filled by Wilfred Rhodes who took 6 for 63 in the first match of the 1898 season and, by the end of the season, he had claimed 154 wickets. So began one of the most illustrious and record-breaking careers in cricket. He was to take 100 or more wickets 23 times, and in three of those seasons he exceeded 200 wickets. He achieved the "double" in 16 seasons, a record that is never likely to be beaten and, in all, he reached 1,000 runs 20 times. His total of 4,024 wickets is a world record.

He made his Test debut at Trent Bridge in 1899. It was the first Test to be played at the ground, and it also marked the end of W.G. Grace's Test career. Rhodes had match figures of seven Australian wickets for 118. He also played in the first Test staged at Edgbaston in 1902, when Australia were bowled out for 36 – Rhodes took 7 for 17. Better was to come. On his first tour of Australia in 1903-04, he took 7 for 56 and 8 for 68 to bowl England to victory in the Melbourne Test. When he went to Australia eight years later, he was Hobbs's opening partner, and the pair established an Ashes record at Melbourne in the fourth Test when they put on 323, Rhodes making 179. The record stood for 77 years.

BARRY RICHARDS

Born: 21 JULY 1945, MORNINGSIDE, DURBAN, SOUTH AFRICA
Teams: NATAL (1964-65 TO 1982-83); GLOUCESTERSHIRE (1965); HAMPSHIRE (1968-78); SOUTH AUSTRALIA (1970-71); TRANSVAAL (1970-71)
First-class: 339 MATCHES; 28,358 RUNS, AVERAGE 54.74; 77 WICKETS, AVERAGE 37.48
Tests (1969-70): 4 MATCHES; 508 RUNS, AVERAGE 75.57; 1 WICKET, AVERAGE 26.00

In the opinion of many, Barry Richards was unquestionably the finest batsman of his generation. An aggressive, right-handed opening batsman with total command of every shot, he adorned county cricket for a decade, and his first-wicket partnership with Gordon Greenidge was largely instrumental in bringing Hampshire the County Championship and two Sunday League titles.

Barry Richards: the finest of his generation.

If he had a fault, it was that it all seemed to come so easily to him that at times he appeared lackadaisical. A thrilling batsman, he hit 325 on the opening day of the match between South Australia and Western Australia at Perth in 1970-71. He finally made 356. He scored 1,000 runs in a season five times in South Africa and nine times in England. He was also a useful off-break bowler.

His Test debut in 1969-70 saw him score two centuries in seven innings against Australia and average 75.57 for the series. That was to be both the beginning and the end of his Test career, for these were South Africa's last Tests before their exclusion.

VIV RICHARDS

SEE PAGE 226

VIV RICHARDS
Arrogant Destroyer

FIRST-CLASS CAREER
(1971-72 to 1992-93, 507 matches)
Batting: RUNS 36,212; AVERAGE 49.33;
HIGHEST SCORE 322; CENTURIES 114
Bowling: WICKETS 223; RUNS 10,070;
AVERAGE 45.15; BEST 5-88
Catches: 464

TESTS
(1974-75 to 1991, 121 MATCHES)
Batting: RUNS 8,540; AVERAGE 50.23;
HIGHEST SCORE 291; CENTURIES 24
Bowling: WICKETS 32; RUNS 1,964;
AVERAGE 61.37; BEST 2-17
Catches: 122

Viv Richards: a swashbuckling batsman who could dominate any attack in the world.

Viv Richards was the best batsman of his generation, and one of Wisden's five cricketers of the 20th century. An aggressive batsman who did not wear a helmet, he could completely dominate bowlers and his swashbuckling attitude around the crease exuded arrogant confidence. He was also a useful right-hand bowler of medium pace or spin, a brilliant fielder and a successful captain.

He made his first-class debut for Leeward Islands in 1971-72, was chosen for combined Islands and in 1973 was sent to Alf Gover's cricket school in England. In 1974 he joined Somerset and over the next dozen years helped establish the county as a force in English cricket. He enjoyed an outstanding season in 1977, when he made 2,161 runs, average 65.48.

He also hit a record 26 sixes in the Sunday League.

Richards was a surprise choice for the West Indies tour of India and Pakistan in 1974-75, beginning his dominance of the world's bowlers in his second Test, when he made 192 not out, with six sixes and 20 fours.

His Test innings in 1976 were: 44, 2, 30, 101, 50 and 98 (in Australia), 142, 130, 20, 177, 23 and 64 (against India in the Caribbean) and 232, 63, 4, 135, 66, 38 and 291 (in England). This made a record total for a calendar year of 1,710 runs, average 90.

Brilliant fielding by Richards in the first World Cup final in 1975 (three run-outs) helped the West Indies win, and his 188 not out in the 1979 final helped them keep the

trophy. In 1980-81, Richards' home town of St Johns provided the West Indies with their first New Test venue for over 50 years and Viv inevitably celebrated with a century, his 14th in Tests.

Against England at Old Trafford in 1984, going in at 11 for 2, he scored 189 not out, setting a new record for one-day internationals.

Richards took over from Clive Lloyd as captain of the West Indies in 1984-85 when his century in the third Test against New Zealand secured the series. In an awesome display of hard hitting against England in Antigua in 1985-86, he scored a second-innings 110 not out, reaching 103 in 56 balls, beating the previous fastest century scored in Test cricket by 11 balls. In 1987, he scored a World Cup record score of 181 against Sri Lanka.

For Somerset, Richards made his highest score of 322 against Warwickshire in 1985. He retired from Test cricket in 1991, having led the West Indies 450 times. He was the first West Indian to score 100 centuries altogether, and retired from the game in 1993. He excelled at other sports and played in the football World Cup qualifiers in 1974.

1952
Born Isaac Vivian Alexander Richards on 7 March at St John's, Antigua, West Indies

1971-72
Made his first-class debut for the Leeward Islands

1974-75
Made Test debut in first Test v India at Bangalore on 22 November, scoring 4 and 3. He went on to score an unbeaten 192 in the second Test

1974
Played for Somerset in the County Championship in England and starts an association with the county that lasts for 15 years

1976
Made a record aggregate for a calendar year of 1,710 runs in Tests

1981
In the first-ever Test match in his home town of St John's, he scored 114, three days after his marriage, March 27-April 1

1986
Scored the fastest century in Test cricket, reaching 103 in 56 balls, v England in St John's, Antigua, April 11-16

1987
Hits World Cup record score of 181, v Sri Lanka at Karachi on 13 October

1998
He was knighted for services to cricket

RICHIE RICHARDSON

Born: 2 JANUARY 1962, FIVE ISLANDS VILLAGE, ANTIGUA
Teams: LEEWARD ISLANDS (1981-82 TO 1995-96); YORKSHIRE (1994); WINDWARD ISLANDS (1997-98); NORTHERN TRANSVAAL (1996-97)
First-class: 234 MATCHES; 14,618 RUNS, AVERAGE 42.40; 13 WICKETS, AVERAGE 33.92
Tests (1983-84 to 1995-96): 86 MATCHES; 5,949 RUNS, AVERAGE 44.39; NO WICKETS FOR 18 RUNS

A shy, modest and courteous man, Richie Richardson succeeded Viv Richards as captain of Leeward Islands and of the West Indies. A right-handed batsman of immense talent and great eagerness to hit the ball, he took some time to prove himself at Test level. He hit two centuries against Australia in 1983-84, but he failed to do himself justice in England the following summer, although his ability was apparent. When he made his third trip to England in 1991, he showed that he had mastered the slower wickets and topped the Test batting averages. He now began to thrive, and hit his eighth Test hundred against Australia in 1992-93, and led the West Indies to victory in the series. In all, he scored 16 Test centuries, but one of his greatest innings was a captain's 69 on a pitch described as "diabolical" at Edgbaston in 1995. He batted for over four hours to ensure an innings victory when England were dismissed for 89.

He was hugely successful in one-day internationals, but the pressures began to tell on him. He left Yorkshire because he was exhausted and ordered to rest for six months. He was reinstated as the West Indies' captain far too quickly and failure in the World Cup in 1996 led to him relinquishing the captaincy and leaving Test cricket. He played for Northern Transvaal in 1996-97, but averaged only 23.09, then the following season joined Windward Islands, whose side had fallen on hard times. Again he failed to reproduce his old form and Windwards failed to win a single game.

ANDY ROBERTS

Born: 29 JANUARY 1951, URLINGS VILLAGE, ANTIGUA
Teams: LEEWARD ISLANDS (1969-70 TO 1983-84); HAMPSHIRE (1973-78); NEW SOUTH WALES (1976-77); LEICESTERSHIRE (1981-84)
First-class: 228 MATCHES; 3,516 RUNS, AVERAGE 15.69; 889 WICKETS, AVERAGE 21.01
Tests (1973-74 to 1983-84): 47 MATCHES; 762 RUNS, AVERAGE 14.94; 202 WICKETS, AVERAGE 25.61

Andy Roberts was the third West Indian to claim 200 Test wickets and, at his peak, he was considered to be one of the two or three best fast bowlers in the world. He reached 100 Test wickets more quickly than any bowler had done before, although his record was later beaten by Botham. He was a great favourite with Hampshire, and he played a major part in their Sunday League triumphs. In 1974, he took 119 wickets, average 13.62, in 21 matches for the county in first-class cricket and was the most feared bowler in the land. His Test debut had come against England the previous winter, but it was in India in 1974-75, that he really established himself. He captured 32 wickets in the series, and at Madras he had match figures of 12 for 121. His best bowling came in Perth a year later when he took 7 for 54 in the second innings to give the West Indies victory.

He joined Packer's World Series along with the other West Indian cricketers, and he was never quite the same afterwards. He assisted Leicestershire on a part-time basis, appearing in 36 matches, and later coached the West Indian team.

JACK RUSSELL

Born: 15 AUGUST 1963, STROUD, GLOUCESTERSHIRE
Teams: GLOUCESTERSHIRE (1981 TO 2004)
First-class: 465 MATCHES; 16,861 RUNS, AVERAGE 30.93; 1,192 CATCHES, 128 STUMPINGS
Tests (1988 TO 1997-98): 54 MATCHES; 1,897 RUNS, AVERAGE 27.10; 153 CATCHES, 12 STUMPINGS

At the age of 17, Jack Russell became the youngest keeper to represent Gloucestershire. Within a few seasons he was considered the best wicket-keeper in England, but his selection for Tests was blocked simply because of the preference for batsmen-wicket-keepers.

In the final Test of 1988, against Sri Lanka, Russell confused the experts by scoring 94, the highest in the whole game. He was chosen for all the Tests of the 1989 Ashes series and continued to confound, by coming second to Robin Smith in England's batting averages. During 1998-90 his ability was such that more than one critic rated him the best keeper in the world. He toured the West Indies in the early months of 1990, and won more plaudits as both keeper and batsman. However, in 1993 and 1994 he was dropped in favour of Alec Stewart – "an illogical snub" was the press term. In 1998, he announced his retirement from Tests, but continued with Gloucestershire until 2004. He is also well-known for his artistic talent.

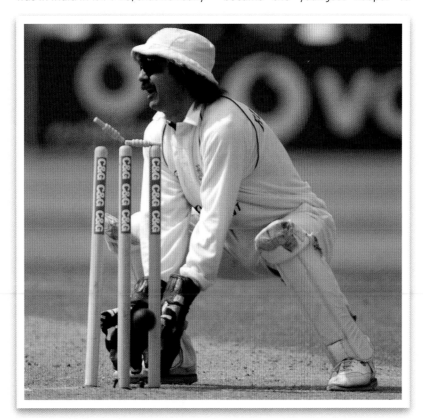

Jack Russell: when he was in his prime, many regarded him as the best keeper in the world.

SALIM MALIK

Born: 16 APRIL 1963, LAHORE, PAKISTAN
Teams: LAHORE (1978-79 TO 1985-86); HABIB BANK (1982-83 TO 2000-01)
First-class: 269 MATCHES; 16,586 RUNS, AVERAGE 45.94; 93 WICKETS, AVERAGE 41.58
Tests (1981-82 to 1998-99): 103 MATCHES; 5,768 RUNS, AVERAGE 43.69; 5 WICKETS, AVERAGE 82.80

An exquisite stroke-maker, Salim Malik was a right-handed batsman who became the youngest player to score a hundred in his first Test match, 100 not out against Sri Lanka in March 1982. He was a big success in England in 1987 - scoring 99 at Headingley and 102 at The Oval - and was even more successful five years later.

He assisted Essex for two seasons and scored heavily in 1991, sharing in a fourth-wicket record stand of 314 with Nasser Hussain at The Oval and ending the season with 1,972 runs. After Salim had been made captain of Pakistan in South Africa and Zimbabwe, he faced allegations of bribery which led to his suspension for some time. He regained his place in the Pakistan side, where he showed that he had lost none of his ability to play as his side required.

Justice Qayyam's enquiry into match fixing, however, recommended a life ban on Salim in May 2000.

KUMAR SANGAKKARA

Born: 27 OCTOBER 1977, MATALE, SRI LANKA
Teams: NONDESCRIPTS (1997-98 TO 2007-08); WARWICKSHIRE 2007
First-class: 179 MATCHES; 12,628 RUNS, AVERAGE 48.01; CAUGHT 323, STUMPED 33
TESTS (2000-01 TO 2010-11): 94 MATCHES; 8,244 RUNS, AVERAGE 57.25; CAUGHT 163, STUMPED 21

A left-hand batsman and wicket-keeper who has occasionally bowled a right-arm off-break, Sangakkara was a 22-year-old law student when he made his first-class debut for the Nondescripts. An elegant batsman, he switched law for cricket, and in 2006-07, for Sri Lanka against a far-from-weak South African attack, he scored his highest innings, 287, joining his friend and captain Mahela Jayawardene (374) in a record stand for all first-class cricket of 624 for the third wicket. He took over from Jayawardene as Sri Lanka's captain. He has excelled in limited-overs cricket and in the IPL, but he is also a great Test batsman, as his average of 57.25 confirms.

SARFRAZ NAWAZ

Born: 1 DECEMBER 1948, LAHORE, PAKISTAN
Teams: LAHORE (1967-68 TO 1984-85); PUNJAB UNIVERSITY (1968-69 TO 1971-72); NORTHAMPTONSHIRE (1969-1982); PUNJAB (1974-75); RAILWAYS (1975-75); UNITED BANK (1976-77 TO 1977-78)
First-class: 299 MATCHES; 5,709 RUNS, AVERAGE 19.35; 1,005 WICKETS, AVERAGE 24.62
Tests (1968-69 to 1983-84): 55 MATCHES; 1,045 RUNS, AVERAGE 17.71; 177 WICKETS, AVERAGE 32.75

Sarfraz Nawaz was a high-class, fast-medium pace bowler who was only the third Pakistani cricketer to take 100 Test wickets and score 1,000 Test runs. He had an impressive Test career, but it was punctuated by injury and arguments with the Pakistan Board of Control. He was never far from controversy. When Allan Lamb asserted that he was the bowler who taught others how to scratch one side of the surface of the ball, Sarfraz took legal action, but did not pursue the case to the full.

In March 1979, at Melbourne, Pakistan celebrated their 100th Test by beating Australia. It was a most unlikely victory, for Australia needed 77 to win and had seven wickets in hand with time to spare. Sarfraz then produced one of the greatest spells of bowling in Test history, taking those seven wickets in 33 balls while he conceded one run. He finished with 9 for 86, and Pakistan won by 71 runs. In the next Test, he caused a furore when he successfully appealed for "handled ball" against Hilditch when the batsman picked up the ball and tossed it back to him.

VIRENDER SEHWAG

Born: 20 OCTOBER 1978, DELHI, INDIA
Teams: DELHI (1997-98 TO 2008-09); LEICESTERSHIRE (2003); DELHI DAREDEVILS (2008-09)
First-class: 151 MATCHES; 12,199 RUNS, AVERAGE 50.61; 104 WICKETS, AVERAGE 39.83
Tests (2001-02 to 2010-11): 86 MATCHES; 7,611 RUNS, AVERAGE 53.59; 39 WICKETS, AVERAGE 42.12

The highlight of Sehwag's career thus far came at Multan in March 2004, when he became the first batsman to hit a triple-century in Indian Test cricket. This innings of 309 contained six sixes and 39 fours and was made off just 375 balls. It was compiled against Pakistan in Pakistan – India won the game by an innings. Sehwag had also been successful in the one-day series which preceded that Test.

Sehwag had originally made his name as a very competent all-rounder in the 1998 Under-19s World Cup, but his bowling faded away, so that on his Test debut in November 2001, v South Africa at Bloemfontein, he scored an outstanding century full of exquisite cover drives. From that moment he became a permanent member of the Indian Test squad. Coming to England for the 2002 tour, he made a brilliant 106 in the Trent Bridge Test. His great enthusiasm for the game can get out of hand. He received a one-match ban for excessive appealing and this caused ructions, with the Indian Board defending Sehwag – in the end diplomacy won the day! In addition to his batting he bowls off-breaks and usually fields in the slips.

SHOAIB AKHTAR

Born: 13 AUGUST 1975, RAWALPINDI, PAKISTAN
Teams: PIA (1994-95 TO 1995-96); RAWALPINDI (1994-95 TO 2006-07); ADBP (1996-97 TO 1997-98); KRL (2001-02); SOMERSET (2001); DURHAM (2003-04), WORCESTERSHIRE (2005), KOLKATA KNIGHT RIDERS (2008), SURREY (2008),
First-class: 133 MATCHES; 1,670 RUNS, AVERAGE 12.27; 467 WICKETS, AVERAGE 26.26
Tests (1997-98 to 2007-08): 46 MATCHES; 544 RUNS, AVERAGE 10.07; 178 WICKETS, AVERAGE 25.69

The "Rawalpindi Express" is the most talked-about fast bowler currently playing in top-class cricket. From the moment he made his Test debut, he seemed to have one ambition, to bowl at 100 m.p.h. In trying to achieve this goal, Shoaib has alternately been the recipient of bouquets and brickbats in equal measure.

He came to England with Pakistan A in 1997 and the press described him as the find of the tour, but in 1997-98 instead of joining the Pakistan one-day squad, he was ignored – indiscipline and misbehaviour on the England trip were the reasons given for his ommission. He did later travel to South Africa, but once again reports of indiscipline emerged. Doubts about his action were cleared by the ICC in May 2001 and, a year later, it was announced that he had broken the 100 m.p.h. barrier, though in the same year he was involved in a ball-tampering

Virender Sehwag: the fast-scoring opening batsman of the Indian team.

controversy. His career continues its see-saw course – playing against England in 2005-06 he seemed to be a reformed character and bowled impressively in the Tests. He failed a drugs test in November 2006 but was exonerated on appeal. Although he ceased playing Test Matches in 2008, he appeared in ODIs for Pakistan in 2010-11.

RAVI SHASTRI

Born: 27 MAY 1962, BOMBAY, INDIA
Teams: BOMBAY (1979-80 TO 1993-94); GLAMORGAN (1987-91)
First-class: 245 MATCHES; 13,202 RUNS, AVERAGE 44.00; 509 WICKETS, AVERAGE 32.89
Tests (1980-81 to 1992-93): 80 MATCHES; 3,830 RUNS, AVERAGE 35.79; 151 WICKETS, AVERAGE 40.96

Ravi Shastri is the only batsman other than Gary Sobers who has hit six sixes in one over. He scored 200 not out for Bombay against Baroda in 1984-85, and hit 13 sixes, six of them in one over. It was the fastest double-century on record, 113 minutes, and the runs came off 123 balls.

A tall, calm and composed right-handed batsman, he won his first Test cap as a slow left-arm bowler. He was flown to New Zealand as a replacement in February 1981 and, just short of his 19th birthday, took six wickets in the match, including three with his last four balls in the second innings. In spite of these achievements, he never quite reached the peak expected of him. His bowling lacked variety and subtlety in flight, but he became a reliable opening batsman. He was seen as captain-elect of India but, in the event, led his country in only one Test. He played a fine innings of 187 against England at The Oval in 1990, and made 206 against Australia at Sydney in 1991-92.

He did well with Glamorgan and was immensely successful in one-day internationals. He was only 30 when he retired and he later became a well respected television commentator.

ALFRED SHAW

Born: 29 AUGUST 1842, BURTON JOYCE, NOTTINGHAMSHIRE
Died: 16 JANUARY 1907, GEDLING, NOTTINGHAMSHIRE
Teams: NOTTINGHAMSHIRE (1864-1897); SUSSEX (1894-95)
First-class: 404 MATCHES; 6,585 RUNS, AVERAGE 12.44; 2,026 WICKETS, AVERAGE 12.13
Tests (1876-77 to 1881-82): 7 MATCHES; 111 RUNS, AVERAGE 10.09; 12 WICKETS, AVERAGE 23.75

Alfred Shaw sent down the first ball to be bowled in Test cricket and appeared in seven of the first eight Test matches. He made two tours to North America and was involved with four tours of Australia, captaining the 1881-82 side. For a long period during his career he was, without question, supreme among slow bowlers, so relentlessly accurate that he bowled more overs in his career than he conceded runs.

A natural leader of men, with a strong personality, Shaw captained Nottinghamshire to four successive championship titles, 1883 to 1886, after which his connection with his native county virtually ended and he was employed to coach young Sussex cricketers. After six years' absence from county cricket, he reappeared for Sussex in 1894 at the age of 50.

He was a strong upholder of the rights of the professional cricketer and did much to help his fellow men. He refused to tour Australia with Grace's side in 1875 because the professionals were to be allowed only second-class facilities, and he led a strike of Nottinghamshire professionals six years later. His faction demanded a formal contract of employment which would guarantee an automatic benefit at the end of an agreed span of years.

This was seen as anarchy by the Nottinghamshire committee who dropped the offenders, confirmed in their belief that it would be better to have an amateur captain. There was a reconciliation eventually, but Shaw's team-mates pointed out that the county went into rapid decline when he was no longer at the helm.

BOBBY SIMPSON

Born: 3 FEBRUARY 1936, MARRICKVILLE, NEW SOUTH WALES, AUSTRALIA
Teams: NEW SOUTH WALES (1952-53 TO 1977-78); WESTERN AUSTRALIA (1956-57 TO 1960-61)
First-class: 257 MATCHES; 21,029 RUNS, AVERAGE 56.22; 349 WICKETS, AVERAGE 38.07
Tests (1957-58 to 1977-78): 62 MATCHES; 4,869 RUNS, AVERAGE 46.81; 71 WICKETS, AVERAGE 42.26

A most dependable right-handed opening batsman, useful leg-break and googly bowler and one of the finest slip fielders the game has known, Bobby Simpson had a Test career that was divided into two distinct parts. When he became captain of Australia in 1963-64, he had not recorded a Test match century, and it was not until his second tour of England in 1964, in the fourth Test at Old Trafford, that Simpson reached three figures; it was his 52nd Test innings. He and Lawry put on 201 for the first wicket, and Simpson went on to score 311, the highest score by an Australian Test captain and the longest innings played against England, 762 minutes. He followed this with a century in each innings against Pakistan at Karachi in 1964-65. Three years later, he announced that he would retire at the end of the season. He scored hundreds in the first two Tests against India and stood down. Recalled for the fourth Test as a farewell gesture, he had match figures of 8 for 97.

He became director of a successful public relations business, and it was believed his career was over. In 1977-78, however, Australian cricket was ravaged by the Packer affair and the defection of the leading players. Simpson came out of retirement to lead Australia against India. Superbly fit in his forties, he hit two Test centuries and won the series. He was less successful in the Caribbean, and with the war with Packer resolved, the Australian Board no longer had need of him.

He held strict, traditional values in attitude, fitness, dress and behaviour, and he became coach to Allan

Border's side of the late 1980s. He also coached Leicestershire for two seasons.

GRAEME SMITH

Born: 1 FEBRUARY 1981, JOHANNESBURG
Teams: WESTERN PROVINCE (2000-01 TO 2006-07); SOMERSET (2005), CAPE COBRAS (2007-08 TO 2009-10) RAJASTHAN ROYALS (2008-09)
First-class: 129 MATCHES; 10,644 RUNS, AVERAGE 50.92; 11 WICKETS, AVERAGE 98.09
Tests (2001-02 to 2010-11): 90 MATCHES; 7,445 RUNS, AVERAGE 50.30; 8 WICKETS, AVERAGE 104.00

Graeme Smith made his Test debut v Australia at Cape Town in March 2002; he scored a very useful 68. In the one-day internationals that came after the Tests, he was picked for the final four games, registering innings of 41, 46, 84 and 73. His talent was patently obvious; he had secured his place in the national side. Just a year after his Test debut, he became South Africa's captain, the youngest in that country's history – he

Graeme Smith: South Africa's youngest captain.

replaced Shaun Pollock who had led a failing side in the 2003 World Cup, held on home ground. Picked to lead South Africa on the 2003 tour to England, he began by demonstrating his authority, refusing to include the controversial Klusener in the squad.

In England he was South Africa's dominant batsman, hitting double-centuries in successive Tests and ending the series, which was tied, with an average of 79.33. He raised eyebrows at press conferences by having the team psychologist sit next to him. 2004 saw South Africa's success begin to fade, but he had the pleasure of leading his country to victory in a one-day match v Australia. In 2005 he captained Somerset, but played in just four Championship games – however, he did hit 311 v Leicestershire.

JOHN SNOW

Born: 13 OCTOBER 1941, PEOPLETON, WORCESTER
Teams: SUSSEX (1961-77)
First-class: 346 MATCHES; 4,832 RUNS, AVERAGE 14.17; 1,174 WICKETS, AVERAGE 22.72
Tests (1965-76): 49 MATCHES; 772 RUNS, AVERAGE 13.54; 202 WICKETS, AVERAGE 26.66

Among the greatest of English post-war fast bowlers, John Snow was also among the most moody and most prone to brushes with authority. While not possessing a classical action, he was rhythmical and intelligent. He was raw when he first played for England in 1965, and did not go to Australia the following winter. He took 12 wickets in three Tests against the West Indies in 1966 and played a major part in England's victory in the final Test, not least because he scored his maiden first-class 50 and shared a last-wicket stand of 128 in 140 minutes with Higgs.

In the West Indies in 1967-68, he was outstanding, taking 7 for 79 at Kingston, 10 for 142 in the match at Georgetown, and finishing the series with 27 wickets in four Tests. Yet perhaps his greatest performance was in Australia with Illingworth's

side in 1970-71, when England regained the Ashes and he took 31 wickets, including a Test-best 7 for 40 at Sydney. Controversy struck the following summer when he barged into Gavaskar in the Lord's Test and was banned for one match. He lost his appetite for county cricket, joined World Series Cricket, published two volumes of poetry and an autobiography called *Cricket Rebel*. He played Sunday League cricket for Warwickshire in 1980.

GARFIELD SOBERS

SEE PAGE 231

F.R. SPOFFORTH

Born: SEPTEMBER 1853, BALMAIN, SYDNEY, NEW SOUTH WALES, AUSTRALIA
Died: 4 JUNE 1926, DITTON HILL LODGE, LONG DITTON, SURREY
Teams: NEW SOUTH WALES (1874-75 TO 1884-85); VICTORIA (1885-86 TO 1887-88)
First-class: 155 MATCHES; 1,928 RUNS, AVERAGE 9.88; 853 WICKETS, AVERAGE 14.95
Tests (1876-77 to 1886-87): 18 MATCHES; 217 RUNS, AVERAGE 9.43; 94 WICKETS, AVERAGE 18.41

Tall, intelligent, able to vary speed, cut and swerve, Spofforth was basically a fast-medium pace bowler. He refused to play in the first Test match of all in 1876-77 because his wicket-keeper Murdoch was not chosen, but he appeared in the second. It was in the third Test in January 1879 at Melbourne that he really made his mark, taking 6 for 48 and 7 for 62 as Australia won by ten wickets. This came as no surprise, for "The Demon" had routed the MCC at Lord's in 1878, taking 6 for 4 and 5 for 16 as the Australians won in a day. His record in England was phenomenal, and in 1884 he took 207 wickets, averaging 12.82.

He had lost some of his demon by 1887 and emigrated to England the following year. He played for Derbyshire from 1889-91, captaining the side in 1890, but the county did not have first-class status at that time.

BRIAN STATHAM

Born: 17 JUNE 1930, GORTON, MANCHESTER, LANCASHIRE
Died: 10 JUNE 2000, STOCKPORT, CHESHIRE
Teams: LANCASHIRE (1950-68)
First-class: 559 MATCHES; 5,424 RUNS, AVERAGE 19.80; 2,260 WICKETS, AVERAGE 16.37
Tests (1950-51 to 1965): 70 MATCHES; 675 RUNS, AVERAGE 11.44; 252 WICKETS, AVERAGE 24.84

For a period of more than ten years, Statham was one of England's great opening bowlers, forming lethal partnerships with both Trueman and Tyson. He bowled right-arm with a fluid, easy action and was relentlessly accurate. He was honest, loyal and reliable, a great teamman who, reluctantly, captained Lancashire from 1965 to 1967.

Flown to Australia as a reinforcement in 1950-51, he made his Test debut in New Zealand and claimed Bert Sutcliffe as his first Test wicket. He did not really establish a regular place in the England side until the tour of the Caribbean in 1953-54, and it was in Australia a year later that he and Tyson bowled England to victory. A few months later, he showed the English public his prowess with a Test-best 7 for 39 against South Africa at Lord's. He played for England until the Oval Test against South Africa in 1965, and in this last match took 5 for 40 and 2 for 105.

A left-handed batsman, he was capable of useful tailend innings, and was a fine fielder in the deep. He took 100 wickets in a season 13 times and performed the hat-trick on three occasions.

Brian Statham: a reliable and accurate right-arm fast bowler for England for 15 years, during which time he formed deadly opening partnerships with both Fred Trueman and Frank Tyson.

GARFIELD SOBERS
The All-round Great

Garfield Sobers: a team in himself.

Sobers began his first-class career when he was not yet 17. Less than a year later, he was in the Test team against England, batting No. 9. He made 14 not out and 26 and took four wickets. The following year against the Aussies he scored 231 runs and took six wickets. All the time he was learning the craft that made him a master left-hand batsman on all types of wicket. At that time, he was bowling orthodox left-arm spin.

It was the visit to the West Indies of Pakistan in 1957-58 which really made Sobers' name. In the third Test at Kingston, he made his first Test century, and then went on and on until captain Gerry Alexander declared at 790 for 3, the West Indies' highest score. Sobers himself had made 365 not out, the highest score ever made in a Test. In the next Test, he got 125 and 109 not out.

Instantly famous, he cashed in at first by signing as a professional for Radcliffe and it was there that he developed a new bowling skill, left-arm medium-fast swing bowling. However, on tour in India, he found the pitches unresponsive and tried out his left-arm off-breaks and googlies. His batting did not suffer and, with centuries in the first three Tests, he took his record to six centuries in six successive Tests.

When England arrived in the West Indies in 1959-60, Sobers first hit them for 154 when playing for Barbados, then in the first Test in Bridgetown, he scored 226. He amassed 709 runs in the series, averaging 101.28.

In the winter, he played in the famous series in Australia which began with the tied Test. He took 15 wickets in this series and from then on his bowling began to pay dividends - in the 1961-62 series against India he took 23 wickets, his best in a single series. That year, he signed for South Australia, for whom he played 26 matches in three seasons.

After a successful tour of England in 1963, he was captain of the West Indies for the visit of Australia in 1964-65, and won the series 2-1. He had a superb tour of England in 1966, scoring 722 runs, average 103.14, and taking 20 wickets. The West Indies won 3-1 and three times Sobers passed 160. In the Lord's Test, with the West Indies 95 for 5 in their second knock, only nine ahead of England, Sobers (163 not out) was joined by his cousin David Holford (105 not out) and the two added 274 unbeaten to turn the series. He agreed to play for Nottinghamshire in 1968, a spell which was to last seven years.

Meanwhile, England won the 1967-68 series in the West Indies 1-0, after a generous Sobers' declaration at 92 for 2, leaving England to get 215. They did so, for which Sobers was much criticized.

Sobers announced his arrival in county cricket in typical fashion.

At Swansea in August, against Glamorgan, he hit every ball of the six-ball over from Malcolm Nash for six.

Sobers began to suffer injuries in 1972-73 and did not play in the home series against Australia, relinquishing the captaincy of the West Indies. He was back in the side for the tour of England in 1973, scoring 150 not out at Lord's. On England's visit in the winter, Sobers became the first batsman to pass 8,000 runs in Test matches during his innings in the second Test. He was the second player (after Richie Benaud) to score 2,000 runs and take 200 wickets in Tests. He was knighted in 1975. He has suffered operations to knees and eyes in retirement, but retains his immense popularity.

FIRST-CLASS CAREER
(1952-53 to 1974, 383 matches)
Batting: RUNS 28,315; AVERAGE 54.87; HIGHEST SCORE 365 NOT OUT; CENTURIES 86
Bowling: WICKETS 1,093; RUNS 28,941; AVERAGE 27.74; BEST 9-49
Catches: 407

TESTS
(1953-54 to 1973-74, 93 MATCHES)
Batting: RUNS 8,032; AVERAGE 57.78; HIGHEST SCORE 365 NOT OUT; CENTURIES 26
Bowling: WICKETS 235; RUNS 7,999; AVERAGE 34.03; BEST 6-73
Catches: 109

1936 Born Garfield St Aubrun Sobers on 28 July at Bay Lane, Bridgetown, Barbados	**1952-53** Made his first-class debut for Barbados	**1954** Made Test debut in final Test v England at Kingston, 30 March-3 April. He scored 14 not out and 26 and took four wickets.

1958 Passes 1,000 runs in Test cricket during the home series with Pakistan	**1958** Broke record for highest Test score when making 365 not out v Pakistan at Kingston, 26 February-4 March

1960 In series against England, January-March, he scored 709 runs, average 101.28, including 226 at home ground of Bridgetown	**1965** Took his 100th Test wicket, in his 48th match, v Australia at Sabina Park, Jamaica	**1968** Played what some thought his greatest innings, at Kingston, 113 not out on a bad wicket interrupted by severe crowd rioting v England, 8-14 February

1968 Established a first-class record by hitting six sixes off an over for Notts against Glamorgan, Swansea, 31 August-2 September

ALEC STEWART

Born: 8 APRIL 1963, MERTON, SURREY
Teams: SURREY (1981-03)
First-class: 447 MATCHES; 26,165 RUNS, AVERAGE
40.06; CAUGHT 721, STUMPED 32
Tests (1989-90 to 2003): 133 MATCHES; 8,463
RUNS, AVERAGE 39.54; CAUGHT 263, STUMPED 13

The son of Surrey and England opening batsman Mickey Stewart, Alec joined the Surrey staff in 1981 as a wicket-keeper-batsman, making his debut that season. A superb timer of the ball, he relied on a good eye and scored heavily through the covers and off the back foot. It was not until he was nearly 27, however, that he forced himself into the Test team, touring the West Indies in 1989-90.

For the fifth Test against the West Indies in 1991, he was also asked to keep wicket. In the Test with Sri Lanka which followed, he was chosen as a batsman and made his first Test century at No. 3. He was vice-captain to Gooch on the tour to New Zealand in 1991-92, then after an excellent World Cup he made 190 in the first Test against Pakistan and in the second at Lord's became the sixth Englishman to carry his bat in a Test. When Gooch was ill, he captained England in a Test in India in 1992-93, and for the following Test in Sri Lanka. The selectors, however, could never decide whether to play Stewart as a pure batsman or as wicket-keeper-batsman.

Played as an opener only in the West Indies in 1993-94 he was superb, scoring 118 and 143 at Bridgetown to enable England to inflict a first defeat on the West Indies there in 59 years. Stewart improved his Test average to an excellent 46 before reverting once again to becoming England's regular keeper, since when his average steadily dropped to just below 40.

Long captain of Surrey, Alec Stewart became captain of England in 1998 and retained the highest standards in all three of his roles.

Alec Stewart: wicket-keeper, batsman and captain.

DALE STEYN

Born: 27 JUNE 1983, PHALABORWA, SOUTH AFRICA
Teams: NORTHERNS (2003-04, 2010-11); TITANS (2004-05
TO 2009-10); ESSEX 2005; WARWICKSHIRE 2007
First-class: 85 MATCHES; 1,124 RUNS, AVERAGE 14.22;
392 WICKETS, AVERAGE 24.28
Tests (2003-04 to 2010-11): 46 MATCHES; 620
RUNS, AVERAGE 13.77; 238 WICKETS, AVERAGE 23.21

Dale Steyn is a tall, very fast right-arm bowler, with the ability to swing the ball both ways, who has added accuracy and a fast bowler's mean streak to his natural great pace. A year after making his first-class debut, he was in South Africa's side against England at Port Elizabeth in 2004-05. He was soon taking Test wickets, but really came of age as a dangerous fast bowler in all senses when New Zealand toured South Africa for a two-match series in 2007-08. On the first day of the second Test a short ball struck Craig Cumming in the face, sending him into intensive care. Steyn was the Man of the Series, having taken ten wickets in each match. In 2008, he became the quickest South African bowler to reach 100 Test wickets. Wickets continued to come in big batches: ten in a match when South Africa won a series in Australia in 2008-09; 15 in the series against England in South Africa the same season; 15 against the West Indies in 2009-10; and 21 in three Tests against India in 2010-11. In April 2011 he was ranked the world's top Test bowler in the ICC rankings.

ANDREW STRAUSS

Born: 2 MARCH 1977, JOHANNESBURG
Teams: MIDDLESEX (1998-2010)
First-class: 208 MATCHES; 14,715 RUNS, AVERAGE 42.28;
3 WICKETS, AVERAGE 46.66
Tests (2004 to 2010-11): 82 MATCHES; 6,084
RUNS, AVERAGE 43.14; NO WICKETS

In 2004, when England were due to play New Zealand at Lord's, Vaughan twisted his right knee during net practice. Strauss, though not in the 13-man squad for the England side, was chosen to replace Vaughan. Strauss hit 112 and helped stand-in captain, Trescothick, to add 190 for England's first wicket. In the second innings, Strauss made 83 not out. Runs continued to flow from his bat throughout 2004 and by the end of that memorable calendar year he had 971 Test runs to his name at an average of 60.68. Vaughan had returned to the team and Strauss really filled the vacancy left by the retirement of Nasser Hussain.

His career showed no signs of slowing down during the 2005 Ashes series, since he made 106 at Old Trafford and 129 in the final game at The Oval. He succeeded Kevin Pietersen as England's Test captain at the beginning of 2009. He led England to Ashes victory in Australia in 2010-11.

Although born in South Africa, Strauss was educated at Radley College and Durham University. Later, as a student, he represented British Universities in the B&H Cup, but did not play regularly in county cricket until he graduated. A left-handed bat, he is also an excellent cover fielder.

After being succeeded by Nasser Hussain, he was named Man of the Match in his 100th Test, coming in on a hat-trick and scoring 105 against the West Indies at Old Trafford in August 2000.

HEATH STREAK

Born: 16 MARCH 1974, BULAWAYO, RHODESIA
Teams: MATABELELAND (1993-94 TO 2003-04);
HAMPSHIRE (1995); WARWICKSHIRE (2004-07)
First-class: 175 MATCHES; 5,684 RUNS, AVERAGE 26.31;
499 WICKETS, AVERAGE 28.76
Tests (1993-94 to 2005-06): 65 MATCHES;
1,990 RUNS, AVERAGE 22.35; 216 WICKETS,
AVERAGE 28.14

Inheriting the love of cricket from his father, who represented Rhodesia (Zimbabwe), Streak showed talent as a fast bowler from an early age. Before he was 21, he had captured 43 Test wickets at an impressive average of 19 runs each. The family had a cattle farm about an hour's drive out of Bulawayo and though politics was beginning to encroach, the future, in 1994, looked bright for young Streak. To gain experience he came to England to play for Hampshire in 1995, taking 50 Championship wickets. In 2000, Streak was a member of the Zimbabwean team on its first full tour to England. Despite the now-increasing political pressure, the team performed better than many had predicted and Streak was singled out as their best bowler; his movement off the wicket and deceptive pace had England's leading batsmen deceived. Later that year he was appointed as Zimbabwe's captain, an almost impossible task given the dire circumstances – three times since he has resigned and then come back, but he was appointed Warwickshire captain in 2006, and didn't play for Zimbabwe thereafter. He retired after the 2007 season.

BERT SUTCLIFFE

Born: 17 NOVEMBER 1923, PONSONBY, AUCKLAND,
NEW ZEALAND
Died: 20 APRIL 2001, AUCKLAND, NEW ZEALAND
Teams: AUCKLAND (1941-42 TO 1948-79); OTAGO (1946-47
TO 1961-62); NORTHERN DISTRICTS (1962-63 TO
1965-66)
First-class: 233 MATCHES; 17,447 RUNS, AVERAGE
47.41; 86 WICKETS, AVERAGE 38.05
Tests (1946-47 to 1965): 42 MATCHES; 2,727
RUNS, AVERAGE 40.10; 4 WICKETS, AVERAGE 86.00

Bert Sutcliffe was the finest New Zealand cricketer of his generation and must rank as one of the best left-handed batsmen of the period. He had a cheerful disposition and was a thing of beauty with a bat in his hands. He was stylish, correct and joyful. He made his Test debut in March 1947, when he shared an opening stand of 133 with Walter Hadlee against England. Sutcliffe made 58, and his class was obvious. He was an outstanding success in England in 1949, scoring 2,627 runs on the tour and averaging 60.42 in the Tests, with a century at Old Trafford. In 1952-53 he hit 385 for Otago against Canterbury, and three years earlier had hit 355 for Otago against Auckland. These remain the two highest individual scores to be made in New Zealand.

He captained New Zealand in four Tests between 1951 and 1954, but captaincy was not a job he relished, and it is significant that his best Test score, 230 not out against India in Delhi in 1955-56, came after he had relinquished the leadership. Sutcliffe retired from Test cricket in 1958-59, but was persuaded to return in 1964-65. He made 151 against India in Calcutta. His final Test was in England in 1965. He proved to be a fine coach.

HERBERT SUTCLIFFE

Born: 24 NOVEMBER 1894, SUMMERBRIDGE, HARROGATE,
YORKSHIRE
Died: 22 JANUARY 1978, CROSS HILLS, YORKSHIRE
Teams: YORKSHIRE (1919-45)
First-class: 754 MATCHES; 50,670 RUNS, AVERAGE
52.02; 14 WICKETS, AVERAGE 41.21
Tests (1924 to 35): 54 MATCHES; 4,555 RUNS,
AVERAGE 60.73

Herbert Sutcliffe's career fits neatly into the period between the two wars, and he averaged 1,000 runs in a season every year from 1919 to 1939. He made only a brief appearance in 1945. He was unquestionably one of the greatest opening batsmen of all time with an outstanding Test record.

Technically sound, neat, determined and totally unflappable, he batted right-handed, was at home on any wicket and shaped his game to the occasion. His opening partnership with Hobbs in the England side is legendary, and his county partnership with Holmes was equally famous. He served as a mentor to the young Len Hutton.

The first of his 15 three-figure Test opening partnerships with Hobbs came in his debut Test against South Africa in 1924. In the next match, they put on 268, and Sutcliffe made 122, the first of his 16 Test centuries. He scored a century in his first match against Australia, a century in each innings in his second, and in the fourth match of the series became the first batsman to hit four centuries in a rubber. Most famously, at The Oval in 1926, when England regained the Ashes, Hobbs and Sutcliffe made 172 on a sticky wicket. Sutcliffe ended with 161.

In 1930, at Leyton, Sutcliffe and Holmes scored a world-record 555 for the first wicket against Essex. Sutcliffe made 313. His last Test was against South Africa at Lord's in 1935, although many felt he should have been retained longer. Once offered the captaincy of Yorkshire, he refused, unwilling to break the amateur tradition.

GRAEME SWANN

Born: 24 MARCH 1979, NOTTINGHAM
Teams: NORTHAMPTONSHIRE (1998-2004);
NOTTINGHAMSHIRE (2005-10)
First-class: 207 MATCHES; 6,890 RUNS, AVERAGE 26.60;
577 WICKETS, AVERAGE 31.94
TESTS (2008-09 TO 2010-11): 29 MATCHES; 741
RUNS, AVERAGE 24.70; 128 WICKETS, AVERAGE 28.10

Graeme Swann impressed as a 19-year-old in his first-class debut season for Northants, scoring a century against Leicestershire. His batting was a bonus, as his principal role was as a skilful off-spinner. He had a successful tour of South Africa with England's A team,

and was in the England squad for the last Test against New Zealand in 1999. He failed to gain a place, and had to wait nearly ten more years for his Test debut. Some put this down to his confident, outgoing personality, which was interpreted by some in authority to be cockiness. He switched counties to Nottinghamshire in 2005, and played a big part in their Championship victory. He was recalled to England duty in one-day matches, for which his aggressive style is well suited, and eventually made his Test debut in India in 2008-09, taking two wickets in his first over (only the second time this has ever happened). Taking a wicket in his first over of a spell of bowling became a habit with him. He produced crucial performances in England's Ashes-winning campaign in 2009, and then took 21 wickets in the tour of South Africa which followed. His 54 Test wickets in 2009 helped him to climb to number two in the ICC Test rankings by 2011.

MAURICE TATE

Born: 30 MAY 1895, BRIGHTON, SUSSEX
Died: 18 MAY 1956, WADHURST, SUSSEX
Teams: SUSSEX (1912-1937)
First-class: 679 MATCHES; 21,717 RUNS, AVERAGE 25.04;
2,784 WICKETS, AVERAGE 18.16
Tests (1924 to 35): 39 MATCHES; 1,198 RUNS,
AVERAGE
25.48; 155 WICKETS, AVERAGE 26.16

Son of a Sussex cricketer who played one match for England, Maurice Tate was a great medium-pace right-arm bowler and a great character. He began as an off-break bowler, but became a seam bowler of brisk pace after the Second World War. Some insisted his deliveries gathered pace off the wicket. Few bowlers have used the seam to such good effect; very few have been as popular. He was also a most capable lower middle-order batsman, good enough, in fact, to score 100 not out against South Africa at Lord's in 1929.

Tate's Test debut was sensational. At Edgbaston in 1924, he and Arthur Gilligan bowled South Africa out for 30 in 12.3 overs. Tate took 4 for 12 and had 5 for 83 in the second innings. He took 30 wickets in the series and created a record with 38 wickets in Australia the following winter. He was England's leading bowler of the time before the pace of Larwood.

He completed the "double" eight times, and in three of those seasons his 1,000 runs were coupled with 200 wickets. He was held in great affection by the public.

HUGH TAYFIELD

Born: 30 JANUARY 1929, DURBAN, SOUTH AFRICA
Died: 25 FEBRUARY 1994, PIETERMARITZBURG, SOUTH AFRICA
Teams: NATAL (1945-46 TO 1946-47); RHODESIA (1947-48 TO 1948-49); TRANSVAAL (1956-57 TO 1962-63)
First-class: 187 MATCHES; 3,668 RUNS, AVERAGE 17.30; 864 WICKETS, AVERAGE 21.86
Tests (1949-50 to 1960): 37 MATCHES; 862 RUNS, AVERAGE 16.90; 170 WICKETS, AVERAGE 25.91

Hugh Tayfield was a very fine off-break bowler whose 170 wickets in Test cricket was a South African record. He played in all five Tests against Australia in 1949-50, and took 7 for 23 at Durban when he and Mann bowled the opposition out for 75. Surprisingly not chosen for the tour of England in 1951, he was flown out as a replacement, but did not play in a Test. In Australia in 1952-53 he thrived with a record 30 wickets, and at Melbourne he bowled South Africa to victory with 13 for 165 in the match.

Success continued unabated, and when South Africa came to England in 1955 he became the first bowler from that country to take 100 Test wickets. He took 26 wickets in the series and had astonishing figures in the second innings at The Oval when he took 5 for 60 in 53.4 overs of which 29 were maidens. England suffered more at his hands in South Africa in 1956-57, when he established a record with 37 wickets

in the rubber, including his career-best 9 for 113 in Johannesburg.

MARK TAYLOR

Born: 27 OCTOBER 1964, LEETON, NEW SOUTH WALES, AUSTRALIA
Teams: NEW SOUTH WALES (1985-86 TO 1998-99)
First-class: 253 MATCHES; 17,415 RUNS, AVERAGE 41.95; 2 WICKETS, AVERAGE 38.50
Tests (1988-89 to 1998-99): 104 MATCHES; 7,525 RUNS, AVERAGE 43.49; 1 WICKET, AVERAGE 26.00

A left-handed opening batsman and brilliant slip fielder, he forced his way into the Australian side against the West Indies in 1988-89, and scored 136 in his first Test against England the following summer. He and Geoff Marsh became a formidable opening pair and, at Trent Bridge, they established a record with a stand of 329. Taylor hit 219. He finished the series with 839 runs, an aggregate exceeded only by Bradman and Hammond in rubbers between England and Australia.

When Marsh retired, Taylor continued to flourish with Slater as his partner, and he succeeded Border as Australia's captain. He helped maintain Australia's supremacy in world cricket with home and away series victories against the West Indies and triumph over Atherton's side in 1994-95.

After a period of bad form – while captain of the 1997 Australian side

Mark Taylor: he equalled Bradman's Test record, and declared.

to England, he actually dropped himself from the one-day squad – he ended his Test career in a blaze of glory, while captaining his country to Pakistan. Australia won the series and Taylor hit 334 not out in the second Test at Peshawar. Returning to Australia he announced his retirement and took a job promoting the Sydney Olympics.

SACHIN TENDULKAR

SEE PAGE 235

JEFF THOMSON

Born: 16 AUGUST 1950, GREENACRE, SYDNEY, NEW SOUTH WALES, AUSTRALIA
Teams: NEW SOUTH WALES (1972-74); QUEENSLAND (1974-75 TO 1985-86); MIDDLESEX (1981)
First-class: 187 MATCHES; 2,065 RUNS, AVERAGE 13.58; 675 WICKETS, AVERAGE 26.46
Tests (1972-73 to 1985): 51 MATCHES; 679 RUNS, AVERAGE 12.81; 200 WICKETS, AVERAGE 28.00

Jeff Thomson made an inauspicious start in Test cricket when he played against Pakistan in 1972-73, but two years later, after he had moved to Queensland, the selectors recalled him. The result was devastating as he and Lillee, with whom his name was to be permanently associated, demolished England. Thomson, bowling at a great pace, took 3 for 59 and 6 for 46. He finished the series with 33 wickets in nine innings. A few weeks later, he was in England for the World Cup and a four-match series and, if not quite so potent as in Australia, he and Lillee again destroyed England. Back in Australia the following winter, 1975-76, he and Lillee outbowled their West Indian counterparts and swept Australia to a 5-1 series victory.

Thomson joined World Series Cricket, then retracted, and then rejoined. He played for Middlesex in 1981, but injury restricted him to eight matches. He was recalled to the Test scene in 1985 after three years' absence, but the old bite had gone.

SACHIN TENDULKAR
The Boy Master

FIRST-CLASS CAREER
(1988-89 to 2010-11, 280 matches)
Batting: RUNS 23,585; AVERAGE 59.86; HIGHEST
SCORE 248 NOT OUT; CENTURIES 78
Bowling: WICKETS 70; RUNS 4,280;
AVERAGE 61.14; BEST 3-10
Catches: 174

TESTS
(1989-90 to 2010-11, 177 MATCHES)
Batting: RUNS 14,692; AVERAGE 56.92; HIGHEST
SCORE 248 NOT OUT; CENTURIES 51
Bowling: WICKETS 45; RUNS 2,388;
AVERAGE 53.06; BEST 3-10
Catches: 106

At 15, Tendulkar made his first-class debut for Bombay, and scored 100. At the end of the season he averaged 64.77. In 1989-90, he became the youngest player to score a 50 in a Test. In the tour of England in 1990, the 17-year-old saved India at Old Trafford with his first Test century, an unbeaten 119. He was the youngest player to score a Test century in England. By the time England toured India in 1992-93 the boy wonder showed his adult mastery with his fifth Test century, a career-best 165.

Tendulkar, like Gavaskar before him, is diminutive, but compact and muscular. He loves fast bowling and plays spinners with careful correctness, but does not let any bowling subdue his aggression.

In 1992, the 19-year-old Tendulkar

Sachin Tendulkar: holds the record for the most centuries in Test cricket with 51.

was the first overseas player to appear for Yorkshire. The young master coped well with the damp conditions, making 1,070 runs.

Outstanding innings came regularly from Tendulkar. In 1996 he was appointed captain of India for the first time, aged 23. This was only the first of at least three spells as captain.

In 1997-98, the cricket world enjoyed the spectacle of the contest between the master batsman and the spin king, Shane Warne. Tendulkar was superb. An unbeaten 155 in the second innings of the first Test turned a first-innings deficit into a 179-run win, and an eventual 2-1 series win. Tendulkar made 336 runs in five innings for an average of 111.50. Warne's wickets cost 54 runs each.

In 2000-01, his mastery of Warne and 126 in the deciding Test helped win an amazing series against Australia. In 2003-04, his 194 not out helped India win in Pakistan for the first time in 20 attempts. Eventually, in 2005-06, he became Test cricket's most prolific century maker with his 35th hundred.

For all his adulation, Tendulkar remains a private man: "I am a normal person who plays cricket," he says.

1973	**1988**	**1989**	**1990**
Born Sachin Ramesh Tendulkar, on 24 April in Bombay, India	Made his first-class debut for Bombay at the tender age of 15	Made Test debut against Pakistan aged 16 against bouncers from Imran, Wasim and Waqar at Karachi, 15-20 November. Scored 15, but scored 59 in the second Test	Made first Test century, 119 not out in fourth innings to earn India a draw v England at Old Trafford, 9-14 August, the youngest to score a Test century in England

1992	**1996**	**2000-01**	**2005-06**	**2007-08**
Became the first overseas player to play for Yorkshire. Ended the season with 1,070 Championship runs	Appointed captain of India aged 23 in August, after scoring 428 runs in five Tests on tour of England, averaging 85.60	Scored 194 not out in India first-ever Test victory in Pakistan, adding 336 with Virender Sehwag, Multan, 28 March-1 April	Took Sunil Gavaskar's record when scoring his 35th Test century, 109 v Sri Lanka at Delhi on 10-14 December.	Passed Brian Lara as all-time leading run-scorer in Tests

Jonathan Trott: carving out a reputation as a proven run-scorer.

JONATHAN TROTT

Born: 22 APRIL 1981, CAPE TOWN, SOUTH AFRICA
Teams: WESTERN PROVINCE (2000-01 TO 2001-02); WARWICKSHIRE (2003-10); OTAGO (2005-06)
First-class: 161 MATCHES; 10,748 RUNS, AVERAGE 45.73; 56 WICKETS, AVERAGE 44.12
Tests (2009 TO 2010-11): 18 MATCHES; 1,600 RUNS, AVERAGE 61.53; 1 WICKET, AVERAGE 86.00

Jonathan Trott was born in South Africa and made his first-class debut there but, holding a British passport, he soon came to England to play for Warwickshire. He claims ancestry with Albert and George Trott, the 19th century Australian Test players. He made 245 for Warwickshire's second XI on his debut in 2002, and 134 on his Championship debut the following season. He is a meticulous and correct right-hand batsman, who takes his time in preparation at the crease, and also a useful medium-pace right-arm bowler.

He was called up for the decisive fifth Test of the Ashes series in 2009, and made 119 in the second innings as England regained the urn. He toured South Africa without much success apart from a vital 69 in the first Test, but in 2010 scored 226 against Bangladesh at Lord's. He continued his successes on the Ashes-retaining tour of Australia in 2010-11, with 135 not out of England's 517 for 1 declared at Brisbane, and 168 not out at Melbourne. He scored 445 (av 89.00) in the series.

FRED TRUEMAN

Born: 6 FEBRUARY 1931, STAINTON, YORKSHIRE
Died: 1 JULY 2006, SKIPTON, YORKSHIRE
Teams: YORKSHIRE (1949-68)
First-class: 603 MATCHES; 9,231 RUNS, AVERAGE 15.56; 2,304 WICKETS, AVERAGE 18.29
Tests (1952-65): 67 MATCHES; 981 RUNS, AVERAGE 13.81; 307 WICKETS, AVERAGE 21.57

A genuine, whole-hearted fast bowler whose belligerence made him feared by batsmen and whose outspokenness and reputation caused him to clash with authority more than once and to miss tours and Tests he might have played in, Freddie Trueman was one of the game's great bowlers, fit to rank alongside Hadlee, Lillee and the rest.

Initial raw pace was augmented by subtlety, and he made a dramatic entry into Test cricket in 1952. He took three Indian wickets for 89 in the first innings and 4 for 27 in the second. Three of these came in eight balls and left India 0 for 4.

This was on his home ground of Headingley, and there were eight wickets at Lord's and nine at Old Trafford where his first-innings 8 for 31 remains the best analysis against India and was the best of Trueman's Test career. Another five wickets in a rain-ruined final Test meant 29 for the series.

Thereafter things did not go so smoothly. He helped England regain the Ashes in 1953, with 4 for 86 in the deciding match of the series, but it was the only Test in which he appeared. He fared poorly in the Caribbean and gained adverse publicity, with the result that he missed the tour of Australia in 1954-55, and it was not until 1957 that he re-established himself and was a permanent fixture in the England side.

For Yorkshire, Trueman was a leading force throughout his career. He took 100 wickets in a season 12 times and took a hat-trick four times. He was in seven championship-winning sides – Yorkshire did not take the title again until 2001. He was a very useful aggressive batsman and a brilliant close-to-the-wicket fielder.

At The Oval in 1964, Neil Hawke, the Australian, was caught at slip by Cowdrey off Trueman, who thereby became the first bowler in Test history to take 300 wickets. His international career ended the following season.

Trueman played Sunday League matches for Derbyshire in 1972, and became a noted commentator. He was also much in demand as an after-dinner speaker.

MARCUS TRESCOTHICK

Born: 25 DECEMBER 1975, KEYNSHAM, BRISTOL
Teams: SOMERSET (1993-2010)
First-class: 271 MATCHES; 18,042 RUNS, AVERAGE 41.09; 36 WICKETS, AVERAGE 43.08
Tests (2000 to 2006): 76 MATCHES; 5,825 RUNS, AVERAGE 43.79; 1 WICKET, AVERAGE 155.00

A prolific batsman at England Youth levels, Trescothick captained England Under-19s to the West Indies in 1994-95, having already made his first-class debut for Somerset in 1993. Although Somerset retained him in their side through the mid-1990s, he had a rather lean time for one who promised so much. In the summers of 1996, 1997 and 1998, his Championship batting average did not reach 30.

A welcome improvement in 1999 saw Trescothick picked for England A in the winter of 1999-2000, but even then his best first-class innings was a mere 45. His form in county cricket, however, continued to improve in 2000 and he was picked to replace Ramprakash for the fifth Test. Opening the innings with Atherton, he hit a sound 66, then made 78 in the final Test. The following winter he was one of the few successes on England's tour to Pakistan and Sri Lanka – for example, he scored 122 and 57 in the first Test v Sri Lanka, when Muralitharan bamboozled everyone else. Since that series he has been an England regular, playing through the memorable 2005 Ashes series. He was unfortunate to be forced home owing to family problems during the 2005-06 Test series and he retired from Test cricket.

HUGH TRUMBLE

Born: 12 MAY 1867, ABBOTSFORD, MELBOURNE, AUSTRALIA
Died: 14 AUGUST 1938, HAWTHORNE, MELBOURNE, AUSTRALIA
Teams: VICTORIA (1887-88 TO 1903-04)
First-class: 213 MATCHES; 5,395 RUNS, AVERAGE 19.47; 929 WICKETS, AVERAGE 18.44
Tests (1890 to 1903-04): 32 MATCHES; 851 RUNS, AVERAGE 19.79; 141 WICKETS, AVERAGE 21.78

Hugh Trumble was a right-arm medium-pace off-break bowler and sound middle-order batsman. He had prominent ears and a large nose, and he usually wore a large stetson. Grace said he was the best bowler Australia had ever sent to England, and Fry believed him to be not only one of the greatest bowlers, but also a master of field placing and a wonderful judge of the game. The first of his five tours to England was in 1890 when he did little, but thereafter he was immensely successful. In 1901-02 he took a hat-trick at Melbourne against England and, two years later, on the same ground, he took another hat-trick when he took seven English wickets for 28 in what proved his last first-class match.

At The Oval in 1902, he took 8 for 65 and 4 for 108, and scored 64 not out and 7 not out to become the first Australian to take ten wickets and score 50 runs in a Test. He captained Australia in two Tests.

VICTOR TRUMPER

Born: 2 NOVEMBER 1877, DARLINGHURST, SYDNEY, NEW SOUTH WALES, AUSTRALIA
Died: 28 JUNE 1915, DARLINGHURST, SYDNEY, NEW SOUTH WALES, AUSTRALIA
Teams: NEW SOUTH WALES (1894-95 TO 1913-14)
First-class: 255 MATCHES; 16,939 RUNS, AVERAGE 44.57; 64 WICKETS, AVERAGE 31.37
Tests (1899 to 1911-12): 48 MATCHES; 3,163 RUNS, AVERAGE 39.04; 8 WICKETS, AVERAGE 39.62

Trumper's figures cannot compare with those of Bradman, yet there is a unanimity of opinion that he was the greatest batsman Australia produced before the arrival of Bradman. Right-handed, effortless, perfectly balanced and supple, he moved into his shots with a grace that bewitched all who saw him. He was modest, kindly and immensely popular. Arthur Mailey described the effect that Trumper had on people when he recalled, as a junior, bowling the great man and feeling that he had killed a dove. He scored 0 and 11 in his first Test, and in his second, at Lord's, he made a chanceless unbeaten 135. He was 21.

Marcus Trescothick: after an outstanding five seasons his career ran into problems.

By the end of that tour, he was opening the innings, and when Australia arrived in England in 1902 he was supreme. At Old Trafford, he reached his century in 108 minutes before lunch on the first day.

In 1903-04, at Sydney, he reached his century in 94 minutes and, batting No. 5, he got 185 not out. He made another century in the same series. Seven years later, South Africa visited Australia and Trumper scored 159 at Melbourne and 214 not out, a Test record for Australia at the time, at Adelaide.

He died of Bright's disease in 1915, and a country mourned.

CHARLES TURNER

Born: 16 NOVEMBER 1862, BATHURST, NEW SOUTH WALES, AUSTRALIA
Died: 1 JANUARY 1944, MANLY, SYDNEY, NEW SOUTH WALES, AUSTRALIA
Teams: NEW SOUTH WALES (1882-83 TO 1909-10)
First-class: 155 MATCHES; 3,856 RUNS, AVERAGE 15.54; 993 WICKETS, AVERAGE 14.25
Tests (1886-87 to 1894-95): 17 MATCHES; 323 RUNS, AVERAGE 11.53; 101 WICKETS, AVERAGE 16.53

Short and thick-set, Turner bowled fast-medium and shot to fame when he took 17 wickets against Alfred Shaw's England side in 1881-82. This feat was for Twenty-two of Bathurst, and by the following season he was in the NSW side. On the occasion of his Test debut at Sydney in 1887, he took 6 for 15 as England were bowled out for 45, their lowest-ever score against Australia. From this moment, the legend of "Turner the Terror" was born. In his next two Tests against England, he took nine wickets and 12 wickets, and his first three Tests in England in 1888, brought him 21 wickets in four innings. Yet England still won the series.

He formed a lethal partnership with Ferris, and on that 1888 tour they took 534 wickets between them in all matches. In 1887-88, Turner had become the first bowler to take 100 wickets in an Australian season.

In 1894-95, having taken 11 wickets in two Tests against England, he was dropped. Reinstated for the fourth Test, he took seven wickets as Australia won by an innings, but he was dropped again. Belatedly receiving an invitation to tour England in 1896, he declined through pressure of business and passed out of Test cricket.

GLENN TURNER

Born: 26 MAY 1947, DUNEDIN, NEW ZEALAND
Teams: OTAGO (1964-65 TO 1982-83); NORTHERN DISTRICTS (1976-77); WORCESTERSHIRE (1967-82)
First-class: 455 MATCHES; 34,346 RUNS, AVERAGE 49.70; 5 WICKETS, AVERAGE 37.80
Tests (1968-69 to 1982-83): 41 MATCHES; 2,991 RUNS, AVERAGE 44.64; NO WICKETS FOR 5 RUNS

Glenn Turner is arguably the greatest batsman New Zealand has ever produced – and certainly the country's best professional. He is the only New Zealand batsman to have scored more than 30,000 runs in his career and the only New Zealand batsman to have scored a hundred centuries (103). His 100th hundred came in his last season with Worcestershire in 1982, when he hit the highest score of his career, 311 not out against Warwickshire at Worcester.

Turner was the total professional cricketer. He dedicated himself to cricket, working tirelessly to earn his fare to England and joining Worcestershire to learn the game in the hard grind of county cricket. He never forgot a lesson, and he developed from the "strokeless wonder" of his early days to a free-scoring opening batsman capable of making runs as quickly as anybody. He began his Test career with a "duck" against the West Indies in 1968-69, but in his second Test he

Glenn Turner: he could hardly hit the ball off the pitch in his younger days, but hard work saw him develop into an attractive batsman.

hit 74, and New Zealand won. His first Test century came in Pakistan in November 1969, when he batted over seven hours for 110.

It was in the 1971-72 series in the Caribbean that Turner established himself as one of the most accomplished batsmen in world cricket. He hit 672 runs in the series, including two double-centuries, at an average of 96.

On the tour of England in 1973, he reached a thousand runs by the end of May, the only New Zealander to have achieved the feat, but he disappointed in the Test series. He led New Zealand in the World Cup in 1975, and in the series against India which followed.

In 1978, he decided to give all his efforts to Worcestershire, and the first rift occurred between Turner and the New Zealand authorities. He did return to Test cricket, but his relationship with the New Zealand Board was never an easy one. He saw them as amateurs in a professional world.

He subsequently managed and coached New Zealand sides, but he was replaced in 1997, mainly because many considered him too authoritarian and too demanding while stinting with praise.

Whatever his failings as a coach, Glenn Turner remains one of the most dedicated, most professional and most successful cricketers in New Zealand's history, and it is unlikely that his records will ever be beaten.

FRANK TYSON

Born: 6 JUNE 1930, FARNWORTH, LANCASHIRE
Teams: NORTHAMPTONSHIRE (1952-60)
First-class: 244 MATCHES; 4,103 RUNS, AVERAGE 17.09; 767 WICKETS, AVERAGE 20.89
Tests (1954 to 1958-59): 17 MATCHES; 230 RUNS, AVERAGE 10.95; 76 WICKETS, AVERAGE 18.56

Tall and strong, "Typhoon" Tyson was, for all too brief a period, the most aggressive and lethal fast bowler in the world. His exceptional speed was recognized from the start of his career, but his run-up was excessive and his accuracy was not always to be relied upon. He was chosen to tour Australia in 1954-55 ahead of Freddie Trueman, and made his Test debut against Pakistan shortly before the party left for the southern hemisphere. He took four wickets in the first innings, but England lost.

In the first Test, at Brisbane, he took 1 for 160, and England lost by an innings but, in the second match, at Sydney, he had 4 for 45 and 6 for 85. He bowled with amazing stamina and great speed, and England won a remarkable victory. He took 17 wickets in the remaining Tests and England went on to win their first rubber in Australia for 22 years and so retain the Ashes. He bowled with considerable success against South Africa the following summer, but wear and tear and injuries took their toll, and he played in only a handful of Tests before his retirement.

An English graduate from Durham University, he settled in Australia where he taught, coached, wrote and commentated on the game.

POLLY UMRIGAR

Born: 28 MARCH 1926, SHOLAPUR, MAHARASHTRA, INDIA
Died: 7 NOVEMBER 2006, BOMBAY
 Teams: PARSEES (1944-45 TO 1945-46); BOMBAY (1946-47 TO 1962-63); GUJARAT (1950-51 TO 1951-52)
First-class: 243 MATCHES; 16,155 RUNS, AVERAGE 52.28; 325 WICKETS, AVERAGE 25.68
Tests (1948-49 to 1961-62): 59 MATCHES; 3,631 RUNS, AVERAGE 42.22; 35 WICKETS, AVERAGE 42.08

A tall, forceful batsman, medium-pace bowler and splendid fielder, "Polly" Umrigar was a dashing cricketer who led Bombay to five successive Ranji Trophy triumphs at the beginning of their period of dominance in the competition. He was the leading Indian batsman of his generation and made his Test debut in 1948, but he had to wait until the last match of the series against England in 1951-52, for his second cap. He hit 130 not out, India

won by an innings and Umrigar's international career was launched.

He had a wretched time in England in 1952, as did other Indian batsmen, but he topped the averages in the inaugural series with Pakistan in 1952-53. In the first Test against New Zealand at Hyderabad in 1955-56, he made India's first double-century in Test cricket, 223. He later took over the captaincy and won the series. He led India in eight Tests and hit 12 Test centuries.

Derek Underwood: the Kent player led the England spin attack for 15 years.

DEREK UNDERWOOD

Born: 8 JUNE 1945, BROMLEY, KENT
Teams: KENT (1963-87)
First-class: 676 MATCHES; 5,165 RUNS, AVERAGE 10.12; 2,465 WICKETS, AVERAGE 20.28
Tests (1966 to 1981-82): 86 MATCHES; 937 RUNS, AVERAGE 11.56; 297 WICKETS, AVERAGE 25.83

Derek Underwood was the leading spin bowler in England for nearly 20 years. Left-arm, he bowled at a pace quicker than most spinners, but he combined accuracy with variety and was a danger to batsmen

on any wicket. His career began sensationally for he was the youngest player to take 100 wickets in his debut season, but he was wicketless on his Test debut, against the West Indies, three years later. The following year, 1967, he had his first five-wicket Test haul, against Pakistan, and in the final match of the Ashes series in 1968, bowled England to victory at The Oval with 7 for 50 in the second innings. He continued to thrive and on damp wickets he was unplayable. He established records against New Zealand, and at Lord's in 1974, became the only English bowler to take 13 wickets in a Test against Pakistan. His 8 for 51 in the second innings was a record.

His partnership with wicket-keeper Knott was vital and, but for the fact that Underwood became involved with World Series Cricket and a rebel tour to South Africa, he might well have become the leading wicket-taker in Test cricket.

ALF VALENTINE

Born: 28 APRIL 1930, KINGSTON, JAMAICA
Died: 11 MAY 2004, ORLANDO, FLORIDA, USA
Teams: JAMAICA (1949-50 TO 1964-65)
First-class: 125 MATCHES; 470 RUNS, AVERAGE 5.00; 475 WICKETS, AVERAGE 26.21
Tests (1950 to 1961-62): 36 MATCHES; 141 RUNS, AVERAGE 4.70; 139 WICKETS, AVERAGE 30.32

Tall and slim, Alf Valentine was a slow left-arm spinner who arrived in England in 1950 with little experience of first-class cricket. He was to take 123 wickets on the tour, 33 of them in Tests. He began with 8 for 104 and 3 for 100 at Old Trafford, but the West Indies lost. The sensation came at Lord's, when he and Ramadhin bowled the West Indies to a famous victory and were celebrated in a calypso.

He showed his real quality with 24 wickets in Australia in 1951-52, when his 6 for 102 in the second innings in Adelaide gave the West Indies their sole victory in the series. He was equally successful against India in 1952-53, but he had declined by the time England went to the Caribbean the following year and was ineffective in England in 1957 and 1963.

MICHAEL VAUGHAN

Born: 29 OCTOBER 1974, MANCHESTER, LANCASHIRE
Teams: YORKSHIRE (1993-2009)
First-class: 266 MATCHES; 16,213 RUNS, AVERAGE 37.01; 114 WICKETS, AVERAGE 46.00
Tests (1999-2000 to 2008): 82 MATCHES; 5,719 RUNS, AVERAGE 41.44; 6 WICKETS, AVERAGE 93.50

Because Vaughan's family moved from Manchester to Sheffield it was with Yorkshire that he became a gritty, unspectacular middle-order batsman. Although he won an Under-15 Cricketer of the Year award and was England Under-19 captain, the unfriendly pitches at Headingley meant that he batted with caution, thus delaying his Test debut until 1999-2000. He was encouraged to develop a more aggressive style by Yorkshire's Australian player Darren Lehmann, transforming his batting and success, especially after he first opened for England in New Zealand in 2001-02. In 14 Tests in 2002 he was England's most reliable batsman, scoring 1,481 runs, average 61.70, with six centuries. Another century in the final Ashes match at Sydney early in 2003 gave him 633 runs for the series, average 58.20, and the Player of the Series award.

He succeeded Nasser Hussain as England captain in the 2003 season, and led England to a 3-0 series win in the West Indies in 2003-04. In 2005, he captained England in the victorious Ashes series. Injuries blighted the remainder of his career and he retired in the middle of the 2009 season.

DILIP VENGSARKAR

Born: 6 APRIL 1956, RAJAPUR, BOMBAY, INDIA
Teams: BOMBAY (1975-76 TO 1991-92)
First-class: 260 MATCHES; 17,868 RUNS, AVERAGE 52.86; 1 WICKET, AVERAGE 126.00
Tests (1975-76 to 1991-92): 116 MATCHES; 6,868 RUNS, AVERAGE 42.13; NO WICKETS FOR 36 RUNS

Michael Vaughan: an astute captain and a prolific run-scorer.

For a decade only Sunil Gavaskar stood ahead of Dilip Vengsarkar as India's most prolific run-scorer in Test history, and only Gavaskar had scored more Test centuries for India than Vengsarkar's 17. He was a batsman of true quality, an artist and fluent stroke-maker who was rushed into the Test side as an opener before his 20th birthday, but who settled to become India's regular No. 3. In 1976-77, he had his hand broken by a ball from Bob Willis, but he established himself in Australia the following season. In 1978-79, he scored two Test centuries against the West Indies and, in Calcutta, where he made an unbeaten 157, he and Gavaskar shared a record unbroken stand of 344 for the second wicket.

In 1979, he made a century in the Lord's Test, and was to repeat this feat in 1982 and 1986 to establish a record. India won the Lord's Test in 1986, and Vengsarkar followed his century with 61 and 102 not out in difficult conditions at Headingley to help India clinch the series. He

captained India in ten Tests and scored centuries against all nations he faced, with the exception of New Zealand.

S. VENKATARAGHAVAN

Born: 21 APRIL 1945, MADRAS, INDIA
Teams: MADRAS/TAMIL NADU (1963-64 TO 1984-85); DERBYSHIRE (1973-75)
First-class: 341 MATCHES; 6,617 RUNS, AVERAGE 17.73; 1,390 WICKETS, AVERAGE 24.14
Tests (1964-65 to 1983-84): 57 MATCHES; 748 RUNS, AVERAGE 11.68; 156 WICKETS, AVERAGE 36.11

An intelligent off-break bowler and fine close-to-the-wicket fielder, Venkataraghavan made his Test debut against New Zealand in 1964-65, and in the fourth and final Test of the series he produced his best performance in international cricket, taking 8 for 72 and 4 for 80 to bowl India to victory. For much of his Test career he vied with Prasanna for the off-spinner's spot in the Indian side, but Venkataraghavan bowled well on the 1971 tour of England and played an important role in India's victory in the series. He captained India in the World Cup in 1975, and also on the tour of England in 1979.

He had productive years with Derbyshire, taking 68 wickets in 1975. He took up umpiring after retiring and is now recognised as one of the world's leading umpires.

HEDLEY VERITY

Born: 18 MAY 1905, HEADINGLEY, LEEDS, YORKSHIRE
Died: 31 JULY 1943, CASERTA, ITALY
Teams: YORKSHIRE (1930-39)
First-class: 378 MATCHES; 5,605 RUNS, AVERAGE 18.08; 1,956 WICKETS, AVERAGE 14.90
Tests (1931-1939): 40 MATCHES; 669 RUNS, AVERAGE 20.90; 144 WICKETS, AVERAGE 24.37

The strength of Yorkshire cricket was founded on sound batting and on great slow left-arm bowlers - Peate, Peel, Rhodes and, in the 1930s, Hedley Verity. Quicker than many of his type, Verity was relentlessly accurate and could spin the ball viciously. He was an intelligent cricketer, dignified and

Daniel Vettori: became New Zealand's youngest-ever Test player when he made his debut in 1996–97.

equable of temperament, who took 100 wickets in a season nine times. In 1935, 1936 and 1937, he exceeded 200 wickets.

On a damp pitch at Lord's in 1934, he took 14 Australian wickets in a day, 15 for 104 in the match, and bowled England to an innings victory. He was a key member of the England side for seven years.

At Headingley, in 1932, he took all ten Nottinghamshire wickets for ten runs, a world record which remains unequalled. He had taken all ten Warwickshire wickets on the same ground the previous season. On 1 September 1939, he took 7 for 9 as Yorkshire beat Sussex at Hove.

During the war, he was commissioned in the Green Howards and was wounded leading his men in an 8th Army attack in Sicily during the invasion of Italy in 1943. He died of his wounds some days later.

DANIEL VETTORI

Born: 27 JANUARY 1979, EPSOM, AUCKLAND, NEW ZEALAND
Teams: NORTHERN DISTRICTS (1996-97 TO 2009-10); NOTTINGHAMSHIRE (2003), WARWICKSHIRE (2006), DELHI DAREDEVILS (2008-09)
First-class: 157 MATCHES; 6,014 RUNS, AVERAGE 30.37; 519 WICKETS, AVERAGE 32.05
Tests (1996-97 to 2010-11): 104 MATCHES; 4,159 RUNS, AVERAGE 30.35; 344 WICKETS, AVERAGE 33.75

First memories of Vettori in England are of the 1999 Lord's Test, when he scored a delightful, though unexpected, 54 and, even more unexpected, New Zealand won by nine wickets. In the fourth Test in the series, Vettori hit another 50 and, more importantly, his left-arm spin captured five wickets – New Zealand won by 83 runs, clinching the Test series. The bespectacled youth, looking more like 15 than his actual 20, had, in 1997, become New Zealand's youngest Test cricketer. He went on to reach 100 Test wickets in record time. A back injury caused him problems in 2003; he did, however, come to England a second time in 2004, though he returned early with a hamstring injury. Vettori remains an automatic choice for New Zealand's Test and one-day squads, with over 200 one-day internationals to his name. He succeeded Stephen Fleming as captain in 2007-08.

GUNDAPPA VISWANATH

Born: 12 FEBRUARY 1949, BHADRAVATI, MYSORE, INDIA
Teams: MYSORE/KARNATAKA (1967-68 TO 1987-88)
First-class: 308 MATCHES; 17,970 RUNS, AVERAGE 40.93; 15 WICKETS, AVERAGE 48.60
Tests (1969-70 to 1982-83): 91 MATCHES; 6,080 RUNS, AVERAGE 41.93; 1 WICKET, AVERAGE 46.00

Brother-in-law to Sunil Gavaskar, Viswanath was a most attractive and attacking middle-order batsman who hit 230 in 340 minutes on the occasion of his first-class debut for Mysore against Andhra. In 1969-70, he made his Test debut for India against Australia at Kanpur. He was out for 0 in the first innings but made 137 in the second. It was the first of 14 Test hundreds, and only against Sri Lanka did he fail to score a century. He played in a record 87 consecutive Tests for India and captained them on two occasions.

A kind and gentle man, characteristics reflected in his delightful batting, he toured England four times and played in all the Tests on those tours, but his highest Test score came at Madras in 1981-82, when he added 316 with Yashpal Sharma. His 222 was, at the time, the highest score made by an Indian batsman against England. After retiring as a player, Viswanath became chairman of the Indian selectors.

CLYDE WALCOTT

Born: 17 JANUARY 1926, NEW ORLEANS, ST MICHAEL, BARBADOS
Teams: BARBADOS (1941-42 TO 1955-56); BRITISH GUIANA (1954-55 TO 1963-64)
First-class: 146 MATCHES; 11,820 RUNS, AVERAGE 56.55; 35 WICKETS, AVERAGE 36.25; CAUGHT 174, STUMPED 33
Tests (1947-48 to 1959-60): 44 MATCHES; 3,798 RUNS, AVERAGE 56.68; 11 WICKETS, AVERAGE 37.00; CAUGHT 53, STUMPED 11

In the years immediately after the Second World War, the West Indies were powered by three great batsmen: the Three Ws – Worrell, Weekes and Walcott. In 1945-46, Walcott and Worrell added an unbroken 574 for Barbados's fourth wicket against Trinidad. It was just a sample of what was to come. Walcott was a giant of a man who could hit the ball with tremendous power and could play all the shots. He was also a capable wicket-keeper who kept to the wiles of Ramadhin and Valentine, an excellent slip and a useful medium-pace bowler.

At Lord's in 1950, he scored 168 not out in the second Test and shared a record stand of 211 with Gomez for the sixth wicket. He also dominated the series against England in 1953-54, and against Australia in 1954-55. He made three centuries against England, the highest being 220 at Bridgetown, and against Australia he hit five centuries in the series, scoring a century in each innings of the second and fifth Tests, even though Australia took the rubber by three matches to nil. In all, he hit 15 Test centuries, and his highest score in first-class cricket was the 314 not out which he scored during his record partnership with Worrell in 1945-46, when he was 20 years old.

He played in the Lancashire League in the 1950s, managed several West Indian sides after his retirement and was awarded the OBE for his services to the game. He coached and commentated and was president of the West Indian Board for some years. He became chairman of the International Cricket Council and was knighted in 1994.

COURTNEY WALSH

SEE PAGE 243

DOUG WALTERS

Born: 21 DECEMBER 1945, MARSHDALE, DUNGOG, NEW SOUTH WALES, AUSTRALIA
Teams: NEW SOUTH WALES (1962-63 TO 1980-81)
First-class: 258 MATCHES; 16,180 RUNS, AVERAGE 43.84; 190 WICKETS, AVERAGE 35.69
Tests (1965-66 to 1980-81): 74 MATCHES; 5,357 RUNS, AVERAGE 48.26; 49 WICKETS, AVERAGE 29.08

Doug Walters was an attacking right-handed batsman who delighted with his stroke-play and his sense of adventure. He was also a successful medium-pace bowler. He triumphed in Australia, but crowds in England and South Africa never saw the best of him. He burst upon the scene with 155 on his debut against England at Brisbane in 1965-66, and made 115 in his second Test, at Melbourne. On leave from national service in 1967-68, he made 93, 62 not out, 94 and run out 5 against India. Released for the tour of England in 1968, he was not a success and made three more trips without doing himself justice. He was impetuous, a weakness that bowlers exploited by attacking his off-stump. Elsewhere he thrived.

Against the West Indies in Australia in 1968-69, he scored 118, 110, 50, 242 and 103 in successive Test innings to become the first to score four centuries in a rubber against the West Indies. At Christchurch in 1976-77, he made 250 against New Zealand, his highest Test score. In all, he made 15 Test hundreds.

Clyde Walcott: the burliest and the strongest of the famous Three Ws who revived West Indian cricket after the Second World War, he was a powerful batsman and a surprisingly neat wicket-keeper.

COURTNEY WALSH
Founder of the 500 Club

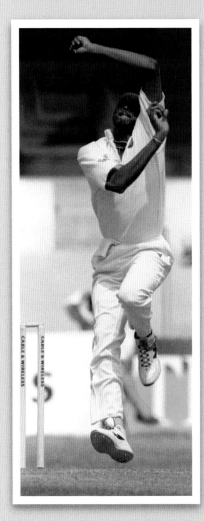

Courtney Walsh: endless resources of energy took him past the 500 Test wicket mark.

Courtney Walsh was the first bowler to take 500 Test wickets. Remarkably for a fast bowler, he captured over 1,800 wickets in all, for the West Indies, Jamaica and Gloucestershire. He bowled 85,443 deliveries, a testament to his dedication, enthusiasm and fitness.

Walsh puts his longevity as a bowler down to a health regimen which he followed from his early days. He made his first-class debut aged 19 in 1981-82 and was in the West Indian party which toured England in 1984, but without playing in a Test. He took 14 wickets in eight other matches and began a 15-year association with Gloucestershire. He began his Test career in the following winter.

At 6ft 51/2in Walsh brought the ball down from about 10ft high. His action was not classical, but it was economical enough to keep him free from serious injury. He bowled very fast, usually just outside off stump and from his height could make the ball rise steeply.

His first big impact in Tests was in Pakistan in 1986-87, after the West Indies had been routed for 53 in the first Test. His 4 for 21 in the second innings helped demolish Pakistan for 77 to tie the rubber. He was the best bowler in India in 1987-88, with 26 wickets at 16.8 in a halved series.

Gradually Walsh came more to the fore in the West Indies fast battery. In the inaugural Test with South Africa at Bridgetown in 1991-92, South Africa began the last day on 122 for 2, needing 80 to win. A spell of 4 for 8 in 11 overs from Walsh left them 54 short. Another last ditch attempt came in 1992-93 in Australia, in the fourth Test at Adelaide, with Australia one up. Walsh came on with Australia needing three to win with one wicket left. A single was scored, but off the fifth ball McDermott edged to the keeper and the West Indies won by one run. They then won the last Test to take the series 2-1.

With England in the West Indies in 1993-94, Walsh was criticized after the first Test for bowling bumpers at England's Devon Malcolm, who returned to England for treatment. In the third Test, England were dismissed for 46 with Ambrose taking 6 for 46 and Walsh 3 for 17. They bowled unchanged throughout the innings. For the final Test, with West Indies 3-1 up, Walsh began the first of two spells as captain. It was the match in which Lara broke the world Test record with 375.

Walsh passed Kapil Dev's record of 434 Test wickets on home soil in Jamaica in 1999-2000 with Zimbabwe the visitors. Against England in 2000 he took 34 wickets, but England won 3-1. His 500th wicket came in the second Test against South Africa in Trinidad in 2000-01.

He retired at the end of the series with 519 Test wickets. His wickets weren't his only Test record. A stylish No. 11 batsman he held the record for the most ducks (43) and the most not-outs (61).

> **FIRST-CLASS CAREER**
> **(1981-82 to 2001-02, 429 matches)**
> **Batting:** RUNS 4,530; AVERAGE 11.32; HIGHEST SCORE 66; CENTURIES 0
> **Bowling:** WICKETS 1,807; RUNS 39,233; AVERAGE 21.71; BEST 9-72
> **Catches:** 117
>
> **TESTS**
> **(1984-85 to 2000-01, 132 MATCHES)**
> **Batting:** RUNS 936; AVERAGE 7.54; HIGHEST SCORE 30 NOT OUT; CENTURIES 0
> **Bowling:** WICKETS 519; RUNS 12,688; AVERAGE 24.44; BEST 7-37
> **Catches:** 29

1962	1981-82	1984	1984	1987
Born Courtney Andrew Walsh on 30 October, at Kingston, Jamaica	Made first-class debut for Jamaica	Made Test debut for West Indies against Australia at Perth, 9-12 November as fourth fast bowler behind Marshall, Garner and Holding. He bowled only in the second innings, taking 2 for 43.	Played for Gloucestershire for the first time in the County Championship, an association that would last for 15 years	Was selected as one of Wisden's five Cricketers of the Year

1997	1998	2000	2001
Took his 350th Test wicket, v Pakistan at Karachi	Played in 100th Test match v England at Georgetown, Guyana, and took his 100th Test wicket against England, 27 February-2 March	Passed Kapil Dev's record of 434 wickets when Zimbabwe's Henry Olonga was caught at short leg to become his 435th wicket, at his home ground, Kingston, 24-28 March. He received £20,000 from gate receipts	Reached 500 Test wickets after dismissing Gary Kirsten and Jacques Kallis in the same over v South Africa in Trinidad, 17-21 March

WAQAR YOUNIS

Born: 17 NOVEMBER 1971, VEHARI, PAKISTAN
Teams: MULTAN (1987-88 TO 1990-91 AND 1997-98);
UNITED BANK (1988-89 TO 1996-97); RAWALPINDI
(1998-99); REDCO (1999-00); SURREY (1990-93);
GLAMORGAN (1997-98); NATIONAL BANK
(2001-02); WARWICKSHIRE (2003)
First-class: 228 MATCHES; 2,972 RUNS, AVERAGE 13.38;
956 WICKETS, AVERAGE 22.33
Tests (1989-90 to 2002-03): 87 MATCHES; 1,010
RUNS, AVERAGE 10.20; 373 WICKETS, AVERAGE
23.56

Many believe Waqar Younis is the best fast bowler to have appeared in Test cricket since the Second World War. He is able to move the ball late both ways at great pace and possesses a deadly yorker. In 1991, playing for Surrey on the unresponsive wickets at The Oval, he was the leading bowler in England with 113 wickets. His Test debut against India at Karachi in 1989-90, had seen him take 4 for 80 and, by the time he had played ten Tests he had 50 victims to his credit. With Wasim Akram, he formed a lethal partnership for Pakistan which is now accepted as one of the great fast-bowling duos of all time. Waqar took a record 29 wickets in a three-match series against New Zealand in 1990-91, and his 100th victim came in his 20th Test. He routed England with a record 22 wickets in 1992, and was devastating again in 1996.

He had a second spell in Championship cricket, for Glamorgan in 1997 and 1998, but in the latter season, he only played four matches before being sent home with an elbow injury. Since then he has not been so successful for Pakistan, though he did play in the 1999 World Cup and captained his country on their 2001 tour of England – his seven wickets in that Test series cost 35 runs each.

JOHNNY WARDLE

Born: 8 JANUARY 1923, ARDSLEY, YORKSHIRE
Died: 23 JULY 1985, HATFIELD, DONCASTER, YORKSHIRE
Teams: YORKSHIRE (1946-58)
First-class: 412 MATCHES; 7,333 RUNS, AVERAGE 16.08;
1,846 WICKETS, AVERAGE 18.97
Tests (1947-48 to 1957): 28 MATCHES; 653 RUNS,
AVERAGE 19.78; 102 WICKETS, AVERAGE 20.39

Johnny Wardle was the best left-arm wrist spinner of his generation, one in a long line of great Yorkshire slow left-arm bowlers. He had an infinite variety of deliveries in his armoury and was a wicket-taker on any surface. He was a hard-hitting late-order batsman and a keen fielder.

He made his Test debut on the 1947-48 tour of the West Indies, but was poorly used by G.O. Allen, and his Test appearances were to remain intermittent for some seasons as he vied first with Jack Young and then with Tony Lock. He played in the first three Tests in 1953 when England regained the Ashes and captured 13 wickets, but he gave way to Lock for the last two Tests.

He was outstanding in South Africa in 1956-57, taking 23 wickets in four Tests, and he played in one Test against the West Indies the following summer, but that marked the end of his international career. He put his name to newspaper articles criticizing the Yorkshire captain and some of his colleagues and was sacked by his county, and the MCC withdrew the invitation he had been sent to tour Australia in 1958-59. To the crowd he had seemed a jolly prankster; many of his team-mates saw a different character. It was a sad end to what had been a fine career.

SHANE WARNE

SEE PAGE 247

SHANE WATSON

Born: 17 JUNE 1981, IPSWICH, QUEENSLAND, AUSTRALIA
Teams: TASMANIA (2000-01 TO 2003-04);
QUEENSLAND (2004-05 TO 2008-09);
NEW SOUTH WALES (2009-10 TO 2010-11)
First-class: 94 MATCHES; 6,921 RUNS, AVERAGE 46.76;
173 WICKETS, AVERAGE 28.46
Tests (1937-56): 27 MATCHES; 1,953 RUNS,
AVERAGE 41.55; 43 WICKETS, AVERAGE 31.41

Shane Watson had to overcome all sorts of physical frailties to build himself into a Test all-rounder. He

Waqar Younis: with Wasim Akram formed one of the most potent new-ball post-war attacks.

began with Tasmania as a hard-hitting middle-order batsman, and right-arm fast-medium bowler. He was the Bradman Young Cricketer of the Year in 2002. Two years later he transferred to Queensland, making his Test debut the same season against Pakistan. He excelled in the Sheffield Shield of 2006, when he scored 203 not out in a total of 900 for 6, as Queensland beat Victoria in the final. His career changed in the Ashes series in England in 2005, when he was asked to open in the third Test, and scored 62 and 53. His five innings in the series ranged from 34 to 62, and he averaged 48.00. He made a habit of scoring 50s but not going to a century, until he finally made his maiden Test century (120 not out) against Pakistan at Melbourne in 2009-10. He was Australia's Player of the Year in both One-Day Internationals and Test Matches for 2010-11 and also won the Allan Border Medal.

WASIM AKRAM

Born: 3 JUNE 1966, LAHORE, PAKISTAN
Teams: PACO (1984-85); LAHORE (1985-86); LANCASHIRE (1988-1997); PIA (1995-03); HAMPSHIRE (2003)
First-class: 257 MATCHES; 7,161 RUNS, AVERAGE 22.73; 1,042 WICKETS, AVERAGE 21.64
Tests (1984-85 to 2001-02): 104 MATCHES; 2,898 RUNS, AVERAGE 22.64; 414 WICKETS, AVERAGE 23.62

Wasim Akram: an inspirational all-rounder who led from the front.

Wasim Akram developed into one of the great all-rounders of world cricket. A left-arm fast bowler with a capacity to swing the ball late either way, in 1996 at The Oval he became the second Pakistani bowler to take 300 wickets in Test cricket. Two months later, against Zimbabwe in Sheikhupura, he hit 257 not out batting at No. 8, a Test record, and shared a record eighth-wicket stand of 313 with Saqlain Mushtaq. He is a ferocious hitter of the ball, unwinding like a spring, and was very effective in one-day cricket.

Wasim Akram formed, with Waqar Younis, one of the most feared fast-bowling partnerships cricket has known. He was captain of Pakistan for 25 Tests, during which time he enjoyed a run of nine wins and two draws, including a 2-0 series win in England. In 1999-2000 – his final season as captain – he became the first Pakistan bowler to capture 400 wickets in Tests.

He was a fine acquisition for Lancashire, particularly effective in the one-day game, helping them to win four limited-over trophies. Wasim's final season in Championship cricket for Lancashire came in 1997, when he broke down after just one game.

MARK WAUGH

Born: 2 JUNE 1965, CANTERBURY, SYDNEY, NEW SOUTH WALES, AUSTRALIA
Teams: NEW SOUTH WALES (1985-86 TO 2003-04); ESSEX (1988-90, 1992 AND 2002)
First-class: 368 MATCHES; 26,855 RUNS, AVERAGE 52.04; 208 WICKETS, AVERAGE 40.98
Tests (1990-91 to 2002-03): 128 MATCHES; 8,029 RUNS, AVERAGE 41.81; 59 WICKETS, AVERAGE 41.16

When English crowds first saw Mark Waugh play for Essex they wondered how on earth he had not claimed a place in the Australian side alongside his twin brother.

He was at last rewarded with a Test cap against England at Adelaide in 1990-91 and made an outstanding 138. He was to remain in the Australian side for the next 12 years. He and his twin brother, Steve, established a world-record fifth-wicket partnership for New South Wales against Western Australia in 1990-91 with an unbroken stand

Mark Waugh: a stylish right-hand batsman who emerged from his twin brother's shadow.

of 464. Mark Waugh himself made 229 not out. It turned out to be the highest score of what was a very distinguished career.

On the 2001 tour of England he played in all five Tests, averaging 86.00 with the bat. If he had a fault, it was that he sometimes gave his wicket away in what seemed a careless or languid manner.

STEVE WAUGH

SEE PAGE 248

EVERTON WEEKES

Born: 26 FEBRUARY 1925, WESTBURY, ST MICHAEL, BARBADOS
Teams: BARBADOS (1944-45 TO 1963-64)
First-class: 152 MATCHES; 12,010 RUNS, AVERAGE 55.34; 17 WICKETS, AVERAGE 43.00
Tests (1947-48 to 1957-58): 48 MATCHES; 4,455 RUNS, AVERAGE 58.61; 1 WICKET, AVERAGE 77.00

Everton Weekes was a brilliant, attacking, right-handed batsman, glorious to watch and one of the legendary Three Ws – along with Frank Worrell and Clyde Walcott.

The first of his 15 Test centuries came in his fourth match, against England at Kingston, Jamaica. This was followed by centuries in his next four Test innings, against India a year later. These included a century in each innings in Calcutta. He was close to hitting six hundreds in successive Test innings, but was run out for 90 in Madras. He established a record in the final Test when he made 56 in the first innings, so becoming the only batsman to hit seven consecutive 50s in Test cricket. He enjoyed a fine tour of England in 1950, and made 206 against them in 1953-54, but returning to England in 1957 he failed to flourish, 90 being his best.

Troubled by sinus problems, he left the Test scene earlier than expected. Like the other two Ws, he was knighted for his services to the game.

BOB WILLIS

Born: 30 MAY 1949, SUNDERLAND, COUNTY DURHAM
Teams: SURREY (1969-71); WARWICKSHIRE (1972-84); NORTHERN TRANSVAAL (1972-73)
First-class: 308 MATCHES; 2,690 RUNS, AVERAGE 14.30; 899 WICKETS, AVERAGE 24.99
Tests (1970-71 to 1984): 90 MATCHES; 840 RUNS, AVERAGE 11.50; 325 WICKETS, AVERAGE 25.20

Tall, with an unorthodox, open-chested action, Bob Willis made himself one of England's greatest fast bowlers, and only Ian Botham has taken more wickets for England.

He first played for Surrey in 1969 and, within 18 months, was on his way to Australia as a replacement for the injured Alan Ward. Surrey's reluctance to give him his county cap persuaded him to join Warwickshire, whom he captained from 1980 to 1984. In truth, he was never a great performer in county cricket, but in Tests no man has given more for his country. At Headingley in 1981, he took 8 for 43 in Australia's second innings to give England victory by 18 runs. He operated with amazing concentration, as if he were a man possessed. The Test arena has rarely seen a better or more passionate display of fast bowling.

He captained England from 1982 to 1984, having been vice-captain on several tours. He has since acted as a commentator and as head of the National Sporting Club.

Bob Willis: one of England's great fast bowlers.

SHANE WARNE
The Spin Doctor

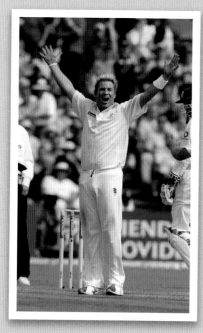

Shane Warne: record-breaking leg-spinner.

Shane Warne is possibly the greatest spin bowler the game has ever seen, and, in 2000, Wisden named him as one of the five cricketers of the century.

His Test debut came in the third Test of the 1991-92 series against India at Sydney, but his first big success came in Sri Lanka the following season, when he snatched victory from Sri Lanka by taking the last three wickets without conceding a run for a 16-run win. Prior to that spell his one Test wicket had cost 346 runs.

It was when he was recalled for the second Test against the West Indies starting in Melbourne on 26 December 1992 that Warne's career took off. He spun Australia to victory, claiming seven wickets for 21 in a final spell. That summer he came to England, and at Old Trafford bowled possibly the most famous ball in Test cricket, his first in a Test in England, an inswinging leg-break which pitched outside Mike Gatting's leg stump and hit the off stump. Later, at Edgbaston, the England skipper Graham Gooch was bowled round his legs by a prodigious leg-break. Warne took a series-winning 34 wickets and set the pattern for his career.

There have been hiccups. In 1995 Warne and Mark Waugh were fined by the Australian Cricket Board for selling information to an Indian bookmaker Then there was a finger operation in 1996, which afterwards gave him pain and caused him to rethink his strategies. In 1998, he suffered a shoulder injury, which meant that when the 1998-99 Ashes series started, he was in the commentary box rather than on the field. His replacement leg spinner was Stuart MacGill. They played together in the first three Tests in the following West Indies tour, but for the fourth, Warne, vice-captain and selector, was dropped, against his will. Australia won the match and the series was drawn 2-2. Back in England for the World Cup he regained his enthusiasm, was leading wicket-taker and Man of the Match in both semi-final and final.

In the series in New Zealand which followed, Warne passed Dennis Lillee's record of 355 Test wickets, becoming Australia's leading wicket-taker. Another finger injury caused another period of rest, but he was back on Australia's losing tour to India in 2000-01.

By February 2003 Warne, with 491 Test wickets, was on his way to Courtney Walsh's world record of 519. However, having declared that the 2003 World Cup would see his last one-day international appearances, he was sent home before a ball was bowled for being caught out for the "reckless act" of taking illegal substances. The ACB banned him for a year. Warne returned to the Test team in March 2004, on a tour of Sri Lanka. In the first Test, he secured the nine wickets needed to become the second bowler to reach 500 and at the series end he had 515.

Warne was at his best on the tour of England in 2005, and became the first to take 600 Test wickets in the third Test at Old Trafford. With 40 wickets altogether and some spirited batting, he shared the Player of the Series award. He retired from Test cricket after the 2006-07 Ashes series having become the first bowler to take 700 Test wickets. Warne captained Rajasthan Royals in the first two IPL campaigns, winning the 2008 competition.

FIRST-CLASS CAREER
(1990-91 to 2007, 301 matches)
Batting: RUNS 6,919; AVERAGE 19.43; HIGHEST SCORE 107 NOT OUT; CENTURIES 2
Bowling: WICKETS 1,319; RUNS 34,449; AVERAGE 26.11; BEST 8-71
Catches: 265

TESTS
(1991-92 to 2006-07, 145 MATCHES)
Batting: RUNS 3,154; AVERAGE 17.32; HIGHEST SCORE 99; CENTURIES 0
Bowling: WICKETS 708; RUNS 17,995; AVERAGE 25.41; BEST 8-71
Catches: 125

1969	1992	1993	1994	1997
Born Shane Keith Warne on 13 September at Ferntree Gully, Melbourne, Australia	Made Test debut v India at Sydney, 2–6 January. He took 1 for 150 (a tired Ravi Shastri on 206) in 45 overs	Famously became the first bowler to clean bowl a batsman with first ball in Ashes Tests, Mike Gatting at Old Trafford on 4 June	Took 100th Test wicket in 23rd Test, v South Africa	Passed 1,000 runs in Test cricket in his 58th Test match

2001-02	2004	2005	2005	2006-07
Took 450th Test wicket in 101st Test match, v South Africa at Durban	Became the leading wicket-taker in Tests, passing Muralitharan, with 533rd wicket, v India at Bangalore, October 6–10	Became the first to reach 600 Test wickets in Ashes Test at Old Trafford, August 11-15. He was joint Player of the Series	Took 96 Test wickets in the calendar year, a record, beating the previous mark by 15	Bowls Andrew Strauss at the MCG in the fourth Ashes Test to pass 700 Test wickets. Retires at end of series.

STEVE WAUGH
Self-made Man

FIRST-CLASS CAREER
(1984-85 to 2003-04, 356 matches)
Batting: RUNS 24,052; AVERAGE 51.94; HIGHEST
SCORE 216 NOT OUT; CENTURIES 79
Bowling: WICKETS 249; RUNS 8,155;
AVERAGE 32.75; BEST 6-51
Catches: 273

TESTS
(1985-86 to 2003-04, 168 MATCHES)
Batting: RUNS 10,927; AVERAGE 51.06;
HIGHEST SCORE 200; CENTURIES 32
Bowling: WICKETS 92; RUNS 3,445;
AVERAGE 37.44; BEST 5-28
Catches: 112

Waugh began as an all-rounder, combining ruthless batting with resourceful medium-paced bowling, but back problems gradually restricted his bowling.

Steve made his debut for New South Wales in 1984-85. He toured New Zealand and Zimbabwe and made his Test debut against India at Melbourne in 1985-86. He did well in a losing series against England in 1986-87, averaging 44 and getting 5 for 69 at Perth, and again, in Australia's World Cup-winning team in 1987. He spent the 1987 and 1988 English seasons with Somerset, scoring 1,314 runs, average 64, in the latter. Nevertheless, he had failed to make a century in 26 Tests when he came to England in 1989, but in the first Test he made 177 not out,

Steve Waugh: led Australia to unrivalled dominance.

and had made 393 runs in the series before being dismissed in the third Test – beating a Bradman record.

Losing his Test place to his twin brother 18 months later, he got his place back, making 100 against the the West Indies pace attack at Sydney in 1992-93. He did well in South Africa and was outstanding in the West Indies in 1994-95 when Australia ended Windies domination of cricket. His 200 at Kingston won the deciding Test.

He became captain of Australia in 1998-99 for the next tour of West Indies and led them in 15 of their record run of 16 consecutive Test wins, as well as their second World Cup success in 1999. He was controversially dropped from the one-day international side in 2002, but continued as Test match captain and led the Aussies to an emphatic Ashes win in 2002-03. Despite Ricky Ponting's success as skipper in the 2003 World Cup, Waugh continued as Test skipper on the tour of the West Indies which followed, winning 3-1. He retired following the 2003-04 series against India in Australia, excitingly drawn 1-1, with a last innings of 80. He has written many books of reminiscences and is connected with a charity for lepers in Calcutta.

1965	**1984-85**	**1985**	**1988-89**
Born Stephen Rodger Waugh on 2 June, at Canterbury, Sydney, Australia	Made his first-class debut for New South Wales: it is the first of 365 first-class games in his career	Made his Test debut against India at Melbourne, 26-30 December. He scored 13 and 5 and took two wickets for 36	Passes 1,000 runs in Test cricket in just his 24th Test when he scores 42 in the first innings v West Indies at Melbourne, 24-29 December

1994-95	**1995**	**1999**	**1999**	**2001**
Passed 4,000 Test runs in match v England at Perth, 3-7 February	Made his highest Test score of 200 at Kingston, Jamaica, in Test that inflicted first series defeat for West Indies in 15 years. He averaged 107.25 in the series	Became captain of Australia on tour of West Indies in Port-of-Spain, 5-8 March. Australia won the Test by 312 runs	Led Australia to second World Cup victory – only one of two players (the other Tom Moody) to play in both World Cup wins	Voted as the Wisden Australian Cricketer of the Year

BILL WOODFULL

Born: 22 AUGUST 1897, MALDON, VICTORIA, AUSTRALIA
Died: 11 AUGUST 1965, TWEED HEADS SOUTH,
NEW SOUTH WALES, AUSTRALIA
Teams: VICTORIA (1921-22 TO 1933-34)
First-class: 174 MATCHES; 13,388 RUNS, AVERAGE 64.99;
1 WICKET, AVERAGE 24.00
Tests (1926-34): 35 MATCHES; 2,300 RUNS,
AVERAGE 46.00

Bill Woodfull was a right-handed opening batsman with so solid and stout a defence that he was deemed "unbowlable". His Test career began on the tour of England in 1926, and he scored centuries in his third and fourth Tests. He was a surprising, and somewhat controversial, choice to lead Australia to England in 1930, but he hit 155 at Lord's and Australia won the series. He was equally successful as captain against both the West Indies and South Africa, but against Jardine's side in the "bodyline" series the outcome was very different.

The son of a clergyman, Woodfull, a teacher, was highly respected by his players, but he was a traditionalist in a changing world. His reaction to Jardine's tactics in 1932-33 was to accuse England of not playing the game, and his attitude virtually assured Australia that they would not be opposed by Jardine and Larwood in 1934. Australia duly regained the Ashes when confronted by a toothless attack and an ill-led side.

A true assessment of Woodfull as a captain is difficult to make, for the achievements of Bradman intrude but, apart from 1932-33, he was successful, and his record as a batsman is impressive.

FRANK WOOLLEY

Born: 27 MAY 1887, TONBRIDGE, KENT
Died: 18 OCTOBER 1978, HALIFAX, NOVA SCOTIA, CANADA
Teams: KENT (1906-38)
First-class: 978 MATCHES; 58,959 RUNS, AVERAGE
40.77; 2,066 WICKETS, AVERAGE 19.87
Tests (1909-34): 64 MATCHES; 3,283 RUNS,
AVERAGE 36.07; 83 WICKETS, AVERAGE 33.91

"There was all summer in a stroke by Woolley, and he batted as is sometimes shown in dreams." So said Robertson-Glasgow, and none who saw the great left-handed all-rounder would disagree with him. He was an exquisite batsman, a slow left-arm bowler and a brilliant slip fielder whose 1,018 catches remain a world record. He scored his runs quickly and gracefully, and he ended his career with 132 centuries to his credit, five of them in Tests. His bowling was a feature of the first part of his career, and he completed the "double" eight times. In four of those seasons, he took 100 wickets and scored 2,000 runs. No other cricketer has achieved this feat on four occasions. He reached 1,000 runs in a season 28 times and, in 1928, went on to reach 3,352. The substance of his Test career came between 1912 and 1926, although he last played against Australia in 1934 at the age of 47.

Frank Worrell: the first regular black captain of the West Indies, whose team revitalized interest in cricket in Australia when they toured in 1960-61.

FRANK WORRELL

Born: 1 AUGUST 1924, BANK HALL, BRIDGETOWN,
BARBADOS
Died: 13 MARCH 1967, MONA, KINGSTON, JAMAICA
Teams: BARBADOS (1941-42 TO 1946-47); JAMAICA
(1947-48 TO 1963-64)
First-class: 208 MATCHES; 15,025 RUNS, AVERAGE 54.24;
349 WICKETS, AVERAGE 28.98
Tests (1947-48 to 1963): 51 MATCHES; 3,860 RUNS,
AVERAGE 49.48; 69 WICKETS, AVERAGE 38.72

After years of discussion and controversy, Frank Worrell was, in 1960-61, the first black man to be appointed captain of the West Indies for more than a single match. He began his career regarded primarily as a left-arm bowler of great pace and movement. He quickly climbed the batting order, for his elegant right-handed batting was stamped with class. He made his maiden century in his second season and scored 131 in his second Test, against England in 1947-48. From that point, he was linked with two other great batsmen, Weekes and Walcott, as a triumvirate – the Three Ws. He and Walcott had already shared an unbroken stand of 574 for Barbados against Trinidad, and Worrell had made 308 not out for Barbados against Trinidad in 1943-44, when he and John Goddard put on 502 for the fourth wicket. Worrell was just 19 years old.

Before he became captain of the West Indies, he had led a Commonwealth side in India and was admired as a man of character and dignity, all grace and charm on and off the field. When he was appointed captain of the West Indies in Australia in 1960-61, the pressure upon him was immense, for the campaign on his behalf had been strong and involved issues outside cricket. His response to the situation was heroic, and the outcome romantic.

The first Test was tied and, although the West Indies eventually lost the series, Worrell and his side left Australia amid tumultuous acclaim. He led the West Indies in two more series and won them both. He had united the side which had once been a group of individuals from different islands vying for supremacy. At the end of the 1963 tour of England, mission accomplished, he retired.

He became a senator in the Jamaican parliament, was knighted and continued as a cricket administrator. Three years after being knighted, he died of leukaemia at the age of 42 and was honoured by a memorial service in Westminster Abbey, becoming the first sportsman to be recognized in this way.

DOUG WRIGHT

Born: 21 AUGUST 21, 1914, SIDCUP, KENT
Died: 13 NOVEMBER 1998, CANTERBURY, KENT
Teams: KENT (1932-57)
First-class: 497 MATCHES; 5,903 RUNS, AVERAGE 12.34; 2,056 WICKETS, AVERAGE 23.98
Tests (1938 to 1950-51): 34 MATCHES; 289 RUNS, AVERAGE 11.11; 108 WICKETS, AVERAGE 39.11

Doug Wright bowled leg-breaks and googlies at medium pace. He had a kangaroo-like approach to the wicket and he was unique among bowlers. He first played for England against Australia in 1938 and took five wickets on his debut, but he was woefully erratic. The selectors kept faith with him over a number of years because he was capable of producing the unexpected that could turn a match. He took 100 wickets in a season ten times, with 177 in 1947 as his best, but a greater measure of his ability to change the course of a game is the fact that he took a hat-trick on no fewer than seven occasions.

A professional cricketer and a man of warmth and honesty, he captained Kent from 1954 to 1956, a difficult time in the county's history.

John Wright: an elegant, hard-hitting left-handed opening batsman who captained New Zealand at a difficult time but nevertheless made over 5,000 runs in Test cricket.

JOHN WRIGHT

Born: 5 JULY 1954, DARFIELD, CHRISTCHURCH, NEW ZEALAND
Teams: NORTHERN DISTRICTS (1975-76 TO 1983-84); DERBYSHIRE (1977-88); CANTERBURY (1984-85 TO 1988-89); AUCKLAND (1989-90 TO 1992-93)
First-class: 366 MATCHES; 25,073 RUNS, AVERAGE 42.35; 2 WICKETS, AVERAGE 169.50
Tests (1977-78 to 1992-93): 82 MATCHES; 5,334 RUNS, AVERAGE 37.82; NO WICKETS FOR 5 RUNS

A man of the utmost courtesy and charm, John Wright was a left-handed opening batsman who became the first New Zealander to pass 4,000 runs in Test cricket. Only Richard Hadlee played in more Test matches for the Kiwis, and only

Martin Crowe and Stephen Fleming scored more runs. Wright had great powers of concentration and was an elegant stroke-maker, exceptionally strong off the back foot, ever popular and always a delight to watch.

He gave Derbyshire outstanding service for 12 seasons, and was a mainstay of the New Zealand side during the finest period of that country's cricketing history. When, in 1987-88, Jeff Crowe lost form and confidence, Wright took over the captaincy of New Zealand, but only on the understanding that Crowe should return as soon as he wished. In all, Wright led New Zealand in 14

Tests but, in truth, he was captaining a great side already in decline.

Wright's Test record was exemplary in that he scored centuries against all six countries against whom he played and maintained a consistent average.

A graduate of Otago University, he was appointed the coach and manager of Kent in 1997, before moving to India to coach the national side in 2000. India won their first three series under Wright, including a 2-1 defeat of Australia, but the Indian Cricket Board demanded he write to explain subsequent poor performances against Sri Lanka and South Africa. His side reached the World Cup finals in 2003, when they were beaten by Australia, and Wright extended his contract by two years soon after.

BOB WYATT

Born: 2 MAY 1901, MILFORD, SURREY
Died: 20 APRIL 1995, TRURO, CORNWALL
Teams: WARWICKSHIRE (1923-39); WORCESTERSHIRE (1946-51)
First-class: 739 MATCHES; 39,405 RUNS, AVERAGE 40.04; 901 WICKETS, AVERAGE 32.84
Tests (1927-28 to 1936-37): 40 MATCHES; 1,839 RUNS, AVERAGE 31.70; 18 WICKETS, AVERAGE 35.66

A consistent and determined batsman and useful medium-pace bowler, Bob Wyatt captained Warwickshire from 1930 to 1937 and Worcestershire from 1949 until 1951. He also captained England in 16 Tests, but he was never fortunate as England's captain nor was his selection as captain a popular one.

He had made his Test debut in South Africa in 1927-28, and made the first of his two Test centuries against the same opposition in 1929. The following year he captained England against Australia in controversial circumstances. Percy Chapman, a national hero, the England captain who had brought back and retained the Ashes, was dropped for the Oval Test and Wyatt was controversially appointed in his place.

Wyatt served under Chapman in South Africa and was vice-captain to Jardine in Australia in 1932-33. When Jardine stood down, Wyatt was named as captain against Australia in 1934, but was unable to play in the first Test because of injury. England were heavily beaten in the final Test and surrendered the Ashes.

He led England to the West Indies in 1934-35, where he made some rather bizarre decisions which turned the tour into something of a disaster. The West Indies won a series for the first time and Wyatt had his jaw broken in the final Test. In spite of this, he captained England against South Africa in 1935. The South Africans won a Test and a series in England for the first time. Wyatt's unfortunate career as England skipper then came to an end. He played under Allen against India in 1936 and was a late call-up for the Australian tour that followed but, in 1938, he announced that he was contracted to write for the *Daily Mail* and was not available for Test cricket.

Never at ease with authority, he resigned the captaincy of Warwickshire when he disagreed with the committee. He became a Test selector for several years and was 56 when he played his last game of cricket. He died less than two weeks before his 94th birthday.

Zaheer Abbas: an outstandingly stylish batsman who, when set, never looked like getting out. He set a world record by scoring a double century and a century in a match four times and in all eight innings he remained unbeaten.

ZAHEER ABBAS

Born: 24 JULY 1947, SIALKOT, INDIA
Teams: KARACHI (1965-66 TO 1975-76); PWD (1968-69); PIA (1969-70 TO 1986-87); GLOUCESTERSHIRE (1972-85); SIND (1975-76 TO 1976-77); DAWOOD CLUB (1975-76)
First-class: 459 MATCHES; 34,843 RUNS, AVERAGE 51.54; 30 WICKETS, AVERAGE 38.20
Tests (1969-70 to 1985-86): 78 MATCHES; 5,062 RUNS, AVERAGE 44.79; 3 WICKETS, AVERAGE 44.00

The first Pakistani batsman to hit 100 centuries in a first-class career, Zaheer Abbas was a player of rare quality with an infinite capacity to entertain with his vast repertoire of beautiful strokes. Initially, he batted in glasses, later changing to contact lenses, but this never handicapped his batting nor his fine slip fielding.

He made a spectacular entrance into Test cricket, scoring 274 at Edgbaston in 1971, his first Test in England and only his second in all. He made 240 at The Oval in 1974 and 235 not out against India at Lahore in 1978. His fourth double-century in a Test match was the most historic, in that he emulated Boycott by scoring his 100th hundred in a Test, 215 against India, again at Lahore. In that series, he became the first Pakistani batsman to score centuries in three successive innings, and he was also the first Pakistani batsman to score 5,000 Test runs. Zaheer set two career records: eight times he scored a century in each innings of a match and four times he made 200 and 100 in a match.

A modest, gentle man, he was immensely popular in his years with Gloucestershire when the county enjoyed a successful time, particularly in limited-overs cricket.

Zaheer captained Pakistan in 14 Tests, taking over from Imran in 1983-84, acting as a buffer between Javed and his critics before relinquishing the job to Javed in 1984-85. He stood down from the national side after the second Test against Sri Lanka in 1985, intimating that he had been forced to retire by certain senior players. It was a sad end to an outstanding career.

6 THE FAMOUS GROUNDS

While Lord's Cricket Ground in London is considered the world headquarters of cricket, Test matches were played at both The Oval and Old Trafford before such games took place at Lord's. The 100th venue staged a Test match in 2009.

It is impossible to say with any certainty which is the oldest ground still used for cricket, if only because early references give such descriptions as Richmond Green, Kennington Common, Dartford Heath, Moulsey Hurst, Penhurst Park, Kew Green, Hyde Park and Clapham Common, but there is no information as to where exactly in these parks, commons or greens the matches took place.

The oldest ground where we have definite knowledge of a match being played approximately where cricket is still played is the Artillery Ground on City Road, Finsbury, London. The match in question was London v Surrey played on 30 August 1730. The following year the first definite reference to a specific match on a current ground is Mitcham v Ewell on Mitcham Green on 2 October 1731.

The Sevenoaks Vine Ground is first mentioned in July 1740, when Sevenoaks opposed London, but it is most probable that the ground had been used some years earlier when Kent played Sussex in Sevenoaks. Extracts from the diary of Thomas Marchant, written between 1717 and 1727, indicate that cricket was played regularly in the Henfield and Hurstpierpoint areas of Sussex between the various villages, and references in documents to matches in Kent and Surrey would seem to imply that similar inter-village matches were being played in those counties. It would, therefore, come as no surprise if evidence emerged proving that a number of village greens in the South East of England, on which cricket is still played, were used for cricket prior to 1730.

Lord's Cricket Ground: it is a dream for anyone who has ever played the game to appear at the home of cricket.

RACECOURSE GROUND, DERBY
Capacity: 9,500
End names: Grandstand End, Scoreboard End
Home team: Derbyshire

GR batting: 273* – EG Hayes,
Surrey v. Derbys, 1904
GR bowling: 10-45 – RL Johnson,
Middlesex v. Derbys, 1994

OLD TRAFFORD, MANCHESTER
Capacity: 19,000
End names: Stretford End, Brian Statham End
Home team: Lancashire

GR batting: 312 – JER Gallian,
Lancs v. Derbys, 1996
GR bowling: 10-46 – W Hickton,
Lancs v. Hants, 1870

EDGBASTON, BIRMINGHAM
Capacity: 21,000
End names: City End, Pavilion End
Home team: Warwickshire

GR batting: 501* – BC Lara,
Warks v. Durham, 1994
GR bowling: 10-51 – H Howell,
Warks v. Yorkshire, 1923

SWALEC STADIUM, CARDIFF
Capacity: 16,000
End names: River Taff End, Cathedral Road End
Home team: Glamorgan

GR batting: 313* – SJ Cook,
Somerset v. Glam, 1990
GR bowling: 10-40 – W Bestwick,
Derbys v. Glam, 1921

COUNTY GROUND, NORTHAMPTON
Capacity: 6,500
End names: Wantage Road End, Abington Avenue End
Home team: Northamptonshire

GR batting: 329* – MEK Hussey,
Northants v. Essex, 2001
GR bowling: 10-30 – C Blythe,
Kent v. Northants, 1907

COUNTY GROUND, BRISTOL
Capacity: 7,000 (15,000 for ODIs)
End names: Pavilion End, Ashley Down Road End
Home team: Gloucestershire

GR batting: 310* – MEK Hussey,
Northants v. Glos, 2002
GR bowling: 10-40 – EG Dennett,
Glos v. Essex, 1906

COUNTY GROUND, TAUNTON
Capacity: 6,500
End names: River End, Old Pavilion End
Home team: Somerset

GR batting: 424 – AC MacLaren,
Lancs v. Somerset, 1895
GR bowling: 10-42 – AE Trott,
Middlesex v. Somerset, 1900

THE ROSE BOWL, SOUTHAMPTON
Capacity: 6,500
End names: Pavilion End, Northern End
Home team: Hampshire

GR batting: 311* – JP Crawley,
Hants v. Notts, 2005
GR bowling: 8-90 – AD Mullally,
Hants v. Warks, 2001

THE OVAL
Capacity: 23,500
End names: Pavilion End, Vauxhall End
Home team: Surrey

GR batting: 366 – NH Fairbrother,
Lancs v. Surrey, 1990
GR bowling: 10-28 – WP Howell,
Australians v. Surrey, 1899

COUNTY GROUND, HOVE
Capacity: 4,000
End names: Cromwell Road End, Sea End
Home team: Sussex

GR batting: 335* – MW Goodwin,
Sussex v. Leics, 2003
GG bowling: 9-35 – JEBBPQC Dwyer,
Sussex v. Derbys, 1906

ST LAWRENCE GROUND, CANTERBURY
Capacity: 15,000
End names: Pavilion End, Nackington Road End
Home team: Kent

GR batting: 344 – WG Grace,
MCC v. Kent, 1876
GR bowling: 10-129 – Jas Lillywhite,
South v. North, 1972

RIVERSIDE GROUND, CHESTER-LE-STREET
Capacity: 5,000 (17,000 for internationals)
End names: Finchale End, Lumley End
Home team: Durham

GR batting: 273 – M Love,
Durham v. Hampshire, 2003
GR bowling: 10-47 – OB Gibson,
Durham v Hants, 2007

HEADINGLEY, LEEDS
Capacity: 14,000
End names: Kirkstall Lane End, Football Stand End
Home team: Yorkshire

GR batting: 334 – DG Bradman,
Australia v. England, 1930
GR bowling: 10-10 – H Verity,
Yorkshire v. Notts, 1932

TRENT BRIDGE, NOTTINGHAM
Capacity: 17,900
End names: Pavilion End, Radcliffe Road End
Home team: Nottinghamshire

GR batting: 345 – CG Macartney,
Australians v. Notts, 1921
GR bowling: 9-19 – J Gundy,
Notts v. Kent, 1864

GRACE ROAD, LEICESTER
Capacity: 12,000
End names: Pavilion End, Bennett End
Home team: Leicestershire

GR batting: 341 – GH Hirst,
Yorkshire v. Leics, 1905
GR bowling: 10-64 – TB Mitchell,
Derbys v. Leics, 1935

COUNTY GROUND, CHELMSFORD
Capacity: 6,500
End names: River End, Hayes Close End
Home team: Essex

GR batting: 275 – GA Gooch,
Essex v Kent, 1988
GR bowling: 9-59 – MS Nichols,
Essex v. Hants, 1927

LORD'S
Capacity: 30,000
End names: Pavilion End, Nursery End
Home team: MCC, Middlesex

GR batting: 333 – GA Gooch,
England v. India, 1990
GR bowling: 10-38 – SE Butler,
Oxford U v. Cambridge U, 1971

Chester-le-Street

Leeds

Manchester

Nottingham

Derby

Leicester

Birmingham

Northampton

Chelmsford

Lord's

Cardiff

Bristol

The Oval

Canterbury

Taunton

Hove

Southampton

ENGLAND

ENGLAND

LORD'S, LONDON

Of the cricket grounds in the British Isles in use today for first-class cricket, Lord's ground is the oldest. The first match on the ground was MCC v Hertfordshire on 22 June, 1814 and the first first-class match was MCC v St John's Wood on 13-15 July the same year.

The present site was the third ground laid out by Thomas Lord. The first, which is now Dorset Square, London, was opened in 1787. Lord had laid out the ground at the behest of the Cricket Club, which met at the Star and Garter in Pall Mall and had in recent years played its matches on White Conduit Fields, Islington. The ground was used until 1810, by which time Lord had already set out an alternative ground at Lisson Grove not far away. However, the building of the Regent's Canal meant that within a few years Lord had to seek a third site off St John's Wood Road, a few hundred yards north-east of the second ground.

The Cricket Club of the Star and Garter adopted the name Marylebone Cricket Club from the district of London in which Lord's was situated and, in 1866, the club bought the freehold of the ground. At this time, the ground was used by the MCC and for such set-piece matches as had traditionally been staged there - Eton v Harrow, Oxford v. Cambridge, Gentlemen v. Players and North v. South. In 1877, the MCC agreed to allow Middlesex County Cricket Club to use the ground for their home fixtures.

The first Test match to take place there was staged on the ground on 21 to 23 July 1884, England beating Australia by an innings and five runs.

In recent years, considerable modernization of Lord's has taken place, culminating in the total refurbishment of the historic Pavilion in 2004-05.

There are few greater venues in world cricket than Lord's, whether you are English or not. In 1990, Graham Gooch set the stage alight with a magnificent first-innings knock of 333 – the highest score ever made at the ground. The England captain also went on to score a century in the second innings.

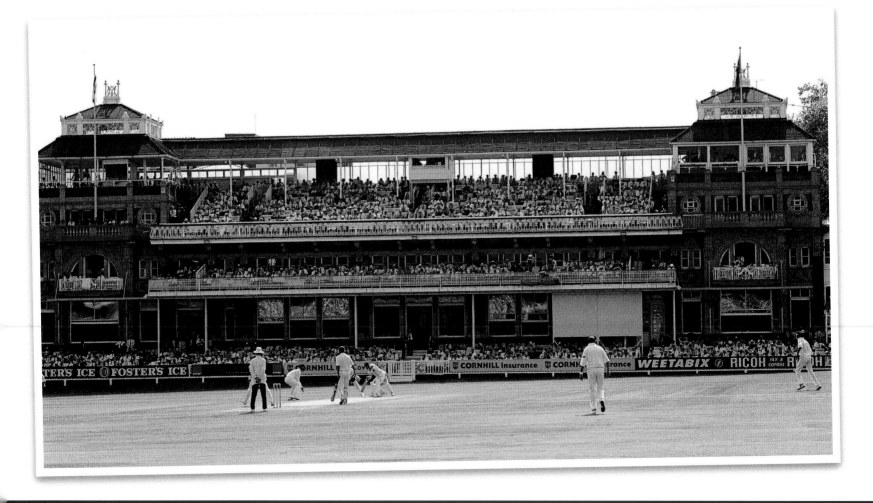

THE OVAL,
KENNINGTON

William Baker, treasurer of the Montpelier Cricket Club, took a lease on 10 acres of ground, then used as a market garden and situated at The Oval, Kennington, one mile south of the River Thames. He converted the land to a cricket ground and the first match was played on the new ground on 13 May 1845. In August of the same year, the Gentlemen of Surrey opposed the Players of Surrey on the ground and, after

the match a meeting was arranged, at which it was proposed to form a Surrey County Cricket Club. The formation duly took place and the Surrey Club played the first first-class match at The Oval on 25 and 26 May 1846. The Surrey Club created an organization for south London similar to the Marylebone Club at Lord's.

The Oval was to become a centre of more than just cricket. The first Association Football match played on the ground was England v Scotland on 19 November 1870.

Within two years, The Oval was recognized as the major football ground in London and, in 1872, the Football Association Cup final, between Royal Engineers and Wanderers, took place there. To soccer were added regular rugby union matches, with the University Rugby Union match being played at The Oval from 1873. England met Ireland in a rugby union match in 1875 but, in 1891, it was decided that the scrummages were damaging the turf too much and rugby ceased to be played there. Soccer

It may have been substantially redeveloped over the years, but The Oval, in Kennington, South London, oozes history.

ceased to be staged on the ground as a regular event after 1895.

The first Test match to be played in England was at The Oval on 6-8 September 1880, when England beat Australia by five wickets. It is still a tradition that the final Test in a five- or six-match series in England takes place at The Oval.

A new stand, costing £24 million, was opened in 2005.

OLD TRAFFORD, MANCHESTER

The ground was formed in 1857 as the home of Manchester Cricket Club; when the present Lancashire Club was formed in 1864, the county made Old Trafford its home. Until recent years the official name of the major club was the Lancashire County and Manchester CC.

The first major inter-county game on the Old Trafford ground was staged on 20-22 July 1865, when Lancashire played Middlesex. Old Trafford became the second ground in England to hold a Test match, when England played Australia in the first of a series of three Tests in 1884. The ground began to build its reputation for rain interruptions immediately – the first day of the first Test was completely washed out.

It was the one major English cricket ground to be badly affected by bombing in the Second World War, but repairs were quickly undertaken when the war ended and it was possible to play one of the Victory Tests there in August 1945. Appropriately, the new press box, opened in 1987, was named after Neville Cardus, whose reputation had been made through the columns of the *Manchester Guardian*. The next major updates came in 2010-11 when the orientation of the pitches were changed and major redevelopment work undertaken.

They say that it always rains in Manchester: well it did for the whole of the first day of the first Test that was ever to be staged on the ground. However, when the sun shines, Old Trafford has been the stage for some magnificent cricket over the years.

TRENT BRIDGE
NOTTINGHAM

This ground, situated in the Nottingham suburb of West Bridgford, was laid out in 1838 by William Clarke. Clarke was the landlord of the Trent Bridge Inn, the ground being in the field at the rear of the Inn; he was also the captain and effective manager of the Nottinghamshire county team. The first first-class match was played on the ground in 1840 when Nottinghamshire opposed Sussex.

The county had previously played their matches on the Nottingham racecourse, but as this was owned by the town council and no entrance money could be charged to spectators, hence the move to the new ground. In the 19th century, the ground was also used at various times by both Nottingham Forest Football Club and Notts County FC. The latter did not leave until 1910 and, in the meantime, two England soccer internationals were staged at the venue in the 1890s.

The first Test match staged on the ground was on 1–3 June 1899 when England drew with Australia. Tests were played in Nottingham intermittently until 1939, and since the Second World War Test matches have been held on the ground in most seasons.

The first Test at the ground took place in 1899 when England played Australia. Twenty-two years later, C.G. MacCartney scored 345 for the touring Australians against Nottinghamshire – it still the highest score ever made at Trent Bridge.

HEADINGLEY, LEEDS

In 1887, a group of sports enthusiasts set up the Leeds Cricket, Football and Athletic Co. Ltd, chaired by Lord Hawke, in order to buy land in the Leeds area for use as a sports field. A 22-acre site was purchased and divided into portions for a variety of sports. The cricket area was officially opened on 27 May 1890 when the local Leeds Cricket Club used the grounds; the first first-class match was in September 1890, a North of England side playing the Australians. In 1891, Yorkshire County Cricket Club played its first first-class game at Headingley and the first Test was on 29-30 June 1899, with England opposing Australia.

At that time, the headquarters of Yorkshire County Cricket Club were in Sheffield. In fact, Sheffield had always been considered the centre of Yorkshire cricket – two grounds had been laid out, one following the other in Darnall, then another appeared in Hyde Park. It was on the Sheffield Hyde Park ground that Yorkshire opposed Norfolk in 1833. In the 1840s, the Hyde Park ground became run down and M.J. Ellison, a keen supporter of Sheffield cricket, organized a meeting to discuss the foundation of a new ground. This materialized in April 1855 as Bramall Lane Cricket Ground. Some eight years later, Ellison was instrumental in founding Yorkshire County Cricket Club and naturally

Sheffield and Bramall Lane were the headquarters of the new club. In 1862, the first soccer match was played at Bramall Lane, which led to the foundation of Sheffield United, and the ground was shared by the cricket and football clubs. The first first-class match at Bramall Lane was Yorkshire v Sussex in August 1855. The first, and only, Test match was played on 3-5 July 1902 when England played Australia. Bramall Lane continued to stage county matches with success through to 1939, but after the Second World War the football club became more and more dominant and the last county match was Yorkshire v Lancashire, 4-7 August 1973.

Headingley, like Bramall Lane, has suffered because of its football connections, but its Test-match status has been maintained to the present day. However, Yorkshire County Cricket Club, at the time of writing, have bought the ground and entered into a deal with a local college for naming rights. It will be known as the Headingley Carnegie Stadium until 2015.

Yorkshire have had, and indeed do have, a number of other famous grounds. Scarborough has been staging an important cricket festival for more than 100 years at its North Marine Road ground. The first first-class match was on 7 September to 9,1874: Yorkshire v Middlesex. For many years, the September Festival comprised a Gentlemen v Players match and a match involving the current touring side.

Another major cricketing centre is Bradford. The Park Avenue ground was opened in July 1880.

The football club which shared the venue fell on hard times in the 1950s and left the Football League, as a result of which the accommodation became increasingly dilapidated. In 1980, the grandstand had to be demolished and, in 1985, the pavilion followed suit. Friends of Park Avenue formed an association to restore the ground and first-class cricket returned in 1992 after a gap of some years. Other grounds which were used by Yorkshire for first-class cricket in 1996 were Acklam Park, Middlesbrough (first used in 1956), Abbeydale Park, Sheffield (first used in 1946, by Derbyshire) and St George's Road, Harrogate (first used in 1882).

Headingley: the stage, perhaps, for the finest performance ever seen by an England player. In 1981, Ian Botham's unbeaten 149 dragged England from the jaws of defeat to set up an astonishing win against Australia. It was one of the most remarkable turnarounds in the history of Test cricket.

EDGBASTON,
BIRMINGHAM

The present Warwickshire County Cricket Club was founded in 1882 and it soon became apparent that the club would not flourish until it established a good ground in the Birmingham area.

William Ansell, the honorary secretary of the county club, was the driving force behind the search for and the acquisition of a suitable site in Edgbaston. The Warwickshire Cricket Ground Co. Ltd was founded in 1885 to raise the necessary capital, and the ground staged its first match on 7 June 1886, with Warwickshire opposing the MCC. The first first-class game came late on in the same season when the Australian touring team played an England XI.

Warwickshire were promoted to first-class status in 1894 and the ground has been the headquarters of the County Championship playing side since it commenced in the competition in 1895.

The first Test match to be played at Edgbaston was on 29-31 May 1902, with England opposing Australia in a remarkable match which saw the touring side all out for 36, their lowest total ever – this in reply to England's 376 for 9 declared. Rain on the last day prevented an England victory. The next Test was in 1909 – again Australia failed badly, being all out for 74. Edgbaston, however, was rarely used for international matches after that until 1957 when the West Indies played England. Since that date, it has been one of the six Test grounds in regular use.

The scene of a world record: in 1994, Brian Lara hit an unbeaten 501 to claim the record first-class score, v Durham.

COUNTY GROUNDS

The non-Test venues in England may seem unassuming at first glance, but history seeps through every blade of grass.

FENNER'S, CAMBRIDGE

F.P. Fenner, the Cambridge Town Club all-rounder, took the lease of a field in Cambridge and opened a cricket ground on the land in 1846.

In 1848, having created what was described as perhaps the smoothest ground in England – being in fact too easy, causing too much run-getting – he sublet the ground to Cambridge University Cricket Club and the first first-class match was staged on the ground on 18-19 May 1848, the university playing the MCC. It has remained the university ground ever since, the university buying the freehold in 1894. Prior to 1848, the university played on Parker's Piece, the first notable match there being against the town club in 1871. A cinder running track was laid out round Fenner's cricket area in the mid-1860s and was used by the University Athletics Club – athletics were staged there until the 1950s.

ST LAWRENCE GROUND, CANTERBURY

The headquarters of Kent County Cricket Club, the St Lawrence ground, was officially opened on 16 May 1847. Immediately prior to 1847, Kent had played on the Beverley Cricket Club ground in Canterbury, but for six years from 1835 the centre of the county club had been at West Malling. The Kent County Cricket Club, on its reformation in 1870, announced that the St Lawrence ground would, in future, be the official county ground. The club purchased the freehold of the ground in 1896. In 1876, W.G. Grace scored 344 for MCC v Kent at Canterbury, this being the highest individual first-class score at the time, and it remains the ground record. By coincidence, the bowling record for the ground is held by W.G.'s brother, E.M. Grace, who took 10 for 69 for the MCC in 1862.

Outground cricket has played an important part in county cricket through history. In recent times, counties have played in fewer and fewer venues beyond their official county homes.

More than anything else the ground was famous for the Canterbury Festival, which for many years involved an MCC-selected England team opposing Kent, followed by two more fixtures; apart from cricket, theatrical performances also played an integral part of the festival.

Kent by no means confined their matches to Canterbury, though, and since the Second World War have staged matches on the following other grounds: Rectory Field, Blackheath; Hesketh Park, Dartford; Crabble ground, Dover; Cheriton Road, Folkestone; Garrison ground, Gillingham; Bat and Ball ground, Gravesend; Mote Park, Maidstone; Lloyds Bank ground, Beckenham; and the Nevill ground, Tunbridge Wells. In recent years, of these only Maidstone and Tunbridge Wells have still found favour.

COUNTY GROUND,
HOVE

The cricket ground of Sussex County Cricket Club since 1872. The first match played by Sussex on the ground was, appropriately, against Kent, the home county's oldest rivals, commencing 6 June 1872.

Sussex have been as unfortunate as Thomas Lord in their battle with building development. Their original ground had been set out at the behest of the Prince of Wales in the 1790s, when he made Brighton a fashionable resort. This ground was taken over in the 1820s by a Brighton businessman, James Ireland, and he was responsible for organizing what is now considered the first match to decide the Champion County of England, in 1825 against Kent. The Prince's ground then became known as Ireland's Gardens. The builders took over the site in the 1840s and it is now Park Crescent, Brighton. Sussex then moved to a new ground in Hove, close to the sea front and known as the Brunswick ground. This opened in 1848 but, in 1871 the builders took over and the site of this ground is Third and Fourth Avenues, Hove. The county's next move was to their present ground, but to further complicate the story, another ground was in operation between 1834 and 1844 which was generally known as Lillywhite's ground and situated where Montpelier Crescent now stands.

Sussex have also played on various other grounds in the county but, by 1996, only two of the old established county venues remained in use for first-class cricket: Horsham (the current ground there has been used by the county since 1908) and Eastbourne (The Saffrons, which Sussex have used since 1897). In addition, the county has been playing matches at Arundel Castle since 1975, when a Sunday League game was staged there. More recently, championship games have also come to Arundel.

COUNTY GROUND,
BRISTOL

Gloucestershire County Cricket Club have used the ground at Ashley Down since 1899. It has, however, had a somewhat chequered history – in 1916, the county club had to sell the ground to Fry's, the chocolate manufacturers, in order to pay off the club's debts. The club regained ownership of the ground in 1932.

In its earliest days, the county club played many of its matches on two school grounds. The one at Clifton College was used from 1871 to 1932, while the one at Cheltenham College, which came into county use the year after Clifton College, has long been established as a ground for an annual cricket festival. In 1882, the county staged its first match on the Spa ground at Gloucester, but this has not been used for county matches since 1923. After that year, the majority of county matches played in the city have been at what is still known, though incorrectly, as the Wagon Works ground.

BATTING
Notable batting records on some current English first-class grounds:

Edgbaston	501*	B.C. LARA, WARWICKSHIRE V. DURHAM, 1994
Taunton	424	A.C. MACLAREN, LANCASHIRE V. SOMERSET, 1895
The Oval	366	N.H. FAIRBROTHER, LANCASHIRE V. SURREY, 1990
Trent Bridge	345	C.G. MACCARTNEY, AUSTRALIANS V. NOTTINGHAMSHIRE, 1921
Canterbury	344	W.G. GRACE, MCC V. KENT, 1876
Chesterfield	343*	P.A. PERRIN, ESSEX V. DERBYSHIRE, 1904
Gloucester	341	C.M. SPEARMAN, GLOUCESTERSHIRE V. MIDDLESEX, 2004
Headingley	339	D.S. LEHMANN, YORKSHIRE V. DURHAM, 2006
Hove	335*	M.W. GOODWIN, SUSSEX V. LEICESTERSHIRE, 2003
Lord's	333	G.A. GOOCH, ENGLAND V. INDIA, 1990
Worcester	331*	J.D.B. ROBERTSON, MIDDLESEX V. WORCESTERSHIRE, 1949
Northampton	329*	M.E.K. HUSSEY, NORTHANTS V. ESSEX, 2001
Cheltenham College	318*	W.G. GRACE, GLOUCESTERSHIRE V. YORKSHIRE, 1876
Scarborough	317	K.R. RUTHERFORD, NEW ZEALAND V. D.B. CLOSE'S XI, 1986
Cardiff	313*	S.J. COOK, SOMERSET V. GLAMORGAN, 1990
Old Trafford	312	J.E.R. GALLIAN, LANCASHIRE V. DERBYSHIRE, 1996
Rose Bowl	311*	J.P. CRAWLEY, HAMPSHIRE V. NOTTINGHAMSHIRE, 2005
Eastbourne	310	H. GIMBLETT, SOMERSET V. SUSSEX, 1948
Colwyn Bay	309*	S.P. JAMES, GLAMORGAN V. SUSSEX, 2000
Fenner's	304*	E. DE C. WEEKES, WEST INDIES V. CAMBRIDGE UNIVERSITY, 1950
Bristol	302*	W.R. HAMMOND, GLOUCESTERSHIRE V. GLAMORGAN, 1934

* Not out

BOWLING
Notable bowling records on some current English first-class grounds:

Headingley	10-10	H. VERITY, YORKSHIRE V. NOTTINGHAMSHIRE, 1932
The Oval	10-28	W.P. HOWELL, AUSTRALIANS V. SURREY, 1899
Lord's	10-38	S.E. BUTLER, OXFORD UNIVERSITY V. CAMBRIDGE UNIVERSITY, 1871
Bristol	10-40	E.G. DENNETT, GLOUCESTERSHIRE V. ESSEX, 1906
Taunton	10-42	A.E. TROTT, MIDDLESEX V. SOMERSET, 1900
Derby	10-45	R.L. JOHNSON, MIDDLESEX V. DERBYSHIRE, 1994
Riverside	10-47	O.D. GIBSON, DURHAM V. HAMPSHIRE, 2007
Edgbaston	10-51	H. HOWELL, WARWICKSHIRE V. YORKSHIRE, 1923
Worcester	10-51	J. MERCER, GLAMORGAN V. WORCESTERSHIRE, 1936
Old Trafford	10-53	J.C. LAKER, ENGLAND V. AUSTRALIA, 1956
Cheltenham College	10-66	A.A. MAILEY, AUSTRALIANS V. GLOUCESTERSHIRE, 1921
Chesterfield	10-66	J.K. GRAVENEY, GLOUCESTERSHIRE V. DERBYSHIRE, 1949
Fenner's	10-69	S.M.J. WOODS, CAMBRIDGE UNIVERSITY V. C.I. THORNTON'S XI, 1890
Canterbury	10-129	JAS. LILLYWHITE, SOUTH V. NORTH, 1872
Trent Bridge	9-19	J. GRUNDY, NOTTINGHAMSHIRE V. KENT, 1864
Scarborough	9-28	J.M. PRESTON, YORKSHIRE V. MCC, 1888
Hove	9-35	J.E.B.B.P.Q.C. DWYER, SUSSEX V. DERBYSHIRE, 1906
Gloucester	9-44	C.W.L. PARKER, GLOUCESTERSHIRE V. ESSEX, 1925
Cardiff	9-57	P.I. POCOCK, SURREY V. GLAMORGAN, 1979

MARRARA CRICKET GROUND
Marrara, Darwin, Northern Territory
CAPACITY: 15,000 (5,000 SEATED)
END NAMES: McMILLANS ROAD END, AIRPORT END
HOME TEAM: NORTHERN TERRITORY

FIRST TEST: AUSTRALIA V. BANGLADESH,
18–20 JULY 2003
FIRST ODI: AUSTRALIA V. BANGLADESH,
6 AUGUST 2003

Darwin

BUNDABERG RUM STADIUM
Cairns, Queensland
CAPACITY: 12,000
END NAMES: CITY END, CLUB END
HOME TEAM: QUEENSLAND

FIRST TEST: AUSTRALIA V. BANGLADESH,
25–28 JULY 2003
FIRST ODI: AUSTRALIA V. BANGLADESH,
2 AUGUST 2003

Cairns

NORTHERN

TERRITORY

QUEENSLAND

AUSTRALIA

WESTERN

AUSTRALIA

BRISBANE CRICKET GROUND
Woollongabba, Brisbane, Queensland
CAPACITY: 42,000 (APPROX.)
END NAMES: STANLEY STREET END, VULTURE STREET END
HOME TEAM: QUEENSLAND

FIRST TEST: AUSTRALIA V. SOUTH AFRICA,
27 NOVEMBER–3 DECEMBER 1931
FIRST ODI: ENGLAND V. WEST INDIES,
23 DECEMBER 1979

ADELAIDE OVAL
North Adelaide, Adelaide, South Australia
CAPACITY: 32,000
END NAMES: CITY END, CATHEDRAL END
HOME TEAM: SOUTH AUSTRALIA

FIRST TEST: AUSTRALIA V. ENGLAND,
12–16 DECEMBER 1884
FIRST ODI: AUSTRALIA V. WEST INDIES,
20 DECEMBER 1975

Brisbane

NEW SOUTH

WALES

SOUTH AUSTRALIA

Perth

Adelaide

Sydney

VICTORIA

SYDNEY CRICKET GROUND
Moore Park, Sydney, New South Wales
CAPACITY: 43,649
END NAMES: PADDINGTON END, RANDWICK END
HOME TEAM: NEW SOUTH WALES

FIRST TEST: AUSTRALIA V. ENGLAND,
17–21 FEBRUARY 1882
FIRST ODI: AUSTRALIA V. ENGLAND,
13 JANUARY 1979

Melbourne

WACA GROUND, PERTH
CAPACITY: 22,000
END NAMES: MEMBERS END, PRINDIVILLE STAND END
HOME TEAM: WESTERN AUSTRALIA

FIRST TEST: AUSTRALIA V. ENGLAND,
11–16 DECEMBER 1970
FIRST ODI: INDIA V. NEW ZEALAND,
9 DECEMBER 1980

MELBOURNE CRICKET GROUND
Jolimont, Melbourne, Victoria
CAPACITY: 96,308
END NAMES: MEMBERS END, GREAT SOUTHERN STAND END
HOME TEAM: VICTORIA

FIRST TEST: AUSTRALIA V. ENGLAND,
15–19 MARCH 1877
FIRST ODI: AUSTRALIA V. ENGLAND,
5 JANUARY 1971

TASMANIA

Hobart

BELLERIVE OVAL
Bellerive, Hobart, Australia
CAPACITY: 16,000
END NAMES: CHURCH STREET END, RIVER END
HOME TEAM: TASMANIA

FIRST TEST: AUSTRALIA V. SRI LANKA,
16–20 DECEMBER 1989
FIRST ODI: NEW ZEALAND V. SRI LANKA,
12 JANUARY 1988

AUSTRALIA

MCG, VICTORIA

The first home inter-colonial match played by Victoria was staged at Emerald Hill on the south side of the Yarra River on 29 and 30 March 1852, in the district now known as South Melbourne, and Victoria's opponents were Tasmania. Within a few years of this game, the ground had disappeared, with a railway line through its centre.

When Victoria faced New South Wales for the first time at home on 26-27 March 1856, the match was staged on what is still Melbourne Cricket Ground. It was on 15 March 1877 that what is now considered to be the first Test match was commenced. The English touring team, under James Lillywhite, opposed Australia. Australia won this historic first match by 45 runs and a return match was immediately arranged on the same ground; this time England won by four wickets. Some spectators accused the England team of deliberately losing the initial match in order to raise the odds on England winning the second so that, with betting a major feature of cricket, the England players could make a killing!

Melbourne: the stage of the first Test match in Australia. The home side won, v England.

SCG, NSW

The first first-class match to be played in Sydney took place on 14–15 January 1857, when New South Wales played Victoria. This game was played on the Domain, the ground having been used for the first time in the previous month.

In 1870–71, the New South Wales v Victoria fixture was moved to the much better ground of the Albert Club. Here spectators had to pay, whereas previously the intercolonial matches in Sydney could be viewed free of charge.

However, in the 1870s, the New South Wales Cricket Association wished to find a new ground and, after various discussions and some objections from the Albert Cricket Ground Company, took over the Garrison ground in Sydney, whose name was then changed to the Association ground. The first first-class match on the Association ground was New South Wales v Victoria on 22–25 February 1878.

The Albert ground itself was sold off as a building site. The Association ground, now known as Sydney Cricket Ground, is still the major ground in New South Wales. The first Test match to be staged there took place on 17–21 February 1882, when Australia beat England by five wickets.

Sydney Cricket Ground: arouses as much sentiment in the minds of the players as Lord's.

ADELAIDE OVAL,
SOUTH AUSTRALIA

The Adelaide Oval has been the principal cricket ground in South Australia since the introduction of first-class cricket to the colony.

In 1871, the South Australian Cricket Club had set about finding suitable land to create a ground for inter-colonial matches and a South Australian Cricket Association was set up to pursue that aim. Land was found in North Park, Adelaide, and the first game was played there on 11 November 1872. It was between British-born and Colonial-born. The first first-class match was against Tasmania in November 1877 – the first time that South Australia opposed another colony on even terms. It was not until 1881 that Victoria played South Australia even-handed at Adelaide and the

Adelaide: there are few more picturesque locations in the world to sit and watch a game of cricket.

first Test match on the ground commenced on 12 December 1884, when England beat Australia by eight wickets.

GABBA, QUEENSLAND

Queensland was created as a separate colony in 1859 and played its first first-class match on 1-4 April 1893 when the home team defeated New South Wales by 14 runs. The match was played on the Exhibition ground in Brisbane which was situated in Bowen Hills. The ground had first been used for a match when the 1887-88 English team had visited Brisbane.

However, in 1896, a new ground was opened at Woolloongabba (more commonly known as Gabba). The first first-class match was played there on 19-22 February 1898, when A.E. Stoddart's team opposed a combined Queensland and Victoria XI. Queensland played its first Shield match there against South Australia in 1898-99 and the Gabba, as it is familiarly called, remains the principal cricket venue in Queensland. The first Test match in the state was not staged at the Gabba, but on the Exhibition ground on 30 November to 5 December, 1928, when England beat Australia

The Gabba had to wait until 1931 before it staged its first Test match – it has played host to them regularly ever since.

by 675 runs. The first Test at the Gabba was Australia v South Africa, commencing 27 November 1931, and every subsequent Brisbane Test has been played on that ground.

WACA, WEST AUSTRALIA

The Western Australian Cricket Association was formed by the leading clubs of Perth specifically to create a good-quality ground within the city. A suitable site was secured in East Perth in 1899, but it took several years to form a practical cricketing surface and the first match on the ground did not take place until the 1893-94 season. The first first-class match was on 3-6 April 1899, when South Australia beat Western Australia by four wickets. In addition to cricket, football was played on the ground and a cycle track was laid round the perimeter.

Western Australia did not join the Sheffield Shield until 1947-48. It was not until December 1970 that the first Test match was played in Perth, Australia opposing England.

TASMANIAN GROUNDS

The two major cricket centres on the island are at Hobart and Launceston. The first first-class match in Australia was staged at Launceston on 11-12 February 1851, with Tasmania playing Victoria - the game was billed at the time as XI of Port Philip against XI of Van Diemen's Land.

The cricket ground used was part of the local racecourse at the time and the Northern Tasmanian Cricket Association, on its formation, took over the ground in 1886-87 - adjacent to the ground cycling, tennis and bowling also took place. A limited-overs international was staged at Launceston in 1985-86 but, since the Second World War, the ground at Hobart has usually taken precedence.

The first first-class match in Hobart was played on 4-5 March 1858: Tasmania v Victoria. It was staged on the Lower Domain ground which was taken over by the Southern Tasmanian Cricket Association in 1869. The building of a railway ended cricket on the ground in 1873 and a new one opened in 1881-82. The first first-class game on the new ground was on 8-9 January 1890, Tasmania v Victoria. This ground is usually referred to as the Upper Domain ground or TCA ground.

A limited-overs international match was played on the ground in 1984-85, but the State government were trying to bring Test cricket to Tasmania and decided that the best prospective venue was the Bellerive Oval. Cricket had been played in Bellerive Park from the 1880s, but the cricket area did not become enclosed until 1947. Major redevelopment of the ground began in 1985 and the first first-class game took place from 23-25 January to 25, 1987, Tasmania playing the West Indies. Continued improvements to the ground led to the first Test match at Bellerive and in Tasmania in December 1989, when Australia opposed Sri Lanka.

Elsewhere in Australia, in 2003 Test matches were staged in Darwin and Cairns for the first time.

BATTING
Notable batting feats on Australia's major grounds:

Sydney	452*	D.G. BRADMAN, NSW V QUEENSLAND, 1929-30
Melbourne	437	W.H. PONSFORD, VICTORIA V QUEENSLAND, 1927-28
Brisbane	383	C.W. GREGORY, NSW V QUEENSLAND, 1906-07
Perth	380	M.L. HAYDEN, AUSTRALIA V ZIMBABWE, 2003-04
Adelaide	369	D.G. BRADMAN, S AUSTRALIA V TASMANIA, 1935-36
Hobart	305*	F.E. WOOLLEY, MCC V TASMANIA, 1911-12

* Not out

BOWLING
Notable bowling feats on Australia's major grounds:

Perth	10-44	I.J. BRAYSHAW, W AUSTRALIA V VICTORIA, 1967-68
Melbourne	10-61	P.J. ALLAN, QUEENSLAND V VICTORIA, 1965-66
Sydney	10-36	T.W. WALL, S AUSTRALIA V NSW, 1932-33
Launceston	9-2	G. ELLIOTT, VICTORIA V TASMANIA, 1857-58
Adelaide	9-41	W.J. OREILLY, NSW V SOUTH AUSTRALIA, 1937-38
Brisbane	9-45	G.E. TRIBE, QUEENSLAND V VICTORIA, 1945-46

**QUEENS SPORTS CLUB,
BULAWAYO**
Capacity: 9,000
End names: City End, Airport End
Home team: Matabeleland

First Test: Zimbabwe v. Sri Lanka,
20–24 October 1994
First ODI: Zimbabwe v. England,
15 December 1996

HARARE SPORTS CLUB
Capacity: 10,000
End names: City End, Club House End
Home team: Mashonaland

First Test: Zimbabwe v. India,
18–22 October 1992
First ODI: Zimbabwe v. India,
25 October 1992

Harare

Z I M B A B W E

Bulawayo

**SEDGARS PARK,
POTCHEFSTROOM**
Capacity: 24,200
End names: Cargo Motors End, University End
Home team: South Africa,
North West

First Test: South Africa v. Bangladesh,
25–27 October 2002
First ODI: South Africa v. New Zealand,
20 October 2000

**THE WANDERERS STADIUM,
JOHANNESBURG**
Capacity: 34,000
End names: Corlett Drive End, Golf Course End
Home team: Gauteng, Transvaal

First Test: South Africa v. England,
24–29 December 1956
First ODI: South Africa v. India,
13 December 1992

**SUPERSPORT PARK,
CENTURION**
Capacity: 20,000
End names: Pavilion End, Hennops River End
Home team: Northern Transvaal,
Northerns

First Test: South Africa v. England,
16–20 November 1995
First ODI: South Africa v. India,
11 December 1992

Centurion

Johannesburg

Potchefstroom

**GOODYEAR PARK,
BLOEMFONTEIN**
Capacity: 20,000
End names: Loch Logan End, Willows End
Home team: Free State

First Test: South Africa v. Zimbabwe,
29 October–1 November 1999
First ODI: South Africa v. India,
15 December 1992

S O U T H

**KINGSMEAD,
DURBAN**
Capacity: 25,000
End names: Umgeni End, Old Fort Road End
Home team: KwaZulu-Natal,
Natal

First Test: South Africa v. England,
18–22 January 1923
First ODI: South Africa v. England,
17 December 1992

Bloemfontein

Durban

**ST GEORGE'S PARK,
PORT ELIZABETH**
Capacity: 19,000
End names: Duckpond End, Park Drive End
Home team: Eastern Province

First Test: South Africa v. England,
12–13 March 1889
First ODI: South Africa v. India,
9 December 1992

A F R I C A

**BUFFALO PARK,
EAST LONDON**
Capacity: 15,000
End names: Buffalo Park Drive End,
Bunkers Hill End
Home team: Border

First Test: South Africa v. Bangladesh,
18–21 October 2002
First ODI: South Africa v. India,
19 December 1992

East London

**NEWLANDS,
CAPE TOWN**
Capacity: 25,000
End names: Wynberg End, Kelvin Grove End
Home team: Western Province

First Test: South Africa v. England,
25–26 March 1889
First ODI: South Africa v. India,
7 December 1992

Cape Town

Port Elizabeth

SOUTH AFRICA

The first Test matches played in South Africa both occurred in March 1889, the first being on St George's Park, Port Elizabeth, and the second on the Newlands ground, Cape Town. These two matches are also considered to be the first two first-class matches played in South Africa. Both of the grounds used are still venues for both Test and first-class cricket.

Port Elizabeth Cricket Club has played at St George's Park from its earliest days and, in 1876, the first major South African cricket competition – the Champion Bat Tournament – was staged in St George's Park, between Kingwilliamstown, Grahamstown, Cape Town and Port Elizabeth. Eastern Province, whose base is Port Elizabeth, played in the Currie Cup for the first time in 1893-94, but the first Currie Cup game at St George's Park was not played there until 1902-03.

Newlands: Table Mountain provides an awe-inspiring backdrop.

The Newlands ground is the base for Western Province. WPCC was formed in 1864 and originally played on Southey's Field, now part of Plumstead, due to city expansion.

They moved to Newlands in 1888, the first match being Mother Country v. Colonial-Born on January 2, 1888.

Western Province entered the Currie Cup in 1892-93 and the first Currie Cup games were played at Newlands in 1893-94, when Western Province, who had won the trophy in 1892-93, retained the title.

Johannesburg was the third South African city to stage a Test match, commencing on March 2, 1896 – with South Africa playing England on what is now termed the Old Wanderers ground. The Old Wanderers ground was required for an expansion of the railway and in 1948-49 Test cricket was transferred to the rugby stadium at Ellis Park, Johannesburg. In 1956-57, the present Wanderers Stadium at Kent Park, Johannesburg, saw its first Test match, South Africa playing England. The ground is also the headquarters of the Transvaal side.

The first first-class match staged in Durban was in April 1885, when Transvaal played Western Province on the Oval, Albert Park. The second was on the Lord's ground in March 1898, and on this ground Durban saw its first Test in January 1910 when South Africa played England. The Lord's ground is now long gone and since 1923 Test matches in Durban have been played on the Kingsmead ground.

In 1995-96, South Africa played for the first time at Centurion, formerly Verwoerdburg. Centurion Park is the headquarters of Northern Transvaal Cricket Union. East London and Potchefstroom staged tests in 2002-03.

ZIMBABWEAN GROUNDS

Three grounds have been used for Test matches in Zimbabwe: Harare Sports Club in Harare and two in Bulawayo, namely Bulawayo Athletic Club and Queen's Sports Club. The highest score in Zimbabwe is 306 by M.H. Richardson in 2000-01 and the best bowling feat is 9-71 by M.J. Procter in 1972-73.

BATTING
Notable batting feats on South Africa's major grounds

Johannesburg	337*	D.J. CULLINAN, TRANSVAAL V. N TRANSVAAL, 1993–94
	306*	E.A.B. ROWAN, TRANSVAAL V. NATAL, 1939–40
	304*	A.W. NOURSE, NATAL V. TRANSVAAL, 1919–20
Worcester, Cape Province	307*	T.N. LAZARD, BOLAND V. W. PROVINCE, 1993–94

*Not out

BOWLING
Notable bowling feats on South Africa's major grounds

Johannesburg	10-26	A.E.E. VOGLER, E PROVINCE V. GRIQUALAND WEST, 1906–07
Cape Town	10-59	S.T. JEFFERIES, W PROVINCE V. OFS, 1987–88

The Wanderers is the third ground in Johannesburg to have been used for Test cricket, after Ellis Park and the Old Wanderers. It first hosted a Test in December 1956 having superseded the Old Wanderers, which is now the site of the local railway station. Two months later Hugh Tayfield took 9 for 113 against England, still the best figures ever recorded by a South African in Test cricket.

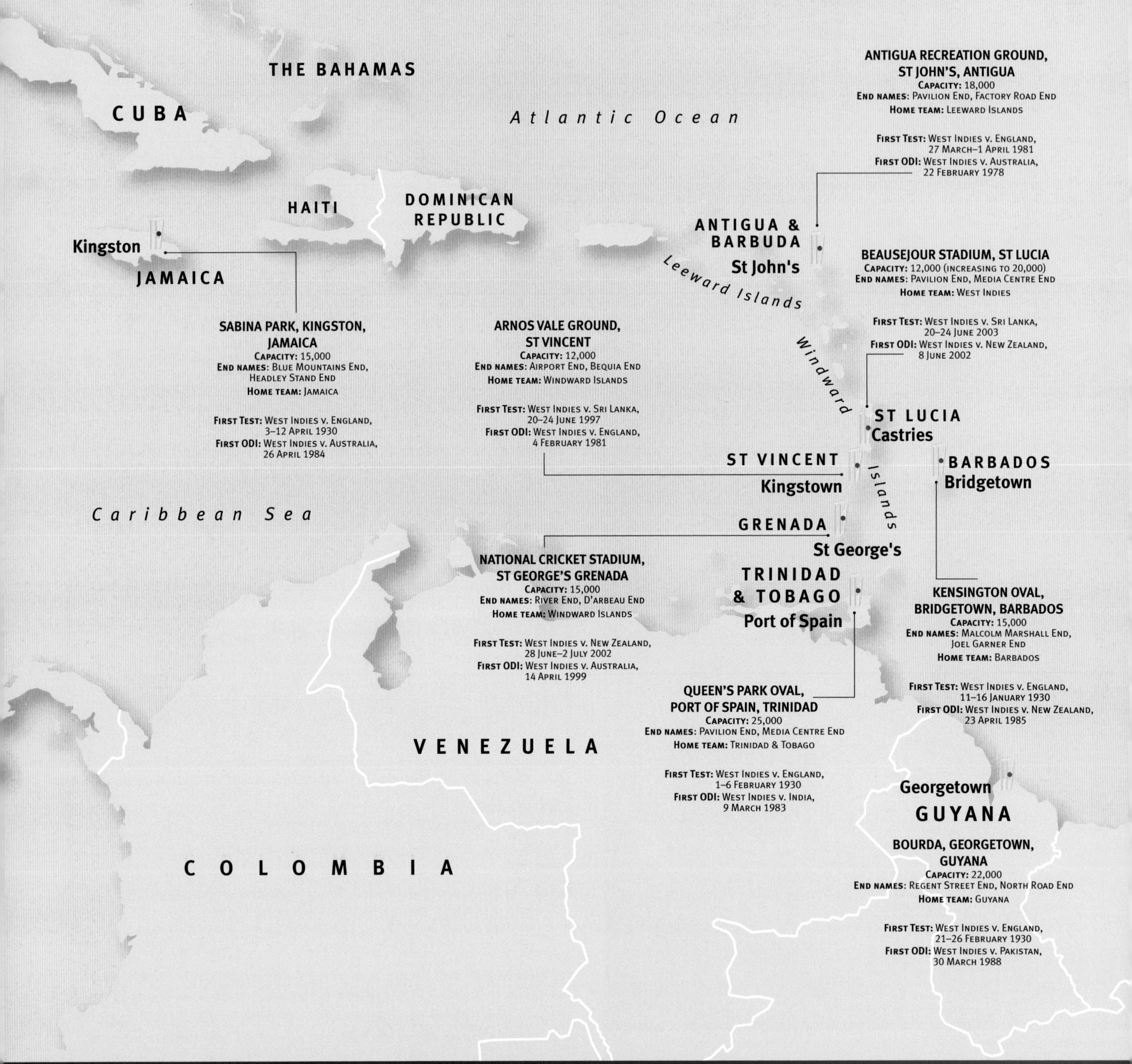

THE BAHAMAS

CUBA

Atlantic Ocean

HAITI

DOMINICAN
REPUBLIC

**ANTIGUA RECREATION GROUND,
ST JOHN'S, ANTIGUA**
Capacity: 18,000
End names: Pavilion End, Factory Road End
Home team: Leeward Islands

First Test: West Indies v. England,
27 March–1 April 1981
First ODI: West Indies v. Australia,
22 February 1978

Kingston

JAMAICA

**ANTIGUA &
BARBUDA**
St John's

Leeward Islands

BEAUSEJOUR STADIUM, ST LUCIA
Capacity: 12,000 (increasing to 20,000)
End names: Pavilion End, Media Centre End
Home team: West Indies

First Test: West Indies v. Sri Lanka,
20–24 June 2003
First ODI: West Indies v. New Zealand,
8 June 2002

**SABINA PARK, KINGSTON,
JAMAICA**
Capacity: 15,000
End names: Blue Mountains End,
Headley Stand End
Home team: Jamaica

First Test: West Indies v. England,
3–12 April 1930
First ODI: West Indies v. Australia,
26 April 1984

**ARNOS VALE GROUND,
ST VINCENT**
Capacity: 12,000
End names: Airport End, Bequia End
Home team: Windward Islands

First Test: West Indies v. Sri Lanka,
20–24 June 1997
First ODI: West Indies v. England,
4 February 1981

Windward

ST LUCIA
Castries

ST VINCENT

Kingstown

Islands

BARBADOS
Bridgetown

Caribbean Sea

GRENADA

St George's

**NATIONAL CRICKET STADIUM,
ST GEORGE'S GRENADA**
Capacity: 15,000
End names: River End, D'arbeau End
Home team: Windward Islands

First Test: West Indies v. New Zealand,
28 June–2 July 2002
First ODI: West Indies v. Australia,
14 April 1999

**TRINIDAD
& TOBAGO**

Port of Spain

**KENSINGTON OVAL,
BRIDGETOWN, BARBADOS**
Capacity: 15,000
End names: Malcolm Marshall End,
Joel Garner End
Home team: Barbados

First Test: West Indies v. England,
11–16 January 1930
First ODI: West Indies v. New Zealand,
23 April 1985

**QUEEN'S PARK OVAL,
PORT OF SPAIN, TRINIDAD**
Capacity: 25,000
End names: Pavilion End, Media Centre End
Home team: Trinidad & Tobago

First Test: West Indies v. England,
1–6 February 1930
First ODI: West Indies v. India,
9 March 1983

VENEZUELA

Georgetown

GUYANA

COLOMBIA

**BOURDA, GEORGETOWN,
GUYANA**
Capacity: 22,000
End names: Regent Street End, North Road End
Home team: Guyana

First Test: West Indies v. England,
21–26 February 1930
First ODI: West Indies v. Pakistan,
30 March 1988

WEST INDIES

The first first-class match in the West Indies was played on the Garrison Savannah ground in Bridgetown, Barbados, on 15-16 February 1865, when the island opposed Demerara. It was not until 1883-84 that a second first-class match took place, and this time at the Wanderers CC ground at Bay Pasture, Bridgetown. The Pickwick CC ground at Kensington Oval saw first-class cricket in 1894-95, when R.S. Lucas's Team visited Barbados. It is appropriate that the first Test in the West Indies should have taken place on the Kensington Oval ground against England in January 1930. Test matches and first-class cricket have been staged regularly on the ground since then.

Georgetown, Guyana, saw its first first-class game on the Eve Leary Parade ground in 1865-66. The present ground, Bourda, was first used for first-class matches in September 1887-88 and the first Test played there was in

The updated Kensington Oval in Bridgetown hosted the 2007 World Cup final.

February 1930, West Indies v England. This remains the principal ground in what was British Guiana, now Guyana.

The Queen's Park Oval in Port-of-Spain is the major Trinidad ground, while Sabina Park is the main venue in Kingston, Jamaica. Both these grounds were first used for Test cricket during the 1929-30 series against England.

The fifth ground in the West Indies to hold a Test match was the Recreation Ground in St John's, Antigua. St Lucia saw its first Test match at Beausejour Stadium in June 2003. St Kitts staged its first Test in June 2006 and new Test grounds opened in Antigua and Guyana in 2008.

St John's in Antigua underwent major redevelopment for the 2007 World Cup.

BATTING
Notable batting feats on major West Indies grounds:

St John's

400	B.C. LARA, WEST INDIES V ENGLAND, 2003–04

Kingston

365*	G.ST A. SOBERS, WEST INDIES V PAKISTAN, 1957–58

Bridgetown

337	HANIF MOHAMMAD, PAKISTAN V WEST INDIES, 1957–58
308*	F.M.M. WORRELL, BARBADOS V TRINIDAD, 1943–44

Port of Spain

324	J. B. STOLLMEYE TRINIDAD V BRITISH GUIANA, 1946–47

* Not out

BOWLING
Notable bowling feats on major West Indies grounds:

Port of Spain

10-36	D.C.S. HINDS, A.B. ST HILLS XI V TRINIDAD, 1900–01

Kingston

10-175	E.E. HEMMINGS, INTERNATIONAL XI V WEST INDIES, 1982–83

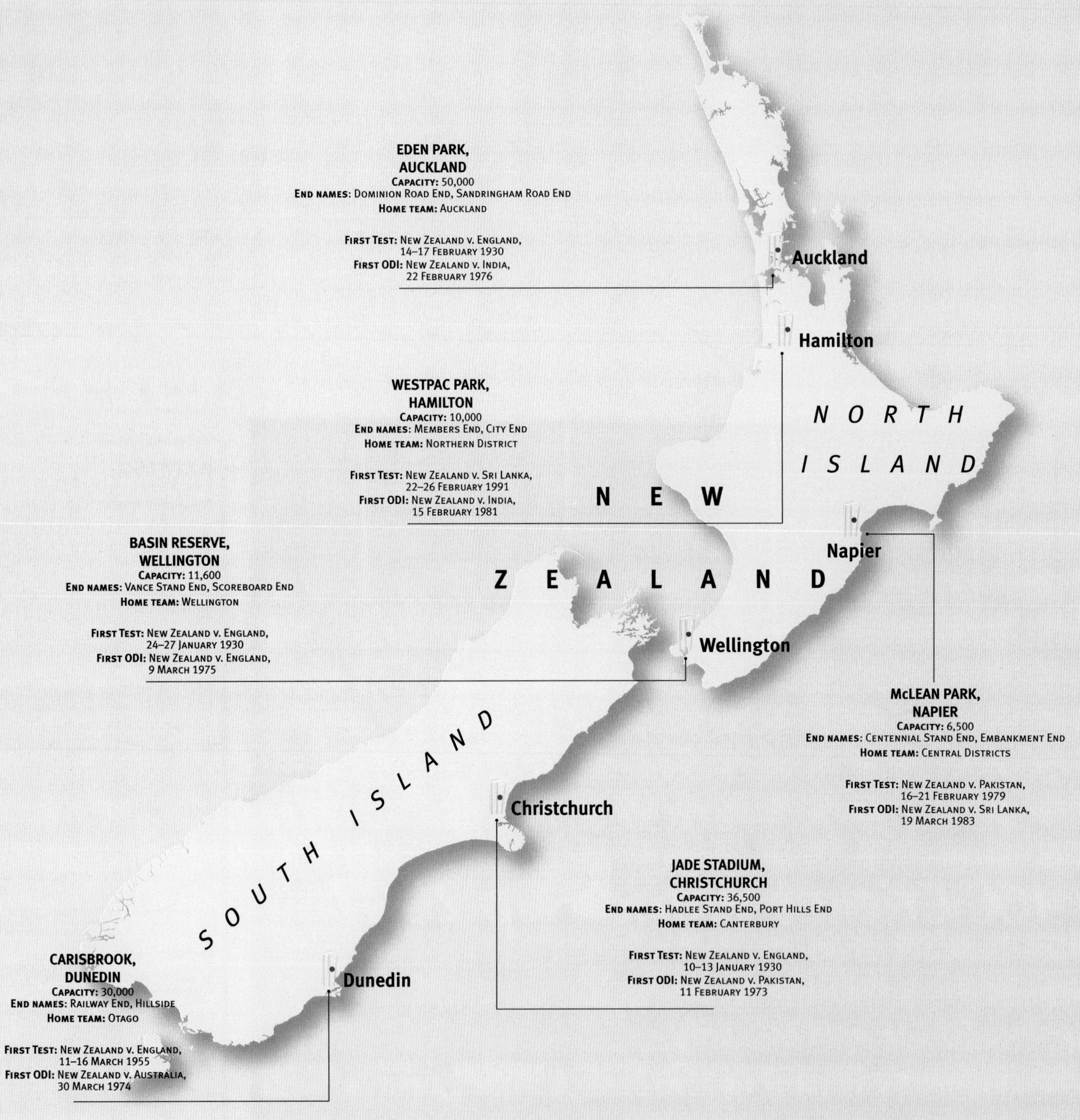

**EDEN PARK,
AUCKLAND**
Capacity: 50,000
End names: Dominion Road End, Sandringham Road End
Home team: Auckland

First Test: New Zealand v. England,
14–17 February 1930
First ODI: New Zealand v. India,
22 February 1976

Auckland

Hamilton

**WESTPAC PARK,
HAMILTON**
Capacity: 10,000
End names: Members End, City End
Home team: Northern District

First Test: New Zealand v. Sri Lanka,
22–26 February 1991
First ODI: New Zealand v. India,
15 February 1981

*N O R T H
I S L A N D*

N E W

**BASIN RESERVE,
WELLINGTON**
Capacity: 11,600
End names: Vance Stand End, Scoreboard End
Home team: Wellington

First Test: New Zealand v. England,
24–27 January 1930
First ODI: New Zealand v. England,
9 March 1975

Z E A L A N D

Napier

Wellington

**McLEAN PARK,
NAPIER**
Capacity: 6,500
End names: Centennial Stand End, Embankment End
Home team: Central Districts

First Test: New Zealand v. Pakistan,
16–21 February 1979
First ODI: New Zealand v. Sri Lanka,
19 March 1983

S O U T H   I S L A N D

Christchurch

**JADE STADIUM,
CHRISTCHURCH**
Capacity: 36,500
End names: Hadlee Stand End, Port Hills End
Home team: Canterbury

First Test: New Zealand v. England,
10–13 January 1930
First ODI: New Zealand v. Pakistan,
11 February 1973

**CARISBROOK,
DUNEDIN**
Capacity: 30,000
End names: Railway End, Hillside
Home team: Otago

First Test: New Zealand v. England,
11–16 March 1955
First ODI: New Zealand v. Australia,
30 March 1974

Dunedin

NEW ZEALAND

which has staged Test matches since January 1930.

The Domain was the major ground in Auckland from 1853, but in the season 1912–13 Eden Park superseded the Domain as the principal first-class venue. The first Test at Eden Park was in February 1930. The ground is used for both cricket and rugby.

McLean Park, Napier, where Central Districts play some of their first-class matches, staged its first Test in February 1979, when New Zealand played Pakistan.

Test cricket has also been played at Hamilton, New Zealand's fifth largest city. It hosted a Test for the first time in 1990–91, when Sri Lanka were in town. It ended in a high-scoring draw and was notable for the fact the New Zealand's Andrew Jones scored a century in both innings. It staged its first one-day international in 1981.

Basin Reserve in Wellington has staged Test matches since 1930. England were the visitors and the match ended in a draw.

New Zealand first-class cricket commenced in Dunedin on 27 January 1864, when Otago played Canterbury. The venue was the South Dunedin recreation ground. In 1879–80, the Caledonian ground in Dunedin was used by Otago, but in 1883–84 the Province played on the Carisbrook ground. It was not, however, until March 1955 that a Test match was played at Carisbrook, when New Zealand played England. Otago now plays at the University Ground in Dunedin. This also is a Test venue.

The ground at Hagley Park, Christchurch, has staged first-class matches, commencing February 1865, but the present main Christchurch ground for Test and for Canterbury first-class games is Lancaster Park. The reason for the switch from Hagley Park to Lancaster Park was that no admission charges could be levied at the former ground. Lancaster Park saw its first first-class match in 1882–83 and its first Test in 1929–30, when New Zealand played England.

The first first-class match at Wellington was Wellington v Auckland on 28–29 November 1873. The principal ground is the Basin Reserve

BATTING
Notable batting feats on major New Zealand grounds:

Christchurch	385	B. SUTCLIFFE, OTAGO V CANTERBURY, 1952-53
Dunedin	355	B. SUTCLIFFE, OTAGO V AUCKLAND, 1949-50
Auckland	336*	W. R. HAMMOND, ENGLAND V NEW ZEALAND, 1932-33

* not out

BOWLING
Notable bowling feats on major New Zealand grounds:

Christchurch	10-28	A.E. MOSS, CANTERBURY V WELLINGTON, 1889-90
Auckland	9-36	A.F. WENSLEY, AUCKLAND V OTAGO, 1929-30
Wellington	9-43	T. EDEN, NELSON V WELLINGTON, 1875-76
Napier	9-47	T.H. DENT, HAWKES BAY V WELLINGTON, 1900-01
Dunedin	9-50	A.H. FISHER, OTAGO V QUEENSLAND, 1896-97

ARBAB NIAZ STADIUM, PESHAWAR
CAPACITY: 30,000
END NAMES: PAVILION END, COLLEGE END

HOME TEAM: PESHAWAR CRICKET ASSOCIATION

RAWALPINDI CRICKET STADIUM
CAPACITY: 15,000
END NAMES: PAVILION END, SHELL END

HOME TEAM: RAWALPINDI

GADDAFI STADIUM, LAHORE
CAPACITY: 60,000
END NAMES: PAVILION END, COLLEGE END

HOME TEAM: LAHORE

IQBAL STADIUM, FAISALABAD
CAPACITY: 22,000
END NAMES: PAVILION END, GOLF COURSE END

HOME TEAM: FAISALABAD

PUNJAB CRICKET ASSOCIATION, MOHALI, CHANDIGARH
CAPACITY: 45,000
END NAMES: PAVILION END, CITY END

HOME TEAM: PUNJAB

BANGABANDHU NATIONAL STADIUM, DHAKA
CAPACITY: 36,000
END NAMES: PAVILION END, PALTAN END

HOME TEAM: DHAKA

NARAYANGANJ OSMANI STADIUM, FATTULLAH, DHAKA
CAPACITY: 35,000
END NAMES: PRESS BOX END, PAVILION END

HOME TEAM: BANGLADESH

MULTAN CRICKET STADIUM
CAPACITY: 18,000
END NAMES: MAIN PAVILION END, NORTH PAVILION END

HOME TEAM: MULTAN

Peshawar
Rawalpindi
Faisalabad
Lahore
Multan
Chandigarh
Delhi

P A K I S T A N

NATIONAL STADIUM, KARACHI
CAPACITY: 50,000
END NAMES: PAVILION END, UNIVERSITY END

HOME TEAM: KARACHI

FEROZ SHAH KOLTA, DELHI
CAPACITY: 30,000
END NAMES: STADIUM END, PAVILION END

HOME TEAM: DELHI

SHAHEED CHANDU STADIUM, BOGRA
CAPACITY: 18,000

HOME TEAM: BANGLADESH

Kanpur

GREEN PARK, KANPUR
CAPACITY: 45,000
END NAMES: MILL PAVILION END, HOSTEL END

HOME TEAM: UTTAR PRADESH

Karachi
Bogra
Dhaka

SARDAR PATEL STADIUM, AHMEDABAD
CAPACITY: 48,000
END NAMES: ADANI PAVILION END, GMDC END

HOME TEAM: GUJARAT

Ahmedabad

I N D I A

Kolkata
Chittagong

EDEN GARDENS, KOLKATA
CAPACITY: 90,000
END NAMES: HIGH COURT END, PAVILION END

HOME TEAM: BENGAL

Nagpur

VIDARBHA CRICKET ASSOCIATION GROUND, NAGPUR
CAPACITY: 40,000
END NAMES: JAIKA END, CHURCH END

HOME TEAM: VIDARBHA

WANKHEDE STADIUM, MUMBAI
CAPACITY: 45,000
END NAMES: GARWARE PAVILION END, TATA END

HOME TEAM: MUMBAI

Mumbai

MA AZIZ STADIUM, CHITTAGONG
CAPACITY: 30,000
END NAMES: PEDROLLO END, ISPAHANI END

HOME TEAM: BANGLADESH

Hyderabad

LAL BAHADUR SHASTRI STADIUM, HYDERABAD
CAPACITY: 30,000
END NAMES: PAVILION END, HILL FORT END

HOME TEAM: HYDERABAD

CHITTAGONG DIVISIONAL STADIUM
CAPACITY: 12,000
END NAMES: ISPHANI END, UCB END

HOME TEAM: CHITTAGONG DIVISION

M. CHINNASWAMY STADIUM, BANGALORE
CAPACITY: 55,000
END NAMES: PAVILION END, BEML END

HOME TEAM: KARNATAKA

Bangalore
Chennai

MA CHIDAMBARAM, CHAPAUK, CHENNAI
CAPACITY: 50,000
END NAMES: ANNA PAVILION END, V. PATTABHIRAMAN GATE END

HOME TEAM: TAMIL NADU

R. PREMADASA STADIUM, COLOMBO
CAPACITY: 35,000
END NAMES: KHETTARAMA END, SCOREBOARD END

HOME TEAM: SRI LANKA

SINHALESE SPORTS CLUB, COLOMBO
CAPACITY: 10,000
END NAMES: TENNIS COURTS END, SOUTH END

HOME TEAM: SINHALESE SPORTS CLUB

P. SARAVANAMUTTU STADIUM, COLOMBO
CAPACITY: 12,000
END NAMES: AIR FORCE FLATS END, PRESS BLOCK END

HOME TEAM: TAMIL UNION CRICKET AND ATHLETIC CLUB

ASGIRIYA STADIUM, KANDY
CAPACITY: 10,000
END NAMES: HUNNASGIRIYA END, HANTHANA END

HOME TEAM: KANDY CRICKET CLUB

Kandy
Colombo

SRI LANKA

Galle

GALLE INTERNATIONAL STADIUM
CAPACITY: 10,000
END NAMES: CITY END, FORT END

HOME TEAM: GALLE CRICKET CLUB

THE SUB-CONTINENT

INDIAN GROUNDS

Something in the region of 300 separate grounds have staged first-class cricket in India, but in a number of towns and cities it is not totally clear which ground was used, mainly because the names of grounds have changed in many cases.

This brief piece on Indian grounds is therefore confined to the major Test match grounds – there have been 20 Test venues so far. The oldest and senior ground for Test cricket is Eden Gardens, Calcutta, where India played England in 1933-34. The Gymkhana ground in Bombay and the Chepauk ground in Madras were also used for Test matches that same season. When the West Indies toured India in 1948-49, the Feroz Shah Kotla ground in Delhi and the Brabourne Stadium in Bombay hosted Tests for the first time. Neither of the two Bombay grounds mentioned is now used for Tests, the current ground being the Wankhede Stadium, first used in 1974-75. The two grounds not so far mentioned which have seen most Test cricket are Green Park, Kanpur and Karnataka CA ground, Bangalore).

Along with the MCG, Eden Gardens remains cricket's answer to the Coliseum. It first hosted a Test in India's early days of Test cricket, when Douglas Jardine's team eased to victory inside four days in 1934. Since then, it has become something of a place of pilgrimage for most international cricketers who see it as the ideal stage upon which to perform. The fanatical crowds add to the atmsophere.

BATTING
Notable batting feats on Indian grounds:

Poona (Pune)
443*   B.B. NIMBALKAR,
        MAHARASHTRA V KATHIAWAR,
        1948-49

Bombay (Mumbai)
377   S.V MANJREKAR,
        BOMBAY V HYDERABAD,
        1990-91

Secunderabad
366   M V SRIDHAR,
        HYDERABAD V ANDHRA,
        1993-94

Bangalore
353   V.V.S. LAXMAN,
        HYDERABAD V KARNATAKA,
        1999-2000

*Not out

BOWLING
Notable bowling feats on Indian grounds:

Jorhat
10-20   P.M. CHATTERJEE,
        BENGAL V ASSAM,
        1956-57

Bombay (Mumbai)
10-78   S.P. GUPTE,
        PRESIDENT'S XI V COMBINED XI,
        1954-55

Jodhpur
10-78   P. SUNDERAM,
        RAJASTHAN V VIDARBHA,
        1985-86

Kotia
10-74   A. KUMBLE,
        INDIA V PAKISTAN,
        1998-99

PAKISTAN/BANGLADESH

PAKISTANI GROUNDS

The first home Test match by Pakistan was played at the Dacca Stadium in 1954-55 – but Dacca is now in Bangladesh. Four other venues were used in the same season for Tests: Dring Stadium, Bahawalpur; Lawrence Gardens, Lahore; Services ground, Peshawar; and National Stadium, Karachi. Only the last has remained a regular Test venue. Lawrence Gardens in Lahore was superseded by the Gaddafi Stadium. The other venue that has regularly seen Test cricket is the Iqbal Stadium, Faisalabad.

Since 1980, other cities which have hosted Tests are Rawalpindi, Gujranwala, Sialkot and Multan. The Services Ground at Peshawar has been superseded by the Arbab Niaz Stadium. The Defence Stadium at Karachi was used in 1993.

SRI LANKA GROUNDS

Since Sri Lanka was raised to Test-match status in 1981-82, four different grounds in Colombo have been used for Test matches, namely Saravanamuttu Stadium, Sinhalese Sports CC, Colombo CC and Premadasa Stadium. Tests have also been played at Kandy, Moratuwa and Galle. The highest innings in Sri Lanka is 340 by S.T. Jayasuriya for Sri

Left: **Stadiums in Pakistan underwent major redevelopment in time for the 1996 World Cup.**
Above: **The magnificent new stadiuim in Dhaka, a perfect stage for the Bangadesh team.**

Lanka v India in Colombo in 1997-98 and the best bowling feat is 10-41 by G.P. Wickramasinghe for Sinhalese SC in 1991-92.

BANGLADESH GROUNDS

The national stadium in Dhaka is the only stadium to have hosted an inaugural Test fixture, for Pakistan in 1954-55 (when Dhaka was the capital of East Pakistan) and 46 years later, on Bangladesh's arrival to Test cricket. Five grounds have staged home Tests.

BATTING
Notable batting feats on Pakistani grounds:

Karachi	499	HANIF MOHAMMAD, KARACHI V BAHAWALPUR, 1958-59
Karachi	428	AFTAB BALOCH, SIND V BALUCHISTAN, 1973-74
Lahore	350	RASHID ISRAR, HABIB BANK V NATIONAL BANK, 1976-77
Peshawar	334*	M.A. TAYLOR, AUSTRALIA VPAKISTAN, 1998-99

*Not out

BOWLING
Notable bowling feats on Pakistani grounds:

Peshawar	10-28	NAEEM AKHTAR, RAWALPINDI B V PESHAWAR, 1995-96
Karachi	10-58	SHAHID MAHMOOD, KARACHI WHITES V KHAIRPUR, 1969-70
Faisalabad	10-92	IMRAN ADIL, BAHAWALPUR V FAISALABAD, 1989-90

INDIAN CRICKET TODAY

The year 2011 shows Indian cricket at its strongest since the formation of the Calcutta Cricket Club at Eden Gardens 219 years before.

Since December 2009 India have been ranked at the top of the ICC Test Championship table. In 2011 they won the World Cup on their own soil. They stage the richest competition in the world, the Indian Premier League. And their great hero, Sachin Tendulkar, was arguably still the world's best batsman 22 years after his Test debut, with more Test runs and more runs in all forms of international cricket than any other batsman - an incredible feat.

Indian cricketers can earn immense riches, and are idolised in a way that in other countries might be reserved for pop stars or film icons. No wonder that all over India children take to the game on any piece of ground available.

Top: **Cricket is the Indian national game. Everyone wants to bat like Sachin Tendulkar.**
Left: **Indian Premier League games attract big crowds and have a carnival atmosphere.**
Inset: **Any patch of open space will do for a game, like this backstreet in Mumbai.**

Above: **Passions always run high when it comes to the Indian national team, as these face-painted kids demonstrate during the 2011 World Cup.**

INDEX

All numbers in *italics* refer to pictures

PICTURE CREDITS

The publishers would like to thank the following sources for their kind permission to reproduce the pictures in this book.

Bridgeman Art Library: /Marylebone Cricket Club: 12B, 13, 15
Getty Images: 27, 99, 149; /AFP: 104; /K Asif/India Today Group: 282L; /Scott Barbour: 93; /Daniel Berehulak: 77; /Hamish Blair: 44, 45TL, 45TR, 60, 78, 101, 107, 113, 124, 174, 260T, 282TR; /Shaun Botterill: 112, 126, 274-275; /Gordon Brooks/AFP: 125; /Randy Brooks/AFP: 137; /Simon Bruty: 192T; /Central Press: 21, 23, 26, 28, 95, 97, 242, 249; /Graham Chadwick/AFP: 74; /Chris Cole: 72, 146; /Mark Dadswell: 265; /Carl de Souza: 35B; /Adrian Dennis/AFP: 273; /Duif du Toit/Gallo Images: 92; /Emmanuel Dunand/AFP: 91TR, 91B; /Rob Elliott/AFP: 76, 282B; /Evening Standard: 185B, 199; /Simon Fergusson: 62; /Stu Forster: 105, 120; /Paul Gilham: 236; /Farjana K Godhuly/AFP: 136; /Laurence Griffiths: 135, 269; /Gianluigi Guercia/AFP: 217B; /Richard Heathcote: 45B, 261; /Julian Herbert: 109, 133; /Mike Hewitt: 88, 129, 150, 213, 221, 280; /A. Hudson/Topical Press Agency: 68; /Francis M.R. Hudson/Topical Press Agency: 42; /Hulton Archive: 18, 19, 140, 147, 185T; /Alexander Joe/AFP: 57; /Naveen Jora/India Today Group: 203; /Paul Kane: 50; /Ross Kinnaird: 151; /Glyn Kirk/AFP: 6-7; /Nick Laham: 117; /Ross Land: 111, 122; /Matthew Lewis: 195; /Joe Mann: 116, 148; /Bob Martin: 110; /Clive Mason: 79; /Marty Melville: 61; /Douglas Miller/Keystone: 65; /Indranil Mukherjee/AFP: 9, 36L, 36R, 70, 91TL; /Adrian Murrell: 31, 46, 52, 73, 82, 98, 115, 145, 200T, 202, 251; /Dennis Oulds/Central Press/Hulton Archive: 141; /John Parkin: 138; /Ryan Pierse: 263; /Adam Pretty: 51; /Aamir Qureshi/AFP: 85; /Ben Radford: 39, 192B, 200B, 206T; /Rischgitz: 10, 12T, 14; /Quinn Rooney: 54; /STR/AFP: 118; /Jewel Samad/AFP: 132, 157; /Dibyangshu Sarkar/AFP: 36T, 37, 69, 123; /Noah Seelam/AFP: 283; /Haider Shah/AFP: 83; /Tom Shaw: 47, 86, 87, 102, 108, 187T; /Jimmy Sime: 24L; /Prakash Singh/AFP: 130; /Dan Smith: 30T; /Cameron Spencer: 3, 103, 264; /Michael Steele: 281; /Carl Sutton/Hulton Archive: 64; /Rizwan Tabassum/AFP: 75; /Frank Tewkesbury/Evening Standard: 43; /Reinhold Thiele: 96; /Bob Thomas: 196; /Bob Thomas/Popperfoto: 90; /Topical Press Agency: 94; /Touchline: 63; /Touchline Photo: 58; /William Vanderson/Picture Post: 56; /Manan Vatsyayana/AFP: 159; /Phil Walter: 114, 119; /Ian Walton: 270-271; /Lakruwan Wanniarachchi/AFP: 131; /William West/AFP: 106, 134, 158; /Greg Wood/AFP: 156; /Jonathan Wood: 53; /Anna Zieminski/AFP: 128
Mary Evans Picture Library: 38
Nottinghamshire County Cricket Club: /Peter Wynne-Thomas: 40
Press Association Images: 16, 29, 34BR, 35T, 160T, 194, 197, 211, 212B, 215, 230, 231T, 231B; /AP: 241; /Gemunu Amarasinghe/AP: 228; /Matthew Ashton: 178; /Mark Baker/AP: 193, 205T, 223B; /Barry Batchelor: 244; /Chris Brandis/AP: 66; /Graham Chadwick: 41, 172B, 177, 255; /K.M. Chaudary/AP: 181T; /Gareth Copley: 201T, 220; /Ben Curtis: 232, 234; /David Davies: 258; /Adam Davy: 256; /Sean Dempsey: 33; /Matt Dunham/AP: 161, 208; /Mike Egerton: 227; /Paul Faith: 81; /Rob Griffith/AP: 209; /Noel Hammond/Africa Visuals: 154, 155; /Jon Hrusa/AP: 139; /Eranga Jayawardena/AP: 219B; /David Jones: 152; /Andres Leighton/AP: 186, 222, 229; /John Marsh: 243B; /Tony Marshall: 188, 252B; /Steve Mitchell: 248T, 252T; /Rebecca Naden: 32B, 166, 170, 183, 266, 267, 279; /Anjum Naveed/AP: 235B; /Phil Noble: 240, 245; /Nick Potts: 160B, 165T; /Michael Regan: 80; /Martin Rickett: 191, 223T; /Rick Rycroft/AP: 184B, 205B; /S&G/Alpha: 17, 20, 22, 24R, 25, 30B, 142, 143, 144, 162, 163, 164, 168, 171T, 171B, 172T, 173, 175T, 175B, 176T, 176B, 180, 182, 189, 190, 204, 206B, 212T, 217T, 225, 226B, 239, 246R; /Ross Setford: 165B, 243T; /Aziz Shah/AP: 84; /Aman Sharma/AP: 34TR, 181B, 210; /Matthew Short: 257; /Neal Simpson: 153, 167, 179, 184T, 187B, 214T, 219T, 224, 226T, 237; /Jon Super/AP: 247T, 247B; /Grant Treeby/World Sport Pictures: 198; /Chris Turvey: 32T, 277; /Phil Walter: 246L, 248B; /John Walton: 201B, 253; /Aubrey Washington: 207, 260B; /Kirsty Wigglesworth: 235T; /Chris Young: 100, 121, 214B; /Obed Zilwa/AP: 34TL
Patrick Eagar Photography: 238, 250
The Picture-Desk: /Eileen Tweedy/Tate Gallery London/The Art Archive: 11

Every effort has been made to acknowledge correctly and contact the source and/or copyright holder of each picture and Carlton Books Limited apologises for any unintentional errors or omissions which will be corrected in future editions of this book.